Map Librarianship

Map Librarianship

An Introduction

Third Edition

Mary Lynette Larsgaard
Map and Imagery Laboratory
Davidson Library
University of California,
Santa Barbara

1998
Libraries Unlimited, Inc.
Englewood, Colorado

Libraries Unlimited, Inc.
P.O. Box 6633
Englewood, CO 80155-6633
1-800-237-6124
www.lu.com

Production Editor: Kevin W. Perizzolo
Copy Editor: Brooke Graves
Proofreader: Felicity Tucker
Indexer: Linda Running Bentley
Interior Design and Typesetting: Judy Gay Matthews

Library of Congress Cataloging-in-Publication Data

Larsgaard, Mary Lynette, 1946-
    Map librarianship : an introduction / Mary Lynette Larsgaard. -- 3rd ed.
      xxix, 487 p.   17x25 cm.
    Includes bibliographical references and index.
    ISBN 1-56308-474-0
    1. Libraries--Special collections--Maps.   2. Libraries--Special collections--Geography.   I. Title.
    Z692.M3L37   1998
    025.2'86--dc21   98-15451
                                                                          CIP

For Phil Hoehn and Stan Stevens,
with thanks

If you look closely,
you'll see in these lines
all your good advice to me over the years.

Contents

Acknowledgments

It is a classic tale among spatial-data librarians that few of us ever received any formal training in working with spatial data. The whole process was learn-as-you-go, with all of the errors that such an inefficient approach implies. This book is an attempt to remedy that situation, to present a how-to-do-it book as much for the librarian who had the job thrust upon her because no one else would touch those awkward, fragile monsters as for the information-science student who has freely chosen to work with spatial data. I have had great help and encouragement in learning how to be a spatial-data librarian, and it is my pleasure to acknowledge that assistance.

The various universities that I have worked in—the now Central Washington State University; Colorado School of Mines; University of California, Santa Barbara—and the many libraries I have visited over the years have each provided me with all the assistance I had the nerve to request. Next are the many, many friends in the field who have helped me over the years. In the last edition, I listed a good many of them—and was horrified to discover that I had forgotten a few! So this time, I shall issue a joint thanks, noting that looking at the bibliography will give the reader the names of many of these stalwart souls.

Introduction

Like its predecessors, the first and second editions of *Map Librarianship*, this volume is intended to serve persons who deal with spatial-data collections, be they students preparing to enter the field, or librarians and others who have just had the responsibility for such collections foisted off upon them. The focus is on theory, techniques, and practices; the volume may be used as a classroom text, a working manual, and a reference source. The author's knowledge of and views on spatial-data librarianship have evolved over—can it be?—nearly thirty years of experience working with these materials, in three United States university libraries, but the points made in this volume very often apply to public and special libraries, and to collections in other countries. Spatial data in school libraries is an area in which the author has no expertise, and it is therefore very seldom mentioned. Architectural plans are also not within the scope of this volume.

After much thought, the author decided to stay with the same title as the first two editions, while at the same time using, when appropriate, the phrase "spatial data," instead of the phrase "cartographic materials," to refer to the materials being discussed. The new phrase is a development of about the last five years; a problem surfaced with persons believing that the word "cartographic" somehow limited the discussion to maps, which it does not.

The object of this volume is to provide timely, pragmatic information, a survey of existing practices, and guidance in choosing specific procedures. It is not concerned with the history of maps, mapping, or map collections except as these may illustrate a point; cartography and interpretation of spatial data are dwelt upon only to the extent that such information is required by any librarian doing reference work in that field.

The arrangement of information in the book parallels the steps a librarian would take dealing with spatial data, starting with selecting and acquiring them. Successive chapters deal with: classification; cataloging; storage, care, and repair; reference services; public relations; and education. Although in theory the last-named chapter should be the first in the book, the author has decided that art should reflect life, which means that often spatial-data librarians learn what it is they are to do after, not before, they begin work.

The text is followed by a bibliography listing items cited, current to July 1997. This in turn is followed by appendices, which provide: lists of CD-ROMs of interest to spatial-data collections; citations to general book-format publications for the collection; citations on projections; citations on cataloging; a sample free-request form; draft cataloging rules for spatial data in digital form; addresses for publishers of globes and plastic raised-relief maps; and addresses of selected suppliers of equipment and supplies. Neither the bibliography nor the appendices of citations are definitive or comprehensive.

There has been some collapsing and deletion of appendices from the last edition; that of citations to monographs and serials in various subjects has been occasioned by the publication of just one superb volume, *Information sources in cartography 1990,* which rendered some of the previous lists mercifully unnecessary. Changes in the spatial-data world, and relative commonness in the library world, rendered unnecessary respectively the list of libraries issuing accession lists and the appendix on collection-development policies. The volume is indexed by author, title, and subject. Abbreviations and acronyms, which as in the rest of librarianship are used extensively, are identified in the list of abbreviations.

The informal writing style of the previous editions has been retained in an effort to make the work as easy to get through as possible, and also to reflect not only the author's turn of mind but also, and more importantly, the fact that the author has found working in the field to be a good deal of fun—hard work, but fun. The author has attempted to make the text and citations accurate; she would greatly appreciate receiving notification of corrections.

The major change throughout the volume is the addition of information on spatial data in digital form, which has meant far-reaching changes throughout the field. Especially the last two or three years, if you took any (printed) issue of a recent library-science periodical and threw it down the stairs, chances are extremely good that it would fall open at an article on digital data in libraries, and it would probably at least mention the World Wide Web. This has meant a very steep learning curve for those of us already in the field, and has been especially difficult for the author, whose idea of user-friendly equipment is a spoon.

A few notes on conventions used for citations:

1. A citation followed by reference to an appendix will be found in full in that appendix; if there is no such phrase, the full citation is in the bibliography.

2. The words "library," "collection," and their plurals are very often assumed to have in front of them the phrase "spatial-data." When libraries in general are referred to, this will be evident from the context; when spatial-data collections are referred to in the same sentence or paragraph, they are specifically identified as such.

3. When multiple citations occur, they are listed in order of importance, or in alphabetical order if order of importance does not apply.

4. When no page number is given, the entire article relates to the subject under discussion.

5. When dates are not available, a best guess has been made. These are indicated by "19_?" or similar convention.

Envoi

Increasingly, the author finds that she thinks of herself as one of the old warhorses of the field; from that point, it is but a short step to such thoughts as "Goodbye, old Paint." Consequently, this will be the last edition of *Map librarianship* that I shall inflict upon the profession. The next time around, it's up to the new kids on the block. I hope you have as much fun as I!

M.L.L.

List of Abbreviations

AAA	American Automobile Association
AACCCM	Anglo-American Cataloguing Committee for Cartographic Materials
AACR	Anglo-American Cataloging Rules; AACR2 is the second edition, AACR2R is the revision of the second edition
AAG	Association of American Geographers
ACIC	U.S. Aeronautical Chart Information Center
ACMLA	Association of Canadian Map Libraries and Archives
ACRL	Association of College and Research Libraries
ADIZ	Air Defense Identification Zone
ADP	automated data processing
AECT	Association for Educational Communications and Technology
AGS	American Geographical Society of New York; collection now at the Golda Meir Library, University of Wisconsin–Milwaukee
ALA MAGERT	American Library Association Map and Geography Round Table
ALCTS	American Library Association's Association for Library Collections and Technical Services
AMS	U.S. Army Map Service
ANSI	American National Standards Institute
ap	aerial photography
APSRS	Aerial Photography Summary Record System
ASCS	U.S. Agricultural Stabilization and Conservation Service
ASDIC	Allied Submarine Devices Investigation Committee
ASTM	American Society for Testing of Materials
AVHRR	Advanced Very High Resolution Radiometer
B&L	Boggs and Lewis
BCR	Bibliographical Center for Research
BGN	U.S. Board of Geographic Names
BIP	*Books in print*

BLM	U.S. Bureau of Land Management
BSI	British Standards Institution
C&GS	United States Coast and Geodetic Survey
C&RL	*College and Research Libraries*
CBI	*Cumulated book index*
CCI	Catalog of Cartographic Information
CDP	collection-development policy
CD-ROM	compact disc, read-only memory
CIA	U.S. Central Intelligence Agency
CIP	Cataloging in Publication
COM	computer output microfiche
CPU	central processing unit
CRT	cathode ray tube
CSB	*Cataloging service bulletin*
CSUF	California State University, Fresno
CUAC	SLAG&M Cartographic Users Advisory Committee; later, Cartographic Users Advisory Council
DD	Dewey Decimal classification
DEM	digital elevation model
DEZ	diethyl zinc
DLG	digital line graph
DMA	U.S. Defense Mapping Agency (now NIMA)
DMAHC/TC	DMA Hydrographic Center/Topographic Center
DMATC	DMA Topographic Center
DOQ	digital orthophotoquad
DOQQ	digital orthophoto quarter-quadrangle
dpi	dots per inch
DRG	digital raster graphic
DUMC	Dutch Union Map Catalogue
ed.	edition
EDP	electronic data processing
EMR	Canadian Department of Energy, Mines and Resources
enl.	enlarged

EOS	Earth Observing System
EOSAT	Earth Observation Satellite Company
ERIC	Educational Resources Information Center
EROS	Earth Resources Observation System
ERTS	Earth Resources Technology Satellite
ESA	European Space Agency
ESIC	U.S. Earth Sciences Information Center (formerly NCIC)
ESRI	Environmental Systems Research Institute
exp.	expanded
FAA	U.S. Federal Aviation Agency
FGDC	U.S. Federal Geographic Data Committee
FID	International Federation for Documentation
FIPS	U.S. Federal Information Processing Standard
FM	field manual
FTU	first-time use
G&M	Geography and Map Division of LC
GB	gigabyte
GIS	geographic information system: an information system in which spatial data stored, retrieved, displayed, and analyzed
GLIS	Global Land Information System
GMD	general material designation
GNC	global navigation chart
GNIS	Geographic Names Information System
GODORT	ALA Government Documents Round Table
GOES	Geostationary Operational Environmental Satellite
GPO	U.S. Government Printing Office
GPS	Global Positioning System
GRASS	Geographic Resource Analysis Support System
GSA	U.S. General Services Administration
GSGS	Great Britain. War Office. General Staff. Geographical Section
GUGK	Soviet Union. Glavnoe upravlenie geodezii i kartografii
HEW	U.S. Department of Health, Education, and Welfare

HMSO	Great Britain's His/Her Majesty's Stationery Office
HUD	U.S. Department of Housing and Urban Development
ICA	International Cartographic Association
IFLA	International Federation of Library Associations and Institutions
IFLAG&M	IFLA Geography and Map Section
IGU	International Geographical Union
IMW	*International map of the world at 1:1,000,000*
IR	infrared
ISBD	International Standard Bibliographic Description
ISBD(CM)	International Standard Bibliographic Description (Cartographic Materials)
JCP	U.S. Congress. Joint Committee on Printing
JNC	*Jet navigation chart*
JOG	*Joint operations graphic*
JSC	Joint Steering Committee for the Revision of AACR
KWIC	key word in context
KWOC	key word out of context
Landsat	Land Satellite, formerly ERTS
LC	U.S. Library of Congress
LCG&M	Library of Congress, Geography and Map Division
LCSH	Library of Congress Subject Headings
LIBER	Ligue des Bibliothèques Europénnes de Recherche
LRTS	*Library resources and technical services*
MARBI	MAchine-Readable Bibliographic Information Committee
MARC	MAchine-Readable Cataloging
MB	megabyte
MCIS	Map and Chart Information System
MIO	U.S. Map Information Office
MIS	Map Indexing System
MLC	minimal level cataloging
MOUG	Map Online Users Group
MR	*Mineral investigations resource map, MR-(USGS)*

MSS	multispectral scanner
NACIS	North American Cartographic Information Society
NAF	name authority file
NAPP	National Aerial Photography Program
NARA	U.S. National Archives and Records Administration
NASA	U.S. National Aeronautics and Space Administration
NCIC	U.S. National Cartographic Information Center (now ESIC)
NGDC	U.S. National Geophysical Data Center
NHAP	National High Altitude Photography Program
NIH	U.S. National Institutes of Health
NIMA	U.S. National Imagery and Mapping Agency
NOAA	U.S. National Oceanic and Atmospheric Administration
NOS	U.S. National Ocean Service/Survey
NTIS	U.S. National Technical Information Service
NUC CM	*National union catalog, cartographic materials*
NYPL	New York Public Library
OCLC	Online Computer Library Center; formerly Ohio College Library Center
ONC	*Operational navigational chart*
op	out of print
OULCS	Ontario (Canada) University Library Cooperative System
PAIGH	Pan American Institute of Geography and History
PAR	Parsons classification
PB	petabyte
PC	personal computer; microcomputer
PERS	*Photogrammetric engineering and remote sensing*
ppi	pixels per inch
PR	public relations
PRECIS	Preserved Context Indexing System
proc.	proceedings
quad	USGS topographic quadrangle
RAM	random access memory
RBMS	ALA Rare Books and Manuscripts Section

RBV	return-beam vidicon
rev.	revised
r.f.	representative fraction, e.g., scale of 1:20,000
r.h.	relative humidity
RLG	Research Libraries Group
RLIN	Research Libraries Network
ROM	read-only memory
RQ	a journal, formerly *Reference quarterly*
RTSD	ALA Resources and Technical Services Division; now ALCTS
RV	Reise und Verkehrsverlag
SAC	*Sectional aeronautical chart*
SCS	U.S. Soil Conservation Service
SGML	Standard Generalized Markup Language
s.l.	*sine loco*; no place of publication given
SLAG&M	Special Libraries Association Geography and Map Division
SLAR	side-looking airborne radar
SMD	specific material designation
s.n.	*sine nomine*; no publisher given
SOLINET	Southeastern Library Network
SSD	standard series designation
SuDocs	U.S. Superintendent of Documents
suppl.	supplement
TB	terabyte
TIGER	Topologically Integrated Geographic Encoding and Referencing System
TM	technical manual (U.S. Department of the Army); technical memorandum; Thematic Mapper (sensor on Landsat satellites)
TOPOCOM	U.S. Army. Topographic Command
TVA	U.S. Tennessee Valley Authority
UBC	universal bibliographic control
UCB	University of California, Berkeley
UCSC	University of California, Santa Cruz
UK	United Kingdom

UN	United Nations
UNESCO	UN Educational, Scientific, and Cultural Organization
URL	universal resource locator
U.S.	United States
USFS	U.S. Forest Service
USGS	United States Geological Survey
USSR	Union of Soviet Socialist Republics
UTM	Universal Transverse Mercator
UV	ultraviolet
vol.	volume
VPF	vector product format
WAC	World aeronautical chart
WAML	Western Association of Map Libraries
Web	World Wide Web
WLN	Washington Library Network
WRS	Worldwide Reference System
WWW	World Wide Web

1

Selection
and Acquisition

Selection

Collection Development Policies
and Acquisition Policies

Although spatial-data collections come in many different sizes, organizations, and facilities, the beginning problem for each is selection, followed closely by acquisition. Selection resolves itself into a question of what sorts of materials your clientele needs, which in turn requires examining the composition of the clientele. Some libraries serve only one or two user groups. For example, a school library knows that its users are students of a given age plus teachers; users of historical-society libraries are interested not only in a given, often relatively small area but probably also in a given time period; and so forth (Loggan 1990). These libraries' needs are limited by level and type of scholastic attainment, or by narrowly defined area or subject, or by a combination of all of the aforementioned.

But for public libraries and university and college libraries, user needs are much wider. A public library, serving as it does the needs of a heterogeneous public of all ages and interests, needs more general maps, recreational maps, and local maps. The academic library serves a clientele that is in the main more restricted with respect to age, but while its primary purpose is to support the curricula, it must bolster the research needs of the faculty; if it is part of a public institution, it often serves the widely varying requirements of off-campus users as well.

Tempting though it may be for a librarian new to a collection immediately to leap in and make changes, it is a far better idea to observe users and use patterns for a few months, paying attention to the most frequently asked reference questions, looking at the refile areas to see which items are most often away from home or in need of repair, and asking those persons who have worked with the collection previously (if anyone is either available or will admit to it) what questions are most often asked. Fairly soon, perhaps within a month if it is a busy time of year (which for public libraries is all year, and for academic libraries is while classes are in session), a general user profile, dependent upon the range of interests of the patrons, will emerge. Thus, in a library serving predominantly an undergraduate college population, at least half the questions may be answered with large-scale topographic maps of the county or state in which the college is located; but in an institution that grants graduate degrees, that portion of the reference questions may be answered by large-scale maps of Nigeria or the Amazon River basin (Brunvand 1991). Entering into informal conversations with repeat users—and for that matter, disgruntled users—about the sorts of materials they would like to see in the collection is a useful device, as is paying attention to seasonal requests such as ski-trail maps in winter and hiking maps in summer.

Sad to say, there are other restrictive factors, far less pleasant than patron needs, that must be taken into account while working on selection policy. Most notable among these are available budget and financial support projections for the future (Koerner 1972, 511). Also to be considered are the strengths and weaknesses of the collection. Does it need shoring up in places? May the library begin collecting in a new area, or at a new scale, or in a material type not previously considered appropriate?

Once the librarian has determined the clientele's needs, it is time to write (and to remember to keep the word-processing file in an obvious place so that one may easily update it) what is variously termed either an acquisition policy or a collection-development policy; which one it is and the details of how it looks will be determined by the institution that holds the collection. The CDP (by whatever name) must be based on the type of clientele (which is dictated by the kind of institution), the information needs of the users, and miscellaneous matters such as consortial agreements and the proximity or lack thereof to other collections (Doehlert 1984, 189–90).

There are some materials—in hard copy or digital form or both, again depending upon use patterns—that almost any collection may profitably obtain. Reference and thematic maps of the Earth as a whole, maps of continents and nations (the 8.5" x 11" maps produced by the U.S. Central Intelligence Agency have saved many a map librarian's hash), topographic series of the world (starting at small scales such as 1:5,000,000 or 1:1,000,000 and progressing toward larger scales as the exchequer permits), a physical-political globe, a reputable world atlas, an atlas of the state in which the collection is located, aerial photographs of the immediate area, and monographs and serials appropriate to the clientele are at the top of the list. Almost no collection can survive without outline and base maps suitable for photocopying or able to be printed out on demand (preferably in color), usually the aforementioned 8.5" x 11" in size. Public-school libraries may find it appropriate to focus on large-scale (e.g., 1:24,000 or 1:25,000, as available) coverage of the local area, a few maps of the state (preferably physical-political), and thematic maps emphasizing the state's prime resources (e.g., a mining map, an agricultural map, etc.) plus the old standby, the road map (Seavey 1980, 42; Kunz 1960, 57). More specific information on all of the preceding is given in the following section on "Spatial Data and Supporting Materials."

The Acquisition Policy

The acquisition policy—which must be a written document on file, not just an oral tradition—should include philosophy and goals, a clear statement of those sharing responsibility for implementing the collection's objectives, an enumeration of the geographical areas to be represented in the collection (in priority ranking, with limiting parameters of subject, scale, and date), a definition of the extent of support materials (such as gazetteers, journals, and cartobibliographies) to be acquired, and a list of materials that are out of scope for the collection. Although the inclusion of digital data as a vital part of almost any collection has considerable implications in many areas—all the way from equipment to staffing to training—these implications are not generally mentioned in the policy. If at all possible, the acquisition policy should be written by the librarian in conjunction with staff members as needed (Schorr 1974b, 30; Koerner 1972, 511).

The Collection-Development Policy (CDP)

Those librarians working in academic libraries or in public libraries that are in consortia (especially when the latter includes a preponderance of academic libraries) will often be dealing with CDPs. Even had relatively hard times not come upon academe, the sheer amount, not to mention the exponential growth, of information (first in hardcopy form and increasingly in digital form through such vehicles as the World Wide Web) would have forced these libraries to work toward cooperative collection development, and to realize that although no one library can be Alexandria, all libraries together can constitute its twentieth-century equivalent (Mosher and Pankake 1983; Dowd 1980; ACM Conference 1976; http://www.alexandria.ucsb.edu). So an important first step before embarking on a library's CDP is to meet with other librarians within the same region or consortium, and in effect to divide up the territory, in meetings that may be faintly reminiscent of Spain and Portugal bisecting the world in the Treaty of Tordesillas in 1494 ("If you'll take Australia, then my library will be responsible for Micronesia") (Christiansen, Davis, and Reed-Scott 1983; *Guide for written collection policy statements 1996*). As a beginning, it is advisable for all concerned to read *Guidelines for collection development 1979* and *Guide for written policy statements 1996*.

Two major problems may immediately arise. One is that there have previously seldom been CDP patterns for anything other than subjects (e.g., geology). The second is harder to tackle. There seems to be a feeling amongst librarians formulating CDPs or coordinating such formulations that CDPs for all the "funny" (here meaning peculiar) formats (e.g., newspapers, manuscripts, government publications, spatial data) should be done last, and that all the subject CDPs should be done first, with apparently no consideration for inclusion of the special formats or categories. Because all of the formats cover many different subjects, this is a strategy doomed to disaster. In advance of any CDP writing within the library as a whole, spatial-data librarians should figure out what subjects should include cartographic materials, then find out which librarians are writing those CDPs, make appointments with them, and bring to the meetings relevant examples of spatial data. If this is not done, the spatial-data CDP will not be consistent with the other CDPs. And if CDPs in state institutions come to have the legal effect of regulations, a spatial-data materials collection could well discover that it has no legal grounds for obtaining certain types of materials. For example, if globes are not specifically mentioned in the spatial-data policy, the collection has no written basis for obtaining them. TAKE NOTHING FOR GRANTED. The spatial-data CDP must be formatted in exactly the same way as the subject CDPs.

The basis of any CDP is the collecting-intensity guide, which is often as follows:

0 out of scope
1 minimal information level
2 basic information level
3 study or instructional support level
4 research level
5 comprehensive level
(Mosher and Pankake 1983, 427)

It may take a librarian several years of working with spatial data, and a few visits to the Library of Congress, to learn what "exhaustive" means; so visiting other collections and getting some perspective as to how different libraries collect, and how much they collect, is necessary. One of the many glories of the WWW is that one may view the CDP of the Library of Congress for Maps, Atlases, and Remote-Sensing Images, and for Geography and Cartography, both formulated in 1995, at LC's Website (gopher://marvel.loc.gov/00/research/collections.catalogs/collections/).

A sense of realism is a *sine qua non* for correctly filling in the collecting-intensity numbers in the CDP. The librarian should cast a cold, analytical look at whether a higher collecting level is justified by present activities and institution plans for the future, and also at whether the collection has the support of the users and library administration. It also helps to figure out, in advance, how much a higher level will cost, not just in dollar terms (easily done even for those of us to whom the phrase "mathematical logic" is a contradiction in terms: for example, for a map series, figure out the total number of sheets in the relevant series and multiply by sheet cost, remembering to guesstimate inflation) but also in storage and staff time (Hagen 1977, 216–17; Seavey 1981 and 1984; and Sutherland 1985).

The main difficulty in fitting what is often very modestly called the Map Room into a CDP format is that almost all spatial-data collections, although composed mainly of maps, atlases, and currently a fair number of CD-ROMs (plus occasionally a few good aerial photographs), encompass not only several different formats (maps, views, sections, and so on; remote-sensing imagery; globes; models; books and serials; all of the preceding but in digital form; etc.), but also many different subjects. Remembering to fit all of those different formats and subjects into the CDP is a demanding task. This fitting-in process becomes most noticeable in the writing of the conspectus, which is composed of classification numbers to be included in the collection. The good news about the conspectus is that LC (Library of Congress) classification, the best classification for spatial data, is preferred. The bad news is that the spatial-data call-number sequence may receive in the conspectus but one line ("G3190-9999"). This is obviously not going to work, so just expand as needed. Fortunately, the RLG (Research Libraries Group) conspectus worksheet, used by many libraries, is quite detailed. See the online conspectus of the University of California/Stanford Map Libraries Group, at the WAML homepage, given in chapter 7 in the section "Continuing Education."

Implied in the CDP will be the collection's withdrawal policy, shown by areas of greatest emphasis, cutoff dates for acquisition, and so forth. A full statement of withdrawal policy is appropriately placed in the Map Room procedures manual because so much of withdrawal is purely mechanical (e.g., keeping only the latest edition of road maps, or of topographic sheets for any but a given area) (Selmer 1979).

The librarian should write CDPs very carefully and in the full expectation of having to live with the policy fundamentally as it is originally written, incorporating changes only when they are fully justified. In all cases, working with other librarians and library advisory boards or with other user groups is a wise idea.

CDPs for Spatial Data in Digital Form

In theory, all it should take to add yet another format to a CDP is a one-line, formal translation of "yes, we collect that also." For an example of an all-purpose phrase, try: "Library collects or provides access to digital data using the same general guidelines and area parameters as are applied to selecting all other formats of spatial data; that is, the data must support the curricula and research of the students and faculty of the University of. . . ." But in practice, more guidance is of assistance in what one author has called "Herding Cats: Options for Organizing Electronic Resources" (Vellucci 1996).

There was a time when libraries were places in which sedate ladies and gentlemen worked. There were settled, traditional methods of performing collection management. Persons working with spatial data had fairly rigid patterns of publication or issuance with which to work—maps, remote-sensing images, book-format materials; government agencies, commercial firms. These patterns existed because of the large investment and long payback period required for mapping surveys and satellite missions. Also, mapmaking and even atlas-making is an expensive enterprise—four-color, large-format printing presses dictate that. In the early and mid-1970s, the use of computing machinery for collecting imagery took a massive step forward, with the launching of the Landsat satellite in 1972 and the ever-increasing experimentation with automated cartography (as evidenced in the Auto-Carto conferences). On the mapping front, by the mid-1980s, Western-world mapmaking agencies were getting closer and closer to using computers to make base-map series, in order to cut revision costs in the long run. But "That was then . . . this is now," and we are up past our eyeteeth in digital data. A brief look at history, using one library as an example: The University of California, Santa Barbara, Library (now the Davidson Library) had, in 1987, a "Collection Development Policy for Computer-Accessed Information," which still reads very well, emphasizing as it does the most important point—that one collects the same subjects in digital format as one does in hardcopy formats, keeping a wary eye on the user- and staff-training, and software and hardware, implications of digital purchases. The Map and Imagery Laboratory (MIL) in the same library had at that time data on diskettes and nine-track tapes. In the early 1990s, CD-ROMs began to appear in map libraries; MIL wrote a stop-gap collection-development statement for spatial data in digital form in late 1991, admittedly only for digital data held in house.The highly attractive concept of graciously allowing someone else to pay for disk space to hold data had not yet appeared. Coincidentally, an *LRTS* article noted the "continued emphasis on electronic formats" (Lehmann and Spohrer 1992, 299). In June 1994, the Library of Congress issued its most recent edition of a collection policy for "Optical and Electronic Computer Files" (gopher://marvel.loc.gov/00/research/collections.catalogs/collections/).

Spatial-data collections have not just been a part of all this, they have been in the forefront. Although digital data is heavily used in many libraries, it has in the not-too-distant past been only in the form of online catalogs and as computer versions of indexes such as *Dissertation abstracts*. It is in spatial data and government documents that actual data in digital form has been, and is still being, most frequently acquired in large amounts—and has been notably so for the past four or five years. This has been caused mainly by the heavy dependence of "map" collections upon federal agencies for spatial data, and the strong move toward digital data by those agencies over the last decade. Also, map librarians are so accustomed to dealing with several different formats that one or two more raise scarcely a ripple of concern—especially when those formats are ones that users and library administration find to be, in some strange way, exciting.

For the last year or two, we are increasingly looking at data available over the WWW. What a marvelous concept! Letting someone *else* store, maintain, and service data! At the base of all this is supporting users' needs, and focusing on information rather than on any one format (McGlammery 1994 and 1995). The next point is, as always, equipment and staff support. Libraries have long been equipped to support users of the book or microform, or in some cases spatial-data hardcopy formats: book stacks, tables, map cases, file cabinets, buildings with appropriate heating or air conditioning, and lighting. Now when we select appropriate data for users, we need to think about the appropriate infrastructure—network connects, PCs/UNIX workstations, Web browsers, cabling throughout the library, speed of transmission of data over each major segment of cabling, and appropriate reference training. Very often, so-called "map collections" are staffed by persons who perform both reference and technical services, so it has been easy for the selection manager to inform the technical-processing and reference staff as to what will be required—just a quick look in the mirror, and it was done.

Now the decision is not whether to collect digital data; it is, for Internet resources, whether to download and keep in house, or to have pointers to those resources. In the latter case, one needs helper software applications to check every address at least once a week and, if it is gone or changed, to notify a human being in order to hunt up the new URL. There are a couple of influences on this decision, which boil down to keeping in house if:

- the item is frequently requested

- the library has sufficient disk space

- the library has slow communications and downloading large files is very time-consuming

- the collection manager has reason to believe that the site is unstable.

Selection is exercised for digital formats as it is for hardcopy formats; although now we carefully scrutinize any licensing agreements, and we view documentation with an eagle eye (bad memories of those expensive, no-catalog-record microform sets tend to make a librarian suspicious). But we still judge the quality of an item by its source's reputation and by reviews. We still may intentionally select poor data so that users may compare it with better data; the object of libraries is for persons to decide for themselves. Users may upon occasion misuse data; some of them have done so with hard copy, and there is no reason to suppose that will change with digital data.

All of which means that a staff that has not increased (and perhaps has even decreased) may as much as double its workload when dealing with digital data as it must do everything from building and repairing Websites to learning the basics of several different software packages and then writing guides for users. At the same time, the demand for information that is available only in traditional formats continues and seems to show little diminution, probably largely because as much as 90 percent of all spatial data is available only in hardcopy form.

Collaboration is now even more important, as we try to provide access to more data, with the same number of staff. An example of this is collaborative building of subject-oriented Internet-resource collections, which is especially important. Let's not all do the same work over and over, the way we did cataloging before USMARC, OCLC, RLIN, and WLN. Let's go at this in a subject/discipline fashion, and divide up the work. As an example of how this may be done, the University of California, Riverside, Library has in InfoMine a setup whereby librarians from several of the UC libraries add what are in effect brief cataloging records on Internet resources to the UCR Web page, INFOMINE (http://lib-www.ucr.edu/).

Spatial Data and Supporting Materials: A Guide Through the Maze

The characteristic of spatial data that can make writing CDPs a bit of a headache—the multiplicity of formats and subjects—has an equivalent effect on actual selection decisions. "So many superb items, so little money" is a good summary. This section works its way through the various types of spatial data (maps, charts, views, sections, diagrams; globes and models; atlases; remote-sensing imagery; digital data) and then through supporting materials (books other than atlases; serials; vertical-file material; and anything left over). The reader should restrain all impulses to panic, and be assured that everything does indeed fit together logically.

Maps, Charts, Plans, Sections, Views, and So Forth

> ❖ *Maps are, in the final analysis,*
> *the way geographers think.*
> —R. Abler 1988

Of all spatial data, the one constituting the bulk of almost any collection is the map and its kindred spirits—the chart, the plan, the section, the view, and the diagram. The word *map* has been defined many times and in many ways. For our purposes, it is the depiction of a geographical area (imaginary or real), usually on a flat piece of paper but increasingly in digital form. The special features of the latter are dealt with in the section on digital data, because the features of any spatial data in digital form are most easily attacked as a whole. A *chart* is a map intended for navigational (aeronautical or nautical) purposes. *Plans* are large-scale (perhaps 1:5,000 or greater) maps, usually of very small areas, such as a small campus, a freeway intersection, or the area upon which a building stands; it stops just short of *architectural plans,* which are plans of a building rather than of the ground upon which the building stands. *Sections* are vertical looks at the Earth (in contrast to the map's horizontal look, as if the viewer were directly above and on a plane perpendicular to the line of sight), and usually are a vertical slice of the Earth; sections are most often geologic (showing layers of geologic formations, like layers of a somewhat gritty cake), but they may be topographic and look like a profile. There is frequently a vertical-scale exaggeration in comparison with the horizontal scale; the Earth's roughnesses (what we in awe call mountains) are slight in comparison to the Earth's overall size. This means that the scale used for the elevation is larger than the scale used for the horizontal distance covered by the slice. The *stratigraphic column*—which shows somewhat stylized geologic formations at a given point in a section— may be included with the section as a type. Usually the columns, which do indeed look like columns, travel in groups; there may easily be twenty or so on a sheet of paper, with the object of showing the changes in geology along an imaginary line drawn on the surface of the Earth. *Views, panoramas,* and the like are maps in which the viewpoint has been shifted from directly above an area to an oblique view, so that there is often a horizon in the depiction; many of these are very close to pictures, and repose beautifully in the borderland between maps and pictures. They are frequently of cities and towns, or of popular recreational (especially mountainous) areas; they tend to have cultural and natural features labeled.

But let us get back to maps, which, because of the substantial portion they compose of almost any collection, merit discussion *in extenso.* There is something about maps that seems to bring about the irresistible urge in their observers to put them into categories, but seldom do the categorizers agree with each other as to what those categories should be. The biggest argument is what is a general map as compared to a thematic map, with able persons taking different points of view. For example, Modelski classifies maps into four broad groups: small-scale general maps of large areas; large-scale detailed topographic sheets; large-scale navigational charts; and thematic maps (Modelski 1977, 143). Farrell and Desbarats, in contrast, consider navigational charts to be thematic maps (1981, 32). Fighting our way through a welter of disagreements, we find that the major difference between the two is that for Farrell and Desbarats a thematic map will emphasize one particular subject, whereas a general map has no such focus but rather is intended to give an overall view of an area. *Information sources 1990* (appendix 2A) has an excellent section, "Part 5, Types of Mapping," with essays and citations to sources of information for large categories of maps, such as earth-science maps.

For our look at the world of maps, we shall use the LC Schedule G classification subject code for maps, largely because it is the best scheme for classifying spatial data, and it behooves a librarian to know it. The version used in this chapter has some terms that are no longer in the current version of Schedule G but are helpful for the purposes of this chapter, and have therefore been left in (see, for example, the expansion of C2). See chapter 2 for a detailed explanation of how the LC subject code is constructed.

First come the maps that receive no subject code in LC classification, the general-reference maps. These are very often planimetric, meaning that they show horizontal locations only, with no indication of elevation. In this group are general maps of countries, such as the excellent ones issued by the U.S. Central Intelligence Agency, and, for LC purposes, the extremely important topographic map series, which are included here because they show both landforms (usually by means of contour lines) and cultural features, and their intent is to provide a general albeit detailed look at a given area. Topographic sheets are used as a basis for all other maps, and are consequently often called *base maps*. A *topographic series* is a group of sheets that depict physical and cultural detail, at scales (at least on a national basis) mostly between 1:10,000 and 1:250,000, with "base map" scales most often between 1:10,000 and 1:50,000. For example, the base map of the United States has for many years been the 1:24,000-scale, 7.5-minute topographic-quadrangle (often called just "quads") series authored and published by the U.S. Geological Survey (USGS)—but there are several other scales, such as 1:62,500 (abandoned), 1:100,000, and 1:250,000. Topographic series are usually issued by either civilian or military governmental agencies, such as national surveys or the mapping divisions of defense departments. Because of their importance, a considerable amount has been written about them (in appendix 2A for summary works, see Bohme 1989-1993 and Larsgaard 1984 and 1993).

Topographic series may be on an international basis, such as the classic sets that almost all collections need:

American Geographical Society of New York. 1948–1975. *World 1:5,000,000*. New York: The Society.

Soviet Union. Main Administration of Geodesy and Cartography. 1965– . *Karta mira 1:2,500,000 = World map 1:2,500,000*. Moscow: The Administration.

International map of the world 1:1,000,000. 1912–1987. Various places: various publishers [done on a national basis]. (For a recent article concerning its demise, see Winchester 1995.)

United States. Defense Mapping Agency. 1946–83? *World 1:1,000,000 (AMS 1301)*. Washington, D.C.: The Agency [earlier sheets under former name, Army Map Service; series cancelled by 1983].

————. 1965– . *Joint operations graphic, JOG (1501)*, 1:250,000. Washington, D.C.: The Agency.

Topographic series are the most basic type of map, accounting for perhaps 75 percent of all map sheets distributed (Winearls 1968, 25).

Also included in the general maps category are city maps, such as those issued by chambers of commerce (see Blachut 1979 in appendix 2A), and celestial charts (see Warner 1979 in appendix 2A).

Moving on to thematic mapping, we need to mention briefly the books on thematic mapping as a whole, which concern how to make such maps (see Cuff and Mattson 1982; Muehrcke and Muehrcke 1992; and Lewis 1977 in appendix 2A); the estimable, invaluable Arthur Robinson wrote a superb work on early (to about 1800) thematic mapping (see Robinson 1982 in appendix 2A). And now let us deal with the various individual kinds of thematic maps.

A   Special category maps and atlases

.A1   Outline and base maps. Cities (collective).
.A2   Index maps.
.A3   Aerial views. Bird's-eye-views.
.A4   Photomaps.
.A5   Pictorial maps.
.A6   Cartoon maps.
.A7   Tactile maps.
.A8   Special geographical names.
.A9   Special formats (e.g., cloth).

With a considerable amount of nerve, LC commences with its wastebasket category, to be used only when an item is not a general map or equivalent, and subject codes in .B through .S do not apply. This catchall classification starts with some tricky terminology for the unwary. In the case of .A1, "base maps" does not refer to the standard topographic series but rather to the kind of maps that are little more than an outline (we all used these in eighth-grade geography), or maps that are in the opinion of the publisher base maps and have the word "base" as part of the title or subtitle. Facts on File and World Eagle have both issued loose-leaf sets of base maps; see in appendix 2A entries under "World Eagle" and *Historical maps on file, Maps on file, Outline maps on file*, and *State maps on file*. USGS calls some of its state maps "base maps."

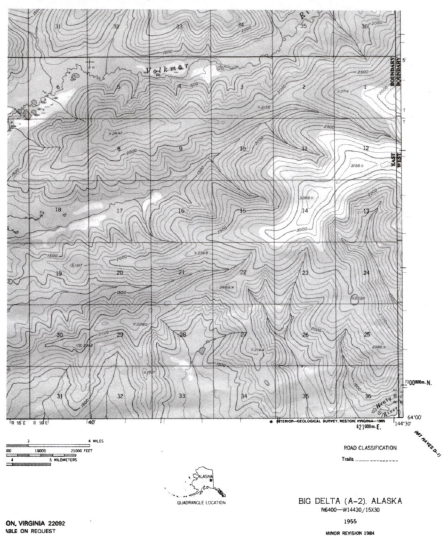

Figure 1.1. USGS topographic map. United States. Geological Survey. 1985. Big Delta (A-2), Alaska. Minor rev. 1984. Scale 1:63,630. Reston, Va.: USGS.

A librarian soon learns—and hopes ardently—that where maps are, indexes often follow. Any group of maps having a large number of separate sheets (say, more than four) either has or needs an index, which brings us to .A2, to be used only for topographic-series indexes; all other indexes are classed by subject (e.g., a geologic map index is classed at .C5). An *index* is a map of an area covered by a group of maps with an overlay, sometimes in a different color, of the locations and numbers or names of the individual maps of the series. Very large map series, or groups of series that nest together, such as the Canadian National Topographic System (NTS), may have an index to the indexes, a situation that any librarian seasoned by bibliographies of bibliographies can accept with equanimity. Indexes should be filed with the series they index if at all possible; because manual indexes are very time-consuming to fill in, open-stack collections often keep manual indexes heavily guarded in the workroom. It would be ideal to have the index online; Christopher Baruth of the American Geographical Society Collection (Golda Meir Library, University of Wisconsin–Milwaukee) has done some work in this area with his software, Geodex, which is intended for the creation of sheet-level, brief bibliographic records for map series. This section now also includes "Digital maps" at .A25; these are discussed in the section on digital data.

.A3 includes the previously mentioned views; these are not as frequently published as they were in the late nineteenth and early twentieth centuries, except for recreational areas (see Hebert 1984; Hyde 1988; and Reps 1984 in appendix 2A). This also includes axonometric maps (large-scale, very detailed maps of cities in which buildings are shown in perspective), such as those by Bollmann, David Fox and Kistler. The next subject code, .A4, is really a format and thus is treated with the larger category to which it belongs—remote-sensing imagery—later in this section.

The remaining subject codes in .A (.A5, .A6, .A7, .A8, and .A9) are the "fun" maps: pictorial maps (drawings of products produced in a given state, etc., mostly for elementary schools); cartoon maps, including cartograms; and cartographic materials in special formats. For a general work on pictorial maps, see Holmes 1991 in appendix 2A; for fabric maps, see Bond 1984 and Doll 1988; for tactile maps, United States LC National Library 1987; and for mental maps Peterson 1987 and "Vertical" 1985. For more information on tactile maps, see the section titled "Relief Models" further on in this chapter. Mental maps are of the type that show the New Yorker's view of the rest of the world; the area is depicted in a mentally realistic rather than a physically realistic way, or a quantity of a subject is depicted through sizing an area according to the quantity involved. One of the first of these to gain wide circulation was:

> British Columbia. University. School of Community and Regional Planning. 1971. *Isodemographic map of Canada*. One square inch represents 60,000 people. Ottawa: Department of Fisheries and Forestry.

Category .A8 refers to maps concerning place names of special historical, national, or religious significance, e.g., Santa Claus.

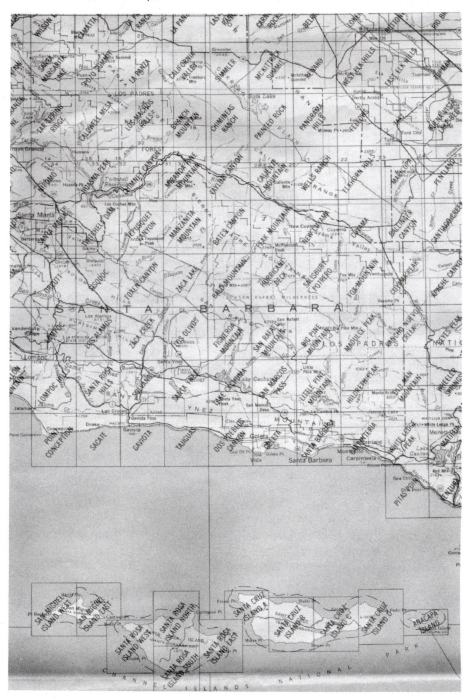

Figure 1.2. USGS topographic-quadrangle index. United States. Geological Survey. 1996. California: index to topographic and other map coverage. Reston, Va.: USGS.

B Mathematical geography

.B1 Astronomical observatories and observations.
.B2 Movements of the Earth.
.B3 Geodetic surveys.
.B5 Surveying.
.B7 Cartography.
.B8 Comparative area maps.

Maps in this group are relatively few, with the most common being time-zone maps, triangulation diagrams, and those noting the extent of surveys or giving examples of projection types. The map most often seen by librarians in collections in the United States is the U.S.-depository map (in various editions) from the U.S. Department of State, *Standard time zones of the world*; but encyclopedias often have time-zone maps if the depository map is not readily available. For a history of the rectangular survey in the United States, see White 1983 in appendix 2A; see the most current publications list of the U.S. National Geodetic Survey for a list of publications, and especially its reference work, *Geodetic glossary* (1987, appendix 2A). For publications on projections, see appendix 2B; for a bibliography on surveying, see Grewe 1984 in appendix 2A.

C Physical sciences

.C1 General.
.C18 Relief models. Raised relief globes.
.C2 Physiography.
.C22 Relief features.
.C221 Spot heights. Elevations.
.C222 Contours. Form lines.
.C223 Hachures.
.C224 Shaded relief.
.C225 Gradient tints. Layer tints.
.C227 Landform drawings. Trachography.
.C228 Anaglyphs and stereographs.
.C229 Bathymetry. Soundings. Bottom characteristics.
.C23 Caves.
.C28 Ground characteristics. Surface quality. Terrain studies.

This is a large and very important section of the LC subject code, so we will look at it in segments. First of all, note that relief models and raised-relief globes (the latter are rare) have the LC subject code .C18; these are dealt with in the section in this chapter on globes and models. .C2 includes profiles and diagrams that do not exhibit geologic information. In appendix 2A, see for geomorphological mapping Allen 1972, Applied 1988, High mountain 1987, *Manual* 1972, Problems 1963, and Verstappen 1977a and 1977b.

Relief features have been depicted in many different ways over the centuries; the .C22 section mentions the most well-known ones. Spot heights, or elevations, are most useful in combination with other methods, such as contouring and hachuring. Indeed, for all except the landform drawings and the anaglyphs, relief-feature types are mainly used on general maps, rather than being the only information given; that is, a map with just spot heights on it, or just contours, or just hachures, would be unusual.

Figure 1.3. A profile. [Fig. 25] Profile along line A-B, pl. XI. Vertical scale about two and one-half times the horizontal. In Salisbury, R. D., and W. W. Atwood. 1908. The interpretation of topographic map, p. 47. (U.S. Geological Survey Professional Paper 60). Washington, D.C.: GPO.

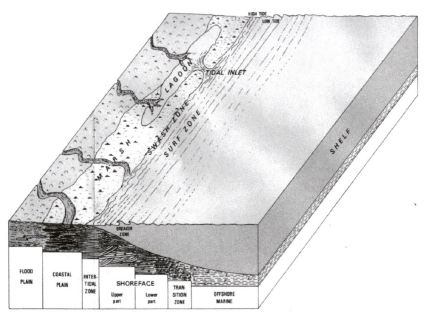

Figure 1.4. A diagram. Mytton, J. W., and G. B. Schneider. 1987. Interpretive geology of the Chaco area, northwestern New Mexico. Scale 1:24,000. Reston, Va.: USGS.

Contour lines are presently the most used form of cartographic relief portrayal because they represent form relatively well and because they give a quantitative altitudinal value to a large number of points. This is a radical about-face from the very early years of topographic mapping, when the French national survey painstakingly used contour lines to derive hachures but then left the contour lines off the final maps. *Contour lines* are curves produced by the intersection of imaginary horizontal planes at a selected interval with the three-dimensional shape of the terrain; they are usually shown in brown. *Form lines,* which look like dashed contour lines, are contour lines that have been sketched in through general observation rather than instrumentally determined by exact measurement.

Hachuring, a system in which light is assumed to fall in vertical rays upon slopes (the illumination received by each slope varying in proportion to its divergence from the plane of the horizontal), was much used on official national topographic sheets in Europe during the nineteenth century; currently it is used, for example, by the National Geographic Society, some European topographical surveys, and the U.S. Forest Service. When poorly done, hachuring gives a map the appearance of having caterpillars firmly affixed to its surface. Shaded relief gives a realistic appearance, and is commonly used with contouring.

Gradient tints or, as they may occasionally be called, *hypsometric tints,* use different colors and shades, usually between widely spaced contour lines, to show elevation. There is a chance for serious user misinterpretation when, as so often happens, green is used to show lower elevations: the credulous user may believe that Death Valley is verdant.

Landform drawings may be taken to include the hill and mountain profiles (sometimes called "sugarloafs") in early maps, but the term is most often applied to the more sophisticated twentieth-century versions of physiographic sketching, as epitomized by the works of Erwin Raisz and A. K. Lobeck; *trachography* refers to the type of careful, evocative landform drawings done by Raisz. See Larsgaard 1984, 9–l8 (appendix 2A), for a fuller discussion of relief methods.

Anaglyphs are seldom seen these days, and when seen are considerable fun to look at but a little hard to believe. The idea here is to have the right component of an image printed in one color (usually red) upon the left component (usually blue), so that a three-dimensional effect is produced when the user looks through correspondingly colored filters of a pair of spectacles. Viewed without the spectacles, an anaglyphic map looks like a case of extremely bad registration; with the glasses, the appearance is highly effective. For an example of this type of map, see:

Cygnus Graphic. 1988. *The Grand Canyon of the Colorado River.* 1:300,000. Phoenix, Ariz.: Cygnus Graphic. (*Cygnus Graphic OPTI-RELIEF map*)

A stereograph may be either a pair of stereoscopic images (the stereoscopic effect is frequently used for viewing aerial photographs), or it may be an image composed of two superimposed stereoscopic images, which produces a three-dimensional effect when viewed with a stereoscope.

Although in theory .C229 includes both nautical charting and depictions of the morphology of the ocean bottom, in practice nautical charts are classified at .P5. The morphology of the ocean bottom has been of considerable interest, at least to scientists, for many years. This interest dates back to the laying of cable on the Atlantic Ocean floor, which was made possible, at least in part, by Matthew Fontaine Maury's producing the first map of the floor of the North Atlantic Ocean (James and Martin 1981, 151, in appendix 2A). In this century, the maps of ocean floors published by the National Geographic Society (Atlantic Ocean floor, 1968; Indian Ocean floor, 1967; Mediterranean floor, 1982; and Pacific Ocean floor, 1969) are of substantial interest to the general public. The works of Bruce Heezen (deceased) and Marie Tharpe, upon which the Society's maps are based, are many in number and thus will not be listed here; suffice to say that the name of either or both on an ocean-floor map is an imprimatur of skill and experience.

Cave maps (.C23) are not especially common and are most likely to turn up in studies of karst topography, where the limestone is often honeycombed with caves. For a brief survey article on cave mapping, see Gale 1983 in appendix 2A. One would appreciate seeing articles or monographs on cave maps of various countries, such as the article by John Dunkley, "Maps of Australian caves and karst" (Dunkley 1996). .C28, terrain studies and ground characteristics, is another relatively little-used classification number. It is apparently intended for physiographic maps that do not fit neatly into any of the rest of the classification.

C3   Hydrology
.C31   Hydrographic surveys. Status. Progress.
.C315   Drainage basins.
.C32   Floods.
.C34   Ground water.
.C35   Water composition and quality.
.C36   Mineral water.
.C38   Glaciers.

The most common type of hydrologic map shows drainage of rivers and streams, closely followed in popularity by maps of ground water, water quality, and glaciation. Librarians working in flood-prone areas may find relevance (if not relief) in Burkham 1978 and Guide 1988 in appendix 2A. .C34 and .C35, maps of ground water and water quality, have become increasingly important, the former for the dry southwest and the latter for urban areas. .C38 may apply either to maps showing locations of glaciers, or to maps showing the results of glaciation or paths of past glaciers.

.C5   Geology. Hydrogeology.
.C51   Geological surveys. Status. Progress.
.C55   Dynamic and structural geology. Tectonics.
               Earthquakes (seismology). Vulcanology.
.C57   Stratigraphy and paleontology. Historical geology.

Of all the series based on topographic map series, geologic maps are the most common, and because of this the literature on geologic maps and mapping is extensive. One of the unique characteristics of geologic maps in the world of science, where physics or chemistry journals more than five years old may often be exiled to remote storage, is that a geologic map that is done correctly is, at least in terms of the average human lifespan, good forever. Series of geologic maps are most often published by national and state geologic surveys; geologic maps frequently accompany periodical articles on the geology of a given area. In recent years, state geological surveys in the United States have mimicked the USGS by issuing their own open-file reports, and very often a substantial proportion of the reports actually consists of maps. Geologic maps are often published as part of book-format items, such as periodicals or geological-survey bulletins, and there is an extensive literature of geological-publication indexes. For some of the more prominent works on geologic maps, see in appendix 2A the following: Alaska 1983, Barnes 1991, Bennison 1975, Blackadar 1979, Blyth 1965, Bolton 1989, Boulter 1989, Larsgaard 1990,
     Maltman 1990, Mosely 1979, Thomas 1977, Vossmerbaumer 1983, and Ward, Wheeler, and Bier 1981. For works on the use of remote sensing in geology, see especially Siegal and Gillespie 1980 in appendix 2A. As may well be imagined from the previous sampling of books on geological mapping, the list of periodical articles on geological mapping is enormous; Crotts 1981—in appendix 2A—is representative of the articles concerning one geographic area. See the *1996 World geologic cartobibliography* (which includes monographs and periodical articles) at the author's homepage, http://www.library.ucsb.edu/people/larsgaard/ .
     Geological-survey status maps are issued by national geologic surveys to show the progress of their work, which seems to take place in geologic time rather than human time. Maps showing dynamic and structural geology, .C55, are maps showing tectonics, faults, and earthquakes; often the phrase "structural geology" will be in the title of such a map. Stratigraphic and paleontological maps are not as frequently in evidence as are geologic sections and stratigraphic columns, which show the stratigraphy (geologic layers) at a given point, cutting vertically into the Earth. Collections with stratigraphic columns should also possess the North American Stratigraphic Code in some convenient spot in their files (see North American Commission on Stratigraphic Nomenclature 1983 in appendix 2A).

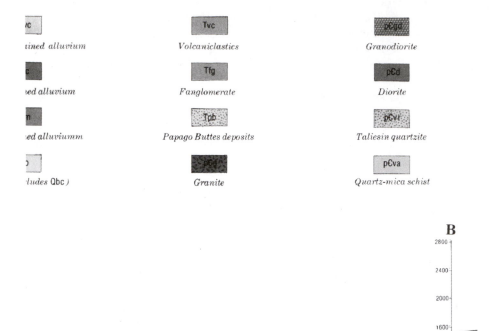

Figure 1.5. A geologic section. Christenson, G. E., D. G. Welsch, and T. L. Pewe. 1978. Environmental geology of the McDowell Mountains area, Maricopa County, Arizona (geologic & landforms maps). Scale 1:48,000. Tucson, Ariz.: State of Arizona Bureau of Geology and Mineral Technology.

.C7   Oceanography.
.C72   Temperature of ocean water.
.C73   Salinity and density of ocean water.
.C74   Icebergs.
.C75   Ocean currents.
.C76   Ocean tides.
.C8   Meteorology and climatology.
.C81   Climate classification systems.
.C82   Atmospheric temperature.
.C83   Insolation and radiation.
.C84   Atmospheric circulation. Wind systems.
.C842   Atmospheric pressure. Surface winds.
.C86   Storms.
.C87   Atmospheric electricity.

.C88   Atmospheric moisture and precipitation.
.C882   Dew. Fog. Frost. Cloud cover.
.C883   Rain.
.C884   Snow.
.C885   Hail.
.C886   Droughts.
.C887   Rainmaking.

Oceanographic maps, as defined in .C7, are presently not as common as maps depicting the morphology of the ocean bottom; but with the increasing interest in mining and farming the ocean, such maps may be produced more frequently. Maps of meteorology and climatology, in contrast, come in droves; the old statement that everyone talks about the weather but no one ever does anything about it is only partially true—we map it very frequently indeed. For monographs on the subject, see Hatch 1983 and Oliver 1973 in appendix 2A; for examples of periodical articles, see Lamb 1983 and Ristow 1960 in appendix 2A. For the application of remote-sensing techniques to climatology, see as an example Barrett 1974 in appendix 2A.

.C9   Geophysics.
.C92   Radioactivity.
.C93   Terrestrial magnetism.
.C95   Gravity.

Because of the extensive use of geophysical maps of oil and gas exploration, libraries may easily accumulate large stacks of, say, magnetic maps. For examples of monographs on geophysical maps, see Bankey and Anderson 1995, Bibliographies 1986, Bibliographic guide 1981, and Vacquier et al. 1951 in appendix 2A. Magnetic declination (that is, the difference between true north and magnetic north) changes over time, as magnetic north drifts; to find magnetic declination for any point in the United States, get in touch with the GEOMAG office at USGS.

D Biogeography

.D1   General.
.D2   Plant geography.
.D4   Animal geography.
.D5   Wildlife conservation and reserves.

Biogeographical maps are more likely to be done by individuals than as massive government projects like the topographic, geologic, and magnetic series, although the recent founding of the U.S. National Biologic Survey is an encouraging change. The two most prominent names in writing about vegetation mapping are De Laubenfels and Kuchler; the former has written a survey work, and the latter is deeply involved in vegetation-map bibliographies. See in appendix 2A De Laubenfels 1975, France 1961, International classification 1973, Kuchler 1967, Ozenda 1986, and Vegetation 1996.

E   Human and cultural geography. Anthropogeography. Human ecology

.E1   General.
.E15   Archaeology.
.E2   Population.
.E3   Languages.
.E4   Religions.
.E5   Medical geography.
.E6   Social and cultural geography.
.E63   Recreation. Sports.
.E635   Tourism. Tourist maps.
.E7   Material culture.
.E9   Slavery.

Although maps on population and tourism are often issued by governmental or nonprofit organizations, the other categories of this delightful area—containing subjects that are in some cases difficult to map—tend to be done by nongovernmental organizations (excluding state university geography departments). For a brief explication of the statistical mapping done by the U.S. government, see Meyer, Broome, and Schweitzer 1975. Maps on population and recreation, and maps for tourists, are among the most often encountered E maps. Architectural plans may occasionally make their way to libraries, but mainly in archival collections. See Cartographic information 1995 in appendix 2A for a periodical issue on architecture and cartography.

F   Political geography

.F1   General.
.F2   International boundaries.
.F3   Sovereignty.
.F5   International relations.
.F7   Administrative and political divisions.
.F8   Government.
.F9   Political campaigns.

Very often the type of information in .Fl, .F2, and .F7 is shown on general maps (the sort with no subject code classification); maps showing only the information above tend to be somewhat rare, except for those concentrating on administrative and political divisions.

G   Economic geography

.G1	General.	
.G2	Economic regions.	
.G3	Natural resources.	
.G4	Land.	
.G43	Land use.	
.G44	Zoning.	
.G45	Planning.	
.G46	Cadastral maps.	
.G463	Land ownership.	
.G465	Land grants.	
.G47	Real property tax.	
.G475	Insurance. Fire protection.	
.G5	Public lands.	
.G52	Parks and monuments.	
.G54	Cemeteries.	
.G6	Ethnic reservations.	
.G8	Labor.	

The G subject area is yet another subject category in which publication is often by the government, and the number of maps issued in it has increased greatly over the last twenty years; population has increased while the land available has remained very much the same. Whereas maps in .G1, .G2, and .G3 are not particularly common, .G4 is a bonanza, marked by such map series as:

> United States. Geological Survey. [1976?]– . Land use series, map L- . Reston, Va.: USGS. [1:250,000 and 1:100,000, in two series]

For a glossary of terms for land use mapping, see *Land use and natural resource mapping* 1983 in appendix 2A; for the key to the land-use classification system used in the L-series, see Land use 1976 in appendix 2A. Maps showing land ownership have been of paramount importance for centuries, and this series is no exception. Maps held by such government agencies as county assessors fall into this category. For works on cadastral maps generally, see in appendix 2A Cazier 1976; McEntyre 1978; Hawes 1977; Stephenson 1967; and C. A. White 1983.

But the sleeper in this group, the one that has a substantial literature all its own, is .G475, which includes the fire-insurance maps that were made by the Sanborn Company, predominantly during the nineteenth and early twentieth centuries. The purpose of these maps was to show in how much hazard of being burned down a given building was; in the process, the company did extremely detailed mapping that included what every building in a town was used for, and produced maps that are treasured and heavily used by scholars in many different disciplines. The maps were also revised often, so scholars may now have comparative looks at a given small area. Sanborn Maps was recently purchased by EDR. See in appendix 2A Breese 1995; Creason 1993; Hayward 1977; Hoehn 1976–77; Keister 1993; Manning 1994; Oswald 1997; Perry 1992; Post 1984; Rainville 1996; Sanborn Map Company 1960; Shkurkin 1993; and U.S. LC 1981.

We finish off the G section with maps on public lands and ethnic reservations as more common than those on business and professional organizations or labor. The U.S. National Park Service publishes many brochures that include maps of parks, and also maps of areas of the United States showing public lands.

H   Mines and mineral resources

.H1   General.
.H2   Metallic group.
.H5   Nonmetallic group.
.H8   Petroleum and natural gas.
.H9   Coal.

Maps of states and countries showing mineral resources are quite common, but at least those for U.S. states tend to be several years old; for a bibliography of state mineral resource maps, see Larson 1984 in appendix 2A. For an excellent general work on mine maps, which includes mine map symbols (pp. 388–406), see Williams 1983 in appendix 2A. Some of the older USGS MR- maps also include symbols; for glossing of these symbols, see *Encyclopedia of field and general geology* 1988 in appendix 2A.

J   Agriculture

.J1   General.
.J2   Systems of agriculture.
.J3   Soils.
.J4   Soil conservation. Reclamation. Irrigation. Erosion.
.J5   Animal husbandry. Livestock.
.J6   Crops.
.J7   Vegetables.
.J73   Fruits.
.J78   Industrial agricultural products.
.J89   Other plants.

Of this group, the most frequently encountered are the soil maps, prominently exemplified by the U.S. Soil Conservation Service's *Soil surveys* (Superintendent of Documents number A 57.38); the *Soil surveys* are usually text with a large number of maps appended, although sometimes the text and loose maps are inserted in large, tough envelopes. SCS occasionally issues "Status of soil surveys." See in bibliography Brunner 1990; Sombroek 1983; and Wisconsin 1993.

K Forests and forestry

The U.S. Forest Service issues individual maps of the national forests of the United States. These are very often classed as general maps, because this classification number is for spatial data focusing on flora rather than on administrative areas.

L Aquatic biological resources

This classification is reserved for biological resources of the waters, such as aquaculture.

M Manufacturing and processing. Service industries

Spatial data showing the distribution of given industries not elsewhere addressed within the classification's subject code—e.g., garment districts—are classed here.

N Technology. Engineering. Public works

.N1	General.
.N2	Hydraulic engineering. Dams.
.N3	Power.
.N32	Steam. Geothermal steam sources.
.N33	Water power.
.N34	Wind power.
.N35	Nuclear power.
.N36	Solar power.
.N4	Electric utilities.
.N42	Gas utilities.
.N44	Water utilities.
.N46	Sewerage. Waste disposal.
.N85	Pollution and pollution control.
.N852	Air pollution.
.N854	Pollution of land.
.N856	Water pollution.
.N858	Noise pollution.

Although the number of maps produced in categories K, L, and M has held steady (with maps of forestry rather more common than those in the L and M categories), the maps in the N category have increased over about the last ten years or so, especially those having to do with geothermal power, nuclear power, and solar power. Electric-utility maps of the United States have been issued with some regularity by the Federal Power Commission (or whatever agency may at a given moment have taken over its responsibilities) since the 1950s or 1960s.

P   Transportation and communication

.P1   General.
.P2   Roads.
.P3   Railroads.
.P4   Pipe lines.
.P5   Water transportation. Nautical charts.
.P6   Air transportation. Aeronautical charts.
.P7   Space transportation.
.P8   Postal service.
.P9   Communications.

Once again we come to a subject area in which a good many maps are issued, largely but not totally in the form of series. Road maps, usually those by state highway (or transportation) and commerce departments and by commercial firms, are ubiquitous in almost any map collection; their status has risen because they are no longer being given away free by gasoline stations (Harding 1984). Road-map history in this country began in the early 1900s, with road maps being given away at gasoline stations by about 1930. More than 250 million maps were printed in 1972, at the height of this pleasant custom ("Rapid rise" 1990). Currently, state highway or commerce departments still hand out free road maps. Characteristically, a road map issued by a state highway department has the following (Ward 1977, 6):

- main map of the state

- inset maps of major metropolitan areas

- tables of intercity distances

- gazetteers

- table of state park facilities

- photographs of state emblems

- some "promotional prose"

- a portrait of and friendly message from the governor.

By 1968, at least 210 million road maps had been produced, largely by companies such as Gousha, Rand McNally, General Drafting Company, Diversified Map Corporation, National Advertising Company, and the National Survey (in Vermont) (White 1970b, 7). The ubiquity of highways and automobiles means that locally produced street maps for major metropolitan areas—e.g., Arrow for Boston, Hagstrom for New York, ADC (formally the Alexandria Drafting Company) for the D.C. area, Franklin for Philadelphia, Dolph's for Miami, Mapsco for Dallas, Creative Sales Corporation for

Chicago, Thomas for metropolitan areas in the state of California, and so on—are essential purchases for map libraries. Folk wisdom has it that some of the most frequently stolen books in Los Angeles bookstores are the Thomas Guides; map libraries are hereby given fair warning. To subscribe to an electronic mailing list whose focus is road maps, send e-mail to majordomo@teleport.com and type as the body of the message "subscribe roadmaps-l". For a history of road maps to the early 1960s, see in appendix 2A Ristow 1964a; see also Arnaud [1996?], and for strip maps Cole 1995 and MacEachren and Johnson 1987, all in appendix 2A.

Railroad maps have also received considerable attention, largely because the heyday of the railroads in the United States—the second half of the nineteenth and the early part of the twentieth centuries—happens to be a time period that persons working on history and genealogy in the United States find especially relevant. For works on nineteenth-century railroad maps in the United States, see Modelski 1984 in appendix 2A.

And now we come to the series part of this subject code: P5, nautical charts, and P6, aeronautical charts. *Chart* refers to a map used for navigation, either on water or through the air. Persons interested in making it safely from one spot to another are, sensibly, deeply interested in the charts that will get them there; because the vehicles in which such persons are encased carry materials and information of interest to all of us, almost every nation has some agency or agencies concerned with charting. As an example, the United States has the Coast and Geodetic Survey (a return to its first name, after time spent as the National Ocean Service and the National Ocean Survey) for nautical charting of native waters, and for foreign waters the National Imagery and Mapping Agency (NIMA; mainly the Defense Mapping Agency's Hydrographic/Topographic Center, itself formerly the Naval Oceanographic Office, at least in part). Nautical charts have the status at sea that topographic series have on land, and therefore the literature on them is extensive. The publications of the International Hydrographic Organization are very helpful for finding out about status and current charting efforts. In appendix 2A, see Howse and Sanderson 1972; Karo 1956; Langeraar 1984; Lefkowicz 1995; Maritime 1986; Ringold and Clark 1980; Simpson 1983; Taylor 1956; US National Ocean Survey 1979; and UN 1956 for general studies. For a brief history of U.S. nautical charting, see Adams 1941 in the bibliography and Shalowitz 1957 in appendix 2A. These charts are considered so essential that the series scarcely even have names. For many years the Coast and Geodetic Survey's series was the "C&GS" series, but, at least in some cases, it seems to have reached the NIMA stage; that is, the librarian must be able to recognize the format—a map depicting an area with a substantial amount of water and a few lonely little spots of land, with a number (often in the thousands) at all four corners just outside the neatline. Aeronautical charts get far less printed interest (which is peculiar, considering the number of airplanes taking off and landing on any given day on planet Earth); see in appendix 2A Schiff 1989, and the most current edition of the National Ocean Service's *Aeronautical chart user's guide*.

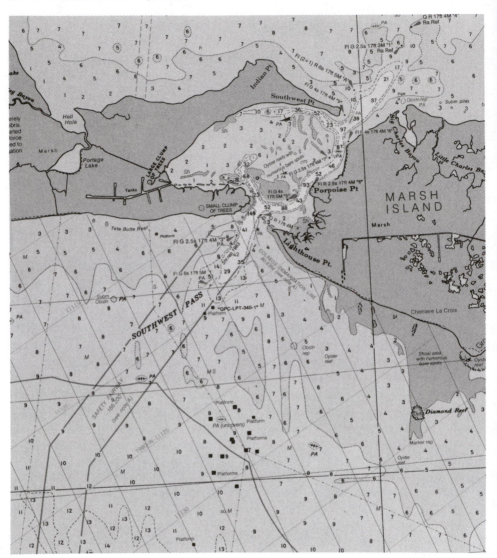

Figure 1.6. A nautical chart. United States. National Ocean Service. 1996.
11349, Vermilion Bay and approaches: United States–Gulf Coast, Louisiana.
Scale 1:80,000. Washington, D.C.: NOS, Coast Survey.

Figure 1.7. An aeronautical chart. United States. National Ocean Service. 1997. Great Falls: aeronautical chart. 52nd ed. Scale 1:500,000. Rockville, Md.: NOS.

Because oceans—either of water or of air—change frequently, charts are very often revised, and this is doubtless why charts, or at least nautical charts, were among the very first large map series to be put on microform. Another major reason is that although nautical charts are in color, black, white, and gray are the most heavily used colors (the "C&GS" series is prone to yellow) and therefore such charts are well suited to black-and-white microform. By whatever name (if any) and in whatever format, charts are useful in any general library, even—or perhaps especially—in landlocked states; the number of times when map users situated in Colorado need to see maps of the island of Diego Garcia in the Indian Ocean, or perhaps one of the Bahamas, is far more than one would ever have suspected.

Q Commerce and trade. Finance

.Q1   General.
.Q2   Business statistics.
.Q3   Movement of commodities.
.Q4   Marketing.
.Q5   Tariffs and other trade barriers.
.Q8   Finance.

R Military and naval geography

.R1   General.
.R2   Military and naval districts and establishments.
.R3   War strategy and tactics.
.R4   Defenses. Fortifications.
.R5   Logistics.
.R6   Civil defense.
.R7   Peacetime military operations.
.R9   Property in war.

The Q and R categories are not much used unless one is working in a library that specializes in one of these topics. Of the two, military maps are more inclined to float across the librarian's desk.

S Historical geography

For this subject area, LC has assigned codes according to area. Thus, world history is:

.S1   General.
.S2   Ancient history.
.S3   Medieval history (476–1453).
.S4   Modern history (1453–).
.S5   Seventeenth through nineteenth centuries.
.S7   Twentieth century.

whereas United States history is:

- .S1   General.
- .S2   Colonial period.
- .S3   Revolution, 1775–1783.
- .S4   1783–1861.
- .S5   Civil War, 1861–1865.
- .S6   1865–1898.
- .S7   1898–1945.
- .S8   1945– .

These are maps that deal with the time period specified, *not* maps that were constructed at that time. The former type of map is relatively common, especially in the United States for wartime periods. And this, the last of the subject codes, serves nicely to lead us into a very special category of maps for which there is no subject code—the rare map.

Rare Maps

Definitions as to what constitutes a rare map vary from country to country, depending upon the history of that country. For the United States, any map published prior to 1900 (and for that time period especially maps of the western United States) should be considered to fall into this category—probably disintegrating as it descends, if it was published during the nineteenth century or in newsprint. In Great Britain, 1825 is the cutoff date for rare maps (British Standards Institution 1975, 3). For historical societies and archival collections, such maps constitute the collection, but for most libraries these maps are a luxury unless they depict an area of local interest.

Rare maps are not only of scholarly use as historical documents, but also are quite often uniquely beautiful objects. Rare-map acquisition takes place in an atmosphere of spiraling prices and *caveat emptor*. If part of a library's policy is to purchase rare maps, the librarian should either acquire a love for and knowledge of rare maps, and the canniness to purchase wisely, or delegate the task to someone who is familiar with the field. The general goal is to find maps that are the "first" (e.g., first map showing a given area with a given name), in good condition, and preferably aesthetically pleasing. *Mercator's world,* and before it *Map collector,* have sections on maps recently sold and their costs; *American book prices: Current* every year has "Part II, books, broadsides, maps & charts." Once such maps are acquired, they must be closely guarded, as their value is increasing apparently exponentially rather than arithmetically (*Antique map price* 1993– in appendix 2A; Beresiner 1983; Pearson 1979; Cohen 1966, 2; and Kiraldi 1973).

There is a considerable body of literature concerning pre-1900 maps; it is a literature about which many harsh words have been said, of which some follow:

> Whether a literature with this degree of eclecticism can be described at all in terms of a functioning network of historiographical and methodological conceptions is difficult to say. Much work has been undertaken in isolation and in oblivion of any grand paradigm (Blakemore and Harley 1980, 3, in appendix 2A).

For an excellent guide to the literature, see "Part 2, History of Cartography," in *Information sources in cartography* (1990) in appendix 2A. Librarians must exercise caution, not only in purchasing such maps, but also in believing what is written about them.

If such problems exist, why bother with them? The underlying reason is their beauty. Many of them bring to the mind and heart that uplifting feeling of happiness that comes from seeing something that is both lovely and useful—although the latter is most likely to appear either in nautical charts or in maps from the mid-eighteenth century on. Aside from their beauty, these maps are valuable research tools. Merely by existing, they evoke a time period and an attitude toward geography and life itself. When dealing with genealogical reference questions, they are invaluable, as they may contain names for locales that have long ceased to exist except in memory (Collins 1977, 10). In the United States there are many important pre-1900 map collections, which include (and the following is just a sampling of the best-known collections) the Library of Congress's Geography and Map Division, the Hermon Dunlap Smith Center for the History of Cartography (Newberry Library in Chicago), Bancroft Library (University of California at Berkeley), and the Henry E. Huntington Library and Art Gallery (San Marino, California).

What if your library does not have a recently deceased rich uncle, and yet the library users persist in asking questions that can be answered only by the rare maps your library cannot afford to buy? Relax; you're in luck because there are many facsimiles or slides available for purchase at reasonable prices (see Noe 1980 in appendix 2A for a list of some dealers). The value of a facsimile is increased if it is accompanied by a text (ca. 3,000–4,000 words) that provides: a discussion of the map and its characteristics; a biography of the cartographer; details of production of the original map; an assessment of the accuracy of the map; the bibliographical history of the map; an assessment of detail; a bibliography of works relating to the map and to the cartographer; and an index if the text is of any length. The location of the original should be given, and either the scale of the facsimile should be equal to that of the original, or a constant reduction scale should be stated somewhere on the map. Facsimiles are seldom so fulsomely accompanied, and the librarian's attention is perforce directed primarily to the facsimile itself, which should correspond as closely as possible to the original and should be well reproduced, with accuracy and printing clarity (Fairclough 1972, 293–94; and Koeman 1964). Even entire atlases are published in facsimile, most notably by Theatrum Orbis Terrarum, in Amsterdam.

Facsimiles are worth buying when: they are of areas and subjects frequently requested or related to research, they fill an important and embarrassing gap in the collection, the rarity and price of the publication puts purchasing the original in the same realm of probability as that of the library purchasing a yacht, and libraries in the same region are similarly impoverished (Fairclough 1972, 291–92).

Globes

❖ *Globes are not only decorative and somehow comme il faut for a map library, they are also useful.*
What a treasure for a Roman soldier the brass globe of Archimedes!
By cutting it in two he could make at once a couple of camp-kettles . . .
—Kohl 1857

The globe—and more importantly, the sphericity of the Earth—has so long been taken for granted that this device, with "the greatest utility of any visual aid in geography," goes in grave danger of being occasionally ignored (McKinney 1969, 183). The globe is the most accurate representation of the world (albeit on a very small scale) in that it uses a three-dimensional surface to represent a three-dimensional surface. Celestial globes are more common in map libraries than are orreries, which are more used as teaching tools for explaining the solar system.

Although few libraries can afford a Rand McNally six-foot-diameter monster, almost any library needs two terrestrial globes (one physical, such as the National Geographic globe showing relief both of land and of the ocean bottom, and one political, such as those put out by the Society, Replogle, and Nystrom), a moon globe, and a celestial globe (Koerner 1972, 514 and McKinney 1969, 187).

Globe-making is very specialized work, and relatively few firms perform it. Globes may be made by hand mounting (very expensive and specialized work), or by machine mounting, which is far more common. In the first case, a map is printed on 30°-wide gores, then cut out and pasted by hand onto spheres. Far more often, a map is printed as an interrupted polar projection (resembling a propeller with twelve blades and called a *rosette*) with each map glued to chipboard, die-cut into a rosette, and then glued to another rosette (a shaped piece of chipboard with overlapping seams) before a hydraulic press forms it into a hemisphere; the two hemispheres are then joined at the Equator with tape, which may mean a slight misalignment at the seams that does not show on smaller globes. To make plastic, raised-relief globes, a map is printed on a sheet of plastic, and then vacuum-formed into hemispheres (Coombs 1981, 503).

Globes may be mounted on a full meridian axial (fixed at 23½°), a half-meridian axial, in a gyro mounting, or in a free cradle. Globes that light up from the inside are effective, but be sure that directions on how to change the bulb when it burns out are filed in some logical, quickly findable place.

If a library requires other than the standard physical or political globes, there are of course firms more than happy to take the money. For example, globes of the moon come from National Geographic, Panoramic Studios, and Replogle, among others; projection teaching models from Hubbard; and celestial globes from, again for example, Rand McNally and Replogle (Coombs 1981, 506; Briesemeister 1957; and McKinney 1969). Geologic globes are also available sporadically.

Globes are expensive purchases, and the librarian will need to select carefully. The most common globe sizes are, in diameter, 12 inches and 16 inches; sizes vary from three inches (bought in your neighborhood stationery store, and good for sharpening pencils) to as large as a purchaser is willing to pay for (a globe on display in Paris some years ago was large enough for a table of bridge and the necessary players inside). Get as large a globe as the budget allows; the larger the globe, the more legible the lines and lettering. In addition, a big globe is an attention-getting device, and well worth the money on that basis alone. As in purchasing maps, look for a reputable firm. See appendix 3 for U.S. globe and plastic-model dealers. For works on globes, see Bertele 1961, Dekker and van der Krogt 1993, *Globusfreund* 1951–, Stevenson 1971, and Yonge 1968, all in appendix 2A.

Relief Models

Relief models may be constructed of *papier-maché*, plaster, or plastic, currently most likely to be the last of these. The first two—heavy, expensive, and hard to display and store—were the predecessors; plastic models remain difficult to display and to store, but since the use of plastics for models was introduced in the 1940s, at least we have light awkward items instead of heavy awkward items (Stanley 1949; Wilson 1949; and Ryerson 1983). Plastic is also much easier to keep clean, so if models are kept on extra-wide shelves and over the years get dusty, it's quick and easy to take a damp sponge to them and refile after they're dry.

A special kind of raised-relief map is that intended for use by the blind. Although there are several types of maps for use by the blind—including Braille, large-print, and sound—the most frequently made seems to be tactual or tactile maps (Chang and Johnson 1976; Forman 1979, 13; Barnes 1979a and 1979b; Lederman 1979; and Now bump-maps 1977).

For book-length discussions of such maps, see in appendix 2A Kidwell and Greer 1973; Sherman 1978; and Wiedel 1983. For a directory of tactile map collections, see in appendix 2A International directory of tactile map collections 1985. For a list of firms issuing models, see appendix 3.

Atlases

Atlases are bound or boxed collections of maps, usually with the maps in one style or format, fairly uniform in scale, with a thematic or areal focus, and generally provided with an index (Walsh 1973, 3, in appendix 2A). The practice of issuing bound collections of maps originated in the middle of the sixteenth century in Europe; the word *atlas* first appeared on the title page of a work published by Gerardus Mercator sometime between 1585 and 1595. By the seventeenth century, both word and form were firmly established, and today the need for atlases in almost any library is well recognized (Gómez-Ibáñez 1969, 625 in appendix 2A; Cobb 1972; and Cobb 1973, 16).

There are three main types of atlases: general-reference world atlases; government-sponsored areal atlases (national, state, provincial, county, or even city); and thematic atlases dealing with a single subject (e.g., soils, geology, minerals). Every library needs at least one of the general-reference atlases. The most current edition of any of the following atlases—the flagship atlas for each publisher—will constitute a good purchase for almost any library: *Goode's world atlas*; Hammond's *Atlas of the world*; *National Geographic atlas of the world*; Oxford University Press's *Atlas of the world*; Prentice-Hall's *International atlas*; Rand McNally's *New international atlas*; and *Times atlas of the world*. The last mentioned is considered the premier world atlas, but it is essential to match your users' needs against how different atlases present information, and then make your choice. A copy of a current Rand McNally *Commercial atlas and marketing guide* is essential for almost any collection located in the United States. For atlases for children, see Cy Behroozi's very helpful 1993 article (appendix 2A) for ideas as to what to look for in children's atlases. The 1993 "World atlas comparison chart" compiled by Jim Walsh also gives the overworked librarian a good overview.

Government-sponsored atlases are collections of thematic maps of a governmental unit, with maps usually representing at the very least the geographical environment, population, and economy of that unit; because such atlases are a status symbol for the unit and the country, the atlases tend to evidence a high cartographic standard and are usually compiled and published by an agency of the political unit depicted. Not only are these atlases symbols of national and scientific prestige, they also serve useful purposes as teaching devices, planning instruments, and indicators of needs for future study and development for the unit in question. For any library they are superb one-volume reference tools (Neville 1982; in appendix 2A, Kent 1986; Kent and Tobias 1990; Pugliese 1987; and

Purpose and use 1979; National and regional 1964; and Stams 1980?). A definitive and continually updated bibliography of national and state atlases does not currently exist; but the classic compilations of reference tools, such as *Guide* 1996, make the effort.

An example of a national atlas, and of the trials and tribulations involved in putting one together, is the once long-awaited and now long out-of-print *National atlas of the United States of America*, which was issued by the USGS in 1970; USGS has a project to issue it in digital form, perhaps on CD-ROM or over the Web. In process since 1950, upon its completion the price tag was $100 (U.S.-depository libraries received it free if they had been wise enough to select I 19.2, the Superintendent of Documents class number under which it was issued); its publication was tragically soon followed by the death of its editor, Arch Gerlach. It is a handsome volume with gray-bordered pages and only occasionally garish colors (most notably in some of the geologic sheets).

Regional, state, provincial, county, and even city atlases appear at least as frequently as do national atlases. For example, Canadian provinces and U.S. states have been putting out their own atlases with blessed rapidity. There have been two updates (in appendix 2A, Ives 1988; and Schwartzkopf 1989) to two bibliographies of state atlases issued in 1983 (in appendix 2A, Cobb and Ives 1983; and Czerniak and Perrone 1983).

Thematic atlases are acquired as their subject or areal coverage matches the collection profile of the prospective purchasing library. Thematic atlases emphasizing almost any topic may be issued, from linguistic atlases to geologic atlases; the only points they seem to have in common are that they are composed of maps; that they are either heavy or awkward to handle or both; and that they are fascinating to look through, whether or not the peruser knows anything whatsoever about the subject matter. A type of atlas of special interest to those libraries collecting, or wishing they could afford to collect, rare maps is the facsimile atlas (appendix 2A, Podell 1994).

Remote-Sensing Images

Remote sensing is the practice of obtaining, from a distance, reliable information about the properties of the surface of the Earth. Sensors and other techniques generally use the electromagnetic spectrum, and the most important ones, such as aerial photography and Landsat imagery, seem to have as their primary purpose the extension and enrichment of the abilities of the first remote sensor—the human eye. Chapter 10 ("Cartographic applications of satellite remote sensing") of *Information sources 1990* (appendix 2A) gives an excellent summary of the remote-sensing world for its time; the most current edition of the *Manual of remote sensing* is a vital reference work for these materials. There are many different kinds of remote sensors and remote-sensing products; the main ones are cameras (producing photographs), electron imagers, thermal imagers and scanners, multispectral scanners, microwave sensors, sonar, and gamma ray sensors. The products that librarians are most likely to see are photographs, multispectral-scanner images, and radar images. The EROS Data Center and its GLIS (Global Land Information System) are presently the best first stop for finding out about almost any kind of aerial photography or satellite imagery produced within the United States:

custserv@edcserver1.cr.usgs.gov

or

http://edcwww.cr.usgs.gov/Webglis/ .

Remote-sensing imagery is divided up according to the area of the electromagnetic spectrum at which the given sensor is aimed:

SENSOR	WAVELENGTH
radar	0.3–300 cm
microwave	0.3–300 cm
thermal IR	3–5 μm, 8–14 μm
reflected IR	0.7–.3 μm
infrared	0.7–100 μm
visible	0.4–0.7 μm
photographic	0.3–0.4 μm
ultraviolet	3nm–0.4 μm
x-ray	0.03–3nm
gamma ray	less than 0.03 nm

Aerial Photographs

In the remote-sensing field, aerial photographs are the most common in libraries. Because of the expense (variable, but at least several dollars for one nine-inch black-and-white contact print), and because of the large number of prints required to cover an area even the size of a county, and also because of the frequency with which photos are retaken, aerial photographs are good purchases only for the areas of greatest interest to users. In the past, large numbers of photographs were usually acquired by obtaining superseded photographs from a government agency, such as the U.S. Forest Service. Even if the photographs may be acquired free, the indexes (which are uncontrolled photomosaics) very often cannot. Free or not, aerial photographs take up a considerable amount of space (whether they are kept in file cabinets or in boxes on standard stack shelving), so most libraries are advised to begin with detailed coverage of the local area—expanding this to repeat coverage of the county (Panel on Aerial Photography 1971, 1–9; and Koerner 1972, 513–14). USGS began a National High Altitude Photography program (NHAP) in 1978, under which it systematically acquired photographic coverage (both black-and-white—1:80,000-scale—and color infrared—1:58,000-scale) of the 48 conterminous states, each photograph covering about 72 square miles. In 1987, the program changed to NAPP—National Aerial Photography

Program—the scale to 1:40,000, and area covered per frame to about 32 square miles. Photographs acquired as part of this program must have no cloud cover, minimal haze, a sun angle of at least 30° to minimize shadows, and be taken from an aircraft altitude of 40,000 feet above the mean terrain. Librarians interested in obtaining such photographs should send to USGS, or direct to the EROS Data Center (Sioux Falls SD 57198; (http://edcwww.cr.usgs.gov/Webglis/glisbin/search.pl?NAPP), for the most current fact sheet and price list.

Aerial photography may be obtained by purchasing or receiving as a gift existing coverage (the route most libraries would prefer to take), by contracting with an aerial photographic firm, or by flying the coverage oneself (Stone 1960, 19). To purchase existing aerial photographic coverage, it is first necessary to discover who holds the negatives—and this may be the hardest part of the whole process. Most aerial photography is flown for or by federal and other governmental agencies, and so much has been done that there are too many projects for manual indexing. The Earth Sciences Information Center (ESIC; formerly the National Cartographic Information Center, NCIC) has attempted since 1975 to provide computer indexing by having all federal agencies that take or contract out aerial photography supply data concerning their projects to a central database maintained by ESIC. The data is maintained and updated on the computer, with indexes to this Aerial Photography Summary Record System (APSRS) being formerly summarized themselves in a number of catalogs (each dealing with a strip of the United States), then on microfiche, and to be available only over the Web after January 1, 1998. The microfiche sets are COM fiche listing amount of cloud cover, camera used, specific scale, date of coverage, and agency project codes. Addresses for agencies or firms holding the coverage are given so that the prospective users may make arrangements with the appropriate agency for print purchases.

The most prominent air-photo agencies have been the U.S. Agricultural Stabilization and Conservation Service (ASCS), USGS, and the U.S. Forest Service (USFS). Other important source agencies are state highway, natural resources, and transportation departments, and county and state mapping agencies.

Before APSRS, the three most important tools for the map librarian wishing to purchase aerial photography of the United States were: *Status of aerial photography* (a map published by USGS); *Status of aerial mosaics* (also issued by USGS); and *ASCS aerial photography status maps*. Both USGS status maps were issued annually and were keyed to a list of U.S. agencies listed at the bottoms of the map. The agencies listed were ASCS, the Soil Conservation Service (SCS), the Forest Service, USGS, the Bureau of Land Management (BLM), the Tennessee Valley Authority (TVA), the National Ocean Service (NOS), and a miscellaneous category—state, commercial, and other. Requests for specific information were to be directed to the agency indicated as holding the film negatives.

Figure 1.8. An aerial photograph. [Frame] BTM-6K-25, 2-24-54. From flight: Pacific Air Industries. 1954. BTM [PMA 6-53 DC Item no. 3.] [Washington, D.C.: Production and Marketing Administration]. Scale 1:20,000.

Figure 1.9. A photomosaic index. Aero Service Corp. 1956? *Monterey County, California, scale 1:20,000.* Scale [of index ca.1:63,360]. [Washington, D.C.?]: U.S. Commodity Stabilization Service.

The third publication, by ASCS, gave detailed information on aerial photographic coverage by state, all of the film being held by ASCS. In this index, page-sized maps of each state showed county boundaries and names with, for each county, the date of the latest photographic coverage, the scale, the lens size, and the number of photo index sheets given, all in code. For example:

74 year	=	(1974)
4WA 4	=	number of photo-index sheets
W	=	lens (6-inch)
A	=	scale (1:40,000)

On the back of each state map were keys to symbols and the addresses to use in requesting information about ASCS aerial photography. Also included in this publication was a U.S. map indicating other agency aerial photography available through ASCS. The librarian should keep in mind that over the past few decades ASCS has been the Agricultural Adjustment Administration and the Commodity Stabilization Service, and should not be surprised by future name changes, or even by the disappearance of the agency (Stone 1960, 22). ASCS county index mosaics may be inspected at local ASCS offices; more than one index will often be required for a county. The indexes have on them the numbers (e.g., roll and exposure) needed for ordering the aerial photographs. Aerial photographs are usually 9" x 9" contact prints, but for a price many variations are possible. ASCS has a code list that gives, for each county in the United States, a three-letter code (e.g., BTM is the symbol for Santa Barbara County, California); these codes form the first part of the flight "name" or identifier. For most current information, librarians should request (or find on the Web) the latest version of the brochure *ASCS aerial photography*.

To find out about holdings of libraries and some government agencies, see Larsgaard 1991. Some state agencies are making their holdings lists available over the Web, such as the *Wisconsin catalog of aerial photography*, available over the Web at http://feature.geography.wisc.edu/sco/apsi/wicap/aerial.html .

The library interested in older aerial photographs must turn to the Center for Cartographic and Architectural Archives of National Archives, which receives photography in waves from other federal agencies as the photography "ages" (the magic number is 50 years of age). Its holdings date from about the mid-1930s. Currently the Archives contracted out reproduction of the aerial photography that it holds, and the prices have risen since this contractual agreement began.

It is difficult for a private citizen of one country, in an unofficial capacity, to obtain good large-scale aerial photographs of foreign countries. Buying Landsat imagery (to be discussed later in this section on remote sensing) from EOSAT may be the only option, but it is worth taking a look at Hyatt 1988b (appendix 2A), relatively old though it is, at least to get an indication of the possibilities for obtaining such photography. Given that a 1:20,000-scale aerial photograph covers 21 square kilometers, whereas a 1:1,000,000-scale Landsat scene covers 34,000 square kilometers, it is obvious that for users who require detail an aerial photograph is the desirable format, although with the new one-meter-resolution satellite images, this may change (Lillesand and Kiefer 1987, 513-17; Corbley 1996).

It is a bit difficult to figure out where in this chapter to insert *orthophotomaps*, mosaicked, rectified (distortion removed) aerial photographs that are presented in map format (Thrower and Jensen 1976 in appendix 2A). This is particularly so now that USGS's chosen vehicle for distributing orthophotos is in digital form, generally on CD-ROM as digital orthophotoquads (DOQs).

Photographs from Space

Another category is what the Library of Congress Subject Headings (LCSH) refer to as "Photographs from space," and this describes them as well as anything else. They are differentiated from aerial photography in that they are usually (but not always) products of handheld cameras, from a platform that is at a far higher altitude than airplanes can attain. Primary examples of this are photographs from the manned space projects such as the space shuttles (see Cloud 1995 in appendix 2A for a summary), and from so-called "spy planes" (U2s, Blackbirds, and so on). About 800,000 of the latter from the 1960s and 1970s were declassified and made available to the public by an Executive Order of President William Clinton dated February 22, 1995. The most current version of the USGS flier, "Declassified intelligence satellite photographs," is a good summary of what is available. Many of these images are available over the Web; see, for example, the space shuttle images at http://images.jsc.nasa.gov/html/home.htm , or search at such sites as telnet sseop.jsc.nasa.gov and http://ersaf.jsc.nasa.gov/sn5.html .

Slides

Although aerial photography is the most frequently found photography in libraries, 35mm slides of maps have been surrogates for rare maps for some years, and are used so much in paper presentations that the first words out of many speakers' mouths are, "Would someone please turn out the lights and turn on the slide projector?" Slides of rare maps may be duplicated and sold by the library holding the maps; some national libraries have had this service for years. The problems of copyright must be kept in mind if such a practice is followed (Best 1963; and Maling 1966). Currently libraries are using the Web to display surrogates of their maps; interestingly enough, one of the primary methods of doing this is to scan slides.

Electron Images

We are still in the realm of cameras, or at least something similar to them, with electron-imaging systems. These systems frame an image on a photoelectric surface, much as a photographic system frames an image on a photochemical surface (film). The television camera is an electron imager; it "forms frame images of the field of view by sweeping an electron beam in a horizontal-line (raster type) pattern across a photosensitive layer onto which the image has been focused" (Smith 1977, 205, in appendix 2A). The major difference between photography and electron imaging is that in the latter case the images are electronically rather than chemically processed, and may be transmitted rapidly (again electronically) from the sensor to the receiving station, or may be stored on magnetic tape. The best known of the electron imagers is the return-beam vidicon (RBV), largely because such an instrument was on a Landsat satellite, and therefore such imagery is available for purchase from the EROS Data Center.

Thermal Images

Now we are very firmly out of the photographic realm as far as equipment and instrumentation are concerned, although the final product of these systems may either look like a photograph or be a photograph; in the latter case the data is presented as a photograph because of the human race's familiarity with that format. But in the main what we are talking about is imagery, not just that one subtype of imagery called photography.

Infrared (IR) systems may be either electrooptical or optomechanical; all are dependent upon the theory that the intensity of radiation emitted from an object is proportional to the fourth power of the absolute temperature of the object, and directly proportional to emissivity. Also, all have an optical head for receiving IR radiation plus a display for a visible image, connected by electronics for passage of electrical signals from the detector element to display input. Display may be in the form of magnetic tape, videotape, photographic film, or television tube (Townshend 1981, 20, appendix 2A). Equipment—such as radiometers, spectrometers, and interferometers—is sophisticated and expensive, and relatively few libraries will have such imagery.

Multispectral Scanners

Multispectral scanners (MSS referring to the sensor carried by the first several Landsats) are a classic example of the whole being greater than the sum of its parts, or of each part considered separately; the scanner operates by measuring the radiant flux from a large number of spectral bands scattered from the Earth's surface. A scanner is quite complex; its two basic sections are a scanning section (which includes the collecting optics) and a spectrograph section (which includes the detectors). The first section is very similar in operation and motion to IR scanners, and the second acts as a spectrometer, that is, observing the spectra gathered. The rotating mirror in the first section focuses the radiation energy emanating from the Earth onto a field stop, which serves as an entrance slit to the spectrometer section; the light is collimated (the rays are made parallel), passed through the dispersive element, and focused on an array of detectors, with each detector collecting a separate light spectrum band. The light photons striking the detectors generate electrical signals that vary in intensity according to the amount of thermal energy coming from the small part of the Earth being viewed by the mirror.

These signals are converted to beams of electrons and can generate visible light when directed onto the face of a cathode-ray tube (CRT), thus painting a line of imagery across the face of the tube. This line of imagery corresponds to the line of terrain just scanned by the mirror. An image of these visible lines may be recorded on film, or the signals may be recorded on magnetic tape. The latter is preferred because converting the original electronic signals into a fluctuating, traveling light spot used to expose film line-by-line entails loss of data; the number of signal level steps that can be extracted from the record is greater than the number of density levels that can be recorded on film (in appendix 2A, see Johnson 1969, 201; and Smith 1977, 210–11). Not bad for an instrument originally designed as a thermal IR imager (Barrett and Curtis 1976, 15, in appendix 2A). MSS and the Thematic Mapper (TM) made their ways to fame as sensors on the Landsat series of satellites, and the AVHRR passive scanning radiometer is a sensor on the TIROS spacecraft, which began in 1979; more on Landsat later, in the section on specific systems. The trend in this area during the 1990s is toward the collection for public use of higher resolution images (one-meter resolution as the touchstone), and toward commercialization of these efforts, with Lockheed Martin, Ball Aerospace, and Boeing each involved in satellite initiatives (Corbley 1996).

Microwave Images

This area is somewhat misleadingly named; although these waves are small compared to radio and television waves, they are extremely large compared to wavelengths in the visible portion of the electromagnetic spectrum. Microwave sensors for our purposes here are either passive (e.g., microwave radiometers) or active (e.g., radar imagers, scatterometers, altimeters, etc.). Most important for library collections are the active systems, and the most important within the active area is *radar* (radio detection and ranging), which uses either pulsed or continuous radiation to illuminate a target, and then receives and displays the scattered or reflected radiation. Radar's major advantage is that, because it is an active sensor, it is all-weather, day-and-night, in operation. One of the most important of the radars is SLAR (side-looking airborne radar), which was developed for military purposes in the 1950s (in appendix 2A, Barrett and Curtis 1976, 69). Radar imagery looks like an aerial photograph of a physiographic drawing; for an example, see USGS's Radar Image Mosaic series. USGS currently has fairly extensive holdings of SLAR; inquiries should be made to the EROS Data Center. Radar is most important in the mapping arena as a basis for topographic mapping; the Amazon Basin was first mapped with any degree of accuracy in Projeto RADAM Brasil, which utilized radar coverage.

Gamma Ray Images

Gamma radiation is emitted by an atomic nucleus. Mineral-exploration methods for airborne and ground radioactivity measure the gamma radiation of radioactive elements, and are used predominantly to prospect for uranium and thorium, although they may also be used to prospect for marine phosphate deposits (which contain small amounts of uranium) and for titanium (found in thorium- and uranium-bearing placers and beach sands). Libraries tend to collect very little of this kind of imagery.

Sound Traces

Seismic exploration, the predominant geophysical activity, is the third of the trio of most used geophysical exploration methods, the other two being aeromagnetic and gravity surveying. It is based on the idea that artificially generated shock waves, reflected through or off layers of the Earth, will travel at different speeds through the rock depending on rock type. For example, the speed of seismic waves is 23,000 feet per second in igneous rock, as compared to 4,000 feet per second in sedimentary rock. Seismic waves are generated by an energy source and then detected by arrays of sensitive receiving devices, such as geophones.

Sonar (sound navigation and ranging) started out in life as ASDIC (Allied Submarine Devices Investigation Committee) during World War I. About or just after World War II, it received its present name. The majority of its uses in the past have been underwater, but it can also be used in the atmosphere. An example of its use is mapping the sea floor (see EEZ-SCAN program 1983).

Specific Remote-Sensing Systems

This is a large and flourishing area, so the following gives only the general outlines of what is available. Of all of the nonphotographic systems, Landsat (land + satellite) is the most successful of the satellites, and the first to use an MSS. All by itself, the Landsat series of satellites has caused more trees to be cut down and turned into paper—so that persons, lost in awe at the thought of this new toy, could write about it—than any of the other remote-sensing satellites. The two most helpful items in this ocean of publications are the *Landsat data users handbook* and Nicolas Short's tutorial workbook (see in appendix 2A USGS 1979 and Short 1982). Landsat-1 was launched in 1972, Landsat-2 in 1975, Landsat-3 in 1978, Landsat-4 in 1982, Landsat-5 in 1984, and Landsat-6, a failure, in 1992 (Short 1982, table I-I, in appendix 2A). The major changes came with Landsat-4; it had no RBV or data tape recorder, but it did have a new sensor, the Thematic Mapper (TM), which had seven channels of spectral ranges instead of the four of the MSS.

Besides the technical changes, Landsat-4 was notable for opening a time period of administrative and policy changes. The aim for this and future Landsats was that they be self-supporting—no minor task when the cost is in the millions or billions of dollars. On 1 October 1982, the U.S. National Oceanic and Atmospheric Administration (NOAA) took over the funding and management of archival Landsat imagery from the U.S. Department of the Interior; in January of 1983 the transfer of Landsat from Interior to NOAA was completed. Meanwhile, Landsat-4 was having operational problems, so Landsat-D was launched 1 March 1984 (that's Landsat-5, as soon as it got off the ground). The U.S. government was working to get the aforementioned full-cost recovery, and seemed to be having problems with how much federal subsidy had to be included in the deal; by late 1984, only Eastman Kodak was still in the proposal process, and there were rumblings from academia and elsewhere on the order of, "If the government routinely funds expensive data collection programs such as topographic mapping, why doesn't it fund Landsat?" (Aronoff 1985 in appendix 2A). When the dust had settled, EOSAT (Earth Observation Satellite Company) was the commercial firm selling Landsat imagery; federal funds continued to be supplied to assist in the support of new satellites (Eisenbeis 1995). There were changes over the years, and in 1990 an agreement was made to transfer imagery more than two years old to the EROS Data Center. The launching of Landsat-6 on October 5, 1993, reminded those who saw it of those lines of poetry, "I shot an arrow into the air/It fell to Earth I know not where," for the satellite disappeared into the clouds and was never heard from again. Landsat 7 is scheduled for launch in 1998; for more information, see the Website http://fdd.gsfc.nasa.gov/mission/landsat7.html .

Through all of this, Landsat imagery remained, next to aerial photography, the remote sensing a library was most likely to have; but as the prices tripled with the move toward cost recovery, library purchases were drastically curtailed. Libraries have been able to afford the various mosaics of Landsat images (usually done for states or nations) and publications of USGS that for various reasons have imagery as a part of them. One excellent example of the latter is:

United States. Geological Survey. 1984. *Landsat Thematic Mapper (TM) color combinations, Washington, D.C., and Vicinity.* (Miscellaneous investigations, map 1-1616). Reston, Va.: Author.

Of all the other many satellites orbiting about above us—one wonders why they aren't crashing into each other all the time—the other major U.S. series of immediate impact on everyday life is the weather satellite series, most notably the GOES (Geostationary Operational Environmental Satellite; first launched 1975). The most current is GOES-9, launched in 1995, orbiting at an altitude of 22,300 miles. The quarterly periodical *Earth system monitor,* 1990– , is devoted to NOAA's data and information services, and provides highly informative updates to that agency's data services, including such information as the Web address for the Historical GOES Browse Server (http://www.ncdc.noaa.gov/psguide/satellite/goesbrowse/gb.html) (see vol. 7, no. 4, p. 16). This imagery is seen every night on television by millions of persons, and is thus so common that it is not routinely collected by libraries, except in the form of weather maps from the Department of Commerce. The next big effort on the horizon is EOS (Earth Observing System), to be composed of space-based observing program, data and information management system, and research program (Stephenson 1990). It is estimated that the system will generate one terabyte *per day* of data. See the EOS periodical *The earth observer* (1989–) for current information.

The European Space Agency (ESA), a consortium of European countries, is active in the remote-sensing area. The French satellite SPOT (Système/Satellite Pour l'observation de la terre) has established itself as providing excellent images; it uses a so-called "pushbroom" MSS-like sensor. Canada's RADARSAT (launched 1995) uses Synthetic Aperture Radar (SAR) rather than SLAR. India's IRS-1C (India Remote-Sensing Satellite; launched 1995) has three sensors with different resolutions (from coarse to relatively high resolution—Wide Field Sensor with 70-meter resolution; Linear Imaging Self-Scanning Sensor with 23.5-meter resolution; Pan camera with 5.8-meter resolution) that can provide respectively images of broad areas (as AVHRR and GOES do), urban areas, and relatively small areas (Corbley 1997a and 1997b). After the breakup of the former Soviet Union, high-resolution images from Russia came on the market as SPIN (spin-2@nando.net).

Spatial Data in Digital Form

❖ *The procurement of forms of electronic map publishing*
presents map curators with major problems.
—Margaret Wilkes, in Joint Scottish ... (1987, 92)

❖ *[Cover of PC TRANS, summer 1992]*
"Coping with Computer Obsolescence"
[depicts person putting goldfish food
into a computer monitor that has become a fishbowl]

This has been an area of explosive growth, in all fields—data, software, and hardware—during the last ten years. The following is a summary of the situation at the time of writing. The surest things about it are that matters will change, and that spatial-data collections increasingly will have, as their most important part, access to digital data and appropriate software and hardware so that the user may obtain exactly the map needed (Cruse 1984). Those of us who have had our fair share of questions on the order of, "I need a map of Patagonia, showing rivers and towns only, on a sheet of paper ten inches by five inches," are actively enjoying this—even as we try to fit learning the software into an already full schedule. More of this in chapter 7, on education. It isn't just us librarians who are thinking data-software-hardware-oh, -no; geography departments the world over face what are in many ways the same challenges (Planning 1993).

A bit of background here on why cartographic databases were so warmly welcomed in the map world. *Digital mapping,* or computer mapping, is the process of making all or part of a map using a digital computer. The advantages of using a computer to do mapping are several, and are very similar to the advantages for using a computer to do any highly repetitive, detailed task: the data may be stored in such a way as to provide flexibility; the response time is greatly decreased; and, most important, maintenance of a previously established database is relatively quick and simple. The last point needs some elaboration.

Making large-scale topographic maps is an expensive and time-consuming process. And no sooner has a sheet been published than it is time to revise it. How much easier to keep map sheets up-to-date if all the data for each topographic sheet was collected in digital form! Then, when there were changes, one would just make the changes in the database, instead of having to redo the entire map. A national survey might reach the point where it no longer had to print map sheets, but could either produce sheets on demand, or sell its database and leave map production to the purchaser. This seeming chimera has tempted the national surveys since at least the mid-1960s. The problem initially, and through the early 1970s, was the state of the hardware art: computer memories were too small. For example, one digitized topographic map would take up the same amount of computation space (about 100–200 million bits) as did one book, which meant that in the 1960s digitizing one topographic sheet pretty much exhausted a computer's memory space. But the whole idea was so attractive, and could save so much time and money, that the surveys kept plugging away at it. As a sure sign of legitimacy, there came into being symposia, such as the International Conference on Computer-Assisted Cartography (Auto-Carto for short) devoted to computer cartography. Then computer memory sizes began to increase exponentially, and hardware and software became more and more capable of dealing with large datasets. Now we are to the point that virtually all the major national surveys use digital databases in some form. The British Ordnance Survey, which began digitizing its 230,000-sheet *oeuvre* in 1973, completed this mammoth task in 1995, and the Topografische Dienst Nederland was planning on having all its 1:10,000-scale maps in digital form by the end of 1997. The hydrographic surveys, which need to revise large numbers of sheets regularly, and whose data is collected in digital form anyway in many cases, are particularly pleased (McGrath and Opalski 198_?, in appendix 2A).

Of course, problems do not magically disappear; instead, new ones take the place of the old—rather like new diseases settling comfortably into a niche formerly held by an eradicated illness. For example, in the last few years USGS has been trying to figure out how to copyright its in-process topographic database. The problem is that the *Code of federal regulations* states that U.S. government documents may not be copyrighted. And so the battle is joined, with the whole matter of copyright being of primary interest; see chapter 5 on reference for more comment.

The number of publications on digital data and how to utilize it easily rivals that of the number on the history of cartography—no mean feat. The best way to swim through this sea of information, hardcopy and online, without drowning is to divide it into the aforementioned areas of data, software, and hardware, and in that order. Data is selected in accordance with the needs of one's users; the type of data dictates the types of software needed, and data and software inform us as to the type of hardware required to manipulate and serve out the data.

Data

Digital spatial datasets tend to be large, forcing the librarian to learn the meanings of the words *megabyte* (MB; 1 million bytes), *gigabyte* (GB; 1 billion bytes), *terabyte* (TB; 1 trillion bytes), and even *petabyte* (1 quadrillion

$[10^{15}]$ bytes). To put this into physical terms, one terabyte of data can be stored in about 7,000 9-track tapes; 5,000 3480 cartridges; 500 CD-ROMs; or 200 8mm cassettes. Formats to hold digital data have moved from diskettes—never very satisfactory, given the maximum for most users of 1.44MB—to the current media of choice, CD-ROMs and magnetic tapes in cassette form. CDs hold sway in the PC world and to some extent in the UNIX-workstation arena also, although the switch from 9-track tapes (as of August 31, 1997, USGS no longer distributes data on 9-track but instead uses CD, 8mm tape cartridge, 3480 tape cassette, and custom Internet download) to cartridges and cassettes has meant that the latter are still heavily used on minicomputers. Although other options, such as videodisks, exist, they are seldom encountered in the spatial-data world. Videodisks were mentioned in the mid-1980s in projects for U.S. nautical charts and Canadian topographic sheets (1:1,000,000 and 1:250,000), but little has been reported recently on their use (see *FDC Newsletter* 2 [Spring 1985]: 3).

Spatial data is generally put into digital form in one of two ways: scanning using a scanner (resulting in a raster file); or digitizing using a digitizer (resulting in a vector file). It is important not to use the word "digitizing" as if it meant "putting into digital form using any method." *Raster data* is pixel (picture-element) in nature, with rows and columns of what are basically small squares; the size of the pixel is related to the resolution in dpi (dots per inch) of the scanner, with each dot being a pixel. This is a very simplified way of looking at matters, incidentally, but it is sufficient for our purposes at this point; keep in mind that scanners scan at a resolution of pixels per inch, and printers print at a resolution of how many dots per inch are delivered to the paper. For example, digital raster graphics (DRGs) are released at 250 dpi, even though they may be scanned at resolutions of up to 500 ppi (pixels per inch). Remember, the size of the item being scanned is an important matter here: 4,000 pixels by 4,000 pixels means one thing for a hardcopy map that is 4' by 5', and something else altogether—much higher resolution—if the item scanned is a 9" x 9" aerial photograph. It's always a matter of elementary-school math—size of the item scanned times the number of ppi per inch. Thus, for a 22" x 27" map—the size of a USGS topographic quadrangle—scanned at 250 ppi is (22" x 250 ppi) x (27" x 250 ppi) = 37,125,000 pixels. An 8-bit pixel yields 256 brightness levels, which means 37.125 MB (8 bits in a byte).

What does "8-bit" display (256 colors), sometimes called bit depth, mean? Well, first of all, it's more affordable than 32-bit displays, but 32-bit is preferable. Why? Each pixel on the screen in an 8-bit display has eight locations in memory for grayscale or color information. Therefore, each pixel can be one of 256 different colors, because the 8 bits of information can be combined in 28 unique combinations. The human eye can distinguish a maximum of about 300 shades of gray, so if your users are dealing with grayscale, 8-bit is fine. But to give the full tonal range and color (of scanned color photographs, for example), a system needs 32 bits of memory for each pixel, a total of 16,777,216 possible colors. The reason you see references to "24-bit" color displays is because in 32-bit color systems

> . . . only 24 of the memory bits for each pixel are routinely used to display color on the screen ... . In 24-bit displays, three blocks of 8 bits each are assigned to handle the three primary colors used in television or computer displays: red, green, and blue. The 8 bits of information above the 24 bits of color information are called an "alpha channel," and are reserved for special-effects information such as transparency, or for combining video images with computer images. With 24-bit color displays, you see virtually photographic render-ings of color images (Lynch 1994, 32).

Some common raster file formats are TIFF (Tagged Image File Format; actually a family of files), BMP (BitMapPed image format), GIF (Compu-Serve Graphic Image Format), JPEG (a lossy compression format; Joint Photographic Experts Group), PICT (Lotus 1-2-3 picture format), TGA (Truevision Targa format), and LAN (ERDAS files). There are many more; see Rimmer 1992 and Murray 1994. Remote-sensing images collected in digital form in the first place (e.g., Landsat satellite images) are the vast majority of the time in raster form. *Vector data* is point/line/polygon data, with lines connecting points and forming polygons, and attributes attached to the points, lines, and polygons. Some common vector file formats are DLG, DWG and DXF (both originally of AutoCAD), TIGER/Line, and VPF.

Increasingly over the past ten years, and especially in the last five, spatial data in digital form is coming to the forefront in what we so modestly term "map libraries." As a sign of the times, *Library literature* has, under the heading "Information systems—Special Subjects" a sub-heading "Maps and globes," replete with citations to electronic atlases and other variants on the theme of spatial data in digital form. The most recent demand—tied directly to the development of the Web—is for such data to be available over the Internet. This data is obtained either as a physical product (such as a CD-ROM) and kept in-house, or over the Internet (and which, once obtained, can if needed become a physical product in-house); many data sets are both.

A few words on spatial datasets available over the Web are in order at this point. This is an area rife with publications, many of them excellent, as for example issue number 26, winter 1997, of *Cartographic perspec-tives*, all four of whose feature articles offer guidance on using the Web to a users' best advantage ("Cartography and the Internet: introduction and research agenda" by Michael P. Peterson; "Geographic information retrieval and the World Wide Web: A match made in electronic space" by David Johnson and Myke Gluck; "Cartography on the Internet:

Thoughts and a preliminary user survey" by Mark Harrower, C. Peter Keller, and Diana Hocking; and "Life after lectures: The Internet as a resource for a senior undergraduate GIS course" by Janet E. Mersey). The wise librarian keeps the eyes peeled for lists of digital data relating to geographic areas, such as:

- a base-data list for topographic data, compiled by University College, London, available free in the early 1990s from Sue Alstad, Information Scientist, HUGHES STX Corporation, South Dakota Operations, EROS Data Center, Sioux Falls, SD 57198

- periodicals issued by U.S. government agencies that supply spatial data in digital form, such as NOAA's *Earth science monitor* and USGS's: *JEI news*. 199?– . College Park, MD 20742-3281; Joint Education Initiative Office, University of Maryland

- F. Provost, P. Nieuwenhuysen, and W. W. de Mes, *Information related to water and the environment: Databases available on-line and on CD-ROM*. Paris: UNESCO (IHP-IV Projects M-2.1 and M-2.2), 1992. Free copies available from: Director, Division of Water Sciences, UNESCO, Place de Fontenoy, 75700 Paris, France

- Bill Thoen, *Internet resources for earth sciences*. Colorado Springs: University of Colorado, 1992– (available csn.org in COGS directory)

Over a period of about four years, the author feverishly collected every Website displaying spatial data that she could find, being especially pleased to find sites that are themselves compilations of sites, such as:

- from Sol Katz, U.S. Bureau of Land Management, ://.blm.gov/pub.gis.nsdi.html

- from Pieter van der Krogt, University of Utrecht, http://kartoserer.frw.ruu.nl/html/staff/krogto/maphist.htm and from the same server, Odden's Bookmarks, http://kartoserver.frw.ruu.nl/html/staff/oddens/odens.htm

- the University of Arkansas, http://www.cast.uark.edu/local/hunt/index.html

- the Center for Global and Regional Environmental Research, Iowa State University, http://www.cgrer.uiowa.edu/servers/servers_references.html

- the Map Collection at the Perry-Casteñada Library, University of Texas,
  http://www.lib.utexas.edu/Libs/PCL/Map_Collection/

- and naturally, from Yahoo,
  http://www.yahoo.com/yahoo/ (see also under
  /Regional/Countries/[country_name]/Business/
  Companies/Navigation/Maps/).

These are in the process of being entered at a list that is continually being updated: http://www.sdc.ucsb.edu/ . What we all want is a robot to do this searching for us, getting zero false hits (Beard 1993; and Crampton 1995). In time . . . .

Some Websites allow map-building over the Web. See especially http://www.mapquest.com , http://www.mapguide.com , and http://www.tiger.census.gov .

Some basics about downloading spatial data from the Web: Here as in the rest of life, it's important to *plan ahead.* Set up a directory on your computer for downloading files to—e.g.: c:\mil\mary\maps\. Be sure you know how much space you have available; most spatial-data files are quite large and you may have to clear off the disk before you download. CAUTION: I don't think we're in Diskette Land any more, Toto. Images that come over the Web as part of a homepage tend to be small enough that, yes, you can download to a diskette if you prefer. Just be aware that when you get a file from an ftp site, you are probably talking BIG. Also, there's the problem of inadvertently downloading a virus along with the file you wanted, so have software to check for viruses. Know what file types the software you have will work with. For example, if you have Adobe Photoshop, you will need to have files in such formats as BMP, GIF, EPS, PCX, PICT, TIFF, and a few more, or you will need to have file-conversion software. Some images print when you issue a simple print command from the browser's command bar, and some don't. You may need to place the mouse on the map, click the right mouse button, save the file (possibly as some other format—for example, Encapsulated Post-Script) to disk, and then import it into software that simultaneously handles that file format and allows you to print out.

One of the wonders of the Web is that we can use anonymous ftp without having access to a UNIX networked workstation. As an example of how this works, go to http://geohazards.cr.usgs.gov/eq/ and then to the Anonymous Information.

When dealing with electronically available information, one is looking at not only a substantial number of what are analogous to individual publishers, but also at two entities that are analogous to vendors—that is, they bring in data from other servers. The latter are WAIS (Wide Area Information Servers) and browsers such as Netscape, in which one searches a variety of databases through one interface. Netscape and similar browsers are so widely used, appreciated, and enjoyed that there is no point in discussing them. The WAIS protocol began as a project of Thinking Machines, to create a system that allows a user to access and manipulate many different kinds of data through one interface. For information on WAIS, see:

- Sally Bates, "The Internet: New WAIS to gopher information," *UNIDATA newsletter*, fall 1992, pp. 1–5.

- Brewster Kahle (Thinking Machines), at: brewster@think.com.

- Mary Lukanuski, "Help Is on the WAIS," *American libraries*, October 1992, pp. 742–44.

- USENET newsgroups under comp.infosystems on the Internet.

Now to the actual datasets. None of these listed pretends to be a definitive list, but this sampling includes those datasets that a spatial-data librarian from the United States is most likely to know about (e.g., sets issued by the federal government; widely advertised commercial sets from the United States and major publishers in other countries; etc.) The caveat is that Web sites do evanesce and change URLs. This list does not include library spatial-data scanning projects; for example, LC Geography and Map Division is planning on scanning 60,000 to 80,000 maps over the next several years as part of LC's National Digital Library project. Unfortunately, there is no registry of such projects, and it is very much needed, to keep us from doing duplicative scanning and digitization. There is a possibility that the University of Arizona's Image Clearinghouse will serve as such a (voluntary) registry.

1. World data sets. Possibly by the year A.D. 2020, we will have high-resolution (e.g., one-meter resolution) datasets available for all of the Earth's land surfaces; the following is what is available now.

    a. Maps.

        i. Base data.

            (a) *World Data Base* I and II: generated from 1:1M ONCs; available through NTIS and from some commercial vendors; usually in magnetic-tape form. *WDBI*—originally generated by the CIA—is available on the Internet from hanauma.stanford.edu World_Map directory); *WDBII* is much more usable (translation: heavy-duty programmer assistance not needed)—available from EROS in Sioux Falls, South Dakota (425MB, 170MB compressed).

            (b) *MundoCart*: also generated from 1:1M base data; work originally done by Petroconsultants; now marketed by

Chadwyck-Healey; CD-ROM; see *Information services* and use vol. 9, pp. 139–47 for a review.

(c) *DCW (Digital Chart of the World)*: done under contract by Environmental Systems Research Institute (ESRI) for the U.S. Defense Mapping Agency (DMA); available initially in VPF format (as per DMA's specifications), now commercial vendors are issuing it in formats usable by their software—e.g., ESRI has it in ARC/INFO format, American Digital Cartography (ADC) has it in MapInfo format, and DXF (AutoCAD) format either is available now or soon will be. Recently NIMA has issued Vector Map Level 0 (VMAP) to replace it.

(d) *ETOPO5*: digital relief of the surface of the Earth, with grid spacing of five minutes of latitude by five minutes of longitude; sold by U.S. National Geophysical Data Center (NGDC).

(e) World Vector Shoreline (WVS): DMA product, available for public sale; contains shorelines, international boundaries, and country names; originally on magnetic tape, now available on CD, at least in prototype.

(f) various atlases in CD form, such as those marketed by the National Geographic Society, Microsoft (*Encarta*), and products such as *PCGlobe*.

(g) *TerrainBase* global DEMs (digital elevation models); NGDC.

(h) *Global Relief* CD-ROM: available from NGDC.

ii. Thematic data. There are many of these; see the CD list of the Map and Imagery Laboratory, Davidson Library, University of California at Santa Barbara, in appendix 1.

b. Imagery. Again, a selective listing; see "Remote-Sensing Images" portion of this chapter, and CD list in appendix 1.

i. Landsat.

ii. SPOT.

iii. EOS (to come).

iv. AVHRR (Advanced Very High Resolution Radiometer). For example, the 1990 conterminous U.S. AVHRR dataset; proposed is a global land 1-kilometer dataset (by the International Geosphere-Biosphere Program, Data and Information Systems Pilot Group, USGS Global Change Program, NASA, NOAA, EEC, ESA).

v. All the various NASA CDs related to space travel—Magellan and Galileo (Venus; Earth, Moon), etc.

Great Basin Geoscience Data Base

By
Gary L. Raines, Don L. Sawatzky,
and Katherine A. Connors

U.S. GEOLOGICAL SURVEY DIGITAL DATA SERIES DDS–41
1996

Figure 1.10. CD-ROM. Raines, Gary L., Don L. Sawatzky, and Katherine A. Connors. 1996. *Great Basin Geoscience Data Base. (U.S. Geological Survey Digital Data Series* DDS-41). Reston, Va.: USGS.

2.   United States. As with hardcopy data, so with digital data; map libraries are heavily dependent upon federal agencies for datasets. The federal government as a whole, spearheaded by USGS and NIMA (absorbed DMA), is working on a National Digital Cartographic Data Base (NDCDB; 1:24K, 1:100K, 1:2M; SDTS format, DLG-E data structure) (Research and development 1991, 11). See the *Manual of federal geographic data products* for much more.

a. USGS. USGS has, from the very beginning of spatial data in digital form, been heavily involved; see, for example, its 1989 publication, *Sources for digital spatial data*. Citations to remote-sensing images, paper maps, DRGs, and DOQs are on the Global Land Information System (GLIS), at http://edcwww.cr.usgs.gov/webglis . The agency's many helpful brochures, some of which have as a heading

"USGeoData" (e.g., *Digital Cartographic and Geographic Data*; *Catalog of Digital Data*), are in the main available over the Website, http://www.usgs.gov .

i. DEMs (digital elevation models). Raster elevation data from topos (1:24K; 1:250K); complete for 1:250K. 1:24K was 41 percent complete as of January 1991.

ii. DLGs (Digital Line Graphs). Vector line data from topos; main scales are 1:100K and 1:2M; data categories for 1:100K are Public Land Survey System, boundaries, transportation, hydrogra - phy, and hypsography. Current standard is DLG-3, with information derived from topo sheets; to come is DLG-E (Enhanced), which is designed to support "enhanced" cartographic and GIS applications; its source data are published maps, existing DLG-3 data, and imagery sources. Some commercial firms, such as American Digital Cartography, sell digital versions of some topos.

iii. DOQs (Digital Orthophotoquads). "Digital image of an aerial photograph with displacements caused by camera angle and ter - rain removed" (from the USGS Fact Sheet of the product's title); issued initially in "county format" on CD; all quarter quads (at a scale of 1:12,000, with one-meter resolution) for a county are present but they are not mosaicked into a seamless image. DOQQs are uncompressed digital orthophoto quarter-quadrangles. These are issued in compressed form (JPEG or lossless, as requested) so that (in most cases) one county will fit on one CD (56M per quarter quad and 224M for a full quad means 3.4 gigabytes for an average 15-quad county if uncompressed); decompression software will be included on the CD. An estimated 12,000 CDs will be issued. Initially intended to be released to U.S. de - pository libraries, with only regional depositories receiving one copy of each CD and other depositories being entitled to select CDs for one state, the distribution was on hold by early 1997 (Manzer 1995).

iv. DRGs (digital raster graphics). Scans of each topographic quadrangle, on CD, arranged in 1:250K blocks of quadrangles (1:24K, 1:100K, and 1:250K quads for a given area). A scan (at 250 dpi) of each map is stored as a compressed TIFF file, with files ranging in size from about five to about 15 MB; a 10 MB compressed TIFF file will ex - pand to about 40 MB. These were initially distributed through the U.S. depository program; several problems developed (e.g., errors in the GEOTIFF files that are to be used to knit scans of adjacent areas to - gether; a full realization of how much it was going to cost to produce all those CDs), and it went on hold by early 1997.

v. And many more. USGS has been heavily involved in digital data for some years (cf. *Scientific and technical, spatial, and biblio-graphic data bases and systems of the U.S. Geological Survey,* 1983 [1984?]). USGS's Geologic Division alone had, in the late 1980s, about 150 databases and systems, e.g., National Coast Resources

Data System; Index to Geologic Maps (GEOINDEX); Geologic Names of the United States (GEONAMES); etc. (Davis 1990, 22–23). GNIS—the geographic-names database for the United States—has every name from every topographic quadrangle included in it. It thus includes names not necessarily accepted by the U.S. Board of Geographic Names.

   b. U.S. Bureau of the Census (USBC).

      i. TIGER (Topologically Integrated Geographic Encoding and Reference files). Generated for the 1990 Census by USGS for USBC, from the 1:100K quads (planimetric data only), and issued in up-dated form very nearly every year since. The 1980 Census generated GBF/DIME files (Geographic Data Base/Dual Independent Map Encoding), which are nowhere nearly as extensive as the TIGER files, either in geographic coverage or in amount of data per file. Many commercial firms have seized eagerly upon the TIGER files as a source for added-value products; Census has available on demand a list of firms that have registered with Census as working with TIGER. A sampling of these firms includes Klynas (Streets), Etak (MapBase), and Geographic Data Technology (DYNAMAP/2000); there are many, many more.

      Census started out not providing any software for TIGER, leaving that void to commercial firms to fill; it became obvious that was not working very well, so for several years, Census has provided a software called LandView. See the following Websites for help or tutorials:

   nsus.gov/geo/www/tiger/lv2_doc.html
   nsus.gov/geo/www/tiger/lv2tutor.html

   c. U.S. Soil Conservation Service. SCS is deeply involved in a digital soils-mapping program; see the excellent pamphlet (free) from the Wisconsin State Cartographer, called *Wisconsin soil mapping*. USGS has also issued a helpful brochure (*Digital soils data*). The nationwide, 1:250K database is called STATSGO. As new soil surveys are produced, they are put into digital form.

   d. NGDC. Map librarians have come almost to expect a flier or two a month from these people in Boulder about some new, must-have product of spatial data in digital form. In the world-datasets portion of this is the *Global Relief* CD; on the U.S. side is, for example, the 30-Second U.S. topography data for personal computers *(TOPO-30)*.

e. U.S. Bureau of Land Management. General Land Office Automated Records Project puts, on CD, pre-1908 homestead and cash entry patent and cadastral survey plat index.

f. And just about every other federal agency you can think of that deals with spatial data. For example, the Forest Service actively pursues GIS applications in forestry. Kilauea volcano data on CD was just issued by NASA this year, as were the Oregon Transect Ecosystem CDs.

g. Many, many atlas and travel products, most based on federal products such as TIGER files; e.g. DeLorme (*Street Atlas*; *Map'n'Go*), Rand McNally (*TripMaker*), Microsoft (*Automap road atlas*), etc.

3. State and local products. Many geological surveys have digital data files and products; on the local side, the heavy use here is existing landbases, especially cadastral, and those agencies dealing with the provision of services (police; fire; utilities). Also, federal agencies frequently issue datasets related to a given state (as the two examples given in the last paragraph), for example, Minnesota Aeromagnetic Data (2 CDs; DOS; Windows). For example:

   NORTH CAROLINA

   —*North Carolina geographic data catalog. 1995. Raleigh: State of North Carolina Center for Geographic Information and Analysis.*

4. Commercial firms. There are many of these, and they're multiplying; the afore-mentioned DeLorme, Geovision, etc.

5. Non-United States. And here the author is reduced to supplying lists of sources! Not given are the standard publications lists of national topographic and geologic surveys, which frequently contain listings of data available in digital form.

   FRANCE

   —*Catalogue des sources d'informations géographiques numériques de niveau national. 2d ed. 1995. Paris: Conseil National de l'Information Géographique and Association Française pour l'Information Géographique.*

   GREAT BRITAIN

   —Data Consultancy (URPI Group Ltd., 7 Southern Court, South Street, Reading RG1 4QS): two titles of interest:

a. *Data set news*

b. *Spatially referenced data sets catalogue: Including maps, boundaries and databases*

—Data directory. 1997. *Mapping awareness* 11(6): 33–35.

—Finch, Sara. 1987. *Cartographic and remote-sensing digital databases in the United Kingdom*. (BL Information Guide 6). London: BL Research and Development Department.

—Gittings, Bruce. 199?– . *Catalogue of digital elevation data*. Department of Geography, University of Edinburgh, Drummond Street, Edinburgh EH8 9XP, SCOTLAND.

—O'Carroll, Paul. 1994. *Directory of digital data sources in the UK*. Oxford, U.K.: Oxford Brookes University.

—SINES (Spatial INformation Enquiry Service): computerized directory of spatial datasets held by U.K. government agencies; free service run by Ordnance Survey, on behalf of the Department of the Environment.

—Wolf, Michael; and Duncan Wingham. 1992. *WP4010: A survey of the world's digital elevation data*. Dorking, Surrey, U.K.: Mullad Space Science Laboratory with the Department of Electronic and Electrical Engineering, University College London.

Software

There are three different categories of software here: image processing; GIS (geographic information system); and everyone's favorite category, other. Those of us who remember the early days sigh after USGS's noble 1987 effort, *Sources for software for computer mapping and related disciplines*; since that time, no one has been brave enough to issue another. What follows is not a definitive list, but rather more common software of the time; versions and prices rapidly change and thus are not usually mentioned here. Some vendors, such as ESRI, have in the past been generous about giving out discounted software and licenses to institutions of higher education; check around, see what's running and what deals are already in place. You may well be able to piggyback onto them for a relatively small amount of money (e.g., the DEC software library on your campus; existing ESRI arrangements); *but* it's worth your time to check and make sure that's the best deal—perhaps the firm has special lower pricing for libraries (or perhaps you can persuade it that it should have).

Let's start with image-processing software.

Image-Processing Software

Image processing is the manipulation and interpretation of graphics (any graphic—art object, map, whatever) in digital form, using a computer. Image-processing software works with raster (pixelated) files. Commonly used techniques are:

- rectification and restoration: manipulating raw data to correct distortions and fit the image to a map base

- enhancement: any process that sharpens or brings out more clearly detail of interest to the user

- classification: assign pixels (picture element; smallest non-divisible element of a digital image) to thematic categories (e.g., land-cover classes)

- data merging: merging different types of image data (e.g., Landsat TM with SPOT).

Image-processing software for scientific analysis differs from graphic-arts image-processing software in that the former includes many routines for image interpretation and analysis. But a good graphic-arts image-processing program (e.g., Adobe Photoshop; http://www.adobe.com) will contain many of the same image-enhancement routines found in scientific image-processing software in the following list:

- ERDAS; ERDAS Imagine: for PC, Sun, DEC platforms. ERDAS Inc., 2801 Buford Highway NE, Suite 300, Atlanta, GA 30329; http://www.erdas.com ; comes in modules, with each module separately priced; educational discount—a "bundle" for the PC of CORE, raster GIS modeling, and image processing.

- IDRISI: DOS, Windows. IDRISI Project, Graduate School of Geography, Clark University, 950 Main Street, Worcester, MA 01610; http://www.idrisi.clarku.edu ; because it was originally written for and is maintained by a university geography department, this is a good choice for a library serving academia.

- IMDISP (Interactive Image Display program): DOS. Derived in 1989 from VICAR (mainframe software from Jet Propulsion Lab's Video Image Communication and Retrieval System); comes with some U.S.-government-issued CDs; generally available off the Web from different sites; do a Web search on IMDISP and see what's available; for example, in 1997, http://nssdc.gsfc.nasa.gov/cd-rom/software/imdisp.html .

- xv: UNIX. Inexpensive (ca. $25 in mid-1990s); license from John Bradley, 1053 Floyd Terrace, Bryn Mawr, PA 19019; bradley@cis.upenn.edu .

- EXCEL. May sound strange, but there are reports of version 6.0 serving as a teaching tool (e-mail, as of 30 January 97, Pine.SOL.3.95.970126152583.29320F-100000@maps.lib. umich.edu , from C.E. Olson).

GIS (Geographical Information System) Software

Some GIS users still hold the (subconscious) opinion that information provided by a computer is somehow inherently correct (Ian Denness, 1997. Some data is more equal than others. *Mapping awareness* 11(7):26). Any librarian dealing with or reading about cartographic databases will be ineluctably drawn into geographic information systems (GIS), "data management systems that capture, organize and use spatial data utilizing the computer" (Gates and Neil 1980, 105). GIS software may be thought of as a computerized system to capture, analyze, and display spatial data, which does so by integrating a wide range of data (e.g., maps; remote-sensing images; attribute data—numerical or descriptive data that is geo-coded). Another way to view it is as many different layers of information for one given geographic area. GISs tend to have extensive I/O (input/output) and heavy CPU requirements. A GIS should be able to:

- work with large, heterogeneous spatial databases

- query databases about the existence, location, and characteristics of a wide variety of objects

- operate efficiently

- be tailored (both to applications and to users)

- "learn" about data and a user's objectives

- supply a readily interpreted output product.

Its five essential parts are data acquisition, preprocessing, data management, manipulation and analysis, and product generation. See the most current edition of USGS's colorful poster/brochure called *Geographic Information Systems* if you'd like more information but not too much more; there are several GIS introductory texts out (e.g., Star and Estes 1990, in appendix 2A).

Prices for software are what your library can negotiate; if your library is a member of ARL, it's worth getting into the ARL/GIS Literacy Project—ArcView software and some data (at least in the past) come free to the library, but the library must make the commitment to get appropriate hardware:

- ARC/INFO: with its viewing module for ARC data, ArcView; DOS, UNIX. Environmental Systems Research Institute (ESRI), http://www.esri.com

- Atlas/GIS: Windows for DOS. Software now owned by ESRI

- AutoCAD: PC and UNIX. AutoDesk (http://www.autodesk. com). Engineering-drafting software, and thus not true GIS

software, but allows the construction of layers that could be
used in a GIS (e.g., ESRI's module ArcCAD) software product

- GRASS: Geographic Resource Analysis Support System; UNIX.
  A public-domain program that is relatively little heard of at the
  current time; associated primarily with the U.S. Army's Corps
  of Engineers; homepage at http://www.ceer.army.mil/grass/
  GRASS.main.html . For a manual, see: Westervelt, J. D. 1989.
  GRASS user's reference manual. Champaign, Ill.: U.S. Army
  Construction Engineering Research Laboratory

- IDRISI: see image-processing software above. IDRISI has elements of GIS software

- MapInfo: DOS. MapInfo, http://www.mapinfo.com

- and more, e.g., Caliper (http://www.caliper.com)

"Other"

As one might expect, this is the nine-tenths of the iceberg that make
all that software and data usable. At the base of everything is the operating
system, with all it takes to keep it going—DOS, UNIX, Ethernet and other
networking software, Windows and Windows NT, security, anti-virus, and
so forth. A very helpful guide to network communications is the most
current edition of Lantronix's *Ethernet tutorial & product guide*
(http://www.lantronix.com ; 15353 Barranca Parkway, Irvine, CA 92618).
Hint: a T1 is 1.544 MBPS (megabytes per second) Internet access.

An essential for any facility dealing with spatial data in digital form is
compression/decompression software, e.g., PKZIP and PKUNZIP ($47 from
PKWare Inc., Brown Deer, WI). Two terms you may see used here are *lossless*
and *lossy* techniques; the first produces compressed files that can be
decompressed into files identical to the original (compression ratios of 2:1
to 10:1 for text and software, less than 2:1 for digital orthophotos, for
example). Lossy software produces compressed files that decompress into
close representations of the original, with ratios of 5:1 up to 30:1 or more
(for example, for digital orthophotos, 10:1 to 15:1 are recommended).

Another essential program is that for file conversion. If the rule with
maps is "Whatever the user needs is at the intersection of four topos," the
rule with digital data is "Whatever form or format you have it in, the user
needs it in some other form or format." There is, for example, Image
Alchemy (Handmade Software, Inc.; 15951 Los Gatos Blvd., Suite 17, Los
Gatos, CA 95032; http://www.handmadesw.com). Handmade's
homepage has a page about running Image Alchemy over the Web, so
you may convert a file right there and try it out. Conversion software for
Unix is available from the San Diego Supercomputer Center.

As part of the new Murphy's Law for spatial data in digital form—
whatever form you have it in, users need it in something else—we have

progressed through "if you have it in hard copy, users need it in digital form (scanners; digitizers)," "if you have it in digital form, users will need hard copy (printers of various capabilities)," and "whatever file format you have it in, users will need it in something else (file-conversion software such as Image Alchemy)"; now we progress to the translations from one base to another. Keep your eyes open for such software as:

> Botz, Maxwell K. 1969. *Conversion of section-township-range to latitude-longitude—A computer technique. (Special publication* vol. 48). Butte: Montana College of Mineral Science and Technology.

> PLANE-PC, interactive grid coordinate conversion for personal computers. 1984– . Reston, Va.: USGS.

There are many other kinds of software of interest to the spatial-data collection—visualization software; mapping software (e.g., Harvard Graphics); clipart; compound-document software; word-processing; desktop-publishing—and on and on. When the need arises, the librarian will probably find there are several competing software packages available. User testing is an important first step before purchasing.

Hardware

Hardware requirements are driven by the needs of your users, the large size of digital spatial-datasets (e.g., 100M for the Los Angeles County TIGER/Line boundary files), and by the complexity of the applications (and therefore of the software) that the users need. The following hardware requirements will change as computers become more powerful.

The basic level starts out with a CPU (central processing unit) of some kind—microcomputer (PC/Mac), minicomputer (workstation), mainframe. Micros and minis are getting closer and closer together, and may at some point merge into one large, amorphous glop. There is strong feeling—due to painful experience—that running GIS software and datasets on a PC (even a 586) is less than satisfactory, and that what best performs effective image-crunching is a workstation; this attitude is changing as PCs get more and more powerful and software writers find slick ways to get around DOS's RAM limit. The catch here is that although PCs are less capable than workstations, they are less expensive and much less difficult and complicated to deal with than are workstations. For example, anyone who can insert diskettes in a drive and type "install" can install software on a PC; DOS is set up so that mere mortals—even mechanical incompetents—can deal with it. More sophisticated operating systems, such as UNIX, are a completely different matter; loading software, especially operating-system software, is a job for an expert. Loading applications software is marginally easier, but in both cases one is dealing with such matters as license managers, so even administratively it is more complex. Having networks—into which one is inevitably sucked when one goes the workstation route or when one has an urge to surf the Web via browser—complicates matters even more. In a draft version of *Recommended minimum specifications for public access work stations in Federal depository libraries* (e-mail from Diane L. Morey, March 21, 1997, dmorey@gpo.gov , of the U.S. Government Printing Office; no message-id; view at http://www.access.gpo.gov/su_docs/dpos/spatial.html), some new specifications came out:

> IBM-compatible Pentium chip, 133Mhz (minimum). Megahertz means "clock speed, expressed in terms of megahertz, or millions of cycles per second. How many times per second electricity cycles through the chip's circuitry is an important measure of microprocessor performance" (Microprocessor . . . 1994, 14)

> Ports: one serial; one Universal Serial Bus; one parallel; one P/S-2 mouse; one SVGA video

> I/O bus: PCI/ISA

> Drive bays: one 3.5" high-density drive; three 5.25" HH externally accessible drives; two 3.5" HH internal drives

> RAM: 24MB minimum, 48MB recommended

> Hard-disk drive: 3 gigabyte capacity, partitioned into two 1.5 GB drives; IDE or SCSI interface

> Floppy disk: 3.5" 1.44MB drive

> CD-ROM drive: 4X speed minimum, 8X or higher speed recommended; should support all available standard CD formats

> Monitor: 17" Super VGA (SVGA) multimedia monitor, 0.28 or smaller dot pitch; 21" SVGA compatible for spatial data, with at least 70MHz vertical-refresh rate, 1024x768 resolution non-interlaced, 0.28 or smaller dot pitch, and display card that supports 1024x768 resolution at 70 MHz or faster

> Video: 64- or 128-bit PCI interface SVGA controller; 2MB Windows RAM (WRAM) or Video RAM (VRAM), expandable to at least 4MB WRAM or VRAM; recommended—MPEG hardware acceleration; Sound Blaster 16 or better or compatible

> Printer: ink jet or laser that supports PostScript; 10MB memory minimum; for spatial data, color ink-jet plotter, 36" 300dpi, 68 MB or more memory, or access to comparable networked printer

> Pointing device: Microsoft-compatible mouse or other compatible pointing device

Internet connectivity: local-area network with TCP/IP (strongly recommended) or dial-up SLIP/PPP connection using 33.6kbps or better modem (internal modem advisable)

Operating system: MS-DOS 6.22 with Microsoft Windows for Workgroups 3.11 or Microsoft Windows 95b or Microsoft Windows NT 4.0 Workstation

Communications software: supports multiple file-transfer protocols, several terminal emulations (e.g., VT-100), Hayes AT-compatible modems; data-transfer rates up to 33.6 kbps; manages telnet sessions

Client software: Web browser (e.g., Netscape, Internet Explorer, etc.) with forms support; ANSI Z39.50-compatible, GILS-aware WAIS client

Viewing software: Web graphical browser for both GIF and JPEG graphics; additional PDF (Adobe) and MPEG player, plus viewers for other file formats such as TIFF; for spatial data, GEOTIFF file view and viewing software for raster data, such as Photoshop or PrintShop

Applications software: integrated office suite (e.g., Microsoft Office; Corel WordPerfect)—database, spreadsheet, word-processing; for spatial data, data-manipulation package such as ArcView, MapInfo, LandView, etc.

If you can tell that the work your users need to do is not possible on a PC, the first thing to do is write up a detailed plan of what the users do need. Then consult a systems manager and find out what you need to get the users what they need. If your users' needs mean that you decide to go the network route, you will need a server, which is basically a workstation, of any size, that is built with components that specifically permit it to act as a server. The object of a server is to connect multiple users or provide multiple users with services. Servers are more expensive than standard workstations (strange, you don't look surprised); DOS servers are available. Not surprisingly (once again), networking software isn't cheap either. Be sure to look at the speed of the server's different components; the lowest speed of any one of them is your limiting factor. Be wary; get the smallest (equals least expensive) machine you can get that will do what your users need done. Computer hardware changes very quickly, and you don't want to invest heavily in something, only to find out that two months later it's available for half what you paid for it. Go for the workhorses; leave the cutting-edge equipment to the researchers on campus (Planning 1993).

For a minicomputer (workstation), one is looking at the same general types of software—operating system (UNIX-type operating system, e.g., VMS, SUN-OS), application software, peripherals, and so on. The most difficult part about obtaining the software is paying for it, although wending one's way through inputting the licensing codes can remind you of a visit to the dentist. On the bright side, more and more software (both OS and applications) is coming on CDs, which makes it somewhat easier to deal with.

The advanced applications software should be capable of handling large databases, and the hardware should have speeds of at least 200Mhz. Get the highest-speed processing you can afford. If you don't, you're wasting money—that's the whole point of having workstations. Speedy swapping of data in and out of memory, for example, is essential for the machines to run optimally. Get the sturdiest equipment you can find, and BUY MAINTENANCE—it will save money and aggravation, in the short and the long run, although you will find that difficult to believe when you see the bills for maintenance. *Running workstations is expensive.* At times during the workstation-adding process, you may be reminded of the old saying about owning a yacht (if you have to ask how much it costs, you can't afford it).

You now need a full-time employee (FTE) who loves working with UNIX, believes in backing up the system religiously, and believes even more fervently in having a *written* systems manual (after all, when it goes down—and it will—you won't be able to consult an online manual to figure out how to bring it back up). Actually, you'll need two persons; keeping the systems manager chained to his/her chair at all times is frowned on, so you need backup for when one person is on vacation/sick leave/coffee break/lunch. If you don't have a backup person, the machines will know when Their Master leaves and will immediately fail or start making funny clunking noises—or, more ominously, no noise at all. Write up instructions on how and when to do backup and how to bring the system back up *immediately*; you'll need them.

RAM of 200MB and higher, and at least 100GB of ROM, are important; workstations are memory hogs, which is why they can do so much so quickly. The reason for all this memory space is that, as your mother long ago told you, nothing in this life is free. The elegant, sophisticated, complicated tasks a workstation performs cost, big time, in terms of disk space. The operating system alone can easily be in the hundreds of MB (and will be, if it's UNIX); applications can take from 100 to 600MB; at that rate, 1.5GB goes quickly. You need to have two to three times in swap space what you have in RAM; for example, if you have 30MB RAM, then you need 100–150MB in swap space. Which means that you need to have 1.5–2GB just for software and swap space. Now, what about space for the actual data that you're working with? See why 100GB sounds comfortable? One more time for this important point—get as much disk as you can afford. You will also need tape drives: 9-track is going the way of the dinosaur, but there's still lots of it out there, especially in some areas of the federal government, so be on the safe side and get one; 8mm cassette in whatever the current most popular size is (1.5–20GB; no, that 20 is not a typo). Next comes support for the peripherals noted earlier, with a few extra (and of course expensive) requirements:

> printers (black-and-white laser printer for relatively inexpensive text printing—amazing how this Paperless Society is not quite working out; a color printer with 24MB of memory)
>
> plotter (finally not as finicky and expensive—e.g., $1,000 per month just for maintenance—as they were)
>
> high-resolution, 21" monitor
>
> scanners (up to 11" x17"; oversize).

Printers print out raster-data files; plotters plot vector data. Because the majority of data in GISs is vector data, plotters are often important features in GIS labs. These vector presentations can be rasterized and printed out on a printer.

There is yet one further level—mainframes. While only a few days of working with large spatial-data files will make you lust after a Cray or a Meiko for your collection, stern reality says this is not an area with which you will normally need to concern yourself.

Libraries are accustomed to equipment like map cases or book stacks. You buy them about once every five to twenty years, they never need maintenance, they almost never need repair, and they never need updating. Nothing could be further from dealing with computer hardware and software. Then there's the little matter of who's going to maintain the hardware in a time of diminishing or stable staff numbers to boot. (Words to the wise: SERVICE CONTRACTS, plus basic trouble-shooting training for staff—starting with "make sure it's plugged in and turned on" and building from that.) Over the years, watching in awe (and occasional disbelief or even fleeting horror), this author has come to look upon the computer side of the shop as reminiscent of the title of the Don Henley 1984 song, *Building the perfect beast*. Dr. Frankenstein has nothing on us so-called "map" librarians.

Supporting Materials

Both monographs and serials—and especially, in the latter category, periodicals—are increasingly subject to electronic publishing. Not just supporting materials but spatial data as a category are moving inexorably toward being stored and accessed by computers; librarians not familiar with this trend have been hermits inside a cave for the last ten years.

Monographs

We now happily relapse into the more traditional book-format materials, dealing first with monographs. Chief among these are: works on cartography and the history of cartography; gazetteers; geographical dictionaries; guidebooks, cartobibliographies of the nonserial type; and works on map librarianship. See appendix 2A for general works which this author has found most helpful over the years and the bibliography for works on map librarianship. Of particular use for citations to monographs and serials of interest in cartography is the strongly recommended 1990 work, *Information sources in cartography* (appendix 2A), a gem of a publication that includes survey chapters in such areas as the history of cartography, general works, map production, map librarianship, and various types of maps. Works on general cartography are less abundant than works on the history of cartography; the latter constitute a severe threat to almost any library's budget because they are often beautifully illustrated, and thus a temptation to the librarian to purchase even if the profile of the library does not justify it. Geographical dictionaries, guide-books (such as Baedeker's), and gazetteers are important reference works—geographic dictionaries for ready reference, guidebooks for city plans (keep the old ones for historical maps of cities), and gazetteers for ready reference not only by users but also by catalogers. Cartobibliographies and works on map librarianship are more likely to be encountered in larger or more specialized libraries.

In about 1840, city plans showing some detail became a standard feature in the better guidebooks, such as those by Murray (from 1836 on) and Baedeker (from 1839 on) (Otness 1981, 270–72). So, though it is understood that for geographical and travel reference questions, the most recent work is required, the older editions are excellent for historical information. And in all cases, the maps are just the right size for photocopying (Otness 1972a, 17–23). The librarian has a plethora of guidebooks from which to choose—AAA, Baedeker, Fodor, and Michelin come most readily to mind.

Gazetteers are among the most frequently consulted of reference books in a spatial-data collection. The traditional names are the 1950s *Columbia-Lippincott gazetteer* (to be available in 1998, *finally,* in a new and sure to be much appreciated edition), *Webster's geographical dictionary*, and the *Cambridge world gazetteer* (see appendix 2A). Many libraries supplement these with the index in a major atlas or two, usually the *Times atlas of the world* and the Rand McNally *Commercial atlas and marketing guide*. The latter served for many years as the unofficial gazetteer of U.S. place names, as the U.S. Board on Geographic Names, and although active in publishing gazetteers of foreign countries (see U.S. Board on Geographic Names in appendix 2A), has never published one of the United States. In 1982 the USGS began publishing a national gazetteer (its *Professional paper* 1200). As a stopgap device, USGS had been issuing volumes since the late 1970s in its Geographic Names

Information System (GNIS), as state-by-state lists of computer printout. The *Omni gazetteer* (1991, in appendix 2A) is much used in many libraries; the publisher used as a basis for the volumes the digital tapes of GNIS. Meanwhile, on the foreign front, the Board, in its Foreign Names Branch, continues to work on foreign gazetteers, with an office located in DMA (now part of NIMA), which, under its former name (Army Map Service), had also issued gazetteers, some specifically to accompany map series that the agency had published (U.S. Army Map Service 1946, in appendix 2A).

There are also gazetteers issued by commercial publishers, usually for states or smaller areas (see Proehl and Shupe 1984 in appendix 2A). Like older guidebooks, older gazetteers are valuable, especially for genealogical reference work and for areas, such as Poland and Germany, where borders over the years have been fluid. The gazetteers for both U.S. and foreign names are available over the Web, with the foreign-names portion at http://164.214.2.53/gns/html/index.html and also through the Alexandria Digital Library, http://www.alexandria.ucsb.edu . The U.S. names have been available at different sites over the Web years; the USGS site is http://www-nmd.usgs.gov/www/gnis/ .

Cartobibliographies are at least as important and as needed as any other kind of bibliography because: maps have traditionally not been cataloged; there is no equivalent to *Books in Print* for maps; maps may appear in almost any book or periodical; and maps concerning virtually any subject may be published. For all these reasons, the librarian will find that the Z6026 and Z6027 section of the stacks in an LC-classed library swells perceptibly over time.

Works on map librarianship tend to be primarily of the periodical variety, but there are such bibliographies as Winch 1976 (see appendix 2A) and Watkins 1967, and works on cataloging and classification.

Serials

One of the most striking love-hate relationships in the library world is that between libraries and serials. We can't live with them, we can't live without them, and they are so expensive! All the old clichés about difficulties between men and women fit equally well here, and are evidenced by the rueful affection of the ALA RTSD Serials Section's "Worst Title Change of the Year" awards (criteria: frivolous title change for no apparent reason and producing no advantage; the unnecessary change of an old, respected title; repeated changes, the latest being no better than any other ones; and the *"Et tu, Brute?"* category for library publications— more recently known as the "Snake in the Grass" award) (RTSD *Newsletter* 9 (No. 4, 1984): 41–42). Map librarians are relatively fortunate here; although we require serials just as much as anyone else, at least our old favorites don't change name with every new moon; there seems to be something sobering about mapping a country in blocks six miles by four miles. And compared with the costs of many physical-sciences serials, the prices do not bring the quick intake of breath so commonly heard in serials departments in the last twenty years. So although the literature has grown rapidly since World War II, expansion of titles is relatively slender, and prices seem as reasonable as we can hope.

Now let us view the spatial-data serials world. In 1970 Richard Stephenson published a most helpful article titled "Published sources of information about maps and atlases." Part of the abstract is, regrettably, as true now as it was then, although matters are improving:

> Even though it is a negative note, it is a fact that the map and atlas publishing field is woefully lacking in biblio-graphic controls. Many countries, for example, produce ex-cellent national bibliographies to describe their book trade. Although citations to significant atlases are included in many of these bibliographies, individually published maps are gen-erally excluded. Unfortunately for the harassed map librar-ian, current bibliographic references are scattered—and often inadequate (Stephenson 1970, 87).

Keeping all of the above in mind—and simultaneously keeping a grip on the idea that yes, we do want to continue to work with spatial data—we shall proceed on our serials journey.

In the serials category, we have yearbooks, monographic serials, irregular series, and periodicals. Yearbooks are most notably represented by the *International yearbook of cartography* (see appendix 2A). Mono-graphic series include the extremely important USGS folded-map series (e.g., I, HA, GQ, MF, C, OM, OC, GP), the equivalent state geological survey series (such as the New York State *Map and chart series*), and other series composed of maps (such as the Geological Society of America's *Map and chart series*).

Irregular series take on anything that is not included anywhere else; and with periodicals, we enter the world of publications that are issued more often than once a year. Most important in the irregular category are the catalogs of map publishers and dealers; for addresses for these agencies, see Allin 1982 and *Worldwide directory* 1984 (both in appendix 2A). Increasingly one may find these catalogs over the Web, using the form http://www.[name_of_firm].com . In the yearbook and periodical area, we have the national bibliographies containing map and atlas citations, the cartographic accession lists (in some ways just an extension of the previously mentioned item), and various journals, usually devoted to map librarianship or to geography (Cobb 1977a; Drazniowsky 1967; Salichtchev 1979; Stephenson 1970; and D. A. Wise 1977b, 1978b, 1979a, 1979b). Some journals are appearing on the Web, as for example *Current geographical publications* (http://leardo.lib.uwm.edu/cgp/cgp.html). Some periodicals have special issues on cartographic materials; examples of this are:

AB bookman's weekly 77 (June 9, 1986) [on "Cartography, voyages and travels"]

Drexel library quarterly 9 (4), 1973 [on map librarianship]

Government publications review 10 (4), 1983 [on government mapping]

Library trends 29, 1981 [on map librarianship and map collections]

PERS 45 (12), 1979 [on USGS centennial]

The next step—horrifying, but logical—is to consider periodicals in which articles on mapping may occasionally appear, or that use maps to illustrate articles; such a list would be at least half the size of the most current Ulrich's. The American Geographical Society has nobly taken on the task of indexing maps in books and periodicals (see in appendix 2A American Geographical Society 1968). It is likely that the best way to attack this matter is to be sure that maps in articles are indexed by computer indexing and abstracting services.

Microform

The thought has surfaced that spatial data on microform is an idea whose time has come and gone, because of the many benefits of digital technology; yet there still remain good reasons to collect materials in this format, largely tied to the relative inexpensiveness of the products. Although microform is photography and thus might logically appear in the remote-sensing portion of this chapter, it was first used for text material and only more recently for maps, so it is subsumed under supporting material, even though, like previous sections in this chapter, it overlaps with other sections—indeed, almost all other sections. Serials and monographs have been available on microform for some time because of the considerable savings in purchase cost and storage space that microform brings. The availability of maps on microform is relatively more recent (Knight 1975–1976; Smyth 1977; and Cruse 1980, 1981a–e, 1985a).

The major reasons for microforming maps are: to protect and preserve the originals; to save space by disposing of maps not needed in hard copy and by putting low-use, hardcopy maps in storage; and to facilitate accessibility and wider dissemination (copies easily made, and interlibrary loan a possibility for older or fragile maps). But the special problems involved with microforming maps are such as nearly to make one reconsider:

1. Color carries information; therefore microforms of maps should be in color, and color microform has lower resolution (maps need high resolution) and lower stability than does black-and-white film. The exception to this is Cibachrome, the production of which has toxic byproducts.

2. Maps come in a wide variety of sizes, almost all of them too large for standard equipment.

3. Maps often have very fine lines, poor background contrast, and a wide variety of typefaces on just one map.

4. Because scale is so important, reproduction must be made in such a way that undistorted copies can be made.

5. Maps that have been rolled are difficult to flatten enough to be photographed.

6. What library users want—and consider to be their birthright—is hardcopy reproduction, in color, and preferably full-sized; no such universal, inexpensive reader-printer exists.

(Langelier 1979, 1–2; Grimaldi 198; Goulard 1981; and Hoehn l978a)

No one would have kept on trying were it not for the substantial improvement in color microfiche (as evidenced by the work of such firms as Micro Aero Charts Inc. of Colorado Springs), and also for the nearly simultaneous continuance of both the information explosion and inflation. The latter two combined means that even if libraries have the space to purchase large map series (and they usually do not), they do not have the money—unless said series could be available in microform (Hodur 1984; Sauer 1984; and Stevens 1970). WAML (Western Association of Map Libraries) has an active map-microfilming program, which uses cooperative purchasing and focuses on specific series, such as detailed topographic map series of France produced before and during the Revolution (Cruse 1985d).

The agencies involved in microforming maps tend to be large ones, most notably the U.S. National Archives, USGS, and the National Map Collection of Canada (now part of the Audiovisual, Cartographic and Sound Archives of Canada). The National Archives was among the first to do substantive research on microforming maps and is often quoted, particularly its finding that using 105mm film for maps is greatly superior to using 35mm film. The National Archives has been very heavily involved in reproducing aerial photographs on microfilm (Williams et al. 1984, 1437–39; Taubes 1973; Oman and Taylor 1972; and Ehrenberg 1977).

USGS's major microfilm program was microfilming all of its topographic sheets (1884–), with maps being added periodically; the film used is 35mm, black-and-white, high-resolution film with a reduction ratio of 20X, 500 frames on a roll, available in silver film or diazo film. USGS has issued a publication entitled, *Approximate number of microfilm rolls to cover states, compiled* . . .; any library interested in purchasing such rolls should request the most current edition of the list from USGS (Markham 1978; Faries 1979; and Simmons 1978).

The U.S. Bureau of the Census has put maps on fiche and computer, along with nearly everything else, for obvious reasons. The former U.S. Bureau of Mines microfilmed all the mine maps it could find; the system, which includes computer indexing and hardcopy reproduction, has apparently been relocated in the USGS Denver office (Gait 1970; Eaton and Gait 1968; and Whaite 1965). Probably this is only the tip of an iceberg of federal map microforming, but it gives an idea of what is going on.

Some state agencies microform maps; for example, the Highway Department of the state of Colorado in the past microfilmed not only its own maps but also U.S. Forest Service maps of the state. Doubtless the same sort of situation pertains in other states.

The Université Laval Cartothèque had for ten years (1969–1979) a system called Cartomatique, based on Kodak's Selector Miracode, which allowed automated retrieval of images on 16mm coded microfilm. As a result, the Cartothèque had a microlibrary of 25,000 maps, including maps in theses done in Canadian universities and maps in Canadian periodicals (Tessier 1979b, 23–24). In 1979 the Provincial Archives of British Columbia had about half of the collection on 105mm film (Langlier 1979, 7). On the other side of the ocean, the British Ordnance Survey offered, beginning in 1970, a microfilm service (Maps from microfilm 1976; and Recommendations 1972), and on the other side of the other ocean, the Australian Electoral Office produced a set of microfiche of all Commonwealth electoral maps (Commonwealth electoral maps 1983, 4).

Commercial publishers, such as Microchart Navigation Systems, entered the field, at first with maps in which color is of relatively little importance, but also providing on a contract basis color microfiche of whatever users are willing to pay for.

Miscellaneous

This final category of supporting materials may truthfully be defined as "whatever else the spatial-data library gets stuck with," and can range from rock samples to well logs, stopping along the way at powderhorns, fans, and other unlikely objects that have at some time had a map executed upon them. The librarian should remember that to show surprise upon having one of these strange objects generously bestowed upon the library is a sign of weakness. About the only characteristic that the miscellanies will have in common is that they will be difficult to store.

Acquisitions

Acquisition of materials other than books and serials quickly proves to be one of the sharpest thorns in the librarian's side, not so much from the standpoint of budgetary restrictions (which, like the poor, are always with us) as from the standpoint of finding out what items of interest to the library's clientele are available—before, not after, the items go out of print, if indeed they were available to the general public in the first place: "Map librarians have learned through experience, however, that production and procurement are not synonymous" (Ristow 1974b, 7). The chief obstacles to the aforementioned procurement are: the lack of well-established bibliographic aids corresponding to such publications as *Books in print*; the greater number of sources as compared with sources for books; the ephemeral and documentary nature of some items, such as maps; the vast number of maps published each year (guesstimates range from 60,000 to 100,000), 90 percent of which are probably from governmental sources; the relatively high cost of acquisition in relation to the cost of the item acquired (except for globes and remote-sensing imagery, which tend to be higher in price than other spatial data); the peculiar author-publisher relationship of agencies printing, publishing, and issuing maps; the fact that many maps are analogous to serials in publication; and "the rigid security restrictions imposed upon many of the most accurate, detailed, and up-to-date maps, the dispersed nature of cartographic publication, the paucity of information about map production and the limited number of wholesale or retail distributors" (Ristow 1974b, 7–8). To illustrate just one of these difficulties, a situation equivalent in the book world to purchasing sheets in a map series would be that of a librarian forced to obtain a book by purchasing unannounced pages separately, at irregular and possibly infrequent intervals (Espenshade 1950, 431; Walker 1974, 71; Espenshade 1936, 209; Ristow 1967a, 403; and Modelski 1977). Matters have if anything become worse with the advent of the Web; the only solace—and it might be considered mean-spirited—is that the many checks to acquisition which map librarians struggled with in the hardcopy world now in many cases apply equally to all subject areas.

The only way to overcome these problems is to read anything likely to list cartographic or supporting materials—staying *au courant* of professional and geographical literature; perusing serials for lists of publishers, accessions, and reviews of atlases and maps; and going through publishers' and dealers' catalogs and other libraries' accessions lists, all of which may now be not only in hardcopy but also in digital form. Since there is no *BIP* for maps, the wise librarian will use whatever guides may appear, including *World mapping today* (1987, in appendix 2A), the long out-of-date *Map source directory* (Allin 1982, in appendix 2A) and will also keep a file of vendor catalogs. Firms issuing spatial data seem to be rather shy, so much so that one wonders if they really want to sell their products. Another point is that some of the most unlikely publishers have been known to dabble in maps, usually as an entirely unexpected sideline and perhaps only once, listing the map in their announcements next to such kindred spirits as multivolume works on Voltaire and monographs on quantum physics.

Accessions Lists

With the ubiquity of shared-cataloging sources such as OCLC and the Web, current-accessions lists of other libraries are not as frequently issued or as much used as they were ten years ago. There is a British standard relating to citations in accessions lists; it applies to single-sheet maps, multisheet maps, and maps in series and in atlases, and lists the elements required to describe all kinds of maps (British Standards Institution 1975–). Creation of this standard was precipitated by map librarians and map curators, who requested that the British Standards Institution prepare it; without the use of a standard, the description of a map in one list could be so different from a description of the same map in another list that the reader could be misled into thinking that two different maps were being described, and could therefore order a map already in possession (Bibliography of references to maps 1975, 355).

If one can generate an accessions list from one's current cataloging, a list becomes a useful part of the spatial-data collection's homepage. The primary purpose of an accessions list is to inform users of new acquisitions, but it is also very useful for communicating with other map libraries and with users via a "news and notes" section, which may include such information as maps on one given topic held by the library, important new acquisitions (e.g., a shipment of Landsat imagery), and cartographic news. Users and other libraries constitute two very different audiences, and items that one would scarcely bother to put in a list sent only to the latter (e.g., CIA maps received on depository) are often of considerable interest to the former. The quiet little system of duplicate exchange that we libraries keep up is best kept *sub rosa*, at least insofar as postings to the reflector MAPS-L (maps-l@uga.cc.uga.edu) allow.

Once the librarian has decided to issue such a list, a decision must be made as to how many items to list, in what format, and how to prepare the list. About the only other alternatives are either to have the work done by a utility off tapes (a service OCLC offers), or—ugh—to do it manually by inputting entries onto a PC with word-processing and HTML software and then uploading to the Web page.

The format used in most accessions lists from U.S. libraries is some variant of AACR2, e.g.:

Van Eysinga, F. W. B. Geological time table. Scale not given. Amsterdam: Elsevier, 1975.

G3201.C57 1975.E9

At the librarian's discretion, a citation may also include scale and almost anything else, and the call number may precede it; but the preceding example shows the basics. If the librarian elects to follow the format recommended by the British Standards Institution, here is how it goes. The sequence of descriptive elements in an entry should be:

1. Geographical area or location

2. Subject

3. Title

4. Scale

5. Series designation

6. Number and name of sheet

7. Edition

8. Authorship

9. Place of publication or execution

10. Publisher or printer

11. Date

12. Physical description

13. Additional information (e.g., projection, language, insets)

14. Sources and bibliographical information

15. Lists of sheets

16. Library reference number

For minimum references for modern materials, items 1, 3, 4, 9, 10, and 11 should be sufficient; for modern manuscript maps, items 1, 3, 4, 8, and 11; for early printed maps, items 1, 3, 8, 9, 10, and 11; and for early manuscript maps, items 1, 3, 8, and 11, although other items may be included as necessary. A full reference would look like this:

UNITED KINGDOM.
Aeronautical.
Chart of United Kingdom airspace restrictions, including danger areas.
1:1,000,000 at 56°N. GSGS 5201. Edition 1 GSGS.
Civil Aviation Authority.
Feltham [Mapping and Charting Establishment RE, 1974].
69 x 106 cm.
Marginal list of restricted areas by type, keyed to numbers on map.

A minimum reference would look like this:

UNITED KINGDOM.
Chart of United Kingdom airspace restrictions, including danger areas.
1:1,000,000 at 56°N.
Feltham [Mapping and Charting Establishment RE, 1974].
(British Standards Institution 1975, 3, 7)

The geographical name in the title is to be given in the currently accepted English form; if there is no title, one should be supplied. Non-Roman characters may be transliterated if the script of the original is stated in the section on additional information, and a title in a foreign language may be followed in square brackets by a translation. Scale should be given as natural scale, that is, in a ratio (e.g., 1:10,000). For early maps, the statement of scale is to be given in the form in which it appears on the map. The following names may be given in the description if they are stated on the map or are readily ascertainable:

Printed maps: Surveyor/Author/Editor; Compiler;
Draughtsman/Engraver/Lithographer

Example: By Henry Popple. C. Lempriere inv. & del.
B. Baron sculp. Engraved by Willm. Henry Toms.

Manuscript maps: Surveyor/Author/Compiler; Draughtsman;
Copyist/Director

Example: Surveyed by James Cook, drawn by Richard Pickersgill.
(British Standards Institution 1975, 3)

If any two of the above are given, the names of both may be listed, in the order given on the map; if there are more than two, only the first is to be listed, followed by "and others." If the place of publication is known but not supplied by the map, it may be given in brackets; if it is not known, "[n.p.]" may be put in the appropriate place. The name of the publisher may be given in a shortened form. If date is not known, an approximation should be given, be it only to the nearest century; hyphens may be inserted in place of unknown dates.

The size of the map is to be stated in centimeters, giving first the height and then the width, both to the nearest centimeter. In the case of multisheet maps where size varies, the overall size may be given (e.g., "89 cm. x 108 cm., in 5 sheets"). In the case of map series containing different sizes of maps, the standard size should be given, or, if that does not exist, the size of the smallest and the largest may be given (e.g., "from

10 cm. x 25 cm. to 50 cm. x 55 cm."). If considered important, any or all of the following information may be given: projection; prime meridian; orientation; reference systems such as grids and navigation lattices; number and name of sheet if not supplied earlier; languages besides English; stylistic features, decoration, marginal data, and inset maps; names of persons given in dedications or signatures; information about earlier editions, especially if such items as title have changed; attributions or indications of authorship if not already given elsewhere; and accompanying text. If a map is part of another bibliographical entity, such as another map or a monograph, an analytical note beginning with "to accompany," "in," "inset on," or "on verso of" should be included in notes (British Standards Institution 1975, 3, 5).

National Bibliographies

Another useful source of information for the librarian is the national bibliography, although for the most part, national bibliographies list and describe only books. Some not only include useful descriptions of atlases and maps, but also have special supplementary lists of maps or separate sections or chapters on them, and may even list that "ever elusive price" (Stephenson 1970, 91), thus saving the librarian one step in correspondence. The most useful bibliographies include maps or have separate sections devoted to them, such as those of Great Britain (British Library 1997), the Netherlands (*Bibliography of cartographic materials published in the Netherlands* 1975?–), and the United States. The latter has NUC CM (*National Union Catalog, Cartographic Materials*; see appendix 2C). National bibliographies are listed in the most current edition of the librarian's bible, *Guide to reference books* (1996); Section CL, "Geography," is most enlightening—this section constitutes required reading. A listing of national bibliographies containing references to maps and atlases is in Wise 1979b; for an article on the history of New Zealand's cartobibliography, see Barton 1983.

For a time—1953 to 1955—the Library of Congress issued as part of the U.S. national bibliography a union catalog composed solely of map cites, *Library of Congress catalog: A cumulative list of works represented by LC printed cards, maps and atlases.* Arrangement is by geographic area, with subject and author indexes, the latter of which is convenient because in the map-publishing world the author is frequently the publisher. Even now, these old catalogs are excellent compilations for the reference shelf. Maps were previously included in the main volumes of NUC, with an hiatus in the late 1960s and early 1970s while MARC Map (Machine Readable Cataloging System for Maps) was being organized and implemented. It is thus with considerable pleasure that librarians work with the new *NUC CM*.

Publishers' Catalogs

Catalogs of publishers and dealers—not just those selling only maps, but rather those who do not deal exclusively in books—are a basic acquisitions source. Continuous and persistent searching of each catalog received, building up a substantial file of publishers' catalogs and bookmarked Websites, and getting on the mailing list of any firm even remotely likely to be dealing in spatial data are all essential actions. Several publishers post new arrivals to the MAPS-L reflector (maps-l@uga.cc.uga.edu). Even if the decision is made to purchase maps through a jobber (and even through the major jobbers), it is important to know the price charged by the actual publisher of an item, and to learn about upcoming or in-print items via the original publishers' catalogs. United States' maps are most often purchased directly from a dealer, not through a jobber. The number of jobbers has fortunately increased over the last ten years, with the most active vendors currently being East View (Minneapolis, MN; http://www.eastview.com); Four One (London, Ontario; http://www.icis.net/fourone); GeoCenter (Stuttgart, Germany); GeoPubs (http://www.geopubs.co.uk); Map Link (Santa Barbara, CA; http://www.maplink.com); McCarta (London); Omni (Burlington, NC; http://www.omnimap.com); Stanford International Map Centre (London); and World of Maps (Ottawa; http://www.WorldofMaps.com). A heartening sign is that there are sufficient map publishers that they have their own organization—International Map Trade Association (IMTA)—and their own listserv/reflector (MAPublisher-L@avenza.com).

Frequently it is easier, albeit more expensive, for a small library to purchase all its foreign maps through a jobber rather than to deal separately with several different publishers in several different countries, where English is seldom the native tongue. Jobbers are especially useful: if a small number of maps of each country is being ordered; if a vendor's address is difficult to determine; if the acquisitions department has no one fluent in the language of a country (or at least in reading that language); if the local bank refuses to convert to the country's currency (or, if the bank will do a conversion, it charges five times the cost of the map for a check fee); or if a producer refuses to sell direct to the library (Sivers 1970).

GeoCenter, the largest maps and geography book jobber, was formed in 1971, when the large cartographic houses Zumsteins Landkartenhaus and Reise und Verkehrsverlag (RV) merged; the main activity is now centered in Stuttgart (Wittman 1973, 33). GeoCenter publishes a list of new maps, guidebooks, gazetteers, and any other works on geography; it started out as RV *Kartenbrief* in 1936 and changed name to *GeoKartenbrief* when the houses merged. The base volumes of the firm's catalog, *GeoKatalog*, were completed in late 1983, with—page 1 of *GeoKartenbrief* 298 (October 1983) informs us—costs that included 6,882 man-hours, 48 translations from the Chinese, 1,003 debating hours, 22 serious quarrels, 68,092 hairs ("grey, teared [sic] out)," 31 dissents with the management, 2,259 cups of coffee, 305 bottles of wine, and 469 blow-ups. Considering the enormity of the task, which has resulted in a peerless reference work that no library (even if it never orders anything from GeoCenter) can afford to be without, it is amazing that a few nervous breakdowns were not also a part of the process. What makes *GeoKatalog* so important are its currency, comprehensiveness, and the inclusion of index maps; the latter are sometimes difficult to obtain from national surveys. Edward Stanford (London) at one time issued its catalog, called *International maps and atlases in print*; the most recent volume is 1976 (Winch 1976, in appendix 2A). The best approach when shopping for a jobber is to place orders with more than one and give each a trial period of a year or two.

Any in-depth acquisition of maps of a foreign country will very likely require direct contact with the original publisher. For addresses, the librarian should try *World mapping today* 1987 (appendix 2A). This is fairly old as address lists go, but even though earth-science agencies are immersed in a welter of officialdom with frequent name changes, map-producing agencies are relatively stable both in name and, *mirabile dictu*, address. For example, USGS has been named the U.S. Geological Survey since 1879, and the mere fact that geologic mapping forms one of the smaller parts of its duties has not pushed the survey toward doing something flighty, like changing its name to reflect what constitutes the majority of its work; after all, it is still the national geologic survey, so the name is not incorrect, just understated.

When a librarian deals with virtually any agency of a foreign government, it is not only courteous but also the essence of common sense to correspond in the language of the country; for dealing with Latin American countries, such a practice is essential (see Miranda 1983 for pointers on obtaining publications from Latin American countries). So often are Latin American maps requested by U.S. map users that a few more words on getting such maps are in order.

Bibliographic identification and finding out what exists are just the beginning when it comes to a librarian's problems; procurement is often even more difficult. As a very general rule, in any given Latin American country there will be a primary agency responsible for the bulk of the topographic map production, and probably another agency that issues—carefully—geologic maps; the primary agency may well be a branch of the military, and it usually has all of the military's distrust of the civilian ("Why do you really want those maps?"), an attitude reinforced by the troubled political situation in so many Latin American countries (Bennett 1968, 8–9). In the United States we are fairly casual about maps, after years of buying topographic quadrangles readily; south of the border, maps are considered to be extremely important strategic information. In some cases, maps must be procured in person at the sales office of the agency of issuance, possibly only after the buyer has been frisked; careful advance planning, desiderata lists, and a firm command of native language are essential (Johnson 1974, 40). The prevailing political situation will have an immediate effect on whether maps are for sale at all; if there is any guerrilla activity going on, large-scale maps of the area may prove impossible to obtain. If all of this sounds too rigorous, some Latin American book dealers will handle requests for maps, and, of course, there are the jobbers.

One political situation has redounded to the good of one's ability to collect medium- and large-scale topographic sheets of foreign countries, and that is the change from the Soviet Union to the Commonwealth of Independent States. One of Russia's forays into the strange new world of commerce has been to make available for sale to the outside world the Soviet military general-staff editions of topographic sheets at 1:200,000 (all of Asia and Europe; significant parts of Africa; almost none of South America), 1:100,000 (all of Europe and much of Asia), and 1:50,000 (all of Europe, nearly all of the Middle East, and parts of Asia), and a series of city plans. These were produced by the former Soviet military for its own use and were classified as top secret; indeed, some still are. The sheets in many cases have extensive information on water flow, trees (e.g., types of trees, diameter of tree trunks), etc., printed on the verso. Spatial-data librarians in the United States who had hungered, in the main fruitlessly, after the often classified 1:250,000-scale JOGs issued—better put, authored and printed—by the U.S. military seized upon the 1:200,000-scale series with gladsome cries, wasting no time in digging up all the acquisitions money they could find and purchasing sheets to cover as much of Asia, Africa, and the former Soviet Union as they could afford. The author still remembers the bliss with which she first carefully ripped open the wrapping of the first shipment of the 1:200,000-scale sheets for the former Soviet Union, gazing upon their Cyrillic words with more pleasure than can readily be believed—pleasure that has subsequently been not only justified but repeated by the users of these sheets ever since. The jobber Omni has kindly put examples of these up on the Web at http://www.omnimap.com/catalog/russia/index.htm .

In dealing with foreign maps, it is frequently of assistance to know the general structure of the mapping agencies. See: Nichols 1982 for brief bibliographical notes on the more important mapping agencies; Parry 1983 for general advice on procuring European maps (especially British Ordnance Survey maps); all of the *Government publications review* issue for July-August 1983 (vol. 10, no. 4) for government mapping generally; Bohme 1989–1993 and Larsgaard 1984 and 1993 for histories of world topographic mapping; and Lock 1969 and *World mapping today* 1987 for guides to twentieth-century map production worldwide (appendix 2A for the last four). Issues of the *Bulletin/Newsletter* of the Canadian Association of Map Libraries and Archives frequently carry information concerning mapping agencies in Canada.

Finding out about and dealing with U.S. commercial publishers is much easier, particularly with Allin 1982 (appendix 2A) close at hand, and there are periodical articles that give the history or a profile of specific firms, as for example:

Singer, M. 1987. Wall power [W. Graham Arader III]. *New Yorker*, Nov. 30, 44–97.

Winnett, T. A. 1985. A short history of the Wilderness Press. *WAML Information bulletin* 16: 291–95.

But a special area is that of early maps or, as they are occasionally called, old and rare maps. For discovering addresses of dealers, see especially the most current edition of USGS's flier, "Historic and antique maps," and Ritzlin 1980. If, after viewing the prices, the librarian backs off in horror, the next possibility is to purchase facsimiles; see Noe 1980 (appendix 2B) for a list of facsimiles.

Even with the address lists given in the last paragraph, the librarian is well advised to set up a file of addresses—initially, probably just a file of publishers' catalogs and a set of bookmarks on one's Web browser. Getting this file into existence takes equal parts of persistence, luck, nearly constant reading of both e-mail and hardcopy publisher's catalogs, and the services of steely-fingered and -eyed typists who understand entering information into databases (such as Microsoft Access), sending out reams of free-request forms on the institution's letterhead (see appendix 4 for a sample form) to any likely agency or firm. To summarize from the above, such entities are commercial, governmental, or associational (the last being nonprofit and occasionally but not always governmental). In the governmental category are international, national, county, state, intergovernmental, and city agencies; such agencies will in the main publish maps of their own jurisdiction, although military, state department, and some earth-sciences agencies are often the exceptions that prove the rule. Commercial firms are likely to issue city maps, tourist maps, road maps, globes, atlases, and plastic, raised-relief maps; associations tend to issue maps relating to a given subject (e.g., the Geological Society of America publishes geologic maps and sections), with a good stiff clue as to the subject in the name of the association. That leaves governmental agencies covering the rest of the waterfront.

International agencies are the most restrained, generally limiting themselves to atlases and to thematic maps of relatively large areas; UNESCO seems to be the most active (see Dulka 1986 in appendix 2A for a discussion of maps from the United Nations). National agencies take on the gargantuan jobs of various kinds of detailed surveys—most frequently topographic, hydrographic, and geologic (see the following section on "U.S. Government-Produced Spatial Data"). State agencies most likely to issue cartographic materials such as maps, atlases, and aerial photographs (the last usually for in-house use) are the state earth resources agencies and highway departments. To obtain a list of addresses for state geological surveys, check with the Association of American State Geologists. But there are always other state agencies quietly working away and discovering that a map or atlas is the perfect way to present information: planning and economic development departments; cartography laboratories in university geography departments; some university institutes (such as the University of Colorado at Boulder's Institute of Arctic and Alpine Research); and almost any agency with the word "land" or "resources" in its title. State agencies also occasionally publish guides to state mapping; see in appendix 2A Minnesota State Planning Agency 1977 and Hawaii 1978 for two examples. Sometimes a desperate librarian will chronicle the mapping of a given state (e.g., for Oregon, Trevitt-Clark 1981); such articles may be used, along with the state capital's telephone book (governmental section), to determine the patterns of publication in a given state. These exercises are much less necessary for states that have or have had a state cartographer's office: Colorado, Florida, Idaho, Kentucky, Nevada, Oregon, South Carolina, Washington, and Wisconsin. The most active state cartographer's office is that in Wisconsin (established 1973), which issues a periodical, the *Wisconsin mapping bulletin,* has a Web page (see previous section on "Spatial Data in Digital Form"), and vigorously promotes and documents mapping of and in the state with such publications as county cartographic catalogs (see Reinhard 1978 and 1979).

The most active county agencies are the county engineers and the county highway departments. Planning commissions, whether city, county, or intergovernmental, are much inclined to issue maps. Searching the Web or hunting through telephone books are the easiest ways to find addresses.

U.S. Government-Produced Spatial Data

"Politicians and bureaucrats here often seem to lose their way. But a case can be made that they really have no excuse. More maps are produced in the Washington, D.C. area than perhaps any other place on Earth" (Washington map capital 1986).

Because the U.S. government and the spatial data it produces are of primary interest to U.S. librarians, they merit special attention in this book. There are two major problems in grappling with the mass of federally produced cartographic materials. First, the U.S. government is the largest publisher—hardcopy or electronic—in the world; second, although federal mapping and charting duties are somewhat coordinated, almost any agency can, and at some time may, produce maps (Shill and Peterson 1989, 649). In the early 1950s, a conservative estimate of the yearly distribution of maps of all kinds in the United States was over 500 million sheets, with the U.S. Coast and Geodetic Survey contributing 42 million and USGS about 2 million (U.S. Coast 1951). The present situation, when viewed through the eyes of grateful but fatigued map librarians, is readily believed to be that of at least 160 million sheets per year distributed by the federal government; in USGS's warehouse in Denver, 75 million sheets are in storage (Seavey 198_?, 1). And through the valuable, extensive U.S. depository system (which is discussed later in this chapter, under "Methods of Acquisition"), many of these sheets make their way into libraries. The U.S. government has been in the map-producing business since at least the early nineteenth century, and the passing years have seldom seen a diminution in production (see Strohecker 1955 for 1937–1953 maps and charts).

Over the past ten years or so, a good deal has been published on the provision of federal information in digital form. Two notable early publications are:

United States. Joint Committee of Printing. Staff. 1985. *Open forum on the provision of electronic Federal information to depository libraries, report* . . . Washington, D.C.: GPO.

United States. Congress. Ad Hoc Committee on Depository Library Access to Federal Automated Data Bases. 1984. *Provision of Federal government publications in electronic format to depository libraries*. Washington, D.C.: GPO.

More followed this. With the stupendous success of the Web, combined with the equally stupendous cost of printing and snail-mailing out the multitudinous publications of the U.S. government, the goal became to have all federal information available over the Internet initially by the year 1998, or perhaps by the year A.D. 2000:

Access to and services for Federal information in the networked environment, draft, March 1997. 1997. Coalition for Networked Information.
http://www.cni.org/projects/fedinfo/www/fedinfo.draft.html

Bauman Foundation. 1995. *Agenda for access, public access to Federal information for sustainability through the information superhighway*. [S.l.]: Author.

The primary work of a spatial-data librarian in the United States is to cope with the mammoth production of the U.S. government. The best way to do so is by comprehending the system and patterns of issuance. And the best way to do that is to view map and atlas production agency by agency, taking a leisurely journey through *List of classes of United States government publications available for selection by depository libraries* (quarterly since 1977), which is arranged in order by Superintendent of Documents classification number, that is, classification by issuing agency.

Thus we begin with A (the Department of Agriculture), and immediately come to a prominent map producer, the Forest Service, at A 13.; it issues *Forest visitor maps* and *Travel maps* of national forests, and also a *Primary base series* at 1:24,000. Note that the "compartments" on the USFS maps are geographic units of national-forest administration and inventory. The last mentioned has information content identical to the USGS 1:24,000 national topographic map series, except that information of interest to the Forest Service has been added; also, the color scheme is somewhat different. Although these maps are all available on depository, they may be for sale and in some cases free of charge from the regional offices (of which there are nine), each dispensing maps of a given region.

The Soil Conservation Service (SCS), at A 57., publishes *Soil survey reports*, *Important farmland* maps, and miscellaneous soil maps, such as a soil-survey status map; it also publishes a *List of published soil surveys* (Proehl 1979). The prominent commercial publication, *Guide to U.S. government publications*, which usually is called "Andriot" (see appendix 2A), also lists all soil surveys issued by SCS, noting those in print. Several agencies in the Department of Agriculture, including SCS, the Forest Service, and the Agricultural Stabilization and Conservation Service, are deeply involved in aerial photography, but not as a depository item.

Moving along to the Department of Commerce, we promptly fall into the maw of the Bureau of the Census, now back at its old stand of C3., but briefly in the past at C56., not to mention a few other locations, primarily under the aegis of Interior during the nineteenth century. Seeing this shifting about, we should not be surprised that the publications of the Census Bureau change at least slightly from census to census; in some cases the changes are substantial, and we find ourselves at one with the statement by an Australian librarian concerning that nation's census maps: "Census maps are probably the greatest problem, as the base maps are hard to use, and change from census to census" (Leeuwenburg 1982, 12).

At one time or another, the bureau has published:

County Subdivision Map series
Urbanized Area Map series
Census Tract Outline Maps
County Map series
Place Map series
Place and Vicinity Map series
Metropolitan Map series
Block Statistics maps
Census tracts, defined as central business districts of the largest U.S. cities
GE-50 series, 1:5,000,000
GE-70 series
                              (Marx 1976, 5–6; and Seavey 1982b)

This list is by no means definitive; doubtless there are yet more series lurking out there. To add to the fun, although most reports and some maps are available from the Superintendent of Documents, there are many print-on-demand maps available (in series that were previously available on depository), as well as computer tapes from the Data User Services

Division in Washington, D.C. and very often from the state census data centers. It is thus clear that the real reason for the ten-year gap between censuses is to allow us sufficient time to figure out the publications before the next census—with different publications, of course—is upon us. Some cowardly, twice-burned spatial-data librarians have virtuously insisted that Census Bureau maps be kept in the government-documents departments, on the grounds that users need the maps in order to use the data; documents librarians are generally kind enough to pretend that they believe the reason given for such generosity. For the 1990 census, the bureau very successfully launched the TIGER/Line (Topologically Integrated Geographic Encoding and Referencing System) files, a computer database mapping system for the entire nation (U.S. Congress 1984). In spite of a certain amount of rude remarks about errors (from sources that one does *not* see volunteer to collect all that information on their own), the TIGER files have been a phenomenal success, sucked in by very nearly countless commercial firms and then the manipulated files offered for sale to a demanding public. Although there has been the nasty remark that the Census Bureau always seems to be surprised that every ten years there is yet another census, given the magnitude of the task and the ridiculous situation of an agency saying to prospective employees, "Now, just wait for ten years, and we'll need your services again," the bureau has done excellent work, and is currently planning for the year 2000 census, with the two emphases to be on the maintenance and enhancement of the hugely successful TIGER files and the work on the master address file (a geocoded list of all housing units in the nation).

Also in Commerce is another hotbed of spatial data, the National Oceanic and Atmospheric Administration (NOAA), at C 55. First of its mapping agencies to meet the eye is the aged, invaluable National Weather Service, with its maps and charts at C55.122. Next is the National Environmental Satellite, Data, and Information Service. Its major publication of interest to us is the *Daily weather maps: Weekly series*. Considering that since 1968 it has had listed as authoring agency several different consecutive agencies (Weather Bureau; Environmental Data Service; Environmental Data and Information Service; National Environmental Satellite, Data and Information Service; Climate Analysis Center; and the current agency names on the cover, which include the National Weather Service and the Hydrometeorological Prediction Center & Climate Prediction Center), this contradiction in title and frequency is not surprising. The neophyte librarian is perhaps reeling by now from the complexities and name changes revealed just at the beginnings of this federal map survey; be reassured that after a short time, one becomes not just inured to but rather appreciative of such changes, and considers a month without a name change to be dull.

Next we come to nautical and aeronautical charts, with the aeronautical charts work to report to the FAA, and the U.S. Coast and Geodetic Survey, which has had to make do with a meager three name changes: its current name; National Ocean Survey; National Ocean Service; and the current name once again. Amongst its many publications are:

> Aeronautical charts, most notably:
> Sectional aeronautical chart (SAC)
> Local aeronautical chart
> VFR terminal area chart
> World aeronautical chart (in spite of the name, these presently cover only the United States; an earlier version, WAC, did indeed cover the world)
> Enroute low-altitude and high-altitude chart
> Area navigation high-altitude chart
> Aircraft position chart
> Jet navigation chart (JNC)
> Global navigation chart (GNC)
> Geodetic diagrams (these have been taken over by the National Geodetic Survey)
> Nautical charts of various kinds, most notably:
> Sailing charts
> General charts; [C&GS] series
> Coast charts
> Harbor charts
> Small-craft charts
> Offshore mineral leasing area maps
> Bathymetric map: discontinued as a depository item in 1996
> Topographic-bathymetric maps (done in concert with USGS)
> Tidal current charts: discontinued in hard copy in 1996; available on CD

Here we will delve into NOS's history. It began its life as the Survey of the Coast in about 1807. Its first geodetic surveys began in 1816; by 1836, the name of the organization had been changed to the U.S. Coast Survey, and by 1878 to the U.S. Coast and Geodetic Survey (C&GS). In 1926 Congress directed C&GS to produce aeronautical charts. In 1970, the name was changed to the National Ocean Survey, and the nautical-charting mission was broadened to include charts of the Great Lakes, previously administered by the U.S. Lake Survey (part of the Army Corps of Engineers). In the fall of 1982 NOS became the National Ocean Service (but still NOS); in the same year, the Office of Charting and Geodetic Services (note what the acronym is), within NOS, began to serve as a focus for charting services (U.S. Coast and Geodetic Survey 1951, 61; and Office of Charting and Geodetic Services 1984, 2–3). As a result of going through its own version of interesting times with the push to make the users bear the cost of services, especially the charting services, the digital versions of the charts have been turned over to the Better Boating Administration, through a formal agreement between C&GS and the firm;

all of these digital versions and software to manipulate them are sold as copyrighted items. This is an inappropriate fate for the charts, data for which was collected using taxpayers' dollars, and a court case was brought by DeLorme against NOAA; the two findings of the case were that yes, digital files of the U.S. government are public records, but also (unfortunately) yes, the files fall within Exemption three of the Freedom of Information Act (U.S. District Court 1995).

C&GS is very much involved in automated production of charts, both nautical and aeronautical. It also produces geodetic data (National Geodetic Survey) and miscellaneous pamphlets. For many years the major nautical series was the C&GS series of coastal charts, in a distinctive yellow, black, and white color combination, whose new editions arrived (with almost appalling regularity) in map collections on the depository system. Then, effective 1 July 1974, NOS, in cooperation with DMA Hydrographic Center, began a new national chart numbering system, designed to provide a uniform method of identifying charts for the entire world; effective 1 October 1977, all ordering and distribution was based on the new numbering, a change that left many libraries with an enormous number of charts in the old numbering being very gradually replaced by charts in the new numbering. At first NOS helpfully provided both numbers on new charts, so that the old ones could be easily retrieved and withdrawn; the agency also provided a nautical-chart conversion table, which wise librarians made several copies of, and kept the original locked up in offices.

C&GS issues catalogs and lists of its nautical charts, most notably *Dates of latest editions, nautical charts and miscellaneous maps* (quarterly; now in different versions that incorporate NIMA charts as appropriate) and *Map and chart catalog no. ___* (e.g., 5 is United States, Puerto Rico, and the Virgin Islands, bathymetric maps and special-purpose charts). Its aeronautical charts are of three major types:

> visual: provide information to pilots flying under FAA visual flight rules; complete topographic base (prominent features emphasized), overprinted with aviation information

> instrument: provide information to pilots flying under FAA instrument flight rules; do not show topographic features

> special-purpose charts and related publications: controller charts and supplements, radar video overlays, and digital data (Office of Charting and Geodetic Services 1984, 7–8)

The key to all of this is the *Catalog of aeronautical charts and related publications*, which includes a list of authorized aeronautical-chart agents. By early 1996, the word was out that the aeronautical-charting portion of the survey was to be moved to somewhere in the U.S. Department of Transportation.

The National Geodetic Survey is responsible for developing and maintaining the National Reference System as defined by the two National Networks of Geodetic Control. These horizontal and vertical control systems are the basis for all accurate mapping. Another part of NOAA, the National Geophysical Data Center, issues digital data with impressive frequency plus occasional hardcopy maps—geothermal maps, including individual maps of various western states, and some seismic maps.

We now move into Defense, beginning with another extremely important mapping and charting agency, the former Defense Mapping Agency, subsumed by the National Imagery & Mapping Agency (NIMA). Although the Coast and Geodetic Survey charts navigable U.S. waters and another civilian agency distributes aeronautical charts, NIMA encompasses the military charting and mapping agency, and there is some overlap; for example, *Jet navigation charts (JNC)* and *Global navigation chart (GNC),* are also available from NIMA. Hydrographic charts of foreign waters are NIMA's business, and are available to anyone who requests them (although some, such as those of the Great Barrier Reef, may be restricted). Mapping of foreign lands is something else again; the extremely important *Joint operations graphic (JOG)* 1:250,000-scale series is mapped by NIMA for foreign countries, and the sheets are released by NIMA only if the country involved agrees. At the same time, the country itself may choose to sell or otherwise make available these sheets, and some countries prefer this route; sheets available may well not be available from NIMA, and vice versa. Also, any JOG sheets that come to depository libraries are on loan to the library from NIMA, and may be called back at any time. Besides JOG and charts of foreign countries, NIMA also distributes numerous small-scale maps of the world and of areas of the world, in such series as the *World plotting series.*

NIMA has a complicated history. Let's begin with World War II, at which time the United States found itself embroiled in a world war—with no maps. To quote one military person, "We weren't caught with our pants down, we had no pants at all!" (Hagen 1979a, 3). What was then called the Army Map Service (AMS) sent out a panic call, in such publications as *Publishers weekly,* asking publishers, booksellers, and librarians for loans or contributions of maps covering areas outside the United States (Army Map Service 1942). As Mary Murphy well puts it: "Collection policies at first were simple. AMS took any map from anyone kind enough to give or lend it" (Federal government map collecting 1969, 2). Various college, university, and public libraries donated or loaned large amounts of materials, including maps; only a cynic would say that the libraries were just clearing out their duplicate-exchange backlog (Nicoletti 1971, 2).

The university map-depository program began in 1945, when AMS sought to express its gratitude by making about 5,000 map sheets available to each of 45 institutions. Predictably, the library response was so gratifying, and gratified, that AMS established a formal map depository program for distributing its surplus stocks, including some of the over 900 tons captured during the war; between 1946 and 1950, about 150 libraries each received over 20,000 maps (Stephenson 1979, 119). More than maps were supplied; AMS also put out gazetteers and map symbols books (e.g., US AMS 1948). By 1951 the Korean hostilities had placed such a burden on AMS that the depository program was temporarily halted, and did not start up again until 1956 (Murphy 1976, 17).

In the 1960s, during the heyday of the program, about 200 libraries received maps, and high-ranking officers would visit the libraries on depository inspections. There was a depository newsletter, contributing such information as the news that maps remained the property of AMS, and that many could not be photocopied without AMS's permission. By the late 1960s, it required a great deal of patience and luck to become an AMS depository and receive all those much-needed maps, books, and plastic raised-relief maps (the molds for the latter of the United States were sold to Hubbard in the early 1970s). AMS had a formal College Repository Program agreement, dated 1967, that included not only requirements but also a very brief history, noting that as of 1967 there were 194 library members, and that a total of 3,782 different map sheets had been distributed to each depository from 1958 to 1966, with a single collection then consisting of about 24,000 individual maps and other publications. Each library was receiving about 300 maps a year, which in itself was an irritating point because the number of maps available for distribution was few in number and decreasing each year. A serious problem from AMS's point of view (and one that would become more obvious as the years went by) was that AMS was a military mapping agency that should, at least in theory, have nothing to do with civilians; on the other hand, the depository program's major value was its role as an inexpensive liaison between the agency and the university cartographic community. From the libraries' point of view, the problem was that every year about four libraries would request withdrawal, and about ten would request membership (Nicoletti 1971, 3).

In 1969 AMS became the U.S. Army Topographic Command (TOPO-COM). TOPOCOM was more involved in supplying to libraries maps of varied types, scales, and areas than it was in supplying complete coverage. In 1973 TOPOCOM changed its name to Topographic Center and became a part of DMA (established that same year), with its duty to compile and publish "small, medium, and large scale topographic mapping, thematic mapping, nautical and aeronautical charting for world areas exclusive of the United States" and its various dependencies (Sivers 1974, 39). At the same time that TOPOCOM became a part of DMA, so did the Aerospace Center (formerly the Aeronautical Chart Information Center—ACIC—in St. Louis) and the Hydrographic Center, the latter of which in its turn had included most of the mapping and charting activities of the Naval Oceanographic Office (Nicoletti 1971, 4, 38). In the past, before its various name changes and absorptions, ACIC had provided 100 free aeronautical charts or ONCs (operational navigational chart) per year to requesting libraries, but when DMA formed its new depository program in 1974 (with—you guessed it—a new Terms of Membership publication), to be composed of 250 members maximum, ONCs were transferred to DMA's program (US DMA TC August 1975, 1). The Hydrographic Center had never maintained a formal depository program; with the formation of the new DMA program, nautical charts were included in DMA's shipments (Sivers 1974, 40). It must be emphasized that by the early 1970s DMA saw the depository program as a drain of labor, resources, and materials, and felt that the program had outlived its original purpose and should be phased out (Hagen 1979a, 5). Even during the 1960s, if copies of a map sheet were insufficient to send to all depositories, they were sent to none; nor was the military interested in holding meetings to discuss matters (Hagen 1979a, 10). In the late 1960s the word came that the lettered series (e.g., M301) were to be replaced by JOGs (1:250,000), and that these JOG sheets were not to be a part of the depository from then on (Hagen 1979a, 11). But even with all the problems, shipping lists were always sent out, and claims were honored.

By the late 1970s, approximately 300 sheets per year were being shipped to each library; these sheets were generally small-scale ONCs and the like. DMA's Centers were consolidated into the Hydro-graphic/Topographic Center in September of 1978 (Defense Mapping Agency consolidated 1978), and new terms of membership came out in 1979. The new terms noted that materials would consist of medium- and small-scale topographic maps and charts, with some other publications, and that stock availability had something to do with which sheets would be shipped, to total about 300 sheets per year. All materials, as in the past, were deposited on an indefinite-loan basis, were to be marked as depository, and could not be disposed of without prior DMA approval. DMA's request in return for the materials was that libraries send their accessions lists (annually at a minimum) to DMA.

After a good deal of agitation by libraries, DMA looked into the problem of distributing JOGs to libraries, and in the 8 May 1981 DMA depository newsletter (edition 2, no. 1) agreed to seek approval from participating countries to loan JOGs to depository-program member libraries. Areas excluded were: areas denied to free U.S. access (Cuba, Warsaw Pact nations, the then USSR, China, North Korea, Libya, etc.); areas covered by the Pan American Institute of Geography and History's (PAIGH) 1:250,000-scale series of Latin America; and areas whose medium-scale map coverage was produced by a third nation (e.g., Kenya, Somalia, Yemen Arab Republic) (US DMA TC 1981). DMA was also working on revising its rules so that member libraries could distribute unwanted sets to each other, relaxing rules on circulation to allow for interlibrary loans, distributing more newsletters, and so on. The JOG series (also known as Series 1501) finally began with an April 1983 shipment of western European sheets; this series is not available to nondepository libraries, nor is it for sale by DMA. As a side note, DMA gazetteers for foreign countries now began to enter libraries, primarily through the general U.S. depository. DMA was exceedingly generous about filling in any missing foreign-country gazetteers that a library might need; it would send a list and have the library return it, with missing gazetteers noted, to DMA. The important 1:1,000,000 series, 1301, had been canceled by 1983. Through all of these somewhat difficult times, DMA's liaison persons—such as Ray Lawyer during the 1980s—with libraries were extremely helpful and courteous.

As alluded to earlier, there was a GPO-depository survey of DMA products in 1983, but distribution continued to be erratic. A new survey came out in 1989. NIMA came into being in 1996, composed of DMA, the Department of Defense's Central Imagery office, and the CIA's National Photographic Interpretation Center; its emphasis thus is on imagery.

As was previously mentioned, NIMA's products are aeronautical, topographic, nautical, and miscellaneous, with the last including such items as foreign-country gazetteers. The most useful in many libraries are the aeronautical ONCs (1:1,000,000); whatever JOGs (1:250,000) we are fortunate enough to receive; any of the 1940s through 1960s 1:250,000-scale lettered series (more on these later); the now retired 1:1,000,000 series (1301); the multitudinous world base maps at small scales; and the general nautical charts (for the last, the librarian will need NIMA's *Numerical listing of charts and publications,* and companion volumes *Catalog of nautical charts, region ... ,* in the most current edition). The old lettered 1:250,000 scale (and assorted other) series are still very heavily used in libraries fortunate enough to have them, even though the sheets often date back to the 1950s; any library with these sheets cannot well manage without Joe Crotts's 1977 country index to the series, and Walsh and Hernden's 1983 cross-index on AMS series number to GSGS series number.

That last acronym needs some explanation. During World War II, when AMS was so severely embarrassed by a lack of maps, it was forced to borrow maps from wherever it could; the logical first place to look was the Allies, and the chief mapper of that group was Great Britain. Britain's major mapping service at the time was the War Office's (honesty is refreshing) General Staff, Geographical Section, which soon came to be referred to as GSGS. The GSGS map series that AMS took over and reprinted retained the GSGS number on the pieces, and occasionally did not have the AMS series number printed on them—but then, occasionally they did. Thus indexes by geographic area and GSGS and AMS series number to the many series issued can save the librarian from an early commitment to a state institution for the insane. Even with those superb indexes, the librarian very much needs the following AMS explanation to work through the series in an effective, efficient manner (from Enclosure 5, *Depository newsletter* 9, 1969):

EXPLANATION OF AMS SERIES NUMBERING

The series number or Standard Series Designation, often referred to as the SSD number, identifies a group of maps which cover a particular geographic area, have the same sheet line system, are in the same scale group, and follow the same cartographic specifications.

The series is expressed in one of two forms. Form A, a four number code such as 1301, is used for series at a scale of 1:255,000 or smaller (scale groups 1–4) covering a continent or comparable major area or more than one regional area. It is also used for all world series. Form B, a code consisting of a letter and three or four numbers such as E552, is used for series not extending beyond one regional area.

Form A consists of three parts. The first part is a digit from 1–9 indicating world or the major area as outlined in blue on the Index of Regional Areas. The second part is a digit indicating the scale range as follows:

CODE	SCALE GROUP
1	1:5,000,000 and smaller
2	Larger than 1:5,000,000 to 1:2,000,000
3	Larger than 1:2,000,000 to 1:510,000
4	Larger than 1:510,000 to 1:255,000
5	Larger than 1:255,000 to 1:150,000
6	Larger than 1:150,000 to 1:70,000
7	Larger than 1:70,000 to 1:35,000
8	Larger than 1:35,000 (excluding City Plans and Photo Maps)
9	City Plans (regardless of scale)
0	Photo Maps (regardless of scale)

City Plans and Photo Maps are usually large scale so in effect 8, 9, and 0 are three types of large scale maps. The third part is a two digit sequential number, starting with 01 to differentiate successive series designations in which the first two digits are the same.

Form B consists of four parts:

The first part is a capital letter indicating a regional area smaller than a continent (except for M which is coextensive with 6). The regional areas are outlined in red on the Index of Regional Areas.

The second part is a digit indicating the scale group as in Form A above.

The third part is a digit indicating subregion. These are outlined in green on the Index of Regional Areas. If a series covers more than one subregion or if the region is not subdivided, a zero is used. In most regions there are nine or fewer subregions. However, in areas L and M there are ten, so in these areas the zero may indicate either a specific subregion or more than one subregion.

The fourth part of the number is a one or two digit sequential number starting with 1 to differentiate successive series designations where the first three parts are the same.

If a special series is issued based on a standard series, the standard series number is used with a letter added, e.g., P for plastic relief map. The following examples may help to clarify this explanation:

1101 is a World map at 1:11,000,000 in nine sheets; in this SSD:

1	equals	World
1	equals	Scale group 1:5,000,000 and smaller
01	equals	The first world series issued in this scale group

1103 is a World map at 1:19,000,000 in three sheets; in this SSD:

1	equals	World
1	equals	Scale group 1:5,000,000 and smaller
03	equals	The third world series in this scale group

L542 is a map of Manchuria at 1:250,000; in this SSD:

L	equals	Far East
5	equals	Scale group larger than 1:255,000 to 1:150,000
4	equals	Manchuria
2	equals	The second series on Manchuria in fifth scale group

L552 is a map of Korea at 1:250,000; in this SSD:

L	equals	Far East
5	equals	Scale group larger than 1:255,000 to 1:150,000
5	equals	Korea
2	equals	The second series on Korea in fifth scale group

Q50l is a map of Alaska at 1:250,000; in this SSD:

Q	equals	Alaska
5	equals	Scale group larger than 1:255,000 to 1:150,000
0	equals	Area Q is not subdivided
1	equals	The first series on Alaska in fifth scale group

Q50l P is a Plastic Relief map of Alaska at 1:250,000 based on Q5Ol.

V761 is a map of Wisconsin at 1:50,000; in this SSD:

V	equals	United States
7	equals	Scale group larger than 1:70,000 to 1:35,000
6	equals	Great Lakes Region
1	equals	The first series on this region in this scale group

An additional aid—appropriately a graphic—is AMS's map, *Index to regional areas* (various editions), which gives general letter and number areas.

Arriving at the Army, D 101., we are most interested in the Army Corps of Engineers publications, at D103., primarily with navigation charts of rivers (the Coast and Geodetic Survey is responsible for charts of the Great Lakes and for such major rivers as the Columbia). Here again, as with the Forest Service, we are looking at an agency that has branch offices; these offices do issue publications.

In the E's we are in energy and education and some agency changes. Like many government agencies, the Energy Information Administration has a Maps and Charts number, E 3.21. The Environmental Protection Agency (EP) has maps in its many environmental-impact statements, and of course a Maps and Atlases number, EP 1.99. Then we arrive at FEM, the Federal Emergency Management Agency, with its Amazon of flood-hazard-area maps; FEMA will supply free hardcopy maps of, e.g., specific counties, upon request. FEMA has mapped every flood plain in the United States; these are a perfect example of maps best collected in digital form or on microfiche.

In the GP's, the class number for the Government Printing Office, we come to Subject bibliography SB-183, Maps and atlases (1994–); formerly Surveying and mapping. The General Services Administration is at GS; publications of the Cartographic Archives of the National Archives are at GS 4. See General information leaflet no. 25, Cartographic and Architectural Branch, the 1971 *Guide to cartographic records in the National Archives* (U.S. National Archives and Record Service 1971, in appendix 2A, and Ehrenberg 1976a). As indicated in this chapter's section on remote sensing, the Archives holds a substantial number of aerial photographs.

We pause briefly in the HE's, the Department of Health and Human Services, where relatively few items of interest for spatial-data collections appear; the 1975 *Atlas of cancer mortality for U.S. counties, 1950–1969,* issued by the National Institutes of Health, is one such.

It is when we come to the Department of the Interior (I) that the river of spatial-data publications becomes a flood. USGS is the civilian topographic mapping agency of the United States; as such it compiles and publishes the topographic series of the United States: 1:24,000; 1:62,500 (no longer available for sale); 1:250,000, and in the metric series 1:25,000 (abandoned while USGS completed the 1:24,000 series and possibly not yet revived); 1:50,000 (county map series); and 1:100,000 (see Gilman 1982 for a commentary on the last-mentioned series). Before the joint depository program that began 1 October 1984, the most important map depository program was that offered by USGS, a program probably started sometime between 1900 and 1910. What made the program (which USGS termed "repository" rather than "depository") so important was not just the sheer numbers involved (around 5,000 maps per year) but the fact that the maps involved are base maps. USGS's chief map product is the topographic map, and even after all these years specifically the l:24,000-scale series, which was finally completed in the early 1990s. To complete the approximately 58,000 quadrangles by that time, the survey issued "Provisional edition maps," readily identifiable by the brown "collar" of print in the margins (standard edition is black print); there are several other differences, but the brown print is the most noticeable (Seavey l982c, 53).

Recently the number of USGS maps received on depository has declined from around 3,000 in 1986 to about 1,500 in 1996; this is heavily influenced by the completion of the 1:24,000-scale series. USGS does have a database on diskette of all its topos at all scales; you may either get your own copy from USGS, or view it on Omni's Web page at http://www.omnimap.com/catalog/usgs.htm .

For the latest official word on USGS's work on topographic mapping, see the 1996 document, *The evolution of topographic mapping in the U.S. Geological Survey's National Mapping Program*, http://www-nmd.usgs.gov/misc/evolution.html . USGS also publishes geologic and mineralogic maps (in the GQ, Geologic Quadrangle, series; I, Miscellaneous Investigations series; MF, Miscellaneous Field Studies series; C, Coal Investigation series; GP, Geophysical Investigation series; MR, Mineral Investigations Resources series; OM, Oil and Gas Investigations Map series; and OC, Oil and Gas Investigations Chart series) and hydrologic maps (HA, Hydrologic Investigations series; hydrologic unit maps for each state; water-resources investigations maps for each state; and river-survey maps for selected areas in the western states). In the miscellaneous category are state base and topographic maps at 1:500,000 (many in both a shaded-relief version and a contours-only version) and 1:1,000,000 (planimetric only), and topographic maps of Antarctica. Maps of foreign countries, such as geologic maps of areas of Saudi Arabia, and other planets, such as maps of areas of Mars, are included in the I series, as are some nongeologic maps (e.g., Mars photo maps).

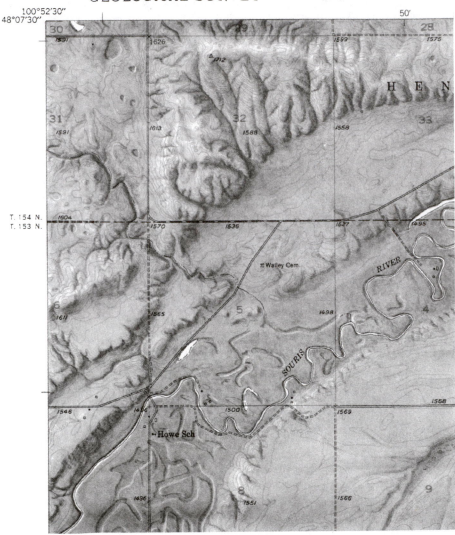

Figure 1.11. Shaded relief and contours used to depict relief. United States. Geological Survey. 1954. Voltaire, N. Dak. Ed. of 1949; shaded relief printed 1954. Scale 1:24,000. Washington, D.C.: USGS.

Next we come to indexes as the map-world means them, graphic indexes to available maps. The most important of these indexes, because it indexes the most important map series, is *Index to topographic maps of* ... (one per state, except for smaller states). This has appeared both as a folded map and as a pamphlet—in the latter case, it first appeared, logically enough, for the state of Virginia (in which the headquarters of the survey is located), in 1981. It apparently was successful, as it was revised in 1984, and a few other states (e.g., Kansas) followed it, with the title *[State] index to topographic and other map coverage*. In the newer form, it was accompanied by a catalog, titled either *Catalog of published maps* or *[State] catalog of topographic and other published maps*. These have since changed in format back to being maps rather than pamphlets. USGS's next important index is *Geologic map index of* . . . (one per state in the main); it indexes not only USGS publications—as the previously mentioned indexes do—but also anything the compiler could find: state publications; periodical articles; theses and dissertations maps; etc. This by no means lists all of the USGS map indexes; generally speaking, there is an index of some kind for every series.

In its book series, USGS publishes many works of interest to spatial-data collections. Its indexes are of especial importance, most notably the monthly *New publications of the U.S. Geological Survey* (now available over the Web at http://www.usgs.gov; annual cumulations). Be warned that the annual cumulations do not include the lists of topographic maps that appear as the last section in the monthly list. One series of special interest to the spatial-data librarian is the *Open-file reports (OFR)* series, which is an agglomeration of text and maps, or just maps separately, which have been done as preliminary work; these come on depository, mercifully on microfiche, as there are a good many of them.

Besides its maps and book series, USGS issues many pamphlets that explain the various map series or some service that the survey offers. These pamphlets are in many cases available over the Web, and are available in hard copy free of charge; the most well known is probably the one entitled "Topographic Maps," which now includes the symbols sheet for the series. The one that gives the best overall look at USGS products is the *Minicatalog of map data*, which provides a poster-type summary of publications. Every library should have one of each of these folders (more, for giveaways to eager map users, would be better), and any library wise enough to select, in the federal depository, I 19.2 (general publications), I 19.79 (maps and posters), and I 19.80 (National Mapping Program) probably will.

In what might be termed the pamphlet category, but of so much importance that they merit a section all their own, are the many indexes that USGS publishes. These include: *Aeromagnetic and aeroradiometric maps and profiles published or open-filed by the U.S. Geological Survey*, one per state; also one per state, except for some smaller states, *List of Geological Survey geologic and water-supply reports and maps*. These index USGS publications only.

Two non-USGS-produced indexes for USGS maps must be mentioned here, largely because they are so much needed: they are Moffat 1986, *Map index to topographic quadrangles of the United States, 1882–1940*, and Stark 1989, *A cartobibliography of separately published*

U.S. Geological Survey special maps and river surveys (both in appendix 2A). For some years, USGS has not noted on its graphic indexes any quads that have been replaced by larger scale quads; yet these smaller scale quads remain in libraries and are often very useful, not only for historical purposes, but also for the person who needs physiographic information for an area located at the corner meeting of four quads. Moffat 1986 magnificently takes care of the problem, with graphic indexes and lists for each state except Alaska (cut out by the end date).

Not content with producing maps, supporting material, and atlases, USGS also: issues geologic sections and columns (usually on its geologic maps); purveys imagery through its EROS Data Center; and maintains the APSRS index, as was noted earlier in the section on remote-sensing imagery. USGS is very active in the remote-sensing field. Aerial photography is one area in which USGS both provides indexes and, through one of its branches, also sells imagery (via 800 number on one's telephone— 1/800/USA-MAPS). The index is the previously mentioned APSRS system; a one-sheet (both sides) publication, "How to obtain aerial photographs" (in the I 19.80 class number) leads the user gently into the system. NHAP and NAPP are sold by USGS's EROS Data Center.

One particular form of aerial photography is distributed to depository libraries: the orthophotoquads and orthophotomaps. To understand why these are made, we need to look at one part of making a topographic map. A major first step in topographic mapping is the taking of aerial photographs of the area to be mapped; but this is just a first step, with a long way to completion. If there is considerable demand for maps of a given area, USGS will issue an orthophotoquad of that area. An *orthophotoquad* is a mosaic of orthophotographs in standard quadrangle format, with little or no cartographic work done. Aerial photographs become orthophotographs by rectification (work performed by a large piece of machinery), which corrects the displacement of images normal to standard aerial photography. Orthophotomaps are far more sophisticated, in that they have had color applied (the o-quads are black-and-white) to enhance ground features, and cartographic symbols have been applied. Orthophotomaps are especially effective for depicting areas of low relief, such as marshes, ocean littoral areas, and the Great Salt Lake flats. And—for one last type of photography that USGS will sell—the survey just happens to have a photographic library (in Denver, Colorado), which holds in excess of 150,000 photographs taken during geological studies of the United States and its territories from 1869 to the present. About 132,000 are black-and-white and the rest are color transparencies (U.S. Geological Survey Photographic Library 1977, 168).

Figure 1.12. Radar image. United States. Geological Survey. 1980. Ugashik area, Alaska: south look, radar stereo image. Experimental ed. Scale 1:250,000. Reston, Va.: USGS.

Another area of remote sensing in which USGS remains very active, in referrals and archiving, is Landsat and other U.S. imagery. The EROS Data Center is the lead agency for this work, with its online search system, GLIS (Global Land Information System). The pamphlet titled "Index of earth resources observation systems" illustrates, in poster form, what sort of imagery is available and how to get hold of it; it continues the tradition of cartography by being not only supremely useful but also quite beautiful. As the reader has by now doubtless come to expect from USGS, the survey has general guides and a set of indexes to Landsat images.

And for a final remote sensing area, there is the side-looking airborne radar (SLAR) program, products of which are available from the EROS Data Center. SLAR data are available for several areas in Alaska and the lower 48 states, with more coverage planned. This imagery is available either as strip images or mosaics, mainly on CD. For a discussion of the SLAR program, see Southworth 1984.

Yet another area where USGS produces large amounts of data is in the digital arena—cartographic, bibliographic, or geographic names. The first named stems from the previously noted situation where USGS is working at having all topographic data for the United States available in digital form. See the previous section on "Spatial Data in Digital Form."

In microforms, USGS primarily works with indexes to the remote-sensing systems, and with the historic file of USGS topographic quadrangles; in both cases, these are accessed through USGS's information arm, now the Earth Science Information Center (ESIC; formed about 1989), formerly the National Cartographic Information Center (NCIC). ESIC has set up affiliates in as many states as possible; these affiliates have the manual and computer-generated indexes and catalogs for existing aerial photography and satellite imagery produced by governmental agencies (Rieke 1984, 134). NCIC was founded in about 1974; its predecessor was the MIO (Map Information Office), which also was far better known by acronym than by full name (Southard 1974, 543). Yes, of course, USGS has a pamphlet describing ESIC and its duties. ESIC's goal is to act as a cartographic-information routing center, dealing not in actual spatial data but in information on how to obtain those materials; hmm, what a concept—sounds rather like a map library sans maps, doesn't it? For information on how USGS works with state mapping advisory committees, see Edwards 1984.

In the miscellaneous category of products, we have USGS's lists, usually state-by-state, of commercial firms that sell USGS maps. USGS also has available symbols sheets for topographic and geologic maps; both are free. And, as a finishing touch, USGS has map exhibits for loan; see "Mapping through the ages—maps and minds" (Mapping through the ages 1984J) for a description of the major exhibit.

It is, in fact, difficult to find a USGS publication that does not hold some interest; USGS has put out everything from the *National atlas of the United States* to the U.S. sheets for the international map of the world at

1:1,000,000. It is impossible to overstate the importance of USGS to U.S. libraries. Its addresses soon become engraved in the librarian's mind; the latest issue of *New publications* supplies them all on the verso of the title page. Certainly there are problems with USGS, but in comparison with the vast amount that the survey does for libraries, and particularly in light of the way in which USGS works with librarians, these are relatively trivial. For example, the shift to metric mapping means a change in the size of the maps and therefore a change in the sizes of map cases that libraries need to hold those maps (USGS shifting 1978, 46). Because USGS is in the main prohibited from advertising (there are exceptions to this), the agency occasionally comes off as extremely shy, as for example during the 100-year celebration in 1979, when only a librarian with the instincts of Sherlock Holmes could have discovered through depository shipments that anything special was going on. For librarians who are still wondering if anything did, see volume 45, Number 12 of *PERS* (1979), which commemorates the USGS centennial. In 1986, USGS consolidated its facilities for distributing materials, closing down its Arlington, Virginia, office and moving all materials to the distribution center in Denver, Colorado, into Building 810. Building 810 and its contents have to be seen to be believed, what with 17 acres under one roof, 2,500 linear feet of shelving 16 feet high, and 100 million sheets representing 70,000 different map titles.

Still in Interior, we come to the National Park Service, at I 29., with its maps and information circulars which when opened up reveal a map. The Board on Geographic Names, at I 33., provides the supremely important foreign-country gazetteers; as was previously mentioned, USGS is issuing the gazetteer for the United States as its *Professional paper* 1200. The Fish and Wildlife Service has the National Wetlands Inventory at I 49.6/7-, available over the Web and in many case in fiche. The Bureau of Land Management (BLM), at I 53., is most obviously represented in map collections by miscellaneous maps and folders, and by its intermediate-scale maps at 1:l00,000, for surface management and surface-minerals management; USGS prepares the base map and sells the final product, while BLM compiles other data. BLM's public-lands background makes its recently issued CDs on that topic of importance.

At last we stagger out of Interior, only to fall into the arms of the Library of Congress. LC publishes many basic works on cataloging, which are discussed in chapter 3 on cataloging. The Geography and Map Division, at LC 5., collects rather than publishes maps; but LC operates a photoduplication service that sells reproductions. The National Aeronautics and Space Administration, at NAS 1., puts out atlas-like publications of remote sensing imagery, primarily of Landsat, and usually in its SP (NAS 1.21) and EP (NAS 1 19) series; particularly with the at least threefold increase in imagery costs during the 1980s (when NOAA was directed to go for cost recovery), this may be the only way in which many libraries can afford to collect Landsat images.

Moving to the Ps, the Postal Service has in the past issued a limited number of state postal maps (P 1.39/2). PrEx (the President's Executive Office) rapidly becomes a favorite number for many cartographic-materials librarians because of the PrEx 3.10/4 CIA maps and atlases, many of which maps, being 8-1/2" x 11", are the answer to a reference librarian's prayers. Another set of base maps, of the same size or smaller and black-and-white (the CIA maps are in color) are the Department of State's *Background notes* for various countries (S 1.123: and S 1.123/2:, indexes), which are brief (ca. five pages or often less) textual summaries of a given country that include maps, simplistic in nature but just right for photocopy. Various international boundary commissions have produced maps also.

The Department of Transportation publishes some maps, perhaps most noticeably in its TD 2.37 class number. The Tennessee Valley Authority, at TVA, is not at present part of the depository system, but has published various topographic maps (1:24,000, by TVA-USGS; map content identical to the USGS 1:24,000 series) and charts and reservoir maps; see Stevens and Malone 1978 for a brief history of TVA mapping.

Occasionally maps are published in Y4., hearings. But the sleeping giant is the serial set (Y 1.1/2)—compilations of House and Senate documents and reports. Especially those from the nineteenth and early twentieth centuries contain many maps within them. An index of the maps included in these documents has been issued by the Congressional Information Service as part of its *CIS U.S. serial set index, part XIV* (four volumes; index and cartobibliography of maps, 1789–1969); Donna Koepp of the University of Kansas has been the driving force behind this monolithic and extremely important project. See Gunter and Shupe 1981 for a discussion of the need for such an index to continue and expand upon the work of Claussen and Friis 1941 (appendix 2A).

As can be seen from all of the foregoing—which, extensive as it is, is by no means exhaustive, but merely hits the high points—it behooves the spatial-data librarian to be on extremely good terms with the documents librarian. In many libraries, the spatial-data collection either is part of documents (perhaps 75 percent of any such collection is government documents), or the spatial-data librarian is the same person as the documents librarian, both of which make matters far easier. The list of items that are quite obviously maps is extensive in itself (see Maps and atlases 1984); it is also extremely important that the documents librarian route to the spatial-data librarian any books relating to cartographic materials; for this to happen, the two librarians need to have some serious discussion and figure out procedure. Some documents librarians say, "Please, take anything you need; I'm out of space here," whereas other documents librarians look with considerable suspicion upon the whole idea of any documents leaving their departments.

Methods of Acquisition

Although the *bête noire* of any spatial-data librarian is trying to find out what was published in time to obtain it, the problem that comes next is the size of the acquisitions budget; somehow, all of us would like to spend at least ten times our allocation. Therefore, obtaining items by purchase is a course of last resort. Although trade books, much remote-sensing imagery, and globes must be purchased, an item issued by a government agency is always fair game for at least trying to receive it free of charge. Following are the major sources for low-cost or free procurement.

Depository Arrangements

The depository system in the United States is the Federal Depository Library Program, administered by the Superintendent of Documents/Government Printing Office.

Effective 1 October 1984, two of the three then-existing map repositories in the country—USGS and the then DMA (now NIMA)—joined the depository program. In June of 1985, a preliminary meeting took place between NOS and GPO. Time marched on; and finally, in November of 1988, NOS phased out its own Library Depository Program and began participating in the GPO Federal Depository Library Program, following Title 44 of the U.S. Code. See the previous section for detailed information on C&GS, NIMA, and USGS.

The New Depository System

All the former depository/repository arrangements are behind us now. Due to the considerable efforts and even more considerable cooperation of many persons in several agencies and associations—most notably USGS, the Joint Committee on Printing (JCP), the then DMA, the Western Association of Map Libraries (WAML), SLA Geography and Map Division (SLAG&M), the Geoscience Information Society (GIS), and ALA Map and Geography Round Table (ALA MAGERT)—all the USGS, NOS, and NIMA depositories were included under the federal depository program; past arrangements have had USGS mailing out the maps, and GPO listing the maps on shipping lists and mailing the shipping lists out, but these are changeable. Map shipments from USGS are signaled not only by USGS being the return address on the mailing labels but also by the word *MAPS* appearing just above the right-hand corner of the library address.

For a brief history on this, we must begin with a meeting at NCIC in Denver on 9 and 10 March 1978, where NCIC and SLAG&M members met to discuss mutual problems. If for no other reason than touring the awesome USGS map sales area in Denver (75 million maps spread over what looked like the equivalent of several football fields, and stacked at least 20 feet high), the meeting would have been well worth it. As it was, it set a tone for good relations and working together that would lead to the joint depository (Cobb 1979a; Larsgaard 1978; and Rudd 1978).

As time went by, SLAG&M formed a Cartographic Users Advisory Committee (CUAC), initially composed only of SLAG&M members, but evolving into the Cartographic Users Advisory Council (CUAC), with members from SLAG&M, WAML, MAGERT, and GIS. This very active committee has made a point of meeting at least once a year with USGS and whoever else was brave enough to meet a pack of map librarians, in the Washington, D.C., area if at all possible (see Stevens 1981a). JCP formed a Map Task Force, speaking with as many federal map-producing agencies as possible (Stevens 1985; and Eisenbeis 1982, 34). In a 26 July 1982 letter from Charles Mathias, JCP Chairman, to heads of all depositories, the intent of incorporating the USGS and DMA depositories into the federal depository program was announced; a questionnaire enclosed with the letter was intended to identify libraries that would be interested in participating in such a program. After all the paper filtered back and was analyzed, the result was Daily depository shipping list no. 18,142 (third shipment of 24 June 1983), which was a survey for DMA maps, and no. 18,143 (fourth shipment of 24 June 1983), which was a survey for USGS maps. Actual shipment of maps was to begin in fiscal 1984, beginning 1 October 1984, and amazingly enough (considering all the paperwork) did so. Librarians who had never before checked off a shipping list had a harried time of it initially; but after all the years when USGS repository libraries complained that one big problem was the lack of shipping lists, it was embarrassing to protest. Both USGS and DMA kindly offered to continue a policy of replacing missing maps (this aside from the claiming done in the first sixty days after an incomplete shipping list has been received) or replacing damaged or lost maps.

The latest developments have all been about making spatial data in digital form available in one's collection and over the Web. These nasty little problems are documented in the previous section, "Spatial Data in Digital Form."

There Are Catches to Everything

Being part of a depository program is not unalloyed joy. A saying among resigned government-documents librarians for years has been, "Depository items are free until they arrive on your doorstep, and then they start to cost." So true. Neither the C&GS nor NIMA depository totals add up to anything particularly onerous (amounting to about 300 maps per year for NIMA, and 100 to perhaps 500 for C&GS—rapidly decreasing with its financial problems); however, USGS's full complement of maps is very close to 1,500 sheets per year, all of which must—at the very least—be stamped, counted, and filed, and according to depository requirements be made accessible (preferably through cataloging). Providing sufficient computer power plus reference assistance for working with spatial data in digital form are neither easily done. Fortunately, the folded maps can go on standard book shelving or in file cabinets, and the CDs into yet more cabinets; but the flat maps must be filed in map cases.

Reverting, with some feelings of financial pain, to map cases, a USGS depository library can count on purchasing at least one set of five-drawer map filing units every four years, which, at a few hundred dollars per file (at the time of writing, about $650, although prices do decrease at certain break points, such as 10 cases) tends to mount up. Speaking of mounting up, that is exactly what the map cases do as the years go by; because of their substantial weight when full, and because of user inconvenience and danger to life and limb, it is inadvisable to stack units more than three or four high; this means that additional floor space—in most libraries at a premium, and therefore expensive—must be available. In one of its previous incarnations, NIMA required that some of its maps be kept in locked cases or in limited-access areas.

Another expense point to keep in mind, particularly with the inclusion of USGS, NIMA, and C&GS depositories under the federal depository program, is that GPO's (or rather its lawyers') interpretation of laws and statutes and so forth is that it is "the responsibility of the library custodians to maintain appropriate insurance to protect the Government's property interest" (see United States government memorandum, dated 12 January 1984, numbered AN-v5n10-7/84; subject is "Responsibility of depository libraries to insure their depository collections"; to the Superintendent of Documents from Mark C. Cramer). This same memo also notes that depository items that require replacement are the financial responsibility of the library. It is essential that the librarian keep a complete file of all depository correspondence; one of the more embarrassing parts of establishing a close working relationship with USGS was that many map collections did not have even a copy of the original repository agreement.

Duplicate Maps

There are other methods of obtaining cartographic materials short of purchasing them; there is, for example, duplicate exchange. Such maps are usually free except for the cost of postage and everyone's time; the former is refunded to the sending institution, in some cases depending upon the amount (e.g., greater than five dollars). Some libraries—staffed by valiant souls who have, if not sufficient, at least some clerical assistance— send out duplicates lists, usually to the listserv/reflector MAPS-L, which is far more satisfactory than the old system of making many, many copies of the duplicates list and then mailing them out to likely victims. These duplicates lists may either painstakingly record each sheet one by one, or, in the lazy-and-harried version (represented by lists sent out in the past by this author), just general categories (e.g., "USGS I's, 790 through 1190, scattered") , leaving the responding library to note which ones it needs. Another route—and one followed increasingly, though perhaps in a mildly surreptitious fashion—is for persons in charge of collections to arrange, at professional meetings, with other collections simply to ship off maps of possible interest to each other, with the full understanding that if the maps are not wanted, they may be unceremoniously tossed into the nearest File 13. The librarians then list on their duplicates lists only those items that are left over after the shipping to corresponding libraries is completed.

There has become recently available over the Web MAPSWAP, for disposing of duplicate maps; see   http://www.norrd.bart.nl/tilde pnugter/ . Here one may offer maps and also post one's want list.

LCG&M Summer Map Processing Project

In yet another category, a trade of labor for maps, is the LCG&M Summer Map Processing Project, now occurring only occasionally, but still well on its way to developing a literature of its own. In exchange for services rendered to the Division, participants sponsored (a polite word for saying that all lodging, food, transport, and salaries are paid by that institution) by libraries (very often college and university) select duplicate maps and atlases from G&M; duplicate stock is mailed off to the sponsoring institution, in the past using Congress members' franks, which latter seem no longer to be available for this purpose.

The project started in 1951 as a result of LC receiving, "on transfer from various Federal libraries and mapping agencies, hundreds of thousands of obsolete maps and charts," so many that the staff was unable to process more than a fraction of the total (USLCIB 34 (34): A-197). To get this massive backlog out of the way, or at least to ascertain its depths, the then Division Chief Arch Gerlach persuaded several institutions to sponsor participants in exchange for the privilege of selecting duplicates for their map collections. For the first 20 years, the project was for 12 weeks, and for the next four years, six weeks. By 1976, the 26th year, more than 1.5 million maps had been distributed in the program (C. Kidd 1977, 31; and *Map librarian in the modern world* 1979, 78). Besides the obvious benefits of large numbers of maps and atlases (picked on one-half day per week), participants also attend weekly seminars put on by LCG&M staff. The projects have come to be regarded as training programs for map librarians, every one of which should seriously consider participating in at least one of them.

Of course, there are some difficulties. The duplicate maps, at least in the past, were selected from foot-high stacks on shelves, in a roughly geographical order that disappeared by the end of the fourth week of the six-week session. Also, hell hath no fury like a librarian scrounging for free maps; as one participant put it, "a mean-mannered middle linebacker with map training would be ideal" for the "chaotic selecting arrangement" (Otness 1971, 16). Highly specialized maps comprise a large portion of the duplicates, and therefore the project is of most value to college, university, and large public libraries. There is also the problem that he who chooses first chooses best, and not everyone can be first; drawing lots is one way to do the pulling in an equitable way (Otness 1971, 19; and Hagen 1970a). It is essential that participants have a very good idea of what kinds of maps are of interest to their libraries, and know enough to stay away from large series unless many of the sheets are available. But all in all, the project is an excellent opportunity for librarians to obtain maps, atlases, and expertise (Strickland 1978).

Gifts of Other Kinds

Gifts may be solicited either specifically or generally, or they may be received with no advance warning whatsoever. In the category of solicitation is the heavily used free-request form (see appendix 4 for an example), which may be used to beg for whatever the librarian has sufficient nerve to try for; particularly in dealing with government agencies, the librarian should always attempt to obtain items free of charge. It is amazing what library letterhead can encourage agencies to give. If the item must be purchased, the free-request form may still be used; on it the librarian is careful to note that if the item is not free, the agency's kindness in notifying the library of the price is appreciated. About once in every one thousand or so free requests, the agency will send both the item and a demand for payment; how this is handled depends on how appropriate and needed the item is, and whether the library has any money left that fiscal year. For free-request forms sent to foreign countries, the form must be in the language of the country if at all possible; forms in French, Spanish, German, and Portuguese constitute the most frequently used of such forms. One option on all such forms is to request to be put on the mailing list for publications announcements; very often such requests are honored.

Almost any sort of spatial data may be requested using the type of form shown in appendix 4. Besides requesting items that the librarian has discovered in a seemingly continuous perusal of periodicals, every library needs to set up a schedule for requesting such items as road maps of states and city street maps. The road map for the library's state of residence must be obtained every year, and larger collections will try to get every state's (and every Canadian province's) road map every year, but small collections may find that once every five years is fine except for their own and immediately adjacent states.

Solicitation programs for city maps are more complicated to set up, although the basic questions—which ones do you need? how often?—are the same. In this case, the librarian needs to decide how many cities in how many states and countries need to be covered and whether the maps are already available over the Web. This is based upon the size of the library, the types of users, and the amount of money available for such city plans as may have to be purchased. Given the variables discussed earlier, it is impossible to give directions for a city solicitation program appropriate to all libraries, but a few generalities do provide some guidance. Most libraries will want to have city maps for their state; these maps are often available from state highway departments, but for a price that may exceed the cost of postage, paper, and typing time, so the library may choose to use the *World chamber of commerce directory* 1980– (appendix 2A) for addresses and do a massive mailing. How many maps the library decides to get for other states and for foreign countries depends in part upon the amount of urbanization; for example, for Albania the library may decide to settle for Tirane, whereas for Great Britain just a map of London is not enough. Perhaps 10 to 15 maps per country (more for heavily urbanized countries or for countries of special interest) are reasonable for a library of 150,000 to 200,000 maps (Armstrong 1978, 4). Five per state is acceptable except for large, heavily populated states, or those of special interest.

In all such decision-making, the librarian must be guided first of all by the users' needs. If the library supports a large urban-studies program, the demand for city maps will be very high; if the library supports a sciences or technical program, the major need is for maps of cities that have large employers in those fields. Once the decision has been made to obtain maps for certain cities, then the librarian needs to decide how often to request them; for all but the largest libraries and the most special cases, once every five to ten years (varying according to staff and budget and, of course, need) is about enough. When sending for city maps, the librarian should tailor a free-request form exclusively for city maps, and should if at all possible enclose a self-addressed mailing label, at least in an initial mailing (D. A. Wise 1981a, 284). Although the library's request is for city maps, the city chambers of commerce will probably also send a good deal of promotional material; the librarian needs to find out, before the requests and the resultant avalanche, if some other part of the library (usually reference) keeps up a file of such material. If all of this seems like more work than it's worth, city maps may be purchased from many firms, e.g., Rand McNally, Michelin, etc.

A library may also receive unsolicited gifts. Persons clearing out their homes and offices in some cases do donate items to libraries. The library may even want to solicit such materials actively, letting users know via the general public-relations handout that gifts are welcome, with the proviso that the giver is responsible for any evaluation by appraisers. Having a list of local appraisers readily available is a wise move.

Purchase

When all else fails, the last resort is purchase. Procedures for purchase are largely determined by the acquisitions department in the library of which the spatial-data collection is a part. Thus, the first move for the librarian is to talk with the head of acquisitions and find out what that department needs to make the order procedure flow as smoothly as possible. If the acquisitions department has a manual that details practices, so much the better. The general procedure is for the spatial-data librarian to make selections and then either to send ordering information (including full address and any ordering peculiarities of the seller) to the acquisitions department, or to generate orders via the library's online system. The spatial-data librarian keeps a copy of the order. The spatial-data librarian should keep readily available ordering information for materials for those hectic times, such as at the end of the fiscal year, when the acquisitions librarian has a large amount of money to spend in a very short time.

Most of the problems with ordering will relate to foreign purchases. One is that if the library is in a relatively small town, local banks may not be willing to issue checks in such currencies as, for example, the Tunisian franc; then the only possibility is to purchase from a jobber. That leads us nicely into the next problem, which is that acquisitions departments far prefer to order from jobbers, because only one order has to be placed and only one check has to be cut. In addition, books are often less expensive when purchased from a jobber than from the original publisher. Just the opposite is true of maps, and if the spatial-data librarian is not on good terms with the acquisition department staff and cannot arrange to have items ordered only from the original publisher, the spatial-data acquisitions budget will disappear faster than summer snow. Here a little give-and-take is important; the spatial-data librarian has to realize that having a banker's check made up in foreign currency costs a minimum of five dollars, and in some cases it is less expensive just to go through the jobber, especially if the orders are, say, ten different maps from ten different countries with ten different currencies.

Evaluation

Spatial-data librarians view with mingled feelings of amusement and yearning the idea that evaluation has something to do with selection. The sad truth is that selection is very often narrowed down to three questions: Does this collection need this item? Is the item available, nonrestricted, and in print? Does the collection have the money to buy it? Except for atlases, globes, and some books, the matter of evaluation seldom enters into it; no matter how poorly designed, sloppily printed, and luridly colored a map may be, if it's the only one on that topic (or the only current one), the library buys it. A map doesn't have to be the best if it's the only, and in demand besides. But who knows, the millennium may arrive, or the librarian may just happen upon the situation where there is more than one map on a given subject—so, just in case, and to be optimistic, following are the evaluative questions for maps, plans, sections, diagrams, and remote-sensing images:

1. Source of map attributes.

Does the publisher have a good reputation?
Is information supplied of sufficient quality and in sufficient quantity?
Is the information up to date?
Can you trust the publisher to put out accurate information?

2. Physical appearance of the map. (Note that this question as-
    sumes the librarian will see the map prior to purchase; un-
    likely, but possible.)

Does it cover the area needed?
How much detail is there—and is it too much or too little for users?
How is color used?
Is it difficult to read place names through the color overlay?
Are text and place names clearly printed, and is registration good?
Are symbols easy to read and adequately explained?
Are scale and north indicated somewhere, somehow?
Is the medium upon which the item is printed durable?
Is the item pleasing to the eye?
Does the item have any special features, such as indexes, mileage
      charts, and so forth, and if so, are they needed? Or are they
      needed but not present?
Is it well designed and well executed? (Harrison 1952, 45; S. Miller
      1971, 134; Nichols 1976, 27; Walker 1974, 70; and Current
      1971, 579)

It is relatively easy to determine whether or not your collection needs
a given item; judging the quality of the item demands that the librarian
understand cartography—design, projections, execution, the map as aesthetic object—and also have seen a large number of spatial-data objects,
to have a context in which to judge an item (Harrison 1952, 46; and
Teggart 1944, 1040–41). But even if the librarian is unable to use these
criteria to select a map, knowing how to evaluate it is supremely useful
for reference work; the librarian can warn the prospective user of pitfalls.
      Evaluating globes is excellently treated in Coombs 1981, which article
is summarized in this chapter's section on globes, and thus is not further
discussed here. Atlases are next in line. Thematic atlases are often one of a
kind; as with maps and remote-sensing images, selection is a matter of taking
what is available. But with the general world atlases, there are so many
available, and purchasing them takes such a substantial part of the budget,
that there is even a book devoted to their evaluation (Kister 1984 in appendix
2A), not to mention a fair number of periodical articles (Porter 1961 and
1975; Schorr 1981; Gómez-Ibáñez 1969 in appendix 2A).
      What makes a good world atlas? As in so many other theaters of life,
time and money—expressed in this case by accuracy, clarity, legibility,
large indexes, attractive color and design, good balance of coverage with
no area slighted, map scales few in number so that areas may be
compared, and sufficiently large scales that some detail may be distin-
guished. Place names should be treated uniformly; projections should be
identified and used appropriately, and nonmap material should be kept
to a minimum (Gómez-Ibáñez 1969, 27, in appendix 2A; Ristow 1945,
54; and Cheney and Williams 1980, 284–85).

Producing an atlas is an expensive process, with much compilation, careful design and graphic work, checking of information, and indexing involved; thus, good atlases are expensive and may cost up to several hundred dollars. Therefore, they should be chosen carefully and compared (if nowhere else, at a larger library) before a choice is made. As a general rule, you get what you pay for when you buy an atlas, but lower-priced atlases are in some cases worthy of purchase, depending upon the users; for example, as was previously noted, *Goode's world atlas* is both good and inexpensive (Porter 1961, 194).

The most important initial consideration is the reputation and competence of the publisher; the average librarian usually does not possess the technical skill needed to judge cartographic fine points. As with any reference work, frequency and thoroughness of revision also have a bearing on purchase. There are certain checks that the librarian can make:

- counting and comparing the total number of map pages

- counting and comparing the number of pages devoted to the United States and the number of pages devoted to Africa—use the following guide to figure out how the page percentages per continent in a given atlas match the percentages of land and population for each continent:

Continent	% of land area	% of population
Africa	23	20
Antarctica	10	0
Asia (including USSR)*	32	58
Europe	8	9
North America	18	5
Pacific Islands	6	0.5
Latin America	14	8
(*USSR	15	6)

- comparing dates of data and of publication

- checking recency of information by looking at place names (for example, in 1993, the former Czechoslovakia split)

- finding out what the sources of information are

- counting the number of thematic maps

- checking to see if surface relief is shown, and if so, in an understandable, meaningful way

- comparing the same area in two or more atlases, observing which atlas is the most detailed, the most legible, the most attractive, the most informative, and the easiest to use

- looking for consistency of scale so that areas may be compared

- checking for nonmap material that is easily found elsewhere and thus qualifies as filler

- making sure that map symbols and abbreviations are explained

- checking the percentage of the total number of pages that is taken up by index (it seems to take an index at least one-third to one-half of the volume to be adequate)

- checking for tipped-in pages, sturdy binding, and attractive appearance (Porter 1961, 195–97; Thatcher 1972a, 133–36; and Schorr 1981, 565–66 in appendix 2A).

The librarian may check for accuracy in detail by looking at a familiar area and checking accuracy and relative completeness for that area. It's always a good idea to read reviews of atlases (MacEathron 1996 and Stout 1977 in appendix 2A). Kister 1984 (appendix 2A) is easy to use and sound in its judgments; many different periodicals also carry reviews as regular features, especially those periodicals devoted to map librarianship and to cartography. Reviews of reference works often include atlases.

Every library needs at least one of the general reference world atlases with an international focus. In the past, and even now, some atlases produced in the United States are visually dull, and may be unbalanced in the amounts of space allotted to various parts of the world; this is due to the relatively unsophisticated audience for which they are intended. The *Rand McNally new international atlas* (1993, in appendix 2A) is a magnificent refutation of statements that all U.S. atlases have to be poor; the *Times atlas of the world* (1985) remains the best English-language world atlas, but the Rand McNally is a close second. Sometimes nominally considered to be a world reference atlas (by virtue in the past of the inclusion of a slender selection of world maps) is the *Rand McNally commercial atlas and marketing guide*. In reality, this annual is very definitely an atlas of the United States, with a wealth of locational and commercial information concerning agriculture, communications, population, retail trade, transportation, trading areas, and much more information about each state. In spite of the aesthetically displeasing dull grayish maps, it is an essential and much valued reference tool for U.S. libraries; even smaller libraries are well advised to purchase an edition about once every five years. Older editions are important for historical research.

The general world reference atlases are needed by almost all libraries. The librarian trying to decide which one, or ones, the library needs should first consider what the library users need; then, by reading reviews and looking at various atlases, decide which atlases satisfy those needs;

and then carefully examine and compare the atlases that are appropriate. After the comparison, a brief check on the health of the budget will supply the final piece of information needed to select the appropriate atlas.

Selecting digital data starts with the same major steps as does selecting any other form of spatial data—that is, first figuring out what user needs are for that geographic area and subject matter and then checking on vendor reliability. Next the librarian needs to find out what software and hardware will be required to use the data, and following that should check to see if the data is available over the Web and decide if use is sufficient to keep a digital copy in house. There are several checks beyond this that will need to be made:

- database not already available through the library's consortial agreements (check pricing—is it more economically sensible to have one license, or to have multi-user licenses?)

- acceptable licensing and use restrictions (for example, if the license does not allow for printing or downloading, the product is useless in a library setting)

- print counterparts, if any

- reasonable customer support (both in terms of hours of availability and of cost)

- "clear and thorough" documentation (Stewart 1987, p. 739)

- trial version available in some form (e.g., sample CD or over the Web)

- includes tutorial

- relatively easy to use, with menus, prompts, on-screen contextual help, error messages that actually give the user a clue as to how to get out of some mess, examples of operations

- easy installation

- easy printing and downloading
  (Stewart 1987; and Znamirowski 1993.)

Selecting digital data available over the Web, either for listing on one's homepage or in the online catalog, involves many of the same judgments, although when the data is taking up space on someone else's hard drive and there is no licensing charge, one's judgment may be solely based on it being spatial data in digital form that one's users might at some time need (Demas, McDonald, and Lawrence 1995).

Conclusion

Selection and acquisition are the most involved and among the most time-consuming of the librarian's duties. They are also among the most important of those duties, and deserve all the attention, concentration, and patience that it takes to perform them properly. The key to this area of work is to know the patterns in issuance of spatial data and supporting material, so that the librarian knows what to look for and where.

2

Classification

Classification Schemes

Although classification of monographs and serials has been accepted practice for many years, nonbook materials do not come off quite so well, a fact with which the cartographic-materials librarian will become all too painfully familiar. What is needed in a cartographic-materials collection is a classification scheme that is: easy to apply; widely used in other libraries; revised periodically; parsimonious in its use of staff time (and that preferably low-priced); and mnemonic and comprehensive, the last not only in terms of subject matter but also in terms of format—for the collection will encompass maps, views, plans, sections, diagrams, remote-sensing images, globes, models, atlases, standard books and serials, and digital materials. Of the following classifications, some are especially formulated for maps, and a few are intended to include all knowledge and formats, although there is some feeling that most classification schemes are intended for text rather than graphic information, and therefore cartographic material may need its own system (Van Snellenberg 1985, p. 35). Usually the term *map* is intended to include views, plans, sections, and diagrams, and even (but erroneously) remote-sensing images—that is, anything that represents a geographic area or area on another planet or elsewhere in the universe.

The first step in classifying a collection is to ask why it is being done at all. A considerable amount of work is entailed, both initially and on a continuing basis. Why not just pile the materials in a corner and walk away, as has been done in the past, and as in effect is often done now on the World Wide Web? The most obvious reason for classing materials is that by systematically arranging them in categories, according to subject or form, the items can be easily retrieved and used, saving much frustration and wasted time on the part of both user and staff.

Although cartographic-materials classification may seem an esoteric subject, the enterprising searcher can find a goodly number of systems—usually focused on maps—from which to choose, including the trusty IWCFIYCUI (if we can find it, you can use it) system. No one scheme is completely accepted by everyone, with some persons even going so far as to state that no one scheme is best suited to all sizes and types of collections (Ansari 1977, 99; White 1959, 154; Bartlett and Marshall 1979, 11). One contributing factor here is that the major class schemes were formulated at a time when cartographic-materials collections were quite small and thus easily ignored. A more recent influence is that computer networking, which points out in a heavy-handed way the virtues of conformity, was completely unknown in earlier days, leaving librarians (including at times library directors) to put together their own little pet schemes. Thus classification in the first half of the twentieth century was largely a matter of personal preference, a *laissez-faire* stance encouraged by the relatively small size of the collections (Letts 1905, 803). A third point deals with the spatial-data user's interests. Although the overall objective of book classification and of nonbook classification is the same—to group like items together by assigning to each a call-number location device—book schemes are theme-oriented, with geographic interest most likely to be subordinate to other subjects, whereas with cartographic materials a user's first interest is area, with other subjects subordinate to area (White 1959, 154). As to whether area is a subject, that's another argument; see chapter 3 on cataloging.

Cartographic-materials classification may be either geographical or non-geographical. Of the geographical systems, there are three types: alphabetic; alphanumeric; and numeric.

Alphabetic Systems

Natural language and abbreviation, grading into each other, are types of alphabetic classification, and are more informal than are the alphanumeric and numeric schemes. One of the main virtues of natural-language classification systems—or, as they are sometimes called, *titling*—is that they are quickly comprehended by the patron, and equally quickly and easily applied by staff, at least up to a point; for this reason, many prominent collections (such as those at the Royal Geographical Society and the University of Washington) have used this system at one time or another (Burkett 1965, 294). Titling is seductive in its simplicity and directness; why unnecessarily translate "the word of your desire into a symbol and back again, multiplying your movement and straining memory, when you can go straight to the word on card or map?" (Prévost

1946, 104). The answer to this is that collections tend to outgrow this system, and then have to be redone when the task has become a mammoth undertaking. The author speaks with particular feeling on this point, having taken over a titled collection of 80,000 sheets and then having to class it all (in LC Schedule G) because the existing system no longer worked on a collection of that size.

Titling is generally used only for maps and their view-plan-section-diagram kin, not for remote-sensing images, atlases, and support material. Titling may be either linear or columnar:

France. Gravity. 1:320,000. Area. Subject. Scale.
sheet 221. 1972. sheet number. date.
(Goodwin 1973)

INDIA	Area
1:500,000	Scale (if part of series)
SOILS	Subject
1968	Date
(Hubbard 1973)	

The latter example is in some ways a verbalization of the Library of Congress (LC) and Parsons systems, to be discussed later.

When titling is used, items classed are filed by continent or convenient physical area, and within these areas alphabetically by political unit. Subjects and areas are selected from a predetermined list, and may be abbreviations. If abbreviations are used, they must be standardized, e.g., "Eufr" for "Europe—France."

An example of an abbreviation system is that set forth by the U.S. National Bureau of Standards in FIPS PUB 10-1 (occasionally revised). Although this standard was originally "prescribed for the interchange of formatted machine sensible coded data between and among agencies and the public" (U.S. National Bureau of Standards 1974– , 1)—that is, for computer applications in government—it does present a ready-made abbreviation system, a list of geographical-political entities, and a code for each such entity. The publication contains a base list (alphabetical by country), a second list (alphabetical by code), and a third list (giving cross-references). An example of a cross-reference to the base list is:

Vanua Levu (island) FIJI (FJ)
(U.S. National Bureau of Standards, 21)

There is also a list of entity additions, deletions, and changes from previous versions of the standard. Some sample entries from the base list are shown on page 120.

Afghanistan	AF
Albania	AL
Algeria	AG
American Samoa	AQ
Andorra	AN

(U.S. National Bureau of Standards 1974– , 4)

The United States is given with no state breakdown, a breach easily filled by using U.S. postal codes for states. Additional codes could be constructed as needed, then noted in the class manual.

Alphanumeric Systems

Many different alphanumeric systems—the most popular of the various types—are extant. As a general rule, these schemes indicate area, and occasionally subject, by number, and subject and author by alphanumeric codes. The better known alphanumeric systems are Library of Congress (LC), Boggs and Lewis (B&L), Dewey Decimal (DD), and American Geographical Society (AGS); another type will be represented by the Parsons system.

The U.S. Library of Congress Classification System, Schedule G

Schedule G of the LC class system contains the best classification scheme for cartographic materials, valiantly attempting to include not only all cartographic materials but also all supporting materials, and generally performing the task fairly well. LC class was created in 1900; the first edition of G came in 1910, with the second edition—which made provision for atlases (in G1001–3035)—in 1928. In 1946 came the preliminary draft for maps, in G3160–9999. The third edition was in 1954, reprinted in 1966, with the fourth edition appearing, much to the relief of cartographic-materials librarians, in 1976. The most current "edition" was to appear in the massive digital version of LC classification schedules as a whole, sometime in 1998 or 1999. This digital version is a database, with 0xx for control information, numbers, and codes; 1xx for classification numbers and terms; 2xx/3xx for complex See and See Also references; 4xx/5xx for tracings; 6xx for note fields; 70x–75x for index term fields (which mirror bibliographic added-entry fields); and 76x for number-building fields, which are specific for classification. This latest version will include all of the geographic-area letter-number codes (for regions, states, and cities) that had previously been available only for states of the United States on microfiche, in the publication *Geographic cutters* (Washington, D.C.: Cataloging Distribution Service, Library of Congress, 1989). There is a proposal at LCG&M (Library of Congress, Geography and Map Division) to do away with the separate atlas portion of the schedule and instead to class atlases at the same numbers as maps (and all other cartographic materials) in the G3160–9999 portion of the schedule. The currently used class area for atlases—which was never as fully carried out as the maps section—is collapsing under the strain of the various changes in political areas over the last five or so years, and includes such irritating matters as classing atlases of the world as a whole in several different sequences, unnecessarily complicating reference work by forcing the librarian to remember to look at several different call numbers. It is also aggravating to have map call numbers structured one way (area, subject, date of situation, author cutter) and atlas call numbers another (area, subject, author cutter, date of publication); after all, atlases are just collections of maps, and therefore should be classed the same way. With the proposed change, staff will need to deal with only one number for one given area, instead of two.

There are several useful publications to assist in the application of LC Schedule G to cartographic materials, beginning with the schedule itself, especially in its new digital format. Librarians may still wish to tear the old 1976 schedule up (or, given an almost unlimited supply of paper, print out the G schedule with its hundreds of thousands of entries), three-hole-punch it, place it in a three-ring binder, and then photocopy 8.5″ x 11″ administrative maps for U.S. states and each foreign country (for different years as appropriate—e.g., maps of Arizona before and after the formation of the new county, with year of formation of that county clearly noted on the new map), inserting them at the appropriate place. This technique will save much time, muttering under one's breath, and seeking out various editions of *Webster's geographical dictionary*. In addition, there are:

a. Library of Congress. 1979. *Shelflist of the Library of Congress: Geography*. Ann Arbor, MI: University Microfilms International.

b. Library of Congress. Geography and Map Division. 1991. *Map cataloging manual*. Washington, D.C.: Cataloging Distribution Service, Library of Congress.

In spite of the second item's title, it does contain extremely useful information on how LCG&M applies class numbers; before its publication, map librarians made use of the photocopied internal manual that the LCG&M catalogers used, with knowledge of the item being folk wisdom that was transferred, sometimes over a congenial glass of wine at a conference, to newcomers in the field. There was for some time no index to the subject codes for maps, nor a list just of geographic areas; this author put together such lists, out of desperation, about fifteen years ago, and they have since been improved upon respectively by LCG&M and by the University of Florida Map Collection.

Table 2.1.
Summary of Library of Congress Classification System for Maps.
Derived from LC classification system, Schedule G, 4th ed.

Universe, solar system	G3190-3192
World	3200-3202
America	3290-3292
Canada*	3400-3654
United States	3700-3702
By states	3710-4374
Latin America	4400-4402
By countries	4410-5663
Eurasia, Afro-Asia	5670-5672
Europe	5700-5702
By country	5720-6985
Commonwealth of Independent Republics	7000-7004
By country	7010-7340
Asia	7400-7402
By country and area	7405-8192
Africa	8200-8202
By country and area	8210-8904
Australasia	8950-9080
By country	8960-9080
Atlantic Ocean	9100-9172
Indian Ocean	9175-9227
Pacific Ocean	9230-9774
Arctic Ocean	9780-9797
Antarctica	9800-9802
Unlocalized maps	9900-9999

*Extensive changes to the Canadian portion of the schedule were proposed and accepted by LCG&M in the early 1980s; these are to appear at some point in a list of additions and changes to the schedule.

In Schedule G, atlases are classed at G1000.3–3122, globes G3160–3182, and maps G3190–9999; views, plans, sections, diagrams, remote-sensing imagery, and models are classed in the maps portion, with subject codes (pages 212–223 of the schedule) taking care of the special aspects of these cartographic materials (e.g., .A3 for aerial views; .C18 for raised-relief models; .C57 for geologic sections). A recently added code is .A25 for digital maps; whether the librarian chooses to use this to indicate that an item is in digital form, or adds as the last line of the call number the digital format (e.g., "CD") is a local option; the librarian may also consider that this is an appropriate place to put maps showing coverage by digital files. In any case, subject codes in A are to be used only when no other subject code (B through S) applies. Each major cultural or political unit of the Earth is assigned a block of numbers, the listing consisting of the letter G followed by a four-digit number. When political areas change name, it's a simple matter just to insert the new name, with relevant dates, in one's schedule; when political boundaries actually change, one must wait until the new class number is issued by LCG&M for a final decision. Sometimes these political changes do require a certain amount of work (trivial in comparison with the wrenching experience undergone by persons actually living in the countries in question); for example, when the Soviet Union split into its constituent republics, the cities that had formerly all been listed as cities of the Soviet Union, in one list, were divided up by new country. Units such as a state in the United States, or a sea in an ocean, are assigned blocks of numbers having the endings either 0 through 4 or 5 through 9. It is important to remember, when viewing which areas get blocks of numbers and which do not, that LC is a reflection of the holdings of LCG&M, with maps of the United States preponderating. Each of these blocks has a range of five numbers if needed; zero and 5 are general maps, 1 and 6 are subject maps, 2 and 7 are regional maps, 3 and 8 are county maps, and 4 and 9 are city maps. Foreign countries for which LC has a large number of maps have more detailed listings than those countries for which LC's map holdings are not so large. Some units, such as oceans, have ranges larger than five numbers.

Table 2.2.
Summary of LC Subject-Code System. Derived from LC classification system, Schedule G, 4th ed.

A	Special categories	H	Mines and mineral resources
B	Mathematical geography	J	Agriculture
C	Physical sciences	K	Forests and forestry
D	Biogeography	L	Fish and fisheries
	D1 General (plant and	M	Manufacturing, processing
	animal distribution)	N	Technology, engineering,
	D2 Plant geography		public works
	D4 Animal geography	P	Transportation,
	D5 Wildlife reservations		communication
E	Human & cultural	Q	Commerce, trade, finance
	geography	R	Military & naval geography
F	Political geography	S	Historical geography
G	Economic geography		

Subject letter/number combinations are not cutters and have no mnemonic significance.

The subject code for the class number is composed of the letters A through S (none of which is mnemonic), followed by numbers representing subtopics. Figure 2.2 shows a subject outline with a breakdown for one subject, D.

Call numbers for maps consist of at least three parts in the LC classification. For example, for general maps with area number ending in 0 or 5:

> G4280   Washington state (area number)
> 1947   Date of data (publication, if no other date given)
> .C7   Cutter for Cram Company

The date in a call number is the date of situation if available, except when a history S letter/number combination is used to indicate subject. In this case, the date of situation is implied by the subject code and the date in the call number is the date of publication.

For a subject map with an area number ending in 1 or 6, with subject codes A through S (subject-code letters may also be assigned to any map with area number ending in 2 or 7, 3 or 8, 4 or 9, but never to one ending with 0 or 5):

> G4281   Washington state (area number for subject map)
> .C5   Geology (subject code)
> 1961   Date of situation
> .U5   United States Geological Survey (authority cutter)

For a regional map with area number endings of 2 or 7, cuttered A through Z:

> G4282   Washington state (area number for regional map)
> .W4   Wenatchee National Forest
> 1959   Date of situation
> .U5   U.S. Forest Service (authority cutter)

Although they are not in the 1976 schedule, codes for national forests and national parks have been established and are given in the digital version of the LC schedules and in geographic cutters.

For most class schemes, the potential for failure or at the very least aggravation is greatest for "fuzzy" boundaries, e.g., nonpolitical regions or features, and especially portions of oceans; LC is no exception to this, but certainly is no worse than others and better than most. The most difficult tend to be when one is classing maps that depict relatively small areas of two countries. When features peskily cross political boundaries, they are classified by the following rules:

1. A feature in two administrative divisions is classified with the division containing the greater portion of the feature.

> G3822   Pennsylvania
> .A5   Allegheny River (located mostly in Pennsylvania but also in New York State)

2. A feature in two administrative divisions, each containing equal parts of the feature, is classified with the first alphabetically. A

local option is to class the item in the area of most interest to the given library.

G3832   Delaware
.D4   Delaware Bay (located equally in Delaware and New Jersey)

3. A feature in three or more administrative divisions is classi-fied with the next larger geographical region which includes the entire feature.

G3707   Eastern United States
.A6   Appalachian Mountains (a feature in more than two states)

A river and a valley are classified together. An island without distinctive number is treated as a regional division of the area of which it is a geographical part. This treatment is also preferred if the island is a political unit:

G3762   Massachusetts (area number for regional map)
.N3   Nantucket Island (NOT G3762.N3, Nantucket County)

As was previously mentioned, an area number with a subarea cutter may take a subject code:

G4282   Washington state (area number for regional map)
.W4C5   Wenatchee National Forest (W4); geologic map (C5)
1984   Date of situation
.G4   USGS (under AACR2, USGS is established not as "United States. Geological Survey." but as "Geological Survey (U.S.)," and the cutter reflects the change)

The call number for a county map, with area number endings of 3 or 8, cuttered A through Z, would be:

G4283   Washington state (area number for a county map)
.K5   Kittitas County (cutter number)
1963   Date of situation
.M4   Metsker Maps (cutter number)

County maps may also take subject codes:

G4283   Washington state (area number for a county map)
.K5C5   Kittitas County (cutter number); geologic map (C5)
1979   Date of situation
.B4   Robert Bentley, geologist

Before we go into the structure of city call numbers, it is important to note that LCG&M has a long-standing program of attempting to have one library in each state put together a list of city cutters for that state, honoring the cutters that have already been applied in LCG&M's USMARC records, and working from the list of city cutters for that state which LCG&M has already used. Most states have been completed.

Call numbers for city maps, with area numbers of 4 or 9, look like this:

G4284	Washington state (area number for city maps)
.E4	Ellensburg (cutter number)
1969	Date of situation
.E4	Ellensburg Chamber of Commerce

City map numbers may also take a subject code:

G4284	Washington state (area number for city maps)
.E4P2	Ellensburg (cutter number); road map (P2)
1969	Date of situation
.E4	Ellensburg City Engineer

A new device for use in classifying smaller political divisions within major political divisions was first presented in the 1976 edition of Schedule G; it is the use of the colon followed by the number 2 (indicating a geographic subdivision) or the number 3 (indicating a political subdivision), and by a cutter for the subdivisions:

G4364	California (area number for city maps)
.L8:2G7	Los Angeles:Griffith Park

.G3804	New York state (area number for city maps)
.N4:3Q4	New York City:Queens

(U.S. LC Subject Cataloging Division 1976, 210)

In classifying series of maps, the date in the call number is replaced by the denominator of the scale minus the last three digits, and preceded by a lowercase letter s; for sets of maps with scales larger than 1:1,000 (e.g., 1:200; 1:950), the denominator of the fraction is treated as a decimal and is preceded by 0 (zero):

G4280	Washington state (area number for general maps)
s25	Series at 1:25,000
.U5	U.S. Army Map Service

G5834   France (area number for city maps)
.P3   Paris
s05   Series at 1:500
.F7   France Institut géographique national

In early editions of the schedule, series numbers were formulated some-what differently; because the old method survives on the LC records produced then, it is well to understand it. Previously, the number 5 came at the end of the first line of the call number:

G4280s
25
.U5

The LC cutter system is somewhat different from the standard cutter tables:

1. After initial vowels

for the second letter:	b	d	l,m	n	p	r	s,t	u-y
use number:	2	3	4	5	6	7	8	9

2. After the initial letter S

for the second letter:	a	ch	e	h,i	m-p	t	u
use number:	2	3	4	5	6	7-8	9

3. After the initial letter Q
   for the second letter,
   always *u* and

for the third letter:	a	e	i	o	r	y
use number:	3	4	5	6	7	9

   for names beginning
   QA-Qt

use:	2-29

4. After other initial consonants

for the second letter:	a	e	i	o	r	u	y
use number:	3	4	5	6	7	8	9

5. When an additional
   number is preferred

for the third letter:	a-d	e-h	i-l	m	n-q	r-t	u-w	x-z
use number:	2*	3	4	5	6	7	8	9

*optional for third letter a or b

(Chan 1981, 84)

LC has very kindly included in the fourth edition of Schedule G a table giving filing arrangement for map classification numbers (excluding author cutters, which are felt to be obvious):

serial map	G38O4.N4 year	New York City
single map	G3804.N4 1974	New York City
set map with definite scale	G3804.N4 s20	New York City
set map with indefinite scale	G3804.N4 svar	New York City
single map showing subject	G3804.N4 P2 1974	road map of New York City
series map showing subject	G3804.N4 P2 svar	New York City road maps
region within city	G3804.N4:2J6 1974	JFK International Airport
region within a city, aerial view of subject shown	G3804.N4:2J6 A3 1974	JFK International Airport
administrative division	G3804.N4:3Q4 1974	Queens
administrative division, subject shown	G3804.N4:3Q4 Pl 1974	transportation map of Queens

(U.S. LC Subject Cataloging Division 1976, 207)

Changes made in the 1976 edition of Schedule G were of five types: correction, updating, expansion, revision, and new devices. Corrections included such situations as differing city cutters. Expansion and updating are considerably more noticeable; geographical place names tend to change frequently, and boundary changes occur every now and again.

The subject heading list was revised; subject letters remain the same, but number breakdowns under letter were in some cases changed and rearranged. Some numbers, such as the Agriculture number for Livestock, were omitted, so it would be advisable for a collection having a considerable number of thematic maps classed with the old subject headings to keep a list of said old headings readily available, unless or until reclassifying of the maps is done. One of the most noticeable subject code changes was that the chronological breakdowns under S (History) were moved from the subject heading tables to the class schedule proper. Thus, the United States, England, Scotland, and Czechoslovakia, for example, each have their own S numbers. There is a general history breakdown under World:

G3201   World by subject
History
     .S1   General.
     .S12 Discovery and exploration.
     .S2   Ancient and classical history.
     .S3   Medieval history, 476–1453.
     .S33 Early medieval history.
     .S36 11th–15th centuries.
     .S4   Modern history.
     .S5   17th–19th centuries.
     .S6   20th century.
     .S65 World War I.
     .S7   World War II.
     .S73 1945– .

It is important to note that in both the subject and the authority sections of an LC class number a decimal point appears immediately before the letter in most cases; this is to ensure, or at least to plead for, proper filing order. Thus .S12 comes before, not after, .S2, as is appropriate for decimal numbers.

An evidence of simultaneous expansion, deletion, and revision is that in the 1976 Schedule G, cutters for regions and cities are different; different cities are given cutters, or no city cutters are given (see Massachusetts in the 1976 and the earlier editions), and emphasis seems to be placed on supplying examples of regional cutters. As formerly, county cutters are given in full.

Revisions in the 1976 Schedule G, at least in the map section (which takes up half of the entire schedule, a considerable increase from its approximate one-fourth of the old), are extensive. Some numbers were deleted or relocated. The scope of "G3235 Water hemisphere" was so confusing that it had never been used by LC, so it was removed. "G6530–6532 Southern Europe. Mediterranean region" caused a problem in that the Mediterranean region cannot be considered synonymous with southern Europe, so that region was moved to G5672.M4, a region of the eastern hemisphere (Hill 1977).

Another basic revision concerned a number of countries divided by Schedule G into arbitrary geographic regions under which subject maps, lists of provinces, and geographic regions were arranged alphabetically by cutter number. This arrangement was awkward both to apply and to use, and tended to separate materials in the files. In addition, political changes often resulted in new states straddling old Schedule G boundaries.

Major countries classified in this way were Italy (G6710–6753), India (G7650–7693), Greece (G6810–6827), and Spain (G6560–6653). In the 1976 schedule, these countries each receive only the basic range of five numbers, under which the lists of subjects, provinces, and regions are arranged alphabetically by cutter for the country as a whole:

> G6710–14   Italy
> 6711.P3   Railroads in Italy
> 6712.E5   Elba
> 6713.F7   Friuli-Venezia Giulia
> 6714.R7   Rome

Nonlocalized maps, placed at the end of Schedule G's section for maps, also had their class numbers much revised:

Previous Schedule G	1976 Schedule G
G9900 Theoretical maps	G9900 Theoretical maps
Class here maps whose primary intent is the illustration or definition of terms and concepts, and maps designed to illustrate methods of mapmaking.	Class maps of a determinable geographic area with the area.
9930 Imaginary maps	9930 Maps of imaginary places
9950 Map samples	
9960 Games	
9970 Maps for the blind	
9980 Unidentified maps	9980 Maps of unidentified places

The primary reason for the changes was that the emphasis, especially in G9950–9970, in the old Schedule G was on format rather than area. Also, "Imaginary maps," which has provided persons classing maps with much innocent fun over the years, was felt to be awkward, as was "Unidentified maps."

The colon was previously mentioned as a new device; another, not as much used because it is primarily in the atlas section of class numbers (where there was not as much room for expansion), is the decimal, which is used as follows:

> G2334.3–34   North Korea, atlases
> G2234.3   General
>   .31   Subject
>   .32   Region or physical feature
>   .33   Administrative division
>   .34   Town

(Hill 1977, 149–54)

An important aid to the classifier is the provision of maps of relatively large geographic areas, such as the United States, divided up into regions with the appropriate class numbers printed in the region. Thus, when a map covering portions of three states arrives, the librarian can see at a glance and with minimal effort in which region it should be classed.

Although atlases are often classed and cataloged by the main cataloging department of the institution of which the cartographic materials library is a part, the atlases fairly often find their way to the cartographic materials collection, and the librarian commanding that area will be better able to find them for requesters if the classification for the atlases is understood. As was mentioned previously, call numbers for atlases are structured differently from those of map numbers. The first line is area (as for maps); the second line is either authority or subarea plus authority; and the third line is date of publication (not of situation, and not on the second-to-the-last line, as it is for maps). If the atlas is regional, the region cutter comes first on line two, followed by authority; if there is a subject, subject letter/number comes first, followed by authority. If both region and subject are present, regional cutter comes first, followed by subject cutter, as is true for maps:

Major area atlas:	G1251	New York state (area number for subject atlases)
	.A5	American Automobile Association
	1974	Date of publication
Regional atlas:	G1253	New York state (area number for counties)
	.M6M7	Monroe County; Monroe County Good Roads Committee
	1974	Date of publication
Regional subject atlas:	G1253	New York state
	.M6P2M7	Monroe County; road atlas; Monroe County Good Roads Committee
	1974	Date of publication

Pages 206 to 211 in the 1976 edition of Schedule G are especially helpful for call number construction; the preceding atlas numbers were taken from page 211.

The major area in which classification problems arise is that of nonpolitical regions (especially as was mentioned previously of oceans), or for political regions for which the library happens not to have an overall map (e.g., the Alaskan boroughs; the Japanese prefectures) readily at hand. But the former is the more troublesome (Mass i Cartagena 1985). Two books listed in appendix 2A may be of some assistance with regions, as they deal with regional limits (U.S. Defense Intelligence Agency l972; International Hydrographic Organization 1953).

One additional complication with the classing of regions is that the U.S. Board on Geographic Names has for some years not established regional geographic names; LC uses the Board as its authority on geographic names, and itself relatively rarely establishes these regional geographic names. Map publishers gaily continue to publish maps of regions whether we have a classification for them or not.

Boggs and Lewis System and the American Geographical Society System

Neither the B&L nor the AGS classification system is part of an overall class scheme (as are LC and DD); instead, both are quite specialized, with B&L allowing for maps, atlases, relief maps, and globes, and AGS for maps, atlases, and reference material. B&L, despite its parentage by persons working for the U.S. Department of State, is more popular in Canada and Australia than it is in the United States; the AGS system is used primarily by the American Geographical Society library. In both B&L and AGS, different areas of the world are represented by numbers:

B&L		AGS	
000	Universe	000	Universe
100	World	050	World
200	Europe	100	North America (excluding United States)
300	Europe	200	Latin America
400	Asia	300	Africa
500	Africa	400	Asia
600	North America	500	Australasia
700	Latin America	600	Europe
800	Australia, New Zealand	700	Oceans
900	Oceans	800	United States
	(B&L 1945, 96)	809	Alabama
		894	Wyoming
			(Drazniowsky 1969, 62–70)

Subjects in both systems are represented by letters, as in the following excerpts from both subject codes:

	B&L		**AGS**
a	special categories	A	physical
b	mathematical geography	B	historical-political
c	physical geography	C	population
d	biogeography	D	transportation, communication
e	human geography	E	economics
f	political geography	F	geophysical
g	economic geography	G	geology
h	history, naval geography	H	hydrology
n	history of geographical knowledge	I	meteorology
p	history	J	mathematical geography

(B&L 1945, 128–40)

K astronomy

L zoogeography

M miscellaneous

(Drazniowsky 1969, 19–20)

The reader will note a striking similarity between LC Schedule G's subject codes (at least through letter P) and the B&L subject codes. Location symbols, designating the type of map (for filing purposes), are used in both systems:

	B&L		**AGS**
w	wall maps	a	wall map
s	sets of maps filed apart	b	sets of maps
r	relief maps	c	regions
g	globes	d	cities

(B&L 1945, 25)   (Drazniowsky 1969, 34)

Following are call numbers in each system for the same map, a wall map of the geology of the United States, published by USGS in 1932:

AGS

w630caq	location, area, subject
800-a	area, location
1932U	date, first letter of author's last name
G-1930	subject, date

In both B&L and AGS, class numbers consist of at least three digits, to which decimals may be added. B&L assigns the numeral 7 to counties in the United States, the numeral 8 to miscellaneous minor regions within a state, and the numeral 9 to cities, instead of using letters as does AGS:

641.7   counties in Maine
641.712 Androscoggin County, Maine
641.8   regions in Maine
641.81   Baxter State Park, Maine
641.9   cities in Maine
641.91   Bangor, Maine

In the B&L system, the numbers to be used following the general city number are determined by the name of the city: for city names beginning with A through B, .1 is used; for those beginning with C through E, .12 is used; and so forth. There is also an expanded city notation; in it, cities beginning with the letters Aa through Ak use .11, and so forth (B&L 1945, 119).

Decimals are used in AGS for islands, gulfs, some cities, and regions, such as the former USSR's Autonomous Soviet Socialist Republics (Drazniowsky 1969, 62–70).

In AGS, atlases are indicated by putting "At." in front of the area number. Reference material is cataloged under the same numerical system, with "R" in front of the area number and a further letter or two-letter combination in front of the date, in place of subject. Thus, an index catalog of Mexican cartography would be classed:

R 210   R for reference; area number for Mexico
Zi-1953   Indexes, catalogs; date

Dewey Decimal Classification (DD)

The most current edition of DD is the 1996 Edition 21. Maps are classed in 911 and 912. 911 is reserved for maps explaining wars; 912 is split up as follows:

912.1001–.1899 Graphic representations of specific subjects in which subject is to take precedence over location; numbers to be used before 912.19 or 912.2–.9. For example, a map of fine-arts centers in France is at 912.17084, not 912.44. Exceptions are such subjects as: tax and real-estate maps and county land atlases, classed at 912.3–.9; tidal atlases treated as nautical charts and classed at 623.89209; and soil surveys classed at 631.47.

912.122 Graphic representations of Biblical areas

912.3–.9 Graphic representations of specific areas
                    (Comaromi and Warren 1982, 419, 525, 912)

912.1001–.1899 is to be divided like 001–899; 912.3–.9 uses area notations.

The first line of a DD call number is the area/subject number, and the second is the cutter for authority:

912.741   Maine (area number)
W29   Waterman

Some libraries have used DD for maps by dropping 912 and putting only the area number on the map (Crutcher and Ledlow 1942, 656; Alonso and Prescott 1977, 47). Another recommendation is to use the divisions under 551.4, dropping the 551.4 and preceding the divisions with an "M" for map:

M1   world as a whole
M2   oceans
M3   ancient countries
M4   Europe
[etc.]   (Snider 1945, 572)

Comparison of Four Alphanumeric Systems

Following is a comparison of map classification systems; one map is classified in each of several systems.

The map:	Washington (State). Division of Mines and Geology. Geological map of Washington. Olympia: The Division, 1961.		
Titling:	WA WASHINGTON (STATE). GEOLOGY GEOL 1:500,000. 1961 1961		
LC:	G4281 .C5 1961 .W3	B&L:	697caq 1961Wg
AGS:	891 B-1961	DD:	912.155797 W317g

The quickest to formulate are the two titling types and AGS; the slowest is DD (at least in part due to the author's lack of familiarity with this system); B&L and LC pack the most information into the call number. For a comparison of seven schemes (area and subject only), including the Universal Decimal Classification, International Geographical Union system, and Parsons, see Merrett 1982, at 20–24.

Other Alphanumeric Classification Schemes

There are, as was noted at the beginning of this chapter, many classification schemes, a respectable number of which include or are limited to cartographic materials, and many of these schemes are alphanumeric. Many use numbers to denote area, as do the aforementioned LC, B&L, AGS, and DD; the Map Collection of the Public Archives of Canada is one such. Others use letter/number combinations to denote area, and because this is different from the Big Four, it deserves some attention.

Perhaps the three most important of the letter/number schemes are those used by military libraries: one devised by Archibald Williams for the U.S. War Department General Staff map collection in 1929 (Murphy 1970, 181); another, a variant of Williams's scheme, which was used by AMS (now part of DMA); and the third, a scheme used by the Great Britain Directorate of Military Survey War Office, usually called Parsons after its progenitor, E. J. S. Parsons; the first edition came out in 1946 with the title *Manual of map classification and cataloguing* (Great Britain 1946; Great Britain 1978–).

The Williams scheme, a form of titling, was initially a simple one that, as the years went by, became more complex. At first, a call number looked like this:

G-127
Turkey

meaning that the map in question was the 127th general map of Turkey received by the library (U.S. War Department 1930, 8–9). A map might be either general (G), covering an entire geographic division; part (P), covering a part of a geographic division; or set (S), maps "planned for an assemblage" (U.S. War Department 1930, 10). But as time went on, the call number became more complicated, with more options for more complete description of the map as other libraries—such as that of the Office of Strategic Services—manipulated it:

US S/25/USGS/62 USGS topo quad, 1:62,500 (L. A. Wilson 1948, 19)

Europe P24-1944-2000   Road map for part of Europe, published 1944, scale 1:2,000,000 (R. White 1959, 156)

In the latter call number, a subject code, with subjects matched to numbers 1 to 30, including some decimal points (25 airports; 25.8 airstrips), has been incorporated (R. White, 1959). Titling has mixed with abstract symbolization and spawned a hybrid.

AMS uses a development of the Williams system, with the same subject-heading structure, coming out with a letter/number coding system whose peculiarity is that it reads from right to left rather than from left to right. Each large geographical area is given a letter classification, for example:

D	Antarctica	K	Near East
E	Caribbean area	L	Far East
F	Mexico	M	Europe
G	Western Africa	N	USSR
H	Eastern South America	P	Northern Africa
J	Western South America	Q	Alaska

(U.S. AMS. Department of Technical Services. Library Division 1966–1967, appendix 1)

and so forth; then each letter is divided into smaller geographic areas, using number prefixes:

1D	Antarctic Peninsula	5D	Coast Land
2D	South Georgia Island	6D	Enderby Land
3D	Crozet Islands	7D	Wilkes Land
4D	Marie Byrd Land	8D	Victoria Land

Great Britain's Directorate of Military Survey (which uses the Parsons system) also has both a letter/number combination to denote area and capital letters to denote major geographical areas:

A	Universe	H	South America
B	World	I	Australasia
C	Europe	J	Pacific Ocean and islands
D	Asia	K	Atlantic Ocean and islands
E	Africa	L	Indian Ocean and islands
F	North America	M	Arctic regions
G	Central America and West Indies	N	Antarctic regions

(Great Britain. Directorate of Military Survey 1946, 3; Candy 1980, 6-1)

Each of these letters is then subdivided with numbers, for example:

    C1 Europe, general

    C2 Europe, seas, gulfs, channels, etc.

    C3 Andorra

    C4 Austria

    C5 Balkans

         (Great Britain. Directorate of Military Survey 1946, 4)

and so forth. The divisions C1 through the end of N are then once again subdivided, again by numbers, which represent compass-point designations, and these numbers are separated from the previous number by a colon:

    :1   Northern

    :2   North-eastern

    :3   North-western

    :4   Eastern

    :5   Central

    :6   Western

    :7   Southern

    :8   South-eastern

    :9   South-western

Librarians otherwise devoted to LC G have been known to eye this with yearning and even envy—though the compass directions are not defined in a diagram, as they should be for maximum consistency in application.

    C1:1   Northern Europe
    C1:2   Northeastern Europe
    C21:3   Northwestern France
    D3:4   Eastern Arabia
    E1:5   Central Africa
    F4:6   Western Canada
         (Great Britain. Directorate of Military Survey 1946, 5–6)

The system does allow for atlas classification; no subdivisions designated by colon numbers are used, with the only hierarchical levels being:

    a   Universe and moon

    b   World

    c   Continents and oceanic areas

    d   Countries and island groups

There is also a secondary classification on the basis of height:

a   up to 23 cm.

b   23–30.5 cm.

c   30.5–37 cm.

d   37–52 cm.

e   52 cm. and larger

f   material filed in "plan presses (e.g., large soft-backed material and loose-leaf atlas plates)"

(Candy 1980, 10-1)

This schedule also includes graphic indexes. An example of province code and nomenclature is:

C4:17   Austria: Vorarlberg province
(Candy 1980, 6-5)

As can be seen by the foregoing, there are many alphanumeric systems; a few more will be very briefly mentioned in the following paragraphs.

The USGS library at Menlo Park devised a system to blend maps in with books, which, in a sample call number, looks like this:

M(200)2	M	=	maps
	200	=	U.S.
	2	=	geology; second line would be author cutter

(Sanders 1970, 11)

The Royal Geographical Society of London uses a scheme dividing collections into four categories: general; divisional; district (precisely defined administrative areas); and special (islands, maps, strip road maps, etc.). In this system, for example, Spain is G.I-20 (Crone 1953, 11). Another scheme is that devised by the Royal Thai Survey Department, which uses an area classification by letter and a subject code by number:

Area classification

X		Space, celestial sphere
G		Globe, earth, world
O		Oceans
E		Eastern hemisphere, Old World
	EU.	Europe
	EUN.	Northern Europe
	.DA	Denmark
	.FI	Finland
	.IC	Iceland
	.NO	Norway
	.SW	Sweden
	EUW.	Western Europe
	[etc.]	

Subject classification

1		Cartography, theory and practice
2		Cartographic products
	2.0	Topographic maps (general maps)
	2.1	Topometric maps, cadastral maps (over 1:10,000 scale)
	2.2	Town plans, city maps
	2.3	Topographic maps, large scale (1:10,000–1:100,000)
	2.4	Topographic maps, small scale (1:100,000–1,000,000)
	2.5	Chorographic maps (scale under 1:1,000,000)
	2.6	Photo maps, picto maps
3.0		Charts (maps for orientation or navigation)
4.0		Maps of the natural environment
5.0		Population maps
6.0		Cultural maps
7.0		Settlement maps
8.0		Economic maps
9.0		Political maps

10.0	Historical maps (maps of historical events)
11.0	Military maps
12.0	Maps of spatial planning
13.0	Other maps, unclassified

(Thailand 1977, 125, 130–31)

Another part of this class system deals with what is called form:

I.   Single map showing a distinct topic in a distinct area, either as a desk or a wall map; D is added for draft, R for rolled.

II. Part of a single map, either an inset map or the portion of an (old or large) map not itself acquired.

III. Map of a map series or of a set of maps (e.g., most large-scale topographic maps).

IV. Single map of an atlas or book that does not "exceed a limited convenient size" with catalog card stating from which atlas, journal, or book the item was extracted.

V.   The atlas.

[and so forth]   (Thailand 1977, 126)

Thus a sample call number is:

G-2.0-V   Globe (G)-topographic map (general map), 2.0-atlas (V)

(Thailand 1977, 127)

Numerical Geographical Classification Systems

Strictly numerical systems of area classification are generally less common than are the alphanumeric systems. The increasing use of computers, the inclination of computers to accept numbers more readily than letters, and an increasing interest in internationally understandable classification systems—for which, in spite of Esperanto, the Arabic number seems to be the only answer—has encouraged their growth.

Geocoding

Geocoding, a quick way of saying "geographic coding," is the devising of geographic reference systems whereby areas are subdivided and coded for purposes of classification. Its two major structural elements are a concept of areal division and some form of coding logic. As such, it is suitable for contributing the area and subject areas of whatever classification schemes are percolating in the mind of the computer-enamored librarian.

There are several different categories of geocoding systems. Geoidentifying systems consist of a set of unique designations for undefined or implicitly defined locations; the U.S. Postal Service's zip code is an example. Geodefining systems, in contrast, provide explicit boundary delineations for the items coded; state-plane coordinate systems are an example of this. Nominal geocodes do not indicate spatial relationships among the units coded; names, name abbreviation, and certain numerical codes fall in this category. Ordinal geocodes indicate relative positions of coded units within spatially related systems; census tracts exemplify this type. Cardinal geocodes indicate relative positions of coded units within a spatially related and incrementally scaled system; geographic coordinates such as latitude and longitude (using plus for northern latitude and eastern longitude, and minus for southern latitude and western longitude) are a classic example of this (Werner 1975, 8–10).

The reader will not be surprised to learn that various agencies of the U.S. government use various geocoding systems. One of the oldest methods of geocoding, latitude and longitude, has long sung its siren song to map librarians: "Perhaps every map cataloger has toyed with the idea of devising a magical system based on latitude and longitude; but when one tries to work it out, one feels like a numerologist and gladly returns to more familiar if less exact terminology" (Anderson 1945, 105).

In any one large series of maps, such as the USGS topo quads, where scale and map size are the same (although physical width varies slightly), it is possible to class the maps geometrically by using tables encoding coordinates of the southeast corner of each map within a degree-square unit (Hubbard 1972, 30; S. Johnson 1977, 115–18; Tobler 1963, 205). To apply this to a collection of topos, first a state index must be marked off in 10 squares, and each square divided into smaller squares numbered from 1 to 64, always in the same order. A typical class number in such a case would be 3096 - 24; this would represent the 24th topo in the latitude 30°N, longitude 96°W degree square. By using this system, the librarian and patron do not have to look in every drawer when the patron wants to see an area covered by more than one topo; and patrons seem to have little or no trouble using the system (S. Johnson 1977, 117). Such a system applied to all maps would make it possible for a librarian to snap her fingers at such problems as country and city name changes, and ill-defined physical regions. No more would the librarian have to make the map or other cartographic material fit into a Procrustean bed of systematic classification.

With all of these lures, several persons have played around with a way to apply a coordinate system to all maps, not just to separate homogeneous series. The existence of computers, which prefer to work with numbers, has made the Perfect Scheme even more enticing, and Hans van de Waal of the Dutch Information and Documentation Centre for Cartography some years ago devised a system for computer use in the Dutch Union Map Catalogue (DUMC) (van de Waal 1974, 167–70).

Universal Decimal Classification (UDC)

One of the few library classification systems that is numeric, geographic, and (as its name implies) intended to cover the entire field of knowledge, is an offshoot of DD—the Universal Decimal Classification. UDC, the most extensively used system in libraries outside of the United States, was formulated by two Frenchmen, Paul Otlet and Henri La Fontaine, who, in the late nineteenth century, took DD and enlarged its range by adding to its enumerated classes and providing a much more extensive apparatus for synthesis, that is, for building class numbers (Rigby 1974, 27). Although correspondence with DD in the first one thousand classes (000/999) has been maintained, constant revision has produced increasingly serious deviation in details (Mills 1964, 9). UDC has developed into a hierarchical, multifaceted, highly specific international (because alphabet- and language-free), complex and detailed classification system (Rigby 1974, 34; Foskett 1973, 20–21). The English edition is:

> British Standards Institution. 1977– . *Universal decimal classification, Classification decimale universelle, Dezimalklassifikation.* 2d. English full ed. London: Author. (BS; 1000) (FID publication; 483).

It is kept up to date by:

> International Federation for Documentation. 19uu– . *Extensions and corrections to the UDC.* The Hague: Author. (FID publication; 248).

UDC begins innocently enough by regarding the whole field of knowledge as unity, and dividing it into ten main classes denoted by decimal fractions .0 to .9, from which the initial decimal point is omitted for convenience:

0	Generalities	6	Applied science
1	Philosophy, psychology	7	Art
2	Religion, theology	8	Language, literature
3	Social science	9	Geography, biography, history
4	vacant		
5	Mathematics & natural science		

> (International Federation for Documentation 1970, 4)

From here on, matters become increasingly complex, for UDC's ability to represent as many different facets as the object to be classified possesses is not without its cost.

The auxiliary tables and signs of association are many, albeit individually simple. The plus sign, +, joins two or more nonconsecutive numbers for subjects:

675+678   Leather and rubber

The diagonal line, /, indicates consecutive numbers:

676/678   Leather, paper, textiles, rubber

The colon, :, denotes a relationship between two or more distinct concepts:

675:93   Leather in history

Square brackets, [ ], may be used as an alternative to the colon:

675[37]   Leather industry instruction; Leather—Study and
                 teaching

The equals sign, =, designates the language; it is used only for very detailed subdivision, where language is important, and refers to the language of the document, not that of the subject. Examples of language codes are: =20, English; =30, German; =40, French; =60, Spanish; =690, Portuguese. Thus:

675=60   Leather, works on, in Spanish (class number in a
                 library in a non-Spanish-speaking area)

Parentheses with 0 enclosed, (0 . . .), are used to indicate the form of a presentation, of which there are, even in an abridged UDC, over a hundred. Some examples are: (03) dictionaries; (05), periodicals and series; (091), historical presentations (Metcalfe 1959, 147–48, Mills 1964, 33; International Federation for Documentation 1970, 9).
Parentheses without an enclosed 0 are used to indicate place:

(21)	land areas	(6)	Africa
(23)	mountains	(7)	North, central America
(26)	oceans	(8)	South America
(28)	rivers	(91/96)	Australia, Oceania
(3)	ancient world	(98/99)	Polar regions
(4)	Europe		

(International Federation for Documentation 1970, 9)

Thus:

675(44)   ·   Leather in France

The parentheses with an enclosed equals sign, (=), are used to indicate race or nationality, with a number from 0 through 9 placed to the right of the equals sign:

675(=027)   Leather among the Arabs
                              (Metcalfe 1959, 146)

A set of quotation marks, " ", is used to enclose time of subject matter:

675"18"   Leather in the nineteenth century
                              (Metcalfe 1959)

Individual names and numbers may be used for final rearrangement or subdivision:

675Smith   Leather, Smith manufacture
                              (Metcalfe 1959, 146)

The point-of-view auxiliaries represented by 00 are used as follows

675007   Leather industry from personnel's standpoint
                              (Metcalfe 1959, 146)

The hyphen analytical or process subdivisions come between point-of-view (which is 00) and the analytical subdivisions (which are 0):

675 78   Leather industry—Safety devices

675 02   Leather dressing
                              (Metcalfe 1959)

An additional auxiliary is the personal classification, -0:

-053.2   Children
-055.1   Men
-055.2   Women
                 (International Federation for Documentation 1970, 10)

The apostrophe also contributes to the complexity of the synthesis:

546.561'131	Cuprous chloride, resulting from the combining of
546.561	Cuprous oxide
546.131	Hydrochloric acid

(Metcalfe 1959)

Now, after that brief run-through of UDC, comes the reason for doing so: the efforts of the International Geographical Union's (IGU) Commission on the Classification of Geography Books and Maps in Libraries, whose final report was made in 1964. In this report it was proposed that 912 represent nontextual representations of a country (as it is in DD), using the UDC auxiliary tables of common auxiliaries of place ( ) and of form (0 . . .). The form numbers used would be:

(084.3)	Maps. Charts. Plans.
(084.3-13)	1:20,000 to larger than 1:75,000 topographic special maps
(084.3-14)	1:75,000 to larger than 1:250,000 topographic general maps
(084.3-16)	1:1,000,000 to larger than 1:20,000,000 Scale may be indicated exactly by adding M and scale minus last three numbers, i.e., 912.30 (084.3M25) for a topographic map of Germany at 1:25,000.
(084.3-221)	Pictorial maps
(084.3-445)	Maps on glass
(084.3-5)	How stored
(084.3-524)	Folded
(084.3-528)	Rolled
(084.3-56)	Mounted
(084.3-568)	Mounted and rolled
(084.35)	Wall maps
(084.44)	Atlases
(084.64)	Three-dimensional representations
(084.643)	Globes
(084.644.4)	Maps or plans in relief

(International Geographical Union 1964, 39; Russia 1970, 256)

For place auxiliary, IGU proposed a classification of physio-geographic areas of the Earth for application in the UDC common auxiliaries of the main units in Annex I (International Geographical Union 1964, 141). The classification completely ignores political boundaries; for example, (7-9.20/.23), British Columbia and Northwestern Canada, extends south through most of Washington state and Idaho. Physiographic features are provided for:

(7-9.240)	Olympic Mountains
(7-9.241)	Oregon Coast range
(7-9.244)	Willamette Valley and Puget Sound
(7-9.246.0)	Cascade range
(7-9.250)	Columbia Plateau

(International Geographical Union 1964, 183)

The IGU Final Report gives some sample class numbers to illustrate their construction:

Vegetation map of Ethiopia:

(63)58.19(84.3)(63)	Ethiopia
58.19	Plant geography
(84.3)	Maps

International geological map (sheet of Europe) at 1:1,000,000:

(4)55(084.3-16)(100) (4)	Europe
55	Geology
-16	Maps of scale groups 1:1,000,000 to 1:20,000,000
(100)	Earth
(084.3)	Maps

(International Geographical Union 1964,41)

In 1966 and 1967, part of the Russian Ministry for Geology—the All-Union Scientific-Research Institute for the Economics of Mineral Raw Materials and Geological Prospecting—published special-subject tables for geology, surveying, cartography, and related branches of science and engineering, with index. See Table 2.1 for the map subject table. The publication also had examples of map numbers constructed according to UDC rules:

914.4:912(084.124)	OR	914.4:912.412.4	Slides, views of France
55(44):912.44	OR	(44)55.912.44	Geologic atlas of France
912.644.4(44):55	OR	9l2.644.4:55(44)	Geologic relief map of France
912.43:55(44)	OR	912.43(44):55	Geologic map of France
912.44:551.58(44	OR	912.44(44):551.58	Climatic atlas of France

(Russia 1970, 256)

Most recently, a new set of auxiliary tables, specifically for cartographic materials, has been proposed. A new auxiliary table for place was prepared, as was one for subjects, linking them with apostrophes to the auxiliary notation of form (084.3):

1. table of places:
   imaginary world
   outer space
   Earth
   oceans and seas
   Asia
   Africa
   Africa
   America
   Oceania
   Antarctica

2. table for subjects:
(084.3'1)	general thematic subjects
(084.3'2)	geodesy, cartography, topography
(084.3'4)	natural sciences
(084.3'5)	landscape, environmental problems, land use, physical planning
(084.3'6)	social subjects
(084.3'8)	multithematic (users) maps

   (Riesthuis et al. 1991)

Table 2.3.
UDC Subject Breakdown for Maps

912.43:008	Civilization
:312	Population
:33	Economic
:338.45	Industrial maps
:35.07	Administrative
:502	Nature (comprehensive)
:502:72	Maps of nature reserves
:527	Navigation
:527.62	Air-navigation
:528.4	Topographic
:55	Geologic
:550.312	Gravimetric
:550.34	Seismological and earthquake
:550.38	Geomagnetism
:550.4	Geochemical
:551.21	Vulcanism
:551.24	Tectonics
:551.32	Glaciological
:551.32	Glacier
:551.35	Ocean floor
:551.4	Physical geography

:551.43	Relief features; hypsometric
:551.46	Oceanological (oceanographical)
:551.462	Ocean floor geomorphology
:551.46212	Bathymetric (depths)
:551.463	Hydrological oceanic
:551.465	Ocean currents
:551.466	Ocean waves and currents
:551.48	Hydrological maps of inland surface waters
:551.49	Hydrogeological
:551.5	Weather
:551.521	Radiation
:551.524	Atmospheric pressure
:551.55	Winds
:551.577	Precipitation
:551.58	Climates and climatic zoning
:551.8	Paleogeographical
:553	Fossils
:577.49	Phenological
:58	Flora
:581.9	Vegetation
:591.9	Zoogeographical
:62	Industries
:620.91	Power resources
:621	Mechanical and metalworking industries
:621.311	Power plants
:622	Mining industries
:625.7	Highways
:63	Agricultural
:631.4	Soils
:631.44	Soil types
:631.61	Clearing and reclamation of virgin lands
:633	Field and industrial crops
:634	Forests
:634.0	Forestry
:635	Horticulture; vegetable growing
:636	Animal husbandry
:639	Game hunting; fishery
:654.1	Telegraph and telephone
:656	Transportation routes
:656.2	Railroads
:656.6	River and sea routes
:656.7	Air routes
:656.8	Mail routes
:661	Chemical industries
:662.6	Fuel industries
:663/665.3	Food industries

:665.3	Petroleum-processing industries
:666	Glass and ceramics industries
:669	Metallurgical industries
:67	Light industries
:674	Woodworking industries
:676	Paper industries
:691	Building-materials industries
:796.5	Tourist maps
:908	Features of a specific country
(075)	School maps
(075.2)	Maps for elementary schools
(075.3)	Maps for secondary schools
(075.8)	Maps for universities

(Russia 1970, 256; International Geolographical Union 1964, 27)

UDC's flexibility means that if the subject of the map is more important than the country, the auxiliary number of place may appear at the end of the entry; if, as is true for most users, the geographic area is more important than the subject, the place number appears before the subject number.

Non-Geographic Classification Systems

Non-geographic classifications may be by subject, date, accession number, provenance, or size. The last mentioned is frequently used, particularly when size and format of maps allow or even necessitate a special type of filing container that utilizes space most effectively. Road maps, for example, because of their folded format, are frequently relegated to a vertical file cabinet. Large wall maps will not fit in map cases unless the maps are folded at least two times, a practice that hastens their dissolution, so they are filed in special holders.

Some snide remarks have been made about filing by size (justly, if size is the only filing parameter): "At the beginning of the nineteenth century, the arrangement of books in the Congress Library [LC] was according to size. . . . It is what might have been expected from a librarian who also held the office of Clerk to the House of Representatives" (Maltby 1975, 118). But some good things may also be said. If maps are filed according to size, not only can space be utilized as much as 30 percent more effectively, but outsize maps are not forced to act as buffers for smaller maps (Ehrenberg 1973a, 57). Topographic quadrangles and other series in which maps are of uniform size may frequently be filed in one specific type of map case; aerial photographs may go in file cabinets or archival boxes.

Arrangement of maps by accession number is espoused by those librarians who believe that it is not possible to file together sufficient maps of like area and subject to justify the time and cost of classification, and that it is far better to put the effort into detailed cataloging; standard classification schemes are believed not to ensure good conservation, and besides, there are always political changes (Christy 1973, 33; Paris 1951, 10). Retrieval of maps is achieved in such a system by consulting a detailed catalog first. The system does economize in some ways on storage, space, time, and money, but money gained by the economical filing system is lost in the amount of time it takes to do detailed cataloging and to retrieve the maps. Moreover, the basic premise—that it is impossible to notate a large portion of maps for any given area and subject so that they will file reasonably close together—is demonstrably faulty (Christy 1973, 33–34).

Although cartographic-materials librarians and cartographic-materials archivists have the same challenge—items with physical forms that present special housing problems—in one respect their collections differ widely. In an archive, the most important aspect of any item, be it monograph, map, or ivory fan, is provenance—that is, origin. Because of this emphasis on origin, maps in cartographic archives are arranged by issuing agency rather than by area, although within a given group, if no original order is obvious, the maps may be arranged by geographic area and then subdivided by subject and date (Ehrenberg 1967, 10 and 1982, 20–21). In the Cartographic Archives of the U.S. National Archives and Records Service, maps are placed in record groups (that is, documentation produced by an administrative unit at the bureau level of 0.5. government); the record groups are subdivided into subgroups, which are records of a specific office or division of an agency, and into series. For example:

> Record group 48. Records of the Office of the Secretary of the Interior
> > Subgroup a. General cartographic records
> > Series 1. Maps of states of the western United States
> > Series 2. Maps of states and territories
> > Series 3. City maps
> > > File 1. Maps of Denver, Colorado
> > > > (Ehrenberg 1967, 12)

Subgroups may be composed of general records, records of central offices, records of regional offices, and records prepared by a predecessor agency. A *series* is a group of maps "composed of interrelated homogeneous filing units arising from organic activities or transactions" (Ehrenberg 1973a, 52). A *file unit* is an assemblage of closely related documents; it may be only one map, or a set of maps. Map series received are normally arranged in the archives in the same order in which the agency maintained them, unless that agency's method of arrangement is illogical and unworkable (Ehrenberg 1973a).

Maps in archives are indexed by means of inventories, special lists, and catalogs; the latter two are generally composed of an introduction, a body of descriptive map entries arranged alphabetically by area and then chronologically, and an index (Ehrenberg 1975, 15).

Maps accompanying reports constitute a special problem, with four possible solutions:

1. File the map, folded up, with the report.

2. File the map flat and therefore separately; write the file number on the map and store by file number; write map number on report.

3. File the map separately, flat (as in 2.); write both the file number and an arbitrary number (starting with 1) on each; file by arbitrary number and have a cross-reference table.

4. File the map separately, flat; but work them into the geographic scheme used for nonarchival maps; have a cross-reference table to get from the file number to the geographic class number.

(Topic IV 1976, 78)

There is considerable discussion as to whether to separate oversized items such as maps from text; maintaining the integrity of the file unit is of primary importance, but there seems little point in doing so if it causes the destruction of items within that unit (Ehrenberg 1982, 19–20).

Archived aerial photographs are stored according to provenance, and within any given group by the numbers on the photographs.

Conclusion

❖ *Classification is thus basically
a subjective process,
despite the apparent objectivity
of the methods employed.*
—Johnston 1968

Perhaps the best way to decide upon a classification system is to peruse the possibilities carefully and then to ask which system is most responsive to the patrons' needs. Area classification is an excellent choice for most libraries because most patrons request maps by area (Special Libraries Association 1956, 4); it is relatively simple to file into and is applicable to the smallest and largest collections alike. Filing solely by subject is appropriate only for those highly specialized libraries that deal with one very small geographical area (for example, historical society libraries), and filing solely by size and accession number ignores the users and their requirements in many ways. Classification and arrangement by provenance is suitable and essential for archives; for other libraries it is inappropriate.

There are many different area classification schemes extant, so the question of what makes one classification better than another immediately arises. A good classification should be inclusive and receptive to new subjects; have a logical system of division and subdivision; be practical; be kept up-to-date with revisions; have a good index; and be capable of providing the user with the desired cartographic materials as quickly and as plentifully as possible while maintaining sufficient control to keep the librarian happy (D. Lewis 1944, 78; Winearls 1975, 35). If anything besides maps is to be kept in the collection—as is almost always the case—the classification scheme should be applicable to every type of material in the library; this last tosses out all but the universal systems (LC, DD, UDC)—but let us look briefly at the others anyway.

Titling makes the most sense as far as the user is concerned; it is far easier for a user to read the name of an area than it is to hunt up the appropriate number for the area in which he is interested. But cartographic control is more easily attained by using numbers; titling is suitable only for small, personal, or ephemeral collections.

UDC is very tempting with all of its faceting possibilities, and is certainly appropriate for a map collection in a library that uses UDC for books, but

> its actual use is not fully explained, and . . . all the issues
> that are implicit in UDC and its makeshifts are not squarely
> faced. The student is left thinking that it is a scientific, near
> perfect system, which he is too dumb to understand (Met-
> calfe 1959, 159).

To put it another way, "simplicity is not a quality which can be claimed for the UDC notation" (Mills 1964, 36). That is a classic understatement: its use of many facet indicators for auxiliaries makes it very mixed when fully used, and the opposite of brief.

When the other numeric systems are considered, geocoding systems provide only the area base number, leaving the librarian to construct the rest of the class system, which is not a good idea. Coordinate indexing is more of a retrieval device to respond to reference questions than a classification scheme.

Of the alphanumeric systems DD is, as has been previously mentioned, inappropriate for cartographic materials. B&L is an excellent system, in some ways like LC, but has not been revised since the mid-1940s and does not seem likely to be; Queens University at Kingston, Ontario, has prepared a revised index to it (announced in *SLAG&MD bulletin* 114: 47 (December 1978)). AGS is easy to apply and has a list of subject headings, but in spite of its parentage it may not supply sufficient differentiation for large collections, and no revisions have been issued.

Because of the widespread use of LC in general libraries in the United States; because LC classification attempts to include all cartographic and supporting materials, and is frequently and regularly updated; because LC has automated the cataloging for its collections, including maps; and because LC is not only *defacto* the national library of the United States but also an international model, LC Schedule G is the best system to use for the classification of cartographic materials. It is the strongest general library classification in existence today, and is being issued in digital form (Parr 1975, 64). Particularly in light of the speed with which libraries, through such utilities as OCLC, are using each others' classification and cataloging, use of a uniform method of classification that happens to be the scheme used by LC—whose shelflist to the late 1970s is available on microfiche—is beneficial to a library and its users. And LC is virtually alone in its sporting attempt to provide a classification niche for all cartographic and all supporting materials. In spite of the fact that LC class was designed and developed by LC for its own collections, it works extremely well for other libraries also.

Certainly LC makes mistakes, such as the LC card sets for AMS series maps of Africa in which the class number was 100 off from the correct class number. But in comparison to its output, LC's mistakes are few in number, and they have the added benefit of giving the rest of us a virtuous glow when we find them. In the cartographic-materials library world, the preeminence of LC must be not only acknowledged but also appreciated, given how much work LC saves all the rest of us. By using LC class, the librarian opens up for patrons enormous potential for national cooperation, from interlibrary loan to online searching, and at a lower processing cost (Schroeder 1981, 424–45).

For many years, cartographic-materials libraries were small, isolated collections, and librarians in the past made up classification schemes or did not classify at all because the collection was so small that it seemed hardly worth the while, not realizing that it is easiest to get a collection classed when it is small.

Although some small, very specialized collections—such as libraries in businesses—may need to devise a special classification for their users (such as the petroleum company library that decided to class all maps by the range and township of the lower right-hand corner, because that is the coordinate system with which petroleum businesspersons work), almost no other library has any good reason to devise its own scheme. Such schemes are seldom well documented and are very likely to be abandoned and the work later done all over again.

At the base of the classification decision is the dichotomy between suitability and practicality. The librarian needs the classification system most suited to the library's clientele and collection, taking into account the time, money, materials available, and also the future of the collection and of the library world. The librarian has a professional duty to give patrons the best possible classification system, and to support national library systems that are of general and specific benefit. LC Schedule G satisfies all requirements better than other classification systems.

3

Cataloging

❖ *The cataloging of maps and atlases differs very little from the cataloging of ordinary books.*
—P. L. Phillips 1921

❖ *Not even the smallest library should now improvise any aspect of cataloging.*
—S. Lewis 1985

History and Background

The cataloging of maps began at the end of the eighteenth century in Dresden, at the *Kurfurstliche Bibliothek* (Electoral Library) in Germany; in the United States, we have nothing quite so early (Bates 1954; Klemp 1982, 22). The earliest map catalog in the United States was produced at Harvard in 1831 (Merrett 1976, 3; Drazniowsky 1975, 299), and was arranged by area. William Hughes first cataloged the British Museum collection in 1843, also using area entry (Merrett 1976, 3). In 1887 Harvard added a second, subject, catalog for maps. Both Harvard and the British Museum carried out recataloging at the end of the century. Since that time and up until LCG&M formulated MARCMap and OCLC brought in the map format, matters went downhill. In many collections catalog entries for spatial data do not exist, a situation that thrusts total dependence for retrieval upon the broad, but not infinitely so, shoulders of the classification scheme, and on the librarian's memory, assuming that the latter is truly an elephant's child.

The reasons for this lack of representation in library catalogs have their roots in economic and mental problems. It is very difficult for librarians to justify taking the time (and therefore the money) to catalog what may seem just one measly sheet of paper. The map and its compatriots have become victims of the seemingly atavistic feeling that the intellectual content and worth of a printed work are best measured by size and weight. Hardcopy maps' strongest point, conciseness, works against their acceptance by catalogers as worthy candidates for "bibliographic" control. It has thus worked to the benefit of spatial data to have so many persons now slaving away at PCs, with digital data, who are immediately struck by the substantial size, even in megabytes, of spatial-data files. A relatively modestly sized map—such as a topographic quadrangle, about three feet by about two feet—when scanned can easily be 100 megabytes, and a Landsat image is about 300 megabytes (Roberts 1962, 12; Special Libraries Association 1966, 14).

Merrett 1976 (3–5) gives an excellent, brief history of British and U.S. map cataloging, tracing it through LC and Anglo-American codes. The continuing thread is that of LC and standard codes stoutly maintaining that maps should be cataloged just like anything else, with author main entry, and the map community just as stoutly maintaining (until about twenty-five years ago) the opposite. Once again automation has come to the rescue here; with the ability to do component-word searching, all on a database rather than flicking through a card file, the two sides have been reconciled and author main entry holds sway.

In this chapter we will be discussing the cataloging of spatial data—maps, views, plans, sections, diagrams, remote-sensing images, globes, models, atlases, and digital data. One of the guiding principles of AACR is to use whichever chapters are appropriate; thus, for cataloging atlases, one uses chapters 1, 2, and 3 of AACR, whereas to catalog digital data one uses chapters 1, 3, and 9.

Purpose of Cataloging

Even more immediately than in the case of classification the librarian will be forced to prove why cataloging the work needs to be done at all (although atlases, by virtue of usually being bound, have escaped the "why-bother?" issue). The purpose of cataloging spatial data, like that of book cataloging, is to make items available for use in an efficient, effective way. It is done by creating a surrogate for the actual item, describing that item, distinguishing it from all others, and making a single, complete record of it, in the form of a unit record, nowadays with very few exceptions in a digital catalog database (Fox 1972, 27; Thiele 1938, 288). In ensuring that the resources of the collection are cataloged, several tasks are accomplished.

First and most importantly, cataloging enables the user (who is, after all, the reason for all our contortions) to discover that the item exists and by what collections it is held. Library users are trusting souls; they believe that if the library has it, it's in the catalog. This is one case where it behooves us to humor them; just because we have them convinced that periodical articles don't appear in the catalog doesn't mean they should be persuaded that several other items don't either. It's amazing how much more use a collection gets when users know it exists; it is quite common for a cataloged collection's use to triple when a substantial portion (the author from her experience estimates about 80 percent) of the collection is cataloged (Buckallew 1986, 2). Cataloging saves a library from the embarrassing experience of having one of its users request on interlibrary loan an item that the first library possesses; the smugness of the librarian of the second library informing the librarian of the first library of this silly occurrence is irritating but justified. With the increasing availability of online catalogs over the Web, users are able to do their hunting twenty-four hours a day, seven days a week (computer systems permitting), instead of only when the map library is open. Some users feel more comfortable using an online catalog than admitting a lack of knowledge to a real human being.

Cataloging gives a much wider choice of approaches to the collection than are obtainable solely from classification. Cataloging complements and in ways overlaps classification. If classification is by area, the catalog assists by providing thematic and author approaches—and provides access to the item which has more than one area on it but is classed by only one area and obeys the law of physics stating that an object may be in only one place at a time. If maps are in a non-geographical arrangement, the catalog is essential for providing access by those two most popular of user-request parameters, area and subject. Cataloging spatial data for a library's union catalog gives the user a chance to find all materials (except periodical articles) on a given area, and that with one fell swoop. If a collection is in closed stacks, then it must be cataloged—either that, or one must make extensive use of divination or creative searching on the line of, "If I were a map of Pemba, where would I be?" (Tanaglia 1977, 17).

As importantly from the technical-processing side, cataloging gives the librarian bibliographic control over the objects. The point of a library is not just to arrange objects in some sort of order, but to know what the library possesses and where it is. A catalog has the additional value of reducing wear and tear on materials; hardcopy maps and images, unlike books, are generally (atlases being the exception that proves that rule) not bound in a protective covering. Further, they are easily damaged, not just by careless use but merely by repeated use and by any but the most careful browsing. For purposes of location, organization, and safekeeping of materials, a catalog is invaluable.

The following may sound strange, but cataloging is more economical than not cataloging. Cataloging time is spent once; reference work with users dealing with uncataloged collections is time spent over and over and over ... You get the picture.

If the positive reasons for cataloging are not enough, consider the negatives. Given that few of our users have second sight, items that are not cataloged are nowhere nearly as often used as are items that are cataloged. And remember, if they aren't used, they stand a good chance, in these days of limited space and no money or space to build larger libraries, of being deemed nonessential—and the spatial-data librarian along with them. Speaking of the librarian, what happens when, through some oversight, the librarian who, in a misguided attempt to ensure job security, has carried around the holdings of the collection in her head, either resigns, dies, or goes off in a huff? The next librarian perforce starts all over again, at the bottom, and the previous librarian may rightly be stigmatized as unprofessional for leaving the collection no better off than it was when she began working on it. The uncataloged collection, like the unindexed periodical, is worthless. Some spatial data may be inexpensive item-by-item, but en masse they are a substantial investment for a library, and thus merit cataloging.

Sadly, a survey in the early 1990s of the cataloging of nonbook materials in Canadian libraries found that of nine types of such materials, spatial data were the least likely to be cataloged, with 80 of 194 libraries having uncataloged collections, and with public libraries least likely to catalog them (Weihs and Howarth 1995, 190).

Cataloging Systems

After the initial suasion to the idea that cataloging is a good thing comes the real fun—deciding how to do the cataloging. There are two sets of major decisions to be made: first, whether to use standard cataloging practices or a nonstandard system (either an existing one or one you make up); and second, whether to use a manual system or an automated one.

Unit Records

During the reign of hardcopy card catalogs, there was a discrepancy between what the oligarchs of library science—ALA and LC—and what the spatial-data community backed for main entry. This discrepancy may be responsible for the "lack of any fully accepted map catalog rules" until the arrivals of USMARC, online cataloging as an everyday matter, AACR2, and relatively soon after *Cartographic materials: A manual for the interpretation of AACR2* (1982) (Drazniowsky 1975, 236). While there is heartening unanimity from about 1900 as to what should be included in a catalog record—call number, area, subject, date of publication, scale, series name, edition, collation (now called physical description), author, and imprint, with secondary importance given to projection, portrayal of language, edition, insets, type of reproduction, size, date of situation, and prime meridian—a substantial difference of opinion immediately arose as to proper main entry, with only LC and AACR1 agreeing with each other as to the virtues of author main entry, and most of the rest of the spatial-data world solidly in favor of area main entry (Phillips 1900, 15; Fox 1972, 27; Daehn 1975, 82–83). Arguments were centered around the map, although many of the comments held true for other spatial data.

Given that a card catalog is arranged in alphabetical order, main entry is the most basic decision that must be made, and thus the fray begins immediately. Those in favor of area main entry start off by saying that a map is both scriptorial and pictorial, combining the features (some sourly say the worst features) of books and pictures, and that a rigid book approach is not practical (Fordham 1927, 4; Fox 1972, 27). Areas of difference between books and maps are many: primary identification of maps is with area rather than with authority, and maps are frequently published by a corporate (often a governmental) body; non-geographic-area subject information is second in significance to area. (There is a disagreement that geographic areas are really subject headings—but after all, they do appear in the Library of Congress Subject Headings, LCSH.) Dates of information and of publication are of unusual significance (for current maps, recency; for historical maps, authenticity): "If an undated book is a nuisance, an undated map, like an undated portrait, is a proper subject of something more than annoyance" (Fordham 1914, 96).

In addition, there is no book counterpart for the very important scale or resolution; size is more important for maps than for books because there is less consistency in dimensions overall than there is for books, and because of the use of maps in displays and scholarly publications. Color is also more important for maps than for books, serving as it does not just for the sake of beauty and ornamentation but primarily for symbolization; in the absence of a tangible title page, the entire map is considered in effect the title page; and maps in an unfamiliar language are more readily understood than are foreign-language books (ALA 1967, 274, 212; Woods 1959, 263–65).

Even among those plumping for area main entry, there was some disagreement over what other items should be included, and in what order items chosen should be placed. The SLAG&MD's Committee on Map Cataloging went for

AREA. DATE. SUBJECT. SCALE. SIZE.
(Special Libraries Association 1956)

while others spoke up for

AREA. SUBJECT. DATE. SCALE. PROJECTION.
(Gerlach 1961)

as more nearly matching the user's needs; and some believed that main entry should be composed solely of area (Prévost 1946, 104; S. Miller 1971, 152).

If area main entry is used, the catalog card answers the primary reference question, for more spatial data is requested by area than any other way, and items of a given area will be brought together in the card catalog—as, of course, they would be brought by subject added entries if main entry were author, but only if the item had no thematic subject. Until LC, in the mid-1970s, began to allow area subject headings for maps with other subject interest, for example:

Geology—Washington (State)—Kittitas County—Maps.
Kittitas County (Wash.)—Maps.

area main entry was especially attractive. Area cataloging is much easier to generate than author main entry cataloging (unless author added entry cards are made, in which case the verification problem is changed only in location on the card, not in work done); existing lists of areas and subjects may be used, and thus student or clerical help can generate cataloging information. If only one entry per map is to be made—as in some form-card systems—the most sought-after entry should be used (Horner 1973, 201). Determination of author, especially for foreign maps, is not always easy; even with U.S.-produced maps, authorship tends to be diffuse (Horner 1973, 200–210). And looking at it from a snobbish point of view, if it was good enough for the British Museum, surely it must have been, at the very least, worthy of consideration (British Museum 1951, 57–58).

On the other hand, patrons are familiar with the widely used author main entry format, even if they don't know what "main entry" means (and they usually don't). Detailed bibliographic reference sources such as the *National union catalog* (with the spatial-data records available not only on microfiche but also through utilities such as OCLC) do exist, so cards could be ordered and time-consuming original cataloging avoided. Although for a time (while LC was working on implementing MARCMap) no LC cards for maps were issued, and for some time after that, for some abstruse reason, the cards could not be ordered, the hiatus was a small price to pay for the result—that of having maps (initially, only single-sheet maps) become part of USMARC, a system that is serving as an international pattern.

If the central cataloging department of a library catalogs the spatial data and the cataloger is accustomed to LC/AACR2 (as the vast majority are), it is most sensible to go the AACR route. Items do not always show well-defined place-name area, and in many libraries they are arranged by area, so that they are retrievable by virtue of classification even if they are cataloged with author main entry and other-subject cards only. And as long as area is given somewhere in the subject headings and the online catalog has component-word searching, it is sublimely unimportant to the patron whether author or area is the main entry, just as long as there is access via area.

Although librarians may in the past have retreated to area main entry for spatial data in the face of the diversity and difficulties of determining authorship, many spatial-data items were cataloged prior to AACR2 using author main entry, even at the cost of increasing numbers of white hairs on the cataloger's weary head. In any case, as was previously noted, if an added-entry card is made in an area main-entry system, the author will have to be verified anyway. Above all, standardization makes cataloging easier to do and to understand; subject headings are available to help the patron find the item required, and the system employed to get that information to the user makes not a bit of difference as long as it works. Librarians, humanistically oriented creatures that they often are, feel that intellectual accomplishment is difficult to attain and that such efforts should be signified by giving author pride of place; more practically, if something is written or made, it has to have an author or maker—it does not just magically appear out of the ether—so authors are the one common element for all such endeavors.

From the main entry skirmish, the librarian proceeds cautiously to the body of the record, and is delighted to find only minor disagreements, of the sort that logically follow from any process—such as cataloging—that appears to be completely objective but in reality has its subjective aspects, and in which a fair amount of autonomy is allowed to the individual participant (an autonomy intentionally increased in AACR2):

> There is some doubt about the type of information re-
> quired, and the order in which it is given, in all catalogu-
> ing... . The hope is that the most required information comes
> early in the entry to obviate the need to scan a great amount
> of unwanted cryptically expressed information and to keep
> the user from being blinded by library science (Horner 1973,
> 208).

Standard AACR Cataloging

❖ *[A cataloger] ... wrote a sort of poem,*
following a set of rules
more rigorous than a villanelle's ...
—Baker 1994

❖ *In so far as we can interpret them,*
we try to follow the
American Library Association cataloging rules
and LC practices for the content of the card ... .
—Galneder 1977

Anglo-American Cataloging Rules (AACR)

The best known of the cataloging systems is AACR, prepared by the Joint Steering Committee for Revision of AACR (JSC), composed of representatives from the American Library Association, the British Library, the Canadian Committee on Cataloging, the Library Association, and the Library of Congress, plus the editors (for the 1978 code, Michael Gorman and Paul W. Winkler). The first AACR, published in 1967, had a woefully inadequate chapter 11, entitled "Maps, Atlases, Etc." It was far too short, had too few examples, implied restricted application, and made an aggravating attempt to differentiate between works in which a subject aspect dominates and those in which a geographic aspect is primary.

The AACR revision, AACR2, was not only published in 1978 but actually had been planned to be published then; it was implemented 1 January 1981. In the interim between publication and implementation, LCG&M began cataloging using revised chapter 6, starting 1 April 1978 (one wonders if the month and day were selected for some symbolic reason). The rest of LC began using revised chapter 6 in September of 1974 (see *Cataloging service bulletin*—better known as CSB—for spring of 1978, 105: 7). The difference between the time LCG&M began using revised chapter 6 and the time the rest of LC did so was justified by the revised chapter having been based on ISBD for books, which could possibly have contradicted the then forthcoming ISBD for Cartographic Materials (ISBD(CM)). In actual fact, revised chapter 6 was more than just based on ISBD: what it did was to incorporate ISBD into the then-current cataloging practices. This was a matter mainly of order of elements and punctuation between elements (to act as a signal, so that a U.S. cataloger working with a record in Sanskrit would know exactly which fields were where).

The main differences are in the punctuation (as previously noted), and in a few other points on the revised card:

1. inclusion of author immediately after title

2. inclusion of publisher immediately after place, even though author and publisher are the same

3. inclusion of "1" prior to "map" in the physical description

4. "col." following "map" rather before it in the physical description

Scale—which under AACR2 moved up to just after the title and author statement—remained a note under revised chapter 6.

Spatial-data cataloging—indeed, cataloging of almost any objects—has been fairly exciting since about 1978, when AACR2 was published. One of the underlying reasons for this has been that with all the arguing and fist-shaking and street-fights concerning AACR2, everyone in the spatial-data library world realized, or began to realize—with a jolt—that cataloging is at the base of everything we do in libraries, and substantially affects how satisfied our users are. In addition, and particularly because of the international cooperative efforts (such as trying to formulate ISBDs that every country could, if not love, at least use), even persons not generally involved in cataloging began to comprehend that cataloging is a mind-cracking, or at least mind-stretching, exercise, and that melding everything together—ISBD, codes such as AACR2, machine formats such as MARC, national practice such as that expressed by LC in CSB, and whatever local practices any given library may have—is a petty trick, and guaranteed to instill humility in the practitioner.

After revised chapter 6 in the order of things came ISBD(CM).

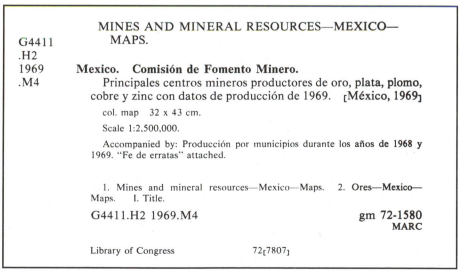

Figure 3.1. An LCG&M catalog card before AACR2.

MINES AND MINERAL RESOURCES—MEXICO—
G4411 MAPS.
.H2
1976   **Mexico.   Comisión de Fomento Minero.**
.M4   Principales centros mineros productores de oro, plata, plomo,
        cobre y zinc, con datos de producción de 1976 / Comisión de
        Fomento Minero. — México : La Comisión, 1977.
          1 map : col. ; 31 x 45 cm.
          Scale not given.
          "Producción por municipios durante los años de 1975 y 1976" on verso.
          Accompanied by: Producción por municipios durante los años de 1975 y
          1976. (p. 2-3 ; 47 cm.)
          1. Mines and mineral resources—Mexico—Maps.   2. Ores—Mexico—
        Maps. ₁1. Mexico—Mines and mineral resources—Maps.   2. Mexico—Ores
        —Maps₁   I. Title.
        G4411.H2 1976.M4   78-693650
                                                              MARC

          Library of Congress   78   MAPS

Figure 3.2. An LCG&M catalog card using revised chapter 6 and ISBD(CM).

International Standard Bibliographic Description for Cartographic Materials (ISBD(CM))

AACR specifies order and format of elements on a catalog record. ISBD specifies the order of elements, except for main entry, which is a national option, and punctuation between elements. Spatial data has its own ISBD, to be referred to hereafter for the sake of simplicity and sanity as ISBD(CM). Formally stated, it:

> . . . specifies requirements for the description and identifica-
> tion of all materials representing, in whole or in part, the
> Earth or any celestial body at any scale, such as two- and
> three-dimensional maps and plans; aeronautical, naviga-
> tional and celestial charts; globes; block diagrams; sections;
> aerial, satellite and space photographs; atlases; bird's-eye
> views; etc.—referred to hereafter as cartographic materials—
> assigns an order to the elements of the description, and speci-
> fies a system of punctuation for that description
> (International Federation of Library Associations 1977, 1)

As is true of the other ISBDs, it is not a format; that is, it does not say that title, place of publication, publisher, and date should be in one paragraph, physical description in another, and so forth. Format is dictated by the cataloging code of the country in which an item is cataloged. National cataloging codes and ISBDs are to be compatible, not synonymous (Stibbe 1977b, 32).

There are two definitions of primary importance that need to be given before we proceed further:

area: a major section of the bibliographic description, comprising data of a particular category or set of categories, e.g., physical description.

element: a word, phrase, or group of characters representing a distinct item of bibliographic information and forming part of an area of the bibliographic description, e.g., dimensions of an item, which is part of the area of physical description.

The areas are: Title and statement of responsibility, area 1; edition area, area 2; mathematical-data area, area 3; imprint area, area 4; physical-description area, area 5; series area, area 6; note area, area 7; SBN, ISBN, and ISSN numbers and terms of availability area, area 8. The AACR2R format for these areas is:

Title and statement of responsibility area.—Edition area.—
Mathematical-data area.—Imprint area.
Physical-description area.—(Series area.)
Note area.
SBN, ISBN, and ISSN number and terms of availability area.

It must be emphasized that ISBD(CM) is not concerned with format, nor with main entry or tracings. The two most noticeable differences from AACR1 order of elements are the move of scale and projection from the notes into the body of the record, and the punctuation, used as a symbol to separate elements and areas. Punctuation used as symbol, not as part of an element, is preceded and followed by a space, with the exception of a period (full stop) and a comma, which are only followed by a space. Punctuation that is part of an element, which may be included at the discretion of the cataloging agency, is given with normal spacing; if symbolic punctuation is included, the prescribed punctuation is still used, even if it results in what appears to be the product of a stuttering typewriter. When is the symbolic punctuation used?

The symbols used in punctuating the ISBD(CM) are the normal signs of punctuation plus the equals sign (=), and the diagonal slash (/). The equals sign precedes parallel titles, parallel series titles or key-title. The diagonal slash precedes the first statement of responsibility.

Point, space, dash, space (. -) is used to separate each area from the next. When, by paragraphing, typography or indentation, an area is clearly separated from the preceding area, the intervening point, space, dash, space may be omitted or replaced by a point (.) given at the end of the preceding area (International Federation of Library Associations 1977, 8).

Capitalization rules of ISBD(CM) state that the first letter of the first word occurring in each area should be a capital; other capitals should follow the usage of the language "in which the information is given (in areas 1, 2, 3, 4 and 6) or in the language of the bibliographic agency (in areas 5, 7 and 8)" (International Federation of Library Associations 1977, 9). As indicated earlier, area 1 is title and statement of responsibility, area 2 is edition, area 3 is mathematical data, area 4 is publication and distribution, area 5 is physical description, area 6 is series, area 7 is notes, and area 8 is SBN, ISBN, and ISSN, and terms of availability.

The detailed elements in ISBD(CM) are intended to cover all possible element occurrences; fortunately, the spatial-data object requiring the use of all these elements will be, we all hope, relatively rare. A library wishing to contribute full-level bibliographic records within the United States or for international exchange must make complete records. Those libraries that do not wish to contribute in these arenas need not prepare records that include all the elements and areas of ISBD(CM), although they should in any case keep the elements and areas in the prescribed order and use the proper punctuation. Fewer and fewer libraries will choose this second option, as worldwide networking proceeds.

Anglo-American Cataloguing Rules, Second Edition (AACR2) and Second Edition, Revised (AACR2R)

> ❖ *AACR2 may take cataloging into the 2lst century, but it will do so flanked by five-foot shelves of manuals, guides, and rule revisions. This may be some comfort to those who fear, like Cutter, "that the golden age of cataloging is over, and that the difficulties and discussions which have furnished an innocent pleasure to so many will interest them no more."*
> —Karrow 1981

Next in our chronological trip through cataloging is AACR2. AACR2 is in many ways a substantial improvement over AACR1, if for no other reason than that LCG&M proposed over fifty changes, ranging from the new chapter title, "Cartographic Materials" (a notable improvement over "Maps, Atlases, Etc."), to an expansion of examples and text (Hill 1977, 151). Apparently LCG&M was never asked to contribute to the first edition (Stibbe 1976a, 27). Admittedly, no other U.S. map librarians had any input into AACR1, largely because so few libraries cataloged spatial data, and if they did, it was all too often cataloged in a nonstandard fashion. Map librarians in many cases did not even know that a second edition was in progress until it was about to be published, and then only because

OCLC's format for maps was finally making it possible to catalog maps relatively quickly; therefore, at last map librarians were beginning to pay attention to cataloging.

The following is by no means a detailed exposition of how to catalog spatial data; for this the librarian must read a copy of the excellent *Cartographic materials: A manual of interpretation for AACR2* (1982). Rather, it is a presentation of the high and low points of cataloging spatial data.

A good deal of cataloging for spatial data exists in pre-AACR2 format, and the librarian performing retrospective cataloging often must use pre-AACR2 records. There are three possibilities in dealing with pre-AACR2 cataloging: change all of it, with no exceptions, to AACR2; accept all LC pre-AACR2 records, and change to AACR2 all non-LC pre-AACR2 records; or accept all pre-AACR2 records. Both the first and second of these options require that the cataloger have a firm knowledge of pre-AACR2 rules in order to be able to transform the existing record. The following comparison points out the differences between the two systems and also depicts how thinking concerning cataloging spatial data has changed over the years.

To begin with, a cataloger working with AACR2 must realize that cataloging spatial data does not mean just reading chapter 3 and having at it. At the very least, the cataloger must have read and understood (the latter being the difficult part) chapter 1 ("General Rules for Description"), chapter 3 ("Cartographic Materials"), chapter 4 ("Manuscripts"), chapter 9 ("Computer Files"), chapter 11 ("Microforms"), chapter 13 ("Analysis"), and all of part 2 ("Headings, Uniform Titles, and References"). This discussion deals only with chapter 3, assuming that the reader has trudged through all of the other chapters mentioned here.

The chapter devoted to spatial data in AACR2 is much larger and more detailed than that in AACR1—27 pages as compared to 10 pages; it has come up in the world, from chapter 11 to chapter 3. But the most important change is the attitude—noted in the introduction (p. v)—that all media are equally deserving of cataloging.

Whereas AACR1 begins by stating that main entry for maps is under the person or corporate body responsible for the informational content, AACR2 deals with main entry in chapter 21 ("Choice of Access Points"), where we are immediately embroiled in the—to spatial-data librarians—infamous 21.1B2, which severely limits those times when a corporate body may be used as main entry. Apparently, this was done to make serials main entry overwhelmingly by title; it reflects "changing interpretations of corporate authorship," especially as shown in such works as Verona 1975 (see appendix 2C; see also Carpenter 1981, 77; Ercegovac 1990b on the concept of map author). Admittedly, with computer manipulation of cataloging data, what the main entry is matters much less in terms of access points, as long as added entry is made for all bodies; but at the time of the discussion, relatively few libraries were working solely with computerized cataloging data. Underlying the whole matter was the belief of spatial-data librarians that a corporate body can (and often does) hold intellectual responsibility for an item and therefore should be main entry. LCG&M issued a cataloging alert, telling librarians that if they were interested in retaining corporate main entry, they needed to speak up (Schroeder l978a, 24–25). After a good deal of discussion, including meetings of the U.S., British, and Canadian map-librarianship community representatives with the Chief of LC's Office of Descriptive Cataloging Policy, Ben Tucker, an addition to 21.1B2 was finally passed by the JSC, adding the following category:

> f) cartographic materials emanating from a corporate body other than a body that is responsible solely for the publication and distribution of the material
> (CSB 14 (Fall 1981): 21–22)

The next area, title and statement of responsibility, remains much the same in AACR1 and 2, except for matters of punctuation and more frequent inclusion of author; edition is also not a matter of difference. It is when we come to scale and projection—which in AACR2 are moved up from the notes to a position just after edition and just before publication data, in a new area (the mathematical-data area, which includes coordinates, an item not even mentioned in AACR1)—that we see massive changes.

Under AACRl, the scale was given in the first paragraph following the collation, and the projection was usually informally given second-note status. *Cartographic materials* (1982, hereafter called the AACCCM manual after the committee that authored it, the Anglo-American Cataloguing Committee for Cartographic Materials) gives excellent instructions on how to determine scale (AACCCM 1982, 164–72). The tool required is a natural scale indicator, which may be obtained from several sources. For a heavy-paper copy, look in the back of Boggs and Lewis 1945, or U.S. Department of the Army 1964 (appendix 2A). Or obtain (for about $10.00) a plastic version (far superior to the paper ones) from:

Dr. Cliff Wood
Department of Geography
Memorial University of Newfoundland
St. John's, Newfoundland AIB 3X9
Canada

For converting obsolete systems of measurements, see Doursther 1965 or Johnstone 1975 in appendix 2C. The scale must be put in the form of what is called *natural scale,* e.g., "1:63,360," which means that one unit on the map represents on the ground the number of units to the right of the colon. This is to be figured out (if not given on the item) by use of the natural scale indicator or by mathematical calculation. The number of inches in a mile is 63,360. If the librarian's natural scale indicator has gone AWOL, this is the figure needed to convert such statements on the map as:

1 inch equals 43.2 miles

to:

Scale [1:2,737,152]

This displays yet another difference from AACR1; in AACR2, if natural scale is not stated on the map, it must be bracketed in the cataloging records.

Another change is that if scale cannot be determined by any of the preceding means, or by comparison with a map of known scale, the statement "Scale indeterminable" should be given. U.S. national policy, as expressed by LCG&M, is that the last named method of determining scale is not worth the time it takes, stopping prior to that point and using the phrase, "Scale not given" (CSB 27 (1985): 53). If there are more than two scales, AACCCM directs that "Scale differs," rather than AACR2's (and AACR1's) "Scale varies," be used; "Scale varies" is to be used for a given map upon which scale varies within the map, e.g., urban-area maps of certain areas in Europe where the central city is at a large scale, with scale decreasing as one gets further away from the city center.

Right after scale in the mathematical-data area in AACR2 comes projection. It is given, as in AACR1, if stated on the map. Following that is the coordinates section; LCG&M's policy is that if the coordinates may be taken directly off the map, they are to be recorded; if not, not. When there are two sets of scales and coordinates, both may be given. Note that 255 is the human-readable MARC field for the mathematical-data area, and 034 is the computer-search field equivalent, which unlike 255 does not include name of projection.

Next is the publication, distribution, etc., area, where again the changes are mainly but not exclusively those of punctuation; because these changes apply to all formats, they are not discussed here. Commercial publishers of maps frequently use date codes; see "Date coding of maps" (1982).

More than just the punctuation has changed in the collation area; its very name is different, and is now "physical description." The differences start at the beginning. Previously, if only one map was being described, it was not necessary to put the number "1" in front of the word "map"; now it is. And AACR2 is not limited to maps; what is now called the specific material designation, SMD ("map" in the last sentence), can now be any number of items. AACR2 gives over twenty of them (3.5B1) and states that if one of the terms is appropriate, another term may be used—this finagling factor was removed in AACR2R. The AACCCM manual urges catalogers to narrow the list of SMDs to nine: atlas; diagram; globe; map; model; profile; remote-sensing image; section; and view (p. 88). Following the SMD are other physical details, such as the number of maps in an atlas, whether the item is colored, or made of some special material (e.g., silk). Then come the dimensions of the item, still in centimeters, and still measured height by width as in AACR1. This is followed by a new area, "accompanying material," which may include such items as texts. Following is a worst-possible-case physical description under AACR2:

> ____ map_ on _____ sheet_ : both sides, ms., photocopy, col., silk, mounted on linen ; _____ x _____ cm. or smaller, sheets _____ x _____ cm. or smaller, folded to _____ x _____ cm., in en-velope _____ x _____ cm. + text (_____ p. : col. maps ; _____ cm.)

The order of information in other physical details (e.g., "col.") is now prescribed; "folded" is now spelled out rather than abbreviated. The physical description of atlases, which was formerly exactly like that for other books, has changed dramatically:

> 1 atlas (152 p.) : col. ill., col. maps ; 32 cm.

After all the changes that have occurred in physical description, it is a relief to go to an area where, once again, relatively little other than punctuation has changed, and that is the series area; the placement of the statement of responsibility changes somewhat, but these are valid for all formats, not unique to spatial data, and will not be covered here.

The next area—and here again, one with several changes—is the note area. As was previously mentioned, scale and projection are no longer notes but are now in the mathematical-data area. Another major change is that while for AACRl there was no particular order of notes (other than that the scale came first and projection very often second), under AACR2 the order is explicit:

Type of Note	Example
Nature and scope (including date of data and relief information)	Shows coal mines. [this information not stated in title] Based on 1971 statistics. Relief shown by contours and spot heights.
Language	Place names in Portuguese. [only if not apparent from rest of description]
Source of title proper Variations in title	Folded title. Panel title: Welcome to Granby.

Parallel titles and other title information	Added title in Italian.
Statement of responsibility	Engraved by S.H. Tuttle.
Edition and history	Sheets in various eds.
Mathematical data	Oriented with north toward lower right.
Publication, distribution, etc.	Maps dated between 1810 and 1910. [Note concerning publication dates: dates-of-situation notes come under "Nature and scope"]
Physical description	Blueline print.
Accompanying material	Each sheet accompanied by geologic sections.
Series	Some sheets have series designation: V882.
Dissertations	Thesis (M.A.)—University of Oregon, 1978.
Audience	Intended audience: Primary schools.
Contents	Includes 7 insets. Includes index. On verso: Cripple Creek - Golden - Idaho Springs. Text and ill. on verso. Contents: Douglas Ranger District - Sneffles Ranger District - Silas Ranger District.
Numbers	Publisher's no.: ZZ-22.
Copy being described and library's holdings	Library's copy annotated in green crayon to show lease holders.
"With" notes	With a separate map on same sheet: Queen Charlotte Range.

(AACR2 1978, 103–8;
AACCCM 1982, 128–50)

The next area under AACR2 is that of standard number and terms of availability, an area not noted for maps under AACR1. In 1977, there was an initiative to formulate an International Standard Cartographic Number (ISCN); for various reasons, including that ISBN agencies feared that maps are reprinted in so many new editions that they would require too many numbers and thus disrupt the whole system, ISCN has not come to light. Thus ISBNs are to be used for spatial data such as maps (van de Waal 1986).

The area following this is for supplementary items that are to be cataloged separately; this is to be used as described in AACR2R 1.9. Next comes the area for items made up of several types of material, to be described as instructed in AACR2R 1.10. The last area is a touchy one, having to do with the description of facsimiles, photocopies, and other reproductions. Whereas AACR2R states that the item in hand is the item to be described, LC has so far clung firmly to the idea of describing the item being reproduced in the body of the record, and describing the copy in hand in a reproduction note.

For the last part of the cataloging record, we have, as previously, the tracings, first subject and then added-entry tracings. The major changes here have been due to the drastic changes in political-body name entries, and this is a most important area for spatial-data librarians. A subject heading for a spatial-data item by definition has to have an area in it, and easily 75 percent of all such materials are issued by government agencies, so either the main entry, some of the added entries, or both will probably be a governmental body. Most helpful in the first case is the most current edition of LC's publication, *Subject cataloging manual: Subject headings*. The cataloger will also find Chan 1986 to be of assistance. Geographic subject headings are a complicated subject; major points to remember are: LC uses names established by the U.S. Board of Geographic Names (BGN); BGN does not establish names for nonpolitical regions, but LC does; and the most noticeable change between AACR2 and pre-AACR2 practice is that the modifying area is now in parentheses:

Jefferson County (Colo.)

not:

Jefferson County, Colo.

Added entries (e.g., other author, other title, series entries) for spatial data follow very closely the practice for noncartographic materials, except that the publisher of a cartographic item is as a general rule traced, whereas a book publisher would not be.

AACR1 did make provision for cataloging spatial data other than maps, especially relief models, globes, and atlases, but the procedure is nowhere near as detailed and obvious. Under AACR2 all spatial data except atlases are to be cataloged using primarily chapters 1 and 3, whereas atlases are to be cataloged using chapters 1, 2, and 3.

AACR2 precipitated a flurry of publication; the librarians who had it the easiest were those who had not cataloged anything since library school (and then not willingly) and had therefore forgotten almost everything about cataloging anyway. These neophytes came to AACR2 with nearly unsullied minds, and could usually accept what to long-time catalogers were mind-boggling ideas. Librarians new to cataloging were probably also in the process of learning not just AACR but also MARC, OCLC, or RLIN format and rules, and local practice, and had no time to get upset about much of anything. A revised edition of AACR2—referred to as AACR2R formally but informally as "AACR two and a half"—was issued in 1988. Although there are many changes from the second edition, the changes to chapter 3 were relatively low-level and easy to understand, and thus are not discussed here.

USMARC (United States MAchine-Readable Catalog Format)

The USMARC formats are standards to be used for representation and communication of bibliographic and related information, in machine-readable form. A quick definition is that USMARC formats are communication formats, for the exchange of bibliographic and related information. The format here meant is the USMARC format for bibliographic data, and specifically MARCMap. Although format integration was completed in 1996, this did not—in spite of its name—mean that all of a sudden we have one gigantic format instead of several large ones. Practically speaking, it seems to mean mainly that all fields are valid for use in all formats, and thus one may use whatever fields one needs in order to describe an item—essential when the item is a serial spatial-data CD-ROM (Format 1992 in appendix 2C).

MARC was originally designed in the late 1960s, with MARCMap being one of the first formats (Carrington and Mangan 1971; LC MARC Development Office 1976). It was at the time, and continues to be, a nearly exact transcription of fields off the catalog card (fields 1xx–9xx; fields for classification numbers, 050–099), with the addition of a large number of what are sometimes called "computer-search" fields (in contradistinction to the catalog-card fields, which are intended to be read by human beings, although they are indeed searched by computer software) in fields 001–049. The maximum size limit of a USMARC record is 100KB; most map records come in at around 700 bytes. For further information on MARC, see LC's Web page (http://lcweb.loc.gov/).

Although there have been many changes and additions to USMARC over the years, we will focus on some recent changes of importance. In 1994, MARBI (the overseeing body for USMARC) approved the fields for cataloging spatial data in digital form; the background of this is discussed later on in this chapter, in "Some Prominent Cataloging Problems," under "Spatial Data in Digital Form." In 1996, the map fields of CANMARC and USMARC were made the same (MARBI proposal 96-8). New fields for remote-sensing images were approved, also in 1996. In 1997, MARBI approved a change that struck a blow in favor of giving content primacy over physical format, as it allowed coding Leader/06 for the content of the item (e.g., a record for spatial data on CD-ROM will be coded for the spatial data, not for computer files, in this one field).

For the last few years in the library world, there have been extensive discussions and some actual use of another format—SGML (Standard Generalized Markup Language)—to carry bibliographic information, for example by the University of Virginia Library (ftp://orion.lib.virginia.edu/library/departments/cataloging/).

Anglo-American Cataloguing Committee for Cartographic Materials (AACCCM)

The next stop on our cartobibliographic trip is the AACCCM and the manual it authored. This requires a look at the history of the committee and why it was formed, which itself goes back to the publication of AACR2 in 1978. As was obvious from the previous section, the changes in cataloging that AACR2 brought forward were extensive in nature and expensive to implement. Because the changes were in many ways so radical, workshops were held throughout the United States and elsewhere. It quickly became evident to spatial-data librarians who had done cataloging that chapter 3, though much improved over the AACR1's chapter 11 (almost embarrassingly so, considering how little U.S. librarians had to say about it), did not give enough guidance, even to an experienced spatial-data cataloger, let alone to a librarian doing such cataloging for the first time. As it happened, the Association of Canadian Map Libraries (ACML; later to become ACMLA, the Association of Canadian Map Libraries and Archives), which had been working for some years on a map-cataloging manual, nobly and sensibly decided in 1979 to turn its work over to an international group, on the basis that only at the international level would such a manual be accepted. The then National Map Collection of Canada forthwith sent out invitations to LC, SLAG&MD, WAML, the British Cartographic Association, the National Library of Canada, the British Machine Readable Records Map Steering Committee, and of course ACML; to the project it also effectively pledged the time, as needed, of three librarians (Hugo Stibbe, Velma Parker, and Vivien Cartmell) plus support staff.

The committee first met 15 October 1979, in Ottawa, at the National Map Collection; the first newsletter was issued 26 October 1979 and included (besides participants' names) a most important signed item endorsing the interpretation of 21.1B2 to permit spatial data entry under corporate body. The Australian Map Curators Circle was invited in late 1979 to participate; Dorothy Prescott represented both the Circle and the National Library of Australia. The National Map Collection of Canada began working on a first draft of the manual in February of 1980. Meanwhile, the newsletter served as a method for listing problems, soliciting answers, and communicating news and notes. The draft came out with *Newsletter* #6, 9 May 1980. By *Newsletter* #7 (15 Dec 1980), the committee had two new members—P. L. Barton for the New Zealand Map Curators Circle, and K. S. Williams for the National Library of New Zealand. In early 1981, the ALA Map and Geography Round Table (MAGERT) joined the committee. The committee decided to meet one time to iron out differences of opinion, 27 April through 6 May 1981, in Washington, D.C.; the final draft of the manual was to be worked over and approved then, and it was. On 2 December 1981, the manual was sent to the publisher. The end result, published in 1982, is excellent, a work that no cataloger can manage without when working with spatial data. The National Map Collection of Canada and Ben Tucker, Chief of the Office of Descriptive Cataloging Policy at LC at the time, are especially to be commended for their efforts above and beyond the call of duty. For reports on the meetings, see Winearls 1981b and Christy 1981.

As time went by, and in particular as spatial data in digital form came to be more and more prominent in collections, it became obvious that it was time for a second edition of the manual. By 1994, work had begun on a new edition, with LCG&M serving as the Secretariat.

Reference Works Needed to Catalog à la AACR2R/LC/MARC/ISBD(CM)

Be forewarned that this will require a large, sturdy bookcase, although having LC's Cataloger's Desktop—and soon, we hope, LC Schedule G—loaded on one's PC helps out, as does the current availability of Schedule G on the ACMLA homepage at http://www.sscl.uwo.ca/assoc/-acml/acmla.html . It is worth the cataloger's time to take a look at the Web for online tools. For example, telnet to locis.loc.gov for such items as LCSH; visit LC's Web page at http://lcweb.loc.gov/ , and take a look at Vianne Sha's *Internet resources for cataloging,* which as of early 1997 were a part of the Website "Internet Library for Librarians" at http://www.itcompany.com/inforetriever/ . The list given in appendix 2C on cataloging reference works is based on the premise that the cataloger is doing standard full cataloging; many of the works are already in cataloging departments, with only perhaps half of the titles, and far less of that in terms of bulk, being items uniquely useful for spatial-data cataloging only. The 1991 *Map cataloging manual* is invaluable when used in tandem with the AACCCM manual.

Beyond these cataloging-focused items, one will need: a recent world atlas—preferably a digital one that gives latitude/longitude coordinates for any point touched by the PC's mouse, so that one may more accurately determine coordinates when they do not appear on the piece; failing the digital atlas, one needs a list of coordinates for foreign countries, states of the United States, provinces of Canada, states of Australia, and counties for the state in which one's library is located; gazetteers, either hardcopy—*Webster's geographical dictionary* or the *Columbia* gazetteer—or in digital form; a natural scale indicator (previously mentioned); and a metal measuring tape marked off in centimeters.

Library of Congress (LC)

LC's importance to the U.S. library world cannot be overstated, and any librarian working with LC cataloging should begin by having a grounding in how LC Processing Services work; reading the most current edition of *The Library of Congress Processing Services: Organization and functions* will do nicely. The next step is for the librarian to realize under what pressures LC operates, working as it does under the gimlet-eyed scrutiny of that most demanding of audiences; demanding for good reasons, which are that cataloging once done should be good for as long as civilization lasts, and also that much of the work done is interdependent, has far-reaching implications, and thus requires a considerable amount of work to redo. LC makes remarkably few mistakes; the one this author has always treasured is the entomological comment on LC card set map 53-695 (for a 1953 National Geographic Society map, Mexico and Central America) where the last note begins with the word "Insects" rather than "Insets."

Even considering that OCLC and RLIN have massive databases that may be less than one-third LC records, librarians finding an LC record have been known to breathe, "Eureka!" Quite simply, LC does the best cataloging of spatial data.

Whilst searching for that elusive LC record, the librarian must keep in mind that the information explosion hit LC at least as hard as anyone else, and that LC has priorities:

Priority 1: materials needed by members of Congress, etc.; CIP materials

Priority 2: high-need or research value English-language material; all currently acquired rare materials

Priority 3: high-need or research value non-English-language material; medium-need or research value English-language materials; added volumes and additions and corrections

Priority 4: medium-need or research value non-English-language material; materials currently purchased for Rare Book and Special Collections Division, as well as selected titles from gift or exchange collections

As of 1983, LC issues Minimal Level Cataloging (MLC) records; these have no class number or subject analysis (CSB 22 (Fall 1983): 69).

Technically, LC's role is in the interpretation of AACRs for U.S. libraries. But it is a much stronger role than the word *interpretation* suggests. AACR proposes, but for U.S. libraries, LC disposes, usually in the pages of CSB, which for some years after the coming of AACR2 was as anxiously—and in some cases as anguishedly—perused as a letter from the Internal Revenue Service.

The portion of LC that is of most interest to spatial-data librarians is the Geography and Map Division, which has often been referred to in previous pages. LCG&M is relatively independent in the LC framework; it is the only reference department that does all its own cataloging and keeps its own shelflist. The division was established in 1897, and began its first "cataloging" with titling in about 1910:

Geographic name

Date

Author

LCG&M's first notable cataloging of maps came after World War II, when it provided cards for AMS depository maps. Since that time, its guiding principle has been to catalog those items that the most libraries are likely to have. MARCMap began in 1968, and was a major step forward for the division. LCG&M catalogs approximately 8,000 titles per year on MARCMap, with a cataloging staff of about 20. LCG&M provides assistance to libraries on an informal basis, in cataloging as in reference work.

Variations on the LC Theme:
Unit-Card Cataloging Systems

Where rules go, exceptions and digressions follow. The human urge to tinker strikes catalogers as often as it does anyone else, and often with deleterious consequences. This sweeping statement is occasioned by the author's having seen—and, painful to admit, having perpetrated one— variations on the LC theme over the last fifteen years; almost without exception (and those mainly in business libraries that have a brisk turnover of stock), such variations are a mistake. They are usually based on the spoken grounds that "our patrons are different," and on the unspoken grounds that the library in question has not reached the point where it requires all the niceties. But it probably will grow, at which point what were formerly considered niceties are clearly seen to be necessities, and then everything will have to be done over again. It is far less expensive to do it right the first time. The main reason for LC being the right way to go is now most obvious because of all the networking going on; underlying that is the fact that cataloging decisions made in AACR2 and by LC are not done by whim, but for very good reasons. So, whenever it occurs to you, dear reader, to make some nice little change in the cataloging rules, think twice and then don't do it; stay with the format we all know and try to love.

That having been said, let's take a look at some of the many variations, starting out close to home and gradually wandering off into the bibliographic equivalent of the Tien Shan. The most harmless variation of the past was the use of different-colored card stock for cartographic materials, e.g., atlases in yellow, series in orange, etc. (Ralli 1979, 240; T. R. Smith 1960, 28; Bakewell 1972, 122). It brightens up the card catalog a bit, which, let us admit, does tend toward the dowdy.

The next step—and this one drastic—was to use area heading, move around scale and physical description, and leave everything else much the same. Perhaps the most venerable of these is that originated by Samuel Boggs and Dorothy Lewis (1945), as expounded in *Classification and cataloging of maps and atlases*. The first line of the record was area, subject, and date (e.g., "Burma. Topography. 1955"). A similar format, guaranteed initially to warm the cockles of any spatial-data librarian's heart, was that put forward by the SLAG&MD's Committee on Map Cataloging in 1953. In this case, the first line of the record was area, date, subject, scale, and size (e.g., "Burma. 1955. Topography. 1:250,000. 18 x 25 cm."). Although it is a logical scheme, cold hard thought will lead the librarian to the conclusion that its adoption, looked at in the long view, would be a mistake. As LC goes, so go we all, albeit occasionally kicking and screaming.

Another prestigious classification and cataloging system, which even includes a subject-heading list, is that propounded by Roman Drazniowsky for the American Geographical Society (revised and expanded edition, 1969). The first line has the familiar area-date-subject crew (e.g., "Burma, 1955, Topography"). Except that it moves author farther down in the body of the card—after scale and projection but before publication information—it is similar to the previous two schema.

There were many, many other cataloging systems in use, mainly on the area-heading line, with greater or lesser degrees of detail below that; paragraphing also tends to vary in these other systems. For examples, see Collison 1957, 80; Kujoth 1968, 274; Lukens 1970, 51; Prévost 1946, 104; Miller 1971, 152 and 1979, 172; Piercey 1974, 104; Galneder 1977, 16; WAML 1973, 9. One fervently hopes that these systems have gone the way of the dinosaur and that they have been replaced by online catalogs following the AACR/USMARC standards that the rest of us now slog through. Isn't there something about misery loving company?

Because of its nonbook, but let it not be said nonprint (except when digital), format, spatial data is frequently considered by audiovisual or multimedia administrators and catalogers to be part of their bailiwick; see Association for Educational Communications and Technology 1972, 31; Beaverton School District 1968, 11; Keen 1955, 16; Weihs 1973, 49; Westhuis and DeYoung 1967, 12, 14; J. T. Johnson et al. 1971, 89, 105–15; Tillin and Quinly 1976, 134–35. Some of these use area headings; others look like simplified AACR style.

Form Cards

Up to about the mid-1980s, a frequent ongoing debate in map-library circles was whether to catalog or brieflist (Buckallew 1986, 2). For some libraries, original cataloging, or even OCLC searching to find records, seems to require an incommensurate amount of effort. Such libraries may turn to form cards—or brieflisting, as it is sometime called—which seem an attractive alternative (Neddermeyer 1973a, 18; Voorhees 1976). Simply by inputting a form on a word-processing file and having a thousand or more forms duplicated in some way, the librarian can fabricate a cataloging system that can be run quickly, inexpensively, and mostly by clerical or student help. A minimum amount of typing time is required, and the typing is mainly a matter of filling in the blanks. Furthermore, the cards thus speedily generated are readily understandable to almost all users because each blank space is labeled—unlike the standard catalog card, where the user had to be able to figure out what is author and what is title and so forth, and was often not very interested in a good deal of the information so expensively provided. Online catalogs generally provide only the minimum of information, and sometimes label the fields provided. If the form card used is one that lists general subject categories, the librarian need not worry about any other subject authority list.

IMAGERY INDEX RECORD

AREA:_____DATE FLOWN_____

_____SCALE OF INDEX 1:_____

_____FILED BY_____

[SEE MAP ROOM INDEXES FOR EXACT COVERAGE]___SPECIAL INDEX LOCATION_____

FLIGHT I.D._____

INDEX: PHOTO MOSAIC_____FLIGHT LINE_____SPOT INDEX_____

    SINGLE PHOTO_____ OTHER_____

IMAGES HELD BY MAP ROOM_____

FORMAT OF PHOTOGRPAHIC IMAGES:

    SIZE_____ ENLARGEMENT_____

    VERTICAL_____ OBLIQUE: HIGH_____ LOW_____ OTHER_____

    FILM TYPE_____ PRINT_____ POS. TRANS._____ NEGATIVE_____

    B/W_____ B/W I.R._____ COLOR_____ COLOR I.R._____ OTHER_____

    _____

    PICTORIAL_____ STEREO_____

    SCALE OF IMAGE AT FLIGHT LINE_____

    GENERATION_____ NOISE_____

FLIGHT ORIENTATION_____

SENSOR: CAMERA SYSTEM_____ LENS FOCAL LENGTH_____

    SCANNER SYSTEM_____

PLATFORM: I.D._____ ALTITUDE_____

CONTRACTOR_____

FLOWN BY_____

ACQUIRED FROM_____ RECEIVED_____

SUPPLEMENTAL DATA:_____

_____

_____

_____

_____

_____

                           ORDER NO._____

Figure 3.3. A sample form card for an aerial-photograph flight—recto; form used at Map and Imagery Laboratory, Davidson Library, University of California, Santa Barbara.

(Lib-564A)

Figure 3.4. A sample form card for an aerial-photograph flight—verso; used at Map and Imagery Laboratory, Davidson Library, University of California, Santa Barbara.

But there are serious drawbacks. Using form cards means that the records do not appear in the main library's catalog; the cards are not compatible with other library catalog cards—not even in size, let alone in layout of information—and are not usually in digital form. Thus the collection's catalog will exist only in the spatial-data collection, which is most convenient for the spatial-data librarian, but to put it mildly incommodes the users, and falls into the category of preaching to the converted. The user can find the collection and the catalog only if he already knows that they both exist, is not too shy to ask, or stumbles across them by accident. There is a limited amount of usable space on the card; there is only one method of entry in most cases (place), and there is no standard form to be used in many different collections, so that libraries cannot easily interchange information (Neddermeyer 1973a, 23). There are many different kinds of form cards, but in the main they vary only in complexity. For examples, see Thailand 1977, 129; Neddermeyer 1973a; Great Britain Directorate of Military Survey 1946, 12; Raisz 1948, 323; Columbia University 1967, example 106; L. Wilson 1948, 16; Colvin 1963, 259; and U.S. AMS Library Division 1964, 9.

Computer Applications

In the preceding pages we have been discussing systems that are manual and result in sets of catalog cards, or in some form of hardcopy cards. The library world has proceeded rapidly—given the enormity of the task—in changing over from manual systems to computer-based systems. Nicholson Baker's 1994 article on the card catalog, "Discards," generated considerable discussion both inside and outside the library world, and makes some valuable points, the most important being that there are still searching tasks that are faster—or possible at all—only in the hardcopy card catalog. Think about all of those "too-many-entries" searches using such subjects as "United States—History," which anyone with tough fingertips and any amount of patience could easily pursue in a card catalog. But the article also includes sentiments that caused this author much hilarity—in particular the idea that hardcopy card catalogs have fewer errors than do online catalogs. Anyone who has ever filed card catalogs, or revised filing—of which this author had more than her fill in the years from 1969 to about 1984—perceives this to be incorrect, a subjective opinion that is borne out by a 1990 study by Gunnar Knutson, in which a new online catalog and an existing card catalog were compared. To no cataloger's surprise, the online catalog was more accurate. As online systems move to the Web and gain the ability to display graphics, they become even more attractive to spatial-data librarians; at last, it is possible to have a user call up a catalog record and go immediately from that to a digital browse graphic of the item (copyright permitting . . .).

Prior to MARCMap and OCLC's bringing up of the map format, automated methods of cataloging were not an option available to most spatial-data libraries; such systems were experimented with and then implemented mostly by large government agencies, such as AMS (now part of NIMA) and LC. But with the latter's inclusion of spatial data in the MARC database, and with the MARCMap format available over the utilities such as OCLC and RLIN, it has become an option that virtually every library now has or soon will. The first edition of *Map librarianship* contains an extensive section on automation of map cataloging prior to the 1980s (pp. 122–47); the second edition covers the 1980s to 1985 in pages 148–50.

One direction taken in the 1980s and early 1990s was seeing if expert systems could be used to assist in cataloging. An important effort in this area for spatial data was Mapper, an experimental, semi-automatic map-cataloging advisor, limited to descriptive cataloging of single-sheet maps issued by the CIA, the National Geographic Society, and H.M. Gousha (Ercegovac and Borko 1992; Ercegovac 1990a).

Several conclusions regarding the shift to automated cataloging may be drawn. In general terms, what computers can do depends on the state of the art, the science of programming, database-software developments, and the speed and memory capacity of the computers. A computer should not merely increase efficiency, but rather should induce a transformation of the institutions and enterprises in which it is installed. In a sort of computer version combining Murphy's Law and the second law of thermodynamics, it almost always takes longer than expected to get a computer to do what is needed; programming and debugging are neither easy nor cheap, what with a worldwide shortage of programmers. More specifically, any U.S. library not using AACR and MARC had better have a very good reason for cutting off its users from a national network. MARC is an evolving, internationally accepted (and modified; e.g., UKMARC) standard, in which digital form millions of records are stored and for which much computer software has been generated. See, for example, Bn-OPALINE, the online catalog of the Bibliothèque nationale de France. It uses INTERMARC as its machine format, and includes, amongst many other items, 80,774 records for "cartes et plans" as of June 1997 (http://www.bnf.fr/web-bnf/catalog/opaline.htm). Compatibility and standardization are essential to alleviate technological lag and to economize. As Parr has pointed out: "The ability and willingness of the general library community to support incompatible applications is limited. The problem of automated cartobibliography must therefore focus on MARC. There is no escaping this" (Parr 1975, 38).

Just to emphasize a point of overwhelming importance—independent development is not a promising route to follow. Even with its warts, MARCMap is the best mode for spatial-data collections to select; systems not compatible with MARC are probably not long for this world, and they render a disservice to library users by cutting them off from national system (Parr 1975, 34–35, 41, 50, 56). Over the years this librarian has read denigrating remarks about MARC. Nevertheless, as the years have gone by, non-MARC systems have usually fallen by the wayside, and have in so doing proved that, in the first place, just possibly persons working on MARC have some faint idea of what they are doing; second, that unless a system is massively supported it cannot survive; and third, that the most profitable expenditure of time is working with the MARC format to make it do what is needed, not in discarding it completely and making up something else altogether.

And speaking of giants, let us give OCLC its due. It was because OCLC incorporated a map format and thus allowed relatively inexpensive, definitely quicker, and easier cataloging of spatial data that collections have been cataloged as much as they have, and that retrospective cataloging occurs as often as it does. It takes approximately seven years of ten hours per week to catalog a 125,000-map collection on OCLC; without OCLC, a lifetime would probably be a good estimate of the hours required. OCLC is an extremely sensible way to catalog spatial data.

Some Prominent Cataloging Problems

Perhaps the only way in which cataloging is like physics is that the theory is easy, but the applications have the potential to drive you crazy. Catalogers have for many years—especially since digital data has become commonplace in many libraries—been proving that they are tough enough to take whatever comes down the pike. It is complex, intricate, demanding work, requiring a knowledge of, and ability to apply simultaneously, AACR1, AACR2, LCSH, LC classification, MARC bibliographic formats (at the least), and local practice. When one is working with spatial data, one also needs to know about coordinates, scale, projections, grids, and digital formats and software (Kollen 1990; Hagen-Lautrup 1989). The bright side is that for dealing with the hardcopy items, one will need a workspace about 12' x 12', and for the digital ones a PC powerful enough to store and manipulate large datasets. Now one is ready to deal with cataloging spatial data, from the everyday, straightforward items ("oh, no, not ANOTHER National Geographic Society map") to the everyday problems.

Archival Spatial Data

This section is intended for use by collections in libraries, not by collections in archives; and the librarian is strongly encouraged first to read Ehrenberg 1982, a reference that enables this discussion to be brief.

The archival map has its own importance, but very often it may be properly understood and interpreted only in relation to accompanying materials, that is, by keeping in mind its provenance. Thus, archival maps are grouped into series according to administrative origin or author. Archives that are solely cartographic—such as that of the Cartographic Division of the National Archives—are described by means of guides and inventories, which, with all due respect to the archival tradition and to the practicalities that have fostered them, are nowhere near as satisfactory to some users as is full cataloging. Although these guides do achieve some form of control over a large number of maps, this control simultaneously puts those maps outside the rest of any library's system, and this is always a mistake. It is best for archival materials in a library to use whatever chapters of AACR2R are appropriate to the material being cataloged (beginning, always, with chapter 1, "General Rules for Description," and proceeding onward as the material dictates), using the archives and manuscript format if preferred over the maps format, and also Betz 1982, *Graphic materials: Rules for describing original items and historical collections*.

Any long-time spatial-data librarian reading literature concerning archives access and cataloging will feel a nostalgia, perceiving the same underlying attitude as was found in spatial-data librarianship publications up to about the early 1970s—something on the order of "We are unique, we are special, we are pushed hard by having too many items to deal with in too little time, and so we will devise our own little system for dealing with the situation." Spatial-data librarians were in the main saved from the horrible situation of having an entire collection accessed by some unique system that would not be kept up by two factors: by being mainly in libraries and therefore tied to standard cataloging, if only by wishful thinking; and by the sheer bulk of material to be accessed. When OCLC made available the map format, the vast majority of collections had not been cataloged in the first place and were a *tabula rasa* as far as any access more sophisticated than asking the librarian if the collection had a certain map.

The same cannot be said of archives collections, which deal with a vast bulk of materials (of all kinds) that surpasses the most nightmarish imaginings of most spatial-data librarians. Many archival collections have set up their own systems for cataloging, systems that, with the advent of the archives and manuscripts format—which itself occurred only because of the AACR2 deep-seated feeling that all material is worthy of access and therefore merits cataloging—may be slowly replaced by full cataloging.

A librarian dealing with an unaccessed archival collection should first do some reading on cartographic archives, starting with Ehrenberg 1982 and moving on to Corsaro 1990, Stibbe 1986, and Tusa 1993. The aim is toward standard cataloging, informed by a background in the basics of cartographic archives. A classification arranged by provenance presents no difficulties because classification is primarily intended to group like materials together—which provenance does, in its own way—and is not inextricably tied to cataloging. Even though it is easier to do LC cataloging along with LC classification, one may certainly be done without the other.

Spatial data kept in an archival collection is often in the position of having to conform to the access system used by the rest of the collection—just as spatial data in a library is well advised to conform to the access system used by the rest of the library. That system is most often, and most sensibly, AACR2R/USMARC/LC.

Brief Cataloging and Cataloging Using Experimental Systems

> ❖ *By September 1990, two things became apparent:*
> *first, the Geology Library owned more than*
> *10,000 maps, and second,*
> *the GEOMAPS database capacity was 9,999.*
> —Baclawski 1992

At one time or another, the spatial-data librarian will look at the stack of items in the to-be-cataloged section, laugh shortly, and look around for quicker ways of getting the work done. MLC and "core" cataloging do have their attractions, specifically a time savings per title of about 17 percent (Kelley and Schottlaender 1996, 258). It makes more sense to get "all" of one's items cataloged to a level that includes information of most use and interest to general users than to have a precious hand-picked few cataloged to a fare-thee-well. Naturally, there are many definitions of what constitutes brief cataloging, even more since the Dublin Core meetings (1994–; http://www.purl.org/Metadata/dublin_core) that have been thrashing out core elements needed to describe resources available over the Internet. LC has its definition, the University of California Libraries has its definition (very similar to LC's), and so on, but they are quite similar except in the terminology used, focusing on areas such as author, title, subject, and local call number, giving short shrift to notes (Freund 1990). For example, the Dublin Core's fifteen fields are, in no particular order: subject/keyword; title; creator/originator; other agent/contributor; publisher; date of issuance of item in its current form; resource type; format; resource identifier; source; language; coverage (spatial and temporal); rights management; description; and relation. First the spatial-data cataloger needs to check with the library's cataloging department and find out what practices are already accepted and in effect for brief cataloging. If there are none, then the cataloger has a long, arduous trail to tread, getting brief-level cataloging stamped "acceptable practice."

Another reaction, occasionally to the "too-much-to-catalog" situation but more often to frustration over not being able to do coordinate searches, is to look at different software (Baclawski 1992; Chu 1991; Fleet 1994; Puntodewo 1991). Coordinates have had a home in AACR and USMARC since 1981, existing both in computer-search fields (034$d,e,f,g) and in a human-readable field (255$c); the problem is that no existing general library-systems software has the option actually to search the 034 fields. Given that very few users come to the reference desk with coordinates in hand—some don't even know what latitude and longitude are—this is an understandable attitude. What users can do is either look up their area in a gazetteer (from which one obtains the coordinates needed) or select an area on a map. Given that what makes spatial data spatial is AREA, there have been many efforts to use it as the first retrieval step; the Dutch system discussed in chapter 2 is one of them (for CARTONET, Morris 1990, Ochman 1978, and Recupero 1992; McGarry 1985; Watt and Browne 1985). Currently the Alexandria Digital Library—one of the six Digital Library Initiatives jointly funded by the National Science Foundation, the Advanced Research Projects Agency, and the National Aeronautics and Space Administration—has as its goal online access to georeferenced information, and thus has primary search by coordinates. It uses USMARC-compatible fields (http://www.alexandria.ucsb.edu/).

Dates

No, not the ones you may have had difficulty getting when you were in high school, but dates of information and dates of publication. What users most need is date of information; what the cataloger can most often provide them with is date of publication. Governmental publications are quite obliging about providing publication dates; commercial map publishers are another matter altogether, leading map catalogers to keep filed at the pages for MARC tag 260$c photocopies of the following periodical articles that tell you how to crack the publishers' codes:

> [Dates on maps in the] *WAML Information bulletin* 6: 15 (1975), 13: 340–41 (1982), and 16: 280–82 (1985)

> "Dating maps." 1990. *U*N*A*B*A*S*H*E*D librarian* 74: 13–14.

> Hoehn, Phil. 1997. "Date codes on maps." Berkeley: UC Map Library. e-mail message of 22 Apr 97, message-id: .OSF.4.90.970422130051.10825A-100000@library.berkeley.edu

> Website: Road Map Collectors of America, http://falcon.cc.ukans.edu/~dschul/rmca/codes.html

It will help the cataloger to have in the everyday cataloging manual (which should be arranged in USMARC field-number order) at 260$c (date of publication) copies of these date guides, plus a list of reunifications and splittings of various countries—e.g., 1990 for the unification of Germany and the division of the former Yugoslavia, 1991 for the breakup of the former Soviet Union, 1993 for the splitting of the former Czechoslovakia, and so forth.

Foreign-Language Cataloging

Bibliographic information from foreign-language materials may often be translated by using foreign-language dictionaries. But occasionally mapping terms are not sufficiently in common usage to be found in a standard dictionary. Then the librarian may turn to AMS's dated but valuable *Glossary of selected map terms relative to authorities, dates, scales, editions, and locations in foreign text maps* (appendix 2A), a 1944-vintage treasure that lists the most commonly used terms by principal foreign-country map publishers, from Bulgaria to Thailand. AMS has also issued glossaries for some individual languages, such as its 1946 *Glossary of Polish map terms* (appendix 2A). Another source for obdurate terms is the *Enzyklopädisches wörterbuch kartographie* (Neumann 1997 in appendix 2A). Or turn to *Languages of the world: Cataloging issues and problems* (1993 in appendix 2C).

Map-Series Cataloging

In the majority of spatial-data collections, at least 60 percent of the holdings, and sometimes as much as 90 percent, will be map series. It is thus singularly unfortunate that AACR2R says not one word about how to catalog such publications. Before the librarian catalogs a map series (a word to the wise: put it off as long as possible), the librarian will need to be able to identify one when seen. Usually this is obvious—if there are so many sheets that the desk upon which they are piled is not readily visible, it's a map series—but the following is intended to offer assistance, and even sympathy, when matters are not so straightforward.

One difficulty is the difference between what the rest of the library world means by *series* and what map publishers and therefore spatial-data librarians mean by that same word. Let us start out with definitions of relevant terms:

> *map series:* A number of related but physically separate cartographic items intended by the producer(s) or issuing body(ies) to form a single group. For bibliographic treatment, the group is collectively identified by any commonly occurring unifying characteristic or combination of characteristics, including a common designation (e.g., collective title, number, or a combination of both); sheet identification system (including successive or chronological numbering systems); scale; publisher; cartographic specifications; uniform format; etc. (AACCCM 1982, 230).

> *series:* A group of separate items related to one another by the fact that each item bears, in addition to its own title proper, a collective title applying to the group as a whole. The individual items may or may not be numbered (AACR2 1978, definition 1, 570).

serial: A publication in any medium issued in successive parts bearing numerical or chronological designations and intended to be continued indefinitely. Serials include periodicals; newspapers; annuals (reports, yearbooks, etc.); the journals, memoirs, proceedings, transactions, etc., of societies; and numbered monographic series (AACR2 1978, 570).

multipart item: A monograph complete, or intended to be completed, in a finite number of separate parts (AACR2 1978, 568).

The first definition will hereafter be what is meant by the term *map series,* whereas the second and third will be what is meant by *book-type series* and *book-type serials,* because maps can and do appear as the latter two.

Our next difficulty is that there is another important type of map—the multisheet single map—that is sometimes easily confused with (and occasionally even grades into) a map series. The reason for the problem is that the map series is actually a type of multisheet single map or, if you will, a type of multipart item, in some ways analogous to the loose-leaf publication in the book world.

One more semantic problem arises. Map series, such as the USGS topographic quadrangles (about 58,000 sheets, many in more than one edition, when completed, or, more correctly, when all sheets have been issued at least once), are in effect a map composed of two or more sheets, which may be used individually. In the early part of this century and in the latter part of the former one, such mapping projects were referred to as the map (singular) of the country. The difference between *map* and *sheet* is important; a map—a bibliographic, monographic entity—may be all on one sheet (itself analogous to a page or a leaf of a book), or it may be composed of many sheets, which could in theory (and sometimes in practice) be taped together, at which point the map would be on one sheet.

Be all that as it may, the differentiation between map series and multisheet single maps is well established in the map publishing and spatial-data library worlds, and is reflected in current cataloging procedures, so a cataloger does need to be able to tell them apart. There are some clues:

Map series:

1. Each sheet has its own border.

2. Each sheet has its own legend, title, etc.

3. Index map on sheets is for contiguous sheets only, not for entire series; or index for entire series is on verso of each sheet; or index sheet is published separately.

4. Each sheet may have a collective title and a sheet title.

5. Each sheet may be used either individually or with other sheets (usually contiguous sheets).

6. The number of sheets usually is relatively large.

7. Sheets may be issued over a relatively long period of time; fifty or one hundred years is not unusual.

8. Sheet numberings tend to be complex (e.g., 76-A-6-III) or to be large numbers (e.g., 3284).

9. A short legend is on all sheets; the full legend is issued on a separate sheet.

Multisheet single map:

1. The border is complete only when sheets are assembled.

2. Full title may appear only when sheets are assembled, or may be given in very small print on all sheets; the legend is on one sheet only.

3. Each sheet has an index map for the entire map.

4. Sheets may have a main title, with individual sheets numbered or given as "North," "South," etc.

5. Sheets are intended to be used together, and cannot be used independently, or at least not easily.

6. There is usually a relatively small number of sheets.

7. Sheets may be issued over a relatively short period of time (e.g., five years), or simultaneously.

There is no list of attributes that either type must have; a simple majority is sufficient. Multiple editions of the same map do not constitute a map series, but they might be construed to constitute a serial. If a group of map sheets may be correctly treated and cataloged either as a map series or as a single map with many parts, choose the method providing the greater access to the user; if both are equally useful, go by the publisher's intent.

A map series may consist of many maps which, taken together, cover a given area, all sheets illustrating the same subject; this is what AACCCM calls a "contiguous-area map series" (such as the USGS topographic quadrangles at 1:24,000 scale). Or it may consist of many sheets, each of which covers the same area but presents a different subject. Or these two approaches may be combined in a given map series. The first type is the most important and the most frequently encountered in almost all collections; generally it is numerically the major portion of collections.

The prime characteristic of this type of series is that a geographic area is covered by individual sheets that are contiguous. There is one fundamental qualification attached to this characteristic, on the basis of which the differentiation between series and nonseries in general, and between multisheet single maps and contiguous-area map series in particular, is made: the primary intent of the mapmaker is to enable the individual sheets of the contiguous-area map series to be used independently of each other. Even though theoretically the individual sheets may be trimmed and mounted for use as an entity, many such series are so large that this would be impractical. The sheets simultaneously exhibit the characteristics of a single independent map and maintain a close relationship with all other sheets in the series.

Most contiguous-area map series are produced and published by a governmental body for areas and regions over which that body has jurisdiction. Some such series are the work of private or commercial firms, usually under contract by a governmental body; some are produced and published cooperatively by a number of commercial firms, but this is rare.

Contiguous-area map series are usually relatively large cartographical works, sometimes totaling as many as 60,000 sheets or more. On the other hand, they may have as few as two sheets. The series as a whole frequently has a series number and a collective title; the individual sheets may be named, designated in some numeric fashion (e.g., numbered, lettered, alphanumerically labeled), or both. The individual sheets are not necessarily published, reissued, or updated at the same time. The sheet designations do not in any way denote the chronology or sequence of publication of the sheets; at any one time one sheet may have been issued a number of times, while another sheet in the same series may have been issued only once or may never have appeared. The lack of contiguous-area sheet coverage extant at any given time does not by itself constitute sufficient evidence that the series is not a contiguous area map series; it is the publisher's intent, as expressed in indexes to the series, that decides the matter.

Contiguous-area map series are often long-range projects. The area to be covered, the sheet layout, the sheet designation system, the cartographic specifications, the revision and update procedures and their cycles, etc., are usually systematically laid out. The sheet characteristics are therefore frequently predictable; this includes uniformity of sheet size, scale, projection, symbolization, color schemes, and other technical cartographic specifications, although national surveys do occasionally change their minds about the aforementioned in midstream. When this happens, individual sheets of contiguous-area map series may look different from those issued earlier, due to the cumulative effect of "minor" changes in technical specifications. Thus currently issued sheets in a series that has been in progress for some time may exhibit considerable change when compared to sheets issued early on in the life of the series.

For most contiguous-area map series, the sheet boundaries are laid out along the lines of a designated grid system, such as latitude and longitude; they may also be laid out along political boundaries, as is the case with USGS's county map series.

Contiguous-area map series are most frequently general geographic maps (e.g., topographic and planimetric national series); some are thematic, dealing with a specific subject such as soils, geology, land use, etc. Of all map series produced today, the contiguous-area map series is the most well known, the most common, the most used, the easiest to identify, and the most often written about in cataloging literature (e.g., McGrath 1985; Moore 1987; Porter 1985). The next two types of map series are not seen quite as often.

In the first of these types of map series, the relationship among the individual sheets is fairly strong, the sheets may be used independently, and area is still quite an important linking factor. But the focus shifts to subject, with a group of sheets, each covering the same area, displaying various themes or different aspects of the same theme (e.g., geology, soils, water supply, climate, etc.). Such sheets will probably all follow the same cartographic specifications. The most obvious example of this is an unbound national atlas, and the dividing line between what is strictly an atlas and what is strictly a map series like this is based heavily on whether or not the maps are bound together and what the intent of the publisher is. Whereas atlases are, fortunately, common, this type of series, equally fortunately, is not, and so the decision seldom has to be made.

Another sort of map series is that in which each of a group of maps shows a common theme (e.g., irrigation potential within a country), but not all of the maps show the same area. These sheets may be at different scales and projections, and may show noncontiguous areas that are usually within a defined geographic entity. In the case of both this type of series and the one previously mentioned, the sheets of the map series will usually be published at the same time, and may not be available separately. The entire series will almost invariably be the work of one publisher, who will indicate the relationship between the sheets by means of designation, sheet identification, or both. Here again, this type of map series is not common, and is very close to a thematic atlas in concept.

Acting as a bridge between map series and book series is yet another type, which the AACCCM manual includes in successively numbered map series. These map series, although covering an area with sheets of a specific scale and following specific sheet lines, take on the quirk of having sheets numbered or lettered in a seemingly arbitrary fashion; USGS's *Geologic quadrangle map*, *GQ*- series, is an example of this.

In the AACCCM manual, such publications as road maps issued by state highway departments in a new edition each year (an annual publication) are considered a type of series; LCG&M considers them map serials. Some libraries, mainly out of desperation, have begun to consider U.S. Forest Service maps for any given national forest—which maps are revised on a relatively regular schedule—to be appropriate material for a map serial. Such treatment is especially apt if the library keeps only the most recent edition of such maps.

Now we come to maps in book series; these are immediately identifiable because they display the same sort of bibliographic data—a numbered series designation, such as *Geologic map 2*, or *Special publication 61*—as do their brothers under the buckram.

Once a map series is identified as such, how may it be cataloged? Most often, and certainly initially, by describing it as a whole, with no contents note; a 505 tag with 58,000 titles seems a bit silly, so holdings for large map series are usually kept on a graphic index rather than on a shelflist (Frost 1989, 47–48). What is called multilevel description—an option given in AACR2 and AACR2R and relatively recently by USMARC with its linking fields, but as yet not available through most local online systems—is a possibility, and with a database of sheet-level records such as Geodex (available from Christopher Baruth, American Geographical Society Collection, University of Wisconsin-Milwaukee Libraries) is an excellent one. Multilevel description has two levels of records, with the first containing elements common to all sheets, and the second containing elements relating to the particular sheet described, with a MARC linking field (772, parent/child) concerning the parent (most notably, and for minimal entry work only, the control number of the parent), and preferably with no information that is common to all children repeated in each child. The example given in AACCCM shows the general pattern:

Parent record:

> Ordnance Survey of Great Britain one inch to one mile map : seventh series. — Scale 1:63 360. — Chessington ; Southampton : 0S, 1952-1974. — 190 maps : col. ; 71 x 65 cm.

Child record:

> Sheet 145: Banbury. — Ed. B. — 1968. — 1 map. — "Fully revised 1965-66."

> (AACCCM 1982, 17)

See Velma Parker's landmark article (1990) for an explanation of how the national map library of Canada has for some years been cataloging using multilevel description.

Note that the other MARC linking fields—773, link to host from part (e.g., one map in an atlas); 775, link to prior edition from newer edition; 776, link to "original" physical form from other forms; 787, nonspecific relationship when none of the other linking fields expresses the relationship— are also of use in spatial-data cataloging. For example, the 775 linking field could be used to link different editions of the same topographic sheet. Barbara Tillett of the Library of Congress has given this whole matter of versions some thought (Tillett 1995); see also Larsgaard 1996b for more detail on multilevel description.

For the more common practice of describing the map series as a whole only, the AACCCM manual gives a brief walkthrough (AACCCM 1982, 181–84); map series are also frequently referred to throughout the manual. As libraries go to automated circulation systems that can handle large numbers of records but not tremendously long individual records, the idea of cataloging map series sheet by sheet becomes more and more attractive. For example, the University of Utah Libraries have sheet-level control for its maps.

Often there are abbreviations of one sort or another on governmentally issued maps. For a guide to these, see the 1986 publication, *Military publishers' designations* (appendix 2C).

More Than One Map on a Sheet

If more than one map is printed on a sheet, several courses of action may be followed:

1. A collective title, if given, may be used in the body of the card, and titles of individual maps given in a contents note and as added entries.

2. If there is no collective title, either several titles may be included as the title, or a title may be devised, or one title may be given in the body and the rest described in notes, with added entries for all titles.

3. If the other maps are important, they may each be cataloged separately, with "With" notes for each one so that all the maps will be linked.

4. Analytic entries may be made for maps other than the one the cataloger decides is the principal map.

Rare Materials

These are usually maps and atlases. The atlases are often facsimiles and almost always expensive; and the wise cataloger with one of these on the desk either waits for LC to do it or uses as a pattern records LC has generated for other facsimile atlases, such as those published by Theatrum Orbis Terrarum some years ago. That leaves the maps.

The first comment on old and rare maps must come from Buffum, speaking about Lloyd Brown's excellent and enjoyable *Notes on the care and cataloging of old maps* (1941): "[It] is a delightful book to know. But when does a map become old?" (Buffum 1977, 47). To which the cynical response is, by the time it gets cataloged, it will be. The reason for this is that the cataloging of rare maps requires extensive knowledge of the rare-map *oeuvre*, and a great deal of care and attention to detail, all of which is fully justifiable in light of the value of the items involved. Because of the maps' financial value and their often fragile condition, handling them is either quite limited or strictly proscribed; and so it is most important that the catalog record give the searcher as accurate a verbal picture of the map as possible, preferably accompanied by a digital scan of the map. Rare-map cataloging is a subfield all its own; helpful guides to it are Robert Karrow's *Manual for the cataloging and maintenance of the cartographic collection of the Newberry Library* (1975b), and Vick and Romero's "Cataloging rare maps" (1990). The AACCCM manual, although occasionally using rare maps as an example or giving an application of a rule to rare items, does not give anything approaching full instructions for cataloging them, nor does it intend to (although plans are that the next edition will do far more in this direction). LC's 1981 *Bibliographic description of rare books* (LC Office for Descriptive Cataloging Policy 1981), although intended primarily for books, is also helpful for working with rare maps. Librarians new to rare maps may also profit by looking at Lee 1955, Verner 1974 and 1976a and b, and in appendix 2A Verner and Stuart-Stubbs 1979, all of which deal with the characteristics of maps and also with cartobibliographical description of rare maps.

One subcategory of map cataloging is that dealing with facsimiles of rare maps. As mentioned previously, the cataloger gives the information on the original of the item only in one specific note, 534. An example of this is:

"Original version: London : Harrison & Sons, Lith., [1899?]"

Remote-Sensing Images

Remote-sensing images, such as aerial photographs and satellite images, also are not mentioned in the AACCCM manual. It will probably be a few years before the new edition of the manual—which will include information on how to catalog them—appears, so take a look at the aerial-photograph portion of the *Alexandria Metadata Manual,* at http://www.alexandria.ucsb.edu/public-documents/metadata/ , as a guide to cataloging aerial photographs. This resource may also be of assistance in dealing with satellite images, as may other sections of this chapter, "Spatial Data in Digital Form" and "Map-Series Cataloging." See also Frost 1989. LCG&M has cataloged mosaicked satellite images (e.g., its satellite-image mosaic of Georgia), and these are excellent patterns to follow.

Reproductions: Micro and Macro

The problem: AACR2R states that the cataloger catalogs the piece in hand, while LC says yes, except for microreproductions and certain forms of macroreproductions, in which case the bibliographic description is based on the original publication and the reproduction (i.e., the piece in hand) is described in a note. As anyone with any library experience could have predicted, the vast majority of U.S. libraries catalog as LC states is best (see CSB 14 (Fall 1981): 56–58 for LC policy more fully stated). Excluded from this directive are macroreproductions that are the only way in which the item is published. For example, some U.S. state and some foreign geologic surveys issue some of their maps only in blueline print, a form of macroreproduction; and commercial petroleum-information firms very often issue maps only as macroreproductions or in digital form. In these cases, the macroreproduction is described. But looking at cataloging microform and the remaining macroreproductions of spatial data, the cataloger runs into a major problem; so seldom in the past have any items other than atlases been cataloged, that the cataloger will in all likelihood seek in vain for catalog copy describing the original, and probably will not have a copy of the original from which to work. To make matters even more interesting, some microform reproductions, and also some macroreproductions, are of pre-1900 maps and atlases, so this problem of cataloging is occasionally intertwined with the next problem on our list of horrifying things to do in spatial-data cataloging.

Retrospective Cataloging

So here many of us are, with spatial data collections that are either uncataloged or where cataloging has just begun. Very quickly we start thinking about retrospective-cataloging projects, outsourcing cataloging, how long it takes to catalog a title, and how much it costs to catalog a title. INSPEL's volume 28, number 1, for 1994 is a gold mine of information on past map-cataloging projects, from the Danish National Bibliography to the British Library's map catalogues (Conversion 1994); see also Armstrong 1994, Campbell 1994, Dinkins 1988, and Sprankle 1991. Following are some useful statistics:

> Ratio of copy cataloging to original cataloging: from 65:35 to 90:10—it depends upon what copy cataloging (which usually means what utility) you have access to, what kind of collection you have, and how long you are willing to wait for copy. For example, if your online catalog already has MARCIVE records for U.S. depository items since 1976 loaded, and you have access to OCLC, you should have a ratio heavily weighted toward the copy-cataloging end. And the United Nations map records have been available on RLIN since mid-1993 (see *RLIN focus* for October 1993, page 7).

Time per title for copy cataloging: five to six per hour.

Time per title for original cataloging: two to three complex items per hour, skidding down to one per hour for something very demanding. Remember, catalogers unfortunately have many other duties besides cataloging, so you are probably looking at 100 to 125 titles per month, perhaps 3,000 to 4,000 titles per year.

Cost of cataloging a title: given only as an indicator, because it varies directly with cost of salaries; $20 for copy cataloging (U Georgia, 1994), $45 for original cataloging (UC Riverside, 1984), $52 (UCSB, 1996).

Spatial Data in Digital Form

So much has happened in this area, and almost all of it since the early 1990s, although we had warmup time with CD-ROMs shyly sliding into our collections and our catalogs (Frank 1993; Kollen and Baldwin 1993; Lai and Wong 1992; Wong 1993). In 1992, the U.S. Federal Geographic Data Committee (FGDC) began work on the *Content standard for digital geospatial metadata,* kicking the process off with the Information Exchange Forum on Spatial Metadata, June 16–18 at USGS's National Center in Reston, Virginia. Work proceeded in the sedate, measured fashion appropriate to cataloging rules—until President William Clinton signed an Executive Order directing, amongst other tasks, that all federal agencies producing geospatial data in digital form catalog (or if you prefer, metalog) it using the content standard—by January of 1995. By June of 1994, the first edition of the standard was available (http://www.fgdc.gov/-Metadata/metahome.html). A second version (in draft form) was issued in spring of 1997. An American National Standards Institute (ANSI) standard followed within a few years, and an American Society of Testing Materials (ASTM) standard, D-5714, in 1996. LCG&M was deeply involved with the creation of the standard, with the result that the new fields were presented by LCG&M to MARBI in the summer of 1994, and were approved as fields in USMARC. The new fields and subfields aimed toward digital spatial data were: 034$s and t, Coded cartographic mathematical data (G-ring latitude and longitude; that is, coordinate pairs for non-rectangle polygons); 037 $g, Source of acquisition (additional format characteristics such as format); 255$f and g, Cartographic mathematical data (Outer G-ring coordinate pairs, and Exclusion G-ring coordinate pairs; the human-readable match to the new 034 subfields); 342, Geospatial reference data, $a through w and $2 (projection, coordinate and grid systems); 343, Planar coordinate data, $a through i (coordinate systems developed on a planar surface); 352, Digital graphic representation, $a through i (raster or vector; qualities of a raster dataset); 355, Security classification control, $a through f plus $6 (just what it sounds like; requested specifically by the military and applicable to all restricted datasets); 514, Data quality note, $a through m (resolution and other measures of accuracy); and 551, Entity and attribute information note, $a through p (documentation of GIS datasets). The new fields were—although a challenge to learn about, understand, and use—a boost to catalogers of spatial data in digital form, who had found chapter 9 of AACR2R to be more suited to relatively small, nongraphic, statistical social-sciences files than to large, graphic spatial data in digital form.

Also in Washington at about the same time, the Library of Congress was holding a Seminar on Cataloging Digital Documents in October of 1994; the moment that most took this author's breath away was when it was suggested that USMARC wasn't forever and we needed to look at moving ahead, perhaps to SGML—and no one in the room fainted, or even looked stunned. Elsewhere in the United States, Idaho and Minnesota were generating their own metadata standards, based on the FGDC standard, with version 4.0 of the Idaho metadata profile appearing in December of 1995, and the Minnesota geospatial metadata guidelines (version 0.4.3) appearing in March of 1996.

Let's just stop a moment here and define *metadata*. The quick definition is "data about data." The longer answer is that it is intended to be more than a catalog record, and yet at the same time it is a surrogate for the actual data. The ICA Commission on the Transfer of Spatial Data defines it as "data that describe the content, data definition and structural representation, extent (both geographic and temporal), spatial reference, quality, availability, status, and administration of a geographic dataset" (e-mail from Jan Smits, 20 Nov 1996, "Metadata and Map Collections," message-id: p02029.AA16461@atlas.sdc.ucsb.edu). Some users of the word limit the data described to digital data, and there is an implication that the producer of the data provides the metadata.

On another front, OCLC's Office of Research, in the spring of 1995, sponsored in the OCLC home offices in Dublin, Ohio, the OCLC/NCSA Metadata Workshop (later named the first Dublin Core meeting) (DC homepage at http://www.purl.org/metadata/dublin_core/), with the idea of getting stakeholders working with data available over the Internet into a large room and not letting them out until they came to a consensus about fields (to be applied mainly by Web page constructors) to describe Web resources. After a few more meetings (University of Warwick, England, in April 1996; once more to OCLC in September of 1996; the National Library of Australia, Canberra, in April of 1997; the National Library of Finland meeting, Helsinki, in October of 1997), there was agreement on fifteen fields: subject; title; creator/originator; publisher; other agent/contributor; date (still under discussion, but not date of data); resource type; format; resource identifier; source; language; coverage (temporal and spatial); rights management; description; and relation. Meanwhile, in ALA, ALCTS had a Task Force on Meta Access, whose charge was to lead the way in defining access and bibliographic-control mechanisms for information on electronic resources. An associated conference was a Joint Workshop on Metadata Registries, July of 1997, at the University of California, Berkeley,

http://wwww.lbl.-gov/~olken/EPA/Workshop/call.html ,

which had as its focus to discuss developing interoperable metadata registries. The new FGDC-generated fields were presented to ALA's Committee on Cataloging: Description and Access (CC:DA) in 1998, in their first step toward being added to AACR. For a 1997 draft of these rules, see appendix 5.

Meanwhile, in Australia, Canada, and Europe . . .

In 1990, the Canada Standards Board's Committee on Geomatics, Working Group on Data Dictionary/Directory and Cataloguing Standards, Working Group 4, Sub-Committee on Cataloguing Standards issued its draft of *Geomatic data sets, cataloguing rules*. It had about it the elements of an idea whose time has come, and also of simultaneous invention. Whatever it was, the release of the FGDC document in 1994 was rapidly followed by a remarkable spate of publications on the topic of metadata for digital spatial data.

In 1995, the Canadian General Standards Board issued *Directory information describing digital geo-referenced data sets* (CAN/CGSB-171.3-94), first in hard copy and later, in 1997, on diskettes. In January of 1995, EUROGI (European Umbrella Organisation for Geographical Information) issued a report, *EUROGI mission to U.S. Federal Geographic Data Committee*, emphasizing the importance of geospatial metadata efforts and the need for such work in Europe. Perhaps not coincidentally, two top-level publications on the international level followed soon after:

1. The ISO (International Standards Organization) TC211 (Technical Committee 211 on Geomatics) metadata standard (committee formed in November of 1995, in draft in 1996, planned "final" release in 1997); the committee had members from FGDC, and one of the group's goals was to keep the ISO and FGDC standards harmonized (Ostensen 1995).

2. CEN/TC 287 (Committee Europeen de Normalisation Technical Committee 287): working draft of *Information geographique, geographic information, geoinformation* was issued 21 September 1995; a version 2 working draft appeared 30 September 1993.

Australia and New Zealand have been extremely active in the geospatial-metadata world, with such documents as *Core metadata elements for land and geographic directories in Australia and New Zealand*, 1996 (http://www.auslig.ogv.au/pipc/anzlic/metaelem.htm).

For links to what is available now, see

http://www.konbib.nl/persons/jan-smits/metadata.htm

and for digital-data schema generally,

http://www.ukoln.ac.uk/metadata/DESIRE/overview/
rev_toc.htm

http://www.alexandria.ucsb.edu/public-documents/metadata/
papers_spatial_data.html

or

http://www.nlc-bnc.ca/ifla/II/metadata.htm .

See Heery 1996 for review of general metadata formats. The *Bulletin of the American Society for Information Science* has several issues on metadata; see, for example, 24(1), October/November 1997.

So we have all these decisions to make—if I find something good on the Web, do I make a link to it from my homepage, or do brief cataloging, and wait for six or twelve months and if it's still there do full cataloging? Actually, these are the same old decisions—is this of sufficient value to spend the time it takes for full cataloging, or is brief cataloging enough for now? We're thinking ahead to when indexes search the spatial data, not just the surrogates for it—searching for image textures that match the textures of the user's needs. We're learning new vocabulary. Chapter 9 of AACR2 was titled "Machine-Readable Data Files"; the revised second edition chapter title is "Computer Files"; and the word on the street is that the new ISBD for computer files isn't "computer files," it's "electronic resources." It isn't cataloging, it's creating metadata, or metaloging; it isn't cataloging, it's knowledge-access management; and so on. Whatever gets us where Melvil Dewey and Charles Ammi Cutter knew we need to get to—matching the reader with his "book."

Conclusion

The librarian with a spatial-data collection is faced with two big decisions: to catalog or not to catalog; and if cataloging, which system to use? The record indicates—more and more clearly over the last twenty years due to the increasing use of automated systems in libraries—that yes, the collection should be cataloged, and the system to be used

must be AACR2/USMARC/LC. Any deviation from this standard cuts users off from a prevailing national and indeed international system, especially considering that computers deal
best with consistency, and that unique systems are very often
going to be abandoned.

We are going to have to learn to be part of larger,
more inclusive systems—even if it is painful. We have jealously guarded our "differentness" as map specialists in the
library world. To enhance accessibility, live with the economy, and the information explosion, we must utilize, support, and push for cooperative efforts such as the Union
Catalog of Maps, cooperative acquisitions, affiliations such
the Research Libraries Co-op, and an expanded national (international) MARC Map system (Hudson 1976, 101).

This quotation, from a paper by Alice Hudson, Chief of the Map Division
of the New York Public Library, has become more on target as the years
have gone by.

It is essential to remember that access systems should be chosen on
the basis of long-term efficiency and effectiveness, not immediate (and
illusory) short-term economy of compilation. In the long run, which is
what libraries are all about, doing something right the first time is least
expensive. Standard cataloging is not easy; a map cataloger with good
historical and geographical background will start feeling comfortable in
about six months, and secure about the work in two years (Alexander and
May 1967, 33). And in terms of expense, think about this: Cataloging time
saved once is reference time spent over and over again—not to mention
the persons who needed a map but did not find it in the online catalog
and never asked a librarian for assistance, who count as our failures. There
is a reason that something as complex and demanding as full cataloging
is done: nothing else is effective, and nothing else, done right (if at all
possible) the first time, continues to serve users for as long as the world
lasts. The wise librarian will not waste time with anything else but the
most economical, effective, efficient way of doing the job—and that is
standard cataloging.

4

Storage, Care, and Repair

> ❖ *One may well imagine*
> *some long-forgotten librarian of Babylon*
> *wondering how he was going to*
> *file a baked clay map into the collection*
> *of incised tablets that were his books,*
> *and realizing, as so many librarians*
> *have realized since,*
> *that maps are a law unto themselves.*
> —D. Mason, 1958

Storage and Preservation of Maps

Storage and preservation of maps is often awarded the palm for presenting the chief problem of administration of spatial-data collections, with cataloging very close on its heels (Brown 1941, 17). The reasons for this are several and, at least on the face of it, dismaying. First, cartographic materials come in a wide variety of formats (both hardcopy and digital) and also of size—flat maps, globes, rolled maps, atlases, remote-sensing images, models, CD-ROMs, and whatever else depicts a geographic area and is awkward to store, especially when compared to books. Second, to paraphrase the Post-Impressionists, first of all a map (and many of its cohorts) is—often—a sheet of paper; the implications of this are discussed in the next section. Almost all spatial data lack protective covering, except for those exceptions that prove the rule (atlases, CD-ROMs in their jewel cases, and some folded maps); paper's flexibility and relatively low tear strength, when compared to, say, the cover of a book, and a paper map's relatively large surface all mean that it is almost defenseless against damage (J. D. Hill 1965, 481; LeGear 1956, viii). When the need to consider economy and convenient arrangement is added to the concern for preserving spatial data from wear and tear, then the aims of storage (to preserve the information, which usually means the surface of the object; to eliminate factors causing damage or strain; and to keep the object as close as possible to the state in which it came from the publisher become problems to consider (Ball 1910, 12; Skelton 1954, 15; Lock 1969, 490).

Paper, Ink, and a Few Enemies

Spatial-data librarians still deal mainly with products on paper, so this is a logical place to start. Although pure cellulose is permanent, raw cellulose fibers contain fats, waxes, and other impurities; the processes by which these impurities, which are harmful to paper, are removed from the cellulose degrade those same fibers (Kathpalia 1973, 31).

Thus paper, the principal medium used in the creation of much spatial data, is an unstable product that has a short life span unless it is properly cared for; it is completely destroyed by fire and water, easily stained or dirtied, and is subject to attack by molds and insects (Pidek 1974, 45; Plenderleith 1969, 41). Libraries have had highly perishable holdings ever since the clay tablet went out of fashion, and even those broke easily (Deterioration 1970, 3). To understand what kind of losing battle they are fighting, librarians need to know what causes deterioration. Factors leading to such deterioration are threefold: those inherent in the material or in the method of manufacture; those due to environment (heat, light, atmosphere, or biological factors); and those due to accidents or to acts of God (Waters 1976, Poole 1976b). A knowledge of the composition of paper and ink is necessary for an appreciation of the first factor.

Paper

In its very early years, paper was under the displeasure of the Christian church because of its perceived Moslem or Jewish origin; any displeasure librarians may feel toward it today are for nonreligious reasons. Paper is composed of matted cellulose fibers held together by the adhesive power of sizing agents such as rosin, starch, and glue. Like so many other staples of Western civilization, it was first invented by the Chinese, in A.D. 105; by the twelfth century, it had voyaged to Spain. Early paper was hardy; specimens from the first century onward survive to the present day.

In its earliest days, paper was made mostly from rags. In the Middle Ages, Renaissance, and Baroque times, the cloth might be bleached by alternate rinses in sour milk and wood ashes, then placed in the bleaching meadows, as was done in England. The action of sunlight and oxygen and the hard-water washings of the rags in the paper mill left calcium and magnesium carbonates in the finished paper—paper that has therefore held up well for 300 to 500 years. In the mid-seventeenth century, problems for future users of paper arose. In 1680 the Hollander beater was invented. Formerly, a wooden stamper was used to beat fibers to be made into paper; the Hollander beater used revolving iron knives and thus introduced iron particles, a catalyst speeding deterioration, into the paper. In another case of success spoiling the product, the demand for books and thus for paper increased with the invention of the printing press and the cylinder press, and with the spread of literacy. There were not sufficient clean rags (nearly the sole ingredient of paper in Europe at that time) to supply the demand, so dirty rags were used. They were bleached not by the sun, but by chlorine, a highly acid formulation, and this was one more factor speeding up paper deterioration. In the early nineteenth century, alum rosin sizing, which converts to sulfuric acid in the presence of moisture, was introduced into paper. Later in the century, about 1860, the final blow was delivered when ground wood was substituted for rags, introducing yet another acidic, and thus deteriorative, element.

Today most paper is made from wood pulp. Mechanical pulp, prepared by grinding wood, is used to make inexpensive papers such as newsprint, guaranteed to turn yellow almost before you have finished reading it; in this paper, "lignin, which holds the fibers together, remains in the paper and turns yellow in sunlight" (*Columbia encyclopedia* 1964, 1597). Chemical pulp is prepared from wood chips boiled under pressure with any of three chemicals (soda, sulfite, or sulfate) to dissolve the lignin binder and leave mostly cellulose. Then the wood pulp is washed, bleached, screened, beaten, and refined; suspended in water, it is poured over a wire screen. As water drains through the screen and is sucked away by pumps, a layer of fibers forms, and a wet felt belt pressed against the screen, or a pressing roll, picks up the paper for feeding through the sets of drying rollers. After this, the paper is passed through a stack of iron rollers called a *calendar*, which press and smooth its surface. To improve the printing, wet and dry strength, and texture, and to produce special properties, mineral fillers (such as clay or starch) are used. Writing papers, which may be all-rag, are always sized; a water-resistant substance such as rosin (still with us) is added to the pulp to prevent the spreading of ink (*Columbia encyclopedia* 1964; DePew 1991, 3–39).

Aging of cellulose is caused by acid-catalyzed hydrolysis (the prime offender), oxidative reactions, photochemical attack, biological attack, and the effects of use (R. D. Smith 1972, 59–60). Like some character in a Greek play, paper has within itself the seeds of its own destruction. Alternatively, it may carry bulwarks against deterioration. If a mill is fortunate enough to receive its water from a river that proceeds from or through limestone bedrock, the resultant paper is assured of a longer life due to the basic (i.e., alkaline, high pH) nature of limestone. Those mills not so blessed can get the same effect by using strong, well-purified chemical fibers, sized with a nonacid substance, with a trace of calcium carbonate added as a buffer against ink acids and atmospheric sulfur dioxide. Permalife is such a paper, with a pH of 8.5; a durable, permanent paper, it retains its original qualities under continued use (*durability*) and resists change over a passage of time (*permanence*) (R. D. Smith 1966, 273).

As one might expect, there is a drawback. Better paper can indeed be produced—at greater initial expense. An enormous expense is that a paper mill must be run on either the acid side or the alkaline side, and the change from one to another may cost in the millions of dollars. In addition, a mill's location determines not only the hardness of its water (the harder the better) but also the kind of wood pulp it gets—southern pine, for instance, gives long-fiber cellulose, whereas hardwoods give short. Also, publishers may not be aware of the magnitude of the problem, understandably being more concerned about publishing something today than wondering what volumes they issued fifty years ago look like now. But more and more papers have a higher pH, with more and more commercial papers up to pH 6.5, and map papers are generally more durable and have greater dimensional stability than do book papers (R. D. Smith 1972, 59).

Ink

Another physical component to be considered is ink. Before 1830 the inks used were India, nutgall, and sepia. India ink, which today's drawing inks match closely (although drawing inks include gum arabic as an adhesive) is black, composed of lampblack or carbon in water; because the carbon is finely divided, it has good penetration into the paper and retains an intense color. Nutgall was made by the action of iron sulfate on oak galls in an acid solution; after a hundred years, this ink turned brown and faded out, leaving an iron salt residue. Such highly acid inks not only faded to yellow but also weakened the paper upon which they were placed (Minogue 1943, 101). Nutgall was a forerunner of this century's iron gallotinate inks, the black and blue record inks; there is very little difference between the black and blue record inks. Sepia ink was made by suspending in water the dried inky secretion produced by a certain cuttlefish (*Sepoidea*), resulting in a brown ink with properties similar to those of India ink. Today no true sepia ink is made, and sepia is used only as a pigment in watercolors (National Archives and Records Service 1975, 2).

With the discovery of coal-tar dyes and the tremendous expansion of the chemical industry, many new inks have appeared, with none exhibiting the resistance to aging of the iron gallotinate. None of these inks holds their pigments in suspension; instead, they contain aniline and other soluble dyes. Printing inks consist of a viscous vehicle, such as petroleum fractions, linseed oil, mineral oil, and synthetics of the alkyd type, used to carry the pigment (generally carbon when the ink is black) onto the paper. Black printing inks are permanent and may outlast the paper on which they are printed (National Archives and Records Service 1975; *Columbia encyclopedia* 1964, 1024; Kathpalia 1973, 45).

Worse, some kinds of photocopying seem to be not just impermanent but downright evanescent. Blueline prints especially are burdens for the librarian; the ink fades in light, and the paper of some of the early photocopiers is so made that it deteriorates almost as quickly as does newsprint. Fortunately, for some years now photocopiers have taken into their maws standard papers.

Deleterious Environmental Effects

Second in the list of factors encouraging deterioration are the environmental effects of heat and light, atmospheric pollutants, and the effects of biologic entities. Let us first consider heat and light.

Heat and Light

Paper deterioration is a chemical process; if any energy input is increased, the process occurs more quickly. For every 20°C drop in temperature, the life of paper is increased eight times; or, for those of us to whom the metric system remains meaningless, for every 10°F drop, the life of the paper doubles (Poole 1976b). Thus in general, the lower the temperature, the better—for the materials, but unfortunately not for staff persons and users.

Light, another energy factor, has many of the same photochemical effects as heat. A photon of light energy is absorbed by a cellulose molecule; the short wavelengths, toward ultraviolet, have the most energy. Light levels for light-sensitive materials, such as paper, should not exceed 55 lux (five foot-candles). All light is damaging to paper, and sunlight is the most damaging; so purchasing fluorescent lights that claim to duplicate sunlight is not a step in the right direction. Solar Bronze or Solar Grey glass for windows will filter out sunlight's ultraviolet rays. Mercury vapor lights give off light that is high in the ultraviolet end of the spectrum; if they are used, an ultraviolet shield around them is essential. Fortunately, although architects like mercury vapor lights because they are efficient and tend to cost less, they are used mainly out of doors, to illuminate large areas.

The incandescent light bulb gives off relatively small amounts of ultraviolet but large quantities of heat. Fluorescent lights seem to be the most frequently used light sources in libraries; tube screens that filter out UV wavelengths may be slipped over the tubes, or fluorescent lights with the UV filter built in or light guards for a battery of such lights may be purchased.

The deleterious effect of light on paper may be even more important than was formerly believed. A large safe, stocked with items at the time of the United States' centennial, was opened during the Bicentennial. The paper items inside, after 100 years of being in a safe that was stored anywhere that was convenient (including, for about twenty years, outside under a staircase in the Washington, D.C., area) were in fairly good condition. The safe was not airtight and certainly not air-conditioned, but it did keep the items dry and out of the light (Waters 1976).

Moisture, Dust, and Dirt

Another environmental factor of great importance is the atmosphere in which the paper is kept and used. The first item of interest in that atmosphere is moisture, measured in a percentage as relative humidity (r.h.)—that is, the amount of water vapor in the air compared to the total amount of vapor the air can hold at a given temperature. The higher the temperature, the more water vapor the air can hold, so relative humidity is directly linked to temperature. In the past, the standard recommendation for relative humidity in libraries was 50 percent, because paper has optimal physical strength at that r.h. But it seems that, although paper is most durable at 50 or 60 percent r.h., its permanence or maximum life is greater when it is stored at lower relative humidities, around 20 percent or thereabouts (R. D. Smith 1972, 62). On the other hand, r.h. that is too low will cause desiccation. Although sources are agreed that high humidity (from 70 percent on up) is injurious to paper—inviting the depredations of mildew and mold—opinion is divided as to lower limits, with from 20 percent to 45 percent recommended for modern papers (R. D. Smith 1972; Plenderleith 1969, 10; Poole 1976b). See the helpful table on page 7 of Reilly, Nishimura, and Zinn 1995 for the relationship between materials' lifetime as plotted against temperature and r.h. A relatively small difference in r.h. can have dramatic results; at 60°F, when r.h. is 63 percent, 1,000 tons of books will absorb 20,000 pounds (10 tons) of water (Plenderleith 1969, 54). Portable hygrometers are useful in measuring humidity.

Remote-sensing images were formerly believed to do best at about 40 to 50 percent r.h. and 60°F or less, but r.h. is now recommended to be about 20 percent. Photographs, being composed of two media (emulsion and base), are much less forgiving than are maps of changes in humidity and temperature; the emulsion takes up moisture more quickly than the base, and then the photos curl. R.h. of about 40 to 50 percent also seems to be very helpful in keeping static electricity at bay in the computer room; no carpeting is important for the same reason.

The chief particulate offenders are dust and sulfur dioxide. Dust and dirt attach by abrasion, and may also carry mold; they must be filtered out by an air-conditioning system, although vacuuming and canopy tops on stacks will help (Poole 1976b). Sulfur dioxide, even in such seemingly minuscule amounts as 0.5 to 1.0 parts per million, is readily absorbed by paper. Once given a home, the gas combines with oxygen and water vapor to form sulfuric acid, which attacks cellulose molecules and breaks down their structure (Minogue 1943, 12).

The answer to atmospheric problems is, as might be expected, an expensive one—air conditioning, with add-ons to neutralize sulfuric acid.

Appropriate filters can remove 95 to 98 percent of incoming dust and dirt; charcoal filters may be used to remove pollutants, but they have the unfortunate characteristic of eventually and all at once dumping their accumulated pollutants into the air. A filter that locks the pollutant gas molecules to the filtering molecules is a better choice (Poole 1976b). Of course, air coming through an air-conditioning plant can be kept at a required r.h., but there will be additional expense in many locations for keeping r.h. at a proper level (R. D. Smith 1972, 62).

It is extremely important to keep temperature and r.h. constant; variations in either cause expanding and contracting paper fibers to rub against each other, thus causing weakening and eventual breaking of the fibers (Plenderleith 1969, 4; Minogue 1943, 12). Any shutdown in an air-conditioning system—and as we all know through sweaty experience, such shutdowns are inevitable—will quickly result in a sharp r.h. change. The ideal air conditioning installation for a library would include heating, ventilation, air filtration, cooling, and humidity control (all within certain narrow specified limits); would be year-round; and would never break down (Deterioration 1970, 72).

Biologic Factors: Fungi Do It, Rats Do It

Biologic factors include fungi (such as those causing mildew and foxing), insects, rodents, and bacteria. The first mentioned, here represented by the ubiquitous mold spores, are encouraged by high relative humidity and by warmth; keeping buildings at below 50 percent r.h. and below 70F will keep the fox away from the page (Poole 1976b). Bacteria are rarely a problem. Many librarians wish they could say the same about insects. Libraries in tropical locations are the most likely to have problems, but silverfish, cockroaches, beetles, and firebrats have an ability equalled only by that of *Homo sapiens* to find a snug ecological niche almost anywhere they chance to find themselves. Insects are particularly prone to sneaking in via shipments from abroad; such boxes should be fumigated before they darken the library's door. Rodents are kept out primarily by good housekeeping, as are insects, but they may get into a building during construction. And if the librarian has the misfortune to join the ranks of the flummoxed, angry few with rats in the map cases, it is time to call the exterminator (Poole 1976b).

Acts of God; or, Is Your Library by Any Chance Located on a Flood Plain in Kansas?

The last set of factors causing deterioration is a mixture of items over which the librarian has in some cases not as much control as we would like. These, the accidental factors, include such disasters as: floods, earthquakes, and high winds; broken water pipes, fires, and vandals; use, overuse, and abuse of maps; and carelessness and apathy on the part of the librarian. The only preparations the librarian can make to guard against the first two categories are to do appropriate readings on disaster planning and salvage, and to formulate a disaster plan. Such plans are often done for the library as a whole, and all that is needed is for the spatial-data librarian to check over the disaster plan and make sure it includes spatial data and the area in which the cartographic materials are located.

A disaster plan is particularly important in light of the fact that a library disaster such as flooding or fire first induces a state of shock in the people involved, to the point that it becomes impossible for them to act rationally, let alone make any plans (Poole 1976b). The visual impact of the damage is too much; very few of us can take the attitude of the little old librarian in the cartoon that came out shortly after a notable California earthquake in the early 1970s. It depicted a sweet little old lady (in actuality as hard as nails) looking at a series of collapsed bookshelves whose contents were tumbled all over the floor, and saying to a much dismayed, younger fellow librarian, "Well, there's no use in crying over spilt milk, so we'll just have to roll up our sleeves and get to work."

The librarian should first make a hazard survey of the area, looking for whatever could cause loss or disorder. Look first at the outside setting of the building, the natural physiographic and climatic hazards. Is the building situated in a flood plain? If so, in the last 100 years how many floods have there been? If there have been two, plan on the eventuality that your library will experience another. Are there dams up river? Are you located in the basement of the library building? How high is the water table? Next, look for hazards in the building, especially such things as plumbing-fire mains and roof drains. Water pipes have been known to break, frequently without warning; if one runs through your map room, a second protective pipe should be put around it, and a piece of gutter under that. If you are involved in the planning of a new building, watch architects and engineers carefully, for they often do not think of the safety of the collections within the building. For example, the architects for the then-new James Madison Memorial Library Building in Washington, D.C., ran a six-inch pressurized fire main right through the map vaults, which contain items worth millions of dollars (Poole 1976b). Check the condition of the roof, and watch for leaks, especially in the vicinity of skylights. When are gutters and downspouts cleaned, if ever? And has someone been unwise enough to clean plastic drainpipes with a corrosive acid that dissolves the pipe (yes, this has happened—the cleaner was accustomed to dealing with metal drainpipes)? Look at the drainage around the building; is there a sump pump? Are basement walls waterproofed? Is there a cooling tower on the roof? If it breaks, 20,000 gallons of water will course through your building and gurgle into your collection (Poole 1976b).

After looking for water hazards, consider fire hazards. Does your staff know how to operate fire extinguishers, or even where they are located? For that matter, do you? A basic element of fire protection is the installment of a sprinkler system. Formerly, sprinklers caused more damage to collections than did the fires they put out, because once turned on, they continued to sprinkle until the main was turned off, and it was recommended that such systems not be used (Minogue 1943, 15). Sprinklers can now be obtained that, unlike their predecessors, will turn themselves off if the temperature falls below 150F for seven seconds. The value of this kind of sprinkling system is apparent—especially since much more is known about recovering paper from water damage (an expertise due in large part to the efforts expended following the disastrous floods, of some years back, in Florence). Given the increase in arson and the speed with which such a system can put out a fire, the sprinkler system's importance cannot be denied. This is particularly true in light of the fact that many state institutions have no insurance; if a state college library goes up in flames, it is at the legislators' discretion that it will be rebuilt and restocked. Check insurance arrangements, if any, closely. What does the insurance cover, and is the policy up to date? Does the library have fire walls and fire doors? Is the fire department familiar with the building? Do fire marshals check it regularly? What about the electrical system? Where is the electric switchboard, and how old is the system?

On to other disasters: Are the bookstacks anchored, cross-stressed, and top-tied so they will not topple? Are large books kept on top of the stacks, from which location they may easily fall and damage not only themselves but the unfortunate person standing underneath them?

Libraries in California have found out more than they ever wanted to know about dealing with earthquake disasters, as witness the photoessay in the *WAML Information bulletin* following the earthquake that wreaked havoc at Stanford (Hagen 1986; Herro 1990; Collins 1996). Bolting five-drawer units together and having a bar that keeps drawers closed are the two main elements of seismic protection.

Do you have a list of telephone numbers to call in case of disaster? Do you know where to get chemicals and preservative materials, and where the nearest industrial-sized freezer is? And how about large fans? (Nagy 1984).

Be sure to include computers and digital data in the disaster plan. Have backup tapes for everything you treasure at some site several miles distant; include with this a list (printed out from time to time from the digital file—after all, you may not be able to get to a working computer) of all computer hardware and software with model numbers and locations. Be prepared to load the backup system; have printed-out instructions (Drewes 1989).

Much of this may seem like overkill for the small collection, or for the collection with few or no valuable rare maps. But consider how much it would cost to replace your present collection; even figuring an absolute minimum of $10 per sheet, it comes to a tidy sum for almost any library, let alone the horrifying thought of replacing atlases (about $200 each, on average) and globes (starting at about $50). No matter how small the collection, a written disaster plan should be formulated, complete with telephone numbers and chain of command.

Recently, preservation has become of obvious importance in libraries, and so librarians are much less hesitant about putting controls on the use of library materials—controls that formerly were only cautiously applied because of the maxim of free access. Eventually, librarians figured out that free access does not mean destructive access; and libraries with rare and archival materials are well advised to look into the possibilities of having all users put on clean white cotton gloves before handling any materials (not just aerial photographs), and being sure that users write only with pencils and do not lean on or trace over the map (Marley and Kohler 1985).

Summary

The ideal map library environment would have: pollutant-free air (which means frequent dusting and vacuum cleaning); total darkness; constant temperature (between 60 and 68F, preferably 60F); constant r.h. (between 20 percent and 50 percent, preferably about 40 percent). It would be housed in a fireproof, vibration-free structure on high ground, said building being equipped with an emergency backup system; all organisms would be absent, especially humans with their dirty, sweaty hands; and it would have "the full cooperation of the Almighty" (Deterioration 1970, 41). Maximum preservation precludes use, but because the purpose of most libraries is to provide materials for use, the librarian must somehow strike a happy medium (in which action there may well be magic involved), making materials available for use but discouraging their abuse and misuse (Preventative 1990).

Everyday Care, Wear, and Tear

Storage

Preservation begins long before spatial data arrives on the scene, first by the materials being printed or otherwise presented on durable, permanent materials, appropriate for use; this can range from low-acid paper (the medium libraries would most like to see), to plasticized or specially treated papers such as Tyvek, a tear- and water-resistant paper by DuPont (these last are most appropriate for maps to be used on canoe trips and the like; see Thompson 1996 for a conservator's analysis of Tyvek), to CD-ROMs. This part of it is usually beyond a librarian's control, except for such matters as setting up good relationships with the major issuers of spatial data and letting the latter know of the library's interest in lasting base materials.

The next step is making provision for proper storage. Librarians have been wondering what constitutes "proper storage" ever since maps first appeared in libraries. For example: "Because the Krigsarkivet has existed since 1805 and since different minds have been at work through the years on the problem of finding the ideal method of storage, the system actually in practice is not uniform" (Steckzén 1950, 14).

In 1856 it was recommended that map cases "should not be higher than a man," and that the maps should be placed flat in broad, commodious drawers (Kohl 1857, 138). In 1891, a group of map librarians suggested portfolios of stout manila paper or of two covers of board joined together by cloth or leather; if the maps were too large for portfolios, they could be tied and folded into bundles, or put in specially constructed cases with drawers (How we keep unbound maps 1891). In the ALA Papers 1894 came a warning not to arrange dissected maps on rollers unless the library had need of a corrugated roof—the long, rolled maps were unwieldy, especially in the confined quarters of the storage rooms.

In 1900 the Library of Congress was putting each sheet map in a thick manila paper folder; the maps were then placed in a series of slide drawers with wooden flaps that swung up automatically when the drawer was opened, and that served as dust protection (P. L. Phillips 1900, 15; Letts 1901). Other libraries of that time, such as the Lenox Library, kept some sheets unfolded in drawers, and some dissected and folded in pamphlet boxes (Letts 1902, 76). In 1903 the John Crerar Library was binding its maps in volumes, first dissecting them if necessary; some of its maps were stored on rolls, others hung on walls or were laid flat on shelves or in drawers (Andrews 1903,23; Hubbard 1903, 28). Even then, there was an awareness that storage for maps was more expensive than that for books. There was a definite opinion that maps should be made to resemble books (e.g., by being cut up and bound or by being folded and placed in book-sized boxes), because such a state was more convenient for the reader and for the librarian (Letts 1905, 805). But by 1908 the opinion again surfaced that maps should be stored flat and not dissected; the opinion was backed up by statements that such dissection affected accurate use of maps for measurement (a fold would cause some distortion also), that it seemed a sort of "wanton mutilation" and a "sacrifice to the dread machine of uniformity and size," and that the maps were more easily stolen if folded up (Drury 1908, 348). Many libraries made a practice of mounting their maps and storing them as rolled maps, thus creating another storage problem, to be discussed later.

By 1910 the vertical file was defended in print; vertical steel files are large and specially constructed for easy vertical access. Maps filed in drawers, in contrast, are difficult to get out and worse to put back, with the desired map always at the bottom of the pile (Windsor 1910). In 1914 one library mounted its topo quads on heavy manila paper, tied them together in groups of ten in the order received, punched holes through them, laced them, tied them, and filed them standing upright in a vertically sectioned cabinet (Storage of maps 1914, 936). Another library filed its topos in pockets of stiff board made by hinging two boards so they were one inch apart at the bottom and two and a half inches apart about twelve inches from the bottom (Treatment 1915, 75). ALA, in a publication that insultingly (if truthfully for the times) included maps with pamphlets "and other minor library material," suggested that sheet maps be dissected, folded, and bound, or put on folders, or filed horizontally (with only one fold) in manila folders (ALA 1917, 25–27). Flat filing in steel cabinets with two-inch-deep drawers was a system that had its adherents in the early l920s; but topos were still in some cases being pasted at the top of pages in loose-leaf manila books in some libraries (Library work 1922, 830). Other libraries placed each map in a folder, as LC had done at the turn of the century (Treatment 1915, 75).

In the early l940s, some libraries stored their maps flat; large steel cases with shallow drawers and ball-bearing suspension slides were recommended, but steel cases were not available for the duration of World War II (Lynn 1940, 397; Ristow 1942, 554). It was recommended that drawers be as shallow as possible, with a maximum $2\frac{1}{2}$-inch depth; if drawers are deeper, it means more pulling and hauling at the bottom maps of any stack (which are, as had been noted forty years earlier, invariably the ones desired), an inefficient and injurious practice, even if folders are used (Brown 1941, 20). In the mid-l940s, some libraries did not use the by-then traditional roller cases for maps, due to lack of space, but continued to dissect maps, put them on rollers, or file them in vertical files (Potterf 1944, 271). In those days wood cases were cheaper than their steel counterparts (Ristow 1946, 1121). By the late l940s, some map curators were brave enough to state flatly that "only flat filing is considered satisfactory" for maps (Winkler 1949, 285). And by the mid-l950s it was obvious to the majority of librarians that the best way to house maps was to lay them horizontally in a map case with shallow drawers; quick-reference maps could be filed in an ordinary vertical pamphlet file (Ristow 1955, 132; F. J. Anderson 1954, 383).

Also in the l950s, vertical map files, in which maps are suspended by clips from rods or held vertically in envelopes or folders, were lauded for being economical in the use of floor space and staff time (Skelton 1954, 15). A large vertical file could hold as many maps as thirty horizontal drawers, was dust-free, and involved less wear on maps; but when folders were full, they became weighty and awkward to lift. Buckram-covered boxes made from heavy cardboard or plywood and placed on roller shelves were another filing suggestion of the time (Spence 1951, 42, 44).

As more and more spatial data in digital form comes into the library, the librarian has two storage decisions to make: where to put the CDs and diskettes; and how much storage to get on the departmental computers. Storing individual CDs one to a case and vertically is the choice of many libraries (Driessen and Smyth 1995, 174). Metal cases with movable dividers, with the CDs and diskettes stored vertically, work well. And as for how much storage on the computer—as the old saying goes, the more the better. Storage in gigabytes is essential at the moment; one expects that terabyte storage will be the next step. See the section on "Spatial Data in Digital Form," especially the subsection "Hardware," in chapter 1 for more comment on this point.

The Decision for Hardcopy Map Storage: Straight Up or Sideways?

At the present time, U.S. map libraries have usually opted for horizontal steel drawer cases, with frequent use of the 50″ x 38″ x 3″ size; these can hold two separate stacks of USGS topos and are large enough to hold most thematic maps either unfolded or only folded once. Any librarian deciding on filing equipment should realize that there are other possibilities, and that the choice of filing equipment will depend on: type of maps to be stored; place of storage; amount of available wall and floor space; desired degree of user access to maps; the collection's overall objective; the way in which the collection is serviced; the collection's present size and future possible expansion; the relative costs of the various types of equipment; the availability of equipment; and the frequency of use of the collection (Ristow 1967a, 409; LeGear 1956, 42; Galneder 1970, 271).

Horizontal Cases

Choosing the type of map filing equipment has to do with style and material; cases may store maps horizontally or vertically, and horizontal cases may be of wood or of steel. The most venerable and popular of the filing cases are the horizontal ones; equipped with shallow drawers, they exhibit the best combination of protection for the maps, accessibility to them, and ease of expansion. Essentially, these are cabinets with large, shallow drawers, usually five to a unit. The units are made to stack on top of one another, so that the height of the cabinets is limited only by: the distance between floor and ceiling; the weight-bearing ability of the floor; whether the library is in a high-risk seismic area (if it is, don't stack the cases more than four high); and the physical agility of library staff to climb ladders (P. B. Lee 1963, 43–44). Indeed, in library circles it is considered that the age and success of a library may be measured merely by counting the number of map cases in a typical stack:

> Two cases high mean a new map library and probably not many maps or map cases. Five cases high mean an old map library and a little old map librarian who thinks that weeding is only done in the garden. A mature map library is

three cases high; just the right height for sorting, easy on the
floor load, and satisfying to the eye (Voorhees 1976, 2).

Three-high cases (this is about 51-inches high) is still about right, especially if the maps are in an open-stack collection and one needs to be
concerned about users damaging themselves while attempting to get a
map out of the top drawer of the top case in a six-high stack.

Horizontal map cases are often advertised as architects' and planners' files, so the librarian seeking out dealers in the Yellow Pages must
look under some subject such as drafting and office equipment. Each
manufacturer has some special features in its cases. The drawers should
be mounted on rollers (steel, not nylon studs, which tend to come out,
and besides, the drawers then have to be greased regularly), with a lock
feature that will hold the drawers in an open position and keep them from
rolling completely out of the cases and onto the consultor's toes. Fabric
dust covers that hook at the front of the drawer: protect the maps from
dust; prevent catching, rubbing, and protruding over the front or the back
of a drawer; and minimize sliding. These covers are to be preferred over
another kind of protection—a 6-inch-wide hood at the back of the drawer
combined with a compressor flat at the front. Drawer dividers are helpful
if large drawers are being used to file two stacks of maps. Some older map
cases have the elegant touch of allowing the front of the drawer, on hinges,
to fall out of the way when the drawer is opened. This makes consultation
of maps much easier, and it is not as liable to make maps cascade onto
the floor as it may seem, but it does mean that the drawers have to be
farther apart, thus reducing filing space. If rare maps are being stored, a
maximum depth for drawers is two inches. Provided the cases are not
stacked too high (and library space being what it is, they usually are), the
tops of these cases may be used as consultation space; when the map
cases are stacked more than two high, the tops may be used as reshelve
stations, or as storage space for globes and gazetteers. Each 2-inch-deep
drawer may hold as many as 300 tightly packed sheets per stack (about
25 sheets per one-fourth to one-eighth inch), but only of same-sized
sheets, like topographic sheets; mounted maps take about one inch for
every 25 maps, and a mixture of various sizes, including folded maps,
will take about one-half inch for every 25 sheets. Horizontal cases come
ready-made in a small assortment of different sizes and colors; they may
be special-ordered in specified sizes and colors as the library's architect
demands and as the budget permits. Many of the different map cases will
interfile with their competitors, but this should not be assumed. Horizontal
files may be put in compact storage; see, for example, the University of
Florida map collection (Armstrong 1992; J. D. Hill 1965, 482–83;
Gerencher 1985; P. B. Lee 1963, 44; Lock 1969, 491; LeGear 1956, 44;
Bartlett and Marshall 1979, 10; Sauer 1971, 52).

The choice between wood and steel has been much simplified in the last forty years or more; wood cases have become far more expensive than steel due to the high cost of cabinetry and carpentry work and of the wood itself. Steel was considered to be the best choice in the first place, mainly because metal is stronger and lighter than wood. But steel locks do jam readily (especially if the case is overloaded); also, in case of fire, paper in wood cabinets only chars slightly, but steel is such a good conductor of heat that the contents of a steel case can be destroyed (the exception here being the vertical Ulrich Planfiles, which are fireproof). Wood used in public places tends not to acquire a patina but to get dirty, unless it is very carefully taken care of; wood drawers generally do not roll on ball bearings, do not have safety stops, are susceptible to changes in temperature and humidity, and tend to warp in the face of large temperature change. Wooden drawers need to be thicker than comparable steel cabinets in order to have the same strength as steel. Unless a library already has wooden map cases which, for reasons of appearance, it wishes to match, steel is the better choice. When steel cases are received, the librarian must check for rust (underneath the top of the rear pocket), make sure the carcass is not dented, be sure that the drawers move in and out, and generally be sure the cases are in good condition (Barton 1982, 595; Nichols 1976, 117–18; Lock 1969, 491; Galneder 1970, 272; Nelson 1943, 468).

Large five-drawer map cases will weigh about 550 pounds, making it close to 1,700 pounds when stacked three high; stuffed-to-the-gills drawers can mean a floor load of over 300 pounds per square foot (Bahn 1961; Galneder 1970).

Vertical Cases

Vertical files, as their name implies, hold maps vertically, using several different systems. Maps (in groups or individually) can hang from hooks or be held by some form of rodlike binder or clasp at the top (suspension files); or they may be filed in racks, troughs (vertical compression files), or suspended folders sliding on rails along the sides of the cabinet. Such files may be from 12 inches to 48 inches wide, 52- to 70-inches long, and are often about 42 inches high, although they may be taller (P. B. Lee 1963, 43; Nichols 1976, 124; C. Stephenson 1983).

All kinds of suspension filing require the addition of a strip of some kind to the top of the map being hung; the strip may be purchased already punched, or it may be punched after application to the map so that the holes will match the clamps or binders in the vertical file. The strip may be applied by hand or by machine; in either case it is advisable that the applier not cover up identifying information on the map. If the information is covered up, then it should be written on the strip. The maps may be suspended in several ways—from long metal clamps or binders in groups of up to 100 maps, or individually by plastic clips fastened by pressure adhesive to the map itself. One particular version of this looks like a medieval instrument of torture, stripped down for twentieth-century use, to encourage borrowers to bring maps back, or maybe not even to take maps out in the first place; it has vicious-looking tusks, in sets of two (opposing each other) attached to the rear of the cabinet and the side door, and may be called, appropriately enough, a double elephant. Some vertical files are so large that they may quite literally be walked into; they may also have wheels and be lockable (Barton 1982, 593; J. D. Hill 1965, 484).

The second type of vertical filing cabinet works by means of spring-compressed pockets. Strong pockets made of heavy manila paper are suspended, sliding on rails at the side of the file. Each pocket or folder holds a group of maps; when one of the maps is desired, the entire folder is withdrawn and the desired map selected. Another type of compressor vertical filing uses "wave-like dividers forming pockets" in the case (Nichols 1976, 125).

Vertical files do have their advantages. They can store 2,000 maps in about half the space it would take to store them in flat files. Within certain narrow limits, maps of different sizes can be filed together in the suspension file without the smaller maps being overlooked and wrinkled or torn. Vertical files are excellent for utilizing narrow spaces where a standard flat file would not fit unless tilted on end (making access difficult), and they are suitable for filing maps of uniform size, such as topographic series of a given country. Patrons especially like the ease of taking topographic sheets out of a vertical file. Vertical files are available in roll-around units, an innovation that horizontal units do not offer; and they "meet the requirements of quick accessibility, of maximum storage space, and of minimum aisle space" (LeGear 1956, 46). They neatly take care of the perennial horizontal file problem—namely, that the map desired is always at the bottom of the pile—by shifting the former bottom to a side; and in the suspension types maps cannot modestly creep to the back as they are wont to do in horizontal files (Bird 1974, 71; McGlam-mery 1982; Perry 1983).

If a pull-out rack holder file is used, the flat top of the metal cabinet can be used as table space; titles or numbers on the side of the map can be read; and a sheet dropped is immediately recoverable. An eight-rack cabinet of this type will hold 1,000 maps. Another very important point, especially for archival or rare collections, is that at least one of the vertical files (Ulrich Planfiles) is fireproof; many years ago, all horizontal steel files were thought to be fireproof but they are not (Jackson 1911, 189).

If a nonsuspension system is used, the maps need no strips added nor holes punched; on the other hand, the vertical suspension method does seem to be an acceptable way of achieving easy access to a large number of sheets of different sizes, and "offering less wear and tear to maps so filed than any other system" (Nichols 1976, 128). Only the map desired is handled, yet a large number of maps are readily browsable. In the main, "vertical files work well when they are moderately full, and when the maps are of a fairly uniform size" (LeGear 1956, 46).

There is a Mr. Hyde side to the vertical file. It takes a considerable amount of strength to slide out the last dozen folders in the compressor files, and this is "backbreaking work, especially for a short person" (LeGear 1956, 46); for this reason, some librarians do not use those last folders, thus losing storage space (Nichols 1976, 124). Patrons are inclined to slide the folders back in the wrong space in compressor files; folders tend to wear at the top and to break through their suspension eyelets. When small maps slip to the bottom of a folder, as they are bound to do in nonsuspension systems, they are crushed, and the resulting bulge makes the folders difficult to extract, not to mention what it does to the maps forming the bulge.

Vertical files are more expensive than horizontal files (in comparative terms—virtually all cases are expensive), but then vertical files hold more maps than do horizontal files. Vertical files cannot be stacked, and generally their tops cannot be used as working space, because in most of them the hinged top is lifted up to provide access to the maps. Besides, the tops of such cabinets (which are in some cases too high and too small to be of much use as working space anyway), complying with nature's abhorrence of a vacuum, are in practice frequently covered with maps and various flotsam and jetsam, rendering the case *hors de combat* until such material is deposited elsewhere—probably on top of an adjoining vertical file.

For all their vaunted capacity, vertical files do not offer as much potential capacity in relation to floor space as do horizontal cabinets, as the latter may be stacked up to the ceiling (Capps 1972 in *Drexel library quarterly* 1973, 68; J. D. Hill 1965, 484–85). Any library having the tusked version has to bolt the cases to the floor so the cases won't topple when the side door is opened for loading the maps; probably the day after the case is bolted down, some maps will fall between the wall and the case, at which point the case must be emptied and unbolted to expose the truants, all of which makes for "a bitter experience" (Barton 1982, 592–93).

Vertical files are more limited as to the size of map they will accept than are horizontal cabinets, and they are not suited to holding groups of different-sized maps. Removing a folder of maps from a compressor file "causes all sheets contained in it to concentrate at the bottom if not to crumple, and because of some maps being smaller than others there is a bulking at the bottom half of the folder" (Nichols 1976, 124). In the suspension file, where many maps are held in one clamp, maps can slide off and fall to the bottom of the case unnoticed; in the individual-map-clip system, a user can draw the map sideways or forward in such a manner as to stretch it against the point of a prong. The type of material forming the strip to be attached to the map and the adhesive to be used may contribute to the dissolution of the map. Tusks can scratch maps and punch holes, maps can slip off the tusks, and only a few maps at a time may be removed. Heavier maps may relatively readily slide to the floor of the case as adhesive dries out (Nichols 1976, 124, 126–27, 129; Barton 1982, 594). From all of this it can be seen that suspension storage, at least of the kind where the strip is applied to the map, is not appropriate for old and rare maps, nor is the compression system (Bartlett and Marshall 1979).

Other Types of Map Filing

Some libraries, especially in Europe, keep maps in portfolios, filed on ordinary shelving. These flip-top buckram boxes are made of two hinged pieces of board, with tapes fastened at the middle of each side and tied to keep the maps from sliding out when the box is moved. These large, book-shaped boxes have served as Procrustean beds for some maps, with the latter being cut to fit the box. The portfolio protects the maps from dust, but unless the entire box is to be carried to a desk, there must be a space immediately adjacent to shelving where it can be opened and the required map withdrawn. Specially constructed boxes may be appropriate for archival situations (J. D. Hill 1965, 485; Kidd 1980, 532; LeGear 1956, 47; Jackson 1911, 190; Lynam 1939, 32–33; Gerencher 1985).

Storing Other Materials

Every library has several different types of items that simply will not fit in standard cases: "Human ingenuity has thus far failed of devising any form of case or rack or portfolio which will accommodate them all together, and yet have them accessible" (Fletcher 1899, 444). These include road maps, aerial photographs, folded maps, rolled maps, plastic raised-relief maps, globes, atlases, and most recently digital data (CDs, diskettes, etc.); we should be grateful that we do not also have sheet music, called "extremely recalcitrant stuff" by one who has handled it (Collison 1955, 5). Vertical file cabinets can handle some, but not all, of these problems. File cabinets are suitable for filing small, already folded maps (such as road maps) and aerial photographs; they are also useful for holding map texts, indexes, and catalogs, and even some of the charts, such as ONCs, that come to the library from the publisher already folded.

Book shelves may also be used; most of the aforementioned items may be put in archival boxes of appropriate size and the boxes on the shelves. The good part about this is that libraries experience a much easier time getting standard book shelving than any of the more esoteric forms of filing equipment. Microform is not much of a problem for the same reason; libraries purchase microform filing cabinets by the score. To store slides, the spatial-data librarian should go in league with the art librarian, and use the same sorts of plastic enclosures (not made out of polyvinyl chloride).

Remote-sensing images of the film type may be stored in protective plastic (e.g., polyester, triacetate, polyethylene, polypropylene; NOT polyvinyl chloride) sleeves, and the sleeved 9″ x 9″ frames put in archival boxes (not just any old cardboard) and thence on standard shelving, or in metal (not wood) file cabinets (Georgenson 1981, 335). Storing frames in paper envelopes may be asking for trouble unless one can obtain adhesive-free paper enclosures; the position of the glued seam and the adhesive used may react with the photograph unless the adhesive is nonhygroscopic and nonreactive (that is, inert). If paper envelopes are used, be sure that the paper has a pH higher than seven; use unbuffered paper for negatives and black-and-white photographs, and buffered papers (alkaline reserve of two to three percent calcium carbonate) for nitrate and acetate film. Better yet, have the nitrate frames reproduced and get rid of the nitrate. If negatives are not placed each in a separate container, they run the danger of some form of deterioration that will be signaled by sticking together or by tarnishing around the edges. If not in protective enclosures, prints may be secured with wide tape made from acid-free paper or polypropylene. Larger versions of remote-sensing images may be stored horizontally in the flat files. Labeling containers of images requires care; do not use felt-tipped or ballpoint pens (the ink may leak through and stain the photo), but rather a no. 2 pencil or India ink on paper, or a film-marking pen on plastic. If one must have identification on the photo itself, use a no. 2 or softer pencil to mark on the back edges (Albright 1997; Anderson and Goetting 1988; Archival storage of photographic materials 1996; CCI notes 1988a, 1988b, and 1988c; Derby 1997; IPI 1993; Eastman Kodak 1979 and 1980; Favier 1986; Hendriks and Whitehurst 1988; Keefe 1990; Swann 1981; Togashi 1997; Weinstein and Brower 1988; Wilhelm 1993).

Plastic raised-relief maps may be stored either flat or hung, depending upon how many of them the library has and the kind and amount of storage space available. If stored flat, either on shelves or in cases (where they take up a large amount of space), these maps must, if left out in the open, have some sort of dust cover, such as the plastic slipcover in which they sometimes arrive from the seller. If hung vertically, they can be hole-punched in the upper margins and then suspended in cabinets from hooks or wires, using "s" hooks or clothespins (Galneder 1970, 272; Bahn 1961 in Drazniowsky 1975, 377). In any case, they will take up an unbelievable amount of space; better to store them as exhibits. Patrons enjoy them and love to touch them; these maps are washable and will need to be dusted anyway, so such handling is fine. Dust them with a soft brush; remove grape jelly and so forth by washing them with a mild detergent and lukewarm water.

Globes are generally also "stored" as display items, and few libraries will have so many of them that they need to worry about classic storage. When not on display, globes can be placed on standard book shelving (double-wide, with adjustable shelving) and covered with transparent plastic or other dust covers, or they may be stored in cabinets or cartons (LeGear 1956, 19).

Atlases come in all shapes and sizes, from pocket to double elephant. Mostly, though, they just keep coming, with the result that the wooden atlas case is rapidly outgrown. At the present high prices of carpentry and wood, few if any libraries can afford to house their entire atlas collection in sumptuous, or even ascetic, wooden cases. Nor is it necessary to do so; the classic wooden atlas cases, with sliding shelves, are best kept in some prominent reference area with heavily used world or local atlases comfortably ensconced on their shelves. The other atlases, particularly if highly specialized, of standard book height or (perish the thought) seldom used, are adequately shelved on standard book shelving, of double width for the large atlases; the shelves for these large atlases should be no more than six inches apart vertically. All atlases except those of standard quarto size or smaller (29 cm.) should be shelved flat, to keep the pages from pulling away from the binding; some libraries file vertically atlases up to 38 cm. high and 34 cm. wide. Get oversize (ca. 11½" x 4" backs) bookends for the atlases. Ideally, these larger atlases should be on the roller-type shelving (made by Reflector Hardware Corporation) that is used at LCG&M; if your library cannot afford this type of shelving, you may eliminate friction damage by placing the atlas on a piece of acid-free heavy paper, and then pulling out the paper (Barton 1982, 596). When obtaining one of the wooden atlas cases, look for a case about 39 to 42 inches high, with a sloping top and a retaining rim, and its shelves about three inches apart, sliding out, and about eighteen inches deep.

Videocassettes, and probably any form of magnetic tape, should be stored vertically, in protective sleeves of some kind, away from hot spots such as heaters. As with remote-sensing images, it is important not to touch the tapes. Tape should be "exercised" once a year, and keep any magnetic fields and such machinery as floor polishers away from it if you treasure the data. Equipment on which it is played should have heads cleaned regularly (Geller 1983).

Digital data has so far not been as much of a problem as other formats we could name. Using the metal cabinets made specifically for holding CDs, and persuading library administration to purchase computers with yet larger and larger hard-disk storage space, has taken care of the matter. Magnetic tape is more sensitive and should be stored in a climate-controlled area. There has been some speculation as to the lifetime of various forms of data on disk. Optical disks with ten years given as a useful life fall far behind CD-ROMs, whose useful life has been given as anywhere from a split second before your dog uses it for a Frisbee to 10 or 100 or 200 years. Apparently there is a danger of the inks in printed matter migrating into the plastic and attacking the metal surface. Most of us are more concerned that hardware to play the discs will become obsolete and vanish long before the data on the disc does the same; so migration of data is more of a focus (Bouley 1992; Cruse 1985c; DeWhitt 1987; Preserving digital information 1996; Stability 1993).

Rolled, or Wall, Maps

❖ *... though we have very many rolled maps*
we do not like them rolled.
—Lynam 1939

All of the foregoing is relatively simple in relation to the final storage problem, the *enfant* (or rather, *gigante*) *terrible* of problem children—the wall, or rolled, map. There are almost as many ways to store wall maps as there are classification and cataloging systems, and each library has been forced to evolve a pet system because few commercial systems are available; there are some racks and pivot filing systems that are commercial products. Rest assured that all of these systems will take a fair amount of space and probably the services of a carpenter. Librarians today agree with a librarian of 1892 in feeling that probably nothing new can be done to make large wall maps less troublesome (Larned 1892, 44). Try not to store them at all, leaving them to academic departments, as a classroom adjunct. If that fails, try the following suggestions.

Rolled maps can be stored horizontally (on shelves, in pigeonholes, or on racks), vertically, or diagonally (in diagonal shelves in a cabinet or in shallow, slanted bins), depending upon the brainstorm of the librarian. As a last resort, they may be cut up and stored flat, on the grounds that they will fall apart if left rolled; this is LCG&M's attitude (Lynam 1939, 33–34). A sampling of possibilities follows. Perhaps the most common method of horizontal storage is the adaptation of the newspaper rack, in which 4-inch dowels, pointing slightly upward at approximately a 60° angle, are affixed about 5-inches apart to a wall, and the rolled maps laid athwart them (Cushing 1924, 557). Open shelves with no end panels, long shallow drawers, the tops of map cases, and cupboards have also been used (Miller 1971, 147). Some maps are mounted on spring rollers in rotary cases, and window-shade rollers have served as the works (Library work 1922, 830; ALA 1917, 25; Winser 1916, 246). Rolled maps may be suspended by small chains from each end of the mounting, on the grounds that filing rolled maps horizontally on pegs causes wrinkles where the maps rest on the pegs (Foncin 1953, 40; LeGear 1956, 16–17). Another way of filing maps horizontally is to put them in tube files, like extremely long pigeonholes, which may be interlocked in stacks; these are available commercially, although plastic racks for wine bottles (ignore the nasty looks you get from the purchasing department when you order them) will also work (P. B. Lee 1963, 44).

Maps may be put into transparent plastic (e.g., static-free polypropylene) tubing of appropriate lengths with caps for both ends (thus water and dustproof), and then filed on warehouse shelving; the plastic tubing is a good idea for use in any system that does not involve a closed cabinet to keep off the dust (Barton 1982, 596; Farrell and Desbarats 1984, 55). Or, in keeping with the name, just hang them on the wall as displays.

The force of gravity means that maps being stored vertically, are subjected to stress, and are more prone to stretch and tear than are maps filed horizontally. Nonetheless, vertical storage solutions have been often, and inventively, used. In some cases they are just the horizontal solution turned on end—as, for instance, the umbrella rack and tubular frames, which are tube files reoriented. Vertical storage of wall maps involves either suspending the map by screw eyes in the ends of the mounting sticks or placing the map on end in a rack, although there are novel alternatives, such as using a series of bicyclist's pant clips mounted on a board on a wall behind a door, with galvanized iron strips over the clips to keep them rigid; the whole affair holds the maps upright (Stoddard 1973, 34; McCune 1952, 301). The umbrella rack/bottle holder form of large wooden boxes divided into squares is popular, perhaps because of the possible alternate uses for the holder; some of these racks are on coasters and may be moved around. Rolled maps may also be placed in regularly spaced countersunk holes in a wood framework (Carney 1908, 54; Thiele 1938, 294; Ristow 1942, 554).

Hanging by means of screw eyes in mounting sticks is a popular method. Here the chief variation seems to be in the framework in which the "s" hooks are hung; some libraries use metal pipe, some sling a board from the ceiling, some use the ceiling as is, some are favored with an elegant cabinet, and some cover the ceiling with soft pine. There is even a hook made especially for the purpose—the Rigid Map Hook by Westermann of Germany (Chatham and Vanderford 1969, 93–95; Collier 1960, 31; Doerr 1960, 34; Bird 1974, 72). In at least one case, rolled maps were hung on the walls surrounding a circular staircase, thus using otherwise wasted space (How we keep unbound maps 1891, 72, 74), but with unpleasant results for the putative users:

> I should not recommend a plan I have seen employed, of utilizing the wall space of a stairshaft for this purpose. It is unsightly and, like happiness, always just beyond reach.
> From an ethical standpoint alone, this plan should be abandoned on account of its injurious effect upon the temper.
> The roller desired hangs temptingly just one step higher than you are, but when that step has been mounted it still dangles out of your reach (Parsons 1895 in Moody 1929, 201).

It is more usual for vertically stored maps to be kept in either a cabinet or a separate room, depending upon the size of the collection. Some wall maps, which may be nine feet wide, cannot be accommodated vertically, particularly if there are seven-foot ceilings in the wall-map room, so such special cases must be stored elsewhere horizontally (Abelson 1954, 11). Once a system for hanging the maps has been devised, a numbering and index system must be figured out to go along with it, unless one has wisely just kept them in class-number order—but then one must also wisely guess correctly where new maps will need to be fitted in, or else resign oneself to frequent shifting. Because rolled maps are somewhat difficult to browse through, they are either hung as they come (with little or no reference to geographical area) and a periodically revised or updated index kept to assist users; or hung in general geographical order with empty hooks left in what the librarian fervently hopes will be the growth areas, and an index kept available and updated as needed.

There are two other methods that may recommend themselves to the librarian. The first is to store them vertically in baskets, next in garbage cans, and then by a logical progression to throw them out (Plunkett and Quick 1968, 12). The next is to refuse to deal with them at all, leaving that to the teaching departments of the university or to the curriculum lab.

Summary

In 1976 P. A. G. Alonso compiled an excellent table of the pros and cons of various kinds of map filing, which is summarized here, with some additions:

> in flat files: good dust protection; have drawers as thin as possible (no more than three inches deep, and preferably shallower) so that materials are easily withdrawn and may be browsed through; tops may be used for study or refile (depending on height); number of cases stacked up limited only by height of ceiling, by load-bearing capacity of floor, and by mountain-goat ability of librarian and users

> horizontally on shelves: dust, tears, yellowing; maps flop off shelf; no study space

> vertically: perhaps not as dustproof as flat cases; odd-sized maps inclined to be damaged; no stacking possible, little or no use of top; excellent for browsing if cases not too full

> boxed or bound after shelving: dissecting first makes for more difficult use and deterioration along edges; compact but hard to use

> rolled: dusty unless covered with plastic or in cabinet; retain curl and are thus difficult to use; compactness almost impossible (Alonso 1976, 80)

Horizontal storage in metal filing cases with large, shallow drawers is best for most flat maps; vertical storage works well for maps of uniform size, especially those used very frequently, although the versions using strips and adhesive should not be used on maps that the library wishes to keep indefinitely. Spatial-data librarians are divided between those who swear by vertical cases and those who swear at them; the balanced view is that for some types of filing—such as topographic quadrangles—they do work well. The matter is somewhat complicated by the fact that it is likely librarians will be coerced by their administrators to pick one style of filing and stick with it; most have therefore chosen the flat files (Dallaire 1974, 45).

Rolled maps are best stored horizontally, because hanging them vertically causes the maps to warp and finally to tear off the mounting sticks. Labels should be put on both ends of each map; otherwise it can almost be guaranteed that whichever end one looks at first will be the unlabeled end. The most favored methods of vertical storage seem to be either on wooden dowels or on warehouse shelving, in both cases protected from dust by plastic tubing (Weihs 1984, 62; Akers 1978, 4).

Globes and plastic raised-relief maps should be stored as display items if at all possible. Remote-sensing images, depending on size, may be stored: in flat map cases (e.g., the large Landsat imagery prints); in archival boxes on bookshelves; in file cabinets (standard aerial photographic prints); or in microfiche cabinets for the smaller images (e.g., 4" x 5"). Atlases over quarto size are best filed flat on standard book shelving, double-width, with the shelves about six inches apart. Microform should be filed in standard microform cabinets, and slides in standard slide holders. Digital data should be stored either in the cabinets designed to hold diskettes, CD-ROMs, and cassettes, or on hard drives.

Handling

Open Sesame—Gently

Preservation begins the moment items are received in the library. Maps should be unwrapped carefully; the unwrapper must observe how the maps are wrapped before flailing in with an X-Acto knife and accidentally slicing through several maps. Spatial data may come in rolls, envelopes, flat packages, boxes, paper bags, triangular containers, and whatever else the publishers' ingenuity can devise (LeGear 1956, 199; Easton 1970, 199). To obtain entrance into these many and varied containers, the librarian will probably use a razor blade in a holder, scissors, letter opener, staple remover, pliers, and imprecations; a screwdriver, clawhammer, or wire cutters may also be needed. Rolled maps require the most caution; frequently the paper covering the maps has been interrolled with the maps themselves. The ends of the roll should be loosened first before the long, sealed edges are broken, so the librarian can determine what system is being used this time.

Maps may also be either rolled around a tube or rolled within the tube (the latter being more common). If rolled within the tube, the maps often stick, usually not at the end of the tube first opened. The canny librarian soon figures out that by balancing the tube in its center with one hand, the heavier end, with most of the maps in it, is easily divined. Both ends of the tube should be checked to determine the end in which the maps are primarily lodged. The end most full of maps should be briskly tapped on the floor, the tube brought horizontal, the inside curls of the maps grasped with the fingers, twisted more tightly, and then the maps pulled out. This procedure will frequently bring errant maps to hand. If the maps do not come out, and particularly if a dent in the tube is observable, the maps are probably well and truly stuck. They can be removed only by cutting along the seam of the tube up to the dent and tearing off the tube in strips as the cutting proceeds. This is not only laborious (map tubes are sturdy), but painstaking because the librarian must be careful not to cut all the way through the tube and damage the maps therein. Occasionally—but not often enough—this onerous process can be avoided by straightening out the dent in the tube, and squeezing the dented area with the fingers in an effort to pop it out. If the maps in the tube are within reach at this point, the librarian may follow standard procedure by grasping the inner edges, twisting the roll so as to tighten it, and gently pulling the maps out, halting if there is resistance (LeGear 1956, 1). When boxes are being opened, it is again necessary not to cut lightheartedly through the tape or the cardboard, since materials may be sited, unshielded, immediately next to the cardboard or tape.

As the maps are unpacked, the librarian should note any flimsy, delicate, or high-use materials that require strengthening or repair, and put them to one side for treatment; some libraries encapsulate any maps that are to be checked out. Any paper clips, staples, rubber bands, or other extraneous material should be removed and if possible some other method of keeping like material together (e.g., putting into a folder; plastic paper clips) used. Maps that are brittle should go into a damp box as quickly as possible, before they are handled and further damaged. Any diazo-produced (brand name, e.g., Ozalid) map will fade in light, and should be put in a folder as quickly as possible; these maps are generally blueline, blackline, or sepia prints, with a preliminary look to them—one color, relatively unsophisticated cartography, and relatively poor quality paper. The librarian will need to carve out of the processing area space for map cases and book shelves to hold just-received items; at least one five-drawer flat file and if cataloging is done in the same area three stacked files are better.

Flattening

After the maps are unwrapped, they should, for ease of processing and their own salvation, be flattened. If the roll is not too tightly curled, it can be flattened by weighting the maps for a few days; these weights can be steel bars (bound with billiard-table cloth to protect the maps), weights used in cartography, or, less formally, several large volumes on the order of bound *Congressional records* or the *Census of India*, or book shelves (wooden ones are best). Maps not too tightly rolled may be reverse-rolled, rubberbanded, and left that way for a day or two; it must be emphasized that this may only be done if the paper is in good condition, and only for maps, not for remote-sensing images. Paper in poor condition will crack when rolled; so will the emulsion of remote sensing imagery. These may be flattened only by the use of the damp box and weights; they will easily take several weeks to flatten enough to file (Bird 1974, 70; Capps 1972 in Drexel library quarterly 1973, 67).

Folded maps should go through the flattening process after being unfolded. Persistent creases can be dampened very slightly with a sponge, or the maps can be placed between slightly damp blotters or cloth. However tempting it may be, maps should not be ironed; the less contact a map has with heat, the better, for heat accelerates dehydration of the paper and lessens its durability (Capps 1972 in *Drexel library quarterly* 1973, 67). After dampening, maps should be weighted and left to dry. Because paper is weaker when wet than when dry, maps should not be handled until thoroughly dry (LeGear 1956, 2-3).

One valuable piece of equipment that is most handy in this initial processing is a humidification chamber or damp box—a box at least 49" x 36" x 8", with a net about half way up on which the maps and so on to be humidified, along with a container with a sponge and some water in it, are placed. The box may be made of transparent plastic or of polyethylene sheeting around a metal or plastic rack; clear plastic makes it obvious at a glance the librarian may tell what's inside; the first one this author saw, at the Colorado Historical Society, was made of wood. These seem not to be commercially available, or at least not in the sizes that spatial-data collections require. It takes approximately one or two months for items placed in the damp box to take up enough moisture so that they may be handled.

If there are not enough maps needing humidifying to justify obtaining a damp box, the librarian can place the maps, loosely rolled, for 24 to 48 hours in a plastic garbage can, with a pint of tepid water in a plastic container in the bottom of the can—the water in a separate container. If the maps are too tall for the top of the container to be clipped on top, a plastic sheet can be draped over all. Be sure to label the top of the container, in large, colorful letters, "This is not garbage! Do not throw it out," and do not place the humidifying chamber anywhere close to wastepaper baskets. This is more decorous than hauling the map home and leaving it in the bathroom (up on a ledge) for a few days worth of showers (BonaDea 1997a; Byers 1997; Steele, Hoff and McColgin 1997).

Stamping

Some sort of ownership stamp is usually applied to library materials, and spatial data is no exception. Opinions vary as to whether old and rare materials should be stamped if it can be avoided; rare-map dealers would rather be able to tell immediately if they are dealing with stolen goods, so the answer is that some sort of property stamp should be applied—a kind of embossing is used in some libraries. If stamping is done, the Assistant Director for Preservation of LC has available a harmless, ineradicable black ink that is as appropriate as any ink will ever be for rare and archival materials. Archival materials should be stamped on the verso, in some area that cannot be snipped off. For all other materials, it is important to select a consistent place, preferably a blank spot on the recto; maps, such as the National Geographic Society's products, that are bled to the edges may be stamped on the verso, as may aerial photographs and other varieties of remote-sensing images that either have no margin on the recto or that have a glossy finish that will not hold a stamp. If the library as a whole has a special method of indicating ownership (such as perforation, embossing, invisible ink), it is best to do as the rest of the library does if at all possible. The ink used should be black; colored inks (especially red) fade. Diskette and cassette labels can be marked with non-ballpoint pens; CDs so far have defeated any stamping techniques, although some libraries have used non-ballpoint pens to label the non-read side (Farrell and Desbarats 1984, 53; Topic IV 1976, 20; Map collections 1979, 6).

The stamp should contain, as a minimum, the name of the institution and the date of receipt—the former for obvious reasons, the latter because it is occasionally necessary to know the date the item came into the library's possession. Have a separate stamp for depository items, with "DEPOSITORY" on the stamp, since such items legally remain the property of the issuing agency, and the librarian must be able to differentiate them from other items.

Filing

After being counted, items should be cataloged, classified, labeled, and sent off to be filed. Labeling may be in pencil or in ink on adhesive labels; label location should be consistent, with the lower left- or the lower right-hand corner often being used. Items should be labeled where the label will be seen; thus, if a map is to be filed rolled, the call number must appear on both of the outside ends. Maps that are folded before they go into the map case need to have a label on the corner that will be the labeling corner when the map is folded, not just on the labeling corner of the map when it is unfolded.

To transport maps from processing area to filing area, one would like to have a book truck wide enough for the job, yet narrow enough to make it through the doors separating the processing room from the map-case room. Media carts and custom-built jobs seem to be the options; dimensions of 42½" high from floor to top of handles, 55½" wide from outside handle to outside handle, and 31½" inches deep are the dimensions of the user-tested special trucks at the Pennsylvania State University Libraries (Andrew 1996).

Maps and remote-sensing images should be filed in protective folders. Folders keep larger maps in a drawer from brutalizing the smaller or more flimsy ones. A folder paper thickness of 0.010-inch is adequate (Stevens l972a, 24). The folders themselves should be labeled, in a lower corner and in the most general of numbers, either in pencil or with a gummed label that can be covered up and replaced with a new one as the library's holdings grow and expand out of their initial folders. Acid-free folders, with a pH of 4.5 or higher, are essential (Galneder and Koerner 1975, 166). Not only do they protect the maps from dust and keep them organized (as would any other folder), they also offer chemical protection, keeping the maps from acidifying, or from doing so as rapidly, since acid migrates from more acidic to less acidic paper (Barrow 1953, 105-7). Remote-sensing transparencies need to be individually filed in clear plastic holders, and then in archival boxes or file cabinets; prints deserve the same attention if the negatives are no longer in existence. Less frequently used film may be stored as roll film, rather than as cut frames.

Depending on the type of maps, up to 50 maps may be put in a folder, but the folders are easier to handle and offer more protection if fewer maps are inserted; more than 50 maps make a folder too heavy to handle. Rare maps should be stored individually or no more than 10 per folder (Raisz 1948, 321; LeGear 1956, 11; Bartlett and Marshall 1979, 10). Maps of fairly uniform size, in series or sets, generally do not need folders (LeGear 1956, 12). Map folders should be about two inches shorter than the inside length and about one inch shorter than the map drawer from front to back; this saves edges and makes the folders easy to manipulate. The folders in any one drawer should be uniform in size (L. A. Brown 1941, 23). Good folders should last from 20 to 50 years (LeGear 1956, 10). Either folders may be purchased cut to map-case or other needed sizes, or libraries may purchase their own, using a roll of acid-free paper.

Map folders, with no map edges protruding, may be filed with the folded edge either at the front or at the back of the drawer. Filing with the fold at the front of the drawer is better for the maps because the user must remove the entire folder instead of being able to rummage through a folder while it is still in the drawer. The problem with rummaging through a folder without taking it out of the drawer is that a map tends to be pulled out, or shoved back in, with no concern for what is happening to the other maps, which may somehow be entangled with it. On the other hand, actively used reference collections may have the fold at the back of the drawer for the very reasons just given against such a practice—the user can look through a folder, provided it is on top or reasonably close to the top, without removing the folder, thus handling and flexing the maps; this works best for uniformly sized maps, with fewer than 30 sheets in a folder. Although folders do slide easily over one another, they are large, and it takes some coordination to remove them if the remover is to avoid dumping maps all over the floor. Filing with the folded edge toward the front keeps maps from tearing and fraying and, since most dust and dirt enter from the front of the cabinet, such a system keeps dust away from the maps more effectively (L. A. Brown 1941, 23).

Shielding materials from light, dust, and frequent handling often takes the form of putting them in folders or cabinets; aerial photographs, as previously mentioned, are often put in vertical files or in boxes. Protecting the emulsion surface is most important with remote-sensing images because emulsion is easily scratched and will crack if the image is folded. Atlases very often provide their own exterior protection, either by being bound or by coming from the publisher in boxes. Those items on display, such as globes and raised-relief maps, do need dusting every now and again.

Oversized Maps

Inevitably there are maps that will not fit into the map cases. There are several solutions to this problem: folding; trimming; rolling; and dissecting. Although a map almost inevitably tears (eventually) where it has been creased, the general feeling is that since map paper is usually high quality, "a single fold does little harm to a map" (Cunha 1971, 107). It is the double and triple folds, where creases intersect, that are so damaging. If the map's margins are quite wide, if the map is a mass-produced item that will be superseded, and if the map is irritatingly only slightly larger than the drawer, the margin can be trimmed off; the NIMA nautical charts apparently are printed on paper that comes in one width only, no matter what the size of the map to be printed on it, and often have an ocean (appropriately enough) of paper surrounding an island of map. If a double or triple fold would be required to make the map fit in the drawer, and the librarian does not believe in keeping rolled maps on the premises, the map may be dissected into pieces small enough to allow the map to fit in the drawer, which is what LCG&M does; here the risk is of slicing place names in half and just generally making the map a little harder to use. If the decision is made to roll the maps rather than to dissect or fold them more than once, the maps may be rolled, but with no less than a three-inch diameter; the rolled map should be protected, with either plastic tubing or linen (Cunha 1971, 107). The above does not relate to rare maps, which should be kept in their original state (if not injurious to the map), stored flat, and not dissected (Bartlett and Marshall 1979; BonaDea 1997b; Treatment 1992).

Back to Filing

Materials should be filed carefully, so that they are not damaged, and accurately, so that they may be found. For example, a map or aerial photograph that is out of place is extremely difficult to find because the items have no spines, and files cannot be read nearly as easily and as quickly as can book shelves. Containers should be kept tightly closed when not in use (to keep out dust and light), and should not be completely full to the top; horizontal map case drawers should be about one-half to three-quarters full. Under no circumstances should one disconsolate corner of a map be left hanging out of a drawer, and care should be taken that front retainers do not crease the maps. Maps of uniform size in a drawer should be neatly stacked and aligned, lined up with the corners of the drawers, for any map edge left protruding will either become dog-eared or be torn off.

When topographic quadrangles are being filed, it is best to arrange the maps to be filed in reverse order, and then to take out of the drawer all maps that would be on top of the first map in the reverse-order stack of maps to be filed; that first map should then be filed in the map drawer. On top of it, all maps coming between it and the next map to be filed should be placed; then the next map to be filed should be put in, and then the next stack of maps that come between the just-filed map and the following map to be filed, and so forth. It would be much easier if these maps could simply be shoved right into a stack of maps; but they crumple up like accordions when that is done.

Libraries with closed stacks are in an enviable position; they may keep all their maps flat and enforce that rule. Libraries with open stacks may have to compromise on this matter, following the rule that if a map is received folded, and the publisher obviously intends that it is to be kept that way (e.g., by having an envelope for the map with considerable bibliographic information on it; see USGS Geologic quadrangle maps, GQ), then it may be best to leave it that way, and file it on standard bookshelves. The primary reason for this is that in an open-stack situation, users often meticulously refold any map with fold marks on it and attempting to stop them from doing so is a losing battle. There are a few desirable side effects of filing folded maps folded; standard book shelving may be used, and such maps may be checked out easily by a computerized checkout system.

While on the one hand a fold at one time inevitably means a tear on that fold at some later time, it does create problems when folded maps are separated from accompanying texts. If the maps are separated from the texts for the sake of preservation of the maps, then in the text there must be printed by the title of the map in the list of illustrations the map's new call number and location. The map in its turn must have the call number (and preferably the author and title) of the text from which it came.

Finally, the User! Who, of Course, Needs a Copy

Sooner or later (sooner, we hope, for the sake of our continued employment), all of this patient, careful filing will be disrupted by that simultaneous *raison d'être* and spanner in the works, the user. Careful use means that the materials are handled gently, keeping in mind that the hardcopy ones very often have no cover. No food or drink should be permitted in the readers' area. Readers must often be cautioned not to fold maps; especially when a user is looking at an area covered by four topo quads, the urge to fold back the margins is hard to resist. Pencils instead of pens (or preferably a PC) are a good idea, as are white cotton gloves if remote-sensing transparencies, or rare materials of any kind, are being used (Guide 1977).

Because of the librarian's ceaseless reading of acquisition publications, sufficient funds to purchase items the librarian believes are needed, and a measure of good luck, the user will find the item he or she needs, and will probably consider it a right, not a privilege, to obtain a photocopy of at least a portion of said item. The user's choices are several: purchase the item from issuing agency; steal the item from the library; or have the item reproduced. The librarian will have appropriate information on how to do the first, will discourage the second, and will be prepared to explain how to do the third.

The most basic preservation of materials once they have been acquired is to hold onto them, and not to allow them to be stolen. There are only two effective ways to do this: have a closed-stack hardcopy collection; and have data available in digital form so that users may have copies as licenses and copyright allow. Read Otness 1988 and Harvey 1997 if you need any further convincing about how rampant stealing of materials in open-stack libraries is. If this persuades you to go the closed-stack route, the next "must" reading is the guidelines that RBMS (ALA Rare Books and Manuscript Section) has prepared for security of special collections (ALA RBMS 1989).

Copyright

On the hardcopy side, many maps, and among these the heavily used topo quads, are U.S. government documents and therefore not copyrighted. But if the item is privately or commercially produced or if it is a government-issued map that is copyrighted (as are, for example, the British topographic series sheets), and if there is any indication that the user plans to use the photocopy in anything other than a "fair use" way, then the user needs to be warned. In many libraries, these legal limitations are posted over the photocopier. It is wise to look very carefully for any copyright symbol on a map, and indeed all other spatial data including satellite images, and to assume that non-U.S.-government-produced maps are indeed copyrighted unless specifically stated otherwise (Ferrazzani and Thiebaut 1993; Questions 1990; Wolf 1992).

Copyright as it applies to digital materials has been an active field of discussion over the past several years, with publications on intellectual property in the digital world (National Humanities Alliance 1997) and copyright and libraries in the digital environment (Risher 1996). This is a very complex area, and comment here will be limited to noting that the wise librarian will pay close attention to any and all copyright and license restrictions on any and all digital data and software (Suchan 1996).

Photocopies and Photographic Copies

Next comes the question of what kind of copy is appropriate. Many libraries have only black-and-white copiers, and only 8½" x 11" and 11" x 17" sizes available, although there may be color, engineering (such as the Xerox 2510, Gestetner 1824ZS, and OCE 7050; copies 36" wide), or blueline (for copying large items in one sheet) copiers elsewhere in town or on campus. For the user rolling in money, there is always photography—which has the virtue of being in color but can easily be several hundred dollars for copying what is to a librarian a medium-sized map (say 3' x 3'). The question of type of copy arises because the same unique qualities that make maps useful and beautiful—legibility, color, fine detail, irregular format, and wide range in type sizes as is suited to the subject—also make maps difficult to copy adequately (Ehrenberg 1973b, 20; Ehrenberg 1976; Hawken 1966, 65; LaHood 1973, 19). Color on maps is not just ornamentation; it carries information, and as such it is often vital. The color and the size create problems when a standard photocopier is used; the absence of color may make the result hard to read, and taping together 8½ " x 11" swaths of photocopy may ruin the user's disposition, not to mention deplete the librarian's tape supply. A compromise is, for maps that the library will check out, for the user to take the map to a commercial reproduction service, and there have a copy made at a more reasonable price than photography. Another road to take is to make in advance color copies of maps for which one knows there will be high usage—such as those accompanying geologic theses and dissertations of the library's local area (Newman 1989).

Yet another option is having the collection placed on color microform, usually on fiche; this has been done for geologic maps and for such map series as the 1:75,000-scale topographic series for the Austro-Hungarian Empire (Scott 1993; Klimley 1993; Maps on microfiche 1988; Mayayo and Lozano 1989; Microfilming 1985). There is some opinion that microform should be an interim step before scanning, since microform has proven to be a mature technology with long-lived products (see Hennenberger 1994, and Martin Gubler and Thomas Klvti's "Colour microfilm as preliminary stage of digital maps," at http://ubeclu.unibe.ch/stub/ryhiner/ry-micr1.html). WAML has an active and successful map microform project, with many series already available; work is done in black and white (Cruse 1985; see any issue of the WAML Information bulletin for a list of titles available). For general background on microform in libraries, see:

Microforms in libraries, a manual for evaluation and management. 1985. Chicago: ALA.

Preservation microfilming, a guide for librarians and archivists. 1987. Chicago: ALA.

Digital Versions

Reformatting, by whatever name, is becoming more and more popular, especially when that reformatting is into digital form. Increasingly a user's first question is, "Is this available in digital form?" and if that answer to that is no, "What's the quickest way I can get it into digital form?" Spatial-data collections thus need to have scanners, digitizers, color copiers, and probably plotters. See in chapter 1 on Selection and Acquisition, the section on "Spatial Data in Digital Form," subsection "Hardware."

The librarian new to the field needs to learn basics of scanning and digitization, and to make decisions as to which items should be put into digital form in anticipation of heavy user demand. Some discussion on hardware and formats is given in chapter 1 on Selection and Acquisition, in the section, "Spatial Data in Digital Form." There are so many useful publications that it is difficult to know where to begin; here are the author's personal favorites:

Allen, David Yehling. 1997. Digital imaging for the rest of us. Kodak PhotoCD and Kodak PRO PhotoCD. *Meridian* 12: 15-18.

Besser, Howard; and Trant, Jennifer. 1995. Introduction to imaging. Santa Monica, Calif.: Getty Art History Information Program. Also available at http://www.ahip.getty.edu/intro_imaging

Digital imaging technology for preservation, proceedings from an RLG Symposium held March 17 and 18, 1994. Mountain View, Calif.: RLG.

Digitizing technologies for preservation. 1996. Washington, D.C.: Association of Research Libraries. (SPEC kit 214)

Ester, Michael. 1996. Digital image collections, issues and practice. Washington, D.C.: Commission on Preservation and Access.

Kenney, Anne R.; and Chapman, Stephen. 1996. Digital imaging for libraries and archives. Ithaca: Cornell University Library, Dept. of Preservation and Conservation.

Klimley, Susan. 1996. Digital preservation: The promise vs. the reality. Geoscience Information Society. Proceedings 26:5-9. For examples of scanned geologic maps from Ms. Klimley's work, see http://www.Columbia.edu/imaging/html/largemaps/oversized.html .

Preserving digital information, report of the Task Force on Archiving of Digital Information. 1996. Washington, D.C.: Commission on Preservation and Access.

Robinson, Peter. 1993. The digitization of primary textual sources: Office for Humanities Communication. (Office for Humanities Communication publications, no. 4)

There is a certain amount of duplication and disagreement amongst these publications, which greatly encourages the librarian to compare and contrast what each is talking about and figure out how it applies to spatial data. A substantial decision is whether one is scanning only to make an item generally available or for preservation purposes, with the idea that the actual item would seldom or never be consulted afterward. The emphasis in spatial-data collections currently is for the first purpose, so there is scanning at, for example, 600 dpi, rather than, say, to a resolution of 12 microns (the size of silver grains in photographic emulsion) which would be required to provide preservation scanning of aerial photographs. Relevant listservs are Imagelib (subscribe at listserv@listserv.arizona.edu) and Photo-CD (subscribe at listserv@info.kodak.com).

A useful list of selection criteria for deciding which items to put into digital form was written by the University of California Libraries Preservation Committee in 1996. The high points are as follows:

- meets information needs of users

- has advocacy from one or more broad scholarly constituents

- has a preservation problem (e.g., at risk of damage or loss because of high use, poor housing, etc.)

- generates institutional prestige

- digital version adds information value over hardcopy version (e.g., greater functionality, such as the ability to manipulate the data)

- contributes to the "critical mass" of digital materials in the subject

- has a commitment from the library to its maintenance over time and across changes in technology (for refreshment and migration as needed) and security threats

- can be adequately captured in digital form

- can be integrated into library service programs

- is accessible from institutionally supported computing platforms and networked environments, conforming to standards in use by the library community

- can be delivered with reasonable speed

- solves technical problems with access to originals or consolidates diverse formats

- is controlled as appropriate by any restrictions to access

- uses an interface easy to master by ordinary users

- has appropriate metadata for identification and search

- can be authenticated.

For an example of one group's draft plan for making spatial data in digital form available to its users, see Larry Carver's 1996 draft of "Alexandria Digital Library for Spatially Indexed Information," at http://www.alexandria.ucsb.edu/tilde carver/ucop3.htm .

Libraries with old and rare maps would be well advised to have the maps scanned into digital form and to have negatives of their maps made, from which copies—often as color slides—can be made on request (Critchley 1970, 68). Another option is to make a photocopy of each map, for patron consultation, so that the original can be protected and preserved. Before any negatives are made, the filming staff should be informed of the large size and value of the maps, and it should be made clear that tacks and tape are vetoed. If a map of considerable value is to be used as a base map and traced, it should first be covered by a heavy-gauge tracing screen (Nichols 1976, 273).

Loaning

Loaning is a form of accelerated aging. Any item to be loaned out must be protected. Globes and plastic models may be checked out in boxes and cartons, while maps, the most often loaned of materials, go out in tubes, and remote-sensing images (positives only, please, never negatives) in stiff envelopes or large-diameter tubes, as is appropriate to the size of the item. Before a map is put into a tube, it must be completely unfolded, or creases will form perpendicular to the fold. If it cannot be completely unfolded, at the very least it must be folded only once and rolled parallel, not perpendicular, to the fold. If the tube is to be mailed, crumpled paper should be placed in one end of the tube, that end taped securely on the outside, the maps rolled and inserted, then crumpled paper put in the remaining open end, and that end also taped securely (Easton 1970, 200). Include with the checked-out map the following list: tips on how to remove and put back in the map tube, and warning that any markings or damage may be cause for replacement (and give cost of a color photocopy of a 4' x 5' map for emphasis).

If at all possible—and it usually is not, because of the large size of maps—the maps should be mailed flat in boxes or cartons, with stiff boards on top and bottom to provide protection. Mounted maps are difficult to roll in a tube because of the extra bulk of the backing; nor is such rolling good for the maps because the curvature places stress on the map, with more pull on the outside of the roll than the inside, and thus the map will begin to tear away from its backing.

When any item is returned from loan, it must be checked for injuries (previous injuries should have been noted on the checkout record); if the maps have ever been folded, tears will appear at the edges of the map on the fold, and should be repaired immediately, before they extend. Many librarians believe that since maps "offer special acquisitions problems, even a map printed in quantity and for sale may be considered difficult to replace and therefore not for loaning" (Alonso 1968, 17). This is an administrative decision that the librarian must make, based on holdings, users, and availability of replacements. Some libraries have a 50-year cutoff rule; any items published more than 50 years before the current year do not get checked out. If the decision is made to loan out materials, the librarian must be sure to have appropriate tubes and boxes available for the purpose.

Barcoding of maps has been done at several libraries, such as those of Johns Hopkins, Pennsylvania State University, the University of Utah, and the University of Kentucky. Because the adhesive of the barcodes is in all likelihood not acid-free, it is best not to barcode rare maps, to say the very least.

Damage and Repair

Damage may be mechanical, chemical, or a combination of the two. In this section only damage to paper will be discussed.

Mechanical Damage

Mechanical damage can result from the actions of rodents, insects, fungi, poor storage, and careless, frequent use; it includes such problems as surface soil, tears, and fungi-inflicted damage. Silverfish are interested in paper's starch and gelatin content, while cockroaches prefer glue and paste, and termites (not being picky) will eat the entire contents of a map drawer with persistence and gusto. Rodents like the multipurpose aspect of paper, not only eating it but also shredding it for their nests. Mold and fungi will, with their powdery deposits, eventually stain paper, and then make it "soft and absorbent as blotting paper" (Capps 1972 in Drexel library quarterly 1973, 66-67), reducing it in time to a pulp. Discoloration and brown spots on old paper, called foxing, are signs of fungi at work some time in the past; it generally occurs along the outside borders of a book and works its way inward (Iliams and Beckwith 1935, 416). Photo-graphs can have tears and scratches; this is especially true of roll film, which can be damaged by roll holders.

Chemical Damage

More destructive than mechanical damage is chemical damage, spe-cifically acidic chemical damage. It is signaled by the discoloration, yellow-ing, and brittleness of paper. Atmospheric impurities, such as sulfur dioxide, contribute to the acidification and thus the deterioration of paper; as was previously noted, excess heat and light accelerate that reaction, besides encouraging mechanical damage, as does excess humidity (Capps 1972 in Drexel library quarterly, 62-65). Photographs can become brown (conditions too moist), yellow and spotty (exposure to oxidizing gases), or yellowish-brown (oxidation again; poor storage); or frames can stick together, either one emulsion stuck to the back of the other or two emulsions stuck together.

Repair

The rules for repair are: first, do not do what you cannot undo; and second, make sure that no information is lost. For the vast majority of libraries, "map repair will be largely confined to mending torn maps" (Royal Geographical Society 1955, 186). For libraries in the past, this meant the surreptitious use of standard transparent adhesive tapes, the mere thought of which makes all paper care and preservation sources draw back in horror (Guldbeck 1972, 66; Minogue 1943, 24; Pidek 1974, 46; Boak 1970, 22; Scriven 1956, 442). In the last twenty years preservation has become a matter of increasing interest to U.S. libraries, and a spatial-data librarian's request for the purchase of acid-free tape will fit right in with what everyone else in the library is ordering. Tape of any kind should never be used on rare, valuable, or archival maps. The solvents required to remove tapes have to be strong and therefore may be quite injurious to the paper; Scotch Magic Mending Tape, in use since 1963, has an adhesive that is almost insoluble in even the strongest solvent (Landers 1970, 466; Alonso 1973, 10; R. J. Lee 1955, 28-29).

Another repair and care action in which most librarians will become involved is the removal of dirt. The best route to follow is to attack—gently—with an art-gum or pencil eraser and a soft brush, or a document cleaning pad (and of course be sure your hands are clean before you start). If the dirt is deeply ingrained, there are those who claim flour or bread may be used to remove it; others believe that flour or bread is not sufficiently abrasive to do anything except cover up the dirt, and would in any case attract insects and rodents (Clapp 1974; Plenderleith 1969, 73; Kidd 1977a, 84). It is while dealing with a map that has been in someone's basement for years, the entire surface of which seems to be covered with dirt, that we may wish that maps were still being printed on linen and silk, and could be washed.

If the librarian has any repairs needed beyond the above, stop: "There may be other things that can be done, but you and I do not know enough about paper and chemicals to do them" (Scriven 1956, 440).

More Advanced Care and Repair

The majority of libraries, even with the increasing emphasis on preservation, are not equipped, with either personnel, equipment, or materials, to do more than the simple repairs described in the previous section. How care and preservation problems may be solved or at least ameliorated will be discussed in the next several pages, but this is most assuredly not a recommendation that the librarian proceed to perform these tasks. Rather, it is to make the librarian aware of the possibilities and thus to be able to have at least some knowledge when discussing a course of action with persons who do conservation work for a living.

If erasing will not clean paper, it may be cleaned by immersing it in water, or by applying local treatment, such as solvents, to specific stains. The first method has a few drawbacks. Inks, for example, must be tested first for waterfastness, with a very small drop of water in an inconspicuous corner, which is blotted after a short time. Color inks are especially suspect. If the ink blurs, all inked portions must be covered with a protective coating, such as a thin solution of cellulose acetate in acetone, before immersion (Minogue 1943, 23). If any part of a sheet of paper needs to be wetted, it all must be, in order to avoid the wrinkling caused by unequal expansion and contraction. The sheer size of most maps makes this a difficult procedure; not only is it hard to obtain the equivalent of a photographic tray in the giant economy size, but it is also difficult to manipulate the support (either glass or heavy plastic) upon which the wet map is placed while it is in the tray. Wet paper, as formerly noted, has little strength, and should not be handled directly; so the map is taken out of the water resting entirely upon a support.

If the difficulties of finding a container can be overcome, the recommended procedure entails soaking the map in cold water for about one hour, followed by drying slightly, placing between blotters, putting weights on top of the blotter sandwich, and leaving the whole arrangement alone for three to four weeks (Scriven 1956, 440). The entire process will take large amounts of space, equipment, skill, and time.

An added problem arises because paper immersed in water loses its sizing (the gelatinous substance added to paper stock to glaze the surface, add strength, and keep the ink from spreading). When washed, paper therefore becomes limp and soft, and needs to be either resized or put in some sort of permanent support. To resize, the paper is immersed in the sizing solution and slid out, and the sheet then put between backing boards and into a finishing press to squeeze out surplus liquid (Lydenberg and Archer 1960, 68-69).

For various stains, certain solvents are recommended:

oil, adhesive tape	carbon tetrachloride; benzene; xylene (especially for tape); trichloroethylene; n-hexane
wax, rubber cement	mixture of benzene and toluene; 1 part acetone plus 3 parts alcohol plus 3 parts toluene
glue	warm water
lacquer	acetone
paint	mixture of alcohol and benzene
shellac	ethyl alcohol

(Boak 1970, 23; Guldbeck 1972, 66; Minogue 1943, 24; Topic IV 1976, 81)

The alert librarian will note that almost all of the solvents just mentioned are not only poisonous but also flammable—not an endearing combination—and should be used only in a well-ventilated room from which all smokers are firmly excluded. The general technique is putting the paper, stained side down, on a white blotter and putting solvent on from the back, perhaps with cotton swabs or cotton wool, and then proceeding to perform such tasks as lifting off tape—slowly and carefully (Lydenberg and Archer I 960, 67).

Treatment of Varnish

Many old maps were varnished in their youth in order to preserve them. With age, the varnish has yellowed, become brittle, and sometimes insoluble. When it can be removed, a painstaking procedure (flooding the map with repeated baths of solvent, then rinsing and bleaching and drying under weights) must be followed. If the varnish resists solvents, hot water will sometimes soften it so that it flakes away; but such a method is not advisable for maps that have colored inks (Plenderleith 1969, 71-72; Map conservation 1976, 44).

Treatment of Foxing

Foxing, caused by dampness, fungal activity, metallic impurities, or decay, leaves dull, rusty patches on paper. The only presently economical way to remove such patches is to bleach with chemicals, such as a two percent solution of Chloramine T, or a two percent solution of sodium chlorite plus five ounces of 40 percent formaldehyde. Since these, like all bleaches, are acid, using them will weaken the paper, and it is often wiser to do nothing other than fumigate (so that the foxing proceeds no further), unless the paper is in otherwise good condition (Lydenberg and Archer 1960, 71; Minogue 1943, 25). Paper disfigured by ink stains, as by foxing, is also better left alone, as any treatment removing the ink will weaken the paper (Lydenberg and Archer 1960, 71).

Treatment of Tears

There are far more sophisticated ways of mending tears than using tape, but they involve painstaking work. The mend should be made with a paper of the same composition as the paper to be mended. The grain of the patch must be aligned with that of the paper; the direction of grain of machine-made paper is found by moistening two edges at right angles, after which the paper swells in the direction across the grain and displays a wrinkled appearance along the edge. For all-purpose mending onionskin paper or Japanese tissue can be used (Scriven 1956, 442).

Paste used in this sort of mending should be homemade wheat paste. Making flour paste is a very personal thing; like gravy, it requires that the maker abhor lumps, be willing to strain, and be ready to make up a fresh batch for each session. Library paste is a slightly dishonorable alternative (Scriven 1956, 442-43; Plenderleith 1969, 86; Waters 1976; Poole l976b).

Once all the materials have been assembled, paste is applied only to the tear, and a piece of the mending tissue about one inch wide is placed over the tear and allowed to dry. Blotters are placed on both sides of the mend, the whole is placed under a weight for a few minutes, and blotters are then replaced as needed at five-minute intervals (Guldbeck 1972, 67; Scriven 1956, 443). Since adhesives and papers react at different rates, and since rare items should be kept in their original state, they should probably not be mended, but rather should have strength applied externally and removably, by such means as polyester encapsulation, a method that will be explained later in this chapter.

Treatment of Mold

If the librarian can catch mold fast enough, it can be wiped off with a cloth dampened in alcohol; if not, and even if so, the paper must be put into a fumigation chamber. Small fumigation chambers can be made of metal boxes with a 40-watt light bulb inside the box, near which a container of thymol is placed; it must be remembered that, just like the molds and fungi, human beings are organic, and what can kill the first two can do the same to the third. Mold spores are in the air everywhere, so fumigation must be followed by proper storage conditions of low humidity and moderate temperature. Mildew disinfectant spray is available for use when storage conditions are difficult to change (Harmon 1993; Poole 1976b; Topic IV 1976, 80; Wellheiser 1992).

Supporting Materials and Backing

Over the years, the concern for lengthening the life of paper has caused the development and use of several methods of reinforcing or supporting paper. Almost all of them require special equipment and some measure of skill and careful handiwork. Some of the more often used of these techniques are inlaying, glazing, sizing, edging, mounting (on silk, Japanese tissue, muslin, jaconet, cardboard, and plywood), lamination, and, in the last twenty years with increasing frequency, polyester encapsulation.

Inlaying is framing a document in permanent paper to protect its edges; considerable practice is needed to do this well, and it does not actually strengthen the paper, but is done more for display purposes. Glazing is the insertion of yellow-colored film between two thin sheets of ordinary glass, and placing the composite in front of items on display. Sizing, to strengthen paper, has been discussed previously. Edging of maps with acid-free tape to reinforce edges has been done with some frequency in spatial-data collections in the past, largely because it is easy to do (Catlin 1976, 60).

The most used method—the first two of which have passed out of use in libraries because of their preservation drawbacks—are mounting, lamination, and (the most recently developed) polyester film encapsulation. It is a pleasure to report that the last named, which is the only one that is immediately reversible, is also the easiest to do.

Mounting

Mounting is like classification and cataloging in that everyone has a favorite method (Thomas and Lloyd 1964; Raisz 1948, 222; Throop 1933, 150; G. Williams 1952, 7; Schmitz 1941, 766; Mackin 1936, 234; Kramer 1952, 21-23; LeGear 1956, 28-35; Wardle 1971, 11-12, 38-43; S. Miller 1979, 175; P. L. Phillips 1921, 15-17; Guldbeck 1972, 68-69; Scriven 1956, 444). Maps have been mounted on linen or other cloth for at least the last three hundred years (Bagrow 1975, 1:16). Documents have been mounted on almost everything—plywood, cardboard, fabric (usually muslin, linen, or jaconet), heavy paper, and window shades. The basic process starts with wetting the cloth and the map, then stretching the cloth on a mounting board, spreading paste on the cloth surface, smoothing and pressing the map with a rubber roller or squeegee, and drying, usually under weights. Almost all of the writers who give directions on how to mount maps begin either with an awesome list of equipment, or an injunction that mounting requires some little skill, or both; they are replete with such instructions as "Mix paste to whipping cream consistency" (G. Williams 1952, 7) and such friendly warnings as:

"It is as well for two persons to work together in making the transfer from table to table; the map must be reversed in order to bring the pasted portion in contact with the cloth, and if the worker attempts the task alone, he may find only two corners in his hands, the rest of the paste-soaked paper having fallen to the floor" (Nute I 936, 60).

Success in this tricky procedure is dependent on the skill of the worker in such matters as keeping the cloth taut and on the accessibility of the work area.

Although cloth is the backing most often used, expert opinion holds that pure rag paper backing, of the same weight as the item being mounted, is preferable. Cardboard and wood should not be used; they contribute to the acidification of the paper (Cunha 1971, 105 Guldbeck 1972, 68-69). Some librarians turned to a special kind of mounting, whose brand name is Chartex. Here the cloth backing comes impregnated with a moisture-proof adhesive (which of course means it is not appropriate for archival materials or indeed anything a library intends to keep for a long time). The map is placed on the cloth and put in a dry mount press, or an iron is applied by hand (yet another no-no). This method does require much less "ingenuity, dexterity, and patience" than does ordinary mounting (LeGear 1956, 26).

To touch briefly on equipment: one item that looms large, literally and figuratively, in any mounting scheme is the mounting table, which should be "as large as there is room for" (Wardle 1971, 11). About I4½' x 6½' would be a minimum area.

A variant of mounting that makes the item more durable but not more permanent is crepelining. Thin silk gauze is put on top, and sometimes also on the underneath side, of a map. Japanese tissue may be used in a similar fashion, giving fair permanence, but the tissue does age, and it obscures printing and detail. In either case, it is a task for skilled labor (Minogue 1943, 30-31).

Plastic raised-relief maps may be mounted by such methods as filling the pockets with foam rubber or plaster of Paris (U.S. AMS 1964, 9, 12).

There are some disadvantages to mounting. It is time-consuming; the soaking of maps may damage color or cause a change in scale; it requires considerable skill to do well, not to mention a large working area and substantial investment in materials; and mounted maps tend to wrinkle, ripple, and billow when subjected to changes in temperature and humidity (S. Miller 1971, 54; Mackin 1936, 234; Kathpalia 1973, 142; U.S. AMS 1964, 4). Experience in working with paper is important, for papers differ, and each reacts differently to moisture, just as the backing's response to moisture differs from that of the map.

Lamination

Lamination is the fusing by heat and pressure of a sandwich of Japanese tissue, acetate, document, acetate, and Japanese tissue, or a sandwich of polyester film, document, polyester film (in its most simplistic version). Cellulose acetate makes a protective covering that is "relatively permanent and resistant to bacteria, fungi, insects, and to gases" (LeGear 1956, 24). It protects the document from dust and liquids, gives added strength, body, and flexibility, and leaves the laminated item thicker, heavier, and easily readable; it seemed not only to reinforce but also to preserve (Snyder et al. l970b, 9; Harrow 1965; U.S. AMS 1961, 8; Nixon 1949).

Lamination was first used on a large scale by the U.S. National Archives in the late l930s and early l940s when that institution, finding itself with large numbers of records and relatively little personnel, needed a mass production kind of preservation; lamination seemed to be the answer. Even then, there were some misgivings: What about the permanence of the laminate? Would it discolor and become brittle? Would the document encased do the same? What about subjecting the documents to the heat and pressure of the laminating press? Why were papers not deacidified before laminating? Was the process reversible? (Evans 1946, 320-21; Nixon 1949, 32-36).

The questioners were right; there are a few flies in the laminate. First of all, any item to be laminated should be cleaned and its inks tested for solubility; if the inks are vagrant, a solution of cellulose acetate dissolved in acetone brushed over the document will lock ink into the paper. Next, and most important, the document must be deacidified (more about this later); if not, it will continue to deteriorate inside its cellulose acetate envelope after lamination, and the deterioration process will be speeded up by the heat of the press. The process is reversible only with difficulty, and lamination with polyester film is almost impossible to reverse.

Polyester-Film Encapsulation

While lamination may be appropriate for materials that the library does not plan to keep, it should not be used for anything else (Cunha 1967, 105; Waters 1975, 19; Poole 1975, 157). LC now recommends the use of polyester-film encapsulation, which, although the finished product may be heavier than lamination and has a gloss, provides a strong, instantly reversible support medium. In this technique the document is protected by an edge-sealed polyester envelope, an envelope that is almost impossible to fracture no matter how rough the handling. The original is not harmed or changed in any way, and the process does not require highly trained personnel; expensive equipment may be purchased (a machine that seals the edges), or double-sided tape may be used. In the early 1980s, many concerns were voiced about encapsulating items that had not been deacidified; after some study, it was determined that putting a piece of buffered paper in with the encapsulated item eliminated the acceleration in the decline of the physical properties of acidic paper upon encapsulation (Marley 1987).

The materials needed for this technique are polyester film (3 mil; 5 and 7 mil for maps larger than about 3' x 4' may be used; 50" wide, 120-pound rolls), and two-sided-adhesive acrylic tape. The film to be used is Type D Mylar (DuPont), Melinex type O (ICI), or Scotchpar (3-M). The film may be purchased directly from the companies, but they usually sell it only in rolls (which may be several hundred yards), so the librarians in any one institution may want to pool their purchase order. The tape is Scotch double-surfaced adhesive type no. 415 from 3-M; here again, the tape may be purchased in bulk from 3-M, or it may be purchased in smaller quantities from preservation firms such as Hollinger. Tools needed are a sharp knife or scalpel, a window-cleaning squeegee, lint-free dustcloths, a rubber roller (brayer), a few two-pound weights with felt or leather on the bottom, and a heavy sheet of paper ruled in squares and covered with plate glass, all on a large table.

For each document to be encapsulated, cut two pieces of film two inches longer and two inches wider than the document. Place one sheet of film on the glass with the two adjacent edges on grid lines, and wipe with lint-free cloth to remove all dust particles and to create a static electric charge. Place a sheet of paper containing an alkaline reserve in the center of the film, and then center the document on the film. Place a weight on it to hold it in position. Place a strip of tape (leaving backing paper on one side) on each of the four sides of the film, leaving one-eighth to one-half inch at each corner for air circulation. Polyester film tends to curl, so place it so that the curved surfaces oppose each other. After dusting the surface of the top sheet of polyester to be in contact with the document, place the film on top of the document and squeegee carefully to force as much air as possible out of the envelope. Place a weight on top; reach under the edge of the top sheet and pull the backing paper from one strip of tape, then from an adjacent strip. Squeegee the film along these two taped edges, and then repeat the process with the remaining two sides. Go over the tape firmly with a rubber roller to make the envelope ripple-free. Trim the envelope, rounding the corners, so that about $\frac{1}{16}$ inch of film remains outside tape lines on all four sides. For more specific details, see LC's Polyester film encapsulation (1980). The whole process will take about half an hour for a 22" x 29" map (Rieke, Gyeszly, and Steele 1984).

Deacidification

Deacidification processes aim to introduce a sufficient quantity of an alkaline chemical into the paper to neutralize the paper's acidic components; the chemical may be aqueous, nonaqueous, or vapor. Aqueous methods mean soaking the paper or spraying it with a saturated solution of water and calcium or magnesium bicarbonate, carbonate, or hydroxide. Nonaqueous deacidification consists of using a nonwaterbased liquid solution of an organic solvent and an alkaline deacidification liquid. Organic solvents wet paper more rapidly, have less distorting effect on the paper, and are easier to dry from the paper than is water (R. D. Smith 1972, p. 63). The vapor method will be explained later, after a brief history of deacidification. Maps that are becoming brittle but are not falling apart may be considered candidates for deacidification.

Three entities—two persons (W. J. Barrow; R. D. Smith) and one institution (LC)—are known for their work in deacidification. Barrow developed equipment for lamination and thus became involved in deacidification; he died in 1967. R. D. Smith runs a firm that sells Wei T'o solutions and sprays. Wei T'o (in aerosol spray cans) stabilizes paper by neutralizing the acids, and by preventing future reacidification; it is nonflammable, nonpoisonous, and nonexplosive, and it's easier to use Wei T'o in preference to making up one's own solutions. LC in its work on a mass deacidification system, the Diethyl Zinc (DEZ) process developed at LC, came head-to-head with Smith. According to Smith, his Wei T'o process provides broader protection against hazards other than deacidification (for example, DEZ does not protect against oxidation); the DEZ process involves a fire hazard that makes it unsafe for use in a library, and Wei T'o is cheaper—the $11 million spent by LC would build a number of smaller Wei T'o systems that would have in toto the capacity of processing a great many more books than the DEZ facility (Fort Detrick in Maryland). LC stated that the DEZ process offers the best answer to LC's problem of salvaging the books it now holds and creating new ones as they come to the library; LC acknowledged alternatives, and itself used Wei T'o in some cases (see Library hotline 14[11 February 1985]:1).

The LC-Wei-T'o wars continued on for a while after this; the reader is referred to Porck 1996 for recent status and to library literature generally for history. Even now, ten years after the original dissension, published statements are still cautious, emphasizing that mass deacidification is not a universal panacea, and that there are several options for deacidification, including DEZ, Bookkeeper, Battelle, and Wei T'o. In the last few years, the Harvard Map Collection has had mass deacidification done on some of its maps. Some map libraries have used the Wei T'o spray and find it an acceptable way to stabilize a map, at a reasonable cost; caution is advised in using it on very rare maps or on blueprints (Harris and Shahani 1994; Porck 1996; Study 1989; Turko 1990).

Care of Other Spatial Data

Atlases require the same sort of care as do other books; the only major difference is that they are usually larger than other books and thus may, through improper shelving and frequent use, need attention more often. Be warned that when they need rebinding, the necessary clipping of gutters will mean the loss of information in many cases. In some cases, one may need to unbind an atlas and encapsulate each page separately, as has been done with the Sanborn atlases at the Library of Congress, and then reassemble, probably in a post binding, or file in map cases (Baynes-Cope 1985; Internationale 1985). Those librarians needing persuasion that restoration of atlases damaged by water or paint should be left to experts need to read Blank 1984, Dahl, Hill and Murphy 1995, Perminova 1994, Sumira 1992 and 1996, and Tracy 1997.

For information on archive conservation and preservation, see Cartographic archives 1982, Managing 1989, and Rhodes 1992.

Globes also present problems of care and restoration; they are susceptible to damage from dust, atmospheric change, humidity, dryness, and careless handling just as are other library materials. Restoration should be handled by experts; see the publication by Internationale Vereinigung Meister der Einbandkunst 1966. Everyday care of a globe is a common-sense matter of dusting, with occasional cleaning with a damp cloth, perhaps moistened with a mild soap if grubby fingers have left their mark.

Plastic raised-relief models also will require dusting and washing if they are on display. Plastic does tend to get brittle with age, and will crack if flexed beyond certain narrow limits; once it is broken, there is little that can be done, at least by a librarian.

Any deteriorating fabric maps around the place? Take a look at *Textiles in the Metropolitan Museum of Art* (1995) to see what you're up against. Although they should still be in good shape; according to an e-mail to MAPS-L on 3 October 1996 from Daniel Jansen, NARA (message-id, 9610031824.AA15502@atlas.sdc.ucsb.edu), the cloth for the World War II maps was tested for resistance to fading, mildew, salt-water degradation, and general weather and passed with "flying colors" (bit of a pun there, given they were used by airplane pilots whose vehicles had crashed).

With remote-sensing images the key point to remember is that the emulsion surface is very delicate, and will scratch and crack under conditions that would scarcely faze a map; color emulsions do not have the longevity of black and white emulsions, and may show signs of deterioration over the years. Photographs with their emulsions stuck together, or emulsion stuck to glass, are something for an expert to deal with. And of course we all know that if any film is other than silver halide, we should not count on keeping it very long. Spatial-data libraries do have microform, and should keep an eye out, reading general library literature to find out what the latest word on preservation of microforms is.

For information on care of digital materials, see in this chapter the section "Storing Other Materials." One special problem relating to conservation has to do with the times when a map is to be framed and put on display. When this occurs, the framing should be museum quality, with acid-free board and tape; the map must not touch the glass, which will conduct moisture and therefore mold. Light will be injurious to the map; some sort of acrylic transparent sheeting should be used as an ultraviolet screen, and the map should be on display for a short period of time. Better yet, have a good color copy of the map made, and display that.

Cheer up, matters could be worse—you could have foam-rubber maps, like the Hoover Institution Archives!

Conservation Experts, Yes—But Where Are They?

Ten years ago, the response to that question was "In England, mostly"; fortunately, there are now a goodly number of trained conservationists on this side of the pond. Frequently in this chapter, either by exact phrase or by implication, the message has been that special repair problems should be left to experts in that field. The problem is that conservators have not been exactly thick on the ground, although matters have improved as libraries have become more preservation-minded. The library looking for a conservator might try the American Institute for Conservation of Historic and Artistic Works, or look in issues of AB bookman; libraries in the same region with established conservation programs may also be of assistance.

There are several conservation centers in the U.S.—e.g., Archival Conservation Center (8225 Daly Road, Cincinnati OH 45231); Canadian Conservation Institute (many useful publications on the care of photographs; 1030 Innes Road, Ottawa K1A OM8); the Northeast Document Conservation Center (http://www.nedcc.org); Rocky Mountain Conservation Center (University of Denver); SOLINET Preservation Services (http://www.solinet.net/presvtn/preshome.htm); Heckman Bindery (POB 89, North Manchester IN 46992)—and in other countries, such as the Centro di studi per lo Conservazione della Carta (Via Festo Avieno, 92, 00136 Roma, Italy). Within the United States, the publications of the Commission on Preservation and Access are extremely helpful, and very often are "must" reading for the spatial-data librarian. The conservation listserv hosted by Stanford—Conservation Distlist, consdist@lindy.stanford.edu—is another good place to keep up to date on what is going on in the conservation-preservation world, and the 1993 Walsh, Hulyk and Barnum "packet" on preservation of government documents is a to-the-point summary of how to find and care for these items.

Moving a Map Library

Moving a map library is just the thing for the jaded map librarian who feels that life is dull and offers no further excitement. Planning a move may seem easy, but as time grinds on and M-Day approaches, and especially during the move, you will have all the excitement and frustration you can handle. Let us start at the beginning, focusing on hardcopy maps—moving traditional materials is dealt with in the standard move literature.

First, plan the move and start saving boxes and packing materials. Planning cuts down on misplaced and damaged items, and results in minimal interruption of services. Join forces with other librarians and persuade management to use professional library movers. If this course is not followed, and non-professional library movers are used—whether they be university physical-plant workers, library staff, or standard movers—the library will be sorry. Money saved will be lost when "helpers" unfamiliar with libraries or with moving fail to grasp the idea that items must remain in order, or drop valuable equipment, such as personal computers. The resultant frayed nerves could damage intralibrary relations and the continued successful operation of the library long after the move. One problem with having library staff help move is that many are women—a worthy sex, but usually not bulging with muscles; and women doing heavy moving may need to take sick leave afterward. Professionals do the job quickly and better than, rank beginners. Public libraries tend to use professional movers; universities and colleges tend to use physical plant, temporary help, and the library staff (Spyers-Duran 1965, p. 4).

A suitable time for moving will be chosen; preferably a period of at least a month during the slowest time of year (such as late summer for universities). A year's notice is preferred but six months will work. You should draw up a diagram of how the move will proceed, based on the number of items and the amount of equipment, taking extensive measurements of the new quarters and the equipment to be moved into it. Take special measurements of doors (of buildings and of elevators) and halls, matched to the dimensions of map cases and other equipment.

A copy of the map collection's moving plan should go to everyone involved, including the director of the library and the foreman of the work crew (Ibid., pp. 1-2; Schuyler in C. Lewis 1963, p. 45). The plan should be clearly and concisely stated, with diagrams. Two weeks before the move, depending on the size of the collection, maps should be prepared. Cases and drawers should be numbered and labeled in one sequence. Drawer interiors should be stabilized and braced even if drawers can be kept horizontal during the move; contents will shift. Drawers with full-sized map folders but without a dust cover can be braced by packing the drawers as full of maps as possible and placing a piece of masonite or a slightly filled full-size folder, with fold to the rear (tucked under the metal hood) on top; interiors may be stabilized using industrial-strength balloons, or packing material such as Styrofoam (Diennes 1995, pp. 20, 24).

If the doors are too narrow for the cases or drawers to be passed through on the level, cases may be gently tipped toward handles to get through, providing the contents were stablized and dust cover are in firmly in place.

Exactly how to move map cases is a problem that has different solutions. The University of Michigan transported cases flat in drawers or in folders on flat-bed dollies; University of Kansas moved cases on dollies, with glazier's suction cups used on some—LCG&M's movers used the latter. At Northwestern University, maps were removed from cases and packed in slit mirror cartons (Koerner 1971, pp. 33-34; Fortney 1971, p. 40; Diennes 1995). Some map-case makers warn that cases and drawers must be moved separately, presumably to keep the metal from warping, so check your equipment capabilities before making a decision. Generally speaking, removing maps from drawers is an unnecessary step; if the cases cannot be moved full, then stack the drawers cross-hatched, on dollies.

A few days before the move, pack up desk contents and supplies, leaving unpacked pressure-sensitive tape, masking tape, rubberbands, pen, pencil, felt-tipped pen, dust cloths, notepad, self-adhesive small notepads, and other supplies or tools that come to mind. Label all boxes and equipment, the latter with felt-tipped pen on masking tape, with the building and room number of the new location. Get out of the movers' way, go the new building with measuring tape, masking tape, felt-tip pen and plan diagram, and with masking tape mark out the location of the map cases, desks, files, and other equipment. It's a good idea to have the area vacuumed. The map librarian should read instructions to check for errors, give the instructions to whoever is in charge of the move, and make sure that everyone understands each other; you should know about union rules as to type of work done, breaks, and hours.

During the move, wear clothes appropriate to ditch digging and other forms of heavy labor—jeans, T-shirts, sneakers or other sturdy, comfortable shoes. Plan on about one day to move and unpack desk and office material, and—depending on methods and skill of the movers—from one to three days to move every 100,000 maps, or about one to two weeks for every 250 map cases (Diennes 1995, p. 16). Each day there should be a staff person on each end of the move—i.e., the packing and picking up, and the unloading and unpacking—to be sure that moving proceeds approximately as planned, and to make emergency decisions. After the move, plan on a couple months of settling in, including those moments when you wonder where you packed something.

Conclusion

Conservation of spatial data depends on using correct methods of handling, storage, and display in conditions inhibiting deterioration (Kathpalia 1973, 182). Librarians should select materials as much as possible with an eye to durability, examine them as they come in, and prescribe conservation treatment if needed before use, provide proper housing and care of materials, assume responsibility for their condition, and decide on policies for treatment, use, and discarding (Deterioration 1970, 182; Rieke 1985). Librarians who believe in planning ahead should, after making sure a disaster plan is up to date, take on a physical-condition-assessment survey; see Allen 1996 for a guide on this.

It would be helpful if preservation needs and information for an item could be in a field or fields on the bibliographic record. Ideally, software could then provide notification of when certain preservation tasks need to be done, as is performed now when single periodical issues are called to bind (Hendriks and Hopkins 1985; Kruger 1988).

Items being considered for repair should first be evaluated. Is it in good condition, sufficiently rare, or important enough to be conserved? Would it be sufficient to preserve intellectual content by scanning into digital form or photographing it for display? Is it frequently used? If repair of a rare item is a necessity, these principles should be observed:

1. the originality of the document should not be disturbed in any way.

2. the repair should be neat, tidy, evident, but not obtrusive.

3. writing, color, and detail should be marred or impaired as little as possible.

4. the process should be reversible.

5. the process should provide maximum reinforcement at minimum cost.

6. materials used for repair should be durable and permanent.
(Kathpalia 1973, 81-84)

When it is decided that an item needs rehabilitation, the librarian should remember that good intentions are not enough:

"Nothing is more bitterly ironic than the well-intended but mistaken steps that are sometimes taken to protect valuable items—makeshift measures that, so far from providing the protection intended, may add to the damage already done by accident or long neglect . . . It is therefore important that the amateur makes no moves in this direction until he knows exactly what he is about" (Scriven 1956, 447).

Another point to consider is use of common items; current map sheets, especially heavily used ones such as topographic quadrangles, are often treated in a cursory way, mainly because they are—at that particular moment—common. The librarian is advised to obtain multiple copies of such high-use items and keep one encapsulated and permanently locked away, for consultation only after all kamikaze copies have fallen apart or disappeared (and they will), and only in a secure room. Without this sort of planning ahead, one year's common item will become next year's rarity, as has happened with so many pre-1920 Canadian and USGS topographic sheets (Layng 1967, 35; Map collections in Canada and conservation 1979).

5

Reference Services

❖ *The user never seems to be satisfied*
with the map as it is,
and there are many ways
he may want to change it.
—Winearls 1975

❖ *Reference is after all,*
the end, the central function
of a map collection.
—Dahl 1975

❖ *But regardless of annual acquisitions,*
regardless of time and staff or funds,
a great number of requests for maps cannot be filled.
—Woods 1954

❖ *In the course of doing the HP and Apple studies,*
and in particular as we analyzed our data,
we were struck by the many crucial tasks
librarians perform that cannot be
handed off to intelligent software agents
or used to inform agent design.
—Nardi and O'Day 1996

The Basics

A librarian must understand the underpinnings of spatial data before he or she can answer questions about them. In chapter 1 the types of spatial data and reference works relating to them were discussed. This chapter concentrates on maps; an understanding of maps enables the librarian to give reference assistance for globes, atlases, remote-sensing images, and spatial data in digital form.

Map Basics

There are many excellent introductory works, ranging from the classic by Greenhood, to the latest classic, Muehrcke and Muehrcke 1992 (appendix 2A), to the many brochures issued by USGS. The only problem is that these books tell the beginning librarian too much about some matters and not enough about others. The following is not intended to replace them, but rather to supply the information that a librarian most needs when answering reference questions, and at the very least to make sure the librarian can understand and explain the legend—a feature that dates, surprisingly enough, only from the early sixteenth century (C. D. Smith 1984).

This section does not give an historical review of mapping. For one thing, this again is more information than a librarian needs initially, and for another, the books dealing with it do so very well, with the oldies still being the goodies—L. A. Brown 1950, Crone 1978, Tooley 1978, and Bagrow 1964 (all in appendix 2A). The superb *Information sources in cartography* (1990; appendix 2A) is a font of citations on the many areas of cartography, and should be consulted for more detail.

There are characteristics common to all or to the vast majority of spatial data and some terms that must be understood to do reference work. The principal ones are: scale; projection; grids and graticules; geodesy; direction; subject represented; and method of reproduction.

Scale and Resolution

Scale is the ratio of distances on a map, globe, relief model, or section (this last being both horizontal and vertical distance ratios) to the actual distances on the ground that the item is representing (AACCCM 1982, 234). A map that is exactly the same size as an area it maps or represents has a scale of 1:1; that is, one unit on the map covers the same area as one unit on the ground (what Lewis Carroll called a really useful scale!). This is not a very practical type of map, so most maps are made at some scale in which one unit on the map represents the area covered by a good many units on the ground. Respectable maps tell the user this by means of what is called the *r.f.* (representative fraction), usually shown as 1:number, instead of as 1/number. The number to the left of the colon is always 1. The units to the left of the colon must be the same as the units to the right, and for us staid U.S. citizens who refuse to clasp metric to our reluctant bosoms, this means the units are inches. There are 63,360 inches to one mile; thus, an r.f. of 1:63,360 means 1 inch on the map represents 1 mile on the ground. The phrases *small scale* and *large scale* are confusing in that they are relative, and they refer to the r.f. as a fraction (not to the size of the number to the right of the colon). Relative means that in Great Britain, which is well mapped (at scales that are as detailed as 1:1,250 for some areas), 1:63,360 is nearly a small scale; in a country that is poorly mapped, and may have only coverage at 1:250,000, 1:63,360 would be a large scale.

GEOLOGIC MAP SYMBOLS

COMMONLY USED ON MAPS OF THE UNITED STATES GEOLOGICAL SURVEY

(Special symbols are shown in explanation)

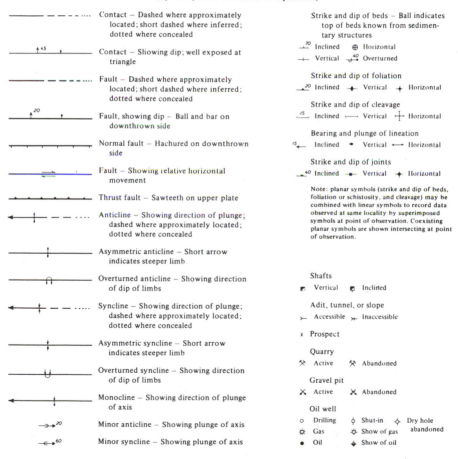

Figure 5.1. Sample of symbols sheet. [United States. Geological Survey. 19— .] Geologic map symbols: commonly used on maps of the United States Geological Survey. [Reston, Va.: USGS].

The second bit of confusion occurs when the user forgets to think of the r.f. as a fraction; for example, 1:63,360 (1/63,360) is a larger scale than 1:250,000 (1/250,000). To no one's surprise, this latter circumstance means that the "smaller scale than" and "larger scale than" phrases are often misused. Remember that maps with a smaller number to the right of the colon cover a (relatively speaking) smaller area—and in greater detail—than do maps with a larger number to the right of the colon. Thus, a map at 1:24,000 covers an area approximately 6 miles x 8 miles, one at 1:250,000 covers an area about 100 miles x 120 miles, and yet each map is on a sheet of paper of about the same size.

One more point here—guaranteed to make those who, like this author, believe that the phrase "mathematical logic" is a contradiction in terms—moan softly. When we deal with scale, we are dealing with an areal measure, and therefore differences in scale are not related as one might perhaps think. For example, a given area at 1:100,000 will cover four times as much area as that same area mapped at 1:50,000, because this is (to repeat) an areal, not just a lineal, measurement. Below is a comparison of various scales and distance covered on USGS quads:

> 1:24,000-scale map: one inch on map represents 2,000 feet on the ground; 49 to 70 square miles per sheet

> 1:62,500: one inch on map represents about one mile on ground; 197 to 282 square miles per sheet

> 1:250,000: one inch on map represents about four miles on ground; 4,580 to 8,669 square miles per sheet

> 1:1,000,000: one inch on map represents about 16 miles on the ground; 73,734 to 102,759 square miles per sheet

> (USGS 1990)

When dealing with geologic sections or with plastic raised-relief models, vertical scale must be measured in addition to horizontal scale. For geologic and other sections, the scale is figured out just as it is for horizontal scale; for models, the scale should be given by the model's maker. In both cases, there will be a considerable difference between the horizontal scale and the vertical scale—with the latter much larger than the former in most cases. The surface irregularities (we call them mountains and hills) of the Earth are so small in comparison to the size of the area mapped and to that of the Earth that they would not show up at all if they were not depicted in an exaggerated form; and thus we have what is called vertical exaggeration, so that Mount Fuji will be appropriately stupendous when shown on a model.

When working with spatial data in digital form, one most often is concerned with resolution, which is usually stated in terms of meters or feet, e.g., "1-meter resolution." This tells the user the size of the smallest object that may be represented or perceived in the data. When one enlarges or reduces a remote-sensing image or map on a computer screen, one enlarges or reduces the scale at exactly the same time—BUT NOT THE RESOLUTION, which remains unchanged no matter how great the enlargement or reduction.

Projection

A map is an attempt at the impossible—trying to put a curved surface or portion thereof on a flat surface. Projections are the way that cartographers grapple with this problem. The best way to visualize what is going on with projections is to wrap a sheet of paper (either as a cone or cylinder, or placed as a tangent plane) around a globe—preferably one with a light bulb inside. This is a simplistic way to look at projections, which are highly complicated mathematical formulae, but for our purposes it will do. Think about what the lines of latitude and longitude will look like when they are projected onto the piece of paper. If a cylinder of paper has been wrapped around the globe, touching the globe at the Equator, the lines of latitude and of longitude will be perpendicular to each other and the lines of latitude always the same distance apart. But the lines of longitude become farther and farther apart as one progresses toward the poles—with the consequent enlargement, far beyond true size, of any land masses toward the poles. And thus we have something like a Mercator projection, perfect for navigation (because it enables all courses to be plotted as straight lines) but misleading on land, and largely responsible for many of us being so firmly convinced that Greenland is far larger than South America.

The example of the cylinder-wrapped globe illustrates two matters to keep in mind when looking at any flat map:

1. When using a projection, one or more of the following properties will be distorted:

    a. distance

    b. angular measurement

    c. area

    d. shape

    Put another way, a projection may show correctly distances OR area OR bearing OR shapes, but NOT all of them at once.

2. The larger the area covered by the map, the greater the distortions; the smaller the area covered (as in, for example, detailed topographic sheets), the less the distortion. The curvature of the Earth's surface is relatively slight in relation to smaller areas.

There are several different ways of grouping projections:

1. Geometrical form (e.g., cylinder, cone, plane)

2. Conformal shape (areas of same shape or size)

3. Graticule lines (curved or straight)

4. Ease of preparation

5. Historical development

6. Appropriateness for larger areas or smaller areas

7. Alphabetical order (mainly, one suspects, for librarians)

8. Aspect or case (where projection is focused, that is, where paper is tangent to globe's surface; main ones are polar, equatorial, and oblique, i.e., focused anywhere except the poles or the Equator)

Which projection to use for a map is dependent on how the map is to be used:

1. Is correct angular representation important? That is, is the user finding a direction or setting a course? This is particularly important for charts, so that all bearings will be straight lines; thus, Greenland is far too large, but the shape (angles) is correct.

2. Is correct shape important? Then choose a conformal or orthomorphic projection, where the meridians and parallels intersect at right angles (as they do on the globe), and on which the scale around any point is the same in all directions. Scale and area increase with distance from the center.

3. Is correct representation of area important? An equivalent, homolographic, or homolosine projection is best; continents toward the poles will be distorted in shape but will maintain correct area.

4. Is correct scale all over the map important? Sorry; only the globe will satisfy this requirement. Scale is most accurate toward the center of a map, and most accurate overall on maps covering a small area (i.e., a map with a large scale).

Two excellent works on projections are Ray 1976 (written for librarians, and including glossary, bibliography, and citations for maps showing various projections) and Alpha 1982 (a poster-type explanation, simultaneously useful and attractive). Both of these works are listed in appendix 2B, a bibliography on projections.

Grids, Graticules, and So Forth

So here we are with a map; it now has a scale and a projection. But how are we to use it if it has no lines, arranged in a grid of some kind, to help us locate places? A *grid* is a network of two sets of uniformly spaced parallel lines, with one set intersecting the other at right angles; it usually, but not always, carries the name of the projection used for the map (e.g., Universal Transverse Mercator grid). When imposing a grid upon a map, the curvature of the Earth is ignored; east-west lines are parallel, and so are north-south lines that are parallel to some central meridian.

A *graticule* is an imaginary network of meridians (running north-south, and not parallel) and parallels (running east-west and parallel to each other) on the surface of the Earth or other celestial body. More familiarly, a graticule is a network of lines, on a map, that represents meridians and parallels, that is, our system of latitude and longitude. Although most users will be familiar with the concept of latitude and longitude, some will not; the savvy librarian will plan ahead and use Steele 1993 as a basis for a guide on the subject.

Most of us are familiar with the latitude-longitude system—the graticule—but grids are a bit tricky, and are very often used on maps. For example, on almost all USGS topographic quadrangles, there are one graticule and two grids, the two grids being the range and township (public land) grid and the Universal Transverse Mercator (UTM) grid. There are also, on some maps, state-plane-coordinate-system grids and national grids. Let's begin with the public land system.

The United States' public land system was devised in 1785 as a means of dividing up land that was part of the public domain. The method used was to divide up the land into six-mile square blocks—*townships*—figured from some base line (east-west) and principal meridian (north-south) with vertical rows known as *ranges*, and horizontal rows known, somewhat confusingly, also as *townships*. Then each six-mile-square township was divided into one-mile-square sections, numbered from 1 to 36; these could be split up into smaller units with cardinal-point designations (e.g., SE corner of the SW corner of Section 23, T3N, R1E, New Mexico Principal Meridian) (Hodgkiss 1981, 31, in appendix 2A). *Ranges* are lines running north-south, *townships* are lines running east-west. The numbering of the sections begins in the upper right-hand corner and progresses in a snake-like maneuver to the lower right-hand corner, ending there with number 36. For public-land maps of Canada, the numbering is just the opposite, beginning in the lower right-hand corner with Section 1 and coiling up to the upper right-hand corner, ending with Section 36.

There are a couple of catches to this. All ranges are to be parallel to all other ranges and all townships parallel to all other townships, so that the range lines and township lines intersect each other at right angles. But the Earth's surface is curved; lines of latitude remain parallel, but lines of longitude get closer together toward the poles. Thus, eventually the system

runs into problems. Because of this, there are thirty-one principal meridians and base lines in the conterminous United States, and three in Alaska;
see, for example, the following map which shows all of them:

> United States. Bureau of Land Management. 1968. *Principal
> meridians and base lines governing the United States public land
> surveys.* Washington, D.C.: Author.

When a patron comes up to the librarian with a range-and-township
location in hand, it is important to know either what the principal meridian
is, or what state the area is in; the petroleum industry and landowners are
most likely to use such citations. Another point to keep in mind—this
when a user needs a range-and-township citation and you can't seem to
find either on the map—is that public land surveys were never done in
the states comprising the thirteen original colonies, Texas, Tennessee,
Kentucky, West Virginia, or parts of Ohio.

The next important grid is the UTM grid system, in which the world
is divided into sixty zones of 6° of longitude each; each zone is numbered
and is itself divided into twenty bands between 80° north and south of the
Equator, with each band allocated a letter. The first part of any UTM
reference is the zone number and band letter. Next, each separate zone
is gridded with 100-kilometer squares, and each square given a two-letter
reference, based on a worldwide letter arrangement; these two letters are
the second element of the reference. The third part is a grid reference,
conventional in nature, based on eastings and northings within the specific
100-kilometer square. *Easting* (the east-west value in a reading) and
northing (the north-south value) refer to locating oneself in each zone.
Easting is the difference in longitude, to the east, from the last preceding
point of reckoning, whereas northing is the difference in latitude, to the
north, from the last preceding point of reckoning. Within each UTM zone,
the meridian in the center of the zone is given an easting value of 500,000
meters; the Equator has a northing value of 0 for northern hemisphere
coordinates and 10 million meters (arbitrary) for the southern hemisphere
(Hodgkiss 1981, 31–32, in appendix 2A). After all of that, one may
wonder why anyone bothers with UTM, and the answer is, because it is
accurate, and enables the user to pinpoint a location—for example, for
targeting artillery (Robinson and Sale 1969, 28).

Let's move on to the next important grid system, though it is scarcely
less complicated—the State Plane Coordinate system. It was devised by
the U.S. Coast and Geodetic Survey in 1933, the objective being to
provide a system of rectangular coordinates with a scale distortion that
would not exceed one part in 10,000. This intolerance for distortion is
why the system was done on a state basis, resulting in 111 separate
projections for the conterminous United States. The 1:24,000-scale USGS
sheets carry tick marks showing locations of this on a 10,000-foot grid.

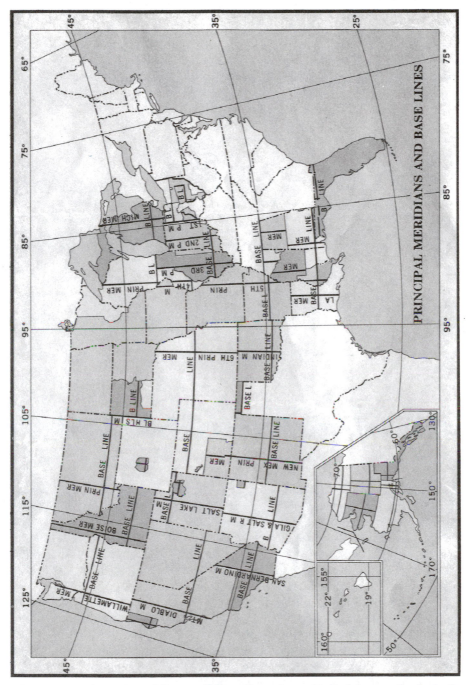

Figure 5.2. Principal meridians and base lines. From: United States. Geological Survey. 1965. United States of America: showing the extent of the public land surveys, remaining public land, historical boundaries, national forests, Indian reservations, wildlife refuges, national parks and monuments. Scale 1:2,500,000. Washington, D.C.: USGS.

UNITED STATES

OF

AMERICA

SHOWING THE EXTENT OF

PUBLIC LAND SURVEYS

REMAINING PUBLIC LAND, HISTORICAL BOUNDARIES,
NATIONAL FORESTS, INDIAN RESERVATIONS,
WILDLIFE REFUGES, NATIONAL PARKS AND MONUMENTS

SCALE 1:2,500,000

1 INCH EQUALS 40 MILES

0	40	80	120	160	200 Miles

0	40	80	120	160	200	240	280 Kilometers

Albers equal-area projection based on parallels 29½° and 45½°

Compiled by the Geological Survey in cooperation with the Bureau
of Land Management, United States Department of the Interior.

1965

LEGEND

National park or monument _o_  National forest _ _ _ _ Indian reservation _o_

National wildlife refuge _o_ Public land _ _ _ _

State capital _ _ _ City, town or village _ _ _ o o

For sale by the Superintendent of Documents, U.S. Government Printing Office, Washington, D.C. 20402 — Price $3.00 per set

National grids are those grids devised by countries for their own national, detailed maps. For example, Great Britain has a national grid which is explained on some of the sheets, specifically the sheets at a scale of 1:625,000. For this system, grid lines are 10 kilometers apart, with marginal numbers by each line denoting distance east or north from the origin of the grid, which is a point southwest of Land's End.

Another grid that the librarian may find reference to is the Marsden Square Identification scheme. This system divides the Earth's surface into geographical areas 10 degrees of latitude by 10 degrees of longitude. The origin for the system is the intersection of the Equator and the Greenwich meridian. The squares are numbered clockwise around the globe, with 36 squares for each 10-degree-latitude band.

Users will from time to time need to convert from one system to another. In preparation, librarians will hoard references to such publications as Botz 1969, which has to do with conversion of public-land coordinates to latitude and longitude.

Geodesy

Now we have a map, which uses a certain projection, at a certain scale, and with a graticule and a few grids. Ah, but there is more. We need to know that the locations on the map (at the moment, horizontal—sometimes called *planimetric*; vertical for elevations) are accurate, that there is what is called *control* (horizontal and vertical). In order to know this, we need to know about geodesy, which determines the exact positions of points and of areas of large portions of the Earth's surface, plus the shape and size of the Earth, and also variations in terrestrial gravity and magnetism.

Triangulation is at the heart of geodetic surveying. Two points, many miles apart, have their latitude and longitude determined very precisely, and the length of the line (base line) between the two is determined equally precisely; the position of a third station is determined by the angle that station's location makes with each end of the base line (here you thought there were no practical uses for trigonometry). This process is continued until the entire arc to be surveyed is covered with a network of triangles, using time and sophisticated instrumentation. Advancements in the latter have been particularly striking in the area of angular measurement, where accuracy had not increased for 150 years until the 1960s, when miniaturization in equipment occurred. During the same decade, electronics (specifically electromagnetics and light waves) came on the scene, and allowed very precise traverse measurements.

In the 1970s, satellite triangulation and electronic-distance measurement enabled geodesists to be on the threshold of accomplishing their goal of establishing a worldwide geodetic network. Satellites were specifically designed to carry instruments to measure variations of the Earth's gravitational field and to determine the exact geographic position of points on the Earth, with the satellite acting as a triangulation point in space, and being photographed against a background of stars in order to compare the relative positions of points on the Earth. The systems are called GPS, Global Positioning System; the two major ones are the Navstar Global Positioning System (run by the U.S. military) and GLONASS (*Global'naya Navigatsionnaya Sputnikova Sistema,* under the Russian *Voenno-Kosmicheski Sily,* that is, Military Space Forces). Three-dimensional, Earth-centered coordinates may now be determined from geometric satellite observations, when combined with the Doppler effect from other geodetic satellite systems. These improvements were much needed; by the mid-1910s, only one-third of the land area of the world was covered by geodetic networks satisfying the then-current requirements. By the early 1980s, satellite geodesy and its earthbound "black boxes" (taking fixes on the satellites) had become an accurate, economical commonplace, ably competing with conventional land techniques in cost and accuracy (Parkinson and Spilker 1996; Larsgaard 1984, 19–20, in appendix 2A).

But why all the fuss? Because accurate maps may be constructed only if they are firmly and precisely "tied" to a location on the Earth's surface. To bring it down to the practicalities of real estate, land ownership measurement requires very precise measurement of the limits of owner-ship; with the use of satellites, relative positions accurate to between 0.3 and 1.0 feet may be obtained (reported in *Wisconsin mapping bulletin* 10, no. 3 [July 1984]). These controls are thus very important in many, many ways. The control data issued, presently by the National Geodetic Survey, is available as horizontal-control data (latitude and longitude) and vertical-control data (elevation). This means that any one map may have two different datums (that surface to which all other points on the Earth's surface are related)—one for horizontal control (e.g., North American datum), and one for vertical control (e.g., mean sea level). A new North American datum—both horizontal and vertical—is being instituted; see especially National Geodetic Survey pamphlets and J. D. Bossler 1982. Yes, this is a complex subject, and it should therefore come as no surprise to discover that ACMLA has a series of articles on geodesy for librarians (Datums 1988 in appendix 2B; Sebert 1983, 1984a, b, and c).

Which Way Is North?

Oh, yes—we also need to know which way is up, or, failing that, which way is north. Ah, but what kind of north do you need?

true north: geographic north—what most people think of when they hear the word north (NOTE: There is not a false north).

grid north: north according to the grid imposed on the map; be-cause grids ignore the curvature of the Earth, this is not the same as true north.

magnetic north: north according to the Earth's magnetic poles rather than its geographic poles; declination from true north is given in mils; one mil equals 1/6,400 of 360 degrees.

Naturally, these three are each different. Once again, USGS and some other publishers take pity on us mortals, and place on their maps a diagram that shows the direction of all three (Fig. 5.1).

Subject Matter

So here we are with our map, with projection, grids and graticules galore, knowing which way is north and that points are located accurately. How about depicting some thematic information? Here is where we get into types of maps, which are covered in chapter 1, so all we need consider is how maps depict a subject. Generally this is explained in the legend; the catches here are that not every map and almost no remote-sensing images have legends, and very large series (especially topographic series) will not have a complete legend printed on every sheet. The legend sheet for each of these series must be acquired as a separate item, and if at all possible in multiple copies. Maps of very small areas, such as of an individual mine, or aimed toward very restricted audiences may not include a legend. So it is a good idea to keep a file of symbol sheets for various topographic series and for various subjects.

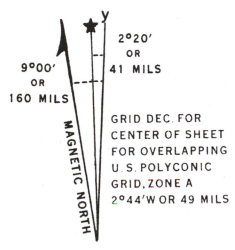

2°20′
OR
41 MILS

9°00′
OR
160 MILS

MAGNETIC NORTH

GRID DEC. FOR
CENTER OF SHEET
FOR OVERLAPPING
U.S. POLYCONIC
GRID, ZONE A
2°44′W OR 49 MILS

**APPROXIMATE MEAN DECLINATION 1946
FOR CENTER OF SHEET
NO ANNUAL MAGNETIC CHANGE**

Use diagram only to obtain numerical values. To determine magnetic north line, connect the pivot point "P" on the south edge of the map with the value of the angle between GRID NORTH and MAGNETIC NORTH, as plotted on the degree scale at the north edge of the map.

Figure 5.3. True north, grid north, and magnetic north. United States. Army Map Service. 1946. Urbana, Md. Scale 1:25,000. Washington, D.C.: Army Map Service.

Let's go a bit further, and look at the words on the map. Place names for the United States are determined by the U.S. Board on Geographic Names (BGN); it also determines the forms of foreign names to be used in the United States. Next, take a look at the map's margins, which may include: title of map or map sheet; title or number of map series; index code of individual sheet; author or authors; imprint; printer and date; survey dates and method of data collection; revisions or overprints; reliability diagram (how accurate the information is); sources and credit notes; magnetic declination; index to adjoining sheets; legend; scale, grid, or coordinates; projection statement; and miscellaneous (Farrell and Desbarats 198, 18). All of this is important, and all should be carefully read.

Methods of Reproduction and Production

Maps most often seen in libraries are printed (black and white, or in color most frequently by offset lithography) or some form of photographic copy (e.g., xerography, diazo, etc.); less common are manuscript maps (done by hand) and those maps produced by a computer mapping program, with the latter becoming more common (Farrell and Desbarats 1984, 17).

Summary

Having plowed through all of the foregoing, a librarian is now able to see why reading a map or other spatial-data item looks so divertingly easy and in actuality takes a bit of effort. Maps are an abstraction and a generalization at the same time, and from a different perspective (directly overhead) than the one from which human beings are accustomed to looking at the world. It all takes some time to figure out. It's advisable to keep a wary eye for publication date and date of data, purpose of the map, and bias of the author and publisher (Obenhaus 1990).

Other Spatial Data

As was previously mentioned, understanding the basics of maps deals neatly with several other types of spatial data—views, plans, sections, diagrams, globes, models, and atlases—and is of some assistance in working with remote-sensing imagery. Panoramas, bird's-eye views, and the like are about halfway between maps and pictures; the user should be wary of scale because such items are liable to vary continuously from the front to the visual rear. Geologic and stratigraphic sections are to be interpreted by the geologists and the geology students who use them. The librarian's chief problem is figuring out a way to indicate that a map has such a section on it, as sometimes all the user needs is the section, and may not be very interested in the map for which the section is a subsidiary part.

Interpretation of remote-sensing images is a field that requires a class or two to understand; here again, the librarian's work is to attempt to have the images needed, and to have them readily retrievable. Once more, USGS comes to the rescue of the beginner in spatial data, with its pamphlet "Aerial photographs and satellite images" (1995)—informative, lovely to look at, and brief. See Lillesand and Kiefer 1994 and Avery 1992 (both in appendix 2A) for details.

Plastic raised-relief maps can be helpful in explaining how contour lines work. By comparing a relief map of an area with an ordinary flat map of the same area at the same scale (e.g., the Hubbard 1:250,000 raised-relief maps of the United States compared with the USGS 1:250,000 topographic sheets of the United States), the user may almost immediately figure out how contour lines work. For globes, just be prepared at some point to explain what the analemma (sun's apparent path in the sky) is.

Another point here—which applies to all spatial data—is knowing where materials not held by the library in question may be obtained. The librarian may reasonably be expected to know where large collections of specific material, on a specific subject, are located, besides being able to inform the user as to where such materials may be purchased.

Reference Desk Basics

Bruno's Laws

1. Never assume.

2. Get off your duff; don't just point.

3. Attempt to answer the original question.

4. Never take anything interesting to read with you to the reference desk.

5. Make it a practice to follow up on unresolved questions.

6. Keep in mind, YOU may have heard the question a thousand times, but it is the first time the user has ever asked it.

7. Dress comfortably.

8. Avoid library jargon like the plague.

9. Be prepared to drop all conversations with colleagues the instant a user shows up.

10. Before coming to the desk, try to take a few minutes for mental calisthenics; the desk shift should be approached for the fun and challenge that it is.

11. Always pass along to colleagues any useful information you encounter in a search.

12. Be as concrete as possible when giving directions.

(Cruse 1995)

The first problem, that of negotiating a reference interview to the mutual satisfaction of the user and the librarian, is the key. Inevitably, striving toward successful reference interviews will lead the librarian, willy-nilly, into the murky depths of another social science, psychology. No one expects a librarian to possess a doctorate in that subject, but a little practical knowledge in the field will be helpful.

A reference interview is, to sink into the dialect, a problem in interpersonal relationships. First of all, consider the user's point of view. The library appears strange; the user does not understand how it operates or why it operates as it does, nor does he particularly want to know; he wants answers to his questions, and is most often unaware of any but the library's most obvious abilities to assist. The user may not know exactly what he needs, or he may have his doubts as to the abilities of the reference librarian (everyone knows that all librarians do is sit and read all day). Most importantly, many of us dislike admitting ignorance—muddling it up with stupidity, which is a different matter altogether—or the need to depend on someone else; most users would often prefer to find what is needed on their own. Thus, the user is in a state of minor tension. He has a question that he doesn't know how to frame, that he wants answered, that is to be answered by persons whom he doesn't know and whom he may see little reason to trust. It is no wonder that many persons never make it to the reference desk. Those few brave souls who do merit a careful effort on our part, not only for their courage, but in the hope that they will tell other persons that we seem to know what we are doing, and seldom bite (Winearls 1974, 16; Penland and Mathai 1974, 51).

So the user finally makes it to the librarian to ask a question. The user's question may be stated in terms of the information needed (the area covered, the subject to be shown) or in reference to a specific item. If the latter, it is advisable to divine if that specific item is needed or if the user believes (perhaps erroneously) that the item will contain the best version of the information sought (Dahl 1975, 6).

Now the librarian must exhibit a list of favorable characteristics as long, if not exactly the same, as a Boy Scout's, going through the stages of approachability, interest, listening and inquiring, searching, and follow-up (*Draft guideline* 1995). The librarian must be approachable, or the patron will never arrive at the reference desk in the first place. When the patron finally does ask questions, the librarian must become the perfect interactive listener. The one big factor at this point that helps make for a successful reference interview is that persons love to talk about themselves and their problems. The librarian clever enough to ask questions defining the user's request in such a fashion that the answer cannot be a straight yes or no will in all likelihood receive at least as much information as is needed to match the user's needs to the collection—at least, as much as the collection will allow. The librarian's talking—until the patron's problem is clearly defined—should be minimal, composed as much as possible of the aforementioned open-ended questions, aimed at encouraging the user to focus his problem, finding out how much information the user needs, and establishing by verbal and nonverbal communication a relationship of frankness and confidence, achieved by virtue of tact, a relaxed manner, and a genuine desire to help (G. B. King 1972, 158–59; Penland and Mathai 1974, 13–14; Farrell and Desbarats 1984, 68).

The librarian should appear to be concentrating totally upon the user immediately at hand, remembering that the library is selling a service, and acting accordingly, even in the most hurried of times. This attention gives a user the luxurious feeling of being important. If the librarian cuts a patron off in the middle of a sentence, the feeling is not reinforced. For the first part of the reference interview, the librarian must try to establish empathy in a very short period of time, not imposing personal values on the user.

One part of the process is remembering that different persons define words in different ways. If there is any chance of confusion in terminology, it should be cleared up quickly. The user focuses on his problem so intently that he is oblivious to the different meanings of and contexts for the words he uses, so the librarian must find out what is really meant when a homonym, or a word like "geography," is used. A frequent example of this is the single most requested, and most misrequested, map—the USGS topographic quadrangle. The United States is nearly unique among nations in having its topographic maps produced by its national geological survey; most nations have both a topographic survey and a geologic survey. It is one of those cases where we could have dispensed with uniqueness because it means that when users ask us for a geologic (or occasionally a geodetic) map, what they often mean is a topographic map.

Once the user's information need has been defined—as precisely as possible in terms of area, subject (the number of times this librarian has been asked for a geologic map of an entire state when what was needed was a topographic map of a quadrangle area does not bear counting), date of data, scale or level of detail, and format—and then translated into libraryese in the librarian's mind, the librarian may go about trying to find materials that will answer the need. The librarian working in an open-stack library is not merely finding the answer to questions, but rather also helping the users to help themselves.

When the time comes to match the user's needs against the materials the library has, matters will be much easier if:

1. the librarian is familiar with the patterns of issuance of spatial data.

2. all of the spatial data possessed by the library is in one place; it is also very helpful if supporting materials—such as

books on spatial data—are in that same area; if a library is paying for a spatial-data librarian, it should get its money's worth.

3. the items are arranged in LC-class number order; pockets of exceptions not only bemuse the user but provide a classic example of the fact that the more places one has to look for something, the less likely one is to find it.

4. all materials are cataloged, and in the library's online catalog; if the book collection in a library were uncataloged, how often would any of it be used, and how difficult would it be to find a specific item? Cataloging is the basis of all reference work, and, once done, substantially increases usage of the materials cataloged.

The librarian should always try the obvious first—the map cases and digital-data files, not just under the class number specifically devoted to the area needed, but also the large series that will be classed under the nation as a whole or under the world. For example, a class assignment demanding a map of Diego Garcia is easily satisfied with the nautical chart of the area, which would be classed with the series to which it belongs, under world oceans as a whole. Next, try atlases; or, if what is needed is a map 8½" x 11" (as it so often is), try the CIA maps of that size (hardcopy or digital), or try the older *Encyclopaedia Britannicas*, where the maps are an austere black and white that photocopies beautifully. If there is nothing so far, then the next step is the appropriate periodical index, since maps are often published as part of a monograph or periodical article. About fifteen years ago, Gary Fitzpatrick researched the amount of times the words "map," "maps," "mapping," etc., appeared in various periodical databases (Fitzpatrick 1983).

The matter of finding spatial data that is issued as part of something else bears a distinct resemblance to a treasure hunt. It would be of considerable assistance just to have individual entries for each map in each atlas in the online catalog (Vick 1987). At some point, we would like to be able actually to search the content of spatial data, not just the surrogates (e.g., catalog records) of that data—that is, retrieving on image content. For right now, many of us will settle for being able to search by drawing a polygon around the area of interest, and then having the software search for citations that cover that area. This is the whole idea behind the Alexandria Digital Library (http://www.alexandria.ucsb.edu)—by late 1998, it should be available for search over the Web (or request a copy of the prototype CD-ROM from this author). *GeoRef* does currently allow coordinate search.

An important part of this whole procedure is that the user is a working part of it. The user may resent the "working" aspect, so there are certain forms of user behavior that the librarian must tactfully but firmly quash.

The librarian should make clear that the librarian will not do the user's work; it is the librarian's job to find items that bear on the question, not to write a paper or to interpret legal phrases. In this vein, it is well for the librarian to remember never to give out unsubstantiated information; if the patron uses such information and disaster ensues, the patron may sue the librarian.

Care must be taken not to swamp the user with far more information than was ever needed; the level of interest—two-page paper or 300-page dissertation—should be pinned down during the initial reference interview. The librarian should be sure that the user knows that a search is ongoing and about how long that search will take if the librarian needs to trek off into the labyrinths of the inner library to find an item. Surely there is little that is more irritating than for a librarian to come back to the map room, covered with dust and glory and bearing information, only to find that the requester has departed: "Woe betide him who panteth after the Hart and waiteth not for the kill" (Gardner and Zeleransky 1975, 326).

If the librarian finds material answering the request, excellent; if not, the librarian must be painfully honest and say, not that the library does not have the item, but simply and truthfully that the librarian cannot find it. And then the librarian should refer the user to a place that will have it.

For medical doctors, the maxim is, "At the very least, do no harm." For us in libraries, it is, "Give out no misinformation; instead, refer the questioner to someone who will know the answer." This means that the most powerful tool the librarian has to answer the tough questions is the addresses (or if you prefer, the coordinates) of other map librarians. See the following directories in appendix 2A: Directory of Canadian Map Collection 1992-; Directory of UK 1995; Guide to U.S. map 1986; O'Connor 1991, and World directory 1993.

One library to be used only as a court of last resort is LC. LCG&M disseminates a fair amount of information, mostly in formal ways such as its Web page and cartobibliographies (under the Superintendent of Documents number LC5.2); its acquisitions lists; periodical articles by its librarians (e.g., Stephenson 1973; Gerlach 1960b; Adkinson 1949; Ristow all); lists of publications (Modelski 1981); exhibits ('Hawaii in Maps' 1948); and guides to services (in several revised editions, and usually entitled something like *The Geography and Map Division, a guide to its collections and services*). We are very fortunate in having LCG&M, for the publications it issues, the cataloging it does, and the assistance it supplies in a multitude of situations.

There are several possibilities for failing to find the item needed: item checked out; item stolen; item misfiled; item doesn't exist; item never possessed by library; or librarian can't find item (Leeuwenburg 1982, 10–11). The first three are self-explanatory. The fourth one does occur commonly and is always a dreadful shock to users who believe that if they need a map, it must exist. An Australian map librarian has noted the response of his users to being told that the Snowy Mountains were not mapped at 1:50,000 or 1:25,000: "Many users simply could not believe this" (Leeuwenburg 1982, 11). This disbelieving response is also common in the United States.

As for the fifth possibility, here we get into the area of interlibrary loan. Frequently libraries do not loan spatial data even to their own users, let alone mail them out. This self-interest is largely because of the fragility of maps, the fact that large series may often be purchased only as a whole (not sheet by sheet), and the large size and hefty price of such items as atlases and Landsat imagery. But it is worth checking, through such systems as OCLC, on the grounds that it never hurts to ask. It may become obvious that, heresy of heresies, spatial data may not provide the best answer to the question; in this case, the librarian should again provide a referral, either to an area elsewhere in the library or to another library in town or on campus. Any referral, of any kind, should always be written down on a piece of paper. If it is merely verbal advice to a patron, the unfamiliar words may either be forgotten or twisted into a completely unrecognizable form.

By the end of a reference interview, the librarian should know whether or not the user got the information required. If the answer is no, the user should have received from the librarian a reference (printed out —not scrawled, and definitely not just spoken) to an agency or person who is likely to have the answer.

Sadly, reference librarians do need to deal at times with problem patrons. Should a negative situation arise, the librarian should act as follows: be empathetic; listen carefully and ask questions nonjudgmentally if clarification is needed; respect personal space, standing at least two or three feet away from the questioner, and at an angle, in a nonchallenging manner; permit the user to vent verbally when possible; set and enforce reasonable limits; try not to overreact; use physical techniques only as a last resort; ignore "challenge" questions; and keep your nonverbal cues nonthreatening (Arterburn 1996, 33).

Users and Map Reading

Before many moons of servitude have passed, the librarian will be able to categorize the types of users the library attracts, and to construct a user profile. This profile may vary somewhat over time (university map collections formerly haunted mainly by geography and geology students and faculty now have landscape architects haunting the premises) and will also be different for different libraries, depending upon each institution's purpose and potential audience. One category, for example, is made up of those who do not know how to read a map but who are interested in using spatial data.

The general public's use of spatial data fluctuates; at the beginning of World War II, a Rand McNally store was crowded with persons "eager to buy anything in stock" (Sudden demand 1939, 882). By the mid-1950s, the pattern in the public attitude toward maps was a "dull background of indifference and ignorance concerning the existence, sources, or uses of maps; and inability to read or interpret accurately the maps that do get attention" (Gerlach 1954, 209). This attitude has improved, with an increasing awareness of maps in fields dealing with environmental data handling and measurement. But Americans in general are less map-conscious than are Europeans, perhaps due to the low status of geography in education at all levels and, until about twenty years ago, a lack of interest in outdoor pursuits (Cobb l977a, 822; Ferro 1980, 173).

As the U.S. Army proved many times, the assumption that any fool can read a map with no introductory explanation is unwarranted (Spellman 1970, 24). Not only can the uninitiated not easily comprehend maps, many times they cannot even refold them; it is amazing how much this latter problem vexes the users' minds. Either such users need to be walked through Otness 1974, or should be told about electronic map displays in automobiles that will guide the driver.

Map reading, beyond such matters as blue signifying water, is seldom taught in schools. A considerably higher level of cartographic under-standing than knowing which is the water is necessary to penetrate that most useful of maps—the large-scale topographic map—and users rarely have that expertise. A permanent display of maps at various scales, and a copy of USGS's poster, *Understanding maps and scale,* will help a great deal, as will a display of a standard 1:250,000-scale sheet of the United States, next to the same area, at the same scale, in a plastic raised-relief map (McDermott 1967, 74; Bergen 1972b, 315–16).

One kind of map reading that can confound even the librarian is the reading of foreign maps. The universality of maps is somewhat overstated. Although contours and rivers are about the same on any map, other signs and symbols, particularly cultural symbols, may present severe difficul-ties, especially if the language is Asiatic. Librarians should either learn just enough of the language to plough through (this usually works for the European languages and for Russian), or should have legend and other salient information on these maps translated, typed up, and identified with the maps' call numbers. Even for maps in English, it is essential to keep legend sheets and appropriate articles on interpretation readily available (Harden 1974, 9–12).

The category of untutored layperson is in startling juxtaposition to that much smaller group composed of scholars who know their subject well, have definite requirements, are prepared to go to a great deal of work, and need either to be only pointed in the right direction, or to receive very detailed information (Winearls 1975, 15). Between these two types is a continuum, and in every case the librarian must delicately discover not only what information is needed, but also how much is required and will be understood. Along the way, the librarian will discover that the utility of spatial data is not restricted to geographers and historians. Frequently the librarian will meet victims of cartophilia like Henry

Drummond, who believed that instead of three or four volumes plus one map, books of travel should have three or four maps and one volume (Moody 1929, 197).

The mind boggles at the uses to which patrons will put spatial data. Occasionally the boggling is due to sheer inappropriateness, such as that of Sunday sailors who take their small boats up the Inland Passage from Seattle to Alaska using only road maps. Or the sea captains who, during the California Gold Rush of 1849, sailed out of New York harbor with "nothing more than an elementary school atlas to guide them around the Horn"—18,000 miles and five months guided by the equivalent of Appleton's school atlases is a frightening thought (L. A. Brown 1942, 144).

Types of Reference Questions

Reference questions follow patterns, both of subject and of scale. Two major categories are general reference questions to ascertain a given fact (e.g., "Where is Lop Nor?"), and research questions, which require much more time (Espenshade 1936, 206). There are several different categorizations of questions; the following is an amalgam:

1. A question about a specific geographic area, with time period implied or stated; this may be for a very large area (e.g., world, continent) or a very small area, or anything between the two

2. A question about a specific geographic area plus specific thematic data, with time period implied or stated

3. A request for a specific item, from a citation

4. A question about spatial-data methodology, technology, or history

5. A request for assistance in interpreting material found

6. A request for referral (including interlibrary loan)

(Kidd and Cardinal 1977, 16–17;
Modelski 1977, 157; Cavanaugh 1983, 16–19)

The purposes for the questions may be that of research, teaching, or recreation (Farrell and Desbarats 1984, 71; Alonso 1975, 11–12). Most common questions focus on the city, county, or state in which the library is located. Locational questions, regarding places, streets, and features, and their proper spelling, are frequent, as are questions relating to distances between two places. An inquiry usually takes the form of a request for a map of a given area or a subject as displayed over that given area, with date of information, scale or resolution, and format (e.g., 8½" x 11"; digital) as qualifiers (Powers 1975, 34; Wallis 1969, 86; Winearls

1974, 12). The following summarizes the most frequently asked questions (these make up about 40 percent or more of the reference questions asked in most university collections), and materials with which they may be answered:

    a. 8½" x 11" format, for photocopying: keep these items on the ready-reference shelf—CIA maps of foreign countries, continents, and regions of the Earth (also available over the Web from the Perry-Casteñada Library, University of Texas, Austin); outline maps of the continents; gazetteers such as *Cambridge world gazetteer* (can't be beat for small maps showing state-level administrative boundaries of foreign countries, but unfortunately does not show cities/rivers/roads), and *Webster's new geographical dictionary* (good for cities/rivers/roads on an 8½" x11" format; political boundaries of state-level areas don't show up well, and in some cases not at all); *Maps on file* (not beautiful to look at, but they photocopy well); *Historical maps on file; State maps on file; Outline maps on file*; street guides for heavily urbanized areas of the state in which the library is located (e.g., Thomas Brothers products for California).

    b. Locating a given place (cultural or physiographic):

    —via hardcopy: for places in the United States, *Omni gazetteer* (vol. 10 is an index of ALL names that appear on ALL topos of the United States; refers you to a volume in the *Omni gazetteer* set, which volume will give, amongst other information, latitude, longitude, and topo quad on which the feature appears). For places in foreign countries, use U.S. Board of Geographic Names gazetteers; to use these lists, you must know what country the place is in, because the gazetteers are arranged by country:

    —via Web: for United States, GNIS at http://www-nmd.usgs.gov/www.gnis/gnisform.html ; for non-U.S. countries, GEOnames at http://164.214.2.53/gns/html/index.html .

    c. Nautical charts: for U.S. waters, the C&GS series (keep multiple copies of indexes available; they are foldout sheets, done by region). For non-U.S. waters, the NIMA nautical charts for foreign waters; index is a series of pamphlets—locate region number at beginning of index and then use region index to locate specific chart.

    d. General map of a relatively small area (ca. 6 x 8 miles) of the United States: USGS topographic sheets.

e. Geologic map of an area in the United States: use the USGS Geologic map index series; done on state-by-state basis.

A most useful article by Leeuwenburg (1982) gives the following statistics concerning breakdown of reference work, which seem to be generally true for many collections:

1. finding maps (50 percent)

2. finding aerial photographs (10 percent)

3. interpreting maps (15 percent)

4. acting as liaison with lecturers (10 percent)

5. presenting reader education classes (5 percent)

6. compiling cartobibliography/availability of maps (10 percent)

Next are types of map searches:

1. simple, specific area (2–10 minutes) (50 percent)

2. area project (15–60 minutes) (20 percent)

3. subject (15–60 minutes) (5 percent)

4. subject area (2–10 minutes) (15 percent)

5. specific projection (2–10 minutes; not searchable in card catalog) (5 percent)

6. form, e.g., Landsat (2–10 minutes; not searchable in card catalog) (5 percent)

Leeuwenberg's library is in an institution of higher education; statistical breakdown of questions would probably be different for public libraries. He found that about 80 percent of the demand was for areas within 200 kilometers of his library; although this seems a bit high, it may be very close to what many collections, regardless of affiliation, experience (Leeuwenberg 1982, 9–10). It is well to note that statistics will be different, not just for different administrative types of libraries but also for libraries that are specialized. For example, the Colorado School of Mines Library specializes in geology and mineral engineering, so subject/area questions are a much higher percentage than is given for Leeuwenberg's institution.

There are some special types of users, and of reference questions, that merit extra attention at this point. A growing interest in outdoor pursuits over the years has most recently displayed itself in an interest in what is called *orienteering*—rather like a car rally, but on foot, through trackless wastes and over cliffs with only topographic sheet and compass for guides (Wexler 1977). Orienteering has discovered its own varieties of Murphy's Laws, most of which librarians already knew about, including the classic one that any area needed will be on the corners of four sheets. Persons doing orienteering will doubtless learn not to trust a map implicitly, and will not believe that all maps are completely accurate; the rest of the population will continue to view maps—if at all—as always correct. Such recreational-map users as these need a large-scale map small enough to carry around in a pocket, showing campgrounds, jumping-off points, access roads, potable water, stream and rapids profiles, and similar information (Donley 1976). As you might expect, USGS has a good one-page brochure on this, "Finding your way with map and compass." Most maps can survive only one wilderness experience (and maybe not that, if the carrier falls into a stream), so these maps should not be checked out unless they have been dissected and laminated. It is preferable for the librarian to be able to refer the user to a local business that sells such maps.

Another frequent question concerns the location of a given cultural or physical feature. First, the librarian should find out if the user has even the faintest idea about which country or state it might be located in. For a specific state, the librarian may try the Web GNIS; the most current Rand McNally *Commercial atlas and marketing guide* (for many years the de facto national gazetteer for the United States); the true official gazetteer, USGS *Professional paper 1200* (being done state by state); or the *Omni gazetteer* (constructed from GNIS, USGS's Geographic Names Information System). If the location is in a state, or in a foreign country but the user doesn't know which one, the index of the latest National Geographic atlas is good for locations in the United States, as are the previously mentioned Web GEOnames gazetteer and the index of the latest *Times atlas of the world*. If the user does know which foreign country the place is located in, then the librarian should go to the U.S. Board on Geographic Names gazetteer series. NIMA issues some foreign-country gazetteers. Both of these sets of gazetteers are depository items.

Another frequent question is what the distance between two points is. If the distance is to be measured on a given map, the user will need an opisometer of some kind; if what is needed is an area measurement, a planimeter is the tool. Or for textual aids, use Fitzpatrick 1986 (appendix 2A) or the most current editions of the *Official table of distances, continental United States . . .* and *Official table of distances, foreign travel* (appendix 2A); or go to the Web and try http://www.indo.com/distance/ . If the latitude and the longitude of the points are known, one may use mathematical formulas, as given in Fitzpatrick. If the latitude and longitude of the point are needed, try the Geo Ruler (Elamco, P.O. Box 301, Lincolnton, GA 30817) or the TopoAid (Stonetree, Inc., P.O. Box 335, Waxhaw, NC 28173).

One reference question this author has received just sufficiently infrequently that each time it is asked, she has to figure it out all over again, is how to apply and derive UTM grid references. Out of this exasperation came the following guide, which uses a UTM template (available from USGS):

The following example uses a 1:24,000-scale topographic quadrangle of the United States, Mt. Baldy, California, 1954.

1. Obtain from MIL staff member template no. 2 and a straightedge.

2. Note information on lower right-hand corner of grid; the last note says, "1000-meter Universal Transverse Mercator grid ticks, zone 11, shown in blue." Look at the neatline of the quad, and you will see blue tick marks; these are 1,000 meters apart. Also note: in the lower right-hand/southeast corner and in the upper left/northwest corner, you see some numbers that contain some numbers larger than others; with "m" at the end of the number:

   se: 441000mE. 3778000mN.

   nw: 443000mE. 3788000mN.

Use the set of numbers closest to the site you are deriving coordinates for; we'll use the se-corner coordinates, to locate the reservoir above the D of "UPLAND." To give a UTM coordinate, FIRST you must know the zone; if it isn't noted on the map (it is in this case—zone 11), MIL staff will find for you a map that has zones on it (3701 B71 1953 .U5). SECOND, you need to derive what are called "easting" and "northing." This is analogous to finding longitude and latitude.

Easting: you can tell from the two figures given with "E" after them that the numbers increase as one goes from west to east. Now, take the template and match the scale of the map with a scale given in corners of template. Place template so that scale of map is same as scale at lower right-hand corner of template (VII), so that "Meters 1000" markings fall exactly on the blue tick marks (arrows on maps).

Easting and northing numbers are ordinary numbers— e.g., 441000mE is 441,000 meters east.

Place template so 1-meter mark is on blue tick mark to left of 441000mE. Now—locate center of reservoir—it's at 480-meter mark. So—KEEPING IN MIND that the easting INCREASES as you go west, and DECREASES as you go east: 441,000mE - 480m = 440,520mE.

Northing: Place template—again with "1:24,000" in lower right-hand corner—so 1 is on blue tick mark at se corner of quad. Now, read UP (since now you're doing a northing) and use a straight edge to locate center of reservoir.

It's at 780 meters. IGNORE the "230,000 feet (s)" marking on the map; this is for the California Coordinate System (zone s).

Now, because the northing numbers INCREASE as you go north, and DECREASE as you go south: 3,788,000 mN - (1,000 + 120m) = 3,776,880 mN.

So the coordinates are: UTM Zone 11, 3,776,880mN, 440,520mE.

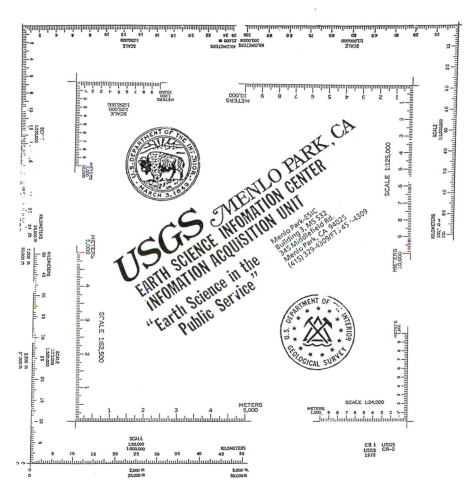

Figure 5.4. UTM template. USGS, Menlo Park.

There, wasn't that simple? See Stott 1977 for more information, presented in a readily comprehensible fashion.

A large and growing area of reference work is that of genealogy. Anyone interested in genealogy would do well to begin by reading the excellent articles by Moffat 1980 and 1981, Flynn 1985, Kidd 1975, Lind

1985 (appendix 2A), Maps can help 1991 (appendix 2A), Morgan 1977, Kersten 1979, Post 1986, and Perry 1992, from which much of the following brief introduction is garnered. Most frequently, genealogical reference work deals with the topic just recently discussed, the "where?" of places. The catch is that it is most often a pre-1900 location, which is trickier to find. Standard gazetteers should always be searched first, in the often vain hope that the place is still in existence and has not changed name. Old atlases of any kind (preferably at twenty- or fifty-year intervals, for as far back as the budget can afford), old city directories, and old topographic sheets are essential; in fact, any sort of pre-1900 publication is almost always helpful. If the library has a collection of pre-1900 maps, these will probably now begin to get more use that may be good for them. Historical maps may provide the only evidence of an event or a place (Cavanaugh 1983, 18; Koeman 1968; Storm 1944; Kidd 1975; F. Woodward 1981; R. B. Collins 1977). Such maps are beautiful in their own right, and have more often been collected for their aesthetic value than for any other reason. Now at last the librarian may point out not just how beautiful they are, but also how useful they are, making that a more practical reason to justify their purchase.

Reference work with digital data is of increasing importance in every collection, especially as the U.S. government soldiers on toward having as much data in digital form by A.D. 2000 as possible, and as the Web becomes more and more important in everyday reference work. The questions fall into these categories: finding out whether spatial data for a given area exists in digital form; finding out if it is available over the Web; finding out about various formats of digital data; figuring out what software one needs to use the digital data; and figuring out how to use the software. In all cases, the canny librarian will speedily write up handouts that give the "how-to" for each of these questions, and have said handouts available both in hard copy and on the spatial-data collection's homepage. Instructions will include: how to use computers within the collection; how to download data (e.g., how to use anonymous ftp); best sites to hunt for data available over the Web; lists of digital data available in the collection, including one specifically for digital data for the county/state in which the library is located; and guides to how to use each of the software packages available in the collection. The first few questions out of a digital-data user's lips after the discovery that the data does indeed exist in digital form are usually, "What file format is it available in?," "How big is the file?" and "What software do I need to use it?" So much has been written on the emergence of spatial data in digital form that it is difficult to limit citations to just a few, but space demands that the list be kept relatively short: Baruth 1993; Bishop and Star 1996 (on digital libraries generally); Lai and Gillies 1991; Lai and Wong 1992; Lamprecht 1986; Making GIS 1995; Map libraries 1993; McGlamery 1995; McGlamery and Lamont 1994; Perkins 1991; Soete 1997; Tatham 1994; and Wong 1993.

Conclusion

As we rush on our way to digital-library/virtual-library/electronic-library nirvana, it is somehow obscurely comforting to know that quality of service remains of primary importance. That quality is composed overall of: good appearance of library's physical facilities, equipment, personnel, and communications materials; library's ability to perform the promised services quickly and dependably; willingness of staff to provide prompt service and to be helpful; high levels of staff knowledge and courtesy; staff ability to be and to convey themselves as trustworthy; and staff ability to provide individual attention to each user (Toward 1997, 241). Reference work, the heart of any library, is a relatively untouched area of study in map-library literature. Spatial-data reference work has much in common with other library reference work, in that it is based on an attempt to find information requested by a user. One major difference is that spatial-data librarians are more likely to do referrals than are other librarians; usually this entails providing the user with purchasing information. But there are more similarities than differences; one major similarity is the good feeling, on the part of both the user and the librarian, when the librarian is able to find absolutely the right—the perfect—item. For all of us who do reference work, that is the goal, and when it is achieved, all the effort is well worth while.

6

Public Relations and Marketing

> ❖ *Designing and implementing a product*
> *(map library service)*
> *is nearly useless without aggressive marketing,*
> *the most underdeveloped area of librarianship.*
> —Yves Tessier, 1983

Communication

Since their inception, libraries have done relatively little advertising or public-relations (PR) work, perhaps from a lingering feeling that it is anti-intellectual, undignified, ill-bred, and above all unnecessary. For, after all, does not everyone know all about a library's services, and is not the library the first and most logical place to turn when in need of information? Unfortunately, the answers to the last two questions have often proved to be "no," leaving libraries at best ill informed about the public mind, and at worst unused. Add to this the general attitude of malaise, if not outright disapproval, on the part of the taxpaying public toward the high price of education *in toto*, and the budgetary emphasis on the bottom line and on immediate returns on investments, with the subsequent poor showing by any institution working toward long-term benefits (some of them hard to measure quantitatively), and it becomes imperative for libraries to get serious about public relations. Libraries must think of public relations not as a slick advertising gimmick but rather as communication with and encouragement of their public, with the aim of forming a positive attitude in that public's mind toward the library. There are now even publications on marketing of libraries; see, for example, *MLS, marketing library services*.

A course in marketing is thus a very good investment for any librarian. While the course is in progress, much of it will immediately seem like common sense: target the markets; research the needs, wants, and values of the markets; keep products current and keyed to the needs of the markets; communicate as effectively as possible; advertise not to the converted alone (to encourage return use) but also to new markets.

Spatial-data collections have several special PR problems. First, they are generally part of a larger institution, so all promotional ventures must be cleared with administration and conform to library practice. If that practice is to do nothing, the librarian may have to employ diplomacy in order to do anything to bring the collection to the public's notice. This leads right into the next problem, which is that the collection may be more in need of PR than any other part of the library. Spatial-data departments seem to be located either in strange, out-of-the-way places in a main library building—say, the sub-basement, or a room accessible only by wending one's way through a labyrinth that makes the walker wish he had remembered his ball of twine (and didn't a bull just roar?), or in a departmental building, in some cases jealously guarded, or even feverishly clutched, by that department. In addition, many collections are still uncataloged or only partially cataloged, so the potential user receives from the main library's online catalog (which the user is firmly convinced contains a record of everything in the library) no hint that such a collection even exists, unless "See" references have been inserted at appropriate places (Fetros 1973, 18; Euler 1972, 46–47). After being for the most part small and often unnoticed until the late 1960s or early 1970s—when the sheer bulk of materials received on depository made them difficult to ignore any longer—spatial-data collections are coming into their own, and can stand some extra promotional work. There is another major point here, at the basis of all we do: why go to all that work to put together a collection if no one knows about it, and no one uses it? And a very closely related point: if no one uses the collection, the librarian in charge of it will soon be joining the ranks of the unemployed (Buckallew 1979, 28).

Before plunging into this, consider one last point: librarians must be convinced in their own minds that they have a service worth selling (and, peculiarly enough, it is something for which the patron has already paid). Most librarians are already firmly convinced of the worth of the library and of spatial data, or they would not be in the field; they aren't in it for the money or *la gloire*—fortunately, since neither will be forthcoming in large amounts. Once confident in the worth of the product, the librarian wonders about what kinds of public relations work to pursue. Here there are two general categories: communications from the library to the user; and vice versa. In the first category are subsumed printed, pictorial, digital, and audiovisual methods of communication; in the second are user studies and questionnaires, which will be discussed later.

Publications

The very first job the librarian should undertake in this area is to get a Web page for the collection up and running, and then to have as many of the collection's publications and handouts as possible available through that Web page. The page should include a brief introduction to the collection, a map of the collection, the aforementioned handouts and publications (or at least citations to them, if copyright does not permit their appearance on the Web), and links to spatial data in digital form.

The textual forms of communication from library to user are, logically enough, those with which the librarian is most familiar. They include the cartobibliography, the accessions list, the promotional brochure, and the "how-to" handout. The cartobibliography is the most onerous to prepare, undertaken only by sterling spirits, and, when done in a detailed, annotated fashion, the most appreciated by the avid user or scholar (Wallis 1969, 86). The way in which one thing leads ever and perfidiously to another is a principle wearily attested to by anyone who has attempted to put together a bibliography. Sir Henry George Fordham discovered this when he decided in 1896 to compile a catalog of Hertfordshire maps, "little conscious of the amplitude such a work could assume" (Fordham reprint 1969, 92). As some slight recompense for his hard work, he is credited with inventing the word "cartobibliography" (Hyde 1972b, 288). Before beginning the donkey work involved in compiling a cartobibliography, it is best to make sure that it has not already been done. If it has not, the budding masochist embarking upon this lengthy, precise bit of work should decide for whom the work is intended (e.g., scholars? general users?), what parameters of area and time are contemplated, taking a sampling to see if initial parameters are too broad; and proceeding— slowly—from there. Changing the idea of audience somewhere along the way, like changing horses in midstream, means that the changer is or soon will be all wet; it leads to having to do work over, or having to scrap what has been done. But when it is finished, a good cartobibliography, like all labors of love, is indeed a joy, of much practical assistance to users, and deserving of a wide audience—if for no other reason than to be sure that some other poor soul does not do it all over again (Chapin 1960; Hyde 1972b; Karrow 1985; Larsgaard 1994; O'Donnell 1992; Powell 1987; Winearls 1976b; Wolf 1986).

There are many forms of citation that may be considered for a cartobibliography; the one chosen will depend upon the purpose and the audience, and thus it is selected after the compiler has decided what the end result is to be. No matter what form one chooses, there will probably be a reader or two who clamors for you to have done it another way. If the object is to provide citations for use in looking up publications in libraries, the system used should be standard AACR2R/LC/ISBD format.

There are many other possible forms of citation—American National Standards Institute (ANSI); British Standards Institution—but the fact remains that if the citations are meant to be checked with library holdings, it is just common sense to have the bibliographic data in the format that libraries use. For many years this author has pondered the stupidity of having bibliographic guides written by nonlibrarians (who frequently leave out such essential matters as series entry, which is often the only entry the library has for an item). It is not too much to ask that at least we librarians should have the intelligence to see that a citation, to be found as quickly and easily (if at all) as possible in a library, must be in standard library format. This point cannot be overemphasized. For a librarian who has never done a cartobibliography before, looking at LCG&M examples, and then embarking on a cartobibliography of local materials—the number-one handout for any collection, since that is what most users request—is the way to begin, being sure that the work includes all formats. For ideas as to pared-down forms and for citing archival materials, see respectively Clark, Larsgaard and Teague 1992 and Archival citations 1983.

Accessions lists, previously discussed in chapter 1, may include news notes, articles on maps and mapping culled from newspapers, notices of tours, and general announcements in addition to the list of new spatial data. These lists are a good PR device, if for no other reason than that a hefty list of new items will convince even casual users that the library is not confining its activities to collecting dust (quietly, of course). These lists also assist the librarian in discovering purchasing patterns, and help the administration to understand what the library is doing with all that money.

There are many other publications that the collection may issue: annual reports; guides to research in various subjects (coupled with classes in various departments if possible); subject analyses of the collection (see especially Buckallew 1983; Bridges, Hinton, and Mason 1978; Heidlage 1980; and The Map Room 1984); guides on where and how to purchase spatial data, especially of the local area (Stark [1981]); guides to using digital data and software; and whatever else the librarian can think of that is of use to the persons who are paying the bills. A good way to figure out what to have handouts on is just to keep track of any questions that get asked more than once a week; they may deserve a handout.

A valuable and very simple kind of printed PR is to be sure that there are good directional signs within the building in which the collection is secreted, and that there is a display of USGS topos of the local area. If the collection's potential users have difficulty finding it, all of the librarian's efforts, all of the maps, and all of the money have been wasted.

Cartobibliographies and accessions lists are of most practical value to the hardened map user. Reaching out to the casual user or the nonuser is a difficult procedure and requires a different approach. One method is the promotional brochure, whose latest variety is the homepage on the Web. Due in part to the high cost of printing and binding, the library handbook of yesteryear has yielded to separate pages for each department of the library, each department's page done in a different color, and all arrayed on a rack prominently displayed in the front entrance of the library, from which patrons may select the needed pages and compile their own handbook.

Although these separates do follow a pattern established by the administration, they can reflect the character of a department. How the separate is organized depends on the library's policies and the librarian putting it all together, but some items that must be included are: location (of course illustrated with a map); hours; scope of the collection; services and staff available; loan period; regulations for users' arrangement of the collection; and, in the case of older, larger libraries such as the British Museum Map Room, history and how to obtain copies through the main library's copy service (although this last is increasingly appropriate for all libraries). It helps to have "SPATIAL DATA," "CARTOGRAPHIC MATERIALS," or "MAPS" in very large type somewhere near the top of the page. All of this now goes quite properly on the collection's homepage on the Web, preferably with a few colorful but small (digitally) graphics. The promotional brochure should speak the language of its audience. The librarian should collect examples of promotional brochures and map-library Web pages, and plagiarize freely from all of them in putting together a brochure. The important points are to keep it simple and colorful, with a minimum of text, and a map of the collection. The hardcopy brochure should be distributed at the main entrance and in the collection proper, and as is appropriate or possible at locations outside the library.

One way to reach potential patrons who do not normally visit the library is through newspaper articles. Local newspapers usually carry notification and explanation of special exhibits in a library; on a college campus, articles on library services may be generated for the college newspaper. When there is an opportunity, such as the Australian map collections had with a nationwide map week, one should seize upon that as a good excuse for publicity (Prescott 1989). The librarian should check with editions of local, campus, and other papers to see what their policies are, and should try to get the library into print in a positive fashion. One way to do this is to get to know the person in charge of public relations at the appropriate institution. Of course, television coverage—which is often more fortuitous than anything else, but may be worked for—gives the library the most exposure.

Yet another way of spreading the word is through periodical articles. Smaller libraries will not be able to obtain the coverage that the large libraries do; NYPL, for example, has been written up in *The New Yorker,* LC in both *Smithsonian* and *The New Yorker*. But all of us can, and often do, write articles for the library press; many librarians have written up their collections (see F. Woodward 1975; Sherwood 1976; Hemperley 1982; Berthelsen 1978; Berthelson 1982; Crone and Day 1960; C. Lewis 1973; Lamprecht 1977; Barkdull 1973; Marshall 1972; Tessier and Kidd

1970; Winearls 1966; Hagen 1967; Griffin 1980; Motteler 1980; Goodman 1955; Baird 1978b; Whistance-Smith 1981; Ansari 1979; Boswell 1976a; and Parsons and Fathers 1968). It helps a great deal if the library has its own periodicals, as does LC—the *Information bulletin* and the *Quarterly*—in which to publicize itself.

Exhibits

> ❖ *Post's Law states that*
> *the map you put on display*
> *will be the very one*
> *someone has come hundreds of miles to consult.*
> —Post 198-?

Pictorial methods of PR are another way of informing the casual user, or the potential user, of the library's existence and services. Most libraries have exhibit areas or cases, and the collection's Web page is an excellent exhibit area for non-copyrighted materials. The librarian should check with the person in charge of displays in the library (ferreting out just who that is may be the hardest part of the whole process) to determine the schedule of displays and discover when the collection may reserve the display area. The librarian might also check with persons in charge of displays in public buildings, such as city halls or shopping centers in the area, as to their display possibilities. Displaying in such areas is highly desirable because it puts the library before a whole new audience, persons who, although they have paid their taxes, probably did not know that the collection existed. Although libraries do not usually have large amounts of unfilled or display space, any large, bare, vertical expanse, be it corridor or the vast surface of a long line of map case backs and sides, is tailor-made for map exhibiting—in the last case, for the cost of magnets alone.

The fundamental purpose of an exhibit is to sell the library and to make the public cognizant of its services (Map exhibits 1958, 12). A theme must be chosen, be it new materials, significant holidays, cartographic rarities, conventions in town, one-man exhibits, cartographic coverage of a given region, an explanation of the use of maps, or political or natural current events. If exhibits are frequently mounted, a cartographic exhibit idea file is a necessity (Ristow 1954, 18-19).

Planning and arranging an exhibit is not easy. One source recommends that the first action a librarian should take—upon being informed that it is her turn to put together an exhibit—is to try to get out of it, and if that fails, to try to get the money to have it professionally done (Map exhibits 1958, 13). These efforts failing—and they usually do—the librarian who realizes that "planning and arranging good exhibits calls for imagination, familiarity with the map collection, desirable display space and equipment, and an abundance of time" (Ristow l967a, 414-15) may resignedly leap into the fray. Simplicity should be a key organizational principle; use as few words as possible, do not try to use too much material, and don't be afraid of empty space. Use informal rather than formal balance, that is, do not exactly balance a display with two 8½" x 11" sheets of paper on one half of the display board and two on the other half. Instead, play color and texture, words and form, against each other to get the desired balance. Unity is linked to simplicity; work with one theme, use as few colors as possible, and use similar (but not exactly the same) shapes to reinforce each other. Have one important item—be it a word or an object—and emphasize it, by encircling it, by setting it apart in an isolated space or against a contrasting color, texture, or value (light, dark). Diagonal designs are usually not wise because they create two awkward areas and also because they direct the eye off the display. Use color to command attention, to clarify, to bring pleasure; use texture to make a contrast, to invite visual or manual inspection; use space to vitalize the display with objects projecting into space, in three dimensions, not just two (Randall and Haines 1961; Stokes 1974; Strickland 1986). The human eye, when looking at a rectangular space, tends to start at the upper left-hand corner and then sweep in a curve to the lower right-hand and then the lower left-hand corners. There should be some sort of order, rhythm, and contrast in the display, but not absolute symmetry. One especially significant item should be emphasized by prominent placement or special lighting.

The exhibit should be designed primarily to give amusement and pleasure, to inspire, to entertain, or to alarm (Dalphin and English 1954, 1466). The display area, its lighting, security, cases, display boards, and frequency of contact with passers-by (we all look twice at something we fall over) should be examined. The backing of the display surfaces is a concern; what will be needed to affix materials to the surface? Tacks? Staples? Tape? Sky hooks? What color is the backing? Neutral and light-reflecting backgrounds are the best (Ristow 1954, 22; Dalphin and English 1954, 1467). Will the display area accommodate only maps, or may the exhibit include many formats? If the latter, book· racks will be needed in addition to colored paper, poster paints, commercial lettering guides or ready-made letters, tape, paper clips, pins, and so forth (Dalphin and English 1954, 1467).

The librarian should seek out far more material than will fit into the display area, so that the best may be selected; the exhibit should be varied but not too much, in order to attract attention but not to confuse. The central theme should be simple, quick, and clear, illustrating places either very familiar or very exotic. The display should not be overcrowded with color or items, and the materials should not be placed too much above or below eye level. Any text should be short and catchy.

If the exhibit is large, benches should be available for those suffering from museum feet. If at all possible, maps should be able to be studied both from far away (for overall effect) and close up (to pick up detail). The items should be protected and insured from and against damage and theft. Light is paper's archenemy, so an exhibit should not be kept up longer than a few weeks. If the items are to be closely inspected, they should be placed behind glass or plastic; peanut butter, mustard, and dirty finger-prints seldom improve an item's appearance or increase its longevity. The exhibit should be open long hours, so that those who work 8:00 a.m. to 5:00 p.m. are not by definition excluded. And perhaps most important, the exhibit should be publicized by whatever means possible: posters, newspapers, newsletters, radio, television, skywriting, whatever is possi-ble and affordable. Putting up an exhibit is time-consuming and there is no point in doing it unless a good many persons view the result. For maximum impact, the exhibit should have clarity and simplicity of message and honesty of presentation, so that persons informed of its existence by publicity will not be disappointed (Ristow 1954, 25; Map exhibits 1958, 12–14). The librarian should also put together an exhibit catalog, which will probably be a cartobibliography plus preliminary text; if the exhibit turns out even better than expected, loan it out (Whistance-Smith 1979; Bent and Blake 1978).

Orientation Lectures and Tours; Classes

Introductory lectures and tours are also of assistance in publicizing the library and its services. Although many libraries, because of a paucity of staff, make an effort to be as "self-help" as possible, an introduction to resources and how to find them is of value even to those suspicious characters who, wherever they may find themselves, frequent libraries. College and university librarians may ensure themselves of captive (soon to be enslaved, if the librarian's peroration is well done) audiences by setting up good relations with professors in geography, marketing, history, geology, and so forth, and showing themselves to be amenable to and encouraging of library orientation tours. If an introductory library-use course is taught at a university or offered at a public library, the librarian should gently bully the teachers into allowing time for a lecture on cartographic materials. The classic library tour—including maps, atlases, remote-sensing imagery, reference materials, and that boon to the map orientation lecture, plastic raised-relief maps—can be slanted to fit almost any subject focus; be sure to have a virtual "tour" of the collection on the homepage. Local maps and the plastic maps always make friends (Batchelder 1981; Weir 1977; Winearls l981a; Leeuwenburg 1982, 13).

Another type of orientation lecture often neglected is that for other librarians. Insist that other librarians, especially those at reference desks, know what the library has to offer, how to explain its services, and when to refer users to the cartographic materials collection (Euler 1972, 46).

Such orientation lectures, or, if there is time and need, seminars, must be more technical than those given to the general users. One such seminar at the Milwaukee Public Library began with an introduction to the map world and definition of terms (especially scale), then proceeded to USGS topos and other high-use series such as DMA, British and Canadian topo series, National Geographic maps, a review of vocabulary, land-ownership maps, fire-insurance maps, charts, and a survey of cartobibliographies (Schwartz 1976, 2–5). In some cases, full-fledged classes may be required, like the one given at the University of Toronto through Continuing Studies during the winter of 1976–1977, which met weekly (Winearls 1977).

Map Societies

One way of bringing spatial data to the attention of the general public is through the map society, which is most popular in larger metropolitan areas. The first U.S. map society was formed in New England in the 1920s, under the name Cartophiles, and operated somewhat erratically until the 1950s. In 1976, the Chicago Map Society made its debut, as did the Historical Map Society of British Columbia. Since then, there has been a pleasant landslide of such societies, with (for example) Delaware Valley, Michigan, New York City, California, Ottawa, and Washington, D.C., following along. The members come from a wide variety of backgrounds; the meetings may be monthly, quarterly, or annually, and some have newsletters. There is now a Website, Map societies around the world, at http://www.csuohio.edu/CUT/MapSoc/Index.htm .

Audiovisual Presentations

If the general library has an audiovisual orientation system, so much the better. Color-slide cameras in conjunction with a tape recorder are sometimes used, as are videotape recorders. Such presentations are in the language of the television-habituated patron; they may be viewed at the patron's convenience, by any size audience; and they do not require a live lecturer who, after the first twenty repetitions of one lecture, is either bored to tears or half insane. Such presentations do lack personal rapport; also, as we all know, machines tend to break down, if not actually self-destruct, and usually at the most crucial moments (Hannabass 1971, 25).

Like exhibits, color-slide/tape presentations need to be well planned and carefully executed, with a clear objective in mind. Because the audience is habituated to television, the presentation must be professional. There must be considerable attention paid to such technical matters as coordination of audio with visual, and there must be some person on the premises who knows, loves, and understands machines. If the general library or the campus has an audiovisual department, the librarian should take the project there, looking for guidance and assistance.

Planning such a project begins with defining audience and objectives, scope, length of presentation (twelve to fifteen minutes is long enough), and general sequence. The amount of money available needs to be taken into account also. Photographs, drawings, maps, charts, and text must be decided on; there will be much reviewing, adjustment, and readjustment. The text, whether spoken or printed, should be concise and clear, and should not be merely a repetition of what is shown visually. Objects depicted on a slide should not be described in detail in text, and spoken narrative should not be exactly the same as printed text. The script should be planned first and the slides fitted to it; it should be conversational in tone. The graphics should be simple, very clear, and of consistent photographic quality; they should be of persons rather than of buildings all alone—and of course duplicates should be made of all the slides. A variety of colorful, pleasing objects should be presented in the slides. Music should be scarce and unidentifiable; it should be eschewed during times of spoken text. Viewing other libraries' presentations is most helpful (e.g., the University of Minnesota; McMaster University) (Gillispie 1983).

A double-spaced, typed copy of the narrative, on cardboard and keyed to the slides, is essential for the reader, who should possess a good recording voice. A minimum pause of two seconds between each slide, with slides on the screen for a minimum of three seconds each, should be budgeted into the time schedule. Touches of humor often improve a presentation. If all this seems like more work than the librarian can bear, SLAG&M has an excellent slide-tape presentation for sale or rent, entitled *Introduction to map libraries*.

User Studies

After discussing the length of time he had spent studying the human psyche, Freud once said something on the order of, "Women, what do they want?" One very important aspect of PR communications is that from users to the librarian—which boils down to finding out what the user wants and needs, preferably before it is requested.

This communication may be in the form of questionnaires, which ask about such matters as: What does the patron use most frequently in the library? Are loan periods satisfactory? What does the user most need that the library does not have? User studies are traditionally a weak point in library service, and spatial-data collections have followed faithfully in the footsteps of general libraries in this matter, with relatively few user studies reported in the literature (Bach 1949, 368; Deckelbaum 1989; Hagen 1970b, 27–30; Ray 1974, 104–9; Bridges 1978; Thatcher 1978b; North 1981; What ... 1978; Collins 1977; Mittra and Ghatak 1993; Seavey and Rex 1992). Even though this is probably only the tip of the iceberg, it seems to be a very small iceberg; most librarians depend on seat-of-the-pants, subjective analyses, an approach that often works well. Simply counting the maps to be reshelved and checking their geographic classification areas provides good feedback, as does checking the types and geographical areas of materials most often loaned out. One possibility for the future is having the computer count the number of times that certain words are used by users pounding away at the computer terminals, accessing the catalog database.

And a Couple of Other Ideas

The following suggestions have been collected from Curtis 1990, Barrow and Hudson 1996, and Villar 1988:

- Have a sale or giveaway of duplicate maps.

- Join non-campus/non-library community activities in related fields (e.g., GIS, city planning, etc.).

- Work with your state geographic alliance.

- Exhibit and speak at local and state historical and genealogical societies.

- Join local user groups, such as Arc/Info user groups.

- Charge non-campus-affiliated users for extended services. Surprise! it will bring in more users.

- Invite effusively happy users to put it in writing, to the library director or president of the campus.

- Participate in regional map societies and events.

- Establish your own friends group (e.g., NYPL Map Division's Mercator Society). CAUTION: Be prepared for large amounts of work—planning and carrying out meetings, publishing a newsletter, sending out Christmas cards. . . .

- Make sure the map collection is in all library and campus directories.

- Have a "constant" exhibit of places in the news.

- Present your spatial-data collection as a potential naming opportunity to the library directory. A naming ceremony and attendant publicity encourage further support by others.

- If you're on a campus, target heavy-use departments. Watch what they are offering as classes, and notify faculty of new materials in their areas. Give demos and introductory classes both inside and outside the library; volunteer to do so. Get involved in student orientations. Meet with individual faculty in a social context (beware of department politics!). Set up "office hours" in the department.

The Librarian

Once a user has finally made it to the collection, the informal communication between user and librarian—as much as the information available—keeps the user coming back. A few basics here deserve emphasis. Courtesy, greeting the user with a smile, honesty about the resources of the collection and the services available, advice on how and where to obtain materials that the library does not possess, and the librarian's abhorrence of the runaround are important. It also helps to have a stack of giveaway materials—such as guides to the collection, indexes, and price lists to frequently used series—ready for the taking (Bergen 1972b, 316).

Conclusion

One worry of librarians has been that active PR will promote more business than the library can handle. As long as librarians do not advertise something they cannot provide or do—which is hardly necessary because just listing the resources available will result in such a detailed enumeration that there is no need to make things up—it is silly to be afraid of success, particularly in times when funding is predicated on that very success. And, as both Buckallew 1979 and Cobb 1984 have noted, there is no point in spending a great deal of time and money in putting together a collection and then sitting there and watching it collect dust.

We must make our collections visible and accessible. The best way to do that is by having the entire collection cataloged, and on the general library online catalog—cataloging time saved once is reference time spent over and over, or, tragically, reference time that is not requested because the users don't know that there is anything about which to ask. Next in line of importance after cataloging are the many methods previously mentioned—a collection homepage on the Web, exhibits, publications, and not only being knowledgeable about our collections but also encouraging their use.

7

Education

❖ *There is a good deal of physical labor connected with the handling of maps.*
—Nelson 1943

❖ *All of this is so close to my heart that I'm sure if anyone cut me open they'd find a map inside, with rivers and roads for veins.*
—Ena L. Yonge 1963, in Ristow 1972b

History and Training

In the early 1900s, most spatial-data collections were administered by persons with varied academic and professional backgrounds, few of whom had any professional training in library science. There is a delightful story—so delightful as to make one suspect that it is apocryphal—that when Lloyd Brown was hired by the Clements Library of American History to work with its maps, he at first protested feebly that he knew nothing much about maps made prior to 1850, in response to which the administrator said, "We have more than 25,000 maps made prior to 1850. We don't know anything about them either. You're hired" (Gillispie 1988). As interest in geography grew in the United States and in its colleges during and between the World Wars, an increasing number of professionally trained geographers, woefully lacking in library science skills, found employment as spatial-data librarians. The only kind of education for such librarians until the 1950s was the kind considered by some to be the best, and by others to be a "very blinkered view"—on-the-job training (Nichols 1977, 24).

Persons became caretakers of maps and their kin usually by accident and under protest, while on their way somewhere else. Traditionally, maps have been the stepchildren of any library. They and their fellow materials, with the exception of atlases (and not all of those), are in nonbook format, and are therefore awkward at best and suspect at worst, as far as the rest of the library world is concerned. Thus anyone who became "stuck with the maps" (and it was often so expressed) either was lowest on the totem pole, or had made the mistake of not being at the meeting where the issue was decided. Librarians who began by finding themselves in a dark, dusty room (probably below ground level, or otherwise relatively inaccessible), staring with dismay or even dislike and horror at a stack of dark, dusty maps, often discovered later that they had become genuinely fond of these bulky, beautiful, supremely useful objects.

It was not until 1950 that some interest was shown in the revolutionary idea of training persons for map librarianship *before*, not after, they became map librarians. A course on maps and cartobibliographic aids was introduced at the University of Illinois in January of that year, taught by James Ranz (Ristow 1978a, 4). This course, intended for geographers and librarians both, was taught thereafter, until 1958, by Bill M. Woods, and in later years by Robert White and David Cobb. William Easton, of Illinois State University at Normal, also taught the course, which for many years remained "the only accredited course in map librarianship available anywhere in the world" (Woods 1971, 1).

The written history of map librarianship education begins, logically enough, just after the first course in the field was initiated, with Woods's seminal article in *Special Libraries* (1952), in which he noted that library schools were finally offering courses in special librarianship. Woods also made recommendations for the curriculum for map librarianship, which— with the addition of a section of digital data—still hold up well nearly fifty years later: introduction to maps and map libraries; cartobibliography (catalogs, periodicals, atlases, geography generally); care and preservation; classification and cataloging; old and rare maps; use of maps; and cartography (Woods 1952). Silence settled once again until Woods's 1956 article, in which he extended his recommendations to include an undergraduate major of 30 to 32 semester hours in geography with special attention to cartography and research, a minor in geology or history, and a foreign language. He closed the article with suggestions that the aspirant consider graduate work in geography and obtain an internship in a cartographic materials collection (Woods 1956).

It was not until the late 1960s that articles on education became relatively frequent, when a veritable gaggle turned up in library literature, dominated by Walter Ristow's survey articles of 1967 (1967a, 1967b) and 1976. In 1967 courses were still offered at only one institution, the University of Illinois, although some slight attention was given to maps in cataloging and technical-processing courses at other schools, and several library schools made provision for directed specialized studies. But things began to pick up. During the fall semester of 1969, Dr. Roman Drazniowsky of the American Geographical Society taught "Map Resources and Map Librarianship" at the Columbia University School of Library Service, one evening a week. "Draz" covered maps as library resources; problems of collecting, conserving, storing, and servicing of maps; and management and administration. The brave souls taking the course had to sprint the distance from the subway to AGS, as this was not a salubrious part of town at night. In Canada in 1969, a committee had been formed to study standards for education of map librarians (Layng 1969, 33).

The 1970s started off well, with the Western Michigan University Department of Librarianship introducing a new curriculum providing courses to develop map librarians. A 36-hour graduate program included studies of the principles of cartography and aerial photography interpretation and concluded with an internship in the university's map library. A course in map librarianship was to be offered in summer of 1970 by Joan Winearls at the University of Toronto. Back again in the States, Catherine Bahn was to teach a maps and charts course (1970–1971) at the Graduate School of the U.S. Department of Agriculture. Way out west, the map librarian at the University of Oregon—Ed Thatcher—offered a seminar on "Map Library Exploration" for new geography graduate students in the fall term of 1971. Internationally, the International Federation of Library Associations (IFLA) had, in 1973, formed a working group on training for map librarianship to investigate the current situation in retraining, to make recommendations, to prepare practical guidelines for map librarians, and to promote and organize seminars (Thatcher 1972b; Zogner 1975; Wallis 1975; Rauchle 1975).

In 1975 Richard Stephenson began teaching a course on map librarianship at Catholic University in Washington, D.C.—a course that he taught into the 1990s. In 1976, Stephenson taught a course on the history of maps and map collecting, following up the 1975 course on map librarianship. Also in 1976, Ristow recommended that, because of the heavy concentration of collections in the northeast United States and the Pacific Coast, library schools in those areas consider introducing map librarianship into their course catalogs. At that time five library schools were offering a course in map librarianship—University of Illinois, University of Toronto, Columbia University, Western Michigan University, and Catholic University—and directed studies and specialized reading courses were available at a number of schools (Ristow 1976). The West Coast had at that time no course offered through the library schools, but the University of Oregon and Southern Oregon College both offered map-librarianship courses taught through other departments by the resident map librarians. By 1978, the number of accredited North American library schools offering at least one course in map librarianship still stood at five—the same five. There were still possibilities for practicums and independent studies at many library schools; the University of Oregon still offered a course (usually taught during the summer); and one course had been taught at the University of British

Columbia (Stephenson 1979, 120–21). By this time, the United States was in transition to a service-oriented information economy, which meant that, at least in theory, library science was the place to be.

In 1980, matters were much the same, having remained at a plateau for more than ten years, with five schools offering at least one course in map librarianship. Beginning in 1980, the University of Wisconsin–Milwaukee began offering a map-librarianship curriculum. In 1981, the IFLA group offered a workshop on map curatorship in Utrecht. And in the fall of 1984 the University of Maryland at College Park announced a dual M.A. in geography and library science (56 credit hours). In 1989, the IFLA Geography and Map Libraries Section offered a workshop in Jamaica (Murphy 1989).

Persons presently planning to become map librarians (any who plan that far ahead!) should major in geography or geology as undergraduates, with a minor in computer science, and take courses in cartography, interpretation of map and aerial photography, use of spatial data in digital form (these are usually billed as GIS courses), UNIX and DOS (use and programming) operating systems, and database management. Regional geography courses are also helpful. The undergraduate years are also an excellent time for the student to take courses in reading knowledge of as many foreign languages as possible; the student should also take basic courses in business administration (e.g., management, marketing, accounting, and so forth). In times past, library schools told prospective students to take whatever they wanted in their undergraduate work; let us hope that those times are long gone, for computer-science and business-administration courses should be demanded by all library schools.

Once in library school, there are two checklists for the student to keep in mind—one relating to information and library science, the other to spatial-data librarianship. For the first, the student should take management courses, either extensions of courses taken in undergraduate school or courses relating specifically to library management. In either case, budgeting must be included. Spatial-data collections are especially prone to being mini-businesses, with the librarian being responsible for effectively managing the collection, its personnel, and its budget. Fair warning is hereby given: any librarian who did not take management courses in graduate school or earlier will suffer for it financially (as will the collection), either by virtue of a lower salary or by having to take one of those expensive management workshops—which the librarian will in all likelihood have to pay for herself. If the library school does not offer management courses, the student should take basic courses offered by the business school of the university.

Other courses that the student would do well to take as an undergraduate (if possible, and if not, as a graduate student), are computer basics, computer programming, and the use of spatial data in digital form. Computer programming is the new *lingua franca*, at least as universal as English, and there is now a worldwide shortage of programming skills. This is the area that has most changed the way job descriptions for librarians are written (Borbely 1985; Corbin 1993; Xu 1996). It is now a commonplace for job descriptions for a "map librarian" to require the ability to install, maintain, and provide reference service for spatial-data software, spatial data in digital form, and the hardware to run it on, and of course to build and maintain a Web page. More and more, words like "cybrarian," "information specialist," "information manager," and "spatialist" better describe the job.

Another course that the aspiring librarian needs seems not yet to exist; that is, a course in reading foreign languages for reference and cataloging. Even though library users are usually conversant only in one language—their native tongue—spatial data with information in a foreign language may be relatively readily used by most persons. Therefore, the librarian will purchase them, and the cataloger will need to catalog them. Most foreign-language courses are more detailed than they need to be, and tend to focus on speaking rather than reading. It is unnecessary to take an entire semester of Italian just to learn how to translate needed elements on a map when the cataloger will probably need to know no more than 500 words, and the acquisitions librarian not many more (unless to translate, and write responses to, letters from across the seas). Catalogers should be able to catalog French, German, Russian, Italian, Japanese, Spanish, and Portuguese maps at the least and, of course, English maps—which means that any prospective librarian had best take both beginning and advanced cataloging, as spatial-data cataloging is discussed only in advanced cataloging classes, and the librarian in charge of the collection is often the only person available to do the cataloging.

The second major focus of study relates specifically to spatial-data librarianship. However such courses are structured, they should include study about spatial data (history, how to interpret them, how they are made, and how to care for and provide service for them), selection, acquisition, classification, cataloging, storage, reference, marketing, preservation, management, and cartobibliography.

The practicalities of the matter are that there are, and will probably continue to be, few classroom possibilities for the prospective librarian to learn about spatial data—and considering the relatively small number of positions that open up each year (from zero to a maximum of six or seven), this is not surprising. It is more appropriate for librarians to learn about different media throughout all of their classes, with finishing-off seminars concerning specific types of librarianship at the end of their course work (Gelfand 1988; Seavey and Clark 1988).

Continuing Education

> ❖ *Librarians and other information professionals*
> *should accept responsibility for their education*
> *throughout their careers.*
> —Educational policy 1996

After the degree, the most valuable learning experience the librarian may have is the work itself, followed closely by attendance at and active participation in professional association meetings and workshops, and by doing research and writing. LCG&M's Summer Map Project, which has become irregular, is an unofficial training ground for the neophyte librarian. Following are the major librarianship associations, divided by area.

International:

Australia: first seminar for mapkeepers held at the National Library, Canberra, 12–13 April 1973; formed Australian Map Curators Circle (later Australian Map Circle, June 1983) (Prescott l973a, 243).

Canada: Association of Canadian Map Libraries (ACML) first meets at Public Archives, June 1968; Society of University Cartographers in Canada first meets at York University, October 1970 (Weissmiller 1972; McGrath 1975, 218; Winearls 1969). Contact the ACML at http://www.sscl.uwo.ca/assoc.acml/ acmla.html .

Great Britain: The British Cartographic Society (founded 1963) established in 1966 a Map Curators' Group; in 1982, the group established a liaison with the Library Association (Wallis 1975, 31). The Society of University Cartographers (SUC) was founded in 1964.

Congress of Cartographic Information Specialists Associations: organized 1988 (Galneder 1989; Baruth 1994).

IFLA's Geography and Map Libraries Subsection (part of Special Libraries Section) formed in 1969; in 1977, IFLA was restructured and G&M became a full section within the Special Libraries Division (Corley 1970, 40; Stephenson 1979, 119; Ristow 1970a and b; Wallis 1981, 109–11, and 1977, 38). Contact G&M at http://www-map.lib.umn.edu/map_libraries.html .

Groupe des Cartothecaires de LIBER: formed in the early 1980s in LIBER—Ligue des Bibliothèques Européennes de Recherche (Farrell 1981).

Netherlands: Werkgroep Kaartbeheer (Working Group on Map Curatorship) of the Netherlands Cartographic Society; established 1975 (van de Waal, 1985).

United States:

ALA MAGERT: founded 1980; http://www.sunysb.edu/libmap/magert1.htm .

Association of American Geographers, Southeastern Division, Committee on Southern Map Librarians (COSML): first workshop held in 1975.

Map Online Users Group: founded 1979.

NEMO: Northeast Map Users Organization: founded 1987; yes, the president's title is Captain NEMO (Northeast 1988).

SLAG&M: began 1941, possibly to be dissolved in 1998; for its history, see Murphy 1982a; for presentations on need for cartographic materials librarians to affiliate with other library associations, see Ray 1981; Stevens 1978c; Fox 1978; Otness 1978a; Cobb 1979c. Contact SLAG&M at http://www.sla.org/membership/divisions/geo-map.html .

WAML: founded 1967, after a meeting in late 1966. Contact WAML at http://gord.ucsd.edu/mw/waml/waml.html .

Another type of organization offering continuing education for the spatial-data librarian is the map society, e.g., British Columbia Map Society, California Map Society (founded 1978), Chicago Map Society (oldest in North America; founded 1976), Delaware Valley Map Society (founded 1983), Michigan Map Society (founded 1977), Washington Map Society. Check the map-society homepage given in chapter 6, in the section on "Map Societies," for current information.

There are many associations dealing with spatial data, not from the point of view of library science:

American Congress on Surveying and Mapping

Association of American Geographers

Geological Society of America

International Cartographic Association

International Conference on Computer-Assisted Cartography (Auto-Carto)

International Conference on the History of Cartography

International Geographical Union

International Map Collectors' Society

International Symposium on Remote Sensing of the Environment

North American Cartographic Information Society: organized 1980

There are also many library associations that are not primarily cartographic (e.g., state and regional library associations), and subject-oriented associations such as the National Online Conferences and the Society of American Archivists.

There are workshops and classes relating specifically to spatial data; general workshops on organizing spatial data are most prevalent, although there have been some map-cataloging workshops, and for the last five years courses on working with spatial data in digital form have been offered. The librarian should also learn about preservation of materials, if this class was not available in the graduate school where the master's degree in library science was obtained (International Seminar 1991). For several years the Newberry Library in Chicago offered its Summer Institute in Cartography, a three-week series of lectures and workshops on the study and use of maps, set up for humanities and social-sciences faculty and for map librarians.

Other major forms of continuing education—previously mentioned briefly, but deserving of emphasis—are research and publication and conference attendance, the first two often being an excuse for the third (and vice versa). Any librarian who wants to stay in the groves of academe had better plan on a fair amount of research, writing, and publication. The librarian already knows how to do research, and how to slave away at boring work for long periods of time—quite an advantage. The next step is knowing how, or learning how, to write. English courses in high school and college should prepare the librarian in the old faithful school of: first tell them what you are going to tell them; tell them; and then tell them what you've told them. Beyond this, what it takes is practice, and being sure to eschew the following rules for poor writing: ignore the reader; be verbose, vague, and pompous; and do not revise (Merrill 1948). The librarian writing book reviews will as a general rule receive a list of rules from the reviewing agency. If not, general practice is to state the purpose of the item reviewed, note its advantages and disadvantages, and summarize, ending by noting the libraries for which the publication is useful.

Presenting one's paper at a conference requires learning a few new rules. First of all, prepare adequately by not only writing the paper but also by presenting it to a long-suffering friend, or by taping the presentation and then listening to it. The written paper and the paper as orally presented should not be exactly the same—the latter should stay away from reciting statistics, use humor when appropriate, and be straightforward and to the point. Next, the speaker should be sure that all pages and all slides and other audiovisual materials have made it to the conference at the same time as the speaker; do not trust any speaking materials to the tender mercies of the airline baggage check. The speaker should organize the talk so that the time allotted for the talk will be all that is used; twenty minutes is about as long as most of us can keep our listeners interested.

The title should be an attention-grabber, and brief to boot. If slides are used, the speaker should be sure that the presentation is a lecture accompanied by slides, not slides accompanied by a casual commentary. The speaker should also take a good close look at the slides to be used: if "you can't see it very well on the slide," don't use the slide. If "the slide isn't very good, but if you look closely, you can see . . .," don't use the slide. If text is being presented on the slide, keep it the largest possible typeface, and keep it sparse; if that is not possible, go the handouts-matched-with-overhead-projector-transparency-or-PC route. If you decide to use a PC, plan on the worst—a network connection like molasses in January; complete failure of all computer systems, including your hard drive—and have a manual backup; overhead transparencies are the best backup option. If your presentation is scheduled immediately after lunch, keep it short and snappy, and if at all possible, do *not* have the lights turned off. If you don't follow these strictures, you deserve to have your presentation marred by the sound of persons snoring, or possibly even falling off their chairs. Do arrange to have someone (probably the program chairperson) turn the lights and the slide projector on and off, and so forth; do not assume that someone will take care of it for you (Effective presentations 1992; Matson 1988).

Another form of writing is that of the grant proposal. It is an unusual librarian indeed who is not involved in writing one of these every few years or so, or even more often. In the past, grants were written most often for retrospective-cataloging projects (see, in chapter 3 on cataloging, in the section titled "Some Prominent Problems," the subsection on "Retrospective cataloging"). More recently, grant proposals are for computer hardware, because the manipulation of spatial data in digital form requires hardware able to handle hefty files, which means large amounts of RAM and ROM, and heavy-duty CPU abilities. There are many guides to assist in writing grants (for example, Ruskin 1995). What is often of most assistance is to read a successful grant proposal to the agency to which one is going to send in a grant proposal; it also is important very often to make and keep up contact with a specific grant officer in the agency.

The newest form of continuing education is subscription to subject-oriented listservs, such as MAPS-L (maps-l@uga.cc.uga.edu). These exist for just about every topic you can think of; the only drawback is that in the first flush of enthusiasm one may sign up for so many as to have in the hundreds of electronic-mail messages per day.

Employment Outlook

Outlook for employment in librarianship, as for employment in any educational or humanities-oriented profession, is a matter in which optimism and realism must be nicely balanced. Things have changed a great deal since the halcyon days when there were more positions than there were librarians (Ristow 1967a, 415). Although there are in the United States and Canada today about a thousand spatial-data collections, the vast majority of the positions connected with these collections are part-time, and the librarian must be ready to assume other responsibilities, such as documents or general reference (Ristow 1976, 41). Another caveat is that although about five to 10 percent of these positions may fall vacant per year on the average, any given year can be feast or famine. The prospective spatial-data librarian does well to become active in professional organizations, especially in the expensive matter of attending conventions, for it is at these conventions that the librarian-to-be will meet persons who will eventually either hire for or vacate a position. It is through getting to know persons that employment is most easily acquired later on. Spatial-data librarianship is still a relatively small field, and it is easy to become acquainted with those librarians who have a great deal of experience and who are likely to be hiring in future.

Beyond the standard courses, librarians will find that working with spatial data necessitates a list of qualities akin to the inventory of a bestiary: strong as an elephant, to lift large stacks of maps and atlases (or even just one atlas at a time); stubborn as a mule while hunting for the answer to a question; diplomatic as the last ten U.S. Secretaries of State, not to mention clairvoyant as a medium and patient as a saint while dealing with a user who either isn't sure what is needed or won't tell you; the nose of a bloodhound while trying to find out where a map might be purchased; the ability to read all languages; the skill of Sherlock Holmes in discerning from patterns of publication where the answer is; and ethics as stable and well founded as the Rock of Gibraltar (Dahl 1983; Yonge 1955b, 23). In addition, the librarian should be able to read truthful statements such as the following, enjoy them, and forge on:

> One of the most common superstitions about library work is that it offers not only a fair social advantage but also a snug haven of rest, relaxation, and perpetual delight to a person fond of literary pursuits. . . . We all know that stern

reality does not sustain this popular view! (J. Christian Bay, "Inspiration through cataloguing," 1916 [from broadside by Harold Otness, Ashland, Oregon]).

"The library keeper's place and office in most countries are looked upon as places of profit and gain." Rather a startling statement to us, who have been accustomed to look upon librarianship as under the special influence of the planet Saturn, which is said to preside over all occupations in which money is obtained with very great difficulty (Garnett 1899, 178).

What assists the librarian in moving onward are the camaraderie of fellow librarians, and the materials themselves. Our meetings with our fellow librarians are an exhilarating combination of hard work and easy enjoyment, and this mixture appears to extend throughout the spatial-data world. The materials themselves—beautiful, awkward, supremely useful—support us well in our continuing project to persuade the rest of the library world that spatial data are not second-class citizens in Alexandria.

Bibliography

This bibliography includes works cited in the text. Other suggested readings are listed in appendixes 2A, 2B, and 2C.

AACCCM 1982. *See Cartographic materials . . .*

AACR2. *See* American Library Association 1978.

Abelson, N. 1954. A method for filing rolled wall maps. *SLAG&MD Bulletin* 15: 10–12.

Abler, R. 1988. Awards, rewards and excellence, keeping geography alive and well. *Professional Geographer* 40 (2): 135–40.

Accession lists from map libraries. 1980. *WAML Information Bulletin* 11: 188–89.

ACM Conference on Space, Growth, and Performance Problems of Academic Libraries, Chicago, 1975. 1976. *Farewell to Alexandria: Solutions to space, growth, and performance problems of libraries.* Westport, CT: Greenwood Press.

Adams, K. T. 1941. Federal surveys and maps. In *The American yearbook, a record of events and progress, year 1940,* 286–90. New York: Thomas Nelson.

Adams, R. 1937. Librarians as enemies of books. *Library Quarterly* 7: 317–31.

Adkinson, B. W. 1949. Library of Congress maps program. *Surveying and Mapping* 9: 130–33.

Aerial photographs and satellite images. 1995. Reston, VA: USGS.

Aeronautical navigation charts: Ideas for their keeping and use. 1996. *WAML Information Bulletin* 27: 122–27.

[AGS Library]. 1978. *University of Wisconsin, Milwaukee UW Memo* 8 (2): [1].

Akers, B. 1978. Care and handling of a map collection. *Map Collector* 4: 2–5.

Albright, Gary. 1997. Care of photographs. *College & Research Libraries* 58:561-63.

Alden, John. 1966. Reproduction vs. preservation. *LJ* 91: 5319–22.

Alexander, G. L. 1959. Some notes toward a history of the New York Public Library Map Room for the years 1923–1941. *SLAG&MD Bulletin* 35: 4–7.

Alexander, J., and B. May. 1967. Cataloguing in the Map Division of the Public Archives of Canada. *ACML Proceedings* 2: 33–34.

al-Hazzam, E. 1973a. Arizona State University, Hayden Library: KWOC index to the map collection. *WAML Information Bulletin* 5 (1): 26–37.

―――. 1973b. KWOC index to the map collection, Hayden Library, Arizona State University, Tempe, Arizona. *WAML Information Bulletin* 4 (3): 48–49.

Allen, R. S. 1996. Map collection physical condition assessment survey, methodology and results. *SLAG&MD Bulletin* 184: 11–27.

Alonso, P. A. G. 1968. Conservation and circulation in map libraries: A brief review. *SLAG&MD Bulletin* 74: 15–18.

―――. 1972. Feasibility study on computer-produced map catalogue. *Australian Library Journal* 21: 245–52.

―――. 1973. Map collections in public libraries: Starting, building, maintaining them. Library Council of Victoria. Public Libraries Division. *Technical Bulletin* 1/73. [2d ed. in Technical Bulletin 3/75.]

―――. 1974. Map collections, map curators and mapkeeping. *Globe* 1: 10–11.

―――. 1975. Notes on map reference work. *Globe* 2: 11–13.

―――. 1976. Map collections in public libraries (in Victoria, Australia): Starting, building, maintaining them. *WAML Information Bulletin* 8: 74–82, 83–92.

Alonso, P. A. G., and D. F. Prescott. 1977. Deweying maps. *Australian Library Journal* 26 (3): 47–52.

American Geographical Society. 1947. Manual for classification and cataloging of maps in the Society's collection. (Mimeographed and offset publication no. 4). New York: Author. [Rev. ed. 1952, edited by E. L. Yonge and M. E. Hartz.]

American Library Association. 1894. *Papers and proceedings of the sixteenth general meeting of the American Library Association, held at Lake Placid, N.Y., September 17–22, 1894.* Lake Placid, NY: Author.

———. 1917. *Pamphlets and minor library material, clippings, broadside prints, pictures, music, bookplates, maps: Preprint of Manual of library economy*. Chicago: Author.

———. 1967. *Anglo-American cataloging rules. North American Edition*. Chicago: ALA.

———. 1978. *Anglo-American cataloguing rules*. 2d ed. Chicago: Author.

American Library Association. Rare Books and Manuscripts Section. Security Committee. 1989. Guidelines for the security of rare book, manuscript, and other special collections: A draft. *C&RL News* 50: 397–401.

American National Standards Institute. Committee on Library Work, Documentation, and Related Publishing Practices, Z39. 1978. *American National Standard for Bibliographic References*. New York: Author. [Excerpt: Appendix A II, Maps. 1978. In *SLAG&MD Bulletin* 114: 28–30.]

Anderson, F. J. 1954. Inexpensive map collection for a small library. *Wilson Library Bulletin* 29: 313+.

Anderson, O. C. 1945. A university library reviews its map collection. *LJ* 70: 103–6.

———. 1950. No best method to catalog maps. *LJ* 75: 450–52.

Anderson, Stanton, and Ronald Goetting. 1988. Environmental effects on the image stability of photographic products. *Journal of Imaging Technology* 14: 111–16.

Andrew, P. G. 1996. A case for moving maps with care: A review of map trucks. *WAML Information Bulletin* 28: 15–23.

Andrews, C. W. 1903. Maps in public libraries. *Public Libraries* 3: 22–25.

Anglo-American Cataloguing Committee for Cartographic Materials. 1980. Committee reports. *WAML Information Bulletin* 11: 117–26. [Also appears as: Minutes of the first meeting of the Anglo-American Cataloguing Committee for Cartographic Materials, Ottawa, Canada, October 1–5, 1979. *ACML Bulletin* 33: 3–22; also in *Globe* 12: 39–62.]

Ansari, M. B. 1977. Compilation and analysis of a state map and aerial photography directory, a Nevada experience. *WAML Information Bulletin* 8: 97–101.

———. 1979. New map room opens at the University of Nevada, Reno. *SLAG&MD Bulletin* 116: 40–42.

Archival citations. 1983. Ottawa: Public Archives Canada.

Archival storage of photographic materials. 1996. Syracuse, NY: Gaylord Bros.

Armstrong, Helen. 1992. Compacting your collection: Innovative strategies in map storage. *SLAG&MD Bulletin* 167: 2–20; errata, 168: 66, 169: 69.

———. 1994. An academic map library loads GPO cataloging tapes: A case study of plans and impacts. *SLG&MD Bulletin* 177: 2–34.

Armstrong, L., and M. T. Pearce. 1976. Preparing acquisitions lists. *SLAG&MD Bulletin* 104: 34–37.

Armstrong, M. 1978. A general town plan acquisition policy for university map collections with special reference to the University of Toronto Map Library. *ACML Bulletin* 29: 1–9.

Army Map Service asks loan of maps. 1942. *Publishers Weekly* 142: 925.

Arterburn, T. R. 1996. Librarians: Caretakers or crime-fighters? *American Libraries* 27 (7): 32–34.

As much to learn as to teach. 1979. Hamden, CT: Shoestring Press.

Association for Educational Communications and Technology. Science Committee. 1972. *Standards for cataloging nonprint materials.* 3d ed. Washington, DC: AECT.

Atlas of cancer mortality for U.S. counties, 1950–1969. 1975. Bethesda, MD: National Institute of Health.

Bach, H. 1949. Library's map room enjoys wide use. *LJ* 74: 368.

Baclawski, D. K. 1992. Inexpensive map and thesis cataloging for the small geology library: A case study of the perils of Pauline on a PC. *GIS Proceedings* 27: 119–24.

Badger, H. C. 1892. Floundering among the maps. *LJ* 17: 375–77.

Bagrow, L. 1975. *A history of the cartography of Russia up to 1600.* Rev. ed., 2 vols. Wolfe Island, Ontario: Walker Press.

Bahn, C. I. 1961. Map libraries—Space and equipment. *SLAG&MD Bulletin* 46: 3–17. [Also in Drazniowsky 1975, 364–84.]

Baird, D. l976. The university library map collection. *Bookmark* 31 (2): 29–31.

———. l978. Checklist of Idaho maps. *Idaho Librarian* 30: 35.

Baker, N. 1994. Annals of scholarship, discards. *New Yorker* 70 (7): 64–86.

Bakewell, K. G. B. 1972. *A manual of cataloguing practice.* Oxford, England: Pergamon Press.

Ball, S. B. 1910. Maps and atlases: Their selection and care. *Public Libraries* 15: 11–15.

Banks, P. N. 1978. *The preservation of library materials*. Chicago: Newberry Library.

Barkdull, M. 1973. National Geographic Society: Cartography Division—Map Library. *SLAG&MD Bulletin* 91: 24–26.

Barnes, R. L. 1979a. Suppliers of graphic products for the blind and partially sighted user. *ACML Bulletin* 32: 20–21.

———. 1979b. Tactual mapping—The state of the art. *ACML Bulletin* 32: 15–20.

Barrow, B., and A. Hudson. 1996. Promoting the map library to your boss and to the public. *SLAG&MD Bulletin* 182: 26–29.

Barrow, W. J. 1953 (pub. 1954). Migration of impurities in paper. *Archivum* 3: 105–8.

———. 1965. Deacidification and lamination of deteriorated documents, 1938–1963. *American Archivist* 28: 285–90.

Bartlett, J., and D. Marshall. 1979. Maps in the small historical society: Care and cataloging. *History News* 34: 9–20. [American Association for State and Local History Technical leaflet 111.]

Barton, P. L. 1981. Map collections and map librarianship in New Zealand: A synopsis. *Library Trends* 29: 537–46.

———. 1982. Map transit and storage. *Archifacts* 22: 591–96.

———. 1983. Aspects of New Zealand national cartobibliography 1933–82. New Zealand Mapkeepers' Circle *Newsletter* 15 (November): 3–9.

Baruth, Chris. 1993. Digital data survey. *SLAG&MD Bulletin* 172: 67–69.

———. 1994. Congress of Cartographic Information Specialists Associations. *SLAG&MD Bulletin* 176: 32–33.

Batchelder, B. 1981. A report on orientation activities in map libraries and collections located in education institutions. *ACML Bulletin* 41: 29–38.

———. 1982. DOBIS/LIBIS and cartographic materials at university libraries in Alberta. *ACML Bulletin* 44: 29–48.

Bates, N. P. 1954. *The history of the classification and cataloging of maps as shown in printed book catalogues of sixteen U.S. libraries issued from 1827 through 1907*. [S.l.]: University of North Carolina, School of Library Science. [thesis].

Baynes-Cope, A. D. 1985. *The study and conservation of globes*. Vienna: Interationale Coronelli-Gesellschaft.

Beard, C. 1993. Exploring the Internet for digital map data. *ACMLA Bulletin* no. 86: 2–11.

Beaverton School District No. 48, Beaverton, Oregon. Director of Instructional Materials. 1968. *Cataloging standards for non-book materials: A complete guide to cataloging non-book materials in the individual school*. Portland, OR: Northwest Library Service.

Beckman, M. 1974. *Automated cataloging system at the University of Guelph Library*. Peoria, IL: LARC Press.

Bennett, C. F. 1968. Notes on Latin American cartography and geography. *SLAG&MD Bulletin* 74: 7–11.

Bent, B. D., and J. Blake. 1978. The Georgia historical map exhibit: What libraries can do to foster statewide interest in maps. *SLAG&MD Bulletin* 112: 57–59.

Beresiner, Y. 1983. *British county maps, reference and price guide*. Woodbridge, Suffolk, U.K.: Antique Collectors' Club.

Bergen, J. V. 1972a. Floor plans: New map library facilities: Western Illinois University. *SLAG&MD Bulletin* 90: 11–19.

———. 1972b. Geographers, maps and campus map collections. *Professional Geographer* 24: 310–16.

———. 1972c. Map collections in midwestern universities and colleges. *Professional Geographer* 24: 245–52.

Berthelsen, B. 1978. The Sparks map collection. *Special Libraries* 69: 164–68.

Berthelson, J. F. 1982. Dartmouth College library map room. *SLAG&MD Bulletin* 128: 61.

Best, T. D. 1963. 35-mm slides of topographic maps: Pitfalls and prospects. *Professional Geographer* 17 (3): 20–23.

Betz, Elizabeth W. 1982. *Graphic materials: Rules for describing original items and historical collections*. Washington, DC: LC.

Bibliography of cartographic materials published in the Netherlands = Bibliografie van in Nederland verschenen kartografische materialen. 1975– . Houten: Bohn Stafleu Van Loghum.

Bibliography of references to maps. 1975. *LRTS* 19: 355.

Bier, R. 1978. On-demand computer cartography and its effect on map libraries. *Special Libraries* 69: 61–65.

Bird, A. J. 1974. Map conservation in an academic geography department. *Aslib Proceedings* 26 (2): 69–73.

Bishop, A. P., and S. L. Star. 1996. Social informatics of digital library use and infrastructure. *Annual Review of Information Science and Technology* 31: 301–401.

Blank, M. G., S. A. Dobrusina, and N. B. Lebedeva. 1984. A search for procedures for restoration and stabilization of 16th and 17th century Netherlands atlases damaged by green paint. *Restaurator* 6 (3–4): 127–38.

Boak, R. I. 1970. Restoration and preservation of maps. *SLAG&MD Bulletin* 81: 21–23.

Boggs, S. W., and D. C. Lewis. 1936. Problems of classifying and cataloging maps. *Public Documents* 1936: 107–15.

———. 1937. Library classification and cataloging of geographic material. *Annals of the Association of American Geographers* 27 (2): 49–67.

———. 1945. *The classification and cataloging of maps and atlases.* New York: SLA.

Bokman, W. 1982. The preservation of photographic records. *ACML Bulletin* 43: 1–5.

BonaDea, A. 1997a. Humidifying and flattening rolled or folded paper materials in the Alaska State Library's Historical Collection. *WAML Information Bulletin* 28: 143–48.

———. 1997b. Safe storage of maps and oversize flat items at the Alaska State Library's Historical Collection. *WAML Information Bulletin* 28: 154–55.

Borbely, J. 1985. Changes in information technology: Its implications for graduate school curriculum. *Online* 9 (2): 126–28.

Borges, J. L. 1964. The library of Babel. In *Labyrinths, selected stories and other writings,* 51–58. New York: New Directions.

Bossler, J. D. 1982. New adjustment of North American datum. American Society of Civil Engineers, Surveying and Mapping Division *Journal* 108 (SU2): 47–52.

Boswell, R. V. 1976a. *Collection for the History of Cartography.* Fullerton, CA: Published by Roy Boswell for the Collection for the History of Cartography, California State University, Fullerton.

———. 1976b. Collection for the history of cartography. *WAML Information Bulletin* 7: i–iii, 1–41.

Botz, M. K. 1969. *Conversion of section-township-range to latitude-longitude—A computer technique.* (Special publication 48.) Butte: Montana Bureau of Mines and Geology.

Bouley, Raymond J. 1992. The life and death of CD-ROM. *CD-ROM Librarian* 7: 10, 12, 14–17.

Bridges, G. 1978. Map use at University College Map Library. *SLAG&MD Bulletin* 111: 10–17.

Bridges, G., S. M. Hinton, and J. Mason. 1978. *Maps and atlases: A cartobibliography*. Swansea, UK: Students' Union Print Room, University College.

Briesemeister, W. 1957. Some three-dimensional relief globes, past and present. *Geographical Review* 47: 251–60.

British Library map catalogue on CD-ROM. 1997. Woodbridge, CT: Primary Source Media.

British Museum. 1951. *Rules for compiling the catalogues of printed books, maps and music in the British Museum*. Rev. ed. London: British Museum. [Reprint of 1936 ed., first ed. 1906.]

British Standards Institution. 1975– . *Recommendations for bibliographical references to maps and charts. Part I. References in accessions lists. Part 2. References in books and articles*. (B.S. 5195). London: Author.

Brown, L. A. 1941. *Notes on the care and cataloging of old maps*. Windham, CT: Hawthorn House.

———. 1942. Special reference problems in map collections. In *Reference function of the library*, 144–62. Chicago: University of Chicago Press.

Brownrigg, E., C. Lynch, and M. Engle. 1984. Technical services in the age of electronic publishing. *LRTS* 28: 59–67.

Brunner, J. R. 1990. U.S./Canada soil map bibliography. *SLAG&MD Bulletin* 160: 1-23.

Brunvand, Amy. 1991. Mental maps and collection development: A view from Colorado. *WAML Information Bulletin* 23: 35–41.

Buckallew, F. 1979. Patronage of the small academic map collection. *Oklahoma Librarian* 29: 28–29.

———. 1983. *Central State University Map Collection: A subject analysis*. Edmond, OK: Central State University Library.

———. 1986. The online catalog and map usage. *MOUG Newsletter* 21: 2–3.

Buffum, C. W. 1972. Map cataloging: An informal review. *SLAG&MD Bulletin* 88: 35–39, 54.

———. 1977. Map cataloging can stand on its own feet. *SLAG&MD Bulletin* 107: 46–48.

Buick, W. G. 1974. Letter to the editor on map classification. *Australian Library Journal* 23: 158.

Burkett, J. 1965. *Special library and information services in the United Kingdom.* 2d ed. London: Library Association.

Byers, Barry. 1997. Relaxing chamber for rolled documents: Some general principles and suggested designs. *WAML Information Bulletin* 28: 139–42.

Cabral, A. de M. 1964. *Tratamento de material cartográfico.* 2d ed. Recife, Brazil: SUDENE.

Campbell, T. 1994. Possibilities for the international sharing of retro-converted map files. *IFLA Journal* 20 (1): 46–52.

Canada. Surveys and Mapping Branch. 1977– . *EMR survey and mapping, numeric map catalogue, alphabetic catalogue (NTS only).* Ottawa: Author.

Candy, B. R. 1980. The development of a new manual of map classification and cataloguing in the Ministry of Defence (UK). *ACML Bulletin* 35: 1–14.

Capps, Marie T. 1972. Preservation and maintenance of maps. *Special Libraries* 63: 457–62. [Rev. ed. in *Drexel Library Quarterly* 9 (no. 4, 1973): 61–70.]

Carney, F. 1908. The storing of topographic and rolled maps. *Journal of Geography* 7 (3): 52–54.

Carpenter, M. 1981. *Corporate authorship: Its role in library cataloging.* Westport, CT: Greenwood Press.

Carrington, D. K., and E. U. Mangan. 1971. *Data preparation manual for the conversion of map cataloging records to machine-readable form.* Washington, DC: GPO.

Cartographic archives. 1982. *Archivaria* 13 (winter 1981/82).

Cartographic materials: A manual of interpretation for AACR2. 1982. Chicago: ALA.

Carver, L. G. 1982. Remotely sensed imagery in a research map library. *ACML Bulletin* 44: 22–28.

Castle, G. 1980. Criteria for determining modes of copying for the average map collection. *ACML Bulletin* 36: 7–9.

Catlin, W. 1976. California State Library and Californian Section Map Collection. *WAML Information Bulletin* 7 (3): 60–64.

Cavanaugh, V. 1983. *A manual for public library map collections in Alaska.* Unpublished ms. for University of Denver Library School, Denver, CO.

CCI/ICC notes. 1991– . Ottawa: Canadian Conservation Institute.

Cerny, J. W. 1978. Awareness of maps as objects for copyright. *American Cartographer* 5: 45–56.

Chamberlain, D. R. 1980. Report on PRECIS and AACR2 at the Map Division of the Provincial Archives of British Columbia. *ACML Bulletin* 37: 34–39.

Chamberlain, G. E. 1951. Binding. *LJ* 76: 1776–79.

Chan, L. M. 1981. *Cataloging and classification: An introduction.* New York: McGraw-Hill.

––––––. 1986. *Library of Congress subject headings.* (Research Studies in Library Science no. 19.) Littleton, CO: Libraries Unlimited.

Chang, C., and D. E. Johnson. 1976. Tactual maps with interchangeable parts. In *Special child in the library*, 79–81. Chicago: ALA. [Reprinted from *New Outlook* 62 (1981): 122–24.]

Chapin, E. L. 1960. The value of cartobibliographies and the technique of their compilation. *Surveying and Mapping* 20: 76–84.

Chatham, R. L., and J. B. Vanderford. 1969. The wall map storage problem: A solution. *Journal of Geography* 68: 93–95.

Cheney, R. N., and W. J. Williams. 1980. *Fundamental reference sources.* 2d ed. Chicago: ALA.

Christiansen, D. E., C. R. Davis, and J. Reed-Scott. 1983. Guide to collection evaluation through use and user studies. *LRTS* 27: 432–40.

Christy, B. 1970. Critique of pure labeling for map collections. *WAML Information Bulletin* 1 (3): 12–22.

––––––. 1973. Map classification: Basic considerations and a comparison of systems. *WAML Information Bulletin* 4 (2): 29–42.

––––––. 1981. Minutes of the second meeting of the Anglo-American Cataloguing Committee for Cartographic Materials (AACR2): Held at the Library of Congress, Washington, DC, April 27–May 1, 1981. *ACML Bulletin* 41: 46–52.

Chu, C.-K. 1991. A HyperCard map information system. *Computer Librarian* 11: 34–38.

Clark, S., M. L. Larsgaard, and C. M. Teague. 1992. *Cartographic citations, a style guide.* Chicago: ALA MAGERT.

Cobb, D. A. 1972. Developing a small geographical library with special emphasis on Indiana. *Focus on Indiana Libraries* 26: 114–20.

––––––. 1973. Selection and acquisition of materials for the map library. *Drexel Library Quarterly* 9 (4): 15–25.

––––––. 1977a. Maps and scholars. *Library Trends* 25: 819–31.

————. 1977b. *OCLC and the future of map librarianship.* Talk given at WAML meeting at the University of Santa Clara [California], 25 March 1977.

————. 1977c. OCLC: Its impact on map librarianship. *SLAG&MD Bulletin* 108: 30–33.

————. 1979a. Map librarians speak out—and United States Geological Survey/National Cartographic Information Center listens. *WAML Information Bulletin* 10: 233–35.

————. 1979b. The politics and economics of map librarianship. *SLAG&MD Bulletin* 117: 20–27.

————. 1979c. SLA or ALA. *Special Libraries* 70: 505–6. [Comment in *Special Libraries* 71 (April 1980): 11A.]

————. 1983a. Current cartographic products of the Western nations. *Government Publications Review* 10: 381–94.

————. 1983b. Map librarianship in the United States: A personal view. *Cartographic Journal* 20: 26–30.

————. 1984. Reference service and map librarianship. *RQ* 24: 204–9.

Cockerell, D. 1920. *Bookbinding, and the care of books.* 4th ed. London: Sir Isaac Pitman and Sons. [Originally printed 1913.]

Cohen, L. 1966. Notes on the antiquarian map trade. *SLAG&MD Bulletin* 64: 2–4.

Collier, J. E. 1960. Storing map collections. *Professional Geographer* 12: 31–32.

Collins, J. 1996. One approach to earthquake preparedness. *WAML Information Bulletin* 27: 128–30.

Collins, R. B. 1977. The nature and requirements of historical map collections. *SLAG&MD Bulletin* 109: 10–23.

Collison, R. L. 1950. *The cataloguing, arrangement and filing of special material in special libraries.* (Aslib Manuals vol. 2). London: Aslib.

————. 1955. *Modern storage equipment and methods for special materials in libraries.* Hampstead, UK: [s.n.]

————. 1957. *The treatment of special material in libraries.* 2d ed. London: Aslib.

Columbia encyclopedia. 1964. New York: Columbia University Press.

Columbia University. School of Library Science. 1967. *Sample catalog cards for use in connection with courses in technical services in libraries and organization of materials.* 4th ed. New York: The School.

Colvin, L. C. 1963. *Cataloging sampler: A comparative and interpretive guide*. Hamden, CT: Archon Books.

Comaromi, J. P. 1976. *The eighteen editions of the Dewey Decimal classification*. New York: Forest Press.

Comaromi, J. P., and M. J. Warren. 1982. *Manual on the use of the Dewey Decimal classification Edition 19*. Albany, NY: Forest Press.

Commonwealth electoral maps. 1983. Australian Map Circle. *Newsletter* 28 (June): 4–5.

Computer maps: A new turn in the road for videodiscs. 1983. *Esquire* 99 (3): 250, 252.

Conversion of map catalogues: Barcelona, August 1993. 1994. *INSPEL* 28 (1): 7–199.

Coombs, J. 1981. Globes: A librarian's guide to selection and purchase. *Wilson Library Bulletin* 55: 503–8.

Corbin, John. 1993. Competencies for electronic information services. *Public-access Computer Systems Review* 4 (6): 5–22. [To obtain this file, send the following e-mail message to LISTSERV@UHUPVM1or LISTSERV@UHUPVM1.UH.EDU : GET CORBIN PRV4N6 F=MAIL.]

Corbley, K. P. 1996. One-meter satellites: Choosing imagery that meets GIS requirements—Part two. *Geo Info Systems* 6 (4): 34–37.

———. 1997a. Regional imagery: Wide-angle advantages, wide-ranging applications. *Geo Info Systems* 7 (4): 28–33.

———. 1997b. Multispectral imagery: Identifying more than meets the eye. *Geo Info Systems* 7 (6): 38–43.

Corley, N. T. 1970. The formation of the Geography and Map Libraries Subsection of the Section of Special Libraries, IFLA: A Canadian view. *SLAG&MD Bulletin* 80: 40–45.

Cornelius, H. F. 1978. Evaluation for map librarians. *Globe* 9: 36–57.

Corsaro, J. 1990. Control of cartographic materials in archives. *Cataloging & Classification Quarterly* 11(3–4): 213–28.

Council on Library Resources, Inc. 1968. *LC Information Bulletin* 27: 148–49.

Cox, C. T. 1971. The cataloging of non-book materials: Basic guidelines. *LRTS* 15: 472–78.

Crampton, Jeremy. 1995. Cartography resources on the World Wide Web. *Cartographic Perspectives* 22: 3–10.

Critchley, W. E. 1970. Old maps: Photocopying helps in using them. *Microdoc* 9 (3): 68–69.

Crogham, A. 1982. *On cataloguing, non-book media and AngloAmerican cataloguing rules.* London: Coburgh Publications.

Crone, G. R. 1936. The cataloguing and arrangement of maps. *Library Association Record,* 4th series 3: 98–104.

———. 1953. Notes on the classification, arrangement and cataloguing of a large map collection. *Indian Archives* 7: 8–13.

Crone, G. R., and E. E. T. Day. 1960. The Map Room of the Royal Geographical Society. *Geographical Journal* 126: 12–17.

Crotts, J. 1977. An index to the Defense Mapping Agency/Army Map Service depository catalogs. *WAML Information Bulletin* 8: 124–32.

Cruse, L. 1980. Collecting microcartography: Sources and prospects. *SLAG&MD Bulletin* 120: 2–26.

———. 1981a. Microcartography. *WAML Information Bulletin* 12: 123–31.

———. 1981b. Microcartography. *WAML Information Bulletin* 12: 335–42.

———. 1981c. Microcartography. *WAML Information Bulletin* 13: 40–50.

———. 1981d. Microcartography and cartographic data bases. *Library Trends* 29: 391–416.

———. 1981e. *Microcartography: Applications for archives and libraries.* (Occasional Paper no. 6). Santa Cruz, CA: WAML.

———. 1984. Softworld: Computers in the map room. *WAML Information Bulletin* 16: 71–77.

———. 1985a. Cartography's photographic revolution: Microcartography. *Wilson Library Bulletin* 60: 17–20.

———. 1985b. Self preservation. *WAML Information Bulletin* 16: 190–92.

———. 1985c. Storage of maps on paper, microforms, optical disks, digital disks and magnetic memories. In *Role of maps in sci-tech libraries,* 45–57. New York: Haworth Press. [Also published as *Science and Technology Libraries* 5 (3).]

———. 1985d. Western Association of Map Libraries' map microfilming consortium. *Microform Review* 14: 99–103.

———. 1988. Microcartography. *WAML Information Bulletin* 19: 87–91.

———. 1995. *Bruno's Laws.* (e-mail message-id: M01928.AA23886@atlas.sdc.ucsb.edu). La Jolla, CA: UCSD Libraries.

Crutcher, L., and E. A. Ledlow. 1942. Solving the map problem. *Wilson Library Bulletin* 16: 656–57.

CSB. *See* United States. Library of Congress. Processing Services. 1978– . *Cataloging Service Bulletin.*

Cunha, G. M. 1971. *Conservation of library materials, a manual and bibliography on the care, repair and restoration of library materials.* 2d ed. Metuchen, NJ: Scarecrow Press.

Current, C. E. 1971. Acquisition of maps for school (and other small) libraries. *Wilson Library Bulletin* 45: 578–83. [Correction in *Wilson Library Bulletin* 45: 737.]

Current and forthcoming courses. 1969. *SLAG&MD Bulletin* 77: 7–9.

Curtis, S. 1990. *Outreach to faculty: Strategies (in no particular order).* [Santa Barbara, CA: UCSB, Davidson Library, Black Studies Collection.]

Cushing, H. G. 1924. How to care for rolled maps and charts. *Public Libraries* 29: 557.

Daehn, R. M. 1975. Maps—The regional approach: A system to share $. *SLAG&MD Bulletin* 100: 74–90.

Dahl, E. H. 1975. Reference services in an archival map collection. *ACML Proceedings* 1974: 5–10.

———. 1983. Ethics and the map custodian. *ACML Bulletin* 48: 38–40.

Dahl, E. H., G. Hill, and M. E. Murphy. 1995. The day it rained all night in the cartographic vault: Lessons in disaster preparedness and recovery at the National Archives of Canada. *ACMLA Bulletin* 94: 1–10.

Dall, Judith A. 1990. The digital orthophoto: The cornerstone of GIS. *ASCM-ASPRS Fall Convention Proceedings* 314–19.

Dallaire, G. 1974. Reproducing and storing engineering drawings. *Civil Engineering* 44 (3): 43–45.

Dalphin, G. R. 1954. More about filing rolled wall maps. *SLAG&MD Bulletin* 16: 10–12.

Dalphin, G. R., and V. H. English. 1954. Geographical exhibits. *LJ* 79: 1466–68.

Data conversion. 1992. *GIS World* 5 (7): 34–43.

Date coding of maps. 1982. *WAML Information Bulletin* 13: 340–41.

Davis, C. 1974. An alternative maps classification. *Australian Library Journal* 23 (2): 71–72.

Davis, Robert E. 1990. *Organization, programs and activities of the Geologic Division, U.S. Geological Survey. (Circular* 1000). Reston, VA: USGS.

Deckelbaum, David. 1989. A user survey conducted in the Henry J. Bruman Map Library, University of California, Los Angeles, Fall 1988. *WAML Information Bulletin* 20: 170–96.

Defense Mapping Agency consolidated—Now the DMA H/T Center. 1978. *WAML Information Bulletin* 10: 54.

Demas, S., P. McDonald, and G. Lawrence. 1995. The Internet and collection development: Mainstreaming selection of Internet resources. *LRTS* 39: 275–90.

DePew, John N. 1991. *A library, media, and archival preservation handbook.* Santa Barbara, CA: ABC-CLIO.

Derby, Deborah. 1997. *Caring for your photographs.* Washington, DC: American Institute for Conservation of Historic and Artistic Works.

Desbarats, A. 1982. Air photographs: Their storage and organization. *ACML Bulletin* 42: 20–23.

Deterioration and preservation of library materials. 1970. *Library Quarterly* 40 (1).

Dewey, Melvil. 1971. *Dewey Decimal classification and relative index.* 18th ed. 3 vols. New York: Forest Press.

DeWhitt, Benjamin L. 1987. Long-term preservation of data on computer magnetic media. Part I, *CAN* 29: 7, 19, 28; Part II, *CAN* 30: 4, 24.

Diennes, J. 1995. Moving the University of Kansas Map Library. *WAML Information Bulletin* 27: 16–31.

Dinkins, R. E. 1988. Map retro on a shoestring. *SLAG&MD Bulletin* 153: 3–10.

Doehlert, I. C. 1984. Basic considerations for development of an effective selection and acquisition policy for an academic library. *WAML Information Bulletin* 15: 188–96.

Doerr, A. H. 1960. Map collections: Another approach. *Professional Geographer* 12: 33–34.

Donkin, K., and M. Goodchild. 1967. A computerized approach to increased map library utility. *Canadian Cartographer* 4: 39–45. [Also in *ACML Proceedings* (1967): 16–23.]

Donley, M. 1976. *Recent cartography in the Pacific Northwest.* Paper presented at WAML Conference, Eugene, OR, 23 September 1976.

Dowd, S. T. 1980. The formulation of a collection development policy statement. In *Collection development in libraries: A treatise*, vol. 1, 67–87. 2 vols. (*Foundations in library and information science* vol. 10). Greenwich, CT: Jai Press.

Draft guidelines for behavioral performance of reference and informa- tion services professionals. 1995. (e-mail message-id 9605021652.AA02628@atlas.sdc.ucsb.edu).

Drazniowsky, R. 1966. Bibliographies as tools for map acquisition and map compilation. *Cartographer* 3: 138–41. [Also as Cartography. 1967. In *Library Trends* 15: 710–17, and in Drazniowsky 1975, 231–40.]

————. 1969. *Cataloging and filing rules for maps and atlases in the Society's collection*. Rev. and exp. ed. New York: AGS.

————. 1975. *Map librarianship: Readings*. Metuchen, NJ: Scarecrow Press.

Drew, F. K. 1960. Maps in libraries. *SLA Georgia Chapter Bulletin* 4 (August): 10–15.

Drewes, J. 1989. Computers: Planning for disaster. *Law Library Journal* 81: 103–16.

Driessen, K. C., and S. A. Smyth. 1995. Cartographic materials. In: *A library manager's guide to the physical processing of nonprint ma- terials*, 43–58. Westport, CT: Greenwood Press.

Drury, F. K. W. 1908. The care of maps. *ALA Bulletin* 2: 347–55.

Dufresnoy, L. 1965. *Catalogue des milleures cartes géographiques générales et particulières*. Amsterdam: Meridian.

Dunkley, John. 1996. Maps of Australian caves and karst. *Journal of the Australian Map Circle* 44: 41–45.

Easterbrook, D. J. 1969. *Principles of geomorphology*. New York: McGraw- Hill.

Eastman Kodak Co. 1979. *Preservation of photographs, F-30*. Roches- ter, NY: Author.

————. 1980. *The care and storage of Kodak color material, E-30*. Rochester, N.Y.: Author.

Easton, W. W. 1967. Automating the Illinois State University Map Li- brary. *SLAG&MD Bulletin* 67: 3–10.

————. 1969. Recent developments in automating the Illinois State University Map Collection. *ACML Proceedings*: 55–71.

————. 1970. Repair and preservation of map materials. *Special Librar- ies* 61: 199–200.

Eaton, W. L., and G. B. Gait. 1968. *Microfilming maps of abandoned anthracite mines, mines in the Wyoming Basin, Northern Anthracite Field*. (U.S. Bureau of Mines *Information Circular* 8379). Pittsburgh, PA: U.S. Bureau of Mines.

Educational policy statement of the Association for Library Collections & Technical Services. 1996. *ALCTS Newsletter* 7 (1): 7–10.

Edwards, L. 1984. The state mapping advisory committee: Its basis and its function in major public mapping programs. *WAML Information Bulletin* 16: 37–53.

EEZ-SCAN program maps sea floor. 1983. *Geotimes* (January): 13–15.

Effective presentations. 1992. [Chicago]: Library & Information Technology Association.

Ehrenberg, R. A. 1967. Map acquisition, arrangement, and description at the National Archives. *SLAG&MD Bulletin* 68: 10–13.

———. 1973a. Non-geographic methods of map arrangement and classification. *Drexel Library Quarterly* 9 (4): 49–60.

———. 1973b. Reproducing maps in libraries and archives, the custodian's point of view. *Special Libraries* 64 (l2): 18, 20–24.

———. 1975. Cartographic archives. *SLAG&MD Bulletin* 99: 2–24.

———. 1976a. Cartographic records in the National Archives. *National Genealogical Society Quarterly* 64: 83–111.

———. 1976b. Photocopying rare maps and atlases. *AB Bookman's Yearbook*, vol. 1: 31–42.

———. 1977. *Conserving a cartographic heritage: Microfilming at the National Archives of the United States*. (International Council on Archives, Microfilm Committee *Bulletin* no. 6). Madrid: Author.

———. 1982. *Archives and manuscripts: Maps and architectural drawings*. (SAA Basic Manual Series). Chicago: Society of American Archivists.

Eisenbeis, K. 1982. Special documents as sources for maps. *SLAG&MD Bulletin* 128: 32–35.

———. 1995. *Privatizing government information: The effects of policy on access to Landsat satellite data*. Metuchen, NJ: Scarecrow Press.

Electronics. 1977. *Science* 195 (4283).

Ercegovac, Z. 1990a. *Research on knowledge-based descriptive cataloging of cartographic publications: An experimental advice-giving system—Mapper*. Los Angeles: UCLA Graduate School of Library Science. [Dissertation.]

————. 1990b. Proposed definitional conditions as a basis to study the concept of map author. *Cataloging & Classification Quarterly* 10 (4): 19–50.

————. 1991. Design, implementation, and evaluation of an experimental cataloging advisor—Mapper. *SLAG&MD Bulletin* 163: 2–29.

————. 1992a. A multiple-observation approach in knowledge acquisition for expert systems: A case study. *Journal of the American Society for Information Science* 43: 506–17.

Ercegovac, Z., and H. Borko. 1992. Performance evaluation of Mapper. *Information Processing and Management* 28 (2): 259–68.

Espenshade, E. B. 1936. Building a collection of maps. *ALA Bulletin* 30: 206–15.

————. 1950. No one source for acquiring maps. *LJ* 75: 43l–34+.

Ester, M. 1996. *Digital image collections, issues and practice*. Washington, DC: Commission on Preservation and Access.

Euler, M. D. 1972. Introducing librarians and students to maps. *SLAG&MD Bulletin* 87: 46–47.

Evans, D. L. 1946. The lamination process, a British view. *American Archivist* 9: 320–22.

Fagg, K. S. 1970. The Rand McNally six-foot geophysical globe: Relief of the floors. *SLAG&MD Bulletin* 81: 29–33.

Fairclough, R. H. 1972. Original or facsimile? *New Library World* 73: 291–94.

Faries, Nancy. 1979. Computers, microforms and the National Cartographic Information Center. *ACML Bulletin* 30: 18–20.

Farrell, B. 1981. European map libraries cooperate: The establishment of the group of map librarians within LIBER—Groupe des Cartothécaires de LIBER. *ACML Bulletin* 38: 39–42.

————. 1982. Telidon and maps: A library experiment. *ACML Bulletin* 44: 15–19.

Farrell, B., and A. Desbarats. 1981. *Guide for a small map collection*. Ottawa: ACML. [2d ed. 1984.]

Favier, Jean. 1986. *Les documents graphiques et photographiques, analyse et conservation*. Paris: Archives Nationales.

Federation of Rocky Mountain States. Information Systems Technical Laboratory. 1978. *Map indexing system user's manual*. Washington, DC: GPO.

Felland, N. 1967. Some history of the Geography and Map Division. *SLAG&MD Bulletin* 76: 2–4.

Ferrazzani, M., and W. Thiebaut. 1993. The legal protection of remote-sensing satellite data. *ESA Bulletin* 76: 61–63.

Ferro, D. P. 1980. Old and new world. *Library Association Record* 82: 171, 173.

Ferro, D. P., and M. Wilkes. 1976. Practical course in map curatorship—Edinburgh, 31st March to 3rd April 1976. *Cartographic Journal* 13: 106.

Fetros, J. G. 1971a. Developing the map collection in smaller libraries. *SLAG&MD Bulletin* 85: 24–28.

———. 1971b. *References for further study of state and local atlases.* [S.1.: s.n.]

———. 1973. Promoting the map collection. *WAML Information Bulletin* 5: 18–22.

Fink, M. E. 1962a. A comparison of map cataloging systems. *SLAG&MD Bulletin* 50: 6–11. [Comments in *SLAG&MD Bulletin* 51 (1963): 7–10.]

———. 1962b. *Map classification at the University of Michigan.* Ann Arbor, MI: University of Michigan.

Fitzpatrick, G. L. 1983. Indirect access to maps via online data base. In *National Online Information Meetings Proceedings, 1983,* 139–46. Medford, NJ: Learned Information.

Fleet, C. 1994. Comparing automated map catalogue systems: A pilot study based in the National Library of Wales. *Program* 28: 223–37.

Fleischer, E., and H. Goodman. 1980. *Cataloging audiovisual materials: A manual based on AACR2.* New York: Neal-Schuman.

Fletcher, R. S. 1899. Maps and charts in the public library. *Public Libraries* 4: 444–46.

Flynn, L. L. 1985. Locating maps for local history research. *Idaho Librarian* 37: 30–31.

Foncin, M. 1953. Some observations on the organization of a large map library. *World Cartography* 3: 33–40.

Foncin, M., and P. R. Sommer. 1957. La Bibliographie cartographique internationale. In l'Information géographique, *La géographie française au milieu du xxe siècle,* 327–29. Paris: J.-B. Baillière et fils.

Fordham, H. G. 1914. *Studies in cartobibliography, British and French, and in the bibliography of itineraries and road-books.* Oxford, England: Oxford University Press. [1969 reprint by Dawsons of Pall Mall, London.]

———. 1927. *Maps, their history, characteristics and uses: A handbook for teachers.* 2d ed. Cambridge, England: Cambridge University Press.

Forman, D. M. 1979. Maps for the blind. *ACML Bulletin* 32: 12–15.

Fortney, M. 1971. Relocation of the map collection at Northwestern. *SLAG&MD Bulletin* 84: 40–42.

Foskett, A. C. 1973. *The Universal Decimal classfication: The history, present status and future prospects of a large classification scheme.* London: Clive Bingley.

Foss, S. W. 1906. The song of the library staff. *LJ* 31: C35–36.

Foster, D. L. 1972. *The classification of nonbook materials in academic libraries: A commentary and bibliography.* (Occasional Paper 104). Champaign-Urbana, IL: University of Illinois Graduate School of Library Science.

Fox, H. 1972. A classification and cataloguing scheme for a small map library. *WAML Information Bulletin* 4: 24–33.

———. 1977. *Designing a cataloging system for maps for computer processing—"One man's experience."* Paper presented at WAML meeting, University of Santa Clara, California, 25 March 1977.

———. 1978. The reorganization of WAML. *WAML Information Bulletin* 9: 188–93.

France. Direction des archives. 1986. *Les documents graphiques et photographiques: Analyse et conservation, travaux du Centre de recherche sur la conservation des documents graphiques, 1984–1985.* Paris: Archives Nationales.

Frank, Steven. 1993. *Cataloging digital spatial data in the information infrastructure: A literature and technology review.* Orono, ME: University of Maine, Department of Surveying Engineering/NCGIA.

Freund, L. 1990. Map cataloging at the Branner Earth Sciences Library, Stanford University. *WAML Information Bulletin* 22: 4–41.

Frost, C. O. 1983. *Cataloging nonbook materials: Problems in theory and practice.* Littleton, CO: Libraries Unlimited.

———. 1989. *Media access and organization: A cataloging and reference sources guide for nonbook materials.* Englewood, CO: Libraries Unlimited.

Gait, G. B. 1970. *Microfilming maps of abandoned anthracite mines. Mines in the Lackawanna Basin, Northern Anthracite Field.* (Information Circular 8453). Pittsburgh, PA: U.S. Bureau of Mines.

Galneder, M. 1970. Equipment for map libraries. *Special Libraries* 61: 271–74.

————. 1977. The recataloging/reclassification project at the Map and Air Photo Library, University of Wisconsin-Madison. *SLAG&MD Bulletin* 108: 15–25.

————. 1982. Recent prices for selected map storage equipment. *SLAG&MD Bulletin* 128: 14–15.

————. 1989. Congress of Cartographic Information Specialists Associations, November 9–10, 1988—Newberry Library, Chicago, Illinois. *SLAG&MD Bulletin* 155: 3–9.

Galneder, M., and A. Koerner. 1975. Maps and map collections. In Grove 1975, 148–70.

Gardner, R. J., and L. Zeleransky. 1975. The ten commandments for library customers. *Special Libraries* 66: 326.

Garnett, R. 1899. *Essays in librarianship and bibliography.* London: George Allen.

Garth, S. L. 1979. Impact of digital mapping on map libraries in the year 2000. *ACML Bulletin* 30: 14–17.

Gates, W. E., and R. J. Neil. 1980. Geographic information systems. American Society of Civil Engineers, Surveying and Mapping Division. *Journal* 106 (SU1): 105–17.

Gelfand, Julia. 1988. Becoming a map librarian: Is graduate library education doing what it should? *WAML Information Bulletin* 19: 220–23.

Geller, S. B. 1983. Care and handling of computer magnetic storage media. (NBS special publication, 500–101). Washington, DC: National Bureau of Standards.

Geographic information systems. 1991. Reston, VA.: USGS.

Geographic information systems and libraries: Patrons, maps, and spatial information. 1996. Urbana, IL: Graduate School of Library and Information Science.

Georgenson, G. S. 1981. Space imagery center: A prototype planetary data facility. In *Picture Librarianship* 328–43. Phoenix, AZ: Oryx Press.

Geoview presents "Moviemaps." 1983. *Resource Development Journal* 2 (4): 3.

Gerber, G. S., et al. 1981. Map storage and care in active collections. *SLAG&MD Bulletin* 125: 15–18.

Gerencher, J. J. 1985. An inexpensive map storage facility. *SLAG&MD Bulletin* 141: 2–6.

Gerlach, A. C. 1954. The public attitude in the United States toward maps [abstract]. *Annals of the Association of American Geographers* 44: 208–9.

———. 1960a. *Geography and map cataloging versus classification in libraries.* Washington, DC: LC.

———. 1960b. The Map Division, Library of Congress. *Geographical Journal* 126: 244.

———. 1961. Geography and map cataloging and classification in libraries. *Special Libraries* 52: 248–51.

Gillispie, J. 1983. Library instruction in a map library via slide/tape. *SLAG&MD Bulletin* 131: 2–13.

———. 1988. Lloyd A. Brown and the Peabody Institute Library. *SLAG&MD Bulletin* 151: 25–31.

Gilman, C. R. 1982. Map commentary: 1: 100,000 map series. *American Cartographer* 9: 173–77.

Goes de Azevedo, R. 1979. International cartographic rules for the demarcation of the Earth's surface. *Journal of Micrographics* 12: 301–3.

Goldhor, H. 1971. *Education for librarianship, the design of the curriculum of library schools.* Urbana, IL: University of Illinois Graduate School of Library Science.

Goodman, M. C. 1955. Map collections in the United States and Canada. *Surveying and Mapping* 15: 31–35.

Goodwin, G. 1973. *Personal letter, March 5, 1973.* Washington, DC: USGS Library.

Goulard, Claude. 1981. Color microfiche: Myth or reality. *IMC Journal* 17 (3): 11–13.

Great Britain. Directorate of Military Survey. 1946. *Manual of map classification and cataloguing prepared for use in the Directorate of Military Survey, War Office.* London: Directorate of Military Survey, War Office. [Occasionally referred to as "Parsons," after the chief compiler, E. J. S. Parsons.]

Great Britain. Ministry of Defence. 1978– . *Manual of map library classification.* Feltham, UK: Author.

Greenberg, G. L. 1982. Map reading tools for map libraries. *WAML Information Bulletin* 13: 290–300.

Griffin, L. 1980. New Zealand map collections. *Special Libraries* 71: 30–36.

Grimaldi, J. E. 1981. Computer-generated color microfiche today. *IMC Journal* 17 (4): 11–13.

Grove, P. S. 1975. *Nonprint media in academic libraries*. (ACRL Publications in Librarianship no. 34). Chicago: ALA.

Guide for written collection policy statements. 2d ed. 1996. Chicago: ALCTS.

Guide to reference books. 1996. 11th ed. Chicago: ALA.

A guide to the preservation of archival materials (Guide pour la preservation des documents archivistiques). 1977. (Catalog no. SA 2-90/1997). Ottawa: Minister of Supply and Services Canada.

Guidelines for collection development. 1979. Chicago: ALA.

Guldbeck, P. E. 1972. *The care of historical collections: A conservation handbook for the nonspecialist*. Nashville, TN: American Association for State and Local History.

Gunter, P., and B. Shupe. 1981. Maps in the U.S. Serial Set, 1817–1917: A statistical estimate. *SLAG&MD Bulletin* 124: 2–7.

Gutsell, B. V. 1967. Some comments on map reference work. *ACML Proceedings*: 47.

Hagen, C. B. 1966a. An information retrieval system for maps. *Unesco Bulletin for Libraries* 20 (January/February): 30–35.

———. 1966b. Maps, copyright, and fair use. *SLAG&MD Bulletin* 66: 4–11.

———. 1967. *An information retrieval system for maps*. Rev. ed. Los Angeles: University of California.

———. 1969. Education and training in map librarianship. *SLAG&MD Bulletin* 77: 3–7.

———. 1970a. LC's summer special map processing project. *SLAG&MD Bulletin* 79: 36–37.

———. 1970b. A survey of the usage of a large map library. *SLAG&MD Bulletin* 80: 27–31.

———. 1971. The establishment of a university map library. *WAML Information Bulletin* 3: 2–15.

———. 1977. Map libraries in the 1970's and the University of California. *WAML Information Bulletin* 8: 200–29.

———. 1979. Map libraries and the armed services—A story of uneven relationships. *WAML Information Bulletin* 11: 3–22.

———. 1982. *Maps: An overview of the producer-user interaction.* Los Angeles: University of California Map Library.

———. 1986. *Seismic dangers and the UCLA Map Library.* Los Angeles: UCLA Map Library.

Hagen-Lautrup, Carlos B. 1989. The LA series and cataloging: A response. *WAML Information Bulletin* 20: 202–4.

Hall, V. S. 1967. *Resume of map project, June 15, 1966–August 15, 1967.* Lexington, KY: University of Kentucky Libraries, Geology Library.

———. 1973. A one-card geographical retrieval system of the cataloging of maps in the University of Kentucky Geology Library. *SLAG&MD Bulletin* 93: 27–54.

Hall, W. L. 1925. A classification for maps. *LJ* 50: 257–59.

Hallen, S. 1991. Finding, evaluating and using existing data sources. *GIS World* 4 (11): 60–65.

Hamilton, E. 1982. The PHOENIX on-line retrieval system and maps. *ACML Bulletin* 44: 49–52.

Hannabass, F. D. 1971. A slide-tape briefing for geographic information. *SLAG&MD Bulletin* 86: 25–30.

Harden, H. H. 1974. How to get more out of your charts. *Aerospace Safety* 30 (6): 9–12.

Harding, K. 1984. Symposium on the marketing of cartographic information. *ACML Bulletin* 51: 74–76.

Harlow, N., and A. H. Horn. 1952. *Reference manual for the classification, cataloging and care of the map collection.* Sacramento, CA: California State Library.

Harmon, James. 1993. *Integrated pest management in museum, library and archival facilities: A step by step approach for the design, development, implementation and maintenance of an integrated pest management program.* Indianapolis, IN: Harmon Preservation Pest Management.

Harris, K. E., and C. J. Shahani. 1994. *Mass deacidification: An initiative to refine the diethyl zinc process.* Washington, DC: Preservation Directorate.

Harrison, R. E. 1943. The war of the maps, a famous cartographer surveys the field. *Saturday Review of Literature* 26 (32): 24–27.

———. 1952. Evaluation of modern maps. *Special Libraries* 44 (2): 45–47.

Harvey, M. 1997. Mr. Bland's evil plot to control the world. *Outside* 22 (6): 96–102, 148–53.

"Hawaii in maps" exhibit opens. 1948. *LC Information Bulletin* 37: 4–5.

Hawken, W. R. 1966. *Copying methods manual.* (LTP Publication no. 11). Chicago: ALA Library Technology Program.

Haykin, D. J. 1951. *Subject headings: A practical guide.* Washington, DC: LC.

Healey, Richard, and Barbara Morris. 1985. *MARC for compatibility: Relational databases for flexibility.* Edinburgh: Department of Geography, University of Edinburgh. [Presented to the British Cartographic Society Symposium, Aberystwyth, 7 September 1985.]

Heawood, E. 1924. The use of watermarks in dating old maps and documents. *Geographical Journal* 63: 391–412.

———. 1930. Reproductions of notable early maps. *Geographical Journal* 76: 240–48.

Hebert, J. R. 1972. Panoramic maps of American cities. *Special Libraries* 63: 554–62.

Heery, R. 1996. Review of metadata formats. *Program* 30 (4).

Heidlage, B. 1980. *Map Study Committee, final report.* (ED 195 255). Columbia, MO: University of Missouri Library.

Hemperley, M. R. 1982. Georgia Surveyor General Department. *SLAG&MD Bulletin* 128: 16–18.

Hendriks, K. B., and D. Hopkins. 1985. *PHOCUS, a bibliographic data base for the conservation of photographic materials.* (Catalog no. SA82-3/1-1985.) Ottawa: Public Archives Canada.

Hendriks, K. B., and A. Whitehurst. 1988. *Conservation of photographic materials.* Ottawa: National Archives of Canada.

Henneberger, B. 1994. Preservation and access of rare maps at the University of Georgia Libraries. *Microform Review* 23: 169–71.

Herro, J. K. 1990. Stanford's earthquake damage. *WAML Information Bulletin* 22: 45–46.

Hewitt, J. A. 1984. Technical services in 1983. *LRTS* 28: 205-18.

Hill, J. D. 1965. Map and atlas cases. *Library Trends* 13: 481–87.

Hill, J. S. 1977. Developments in map cataloging at the Library of Congress. *Special Libraries* 68 (4): 149–54.

Hodur, T. 1984. Color micrographics. *WAML Information Bulletin* 16: 19–25.

Hoehn, R. P. 1977. Collecting responsibilities for cartographic materials, Stanford University and northern campuses, University of California. *WAML Information Bulletin* 8: 185–87.

———. 1978a. Micrographics and maps was the theme of the fall meeting of the Western Association of Map Libraries held at the University of California, San Diego, on October 6 and 7, 1977. *C&RL News* 39: 18–19.

———. 1978b. Used American map price averages 1976–1977. *WAML Information Bulletin* 9: 245–46.

———. 1979. Used American map price averages 1978. *WAML Information Bulletin* 11: 27–28.

Holmes, R. A. 1984. Advanced sensor systems: Thematic Mapper and beyond. *Remote Sensing of Environment* 15: 213–21.

Holway, A. H., and D. Jameson. 1947. *Good lighting for people at work in reading rooms and offices.* Boston: Division of Research, Graduate School of Business Administration, Harvard University.

Hopkins, J. 1973. The Ohio College Library Center. *LRTS* 17: 308–19.

Horner, J. 1973. *Special cataloguing with particular reference to music, films, maps, serials and the multi-media computerized catalogue.* Hamden, CT: Linnet Books.

How we keep unbound maps. 1891. *LJ* 16 (3): 72–75.

Hubbard, A. G. 1903. Cataloging and preservation of maps in Indiana State Library. *Indiana Libraries* 28: 610–11. [Also in *National Association of State Libraries Proceedings* 6: 27–30.]

Hubbard, L. 1972. Two-dimensional access to maps. *SLAG&MD Bulletin* 88: 30–31.

———. 1973. *Interview with author, 12 April 1973.* Seattle, WA: University of Washington Library.

Hudson, A. C. 1976. Conversion to automated cataloging at the Map Division, New York Public Library. *Special Libraries* 67 (2): 97–101.

Hyde, R. 1972a. Librarians and their maps, a look at some of the problems. *New Library World* 73: 287–99. [and comment 73: 343–44.]

———. 1972b. What future for carto-bibliography? *New Library World* 73: 288–90.

Iliams, T. M., and T. D. Beckwith. 1935. Notes on the causes and prevention of foxing in books. *Library Quarterly* 5: 407–18.

India. Imperial Record Department. 1941. *Notes on the preservation of records.* Calcutta: Author.

Instructions to depository libraries. 1984. Washington, DC: GPO.

International Federation for Documentation. 1970. Key to information, Universal Decimal Classification. (*FID Publication*, 466). The Hague: FID.

International Federation of Library Associations. Joint Working Group on the International Standard Bibliographic Description for Cartographic Materials. 1977. *ISBD (CM): International Standard Bibliographic Description (Cartographic Materials)*. London: IFLA International Office for UBC.

International Federation of Library Associations. Special Libraries Section. Geography and Map Libraries Subsection. 1970. IFLA meeting of the Geography and Map Libraries Subsection Sept. 1, 1970, agenda. *INSPEL* 5 (2): 44.

———. 1972. Geography and Map Libraries Subsection, Secretary/Treasurer's report, Budapest, August 1972. *INSPEL* 7 (3&4): 53–54.

———. 1996. [Papers presented at 1989 meetings of the Section]. Paris: Comité français de cartographie.

International Geographical Union. Commission of the Classification of Geographical Books and Maps in Libraries. 1964. *Final report on the classification of geographical books and maps: Presented to XIth General Assembly and IXth International Geographical Congress, London, July–August 1964*. Bad Godesberg, Germany: Institut für Landeskunde.

International Seminar on the Teaching of Preservation Management for Librarians, Archivists and Information Scientists, Vienna, 1986. 1991. *Education and training for preservation and conservation*. Munich: Saur.

Internationale Coronelli-Gesellschaft fur Globen-und Instrumentenkunde. 1985. *The study and conservation of globes*. Vienna: Author.

Internationale Vereinigung Meister der Einbandkunst, Royal Library, Stockholm, September 1966. 1966. *The repair of globes*. London: International Institute for Conservation of Historic and Artistic Works.

IPI storage guide for acetate film: Instructions for using the wheel, graphs, and table, basic strategy for film preservation. 1993. Rochester, NY: Image Permanence Institute, Rochester Institute of Technology.

Ives, P. 1984. *Selected bibliography related to geographic information systems*. [S.l: s.n.].

Jackson, C. P. 1911. Maps: Their value, provision, and storage. *Library Assistant* 8: 184–91.

Johnson, J. T., et al. 1971. *AV cataloging and processing simplified.* Raleigh, NC: Audiovisual Catalogers of North Carolina.

Johnson, P. T. 1974. Sources and methods of Latin American flat map procurement. *SLAG&MD Bulletin* 95: 40–47.

Johnson, S. G. 1977. Geographic arrangement of topographic maps. *Special Libraries* 68 (3): 115–18.

Johnston, R. J. 1968. Choice in classification, the subjectivity of objective methods. *Annals of the Association of American Geographers* 58: 575–89.

Joint Royal Scottish Geographical Society and British Cartographic Society Symposium (1985: University of Aberdeen). 1987. *Cartography: The way ahead.* Norwich, Norfolk, UK: Geo Books.

Jong, G. de. 1948. De Kaartenverzameling. *Bibliotheekleven* 33: 267–81.

Jordan, L. E., and J. Star. 1992. A call to action: standards for the GIS community. *PERS* 58: 863–64.

Juhlin, A. B. 1960. Reproduction—Current practices in map libraries. *Special Libraries* 51: 247–50.

Kaiser, Frances E. 1974. *Handling special materials in libraries.* 76–90. New York: School Library Association.

Kaminstein, A. 1960. Maps, charts and copyright. *Special Libraries* 51: 241–43.

Kantrowitz, M. S., E. W. Spencer, and R. H. Simmons. 1940. *Permanence and durability of paper: An annotated bibliography of technical literature from 1885 A.D. to 1939 A.D.* (U.S. GPO Technical Bulletin 22). Washington, DC: GPO.

Karrow, R. W. 1975a. Hermon Dunlap Smith Center for the History of Cartography at the Newberry Library: Progress and prospect. *SLAG&MD Bulletin* 102: 18–23.

———. 1975b. *Manual for the cataloging and maintenance of the cartographic collection of the Newberry Library.* Chicago: The Newberry Library.

———. 1981. Innocent pleasures: ISBD(CM), AACR2, and map cataloging. *SLAG&MD Bulletin* 126: 2–12. [Rev. version in *International Cataloguing* 12 (April 1983): 10–12, erratum 12 (April 1983): 19.]

———. 1985. The role of cartobibliography in the history of cartography. *ACML Bulletin* 57: 1–9.

Kathpalia, Y. P. 1973. *Conservation and restoration of archive materials*. (Documentation, Libraries and Archives: Studies and Research no. 3.) Paris: Unesco.

Katz, W. A. 1969. *Introduction to reference work. Vol. 1, Basic information sources*. New York: McGraw-Hill.

———. 1982. *Introduction to reference work. Vol. I, Basic information sources*. 4th ed. New York: McGraw-Hill.

Keefe, L. E. 1990. *The life of a photograph: Archival processing, matting, framing and storage*. 2d ed. Boston: Focal Press.

Keen, E. 1955. *Manual for use in the cataloging and classification of audiovisual material for a high school library*. Lakeland, FL: Lakeland High School.

Kelley, S. L., and B. E. C. Schottlaender. 1996. UCLA/OCLC core record pilot project: Preliminary report. *LRTS* 40: 251–60.

Kent, D. 1976. Sign on service station: "Maps Refolded." *Good Housekeeping* 182 (2): 187.

Kersten, E. W. 1979. The obsolete topographic map as a research document. *WAML Information Bulletin* 10: 147–59.

Kett, W. F. 1990. Fifty years of operations by the Mountain Copper Company, Ltd., in Shasta County, California. *California Geology* 43 (2): 105–62.

Kidd, B. 1975. The genealogist and the map curator. *ACML Bulletin* 19: 20–23.

———. 1977a. Cleaning of maps: Note from conservation committee. *ACML Bulletin* 25: 84.

———. 1977b. 3M Micropore surgical tape #1530 pH reading of 6.4 acceptable. *ACML Bulletin* 23: 65.

———. 1979. The National Map Collection, Public Archives of Canada: An update. *SLAG&MD Bulletin* 116: 7–14.

———. 1980. Preventive conservation for map collections. *Special Libraries* 71: 529–38.

Kidd, B., and L. Cardinal. 1977. The map user in libraries and archives. *ACML Bulletin* 23: 12–20.

Kidd, C. 1977. LC Map Processing Project. *Oklahoma Librarian* 27 (January): 28.

Kilmartin, J. O. 1956. Map Information Office. *C&RL* 17 (2): 132–34, 155.

———. 1962. The function of a national map information office. *SLAG&MD Bulletin* 48: 5–7.

Kimberly, A. E. 1932. Deteriorative effect of sulphur dioxide upon paper in an atmosphere of constant humidity and temperature. *NBS Journal of Research* 8 (February): 159–71.

———. 1937. *Summary report of NBS research on preservation of records.* (U.S. National Bureau of Standards Miscellaneous Publication no. 154.) Washington, DC: GPO.

———. 1939. The repair and preservation of records in the National Archives. *Journal of Documentary Reproduction* 2: 68–75.

King, G. B. 1972. Open and closed questions: The reference interview. *RQ* 12: 157–60.

Kingsbury, R. C. 1969. Comparing maps and aerial photographs. *Journal of Geography* 68: 426–49.

———. 1972. Maps and aerial photographs for the small library. *Focus on Indiana Libraries* 26: 107–13.

Kiraldi, L. 1970a. Cooperation between map and document librarians: Common problems and concerns. *SLAG&MD Bulletin* 80: 32–34.

———. 1970b. Courses in map librarianship. *Special Libraries* 61: 496–500.

———. 1973. Old maps on the European market. *SLAG&MD Bulletin* 92: 12–15.

Kirby, R. P. 1970. A survey of map user practices and requirements. *Cartographic Journal* 7: 31–39.

Klemp, E. 1982. On the access to cartographic collections in GDR libraries. *INSPEL* 16: 21–30.

Klimley, S. 1993. Notes from the cutting edge. *Microform Review* 22: 105–7.

Knight, J. W. 1975–1976. Microforms and their application to map collections. *Archivaria* 1: 98–100.

Knutson, Gunnar. 1990. A comparison of online and card catalog accuracy. *LRTS* 34: 24–35.

Koeman, C. 1964. An increase in facsimile reprints. *Imago Mundi* 18: 878–88.

———. 1968. Levels of historical evidence in early maps (with examples). *Imago Mundi* 22: 75.

Koerner, A. G. 1972. Acquisition philosophy and cataloging priorities for university map libraries. *Special Libraries* 63: 511–16.

———. 1971. Floor plans: The new Map Room of the University of Michigan Library. *SLAG&MD Bulletin* 85: 33–38.

Kohl, J. G. 1857. Substance of a lecture delivered at the Smithsonian Institution on a collection of the charts and maps of America. In: Smithsonian Institution. *Annual report of the Board of Regents for the year 1856*, 93–146. (U.S. 34th Congress. 3d Session. Senate Miscellaneous Document no. 54; Serial Set 890.) Washington, DC: A. O. P. Nicholson, Printer.

Kollen, C. 1990. Work flow of map copy cataloging at the University of Arizona. *WAML Information Bulletin* 21: 143–46.

Kollen, C., and C. Baldwin. 1993. Automation and map librarianship: Three issues. *SLAG&MD Bulletin* 173: 24–38.

Kramer, F. 1952. Map mounting procedure. *Journal of Geography* 51: 21–23.

Kruger, Betsy. 1988. Automating preservation information in RLIN. *LRTS* 32: 116–26.

Kujoth, J. S. 1968. *Readings in nonbook librarianship*. Metuchen, NJ: Scarecrow Press.

Kunz, E. F. 1960. Maps for small and medium size municipal and shire libraries. *Australian Library Journal* 9 (April): 56–60.

Lacy, D. 1949. Microfilming as a major acquisitions tool: Policies, plans, and problems. *LC Quarterly Journal of Current Acquisitions* 6 (3): 8–17.

LaHood, C. G. 1973. Reproducing maps in libraries, the photographer's point of view. *Special Libraries* 64 (12): 19, 25–28.

Lai, P., and C. F. Gillies. 1991. The impact of geographical information systems on the role of spatial data libraries. *International Journal of Geographical Information Systems* 5: 241–51.

Lai, P., and M.-K. Wong. 1992. Problems in the cataloging of digital cartographic databases. In *Cataloging heresy: Challenging the standard bibliographic product, proceedings of the Congress for Librarians, February 18, 1991, St. John's University, Jamaica, New York, with additional contributed papers*, 185–96. Medford, NJ: Learned Information.

Lamprecht, S. J. 1974a. Periodical and bibliographic sources for geography book and atlas collections. *WAML Information Bulletin* 5 (3): 46–50.

———. 1974b. The university library map room orientation. *SLAG&MD Bulletin* 98: 31–33.

———. 1977. Goals and objectives for the university library map room. *SLAG&MD Bulletin* 110: 12–15.

———. 1986. The geography librarian and online information retrieval. *SLAG&MD Bulletin* 143: 2–6.

Lancaster, F. W. 1978. *Toward paperless information systems*. New York: Academic Press.

Landers, J. J. 1970. Commentary on mending tape for maps. *Special Libraries* 61: 466.

Landsat II imagery. 1981. *AB Bookman's Weekly* 67: 4931–32.

Langelier, G. 1977. Redistribution. *ACML Bulletin* 25: 8–12.

―――. 1978a. Copyright. *ACML Bulletin* 27: 57–59.

―――. 1978b. Redistribution. *ACML Bulletin* 26: 5–8.

―――. 1979. Microfilming of cartographic documents. *ACML Bulletin* 30: 1–8.

Langston, A. L., and R. Yapkowitz. 1976. California regional classification scheme. *WAML Information Bulletin* 8: 6–16.

Larned, J. N. 1892. Arrangement of maps (Lakewood conference, 4th session). *LJ* 17 (18): 44–45.

Larsgaard, M. L. 1973. Map classification. *Drexel Library Quarterly* 9 (4): 37–47.

―――. 1977. The International Standard Bibliographic Description for Cartographic Materials (ISBD (CM)): A cautious explication. *WAML Information Bulletin* 8: 153–57.

―――. 1978. NCIC/SLA meeting, Federal Center, Denver, March 9–10, 1978: A mutual discovery. *SLAG&MD Bulletin* 113: 3–16.

―――. 1991. Conservation of cartographic materials. In *Conserving and preserving materials in nonbook formats*, 135–45. Urbana: University of Illinois at Urbana-Champaign, Graduate School of Library & Information Science.

―――. 1992. The geographic distribution and organization of remote-sensing imagery in U.S. libraries—A work in progress. *SLAG&MD Bulletin* 166: 7–28.

―――. 1994. Bibliographic control of cartographic materials. *Encyclopedia of Library and Information Science* 53 (suppl.16): 28–38.

―――. 1995. Cataloging geospatial data in digital form. *SLAG&MD Bulletin* 181: 2–22.

―――. 1996a. Cataloging planetospatial data in digital form: Old wine, new bottles—new wine, old bottles. In *Geographic information systems and libraries: Patrons, maps and spatial information*, 17–30. Urbana: University of Illinois at Urbana-Champaign, Graduate School of Library and Information Science.

———. 1996b. *Multilevel description, multilevel inheritance, relations/links: Content and carrier.* Santa Barbara, CA: UCSB Alexandria Digital Library/Davidson Library. http: /www.library.ucsb. edu/people/larsgaard/ .

———. 1997. Access and preservation via digital surrogate for spatial data. *Meridian* 12: 31–36.

Layng, T. E. 1961. Problems in the map room. *Canadian Library* 18: 63–66.

———. 1967. Whither Canadian map libraries? *ACML Proceedings*: 5–8.

———. 1969. Discussion of standards of education and pay for map librarians: Summary. *ACML Proceedings* (1968): 33.

LC. *See* United States. Library of Congress.

LC's mass deacidification process. 1984. *RTSD Newsletter* 9 (4): 37.

Lea, G., J. Shearer, and D. Paterson. 1978. Computerized indexing of the Institute of Geological Sciences (UK) Geological Map Collection. *SLAG&MD Bulletin* 112: 27–46.

LeBlond, R. 1969. Miracode et documentation cartographique. *ACML Proceedings* (1969): 25–36.

Lederman, S. J. 1979. Tactual mapping from a psychologist's perspective. *ACML Bulletin* 32: 21–25.

Lee, P. B. 1960. Copyright—The publisher's viewpoint. *Special Libraries* 51: 244–46.

———. 1963. Map filing equipment. In C. M. Lewis 1963, 43–45.

Lee, R. J. 1955. *English county maps—The identification, cataloguing, and physical care of a collection.* (Library Association Pamphlet no. 13.) London: Library Association.

Leeuwenburg, J. 1982. Map reference work in an academic library. *Globe* 18: 9–18.

LeGear, C. E. 1956. *Maps, their care, repair and preservation in libraries.* Rev. ed. Washington, DC: LC Reference Department, Map Division.

Lehmann, Stephen, and James H. Spohrer. 1993. The year's work in collection development, 1992. *LRTS* 37: 299–313.

Lepine, P. 1981. Past and future: TV networks and computer databases. *ACML Bulletin* 40: 25–29.

Letts, T. 1900. Maps, from the romantic and prosaic standpoints. *LJ* 25: 5–7.

———. 1901. Notes on the care of maps. *LJ* 26: 688–89.

————. 1902. Notes on the cataloging of maps. *LJ* 27: 74–76.

————. 1905. Maps: Handling, classifying, cataloguing. In *International Geographical Congress, 8th, U.S. Report 1904*, 803–8. (U.S. 58th Congress. 3d Session. House Document no. 460, Serial Set 4890.) Washington, DC: GPO. [Also in *American Geographical Society Bulletin* 37 (1905): 485–90.]

Lewis, C. 1973. The new geography department at Lampeter. *Society of University Cartographers Bulletin* 7 (2): 39–41.

————. 1985. Nonprint materials in the small library. *LRTS* 29: 145–50.

Lewis, C. M. 1963. *Special libraries: How to plan and equip them.* (Monograph no. 2.) New York: SLA.

Lewis, D. C. 1944. Maps: Problem children in libraries. *Special Libraries* 35 (3): 75–78.

Lewis, W. S. 1976. Reports/rapports IV, Environment Canada. *ACML Proceedings*: 66–70.

Libault, A. 1955. Classification of maps and geographical publications. *Unesco Bulletin for Libraries* 9 (5,6): 93–95.

Library Association. Media Cataloguing Rules Committee. 1973. *Nonbook materials cataloguing rules.* (National Council for Educational Technology. Working Paper no. 11.) London: National Council for Educational Technology.

Library of Congress footnotes: A conference on automation in federal map libraries. *LC Information Bulletin* 27: 717–18.

Library of Congress geography and maps: An illustrated guide. 1996. Washington, DC: LC.

Library work: Maps, their care and cataloging. 1922. *LJ* 47: 830.

Lochhead, K. 1982. Cataloguing map series. *ACML Bulletin* 44: 10–14.

Lock, C. B. M. 1969. *Modern maps and atlases, an outline guide to twentieth century production.* Hamden, CT: Archon Books.

Loertscher, D. V. 1975. *A nonbook cataloging sampler.* Vol. 5 of *Applications of library science.* Austin, TX: Armadillo Press.

Loggan, K. 1990. How to bring map awareness to your school library collection. *SLAG&MD Bulletin* 160: 24–38.

Low, J. G.-M. 1975. *The acquisition of maps and charts published by the United States government.* Denton, TX: Texas Women's University [Master's thesis in library science. Also in University of Illinois Graduate School of Library Science. 1976. Occasional Paper no. 125, and as ED 101 723 from ERIC.]

Lowcock, E. A. 1967. Map Curators Group Meeting held during the British Cartographic Society Symposium. *Society of University Cartographers Bulletin* 2 (1): 53–54.

Lukens, B. 1970. Arrangement and organization of geologic maps in the library. *SLAG&MD Bulletin* 81: 51–53. [Also in *WAML Information Bulletin* 2 (2): 24–26.]

Lydenberg, H. M., and J. Archer. 1960. *The care and repair of books.* Rev. by J. Alden. New York: R. R. Bowker.

Lynam, E. 1939. The development of symbols, lettering, ornament and color on English maps. British Records Association *Proceedings* for l936: 32–34.

Lynch, Patrick. 1994. A closer look at color displays. *HEPC Syllabus, Technology for Higher Education* 3 (5): 30, 32.

Lynn, L. D. 1940. The care of special materials in the U.S. Coast and Geodetic Survey Library. *Special Libraries* 31: 396–400.

Mackin, J. H. 1936. A method of mounting maps. *Science* 84: 233–34.

MacLeod, B. 1981. Reproduction processes (nonprinting). *ACML Bulletin* 41: 17–19.

Maddox, J. T. 1943. Current new map material worthy of preservation by public libraries. *LJ* 68: 309–12.

Magnan, G. A. 1973. Defense Mapping Agency charts the world. *Engineering Graphics* 13 (3): 6–11.

Making GIS a part of library service. 1995. *Information Technology and Libraries* 14 (2). Entire issue.

The making of a code: The issues underlying AACR2: Papers given at the International Conference on AACR2, held March 11–14, 1979. 1980. Chicago: ALA.

Maksimov, N. P., and F. V. Sidorov. 1970. *Microfilming of maps and drawings (selected parts)—Translation of mono. Mikrofilmirovanie Karti Chertezhei Moscow, 1970,* chs. 1, 2, 4, 7, 9, and bibliography by Eric Peabody. (AD–770 552.) Springfield, VA: NTIS.

Maling, D. H. 1966. Some thoughts about miniaturization of map library contents. *Cartographic Journal* 3: 14–17.

Maltby, A. 1975. *Sayers' manual of classification for librarians.* 5th ed. London: Andre Deutsch.

Managing cartographic and architectural records. 1989. (Instructional Guide Series.) Washington, DC: National Archives and Records Administration.

Manning, M. 1994. Sanborn fire insurance maps: An aid for genealogists. *Illinois Libraries* 76: 101–4.

Manzer, Gary. 1995. Maximizing digital orthophoto use, a technical overview. *GIS World* 8(12) 50–55. December.

Map automation project at the Library of Congress. 1968. *SLAG&MD Bulletin* 72: 19.

Map conservation. 1976. *ACML Bulletin* 24: 44. [Reprinted from *Journal of the Canadian Conservation Institute* 1 (1976): 27–28.]

Map exhibits—Panel discussions. 1958. *SLAG&MD Bulletin* 33: 11–14.

The map librarian in the modern world: Essays in honor of Walter W. Ristow. 1979. Munich: K. G. Saur.

Map libraries in transition: A report on the conference. 1993. *WAML Information Bulletin* 25: 30.

The Map Room and its services. 1984. Edinburgh: National Library of Scotland.

Map types (for "current" maps only). 1972. *ACML Newsletter* 5: 7–11.

Mapes, C. H. 1959. Make your library globe a space age tool. *LJ* 84: 3818–19.

Mapping through the ages—Maps and minds. [1984] (I 19.2:M 32/15.) Washington, DC: GPO.

Maps and atlases available on depository for depository libraries. 1984. In *Instructions to depository libraries*, Appendix C, 30–34. Washington, DC: GPO.

Maps from microfilm service now well established in UK. 1976. *Microinfo* 7 (1): 10.

Maps, globes acquired by G&M. 1976. *LC Information Bulletin* 35: 719.

MARC begins map catalog services. 1973. *LC Information Bulletin* 32: 3–4.

Margary, H. 1973. The facsimile reproduction of early engraved maps. *Society of University Cartographers Bulletin* 7 (2): 1–7.

Market preview. 1981– . Silver Spring, MD: National Microfilm Association. [Formerly titled *Buyers guide to micrographic equipment, products and services*.]

Markham, R. P. 1978. Topographic maps on microfiche. *Journal of Micrographics* 11: 315–18.

Marley, C. 1987. Save it! Conservation/preservation news. *ACML Bulletin* 62: 32–33.

Marley, C., and J. Kohler. 1985. Association of Canadian Map Libraries 19th Annual Conference conservation workshop. *ACML Bulletin* 55: 44–56.

Marsh, S. 1967. Maps, the oldest visual aid and a primary source material. *Journal of Geography* 66: 130–32.

Marshall, B. 1983. Organisation of a small map collection. New Zealand Map Keepers Circle *Newsletter* 14: 3–7.

Marshall, D. W. 1972. Floor plans: The Division of Maps, William L. Clements Library, University of Michigan. *SLAG&MD Bulletin* 89: 41–47.

Martin, L. 1936. A tentative scheme of classification for maps in the Library of Congress. *Public Documents*, 123–26.

Martinson, T. L. 1972. Maps in libraries. *Focus on Indiana Libraries* 26: 103–5.

Marx, R. W. 1976. *The mapping program of the Bureau of the Census*. Washington, DC: U.S. Bureau of the Census.

Mason, D. 1958. *Primer of non-book materials in libraries*. London: Association of Assistant Librarians.

Mason, E. R. 1918. How maps are mounted. *American Printer* 66 (4): 30.

Massó i Cartagena, J. 1985. *Estui sobre la classificació de la cartografia*. Barcelona, Spain: Institut Cartogràfic de Catalunya.

Matson, S. 1986. Speech writing for library conferences. *C&RL News* 47: 497–500.

Maughan, E. K. 1953. Binding maps for easy reference. American Association of Petroleum Geologists *Bulletin* 37: 2051–54.

Mayayo, C. L., and I. Lozano. 1989. The reproduction in microform of the cartographic collections of the Biblioteca Nacional, Madrid. *Microform Review* 18: 135–36.

McCune, S. 1952. A simple map holder. *Journal of Geography* 51: 301–2.

McDermott, P. D. 1967. Map use in our schools. *Journal of Geography* 66: 74–78.

McDonald, G. 1950. Public libraries must have maps. *LJ* 75: 453–55.

MC&G . . . A brief history of U.S. military mapmaking—and the first decade of the Defense Mapping Agency. 1982. Washington, DC: DMA.

McGarry, D. 1981. Responses to a map cataloging questionnaire. *SLAG&MD Bulletin* 125: 32–39.

———. 1985. On the cataloging/cataloguing front. *Base Line* 6 (2): 46–47.

McGlamery, P. 1982. University of Connecticut's map storage equipment. *SLAG&MD Bulletin* 128: 10–13.

―――. 1995. MAGIC at the University of Connecticut: Building the virtual map library. *SLAG&MD Bulletin* 179: 14–30.

McGlamery, P., and M. Lamont. 1994. New opportunities and challenges: Geographic information systems in libraries. *Database* 17 (December): 35–42.

McGrath, G. 1975. Whither cartography in Canada: From under- to over-representation? *Canadian Cartographer* 12: 217–21.

―――. 1985. Cataloguing and marginal information on topographical map series. *The Globe* 23: 39–52.

McGrath, G., and R. P. Kirby. 1969. Survey methods on the use of maps and atlases. *Canadian Cartographer* 6: 132–48.

McGregor, D. R. 1966. Geographical globes. *Cartographic Journal* 3: 7–9.

McIntyre, J. 1976. Practical course in map curatorship. *ACML Bulletin* 21: 11–12.

McKinney, W. M. 1969. The globe. *Journal of Geography* 68: 406–10. [Also in Drazniowsky 1975, 183–92.]

McLaughlin, P. 1971. Federal map libraries and the development of automation standards. *SLAG&MD Bulletin* 86: 21–23.

McNamee, G. 1975. The San Francisco Bay Area Reference Center. *WAML Information Bulletin* 6 (2): 33.

McQueen, L. M. 1977. A proposal for map displays in an academic library. *SLAG&MD Bulletin* 110: 16.

Meine, K.-H. 1968. Report on cartobibliographies. *Canadian Cartographer* 5: 149–53.

Merrett, C. E. 1976. *Map cataloguing and classification: A comparison of approaches.* (Occasional Publication Series no. 7). Sheffield, UK: University of Sheffield Postgraduate School of Librarianship and Information Science.

―――. 1982. *Map classification: A comparison of schemes with special reference to the continent of Africa.* (Occasional Paper no. 154). Urbana, IL: University of Illinois Graduate School of Library and Information Science. [Also as ED 221 195 from ERIC.]

Merrill, P. W. 1948. The principles of poor writing. *Surveying and Mapping* 8: 244–46.

Metcalfe, J. 1959. *Subject classifying and indexing of libraries and literature.* New York: Scarecrow Press.

Meyer, A. H. 1947. A geographic classification of geography material as based upon the Dewey Decimal classification. *Annals of the Association of American Geographers* 37: 219–22.

———. 1971. Resolving parallel problems in geography classification under the Dewey Decimal and Library of Congress systems. *Professional Geographer* 23: 5–10.

Meyer, M. A., F. R. Broome, and R. H. Schweitzer. 1975. Color statistical mapping by the U.S. Bureau of the Census. *American Cartographer* 2: 100–17.

Microfilming of maps and plans: A report. 2d ed. 1985. Hatfield, Hertsfordshire, UK: Cimtech (The National Centre for Information Media and Technology).

Microprocessor technologies, a primer: What makes the new CPUs so fast? 1994. *HEPC [Higher Education Product Companion] Syllabus, Technology for Higher Education* 3 (5): 14–16.

Miller, R. 1978. KWOC index for maps. *WAML Information Bulletin* 10: 34–39.

Miller, S. 1971. *The vertical file and its satellites: A handbook of acquisition, processing and organization.* Littleton, CO: Libraries Unlimited.

———. 1979. *The vertical file and its satellites.* 2d ed. Littleton, CO: Libraries Unlimited.

Mills, J. 1964. *The Universal Decimal classification.* (Rutgers Series on Systems for the Intellectual Organization of Information). New Brunswick, NJ: Rutgers State University Graduate School of Library Science.

Minicatalog of map data. [198_?]. Reston, VA: USGS.

Minogue, A. E. *The repair and preservation of records.* 1943. (*U.S. National Archives Bulletin* no. 5). Washington, DC: GPO.

———. 1945. Some observations on the flattening of folded records. *American Archivist* 8 (2): 115–21.

———. 1946. Treatment of fire and water damaged records. *American Archivist* 9: 17–25.

Minton, J. O. 1978. OCLC map cataloging: An emerging standard practice. *SLAG&MD Bulletin* 113: 25–40.

Miranda, S. 1983. Do's and don'ts when acquiring documents from Latin America and the Caribbean. SLA Florida Chapter *Bulletin* 15 (2): 82–91.

Mittra, D. K. 1968. Maps in libraries, their storage and preservation. *Herald of Library Science* 7: 27–32.

———. 1969. More about processing of maps. *Library Herald* 10: 268–75.

Mittra, D. K., and Ghatak, A. K. 1993. Map collection of the National Library and its users' pattern. *INSPEL* 27 (2): 65–72.

MLS, marketing library services. 1987– . Harrod's Creek, KY.: Riverside Data.

Modelski, A. M. 1977. Maps, charts and atlases. *Encyclopedia of Library and Information Sciences* 20: 117–67.

———. 1981. List of officially published works of the Geography and Map Division. *WAML Information Bulletin* 12: 172–81.

Moffat, R. 1980. Genealogy and maps: Some reference sources. *WAML Information Bulletin* 12: 21–30.

———. 1981. Maps, atlases & gazetteers for genealogical research. *WAML Information Bulletin* 12: 161–65.

Mole, D. 1982. Video discs and maps. *ACML Bulletin* 44: 20–21.

Moody, K. T. 1929. *The library within the walls: Reprints of articles and addresses.* New York: H. W. Wilson.

Moore, B. N. 1981. *A manual of AACR2 examples for cartographic materials.* Lake Crystal, MN: Soldier Creek Press.

Moore, J. A. 1982. Landsat-4 and its Thematic Mapper. *WAML Information Bulletin* 14: 47–51.

Moore, P. 1981. Map societies. *Map Collector* 17: 40–41.

Moore, P. A. 1982. *Bibliography and index. Part 1, Author's index.* (Harvard Library of Computer Graphics, 1981 Mapping Collection, vol. 18). Cambridge, MA: Harvard Graduate School of Design.

———. 1987. Topographic maps in US libraries. *International Library Review* 19: 201–23.

Morehead, J. H. 1983. *Introduction to United States public documents.* 3d ed. Littleton, CO: Libraries Unlimited.

Morgan, G. L. 1977. Notes on genealogy. *Prologue* 9: 178–82.

Morris, B. 1990. PC-CARTONET: A microcomputer version of the CARTONET map library automation system. *INSPEL* 24 (2): 68–73.

Morris, B., and R. Healey. 1985. *MARC for compatibility: Relational data bases for flexibility, a relational data base approach to automated map cataloging.* Edinburgh: University of Edinburgh, Department of Geography.

Morrow, C. C. 1982. *Conservation treatment procedures: A manual of step-by-step procedures for the maintenance and repair of library materials.* Littleton, CO: Libraries Unlimited.

Mortensen, S. A. 1977. *A written map acquisition policy: The standardized compared with actual map library practice.* ED 174 235. Washington, DC: Educational Resources Information Center.

Mosher, P. H., and M. Pankake. 1983. A guide to coordinated and cooperative collection development. *LRTS* 47: 417–31.

Motteler, L. S. 1980. Pacific Scientific Information Center: Geographic emphasis of a Pacific map collection. *Special Libraries* 71: 229–33.

Muehrcke, P. C., and J. O. Muehrcke. 1974. Maps in literature. *Geographical Review* 64: 317–38.

Mukherjee, A. K. 1966. *Librarianship, its philosophy and history.* New York: Asia Publishing House.

Mullen, R. R. 1970. Current status of orthophoto mapping in the United States Geological Survey—1970. In *Proceedings*, 200-2, United Nations Regional Cartographic Conference for Asia and the Far East, 6th, 1974. E/CONF. 57/L.2I. New York: United Nations.

Murphy, M. 1963. Will automation work for maps? *Special Libraries* 54: 563–67.

———. 1970. Map collection prepares to automate, the U.S. Army Topographic Command Library. *Special Libraries* 61 (4): 180–89.

———. 1976. DMATC and the map and chart depository program. *SLAG&MD Bulletin* 106: 13–20.

———. 1982a. 1941–1981: Forty years of the Geography and Map Division in SLA. *SLAG&MD Bulletin* 128: 2–9.

———. 1982b. Workshop on practical map curatorship in developing countries. *SLAG&MD Bulletin* 127: 25–27. [Also in *IFLA Journal* 8: 71–73.]

———. 1989. IFLA Geography and Map Libraries Section workshop. *SLAG&MD Bulletin* 156: 14–15.

Murray, James D. 1994. *Encyclopedia of graphic file formats.* Sebastopol, CA: O'Reilly & Associates, Inc.

Myers, M. J. 1979. The mid-career special librarian, where do we go from here? *Special Libraries* 70: 263–71.

Mysheva, I. A. 1967. Punch cards for retrieval of maps in texts. *Geodesy and Aerophotography* 6: 250–53.

Nagy, T. 1975. Map libraries and the map user: The map users comment. *ACML Bulletin* 17: 26.

———. 1984. Disaster contingency planning for map collections: An ounce of prevention. *ACML Bulletin* 53: 1–30.

Napier, N. 1946. *Library levity.* Seattle, WA: F. McCaffrey at his Dogwood Press.

Nardi, Bonnie A., and Vicki O'Day. 1996. *Intelligent agents: What we learned at the library.* Palo Alto, CA: Xerox Palo Alto Research Center.

National Humanities Alliance. 1997. *Basic principles for managing intellectual property in the digital environment.* http://www-ninch.cni.org/ISSUES/COPYRIGHT/PRINCIPLES/NHA_Complete. html .

Nebert, Douglas D. 1992. Data characteristics and quality: The importance of spatial metadata. *GIS World* 5 (9): 64–67.

Neddermeyer, G. 1973a. Cataloging of a map collection. *WAML Information Bulletin* 4 (2): 18–25.

———. 1973b. Map cataloging—An introduction. *Drexel Library Quarterly* 9 (4): 27–35.

Nelson, Raymond L. 1943. Map storage and distribution. *Military Engineer* 35: 465–69.

Neville, E. P. 1982. A new golden age in map and atlas publishing. *SLAG&MD Bulletin* 133: 12–22.

New committee to establish liaison with USGS/NC1C. 1978. *WAML Information Bulletin* 10: 86.

Newman, L. P. 1989. Color photocopying to reproduce/preserve geologic maps in literature. Geoscience Information Society *Proceedings* 23: 205–8.

Nichols, H. 1976. *Map librarianship.* Hamden, CT: Linnet Books.

———. 1977. Educating the map librarian, a review. *Society of University Cartographers Bulletin* 11: 23–26.

———. 1982. *Map librarianship.* 2d ed. London: Clive Bingley.

Nicholson, N. L. 1973. The evolving nature of national and regional atlases. *SLAG&MD Bulletin* 94: 20–25, 62.

Nicoletti, F. T. 1971. Conference on maps and map librarianship: U.S. Army Topographic Command College Depository Program. *SLAG&MD Bulletin* 86: 2–8.

Nixon, H. M. 1949. Lamination of paper documents with cellulose acetate foil. *Archives, the Journal of the British Records Association* 1 (2): 32–36.

North, G. W. 1981. *Maps: Who uses them?* Reston, VA: NCIC.

———. 1983. Maps for the nation: The current federal mapping establishment. *Government Publications Review* 10: 345–60.

Northeast Map-Users Organization (NEMO), inaugural meeting, October 7, 1987, Storrs, CT. 1988. *WAML Information Bulletin* 19: 96–97.

Now bump-maps help the blind to "see." 1977. *ACML Bulletin* 24: 43.

Nute, G. L. 1936. *The care and cataloging of manuscripts as practiced by Minnesota Historical Society.* (Special Bulletin IV). St. Paul, MN: Minnesota Historical Society.

Obenhaus, Bruce. 1989. Automated map retrieval. *INSPEL* 23 (2): 122–29.

———. 1990. Maps: Knowing enough to help users help themselves. *Research Strategies* 8: 144–49.

Ochman, P. G. 1978. Automated map retrieval. *INSPEL* 23: 122–29.

OCLC, Inc. 1976. *On-line cataloging of maps: Preliminary document.* Columbus, OH: OCLC.

Odell, C. B. 1959. The use of maps, globes, and pictures in the classroom. National Council for the Social Studies *Annual Yearbook* 29: 200–10.

O'Donnell, A. 1992. Cartobibliography: Purpose and rationale. *WAML Information Bulletin* 23: 169–71.

Office of Charting and Geodetic Services. 1984. Washington, DC: GPO.

Ogata, A. I. 1992. Making the most of today's data conversion methods. *GIS World* 5 (3): 82–87.

Olsgaard, J. N., and J. Van Balen. 1978. A case study in promotion and use of the map collection: Travel literature. *WAML Information Bulletin* 9: 105–11.

Olson, E. C., and A. Whitmarsh. 1944. *Foreign maps.* New York: Harper and Brothers.

Oman, R., and C. Taylor. 1972. *Map microfilming feasibility study.* Washington, DC: National Archives and Records Service.

Onsrud, H. J. 1993. *Law, information policy, and spatial databases.* (NCGIA Initiative 16 working paper). Santa Barbara, CA: National Center for Geographic Information and Analysis.

O'Reilly, R. N. 1964. Expansion of class 993.1: New Zealand classification schedules revised (1963) edition. *New Zealand Libraries* 27 (6): 133–53.

Ormeling, F. J., and E. H. van de Waal. 1977. Marginal information on maps. *ACML Bulletin* 24: 5–12.

Ostensen, Olaf. 1995. Mapping the future of geomatics. *ISO Bulletin,* 5–10, December.

Otness, H. M. 1971. A look at the Library of Congress Summer Map Processing Project. *WAML Information Bulletin* 3: 16–19.

———. 1972a. Guidebook maps. *SLA G&MD Bulletin* 88: 17–23.

———. 1972b. How to build a free map collection for a school media center. *California School Libraries* 43 (4): 10–13.

———. 1973. Globes: Current offerings. *WAML Information Bulletin* 4 (2): 5–7.

———. 1974. A primer on map folds and map folding. *WAML Information Bulletin* 6(1): 13–16.

———. 1977. Application for license to reproduce copyrighted map. *WAML Information Bulletin* 9: 18–19.

———. 1978a. The opportunities of realignment, remarks made in the role of devil's advocate. *WAML Information Bulletin* 9: 193–97.

———. 1978b. Random notes of a relieved president. *WAML Information Bulletin* 10: 4–7.

———. 1981. In praise of old guidebook city plans. *WAML Information Bulletin* 12: 268–75.

———. 1988. "Going plating": Stealing maps from libraries. *WAML Information Bulletin* 19: 206–10.

OULCS map project. 1977. *ACML Bulletin* 24: 46.

Palmerlee, A. E. 1967. Automation and map libraries. *SLA G&MD Bulletin* 69: 6–16.

Pan American Consultation on Cartography, 6th, Ciudad Trujillo, 1952. *Acta final.* (Conference and Organizations Series no. 32). Washington, DC: Pan American Union.

Panel on Aerial Photography. 1971. Getting them free: Panel on aerial photography. *WAML Information Bulletin* 2 (3): 1–9.

Parent, Phil. 1991. Digital orthophotography provides a new tool for GIS database integration. *GIS World* 4 (11): 48–49.

Paris. Bibliothèque nationale. Département des cartes et plans. 1951. *Régles adoptées pour la conservation des collections et la rédaction des catalogues*. Paris: Author.

Parker, V. 1983. LC G schedule users conference. *ACML Bulletin* 46: 69.

―――. 1990. Multilevel cataloging/description for cartographic materials. *WAML Information Bulletin* 21: 86–96.

Parr, T. 1975. Automation of cartobibliography, review of MARC for map library information retrieval and cartographic information. *SLAG&MD Bulletin* 100: 26–73.

Parry, R. B. 1983. Selection and procurement of European maps for an American map library. *SLAG&MD Bulletin* 131: 16–22.

Parsons, D. E. 1971. An experiment with a book of maps. *Repairers' News Sheets* 18: 8.

Parsons, E. J. S. 1965. Atlases in facsimile. *Cartographic Journal* 2: 39–42.

Parsons, E. J. S., and B. D. Fathers. 1968. Map Room, Bodleian Library. *Society of University Cartographers Bulletin* 2 (2): 1–12.

Parsons, F. H. 1895. The care of maps. *LJ* 20: 199–201. [Also in Moody 1929, 199–205.]

Patent issued to three employees of LC Preservation Office. 1975. *LC Information Bulletin* 34: 395, 397.

Pearson, L. R. 1979. Yale and Newberry recover stolen maps. *American Libraries* 10: 100.

Pelletier, M. 1981. French map libraries and national and international professional organizations. *INSPEL* 15: 215–18.

Penland, P. R., and A. Mathai. 1974. *Interpersonal communication, counseling, guidance and retrieval for media, library and information specialists*. New York: Marcel Dekker.

Penny, V. 1980. Design of displays and exhibitions. *ACML Bulletin* 36: 1–3.

Perkins, C. R. 1991. The automation of map library routines: Problems and potential. *Program* 25: 223–40.

Perkins, C. R., and R. B. Parry. 1988. Changing patterns of map availability. *International Journal of Special Libraries* 22: 56–69.

Perminova, O. I. 1994. The preservation of leather bindings of cartographic atlases. *IFLA Journal* 20 (3): 306–11.

Perry, A. 1979. Geographers, cartographers, and regional federal archives. *SLAG&MD Bulletin* 115: 2–6.

Perry, J. M. 1982. Vertical map storage. *Special Libraries* 73: 207–12. [Addendum in *SLAG&MD Bulletin* 131: 14–15.]

―――. 1983. Map storage methods: A bibliography. *SLAG&MD Bulletin* 131: 14–15.

―――. 1992. Use of map collections by genealogists: Responses to a survey. *SLAG&MD Bulletin* 170: 22–31.

Petrie, G. 1979. The status of topographic mapping from space imagery. Remote Sensing Society, 5th. *Remote sensing and national mapping, proceedings of conference*, 1–16. Reading, UK: Remote Sensing Society.

Pettee, J. 1946. *Subject headings, the history and theory of the alphabetical subject approach to books*. New York: H. W. Wilson.

Pettit, K. 1966. Maps, microfilm. In *Acquisition of special materials* 144–57. San Francisco: San Francisco Bay Region Chapter of SLA.

Peucker, T. K. 1970. Computer cartography and the map librarian. *ACML Proceedings*: 41–44.

Phillips, B. F. 1973. The computer-produced map catalog: Some considerations and a look at operation. *Drexel Library Quarterly* 9 (4): 71–78.

Phillips, B. F., and G. Rogers. 1968. Simon Fraser University computer-produced catalogue. *ACML Proceedings*: 11–24. [Also in *Journal of Library Automation* 2 (3): 105–15.]

Phillips, P. L. 1900. Preservation and record of maps in the Library of Congress. *LJ* 25: 15–16.

―――. 1921. *Notes on the cataloging, care, and classification of maps and atlases including a list of publications compiled in the Division of Maps*. Washington, DC: GPO.

Phinney, H. K. 1983. Map accessibility. *GIS Newsletter* 85: 4–5.

Pidek, J. 1969. Methods of reinforcing maps. *ACML Proceedings*: 14–17.

―――. 1974. Notes on the preservation and conservation of maps. *ACML Proceedings*: 45–47.

Piercey, E. J. 1974. *Commonsense cataloging, a manual for the organization of books and other materials in schools and small public libraries*. 2d rev. ed. New York: H. W. Wilson.

Planning a computer lab, considerations to ensure success. 1993. *Higher Education Product Companion* 3 (1): 16–20.

Plasker, J. R. 1976. History of geodetic networks. American Society of Civil Engineers, Surveying and Mapping Division *Journal* 102 (SU1): 21–30.

Plenderleith, H. J. 1969. *The conservation of antiquities and works of art: Treatment, repair, and restoration*. London: Oxford University Press.

Plunkett, D. G., and A. D. Quick. 1968. *Cataloging standards for non-book materials: A complete guide to cataloging non-book materials in the individual school*. Tigard, OR: Northwest Library Service.

Polyester film encapsulation. 1980. Washington, DC: GPO.

Poole, F. G. 1976a. Current lamination policies in the Library of Congress. *American Archivist* 39: 157–59.

————. 1976b. *Preservation and Care Workshop, 20–21 August 1976*. University of California at Santa Cruz. Notes.

Porck, Henk J. 1996. *Mass deacidification, an update on possibilities and limitations*. Amsterdam: European Commission on Preservation and Access.

Porter, Donna. 1985. Trials and tribulations—A day in the life of a map cataloguer, coping with series material. *ACML Bulletin* 56: 1–6.

Porter, R. E. 1961. How to select an atlas. *LJ* 86: 3747–50.

————. 1975. How to select an atlas. *LJ* 86: 3747–50. [Also in Drazniowsky 1975, 193–97.]

Post, J. B. 198_? *Map displays in public libraries*. Philadelphia: Free Library of Philadelphia.

————. 1981a. A modern map librarian. *Library Trends* 29: 417.

————. 1981b. Historical map research. *Library Trends* 29: 439–51.

————. 1986. Maps for genealogists. *SLAG&MD Bulletin* 143: 29–32.

Potterf, R. M. 1944. The map collection in the public library, acquisition, cataloging, and care of the collection. *Wilson Library Bulletin* 19: 270–72.

Powell, Antoinette Paris. 1987. Creating a traditional reference tool in the Age of Electronics. *C&RL News* 48: 679–83.

Powers, A. 1975. Map and geographical questions of a general public. *WAML Information Bulletin* 6 (2): 34.

Pratt, E. I. 1955. Standard indexing system for aerial photography. *SLAG&MD Bulletin* 20: 10–14.

Prescott, D. F. 1973a. Map Keepers' Seminar and Workshop. *Australian Geographical Studies* 11: 243.

————. 1973b. Problem of a university map collection. *Australian Library Journal* 22: 303–8.

————. 1975. The bibliographic description of maps. *Globe* 3: 51–63.

————. 1980. AACR2 and maps. *Cataloguing Australia* 6: 58–64.

————. 1989. Promoting maps to the Australian public: Nationwide map week. *INSPEL* 23 (2): 109–21.

Preservation microfilming: A guide for librarians and archivists. 2d ed. 1996. Chicago: ALA.

Preservation of library and archival materials: A manual. 1991. Alexandria, VA: Association of Higher Education Facilities Officers.

Preserving digital information, report of the Task Force on Archiving of Digital Information. 1996. Washington, DC: Commission on Preservation and Access.

Preventive maintenance. 1990. *C&RL News* 51: 408.

Prévost, M. L. 1946. Is classificatory approach the best for maps? *LJ* 71: 93–94, 104.

Proehl, K. H. 1979. The soil survey: An annotated-cartographic tool. *SLAG&MD Bulletin* 115: 18–25.

Pruett, N. J. 1981. A geological perspective: Searching for maps on GeoRef. *WAML Information Bulletin* 13: 1–18.

Pumpelly, J. W. 1964. Cartographic treatments in the production of orthophoto maps. *Surveying and Mapping* 24: 567–71.

Puntodewo, A. 1991. Creation of a map catalogue using CDS/ISIS. *LASIE: Information Bulletin of the Library Automated Systems Information Exchange* 21: 88–105.

Queens University at Kingston, Ontario, has prepared a revised index to Boggs-Lewis. 1978. *SLAG&MD Bulletin* 114: 47.

Questions and answers about map copyrights. Rev. 1990. Kankakee, IL: International Map Dealers Association.

Radway, J. W. 1903. Relief maps and globes. Royal Geography Society *Journal* 22: 575–76.

Ragsdale, R. C. 1957. Topographic maps: File 'em and find 'em! *California Librarian* 18: 163–65, 200–201.

Raisz, E. 1948. Globes. National Council for the Social Studies *Yearbook* 19: 105–16.

Ralli, R. A. 1979. Developing a map collection. *Australian Library Journal* 28: 240–41.

Randall, R., and E. C. Haines. 1961. *Bulletin boards and display.* Worcester, MA: Davis Publications.

Rapid rise and lamentable fall of the free road map. 1990. *San Diego Union*, Saturday, March 10, auto-1.

Ratajski, L. 1977. Model of communication in cartography for adaptation to map librarianship. *ACML Bulletin* 24: 4, cover. [From *Polski przeglad kartograficzny* 2 (3): 97–110.]

Rauchle, N. M. 1975. Towards intellectual foundations of map librarian education. *Australian Library Journal* 24: 94–99.

Rauchle, N. M., and P. A. G. Alonso. 1974. Map staff reference functions and map library systems design. *SLAG&MD Bulletin* 97: 33–38.

Ray, J. M. 1974. Who borrows maps from a university library map collection and why? *Special Libraries* 65 (3): 104–9.

———. 1978. Automated map cataloging with OCLC. *SLAG&MD Bulletin* 113: 76.

———. 1981. G&M: Whence, why, whither? *SLAG&MD Bulletin* 124: 31–33.

Ray, J. M., and A. B. Rubin. 1985. Pay equity in academic libraries, and how do map librarians come out? *SLAG&MD Bulletin* 141: 48.

Ready, W. B. 1967. Punched card and/or computer control of a map collection. *Special Libraries* 58: 365.

Recent practices in map libraries. 1971. New York: SLA. [Reprinted from articles in 1969 issues of *Special Libraries.*]

Recommendations on methods of microfilming maps and plans. 1972. Hatfield, UK: National Reprographic Centre for Documentation.

Recommended minimum technical guidelines for federal depository libraries. 1993. In *Federal Depository library manual* 45–55. Washington, DC: GPO. [Also *Administrative Notes* 14 (19), September 15, 1993.]

Recupero, Lisa. 1992. *Evaluation of programs for the storage and retrieval of cartographic data.* Chapel Hill, NC: University of North Carolina, Graduate School of Library Science.

Reed, S. R. 1978. Library education 1977–1987. *Journal of Education for Librarianship* 19: 87–96.

Rees, G. W. 1972. Pre-education for map librarianship. *WAML Information Bulletin* 3 (3): 3–5.

Reilly, James M., Douglas W. Nishimura, and Edward Zinn. 1995. *New tools for preservation.* Washington, DC: Commission on Preservation and Access.

Reinhard, C. 1978. Wisconsin county cartographic information system. [American Congress on Surveying and Mapping Fall Technical Meeting, October 15–20, Albuquerque, New Mexico.] American Congress on Surveying and Mapping *Proceedings*: 316–21.

———. 1979. Wisconsin county cartographic information system. *SLAG&MD Bulletin* 115: 7–17.

Research and development in the National Mapping Division, USGS: Trends and prospects. 1991. Washington, DC: National Academy Press.

Responsibility of depository libraries to insure their depository collections. 1984. U.S. government memorandum, AN-v5n10-7/84, January 12.

Rhoads, J. B. 1992. Conservation of cartographic materials. *WAML Information Bulletin* 23: 163–67.

Riccoboni, A. 1964. A proposito della "Bibliographie cartographique internationale" e di un progetto per una "Bibliografia cartografica Italiana." Associazione italiana di cartografia. *Bollettino* 2 (December): 35–38.

Richards, E. M. 1933. The storage of maps. *Wilson Library Bulletin* 7: 356–57.

Rieke, J. 1984. Aerial photography: An information tool for the map collection. *WAML Information Bulletin* 15: 129–37.

———. 1985. Keepers of maps: Some advice on preservation. *Wilson Library Bulletin* 60 (October): 25–27.

Rieke, J., S. Gyeszly, and L. Steele. 1984. Preservation of sheet maps: Lamination or encapsulation, a durability study. *SLAG&MD Bulletin* 138: 2–10.

Riesthuis, G. J. A., et al. 1991. New UDC auxiliary tables for cartographic materials and geographic information. *International Forum on Information and Documentation* 16: 30–35.

Rigby, M. 1974. The use of the Universal Decimal Classification in map indexing. *ACML Proceedings*: 25–44.

Rimmer, Steve. 1992. *The graphic file toolkit.* Reading, MA: Addison-Wesley.

Ripin, A. L., and D. Kasman. 1976. Education for special librarianship, a survey of courses offered in accredited programs. *Special Libraries* 67: 504–9.

Risher, Carol. 1996. *IPCC statement: Libraries, copyright and the electronic environment.* New York: Association of American Publishers.

Ristow, W. W. 1942. The library map collection. *LJ* 67: 552–55.

———. 1943. Maps: How to make them and read them: A bibliography of general and specialized works on cartography. *Bulletin of the New York Public Library* 47: 381–86.

———. 1945. A survey of world atlases. *LJ* 70: 54–57, 100–103.

———. 1946. Maps in libraries, a bibliographical summary. *LJ* 71: 1101–7, 1121–24.

———. 1954. Cartographic exhibits. *Surveying and Mapping* 14: 18–25.

———. 1955. What about maps? *Library Trends* 4 (2): 123–39.

———. 1957. Journalistic cartography. *Surveying and Mapping* 17: 369–96.

———. 1963. Maps and map making. *Grolier encyclopedia* 13: 205–9.

———. 1965. Nineteenth-century cadastral maps in Ohio. *Bibliographical Society of America Papers* 59: 306–15.

———. 1966. State maps of the southeast to 1833. *Southeastern Geographer* 6: 33–40.

———. 1967a. The emergence of maps in libraries. *Special Libraries* 58: 400–19.

———. 1967b. Map librarianship. *LJ* 92: 3610–15.

———. 1968. New maps from old—Trends in cartographic facsimile publishing. *Canadian Cartographer* 5 (1): 1–17.

———. 1969. Automated map cataloging at the Library of Congress. *ACML Proceedings*: 37–44.

———. 1970a. Geography and Map Libraries Subsection, International Federation of Library Associations. *International Libraries Review* 2: 387–89.

———. 1970b. International Federation of Library Associations, Special Libraries Section, Geography and Map Libraries Subsection, sessions at Moscow IFLA Conference, 1–5 September 1970. *INSPEL* 5 (3–4): 55–60.

———. 1970c. International map librarianship, IFLA (Moscow), 1970. *SLAG&MD Bulletin* 82: 42–43.

———. 1970d. Theatrum Orbis Terrarum 1570–1970. *Quarterly Journal of the LC* 27: 316–31.

———. 1971. Maps of the American Revolution: A preliminary survey. *Quarterly Journal of the LC* 28: 196–215.

———. 1972a. À la carte: Selected papers on maps and atlases. Washington, DC: GPO.

———. 1972b. Ena L. Yonge 1895–1971. *SLAG&MD Bulletin* 88: 24–29.

———. 1974a. Cartographic information services of the Library of Congress. *American Cartographer* 1: 125–30.

———. 1974b. Map production and procurement today. *SLAG&MD Bulletin* 96: 2–9, 17.

———. 1975. Library of Congress Geography and Map Division Map Processing Project. *SLAG&MD Bulletin* 102: 30–33.

———. 1976. Map library education in the United States and Canada. *SLAG&MD Bulletin* 104: 38–41. [Also in *INSPEL* 11 (3): 95–99.]

———. 1978a. The greening of map librarianship. *SLAG&MD Bulletin* 111: 2–9.

———. 1978b. Worlds of Christmas greetings. *Quarterly Journal of the LC* 35: 234–41.

———. 1979. List of publications. In *Map librarian in the modern World* 1979, 40–46.

———. 1980. *The emergence of maps in libraries*. Hamden, CT: Shoe String Press.

Ristow, W. W., and D. K. Carrington. 1969. Computerized map cataloging project. *INSPEL* 4 (3,4): 74–79.

———. 1971. Machine-readable map cataloging in the Library of Congress. *Special Libraries* 62: 343–52.

Ritzlin, G. 1980. *World directory of dealers in antiquarian maps*. Chicago: Chicago Map Society.

Roberts, J. A. 1962. The topographic map in a world of computers. *Professional Geographer* 14 (November): 12–13.

Robinson, A., and R. D. Sale. 1969. *Elements of cartography*. 3d ed. New York: Wiley.

Robinson, Peter. 1993. *The digitization of primary textual sources*. (Office of Humanities Communications Publications 4). Oxford, England: Office for Humanities Communications.

Roepke, H. G. 1958. Care and development of a wall-map collection. *Professional Geographer* 10 (May): 11–15.

Rogers, J. V. 1982. *Nonprint cataloging for multimedia collections: A guide based on AACR2*. Littleton, CO: Libraries Unlimited.

Rogers, J. W. 1950. Copyright catalog is useful tool. *LJ* 75: 444–46.

Rogers, T. M. 1954. One way of dealing with maps. *Library World* 55: 149–51.

Role of maps in sci-tech libraries. 1985. New York: Haworth Press. [Also published as *Science & Technology Libraries* 5 (3).]

Royal Geographical Society. Library and Map Committee. 1955. The storage and conservation of maps: A report . . . , 1954. *Geographical Journal* 11: 182–89.

Rudd, J. K. 1978. NCIC's Denver meeting for map librarians. *WAML Information Bulletin* 9: 217.

Rudd, J. K., and L. Carver. 1981. Topographic map acquisition in U.S. academic libraries. *Library Trends* 29 (3): 375–90.

Rugg, D. S. 1967. Developing the university map library. *Journal of Geography* 66: 119–29. [Also in Drazniowsky 1975, 490–505.]

Ruskin, K. B. 1995. *Grantwriting, fundraising, and partnerships: Strategies that work!* Thousand Oaks, CA: Corwin Press.

Russia (1923– , USSR) Ministerstvo Geologii. Vsesoyuznyi Nauchno–Issledovatel'skii Institut Ekonomiki. Mineral'hogo Syr'ya i Geologorazvedochnykh Rabot. 1970. *Universal Decimal Classification UDC (Universal'naya Desyatichnaya Klassifikatsiya UDK).* (FID Publication no. 431). Jerusalem: Israel Program for Scientific Translations.

Ryerson, C. C. 1983. Technical note: Improved methods of reproducing large relief models. *American Cartographer* 10: 151–57.

Saffady, W. 1994. *Introduction to automation for librarians.* 3d ed. Chicago. ALA.

Salichtchev, K. A. 1979. Periodical and serial publications on cartography. *Canadian Cartographer* 16: 109–32.

Sanders, W. 1970. Bibliographic control, patron access, and selection of maps in the U.S. Geological Survey Library, Menlo Park, California. *WAML Information Bulletin* 1 (2): 11.

Sandilands, R. W. 1978. Charting by the Canadian Hydrographic Service. *ACML Bulletin* 29: 10–12.

Sandner, F. 1979. A bibliography on the storage and care of non-book materials in libraries with selected annotations. (ED 179 246). Arlington, VA: ERIC Document Reproduction Service.

Satterlee, S. 1970. Sources of free maps from Central America, South America and Africa. *WAML Information Bulletin* 1 (3): 41–47.

Sauer, S. A. 1969. Some thoughts on planning, furnishing and acquisitioning a map library. *ACML Proceedings*: 18–21.

———. 1971. Planning the new map library: A panel presentation. *ACML Proceedings*: 49–53.

———. [1975] *University map libraries in Canada, a folio of selected plans*. London, Ontario: Department of Geography, University of Western Ontario.

———. 1984. Microfiche records of Canadian topographic series. *ACML Bulletin* 51: 32–34.

Sayer, M. 1973. How to start a small map library. *WAML Information Bulletin* 5: 5–11.

Schmeckebier, L. F., and R. B. Eastin. 1969. *Government publications and their use*. 2d rev. ed. Washington, DC: Brookings Institution.

Schmitz, J. M. 1941. Mounting maps on plywood. *Wilson Library Bulletin* 15: 765–67.

Schorr, A. E. 1974a. Map librarianship, map libraries, and maps: A bibliography, 1921–1973. *SLAG&MD Bulletin* 95: 2–35, 39. [Suppl. 1 in *SLAG&MD Bulletin* 107 (1977): 2–18.]

———. 1974b. Written map acquisition policies in academic libraries. *SLAG&MD Bulletin* 98: 28–30.

———. 1975. Lotka's law and map librarianship. *Journal of the American Society for Information Science* 26 (3): 189–90.

———. 1981. General world atlases. *Booklist* 77: 564–67.

Schraubstadter, C. W. 1948. *Care and repair of Japanese prints*. Cornwall-on-Hudson, NY: Idlewild Press.

Schroeder, J. R. 1978a. AACR2 abandonment of corporate body main entry: LCG&M Division position paper. *SLAG&MD Bulletin* 114: 24–27. [Also in *WAML Information Bulletin* 10: 78–81.]

———. 1978b. Announcement from LC. *SLAG&MD Bulletin* 112: 81.

———. 1981. Perspectives on map cataloging and classification. *Library Trends* 29: 419–38.

Schwartz, V. 1976. Map reference seminars at the Milwaukee public library. *SLAG&MD Bulletin* 105: 2–5.

Scott, S. J. 1993. Preservation needs of oversized illustrations in geology master's theses. *LRTS* 37: 73–85.

Scribner, B. W. 1941. *Protection of documents with cellulose acetate sheeting*. (U.S. National Bureau of Standards Miscellaneous Publication Ml68). Washington, DC: GPO.

Scriven, M. 1956. Preservation and restoration of library materials. *Special Libraries* 47: 439–48.

Seavey, C. A. 1977a. Maps in documents. *SLAG&MD Bulletin* 110: 49–51.

———. 1977b. Maps of the American State Papers. *SLAG&MD Bulletin* 107: 28–35; 110: 3–11.

———. 1977c. Wheat to Serial Set conversion chart. *SLAG&MD Bulletin* 108: 37–40.

———. 1978a. Maps as documents/documents as maps. *SLAG&MD Bulletin* 112: 2–18.

———. 1978b. Visual indexes to the LC "G" schedule. *SLAG&MD Bulletin* 114: 17–23.

———. 198_? *Developing the academic map collection.* Albuquerque, N.M.: University of New Mexico.

———. 1980. Inexpensive map collection. *School Library Journal* 26 (10): 42.

———. 1981. Collection development for government map collections. *Government Publications Review* 8A: 17–29.

———. 1982a. *Government map publications: An overview.* [S.l.: s.n.].

———. 1982b. 1980 Census geography and maps. *SLAG&MD Bulletin* 129: 10–26.

———. 1982c. U.S. Geological Survey topo quad count by state. *SLAG&MD Bulletin* 127: 53.

———. 1984. Map collection development planning: Mapkeeper and library administrator working together can tailor a rational acquisition policy. *WAML Information Bulletin* 15: 268–79.

Seavey, C. A., and S. M. Clark. 1988. Library education for work with maps. *Journal of Education for Library and Information Science* 29: 121–26.

Seavey, C. A., and H. F. Rex. 1992. Users and geographic areas of interest in an academic library map collection, 1983–1989: Implications for policy development. *Meridian* 7: 15–25.

Sebert, L. M. 1983. Geodesy for map librarians. *ACML Bulletin* 48: 41–43.

———. 1984a. Geodesy for map librarians. *ACML Bulletin* 50: 8–13.

———. 1984b. Geodesy for map librarians. *ACML Bulletin* 51: 24–28.

———. 1984c. Geodesy for map librarians. *ACML Bulletin* 52: 49–57.

Seldin, D. T. 1978. Library of Congress Summer Processing Project: A participant's point of view. *SLAG&MD Bulletin* 112: 51–56.

Selmer, M. L. 1976. Map cataloging and classification methods, a historical survey. *SLAG&MD Bulletin* 103: 7–12.

————. 1979. A policy for withdrawal from the map collection. *SLAG&MD Bulletin* 116: 2–6.

Seminar on AACR2 (1979: University of Nottingham). 1980. *Seminar on AACR2: Proceedings of a seminar organized by the Cataloguing and Indexing Group of the Library Association at the University of Nottingham, 20–22 April, 1979.* London: Library Association.

Seminar on the Application of Chemical and Physical Methods to the Conservation of Library and Archival Materials, Topsfield, MA, May 17–21, 1971. 1972. *Library and archives conservation.* Boston: Library of the Boston Athenaeum.

Shaffer, N. J. 1988. Maps on microfiche: A success story at the Library of Congress. *Inform* 2: 21–22.

Shannon, M. O. 1983. The state of map acquisitions and reference use in libraries. *Specialist* 6 (July/August): 1.

Sharp, H. A. 1916. The cataloguing and description of maps: Some problems. *Library World* 18: 256–71.

————. 1935. *Cataloguing: A text book for use in libraries.* London: Grafton.

Shepherd, I. K. H., and S. Chilton. 1980. Computer-based enquiries in the map library: The MAPLIB system. *Cartographic Journal* 17: 128–39.

Shera, J. H. 1972. *The foundations of education for librarianship.* New York: Becker and Hayes.

Sherman, J. 1978. Mapping for the blind and handicapped. *WAML Information Bulletin* 9: 153–54.

Sherwood, A. 1976. Maps in the Illinois State Library. *Illinois Libraries* 58: 160–79.

————. 1981a. Bibliography of verification and location tools for Illinois county atlases. *Illinois Libraries* 63: 560–61.

————. 1981b. Status report on the map cataloging project at the Illinois State Library. *SLAG&MD Bulletin* 124: 15–19.

Shill, H. B., and S. K. Peterson. 1989. Is government information in your library's future? *C&RL News* 50: 649–56.

Sijmons, A. H. 1974. Kaartbeheerder, een nieuwe specialisatie. *Geografisch tijdschrift* 8: 460–63.

Simmons, J. 1978. Micrographics in the National Cartographic Information Center. *SLAG&MD Bulletin* 112: 47–50.

Singer, M. 1987. Wall power. *New Yorker* 63 (November 30): 44–97.

Sivers, R. 1970. Resumes from the control of map acquisitions. 1, Control of acquisitions in the Map Room, the University of California, Santa Barbara. *WAML Information Bulletin* 1 (3): 26–28.

———. 1974. U.S. federal map and chart depositories. *WAML Information Bulletin* 6: 37–43. [Later published as Federal map and chart depositories. In *Government Publications Review* 2 (Winter): 9–15.]

Skelton, R. A. 1954. The conservation of maps. *Society of Local Archivists Bulletin* 14 (October): 13–19.

Skogh, H. M. 1941. Maps: Inexpensive and free. *Illinois Libraries* 23 (10): 6–10.

Smith, C. D. 1984. Cartographic explanations before the key. *Map Collector* 26: 38–41.

Smith, D. M. 1974. Cartographic indexing. *Indexer* 9: 18–20.

Smith, R. D. 1966. Paper deacidification: A preliminary report. *Library Quarterly* 36: 273–92.

———. 1972. Maps, their deterioration and preservation. *Special Libraries* 63 (2): 59–68.

———. 1984. Mass deacidification: The Wei T'o way. *C&RL News* 45: 588–93.

Smith, R. F. 1978. A funny thing is happening to the library on its way to the future. *Futurist* 12 (2): 85–91.

Smith, T. R. 1953. Map classification and arrangement at the University of Kansas Library. *SLAG&MD Bulletin* 22: 11–17.

———. 1960. *Map collection in a general library: A manual for classification and processing procedures.* Lawrence, KS: University of Kansas.

Smither, R. E. 1912–1913. The treatment of pamphlets, maps, photographs, and similar items. *Library World* 15: 195–99.

Smyth, A. L. 1977. Change on the way? *ACML Bulletin* 24: 45–46.

Snider, F. E. 1945. Suggested map arrangement for the general library. *LJ* 70: 571–74.

Snyder, D. L., et al. 1970a. Bibliography: Map preservation. *WAML Information Bulletin* 1 (3): 23–25.

———. 1970b. Lamination as practiced in the California State Archives. *WAML Information Bulletin* 1 (3): 8–12.

Soete, G. 1997. *Geographic information systems*. (Transforming Libraries 2.) Washington, DC: Association of Research Libraries, Office of Management Services.

Southard, R. B. 1974. National Cartographic Information Center—A status report. American Congress on Surveying and Mapping *Proceedings* 34: 543–52.

Southworth, C. S. 1984. The side-looking airborne radar program of the U.S. Geological Survey. *PERS* 50: 1467–70.

Special Libraries Association. Geography and Map Division. 1979. Map Librarians' Professional Concerns Committee on Cooperation with the Library of Congress Geography and Map Division. *SLAG&MD Bulletin* 118: 33–41.

Special Libraries Association. Geography and Map Division. Committee on Automation in Map Libraries. 1966. Map libraries and automation, a bibliography compiled by G&M Division's Committee on Automation. *SLAG&MD Bulletin* 66: 14–19.

Special Libraries Association. Geography and Map Division. Committee on Map Cataloging. 1956. Final report. *SLAG&MD Bulletin* 24: 4–9 [comments in 24: 10–12].

A special report, the new OCLC system. 1986. *OCLC Newsletter*, no. 161.

Spellman, L. E. 1970. Value of maps as reference tools. *SLAG&MD Bulletin* 81: 24–28.

Spence, M. R. 1951. *The classifying, cataloging and filing of maps in college and university libraries*. Master's thesis, Western Reserve University, School of Library Science, Cleveland, Ohio.

Spiess, E. 1994. *Some problems with the use of electronic atlases* [paper from the 9th Conference of the European Map Curators Group, Switzerland, 1994]. http: //www.konbib.nl/kb/skd/ liber/overview.htm#subject .

Sporer, A. H. 1983. The impact of digital storage on micrographics storage. *Journal of Micrographics* 16 (2): 41–45.

Spyers-Duran, P. 1965. *Moving library materials*. Rev. ed. Chicago: ALA.

Sprankle, A. T. 1991. Map retrospective conversion: The latest development in one university's map collection. *SLAG&MD Bulletin* 165: 15–18.

Stability of optical disks. 1993. *Commission on Preservation and Access Newsletter* 58: 3–4.

Stallings, D. L. 1966. A look at automated cartographic retrieval. *SLAG&MD Bulletin* 64: 5–11.

Stanford, Edward. 1890. *Methods of map counting with illustrations*. London: Author.

Stanley, A. A. 1949. Plastic relief models. *Surveying and Mapping* 9: 54–60.

Stark, P. L. 1981? *Purchasing maps of Washington: A popular guide*. Ellensburg, WA: CWU Alumni Association, College of Letters, Arts and Sciences, University Library Map Library.

Steckzén, B. 1950. Storage and preservation of maps in Swedish Military Archives. *Indian Archives* 4: 14–19.

Steele, D. 1993. Location grids—latitude and longitude, a training aid for students. *WAML Information Bulletin* 24: 208.

Steele, D., Julie Hoff, and Michael McColgin. 1997. Humidity chamber for flattening maps at the Arizona Department of Library, Archives and Public Records. *WAML Information Bulletin* 28: 149–53.

Stephenson, C. 1983. Storing your maps. *Map Collector* 23: 24–26.

Stephenson, Richard W. 1970. Published sources of information about maps and atlases. *Special Libraries* 61 (2): 87–98+.

———. 1973. The reference facilities and services of the Geography and Map Division, Library of Congress. American Congress on Surveying and Mapping *Proceedings* 33: 365–70. [Also in *Special Libraries* 65 (1974): 227–33.]

———. 1979. Map collections and map librarianship in the United States, a review. *Special Libraries* 70 (3): 117–26.

Stephenson, T. 1990. Imaging, visualization and the challenge of global change. *Advanced Imaging* (July): 59–61.

Stevens, A. R., and D. L. Malone. 1978. Capabilities and services of Mapping Services Branch, the Tennessee Valley Authority. *SLAG&MD Bulletin* 113: 41–48.

Stevens, S. D. 1970. Color microfilming of Sanborn maps for a local history collection. *WAML Information Bulletin* 1 (3): 2–7.

———. 1971. A short history of the Western Association of Map Libraries. *WAML Information Bulletin* 2 (2): 22–24.

———. 1972a. Maps in the local history collection. *WAML Information Bulletin* 3 (3): 17–28.

———. 1972b. Planning a map library? Create a master plan! *Special Libraries* 63: 172–76.

———. 1977a. The Circum-Pacific map project: An introduction and review. *WAML Information Bulletin* 9: 2–10.

―――. 1977b. *The computer-produced map catalog—U.C. Santa Cruz system converts to MARC.* Paper presented at WAML meeting, University of Santa Clara, California, 25 March 1977.

―――. 1978a. California Map Society charts course at its first meeting, May 20, 1978. *WAML Information Bulletin* 9: 240–42.

―――. 1978b. Map collections in the United States and Canada, a directory [review]. *WAML Information Bulletin* 10: 46–50.

―――. 1978c. WAML's questionnaire re: Proposed new organization. *WAML Information Bulletin* 9: 161–87.

―――. 1979. American federation: A proposal to unite all groups interested in cartographic materials. *SLAG&MD Bulletin* 118: 2–6.

―――. 1981a. CUAC meets with DMA and USGS. *WAML Information Bulletin* 12: 113–22.

―――. 1981b. Map and aerial photo collections in the United States: Survey of the seventy largest collections. *Library Trends* 29: 513–36.

―――. 1985. Map librarianship: Suggestions for improvement. *Wilson Library Bulletin* 60: 33–36.

Stewart, L. 1987. Picking CD-ROMs for public use. *American Libraries* 18: 738–40.

Stibbe, H. L. P. 1970. Air photographs in the map library. *ACML Proceedings*: 44–51.

―――. 1976a. *MARC-Maps, the history of its development and a current assessment.* (*Bulletin van de Vakgroep Kartografie* no. 3). Utrecht, The Netherlands: Organization for Information Policy, Geografisch Instituut van de Rijksuniversiteit.

―――. 1976b. *Personal letter, December 24, 1976.* Ottawa: National Map Collection.

―――. 1977a. IFLA Joint Working Group on the International Standard Bibliographic Description for Cartographic Materials, ISBD (CM), Utrecht, November 8–12, 1976. *ACML Bulletin* 24: 30–32.

―――. 1977b. Report on the IFLA General Council and the UNI-MARC meetings . . . . *ACML Bulletin* 23: 25–37.

―――. 1986. International bibliographic standards in cartographic archives: The National Map Collection, Public Archives of Canada, experience. *INSPEL* 20 (1): 5–33.

―――. 1992. Conservation treatment of rare atlases at the National Archives of Canada. *The Archivist* 19 (2): 21–22.

Stoddard, R. H. 1973. *Planning college geography facilities: Guidelines for space and equipment.* (Publication no. 12). Washington, DC: Association of American Geographers, Commission on College Geography.

Stokes, M. 1974. Bulletin board principles. *Audiovisual Instruction* 19 (8): 56.

Stone, K. M. 1960. Procurement of aerial photography. In American Society of Photogrammetry, *Manual of photographic interpretation* 19–26. Washington, DC: American Society of Photogrammetry.

Stoneman, W. G. 1955. Use and appreciation of maps. *SLAG&MD Bulletin* 22: 7–10.

Storage of maps. 1914. *LJ* 39: 936.

Storm, C. 1944. Maps as historical documents. *Publishers Weekly* 146: 2060–65.

Stott, P. 1977. The UTM grid reference system. *Journal of the Society for Industrial Archeology* 3 (1): 1–14.

Strickland, M. 1978. Library of Congress summer project acquisitions. *WAML Information Bulletin* 10: 67–71.

———. 1986. Map displays: A means of promoting map use. *WAML Information Bulletin* 17: 257–60.

Strohecker, E. C. 1955. Guide to federal map and chart publications, 1937–1953: Index. *Aspects of Librarianship* 9. Entire issue.

Study on mass conservation techniques for treatment of library and archives materials. (PGI-89/WS/14). Paris: Unesco. [Also available as ED 325 129.]

Sturges, Paul. 1987. Policies and criteria for the archiving of electronic publishing. *Journal of Librarianship* 19: 152–72.

Suchan, T. 1996. Copyright and cartographic multimedia. *Cartographic Perspectives* 24: 13–23.

The sudden demand for maps. 1939. *Publishers Weekly* 136: 881–83.

Sumira, Sylvia. 1992. "Old globe syndrome" and how to cure it. *Map Collector* 61: 52–54.

———. 1996. Around the world of globes with Sylvia Sumira. *Paper Conservation News* 79: 1–4.

Survey of facsimiles: Maps and atlases. 1974. *WAML Information Bulletin* 5 (2): 31–35.

Sutherland, J. 1985. Collection policies. *SLAG&MD Bulletin* 142: 2–11.

Swann, A. 1981. *The care and conservation of photographic materials.* London: Crafts Council.

Swartzell, A. 1984. Preservation: Deacidification. *RTSD Newsletter* 9 (6): 71–73.

Symposium held on maps, graphics for the visually handicapped. 1983. *LC Information Bulletin* 42: 140.

Tanaglia, B. R. 1977. Catalog card filing arrangement for a geology map collection. *SLAG&MD Bulletin* 110: 17–22.

Tatham, A. 1994. Can the map curator adapt? [Paper from the 9th Conference of LIBER] http://www.Konbib.nl/.kb/skd/liber/articles/2tatham.htm .

Tatham, A. F. 1981. A simple numeric filing system: A comment. *WAML Information Bulletin* 12: 230–37.

Taubes, P. 1973. *Map microfilming project: Methods and equipment for a proposed 105 mm system*. Washington, DC: National Archives and Records Service.

Taylor, R. S. 1968. Question-negotiation and information seeking in libraries. *C&RL* 29: 178–94.

Technical auxiliary equipment for the map library. 1972–1973. *ACML Newsletter* 6 (2): 9–16.

Teggart, R. V. 1944. A university library reviews its map collection: Official sources stressed for both war and peacetime use. *LJ* 69: 1040–42.

Tessier, Y. 1967a. Computer cataloguing: The Laval map library project. *ACML Proceedings*: 24–26.

———. 1967b. Terminologie française se rapportant au domine de la conservation des cartes. *ACML Proceedings*: 48–50.

———. 1973. Cartomatique and the Canadian map user. *ACML Newsletter* 7: 41–42.

———. 1978. Basic maps of Canada and the provinces on microreproduction. *ACML Bulletin* 27: 62.

———. 1979a. De la carte à la cartothéconomie: l'emergence d'un secteur documentaire qui découvre son identité. *Documentation et bibliothèques* 25 (June): 71–80.

———. 1979b. Le système cartomatique: Possibilities of use and evaluation. *ACML Bulletin* 30: 23–25.

Tessier, Y., and J. Winearls. 1970. Map library of the Université Laval. *Special Libraries* 61: 131–32.

Textiles in the Metropolitan Museum of Art. 1995/1996. *Metropolitan Museum of Art Bulletin: winter 1995/96. Entire issue.*

Thailand. Royal Thai Survey Department. 1977. Organization principles of the map catalogue. In United Nations Regional Cartographic Conference for Asia and the Far East, Bangkok. *Proceedings*, vol. 2, 125–33. (E/CONF.68/3/add a). New York: United Nations.

Thatcher, E. 1972a. Guides for atlas-map selection. *Focus on Indiana Libraries* 26: 132–37.

———. 1972b. Toward education in map librarianship, or who else is seminar happy? *WAML Information Bulletin* 3 (3): 2–3.

———. 1978a. A possible final examination for a seminar in map librarianship. *WAML Information Bulletin* 10: 82–86.

———. 1978b. Who uses carto-materials from a university library collection—and why? A note on recent survey. *WAML Information Bulletin* 9: 103.

Thiele, W. 1938. *Official map publications, a historical sketch, and a bibliographical handbook of current maps and mapping services in the United States, Canada, Latin America, France, Great Britain, Germany, and certain other countries.* Chicago: ALA.

Thomas, D., and H. Lloyd. 1964. *Practical storage and use of maps and posters.* (Practical Projects for the School Library no. 1). Stillwater, OK: Oklahoma University Library, Library Education Department.

Thompson, Michael. 1996. Maps printed on Tyvek: A conservator's analysis. *ACMLA Bulletin* 96: 1–5.

Throop, V. M. 1933. Scientific apparatus and laboratory methods: A method of mounting maps. *Science* 78: 149–50.

Tiberio, B. 1977. Publicizing the map collection in the academic library: A facet of aggressive reference service. *SLAG&MD Bulletin* 107: 49–53.

———. 1979.The acquisition of free cartographic materials: Request and exchange. *Special Libraries* 70: 233–38.

TIGER tales. 1985. Washington, DC: Bureau of the Census.

Tillett, B. 1995. *Versions, prepared . . . for the Metadata Workshop, Dublin, Ohio, March 1–3, 1995.* Washington, DC: Library of Congress.

Tillin, A. M., and W. J. Quinly. 1976. *Standards for cataloging nonprint materials, an interpretation and practical application.* 4th ed. Washington, DC: Association for Educational Communications and Technology.

Tobler, W. R. 1963. Geographical ordering of information. *Canadian Geographer* 7: 203–5.

Togashi, R. 1997. Photo essay, aerial photography storage. *WAML Information Bulletin* 28: 59–81.

Topic IV (conservation and preservation). 1976. *Globe* 1: 77–79.

Toward a TQM paradigm: Using SERVQUAL to measure library service quality. 1997. *C&RL* 58: 237–51.

Trabing, W. 1974. Mostly about people—Maps are not for folding. *WAML Information Bulletin* 5 (3): 9. [Also in *Santa Cruz Sentinel,* March 29, 1974, 11.]

Tracy, G. 1997. Treating globes: A rewarding challenge. *Northeast Document Conservation Center News* 7 (2): [1–2].

Treatment of oversized maps. 1992. Andover, MA: Northeast Document Conservation Center.

Treatment of special materials: Maps, storage of. 1915. *LJ* 40: 75.

Treude, M. 1975a. "The Globe," Journal of the Australian Map Curators' Circle, a review. *WAML Information Bulletin* 7: 45–46.

———. 1975b. Reference services with maps. *SLAG&MD Bulletin* 102: 24–29.

———. 1981. Map library users in an academic setting. *Library Trends* 29: 453–71.

Trevitt-Clark, S. 1981. Availability of maps and aerial photos in Oregon. *WAML Information Bulletin* 12: 219–22.

Turko, K. 1990. *Mass deacidification systems: Planning and managerial decision making.* Washington, DC: ARL.

Tusa, R. M. 1993. An overview of applications of automation to special collections: Maps and archives. *Information and Technology for Libraries* 12: 405–11.

Tyner, J. A. 1981. Trends in American atlas cartography. *SLAG&MD Bulletin* 125: 3–14.

UNIMARC: Universal MARC format. 1980. 2d ed. rev. London: IFLA International Office for UBC.

United States. Ad Hoc Committee on Depository Library Access to Federal Automated Data Bases. 1984. *Provision of federal government publications in electronic format to depository libraries.* (98/2, Senate Print 98-260). Washington, DC: GPO.

United States. Aeronautical Chart and Information Center, St. Louis. 1952. *Classification systems for map libraries.* St. Louis, MO: ACIC.

———. 1969. Chart library automation. *Military Engineer* 61: 280.

United States. Army Corps of Engineers. Mobile District. 1981. *Environmental data inventory, state of Alabama.* Mobile, AL: Author.

United States. Army Map Service. 1948. *Greek map symbols.* (AMS Technical Manual no. 25). Washington, DC: Author.

———. 1951. *A researcher's guide to the Army Map Service Library.* AMS 1. (AMS Technical Manual no. 46). Washington, DC: Author.

———. 1961. Preservation of maps by lamination. *AMS Bulletin 37.* Entire issue.

———. 1964. Map mounting. *AMS Bulletin 41.* Entire issue.

United States. Army Map Service. Department of Technical Services. Library Division. 1964. *A simplified map collection system.* Washington, DC: AMS.

———. 1966–1967. *Automation of a map library.* Washington, DC: AMS.

United States. Congress. House Committee on Post Office and Civil Service. Subcommittee on Census and Population. 1984. *Geographic mapping program of the Census, hearing . . . .* Washington, DC: GPO.

United States. Department of Health, Education and Welfare. Office of the Assistant Secretary, Comptroller. Data Management Center. 1973. *Geographical location codes.* (DHEW Publication no. PS-73-11). Washington, DC: GPO.

United States. District Court, District of Maine. 1995. *De Lorne Publishing Company, Inc., Plaintiff, v. the National Oceanic and Atmospheric Administration of the United States Department of Commerce, Defendant;* civil no. 95-44-P-H. [S.l.]: District Court.

United States. Federal Mapping Task Force on Mapping, Charting, Geodesy and Surveying. 1973. *Report.* Washington, DC: GPO.

United States. Fish and Wildlife Service. Region 6. 1980. *The Map Indexing System (MIS), applications guide and coding instruction.* Denver, CO: Author.

United States. General Services Administration. 1984. *Worldwide geographic location codes.* Washington, DC: GPO.

United States. Geological Survey. 1976. *Georgia, satellite image mosaic, 1973–1974.* Reston, VA: USGS.

———. 1990. Map scales and corresponding areas in the ground. *California Geology* 43: 155.

United States. Library of Congress. 1946. *Classification, class G: Maps G3160–G9999.* Preliminary draft. Washington, DC: Author.

———. 1968. *Conference on automation in federal map libraries.* Washington, DC: Author.

———. 1976a. *Collation practice, working draft.* (LC Publications on Conservation of Library Materials, Conservation Workshop Notes on Evolving Procedures, Series 200, no. 1). Washington, DC: Author.

———. 1976b. *Deacidification—methylmagnesium carbonate non-aqueous treatment, working draft.* (LC Publications on Conservation of Library Materials, Conservation Workshop Notes on Evolving Procedures, Series 500, no. 1). Washington, DC: Author.

United States. Library of Congress. Descriptive Cataloging Division. 1949. *Rules for descriptive cataloging in the Library of Congress (adopted by the American Library Association).* Washington, DC: GPO.

United States. Library of Congress. Information Systems Office. 1970. *Maps, a MARC format, specifications for magnetic tapes containing catalog records for maps.* Washington, DC: GPO.

United States. Library of Congress. MARC Development Office. 1976. *Maps, a MARC format, specifications for magnetic tapes containing catalog records for maps.* 2d ed. Washington, DC: GPO.

United States. Library of Congress. Office for Descriptive Cataloging Policy. 1981. *Bibliographic description of rare books.* Washington, DC: LC.

United States. Library of Congress. Office of the Assistant Director for Preservation. 1975. *The physical protection of brittle and deteriorating documents by polyester encasement.* Washington, DC: GPO.

United States. Library of Congress. Processing Services. 1978– . *Cataloging Service Bulletin.*

United States. Library of Congress. Subject Cataloging Division. 1976. *Classification, Class G.* 4th ed. Washington, DC: LC.

United States. National Archives and Records Service. 1971. *Guide to cartographic records in the National Archives.* Washington, DC: NARS.

United States. National Archives and Records Service. 1975. *The rehabilitation of paper records.* (Staff Information Papers no. 16). Washington, DC: GPO.

United States. National Bureau of Standards. 1974– . *Countries, dependencies, and areas of special sovereignty, federal general data standard representation and codes.* (FIPS PUB 10-I). Washington, DC: GPO.

United States. Naval Electronics Laboratory Center, San Diego. 1976? [NELC Research Library Guide]. [S.l.: s.n.].

United States. Panel to Review the Report of the Federal Mapping Task Force on Mapping, Charting, Geodesy, and Surveying, July 1973. 1981. *Federal surveying and mapping: An organizational review.* Washington, DC: National Academy Press.

United States. War Department. General Staff. 1930. *The Williams system of classification, cataloguing, indexing, filing, and care of maps.* Washington, DC: War Department.

United States government publications available for selection by depository libraries. 1960– . Washington, DC: GPO.

U.S. Coast & Geodetic Survey. 1951. *Surveying and Mapping* 11: 61–73.

U.S. Geological Survey Photographic Library. 1977. *WAML Information Bulletin* 8: 168–69.

USGS shifting national mapping program to metric system. 1978. *SLAG&MD Bulletin* 114: 45–46.

Value of metadata: National spatial data infrastructure. 1996?. Reston, VA: USGS.

van de Waal, H. 1974. The application of geographical coordinates for retrieval of maps in a computerized map-catalogue. *International Yearbook of Cartography* 14: 166–73.

———. 1978. Documentational aspects of cartographic materials. *ITC Journal* 1978-2: 284–98.

———. 1981. Information policy and cartographic communication. *INSPEL* 15: 22–33.

———. 1982a. Exchange of map MARC tapes on an international level: A possibility for international cartographic networking. *INSPEL* 16: 256–61.

———. 1982b. Perspectives on cooperation from an international point of view. *ACML Bulletin* 44: 3–9.

———. 1985. Achtergronden en nieuwe ontwikkelingen bij 10 jaar Werkgroep Kaartbeheer [Ten years of the Working Group on Map Curatorship: Backgrounds and new developments]. *Kartografisch tijdschrift* 11 (4): 31–34.

———. 1986. How to use the ISBN on cartographic materials. *International Yearbook of Cartography* 26: 183–88.

Van Snellenberg, J. N. H. M. 1985. Classificatie voor kartografische informatie, [Classification for cartographic information]. *Kartografisch tijdschrift* 11 (4): 35–41.

Vellucci, Sherry. 1996. *IRSQ: Internet Reference Services Quarterly* 1 (4): 9–30.

Verner, C. 1974. Carto-bibliographical description: The analysis of variants in maps printed from copperplates. *American Cartographer* 1: 77–87.

———. 1976a. Carto-bibliography. *WAML Information Bulletin* 7 (2): 31–37.

———. 1976b. Overview and summation. *AB Bookman's Yearbook:* 71–73.

Verner, C., and Stuart-Stubbs, B. 1979. *The northpart of America.* [S.l.]: Academic Press Canada.

Vick, N. 1987. Analyzing atlases. *WAML Information Bulletin* 19: 30–32.

Vick, N., and N. L. Romero. 1990. Cataloging rare maps. *Cataloging & Classification Quarterly* 10 (4): 3–18.

Vietor, A. O. 1950. Faculty, students must have maps. *LJ* 75: 456–58.

Villar, S. P. 1988. Survey of map library outreach and user education. *WAML Information Bulletin* 19: 137–50.

Voorhees, W. D. 1972. A proposed map library survey form. *SLAG&MD Bulletin* 87: 39–45.

———. 1976. Brieflisting your map library, or what to do until you go on-line. *SLAG&MD Bulletin* 103: 2–6.

Walker, B. 1974. Maps. In Kaiser 1974, 69–75.

Wall and movable map racks. 1966. *LJ* 91: 5366.

Wallis, H. 1965. Report on the library classification of books and maps. *Cartographic Journal* 2: 14–15.

———. 1966. The role of a national map library. *Cartographic Journal* 3: 11–14.

———. 1967. Report on the Map Curator's Group. *Cartographic Journal* 4: 11.

———. 1969. Reference work in a map library. *INSPEL* 4 (3–4): 85–88. [Earlier version in Zogner 1971, 111–16.]

———. 1972. Associations for map librarians. *New Library World* 73: 295–96.

———. 1975. The training of map curators in Great Britain. *INSPEL* 10: 28–33.

———. 1976. Education and training of map librarians: Special needs of developing countries. *INSPEL* 11 (3): 100–102.

————. 1977. Geography and Map Libraries Section, IFLA—News. *ACML Bulletin* 24: 37–40.

————. 1981. Introduction to the Geography and Map Libraries Section of IFLA. *INSPEL* 15 (2): 108–13.

Walsh, J. 1990. World atlas survey. *Booklist* 87: 769–73.

————. 1993. World atlas comparison chart. *Booklist* 89: 1, 903.

Walsh, J., and D. Hernden. 1983. Conversion tables from DMA/AMS standard series designation to GSGS numbering and from GSGS numbering to DMA/AMS standard series designation. *WAML Information Bulletin* 14: 118–25.

Walsh, J., B. Hulyk, and G. Barnum. 1993. *Rare and valuable government documents: A resource packet on identification, preservation, and security issues for government documents collections.* Chicago: ALA.

Walter, G. 1983. Are micrographics and optical data disks competing technologies? *Journal of Micrographics* 16 (2): 37–39.

Ward, A. W. 1977. The state of state road maps. *American Cartographer* 4: 5–9.

Wardle, D. G. 1971. *Document repair.* London: Society of Archivists.

Washington map capital of the world. 1986. *Denver Post,* June 29, 8G.

Waters, P. 1973. Deacidification, lamination and the use of polyester film encapsulation at the Library of Congress. *WAML Information Bulletin* 6 (3): 19–21. [Also in *SLAG&MD Bulletin* 99: 46–48, and in *ACML Bulletin* 9: 11–13.]

————. 1975. *Procedures for salvage of water-damaged library materials.* (LC Publications on Conservation of Library Materials). Washington, DC: GPO.

————. 1976. *Preservation and Care Workshop, 20–21 August 1976.* University of California at Santa Cruz. Notes.

————. 1979. Polyester film encapsulation. *WAML Information Bulletin* 10: 117–27.

Watkins, J. B: 1967. *Selected bibliography on maps in libraries: Acquisitions, classification, cataloging, storage, uses.* Rev. ed. Syracuse, NY: Syracuse University Libraries.

Watt, I., and T. J. Browne. 1985. Using computers to catalogue map collections. *Cartographic Journal* 22: 131–35.

Watt, Marcia, and Biblo, Lisa. 1995. CD-ROM longevity, a select bibliography. *CAN (Conservation Administration News),* 61.

Webster, G. 1982. Cartographic materials and MARC. *Cartographic Journal* 19: 60–67.

Weihs, J. R. 1973. *Nonbook materials, the organization of integrated collections*. Ottawa: Canadian Library Association.

———. 1984. *Accessible storage of nonbook materials*. Phoenix, AZ: Oryx Press.

Weihs, J. R., and Lynne C. Howarth. 1995. Nonbook materials: Their occurrence and bibliographic description in Canadian libraries. *LRTS* 39: 184–97.

Weihs, J. R., S. Lewis, and J. Macdonald. 1979. *Nonbook materials: The organization of integrated collections*. 2d ed. Ottawa: Canadian Library Association.

Weinstein, H., and C. Brower. 1988. *The permanence and care of color photographs: Prints, negatives, slides and motion pictures*. Nashville, TN: AASCH Press.

Weir, K. 1977. The teaching library. *SLAG&MD Bulletin* 109: 34–39.

Weissmiller, D. 1971. Do we need a national bibliography of Canadian maps? *ACML Proceedings*: 15–24.

———. 1972. Association of Canadian Map Libraries conference. *Canadian Cartographer* 9: 150–51.

Wellheiser, J. G. 1992. *Nonchemical treatment processes for disinfestation of insects and fungi in library collections*. (IFLA Publications 60). Munich: Saur.

Wellisch, H. H. 1976. *Nonbook materials*. (Student Contribution Series no. 6). College Park, MD: University of Maryland College of Library and Information Service.

Werner, P. A. 1975. *A survey of National Geocoding Systems final report*. (Report no. DOT-TSC-OST-057-74-26). Washington, DC: GPO.

Western Association of Map Libraries. 1973. *Maps in the local historical society*. Stockton, CA: Conference of California Historical Societies.

Westhuis, J. L., and J. M. DeYoung. 1967. *Cataloging manual for nonbook materials in learning centers and school libraries*. Ann Arbor, MI: University of Michigan.

Wexler, M. 1977. They call it orienteering. *National Wildlife* 15 (4): 12–16.

Whaite, R. H. 1965. *Microfilming maps of abandoned anthracite mines: Mines of the Eastern Middle Field*. (Information Circular 8274). Pittsburgh, PA: U.S. Bureau of Mines.

What do people use air photos for? 1978. *SLAG&MD Bulletin* 111: 55.

Whicher, J. F. 1963. Originality, cartography, and copyright. *New York University Law Review* 38: 280–300.

Whistance-Smith, R. 1976. New quarters for the university map collection. *ACML Bulletin* 21: 13–14.

———. 1979. *Maps in the service of administration: Descriptive catalogue.* Edmonton, Alberta: University Map Collection.

———. 1981. In which we serve: Map libraries and our clientele, a report on activities at the University Map Collection at the University of Alberta. *ACML Bulletin* 38: 32–38.

White, J. B. 1962. Further comment on map cataloging. *LRTS* 6: 78.

White, R. C. 1959. The ideal arrangement for maps in a library. *Special Libraries* 50 (4): 154–61.

———. 1970a. Map librarianship. *Special Libraries* 61 (5): 233–35.

———. 1970b. The oil-company road map revisited. *SLAG&MD Bulletin* 79: 7–9.

Wilbanks, T. J., and M. Libbee. 1979. Avoiding the demise of geography in the United States. *Professional Geographer* 31: 1–8.

Wilhelm, Henry Gilmer. 1993. *The permanence and care of color photographs: Traditional and digital color prints, color negatives, slides, and motion pictures.* Grinnell, IA: Preservation.

Williams, G. 1952. Maps in the library. *Aspects of Librarianship* 1: 1–9.

Williams, G. R. 1966. The preservation of deteriorating books. Part II, Recommendations for a solution. *LJ* 91: 189–94.

Williams, J. C., and G. B. Kelly. 1974. Research on mass treatments in conservation. *Bulletin of the American Institute for Conservation of Historic and Artistic Works* 14 (2): 69–77.

Williams, M. W. 1988. Moving a university map collection: The planning and execution of the 1987 move of the Maps Collection of the University of North Carolina at Chapel Hill (MSLS thesis). Chapel Hill, NC: University of North Carolina.

Williams, R. S., et al. 1984. Evaluation of the National Archives to convert nitrate aerial photographs of the United States to a stable-base safety film. *PERS* 50: 1437–41.

Williamson, L. E. 1983. A survey of cartographic contributions of international governmental organizations. *Government Publications Review* 10: 329–44.

Wilson, D. C. 1949. Production of plastic relief maps. *Surveying and Mapping* 9: 183–86.

Wilson, J. P. 1979. Map and chart information storage and retrieval. American Congress on Surveying and Mapping *Proceedings* 39: 390–96.

Wilson, L. A. 1948. Library filing, classification, and cataloging of maps, with special reference to wartime experience. *Annals of the Association of American Geographers* 38: 6–37.

Wilson, M. 1972. Manual of standards and procedures for map libraries: Basic public relations for the map library. *ACML Newsletter* 4 (3): 11–13. [Physical requirements: Planning the map area, ibid. at 14–22.]

———. 1975. Time off at Stanfords. *ACML Bulletin* 19: 6–7.

Wilson, W. K., and B. W. Forshee. 1959. *Preservation of documents by lamination.* (NBS Monograph no. 5). Washington, DC: GPO.

Winchester, Simon. 1995. Taking the world's measure: Cartography's greatest undertaking survived wars and bureaucratic snarls only to die when it was nearly done. *Mercator's World* 2 (6): 56–59.

Windsor, P. L. 1910. A new vertical file for maps. *LJ* 35: 509.

Winearls, J. 1966. Map libraries in Canada. *Cartographer* 3 (2): 163, 165.

———. 1967. Some problems in classifying and cataloguing maps. *ACML Proceedings:* 27–32. [Also in Drazniowsky 1975, 352–58.]

———. 1968. Topographic series in the Map Library of the University of Toronto. *ACML Proceedings:* 25–32.

———. 1969. Highlights of the 3rd annual conference of the Association of Canadian Map Libraries. *Canadian Cartographer* 6: 166.

———. 1971a. Education for map librarianship, a panel presentation. *ACML Proceedings:* 11–14.

———. 1971b. To loan or not to loan. *ACML Proceedings:* 57–59.

———. 1972. Report on map librarianship course at Toronto. *WAML Information Bulletin* 3 (3): 5–7.

———. 1974. Reference work in a current map collection. *ACML Proceedings:* 11–24.

———. 1975. Recent literature on map librarianship. *SLAG&MD Bulletin* 101: 32–37, 48.

———. 1976a. Cartobibliography and map cataloging in Canada. *AB Bookman's Yearbook,* 1976, vol. 1, 63–70.

————. 1976b. Progress in cartobibliography and automated cataloging of maps in Canada. *AB Bookman's Yearbook*, Part 1, 63–70.

————. 1977. Reaching the public: The University of Toronto's course on the history of cartography in the continuing studies program. *ACML Bulletin* 25: 26–29.

————. 1980. Report of the MARC Maps Processing Workshop: Library of Congress Geography and Map Division, June 16–20, 1980. *ACML Bulletin* 37: 9–13.

————. 1981a. Library instruction in the Map Library, University of Toronto. *ACML Bulletin* 41: 25–29.

————. 1981b. Report on the second meeting of the Anglo-American Cataloguing Committee for Cartographic Materials. *ACML Bulletin* 40: 30–33.

Winkler, J. F. 1949. Cartographic record filing in the National Archives. *American Archivist* 12: 283–85.

————. 1952. One solution for the map-handling problem. *American Archivist* 15: 259–61.

Winser, B. 1916. Making maps available. *ALA Bulletin* 10: 245–48.

Winsor, J. 1887. Classing and arranging maps and charts. *LJ* 12: 442.

Wise, D. A. 1976. Cartographic acquisition methods. *SLAG&MD Bulletin* 103: 13–19.

————. 1977a. Addendum to treasure map list. *WAML Information Bulletin* 8: 136–42.

————. 1977b. Cartographic sources and procurement problems. *Special Libraries* 68 (5/6): 198–205.

————. 1978a. Cartographic acquisitions at the Library of Congress. *Special Libraries* 69: 486–89.

————. 1978b. Cartographic sources and procurement problems, appendices. *SLAG&MD Bulletin* 112: 19–26; 113: 65–68; 114: 40–44.

————. 1979a. Cartographic sources and acquisitions techniques. *WAML Information Bulletin* 10: 176–82.

————. 1979b. Cartographic sources and procurement problems, appendices. *SLAG&MD Bulletin* 115: 35–50.

————. 1981a. Cartographic solicitation programs for city maps. *WAML Information Bulletin* 12: 284–87.

————. 1981b. Selected list of major national mapping agencies. *SLAG&MD Bulletin* 126: 19–34. [Erratum in 128 (1982): 18.]

————. 1981c. A selective list of United States publishers and distributors of globes and three-dimensional plastic relief models (maps). *SLAG&MD Bulletin* 126: 35–36.

————. 1982a. A list of national bibliographies and references containing citations on atlases and maps. *SLAG&MD Bulletin* 128: 39–41.

————. 1982b. A selective list of international publishers and distributors of globes and three-dimensional plastic relief models (maps). *SLAG&MD Bulletin* 128: 36–38.

————. 1985. *Cartographic acquisitions: A collection of articles*. Broken Arrow, OK: Clay Cotsha Press.

Withers, M. M. 1992. Moving maps at the Virginia State Library and Archives. *SLAG&MD Bulletin* 168: 24–27, 170: 59.

Wittman, [no first name given]. 1973. Publisher/dealer description: Geo Center: International Map Center. *SLAG&MD Bulletin* 91: 33.

Wolf, D. B. 1992. Is there any copyright protection for maps after Feist? *Journal of the Copyright Society of the U.S.* 39 (3).

Wolf, E. W. 1986. Cartobibliography: Whither and why. *SLAG&MD Bulletin* 144: 28–34.

Wolter, J. A. 1964. The current bibliography of cartography: An annotated selection of serials. *SLAG&MD Bulletin* 58: 9–13.

————. 1973. Geographical libraries and map collections. *Encyclopedia of Library and Information Science* 9: 236–66.

————. 1974. Source materials for the history of American cartography. *American Studies, an International Newsletter, Supplement to the May 1974 American Quarterly* 9 (3): 12–27. [Also in *SLAG&MD Bulletin* 88: 2–16.]

————. 1976. Research tools and the literature of cartography. *AB Bookman's Yearbook*, Part 1, 21–30.

Wong, M.-K. 1993. Exploring the impact of digital cartographic data on map librarianship using data use models. *SLAG&MD Bulletin* 173: 2–14.

Woods, B. M. 1952. Training for map librarianship. *Special Libraries* 43 (3): 87–88, 102.

————. 1954. Map information reference service. *Special Libraries* 45: 103–106.

————. 1956. Map librarianship. *SLAG&MD Bulletin* 23: 9–12.

————. 1959. Map cataloging: Inventory and prospect. *LRTS* 3: 257–73.

———. 1970. A continuing need: Education for map librarianship. *SLAG&MD Bulletin* 81: 28–29.

———. 1971. *Map librarianship, a selected bibliography*. New York: Engineering Index.

Woodward, D. 1979. Hermon Dunlap Smith Center for the History of Cartography: A review of its early development. In *Map librarian in the modern world*, 143–60. Munich: K. G. Saur.

Woodward, F. 1968. Archival maps. *ACML Proceedings* 2: 71–74.

———. 1975. Historical map collections, Special Collections Division, University of British Columbia Library. *ACML Bulletin* 17: 2–3.

———. 1981. Making users aware of archival maps. *ACML Bulletin* 41: 39–41.

Workshop for practical map curatorship in developing countries, Utrecht, 1981: A report. 1982. *INSPEL* 16: 34–39.

Wynar, B. S. 1980. *Introduction to cataloging and classification*. 6th ed. Littleton, CO: Libraries Unlimited.

Xu, H. 1996. The impact of automation on job requirements and qualifications for catalogers and reference librarians in academic Libraries. *LRTS* 40: 9–32.

Yonge, E. L. 1950. These maps are essential. *LJ* 75: 440+.

———. 1955a. The Map Department of the American Geographical Society. *Professional Geographer* 7 (2): 2–5.

———. 1955b. Ten commandments for map librarians. *SLAG&MD Bulletin* 21: 23.

Young, M. J. 1978. *Introduction to minicomputers in federal Libraries*. Washington, DC: GPO.

Znamirowski, Barbara M. 1993. OCUL map group survey: Cartographic software and data profile. *ACMLA Bulletin* 86: 12–16.

Zogner, L. 1971. *Karten in Bibliotheken*. Bonn-Bad Godesberg: Bundesforschungsanstalt für Landeskunde und Raumordnuag. (Karteusammlung und Kartendocumentation, 9).

Zogner, L. 1975. Report on the West Berlin meeting of November 1973 and some further consideration on the training of map librarians. *INSPEL* 10: 33–38.

———. 1979. Training for map librarianship, Working Group in the IFLA Section, Geography and Map Libraries. In *Map librarian in the modern world*, 117–25. Munich: K. G. Saur.

Appendix 1

A Sampling of Digital Data on CD-ROMs and Diskettes

From the Map and Imagery Laboratory, Davidson Library, University of California, Santa Barbara

Atlases/Reference Sources

GIS and Decision Making
a. Subject: geographic information systems
b. Call no.: MIL, DIGT G 70.2 G54 1993 diskette

Manual of Remote Sensing
a. Subject: Earth observing platforms and sensors
b. Call no.: G 70.4 M36 1996 CD

U.S. Navy Marine Climatic Atlas of the World
a. Subject: climate
b. Call no.: G 2801 C8 .U495 1992 CD

Random House Unabridged Dictionary
a. Subject: general
b. Call no.: PE 1625 .R3 1993 CD mil,ref

Skymap for Windows (3 diskettes)
a. Subject: stars
b. Call no.: MIL, DIGT QB 6 S55 1990 diskette

GIS Spatial Data Standards Cataloging
a. Subject: see title
b. Call no.: Z695.6 .T7 1995 CD

Universe

Selected astronomical catalogs—test disk
a. Subject: collection of astronomical data for stellar and nonstellar sources
b. Call no.: 3185 1989 .U5 CD

Solar System

Comet Halley Archive
a. Subject: remote data
b. Call no.: 3187 .H3 A4 1986 .U5 CD

Joint Education Initiative
a. Subject: remote-sensing imagery
b. Call no.: 3191s A4 VAR .J4 CD

Voyagers to the Outer Planets (IMDISP required)
a. Subjects: imagery of Uranus, Saturn, Jupiter
b. Call no.: 3191s A4 VAR .U5 CD

Mission to Jupiter, Galileo (IMDISP required)
a. Subject: imagery of Venus, Earth, Moon
b. Call no.: 3191s A4 VAR .U51 CD

Viking Orbiter Images of Mars
a. Subjects: satellite imagery
b. Call no.: 3192 .M3s A4 VAR .U55 CD

Selected Geomagnetic and Other Solar-Terrestrial Physics Data of NOAA and NASA
a. Subjects: geomagnetic, solar & ionospheric data
b. Call no.: 3192.S8 C1 VAR .U5 CD

Mission to Venus, Magellan (IMDISP required)
a. Subjects: imagery of Venus
b. Call no.: 3192 .V4s A4 VAR .U522 CD

Clementine Mission to the Moon
a. Subjects: imagery of the Moon
b. Call no.: 3196s A4 VAR .U5 CD

World

Digital Chart of the World (DCW)
a. Subject: data from Operational Navigational Charts
b. Call no.: 3200s 1000 .D5 CD

Development of the DCW (Sept. 1992)
a. Subject: none given
b. Call no.: 3200s 1000 .D5 diskette

Digital Chart of the World (DCW) in ARC/INFO format
a. Subject: data from Operational Navigational Charts
b. Call no.: 3200s 1000 .E5 4/93 CD

Digital Chart of the World (DCW) in ARC/INFO format
a. Subject: data from Operational Navigational Charts
b. Call no.: 3200s 1000 .E5 9/93 CD

ArcWorld 1:3M
a. Subject: general
b. Call no.: 3200 1988 .A7 CD

PC Globe
a. Subject: profiles of 77 countries
b. Call no.: 3200 1989 .C6 diskette

Software Toolworks World Atlas
a. Subject: general
b. Call no.: 3200 1991 .E4 diskette

ArcWorld Statistical Sampler
a. Subject: cartographic and statistical data
b. Call no.: 3200 1992 .E55 diskette

National Geographic Picture Atlas of the World
a. Subject: general
b. Call no.: 3200 1992 .N32 CD

Relational World Data Bank II
a. Subject: various
b. Call no.: 3200 1992 .R4 cassette

PC Globe Maps 'n Facts
a. Subject: world atlas
b. Call no.: 3200 1993 .B7 CD

DeLorme Global Explorer
a. Subject: general
b. Call no.: 3200 1993 .D3 CD

Tiled DCW Database & Related Files in ARC/INFO Format
a. Subject: none given
b. Call no.: 3200 1994 .E5 cassette

ArcView for Schools and Libraries/Sample Electronic Atlas & Screen
   Show
a. Subject: none given
b. Call no.: 3200 1994 .E5 diskette

Encarta
a. Subject: Encyclopedia
b. Call no.: 3200 1994 .M5 CD

Earthscapes in Time
a. Subject: general
b. Call no.: 3200 1995 .E2 CD

World Atlas
a. Subject: general
b. Call no.: 3200 1995 .W6 CD

Encarta 1996
a. Subject: Encyclopedia
b.   Call no.: 3200 1996 .M5 Beta CD

Encarta 97 World Atlas
a. Subject: Atlas
b. Call no.: 3200 1996-7 .M5 atlas CD

Global Change Database
a. Subject: various
b. Call no.: 3201s VAR .G5 diskette

Global Ecosystems Database Version 1.0
a. Subject: general
b. Call no.: 3201s VAR .G52 CD

MapArt: Maps for Graphic Design
a. Subject: base and outline maps
b. Call no.: 3201 A1 1995 .C3 CD

SIR-C: Survey Image Product
a. Subject: radar imagery
b. Call no.: 3201s A4 VAR .S5 CD

X-SAR: Survey Image Product
a. Subject: radar imagery
b. Call no.: 3201s A4 VAR .S52 CD

Spot Imagery Coverage of California
a. Subject: satellite imagery
b. Call no.: 3201 A4 1994 .S6 CD

ArcScene World Tour
a. Subject: satellite imagery
b. Call no.: 3201 A4 1996 .S7 CD

Worldwide LANDSAT Data Base Catalog
a. Subject: imagery; 1972-present
b. Call no.: 3201s A49 VAR .L3 CD

Landsat MSS Data Catalog
a. Subject: satellite imagery indexes
b. Call no.: 3201 A49 1996 .L3 CD

Worldwide SPOT Scene Catalog
a. Subject: Remote Sensing—Images—Indexes
b. Call no.: 3201s A49 VAR .S7 CD
NOTE: also SPOTool Coordinate Conversion Utility filed under same
call number as diskette

GeoName
a. Subject: geographical names—non U.S.
b. Call no.: 3201s A8 VAR .G4 CD

ISLSCP Initiative I—Global Data Sets for Land Atmosphere Models
    1987–1988
a. Subject: hydrology, soils, snow, ice, oceans, meteorology,
    vegetation
b. Call no.: 3201 C1 1988 .U5 CD

Global Relief Data from NGDC
a. Subject: physical geography
b. Call no.: 3201 C1 199- .N3 CD

Geomedia
a. Subject: physical sciences
b. Call no.: 3201 C1 1994 .U5 CD

TerrainBase, Worldwide Digital Terrain Data
a. Subject: physical geography
b. Call no.: 3201 C2 1995 .N3 CD

GLOBE: Global Land
a. Subject: physical geography
b. Call no.: 3201 C2 YEAR .U5 CD

World and U.S. Regional Topography
a. Subject: physical geography
b. Call no: 3701 C2 1996 .C5 CD

Q3 Flood Data Demonstration Disk
a. Subject: floods
b. Call no.: 3201 C32 1996 .U5 CD

Earthquake Digital Data
a. Subject: seismology; mag. 5.5; 1980–1985
b. Call no.: 3201s C543 VAR .U5 CD

Global Hypocenter Data Base
a. Subject: seismology; parameters for 438,000 tremors; 2100 bc
   through ad 1988
b. Call no.: 3201 C543 1988 .U5 CD

Greenhouse Effect Detection Experiment
a. Subject: climate
b. Call no.: 3201s C8 VAR .G6 CD

NOAA Weather Charts, Chart Series A
              Surface and Upper Air Weather Charts
a. Subject: climate
b. Call no.: 3201s C8 VAR .N6, Chart A, CD

NOAA Weather Charts, Chart Series B
              Initial Analysis and Forecast Charts
a. Subject: climate
b. Call no.: 3201s C8 VAR .N6, Chart B, CD

Total Ozone Mapping Spectrometer (TOMS) Gridded Ozone data
a. Subject: ozone measurements taken 1978–1988
b. Call no.: 3201s C8 VAR .U5 CD

Global Historical Fields
a. Subject: climate
b. Call no.: 3201 C8 1994 .G5 CD

U.S. Federal Climate Complex
a. Subject: climate
b. Call no.: 3201 C8 1995 .U5 CD

Global Gridded Upper Air Statistics
a. Subject: climatology
b. Call no.: 3201 C8 1980-95 .N3 CD

International Station Meteorological Climate Summary, V. 4
a. Subject: climate
b. Call no.: 3201 C8 1996 .F4

International Satellite Cloud Climatology Project Data
a. Subject: clouds
b. Call no.: 3201 C884 1983-90 .U5 CD

GOES Space Environment Monitor
a. Subject: geophysics
b. Call no.: 3201s C9 CAR .G6 CD

Gravity, Earth System Data
a. Subject: gravity
b. Call no.: 3201 C9 1992 .G7 CD

Toyota Conference Global Environmental Data Sets
a. Subject: ecology
b. Call no.: 3201 D2 1994? .T8 CD

Grid Data Catalogue
a. Subject: index to global resource information database
b. Call no.: 3201 D29 1994? .G6 diskette

Digitized Soil Map of the World
a. Subject: soils
b. Call no.: 3201s J3 5000 .U5 diskette

ARC Digitized Raster Graphics of ONCs
a. Subject: data from Operational Navigational Charts
b. Call no.: 3201s P6 1000 .U51 CD

Microworld Data Bank 1
a. Subject: derived from Operational Navigational CNC charts
b. Call no.: 3201s P6 1000 .U51 diskette

Time Throttle
a. Subject: history
b. Call no.: 3201 S1 1994 .B5 diskette

World Vector Shoreline (Prototype)
a. Subject: shorelines
b. Call no.: 3202 .C6 1989 .U5 CD

USGS Digital Data Series
a. Subject: physical sciences
b. Call no.: 3701s C1 VAR .U5 DDS# CD
    DDS-8: Photographs (earthquakes, volcanoes, geologic hazards,
    and other phenomena)

World—Regions

SIR-C Education Program
a. Subject: satellite imagery
b. Call no.: 3202 A4 199-? .U5 CD

AVHRR CD Browser Ionia
a. Subject: satellite imagery
b. Call no.: 3202 A4 1993? .A9 CD

Compiled Volcanology Data Set Kilauea, Mauna Loa
a. Subject: volcanology
b. Call no.: 3206s C542 VAR .J4 CD

Global Tropical/Extratropical Cyclone Climatic Atlas
a. Subject: climate
b. Call no.: 3256 C8 1996 .U5 CD

NOAA Weather Charts, Series C
   Tropical Strip/Precipitation and Observed Weather
a. Subject: weather
b. Call no.: 3256s C8 VAR .N6 Chart C CD

Polar—Regions

Arctic and Antarctic Sea Ice Data
a. Subject: sea ice
b. Call no.: 3246 C7 1996 .A7 CD

NIMBUS-7 Scanning Multichannel Microwave Radiometer (SMMR)
a. Subject: radiance grids
b. Call no.: 3246s C73 VAR .U5 CD

Historical Arctic Rawinsonde Archive
a. Subject: climate
b. Call no.: 3246 C8 1987 .U5 CD

NIMBUS-7 Scanning Multichannel Microwave Radiometer (SMMR)
a. Subject: brightness temperature grids
b. Call no.: 3277 .A7s C732 VAR .W6 CD

Arctic Data Interactive: A Prototype CD ROM Science Journal
a. Subject: sciences
b. Call no.: 3277 .A7 1990 .A7 CD

Atlas en Reseau des Espaces Mediterraneeas Multimedia. Interactive
   Multimedia Atlas of the Mediterranean.
a. Subject: environment
b. Call no.: 3277.M4 1993 .C5 CD and disk

Monthly Average Polar Sea Ice Concentration
a. Subject: oceanography
b. Call no.: 3701s C1 VAR .U5 CD DDS-27

Antarctic Digital Database
a. Subject: general
b. Call no.: 9085 1993 .B7 CD

DMSP Special Sensor Microwave/Imager (SSM/I)
a. Subjects: ice concentration grids
b. Call no.: 9101s C384 VAR .U5 CD

DMSP Special Sensor Microwave/Imager (SSM/I)
a. Subjects: brightness temperature grids
b. Call no.: 9101s C732 VAR .U5 CD

North America

Geophysics of North America
a. Subjects: topography; DNAG magnetics; MAGSAT magnetics;
   DNAG gravity; isostatic gravity (U.S. only); satellite imagery,
   summer; satellite imagery, fall
b. Call no.: 3301 C9 1989 .N3 CD

Automap Road Atlas (Microsoft)
a. Subjects: roads
b. Call no.: 3301 P2 1995 .M5 CD

Geophysics of North America
a. Subjects: geophysics
b. Call no.: 3301 C9 1990 .H5 CD

ERS-1 Canadian Images
a. Subject: satellite imagery
b. Call no.: 3401 A4 1991 .C32 CD

Forestland Information
a. Subject: forest
b. Call no.: 3401 K1 199- .C3 CD

Territorial Expansion of Canada
a. Subject: history
b. Call no.: 3401 S1 1995 .C3 CD

AVHRR Imagery of Western Canada on CD-ROM
a. Subjects: imagery; 1987–1988
b. Call no.: 3426 A4 1988 .S7 CD

USGS Digital Data Series
a. Subject: physical sciences
b. Call no.: 3701s C1 VAR .U5 DDS# CD
   DDS-7: Digitized Strong-Motion Accelerograms of North and
   Central American Earthquakes 1933–1986

Canada

Digital Bibliographic Index of B.C. Geological Survey Branch Publications
a. Subject: physical sciences—indexes
b. Call no.: 3471s C1 Var B72 1994-13 diskette

Minfile Data 092E—NOOTKA SOUND June 1989
a. Subject: mining data
b. Call no.: 3471s H1 250 .B7 diskette

Minfile Data
a. Subject: mining data for sample area in British Columbia
b. Call no.: 3471 H1 1992 .B7 diskette

Geochemical data for areas in Ontario
a. Subject: geochemical data for lakes
b. Call no.: 3611s C5 VAR .O59 diskette

Wawa Region—Experimental Data Set
a. Subject: physical sciences
b. Call no.: 3612 .N4 C5 1992 .O5 diskette

Kirkland Lake Incentives Program (KLIP)
a. Subject: geochemistry
b. Call no.: 3612 .N4:2 C5 1990 .O5 diskette

United States

DRG Digital Raster Graphic Data Product Development Report
a. Subject: U.S. topos in raster form
b. Call no.: 3700s VAR .U5 DR6 CD

USGS United States 7.5" series
a. Subject: topographic
b. Call no.: 3700s VAR .U5 diskette
NOTE: we have NJ, TX, AK, UT

Digital Orthophoto, USDA SCS-USGS NMD Joint Project
a. Subject: orthophoto; experimental ed. in Dane County WI
b. Call no.: 3700s VAR .U5 7.5 CD

Tiger Files for Goleta CA Quad
a. Subject: TIGER files manipulated by American Digital Cartography
b. Call no.: 3700s VAR .U5 7.5 CA Goleta diskette

Demo Disk, AutoCAD & ARC/INFO
a. Subject: digital maps
b. Call no.: 3700s VAR .U5 7.5 diskette

USGS DEM Quads in ERDAS .LAN Format
a. Subject: LAN format of Carpinteria, Dos Pueblos, Goleta, Santa
   Barbara, Tajiguas
b. Call no.: 3700s 24 .U5 CA Quad name diskette

Digital Elevation Model (DEM) data over Blue Mounds, WI
a. Subject: DEM data
b. Call no.: 3700s 24,250 .U5 DEM - WI - diskette

TIGER FILES
a. *Subject: not given*
   i. Digital Orthophoto Disk of Dane County, Wisconsin
      Call no.: 3700s 100 .U5 WI Dane County diskette
   ii. TIGER for Atlas/GIS (Pre-Census), Santa Barbara County, CA
      Call no.: 3700s 100 .U542 CA SB County Atlas
      diskette
   iii. Streets on a Disk [Santa Barbara County] (Klynas)
      Call no.: 3700s 100 .U542 CA SB County Klynas
      diskette
   iv. TIGER Documents [accompanying text]
      Call no.: 3700s 100 .U543 TIGER DOCS diskette

FEDSTAT/TIGER
a. Subjects: demographic and economic data (e.g., county-city data
   book) from U.S. Census; 1980s, 1990
b. Call no.: 3700s 100 .U54 CD ANNEX

TIGER/Line Precensus Files, 1990
a. Subjects: demographic and economic data (e.g., county-city data
   book) from U.S. Census (from U.S. Statistics FEDSTAT);
   1:100,000-scale planimetric data (TIGER); 1980s, 1990
b. Call no.: 3700s 100 .U542 CD ANNEX (except for CA)

TIGER/Line Census Files, 1990
a. Subjects: demographic and economic data (e.g., county-city data
   book) from U.S. Census (from U.S. Statistics FEDSTAT);
   1:100,000-scale planimetric data (TIGER)
b. Call no.: 3700s 100 .U543 CD ANNEX (except for CA)

TIGER/Line Census Files, 1992
a. Subjects: demographic and economic data (e.g., county-city data
   book) from U.S. Census (from U.S. Statistics FEDSTAT);
   1:100,000-scale planimetric data (TIGER)
b. Call no.: 3700s 100 .U543 1992 CD
NOTE: CA Alameda-Santa Cruz counties are on disk on ATLAS at
/usr/home/atlas1/TIGER

TIGER/Line Census Files, 1994
a. Subjects: demographic and economic data (e.g., county-city data book) from U.S. Census (from U.S. Statistics FEDSTAT); 1:100,000-scale planimetric data (TIGER)
b. Call no.: 3700s 100 .U543 1994

TIGER/LINE 1995
a. Subject: census
b. Call no.: 3700s 100 .U543 ed. 1995 CD

1:100,000-scale Digital Line Graph (DLG) Data
a. Subjects: hydrography and transportation; 1991
b. Call no.: 3700s 100 .U544 hy/tr CD

1:100K DLG CD-ROM Area, Florida (corrected files)
a. Subject: digital line graph; hydrography and transportation
b. Call no.: 3700s 100 .U544 hy/tr diskette

1:2,000,000-scale Digital Line Graph (DLG) Data
a. Subjects: elevation
b. Call no.: 3700s 2000 .U52 CD

GEODisc U.S. Atlas
a. Subjects: general; 1980s
b. Call no.: 3700 198- .G4 CD

PCUSA
a. Subject: general
b. Call no.: 3700 1989 .P1 diskette

SIGCAT/GRIPS (IMDISP required)
a. Subjects: various
b. Call no.: 3700 1989 .S5 CD

GRIPS 2 (IMDISP required)
a. Subjects: various
b. Call no.: 3700 1990? .S5 CD

ArcUSA 1:25M, Conterminous US
a. Subject: general
b. Call no.: 3700 1990 .E5 CD

ArcUSA 1:2M, Conterminous US
a. Subject: general
b. Call no.: 3700 1990 .E52 CD

Software Toolworks U.S. Atlas
a. Subject: general
b. Call no.: 3700 1991 .E4 diskette

Geographic/Map Files, Prototype: Map Metafiles
a. Subject: cartography; 4 counties in Mississippi; 1990
b. Call no.: 3700 1991 .U5 CD

Sample Views for ArcView for Windows
a. Subject: general
b. Call no.: 3700 1992 .F5 diskette

Wessex TIGER 92 U.S. Streets and Boundaries
a. Subject: general
b. Call no.: 3700 1992 .W4

Wessex STF 1a
a. Subject: U.S. demographics
b. Call no.: 3700 1992 .W4 STF1a CD

Tiger 92 Loading Program
a. Subject: Tiger data
b. Call no.: 3700s 1992 .W4 Tiger 92, diskette

Sylvan Ascent, Inc. CD/Maps
a. Subject: physiography
b. Call no.: 3700 1995 .S9 CD

AutoCAD 11,12,13 Demonstration File 48 118-E1, DWG
a. Subject: AutoCAD demo
b. Call no.: 3700 1995 .S9 diskette

TIGER 94
a. Subject: not given
b. Call no.: 3700 1996 .W4 CD

USGS OPEN-FILE REPORT SERIES (formats vary, see individual titles)
a. Subjects: various
b. Call no.: 3701s VAR .U5 CD OFR#
    88-44: Geonames, database of geological names (diskette)
    89-94: Lasergraph (diskette)
    90-250: GSEDIT and GSMEDIT, Screen Edit Programs for
        GSDRAW and GSMAP data (diskette)
    90-269-B: GSPOST, Version 3.0 (diskette)
    90-544-B: Roseau 1x 2 digital data (diskette)
    90-621: Vermont Landslide Map (diskette)
    91-23-B: Analytical Results and Sample Locality Map,
        Livergood 1x 2 Quadrangle, AK Prince Rupert
        Quadrangles, AK (diskette)
    91-283-B: Gold, Mercury, Tellurium, and Thallium
        Data & Sample Locality Map of Stream Sediment samples
        from the Iditarod Quadrangle, Alaska. (diskette)
    91-345: E2MCOD, E2MGSM programs for CD-ROM titled
        1:2M scale DLGs (diskette)

91-376-B: Principal Facts for Gravity Data Compiled for the Bakersfield 1x 2 sheet, CA (diskette)

91-396: Gloria Imagery and Bathymetry from the U.S. EEZ off WA, OR, and CA (diskette)

91-575-B: GEOINDEX database on geologic maps (diskette)

92-292-B: A digital data set of the linear features of the Preliminary Geologic Map of Yucca Mtn., Nye County, NV (diskette)

93-231: Data Software, & Applications for Education and Research in Geology—Virginia (diskette)

94-205: USGS Coal Quality (COALQUAL), version 1.3 see QE 75 .O7 CD 94-205 (diskette)

94-255: Southern Lake Michigan Coastal Erosion Study

95-526: Digital Files of Geological Map Symbols with Cartographic Specifications

94-388: GCIP Reference Data Set (GREDS) (diskette)

95-727: Watershed Boundaries and DEM of Oklahoma see QE 75 .O7 95-727 (diskette)

96-96: Database for a National Mineral-Resource Assessment for Undiscovered Deposits of Gold, Silver, Copper, Lead and Zinc in the Conterminous U.S. (diskette)

97-23: Digital Atlas of Oklahoma

US Counties Database
a. Subject: U.S. counties
b. Call no.: 3701 A1 19— .C6 diskette

MAPExpert
a. Subject: base and outline maps
b. Call no.: 3701 A1 1993 .D4 CD

Cartographic Catalog
a. Subject: indexes (textual)
b. Call no.: 3701s A2 VAR .C3 CD

Generic File Disk (Gene 9402: GEN)
a. Subject: none given
b. Call no.: 3701 A3 1991 .U5 diskette

USGS DOQs
a. Subject: orthophoto quads
b. Call no.: 3701s A4 12 .U5 CD

USGS SLAR Acquisition Program 1980–1991
a. Subject: SLAR imagery
b. Call no.: 3701s A4 250 .U54 CD

Conterminous U.S. AVHRR, 1990 bi-weekly composites
a. Subject: AVHRR imagery
b. Call no.: 3701s A4 VAR .U5 CD

SLAR, Side-Looking Airborne Radar, Joint Earth Sciences (JES-2)
    demonstration disc - (IMDISP required)
a. Subjects: SLAR imagery of selected areas of U.S.; 1980–88
b. Call no.: 3701 A4 1990? .U52 CD

Arc Scene USA Tour
a. Subject: general
b. Call no.: 3701 A4 1992 .E5 CD

APSRS (Aerial Photography Summary Record System)
a. Subjects: U.S. aerial photography database; early 1900s–present
b. Call no.: 3701s A49 VAR .U5 CD ready ref

GNIS (Geographic Names Information System)
a. Subject: geographic names
b. Call no.: 3701 A8 1991 .U5 CD ready ref

United States Place Names
a. Subject: place names; lat., long., elev.
b. Call no.: 3701 A89 19— .T6 diskette

United States Geographical Place Names
a. Subject: place names
b. Call no.: 3701 A89 199- .U5 diskette

GEOID 96
a. Subject: geodesy
b. Call no.: 3701 B3 1996 .U5 CD

USGS Digital Data Series
a. Subject: physical sciences
b. Call no.: 3701s C1 VAR .U5 DDS# CD

DDS-1: National Uranium Resource Evaluation Data for the
    Conterminous Western United States

DDS-2: A Digital Representation of the 1978 Geologic Map
    of Nevada

DDS-3: A Geologic Map of the Sea Floor in Western
    Massachusetts Bay

DDS-5: National Energy Research Seismic Library—Processed
    Seismic Data for 29 lines in the National Petroleum Reserve in
    Alaska.

DDS-6: Stratigraphic Nomenclature Databases for the United States, Its Possessions and Territories

DDS-7: Digitized Strong-Motion Accelerograms of North and Central American Earthquakes 1933–1986

DDS-8: Photographs (earthquakes, volcanoes, geologic hazards, and other phenomena)

DDS-9: National Geophysical Data Grids: Gamma Ray, Gravity, Magnetic, and Topographic Data for the Conterminous United States

DDS-10: Modern Average Global Sea-Surface Temperature

DDS-11: Geology of the Conterminous United States at 1:2,500,000

DDS-14: National; Geochronological and Natural Radioelement Databases

DDS-17: Geology and Mineral and Energy Resources, Roswell Resource Area, New Mexico

DDS-18A: National Geochemical Database . . . Uranium (no scale given)

DDS-18B: National Geochemical Database . . . Uranium (no scale given)

DDS-19: Geology and resource assessment of Costa Rica

DDS-21: Earth Science Photographs from the U.S. Geological Survey Library

DDS-23: Photoglossary of Marine and Continental Ichnofossils

DDS-24: Images of Kilauea East Rift Zone Eruption 1983–1993

DDS-27: Monthly Average Polar Sea Ice Concentration

DDS-30: 1995 National Assessment of U.S. Oil and Gas Resources, Release 1, Release 2

DDS-31: Profiles of Gamma-Ray and Magnetic Data, Western U.S.

DDS-32: Powder River Basin . . . Seismic Profile Data

DDS-35: Digital Map Data, Text and Graphical Images in Support of 1995 National Assessment of U.S. Oil and Gas Resources

DDS-36: Tabular Data, Text and Graphical Images in Support of 1995 Assessment of U.S. Oil and Gas

DDS-37: Data from Selected USGS National Stream Water Quality Monitoring Networks

DDS-41: Great Basin Geoscience Database

3 ARC Second Elevation Data
a. Subject: topography
b. Call no.: 3701s C2 250 .U54 diskette

TOPO30 Region 1 Disk: 30-Second Point Topographic, Database, Latitude 37°- 51° N, Longitude 120°-129° W
a. Subject: topography
b. Call no.: 3701 C2 1992 .U5 diskette

U.S. Digital Topography
a. Subject: topography
b. Call no.: 3701 C2 1994 .U5 CD

U.S. Digital Topography for GIS
a. Subject: physical geography
b. Call no.: 3701 C2 1996 .C5 CD

FIRM-DLG
a. Subject: floods
b. Call no.: 3701s C32 24 .U522 BETA CD

Q3 Flood Data, demonstration disk
a. Subject: floods
b. Call no.: 3701 C32 1996 .U5 CD

NERSL (National Energy Research Seismic Library)
a. Subject: seismicity
b. Call no.: 3701s C543 VAR .U52 CD

Cooperative Summary of the Day
a. Subject: meteorology
b. Call no.: 3701s C8 Var .U52 CD

U.S. Divisional and Station Climate Data and Normals
a. Subject: climate
b. Call no.: 3701s C8 VAR .U55 CD

Hi-Rez Data Climatological Series
a. Subject: 30-year (1951–80) Monthly Means
b. Call no.: 3701 C8 1990 .Z4 diskette
    MIL has CT, MA, RI only

DEFLEC93
a. Subject: gravity
b. Call no.: 3701 C9 1993 .D4 diskette

Geomagnetic Observatory Data
a. Subject: geophysics
b. Call no.: 3701 C9 YEAR .G45 CD

NGB-ARF/ARO National Environmental Database
a. Subject: ecology
b. Call no.: 3701s D2 VAR .N4 CD

National Wetlands Inventory
a. Subject: ecology
b. Call no.: 3701s D2 VAR .U5 CD

1990 Census Transportation Planning Package
a. Subject: human and cultural geography
b. Call no.: 3701s E1 100 .U5 CD

FEDSTAT, Volume 89-1, County Demographic and Economic
   Databases
a. Subject: demography; 1980s
b. Call no.: 3701 E1 1989 .F4 CD ANNEX

Arc Census: pre-release California
a. Subject: census data
b. Call no.: 3701 E2 1992 .E5 CD

Geographic Identification Code Scheme
a. Subject: population
b. Call no.: 3701 E2 1994 .U5 CD

Conterminous U.S. Landcover Characteristics Data Set . . .
a. Subject: land cover
b. Call no.: 3701 G43 1990 .U5 CD

GLO Automated Records Project
a. Subject: cadastral maps
b. Call no.: 3701s G46 Var .U5 CD

National Park Service Digital Raster Images
a. Subject: parks and monuments
b. Call no.: 3701s G52 VAR .U5 CD

USGS Coal Quality (COALQUAL), version 1.3
a. Subject: coal
b. Call no.: 3701 H9 1994 .U5 CD

LandView II: Mapping of Selected EPA-Regulated Sites
a. Subject: pollution
b. Call no.: 3701 N7 1992 .L3 CD

Airline Distances
a. Subject: U.S.—Distances
b. Call no.: 3701 P15 1993? .U5 diskette

TIGER/Census Tract Street Index
a. Subject: roads
b. Call no.: 3701 P2 1990? .U5 CD

DeLorme Street Atlas U.S.A.
a. Subject: roads
b. Call no.: 3701 P2 1991 .D4 CD

Wessex. Tiger 94
a. Subject: roads
b. Call no.: 3701 P2 1994 .W4 CD

Street Atlas USA
a. Subject: roads
b. Call no.: 3701 P2 1996 .D4 CD

Streets Plus
a. Subject: roads
b. Call no.: 3701 P2 1997 .M5 CD

Wessex
a. Subject: roads
b. Call no.: 3701 P2 1997 .W4 CD

Compressed Aeronautical Chart (CAC)—Prototype
a. Subject: aeronautical charts; SE U.S.
b. Call no.: 3701s P6 VAR .U552 CD

NOAA Aeronautical Data Sampler I
a. Subject: airports, air route traffic control centers, airspace fixes,
   Navaids, obstacles, runways; some text
b. Call no.: 3701 P6 198-? .U5 CD

Zipcode Centroids
a. Subject: zip codes (U.S.)
b. Call no.: 3701 P817 199- .S8 diskette

NOAA Aeronautical Data Sampler II
a. Subject: airports, air route traffic control centers, airspace fixes,
   Navaids, obstacles, runways; some text
b. Call no.: 3701 P6 1990? .U5 CD

Southern Appalachian Assessment GIS
a. Subject: general
b. Call no.: 3702.A6 1996 .S6 CD

Cities Below
a. Subject: general
b. Call no.: 3704 1995 .N6 CD

SPOTview Data Sampler
a. Subject: satellite imagery
b. Call no.: 3704 A4 1995 .S7 CD

Sim City 2000
a. Subject: cities
b. Call no.: 3704 N1 1996 .S5 CD

Northern Great Plains, AVHRR data set - (IMDISP required)
a. Subject: Advanced Very High Resolution Radiometer imagery;
   selected months in 1987 and 1988
b. Call no.: 3756 A4 1990 .U5 CD

Alaska AVHRR
a. Subject: Advanced Very High Resolution Radiometer
b. Call no.: 3821s A4 VAR .U5 CD

Spot Imagery Coverage of California
a. Subject: satellite imagery
b. Call no.: 3201 A4 1994 .S6 CD

California Counties as Lat/Lon Polygons
a. Subject: county boundaries
b. Call no.: 3851 A1 1990 .T6 diskette

California Geologic Map Index
a. Subject: geology
b. Call no.: 3851 C59 YEAR .C7 diskette

SJVDP Hypercard Stack
a. Subject: San Joaquin Valley, CA
b. Call no.: 3852 .N2 1991? .U5 diskette

Geologic Remote Sensing Field Experiment [Mojave Desert and
   Lunar Crater Volcanic Fields]
a. Subject: imagery
b. Call no.: 3852 .S46 .A4 1989 .G4 CD

Sample TNT Atlas of San Francisco
a. Subject: general
b. Call no.: 3852.N825 1994? .T7 CD

Alexandria Digital Library Prototype CD
a. Subject: various
b. Call no.: 3852.S8 1995 .A4 CD

Thomas Bros. Air Photo, L.A. and Orange Counties
a. Subject: aerial photography
b. Call no.: 3853 .L6 A4 1994 .C8 CD

Geo-CD 94, LA Quake
a. Subject: aerial photography
b. Call no.: 3853.L6 A4 1994 .D5 CD

Santa Barbara County Shoreline Inventory
a. Subject: ecology
b. Call no.: 3853.S3:2 D2 1994 .C5 diskette

UCSB Library Floor Plans
Auto CAD Version II files
a. Subject: floor plans
b. Call no.: 3853.S3:282:2U5L 1992 diskette

Santa Barbara, CA 1853B, 1877, 1898; TIF from LCG&M
a. Subject: general, historical maps
b. Call no.: 3854.S68 1877 .G6 1995 cassette

Santa Barbara, CA 1889; TIF from LCG&M
a. Subject: general, historical maps
b. Call no.: 3854.S68 1889 .R5 cassette

Stockton, California, 1994
a. Subject: aerial photographs
b. Call no.: 3854.S9 A4 1994 .D5 CD

Washington, DC, USA—The Capitol
a. Subject: digital orthophoto
b. Call no.: 3891 A4 1989 .P4 diskette 2 copies

Atlas of Florida
a. Subject: general, diverse
b. Call no.: 3900 1994 .F5 CD

Interactive Atlas of Florida
a. Subject: general
b. Call no.: 3910 1996 .I5 CD

Topographic Field Trip of Washington, DC
a. Subject: topography
b. Call no.: 3891 C2 1996? .U5 CD

Digital Databases of Illinois
a. Subject: general
b. Call no.: 3940 1994 .I44 CD

Collected Data of the First ISLSCP Field Experiment (FIFE)
a. Subject: imagery and ground measurements
b. Call no.: 3973 .R6s A4 VAR .C6 CD

Digital Atlas of Oklahoma
a. Subject: general
b. Call no.:3701s VAR .U5 CD 97-23

Oregon Transect Ecosystem Research Project (OTTER)
a. Subjects: imagery and ground measurements
b. Call no.: 4182.W45s A4 VAR .O6 CD

South America

USGS Digital Data Series
a. Subject: physical sciences
b. Call no.: 3701s C1 VAR .U5 DDS# CD

DDS-19: Geology and resource assessment of Costa Rica

Europe

ERS-1 SAR Reference Coverage
a. Subject: Satellite Imagery Index
b. Call no.: 5551 A49 1993? .E7 CD

ORFEUS (Observations and Research Facilities for European
      Seismology) NARS
a. Subject: seismology; Western Europe (Spain north to Denmark);
      1/83–2/88
b. Call no.: 5551 C543 1988 .O7 CD

Great Cities of Europe
a. Subject: cities
b. Call no.: 5554 1996 .G7 CD

Great Britain Ordnance Survey
a. Subject: sample cartographic data in digital form
b. Call no.: 5820 1993 .O7 diskette

1854 Cholera Map of London
a. Subject: diseases
b. Call no.: 5864.L7 E51 1854 .S7 1994? diskette

Central Europe Class Project
a. Subject: using Atlas/GIS
b. Call no.: 6040 1991 .P3 diskette

Sweden From Space
a. Subject: satellite imagery
b. Call no.: 6311 A4 199-? .S9 CD

Africa

Africa, National Boundary Files
a. Subject: boundaries
b. Call no.: 7801 A1 19— .M3 diskette

Africa Data Sampler
a. Subject: general
b. Call no.: 7800 1995 .W6 CD

Asia

Sample Satellite Remote Sensing Data
a. Subject: satellite imagery of area in Central Mysore
b. Call no.: 6908.M9:2 A4 1993 .S3 CD

Geological Maps of Japan
a. Subject: geology
b. Call no.: 7071 C5 1992 .J3 CD

Kamchatka: Compiled Volcanology Data Set 3
a. Subject: remote sensing images
b. Call no.: 7513.K35:2 A4 1995? .K3 CD

Australasia

Register of Place Names
a. Subject: gazetteer
b. Call no.: 8940s 250 A8 Victoria gazetteer diskette

Australasia From Space
a. Subject: satellite imagery
b. Call no.: 8941 A4 1986-92 .A8 CD

AusWATCH
a. Subjects: satellite imagery
b. Call no.: 8941 A4 1992 .A8 CD

Geologic Map of Australia
a. Subject: geology
b. Call no.: 8941 C5 1991? .A8 cassette

Oceans

The Ocean CD Browser
a. Subject: geophysics
b. Call no.: 9096 A4 1978-86 .O2 CD

Deep Sea Drilling Project
a. Subjects: marine geologic and geophysical data; selected sites of
   World Oceans; 1968–1987
b. Call no.: 9096 C1 1968 .U5 CD

Ocean Drilling Program
a. Subjects: physical sciences; selected sites
b. Call no.: 9096 C1 1992 .N3 CD

Marine Data Sampler
a. Subject: physical sciences
b. Call no.: 9096 C1 1993 .M3 CD

GEBCO Digital Atlas
a. Subject: bathymetry
b. Call no.: 9096s C2 10,000 .G4 CD

MCSST/Pigment Concentrations
a. Subjects: multi-channel sea surface temperature and
   phytoplankton pigment concentration data
b. Call no.: 9096 C73 VAR .M62 CD

NODC-02 & NODC-03, Global Ocean Temperature and Salinity
   Profiles
a. Subjects: physical and chemical characteristics
b. Call no.: 9096 C73 1991 .U5 CD

Ocean Atlas for MacIntosh (Version 2.5)
a. Subject: oceanography
b. Call no.: 9096 C73 1994 .O8 diskette

TOPEX/Poseidon Mission. PO.DAAC Merged Geophysical Data
   Record from the TOPEX/Poseidon Mission
a. Subject: geophysics
b. Call no.: 9096s C9 Var .U5 CD

GEODAS, Marine Geophysical Data
a. Subject: geophysics
b. Call no.: 9096 C9 1992? .U5 CD

Geophysical Data System for Hydrographic Survey Data
a. Subject: geophysics
b. Call no.: 9096 C9 1996? .U5 CD

NOAA Raster Nautical Chart Image
a. Subject: Nautical Chart 12214, Cape May to Fenwick Island
b. Call no.: 9096s P5VAR .U53 12214 37th ed. diskette

DMSP Brightness Temperature Grids
a. Subject: physical characteristics of oceanography
b. Call no.: 9101s C732 VAR .U5 CD

Tropical Ocean Global Atmosphere (TOGA) Data Sets for 1985–6
a. Subjects: meteorology and oceanography
b. Call no.: 9101 .T7s C1 VAR .J4 CD

Arctic Ocean Snow and Meteorological Observations
a. Subjects: climatology
b. Call no.: 9121 C8 1991 .N3 CD

Eastern Arctic Ice, Ocean and Atmosphere CEAREX-1
a. Subjects: physical sciences
b. Call no.: 9127 .E12 C1 VAR .N3 CD

GLORIA
a. Subject: physical sciences; East coast
b. Call no.: 9182 .C65 C1 198- .U5 CD

SeaView Satellite Imagery of the Southeastern U.S. Coast
a. Subject: satellite imagery
b. Call no.: 9182.F5 A4 1996 .S4 CD

GLORIA
a. Subject: physical sciences; Gulf of Mexico; 1980s
b. Call no.: 9192 .G8 C1 198-? .U5 CD

U.K. Digital Marine Atlas
a. Subject: oceanography
b. Call no.: 9192.N6 C7 1994 .U5 disk

NODC-1 (Experimental Compact Disc), Pacific Ocean
a. Subjects: temperature and salinity profiles; 1900–1988
b. Call no.: 9481 C73 1988 .U5 CD

West Coast Time Series Coastal Zone Color Scanner Imagery, vol. 1, version 2 - (IMDISP required)
a. Subjects: imagery; compressed data; Pacific Coast; 1979–1981
b. Call no.: 9507 .N2s A4 VAR .U5 CD

High Resolution Bathymetry and Selected Geoscience Data for the
   Monterey Bay Region
a. Subject: physical sciences
b. Call no.: 9507 .N2444 C1 198- .U5 CD

USGS Digital Data Series
a. Subject: physical sciences
b. Call no.: 3701s C1 VAR .U5 DDS# CD

DDS-3: A Geologic Map of the Sea Floor in Western
   Massachusetts Bay

DDS-10: Modern Average Global Sea-Surface Temperature

DDS-23: Photoglossary of Marine and Continental Ichnofossils

Appendix 2

Specialized Bibliographies

In appendix 2 are specialized bibliographies: (2A) Monographs, Serials, and Periodical Articles; (2B) Projections; and (2C) Cataloging. These bibliographies list those works focussing on spatial data or spatial-data librarianship that are most often useful in a general spatial-data collection.

Appendix 2A—Monographs, Serials, and Periodical Articles

Ackroyd, Neil. 1994. *Global navigation: A GPS user's guide*. 2d ed. London: Lloyd's of London Press.

Alaska. Division of Geological and Geophysical Surveys. 1983. *Handbook for geologic cartography: Guidelines and graphic techniques for the production of geologic illustrations*. College, AK: Author.

Allen, D. 1972. Geomorphological maps of Canada: A bibliography of Canadian federal government maps. *SLAG&MD Bulletin* 90: 25–43.

Allin, J. 1982. *Map sources directory*. Downsview, Ontario: Map Library, York University Libraries. [Looseleaf; third update 1983.]

American Congress on Surveying and Mapping. 1979? *Bibliographies on surveying, cartography, and geodesy*. Falls Church, VA: Author.

American Geographical Society. Map Department. 1968. *Index to maps in books and periodicals*. Boston: G. K. Hall. [10 vols.; first suppl. (1968–71), 1971; second suppl. (1972–74), 1976; third suppl. (1976–82), 1987.

Antique map price record & handbook. 1993– . Amherst, MA: Kimmel.

Applied geomorphological mapping. 1988. *Zeitschrift für Geomorphologie, Supplementband* no. 67. Berlin: Gebruder Borntraeger.

Arnaud, Alain. 1996? "Road maps and cost of travel." In: International Federation of Library Associations, Section des Cartothèques et Bibliothèques de Géographie, *1989 IFLA, Paris 24–30*. Paris: Comité Français de Cartographie.

Aronoff, S. 1985. Political implications of full cost recovery for land remote sensing systems. *PERS* 51: 41–45.

Association of Canadian Map Libraries and Archives. 1967–1976. *Proceedings*. Ottawa: Author.

———. 1968–1973. *Newsletter*. Ottawa: Author.

———. 1974– . *Bulletin*. Ottawa: Author.

Atlas of state plane-coordinates zones & UTM zones: Western region. 1984. Menlo Park, CA: NCIC.

Australian Map Circle. 1983– . *Newsletter*. Queen Victoria Terrace, ACT: Author. [From 1977 to 1982, issuing agency is Australian Map Curators Circle.]

Avery, Thomas E. 1992. *Interpretation of aerial photographs*. 5th ed. New York: Macmillan.

Bagrow, L. 1964. *History of cartography*. Rev. and enl. by R. A. Skelton. Cambridge, MA: Harvard Univ. Press. [2d ed. 1985. Chicago: Precedent Publishing.]

Bankey, Viki; and Walter L. Anderson. 1995. *A bibliography of some geophysical computer programs, databases, and maps from the U.S. Geological Survey, 1971–1994*. (Open-file Report 95-77). Reston, VA: USGS.

Barnes, John W. 1991. *Basic geological mapping*. 2d ed. (Geological Society of London Handbook Series). New York: Halsted Press.

Barrett, E. C. 1974. *Climatology from satellites*. London: Methuen.

Barrett, E. C., and L. F. Curtis. 1972. *Environmental remote sensing*. London: Edward Arnold.

base line: A newsletter of the Map & Geography Round Table. 1980– . Chicago: ALA.

Batson, R. M. 1987. Digital cartography of the planets: New methods, its status, and its future. *PERS* 53: 1211–18.

Baxes, Gregory A. 1994. *Digital image processing: Principles and applications*. New York: Wiley.

Behroozi, Cy. 1993. Children's atlases: A selected bibliography. *WAML Information bulletin* 25: 23–27. [Also in *NEMO Newsletter* March 1993 and April 1993.]

Bengtsson, H., and G. Atkinson. 1977. *Orienteering for sport and pleasure*. Brattleboro, VT: Stephen Greene Press.

Bennison, George Mills. 1975. *Introduction to geological structures and maps*. 3d ed. (metric). London: Edward Arnold.

———. 1990. *An introduction to geological structures and maps*. 5th ed. London: Edward Arnold.

Berhardsen, Tor. 1992. *Geographic information systems*. Arendal, Norway: Viak IT.

Bertele, H. von. 1961. *Globes and spheres*. Lausanne, Switzerland: Swiss Watch and Jewelry Journal.

Bertin, Jacques. 1983. *Semiology of graphics: Diagrams, networks, maps*. Madison, WI: University of Wisconsin Press.

Bibliographia cartographica. 1974– . Munich: K. G. Saur. [Continuation of *Bibliotheca cartographica* (1957–1972), which itself continued H.-P. Kosack and K.-H. Meine's 1955 *Die Kartographie 1943–1954, eine bibliographische Übersicht*. (*Kartographische Schriftenreihe*, Band 4). Lahr/Schwarzwald: Astra Verlag.]

Bibliographic guide to maps and atlases. 1980– . Boston, MA: G. K. Hall.

Bibliographic guide to the production of local and regional magnetic charts. 1981. (Geomagnetic Bulletin 12). London: HMSO.

Bibliographie cartographique internationale. 1938–1975. Paris: Colin. [*See* Pelletier 1981; Foncin and Sommer 1957; and Riccoboni 1964 for articles on this publication.]

Bibliographies and location maps of aeromagnetic and aeroradiometric publications for the states [of the United States]. 1986. (Open-file Reports 86-525 A-G). Reston, VA: USGS.

Blachut, T. J. 1979. *Urban surveying and mapping*. New York: Springer-Verlag. [1980 Spanish ed.: *Cartografía y levantamientos urbanos*. Mexico D.F., Mexico: Dirección General del Territorio Nacional.]

Blackadar, R. G. 1979. *Guide to authors: A guide for the preparation of geological maps and reports*. Rev. (Miscellaneous Report, no. 29). Ottawa: Geological Survey of Canada.

Blakemore, J. J., and J. B. Harley. 1980. *Concepts in the history of cartography: A review and perspective*. (*Cartographica*, vol. 17, no. 4, Monograph 26). Toronto: University of Toronto Press.

Blyth, F. G. H. 1965. *Geological maps and their interpretation*. London: Edward Arnold.

Bohme, Rolf. 1989–1993. *Inventory of world topographic mapping.* 3 vols. London: Elsevier Applied Science Publishers (published on behalf of the ICA).

Bolton, T. 1989. *Geological maps: Their solution and interpretation.* Cambridge, UK: Cambridge University Press.

Bond, Barbara A. 1984. Silk maps, the story of M19's excursion into the world of cartography, 1939–1945. *Cartographic Journal* 21(2): 141–44.

Bonham-Carter, Graeme. 1994. *Geographic information systems for geoscientists: Modelling with GIS.* 1st ed. Oxford, UK: Pergamon Press.

Boulter, Clive A. 1989. *Four-dimensional analysis of geological maps: Techniques of interpretation.* Chichester, UK: Wiley.

Breese, P. et al. 1995. Sanborn fire insurance maps: Across the curriculum, across the school. *School Library Media Activities Monthly* 11 (January): 26–30.

British Museum. 1967. *Catalogue of printed maps, charts, and plans.* Photolithographic edition to 1964. London: Author. [15 vols.: corrections and additions, 1968; ten-year suppl. (1965–74) published in 1978.]

Brown, B. 1932. *Astronomical atlases, maps and charts: An historical and general guide.* London: Search Publishing.

Brown, L. A. 1950. *The story of maps.* Boston: Little, Brown.

Burkham, D. E. 1978. Accuracy of flood mapping. *Journal of Research of USGS* 6: 515–27.

Burnside, Clifford Donald. 1985. *Mapping from aerial photographs.* 2d ed. London: Collins.

Cambridge world gazetteer. 1990. Cambridge, England: Cambridge University Press.

Cartographic information for architecture. 1994. *Art Reference Services Quarterly* 1(3). Entire issue.

Cartographic innovations: An international handbook of mapping terms to 1900. London: Map Collector Publications, ICA.

Carver, L. G. 1982. Remotely sensed imagery in a research map library. *ACML Bulletin* 44: 22–28.

Castleman, K. R. 1979. *Digital image processing.* Englewood Cliffs, NJ: Prentice-Hall.

Catalog of digital geographic data: New Mexico Resource Geographic Information System Program. 1993. Albuquerque: RGIS Clearinghouse, Technology Application Center, University of New Mexico.

Cazier, L. 1976. *Surveyors and surveys of the public lands*. Washington, DC: GPO.

Chrisman, Nicholas R. 1997. *Exploring geographic information systems*. New York: Wiley.

Clarke, Keith C. 1997. *Getting started with geographic information systems*. Upper Saddle River, NJ: Prentice-Hall.

Claussen, M. P., and H. R. Friis. 1941. *Descriptive catalog of maps published by Congress, 1817–1843*. Washington, DC: Private printing. [Covering 1789–1861 is 1985–announced publication, *Union catalog and subject index of maps published by the U.S. Congress, 1789–1861*. Washington, DC: HistoriConsultants.]

Cloud, John. 1995. Wild blue and yonder improve access to Space Shuttle Earth observations photography. *Information Systems Newsletter* 3: 7–10.

Coastal mapping handbook. 1978. Washington, DC: GPO.

Cobb, D. A., and P. B. Ives. 1983. *State atlases: An annotated bibliography*. (CPL Bibliography no. 108). Chicago: CPL Bibliographies.

Cohen, C. G. 1980. *Shtetlfinder, Jewish communities in the 19th and early 20th centuries in the pale of settlement of Russia and Poland, and in Lithuania, Latvia, Galicia and Bukovina, with names of residents*. Los Angeles: Periday.

Cole, David. 1995. Some further notes on strip maps. *Cartomania* 39/40: 10–11.

Columbia gazetteer of the world. To come 1998. New York: Columbia University Press. [Current ed., 1952.]

Colvocoresses, A. P. 1974. *Remote sensing platforms*. (Circular 693). Reston, VA: USGS.

Congressional Information Service. 1995– . *CIS U.S. serial set index. Part XIV, index and carto-bibliography of maps, 1789–1969*. Washington, DC: Author.

Corbin, J. B. 1965. *An index of state geological survey publications issued in series*. New York: Scarecrow Press.

Cracknell, A. P. 1981. *Remote sensing in meteorology, oceanography and hydrology*. New York: Halsted Press.

Creason, Glen. 1993. The Sanborn fire insurance maps in the Library of Congress by Chadwyck-Healey. *WAML Information Bulletin* 24: 97–101.

Crone, G. R. 1978. *Maps and their makers, an introduction to the history of cartography*. 5th ed. Hamden, CT: Archon Books.

Crotts, J. 1981– . Geologic map index to USGS 7.5' and 15' quadrangles of California. *WAML Information Bulletin* 12: 238–64; 13: 74–100; 14: 32–45.

Cuff, D. J., and M. T. Mattson. 1982. *Thematic maps, their design and production.* New York: Methuen.

Czerniak, R. J., and G. Perrone. 1983. *State atlases, a bibliography.* (Public Administration Series Bibliography P-1213). Monticello, IL: Vance Bibliographies.

Davis, Bruce. 1996. *GIS: A visual approach.* Santa Fe, NM: OnWord Press.

De Laubenfels, D. 1975. *Mapping the world's vegetation: Regionalization of formations and flora.* (Syracuse Geographical Series no. 4). Syracuse, NY: Syracuse University Press.

Deepal, A. 1980. *Remote sensing of atmospheres and oceans.* New York: Academic Press.

Deetz, C. H. 1935. *Cartography.* (U.S. Coast and Geodetic Survey, Special Publication 205). Washington, DC: GPO.

Dekker, E., and P. van der Krogt. 1993. *Globes from the western world.* London: Zwemmer.

Dictionary of geography. 1997. 2d ed. Oxford, UK: Oxford University Press.

Digital elevation models. 1993. (Data Users Guide 5). Reston, VA: USGS.

Digital files of geologic map symbols with cartographic specifications. 1995. (Open-file Report 95-526). Reston, VA: USGS.

Digital image processing. 1992. Los Alamitos, CA: IEEE Computer Society Press.

Digital image processing in remote sensing. 1988. London: Taylor & Francis.

Digital line graphs from 1: 2,000,000-scale maps. 1990. (Data Users Guide 3). Reston, VA: USGS.

Directory of Canadian map collections. 1992. 6th ed. Ottawa: ACML.

Directory of UK map collections. 1995. 3d ed. Kingston upon Thames, Surrey: British Cartographic Society.

Distances between United States ports. 1993. 8th ed. Washington, DC: DMA Hydrographic/Topographic Center.

Doll, John G. 1988. Cloth maps of World War II. *WAML Information Bulletin* 20: 23–35.

Dulka, Michael. 1986. Access to maps and other cartographic publications of the United Nations and its specialized agencies. *WAML Information Bulletin* 17: 215–20.

Earth observer. 1989– . Greenbelt, MD: EOS Project Science Office, NASA/Goddard Space Flight Center.

Ehrenberg, R. E. 1982. *Archives and manuscripts: Maps and architectural drawings*. (SAA Basic Manual Series). Chicago: Society of American Archivists.

Elements of cartography. 1995. 6th ed. New York: Wiley.

Encyclopedia of field and general geology. 1988. New York: Van Nostrand Reinhold.

Examples of environmental maps (exemples de cartes de l'environnement). 1980. Madrid: Instituto Geográfico Nacional.

Falkner, Edgar. 1995. *Aerial mapping: Methods and applications*. Boca Raton, FL: Lewis.

Fisher, H. T. 1982. *Mapping information: The graphic display of quantitative information*. Cambridge, MA: Abt Books.

Fisher, Morris. 1985. *Provinces and provincial capitals of the world*. 2d ed. Metuchen, NJ: Scarecrow Press.

Fitzpatrick, Gary L. 1986. *Direct-line distances*. [In 2 editions: International ed. or U.S. ed.] Metuchen, NJ: Scarecrow Press.

Fordham, H. G. 1914. *Studies in carto-bibliography of Britain and France, and in the bibliography of itineraries and road books*. Oxford, UK: Clarenden Press.

France. Centre national de la recherche scientifique. 1961. *Méthodes de la cartographie de la végétation: Toulouse, 6-21 mai, 1960*. (Colloques internationaux 97.) Paris: Éditions du CNRS.

Fremlin, G., and L. M. Sebert. 1972. *National atlases: Their history, analysis and ways to improvement and standardization*. (Cartographica Monograph no. 4). Toronto: York University, Department of Geography.

Gale, Stephen. 1983. The mapping of caves. *SUC Bulletin* 16(1): 21–23.

Gannett, H. 1884. *A dictionary of altitudes in the United States*. Washington, DC: GPO.

Garson, G. D. 1992. *Analytic mapping and geographic database*. Newbury Park, CA: Sage Publications.

Geocarto international: A multi-disciplinary journal of remote sensing. 1986– . Hong Kong: Geocarto International Centre.

Geodetic glossary. 1987. (U.S. Coast and Geodetic Survey Special Publication 242). Rockville, MD.: National Geodetic Survey.

Geographic notes. 198 –1992/93. Washington, DC: U.S. Department of State, Bureau of Intelligence and Research.

Geographical information systems: Principles and applications. 1991. Harlow, Essex, UK: Longman.

Geographical systems. 1993– . Yverdon, Switzerland: Gordon and Breach.

GeoKartenbrief. 1976– . Stuttgart: Geocenter.

Geo-Katalog. 1975– . Stuttgart: GeoCenter. [2 vols.; Band 2 looseleaf; supersedes *Zumstein-Katalog* and *RV-Katalog.*]

George, W. 1969. *Animals and maps.* London: Secker & Warburg.

GIRAS: A geographic information retrieval and analysis system for handling land use and land cover data. 1977. (USGS Professional Paper 1059.) Washington, DC: GPO.

GIS approach to digital spatial libraries. 1993. Redlands, CA: ESRI.

GIS Europe. 1992– . Lemmer, Netherlands: GIS World Europe.

GIS world. 1988– . Fort Collins, CO: GIS World, Inc.

The globe. 1974– . Melbourne: Australian Map Circle. [Issuing agency formerly the Australian Map Curators Circle (for numbers I–I 8); suppl. is *Newsletter.*]

Der Globusfreund. 1951– . Vienna: Coronelli-Weltbund der Globusfreunde.

Gomez-Ibáñez, D. A. 1969. World atlases for general reference. *Choice* 6: 625–30.

GPS for geodesy. 1996. Berlin: Springer.

GPS world: News and applications of the global positioning system. 1990– . Eugene, OR: Aster.

Greenhood, D. 1964. *Mapping.* Chicago: University of Chicago Press.

Grewe, Klaus. 1984. *Bibliographie zur Geschichte des Vermessungswesens [Bibliography of the history of surveying].* Stuttgart: K. Wittwer.

Grimshaw, David J. 1994. *Bringing geographical information systems into business.* Harlow, Essex, UK: Longman.

Guide to flood insurance rate maps. 1988. (FIA-14). Washington, DC: U.S. Federal Emergency Management Agency.

Guide to U.S. government maps: Geologic and hydrologic. 1975– . McLean, VA: Documents Index.

Guide to U.S. government publications. 1973– . McLean, VA: Documents Index.

Guide to U.S. map resources. 2d ed. 1990. Chicago: ALA.

Hanson, C. R. 1975. *Earth science maps of Wisconsin l818–1974: A bibliography and index.* (Information Circular no. 1). Madison, WI: Wisconsin State Cartographer's Office.

Harder, K. B. 1976. *Illustrated dictionary of place names, United States and Canada.* New York: Van Nostrand Reinhold.

Harley, J. B. 1972. *Maps for the local historian: A guide to the British sources.* London: National Council of Social Service for the Standing Conference for Local History.

―――. 1975. *Ordnance Survey maps: A descriptive manual.* Southampton, UK: Ordnance Survey.

Harvey, P. D. A. 1980. *The history of topographical maps: Symbols, pictures and surveys.* London: Thames and Hudson.

Hatch, W. L. 1983. *Selective guide to climatic data sources.* (Keys to Meteorological Records Documentation no. 4.11). Washington, DC: NOAA, Environmental Data and Information Service.

Hawes, J. H. 1977. *Manual of United States surveying.* Columbus, OH: Carben Surveying Reports.

Hawaii. Department of Planning and Economic Development. 1978. *Directory of Hawaii map sources.* Honolulu: Author.

Hayward, R. J. 1977. *Fire insurance plans in the National Map Collection.* Ottawa: Public Archives.

Hebert, J. R. 1984. *Panoramic maps of cities in the United States and Canada: A checklist of maps in the collections of the Library of Congress, Geography and Map Division.* 2d ed. Washington, DC: Library of Congress.

Heppell, R. C. 1982. *Topographic maps and the local historian.* (Information Sheet 68). Manlius, NY: Regional Conference of Historical Agencies.

Hicks, S. D. 1989. *Tide and current glossary.* Rockville, MD: National Ocean Service.

High mountain cartography. 1987. *Mountain research and development* 7(4). Entire issue.

Historical boundary atlas and chronology of county boundaries, 1788–1980. 1984. Boston: G. K. Hall.

Historical maps on file. 1984. New York: Facts on File.

History of cartography. 1986– . Chicago: University of Chicago Press. [6-vol. general history of cartography: vol. 1, Prehistoric, ancient and medieval Europe and the Mediterranean; vol. 2, The traditional Asian studies; vol. 3, Renaissance and discovery 1470–1640; vol. 4, Science, enlightenment, and expansion, 1640–1800; vol. 5, Nineteenth century; vol. 6, Twentieth century.]

Hoar, G. J. 1982. *Satellite surveying: Theory (geodesy, map projections), applications (equipment operations).* (MS-TM-3346-8l). Torrance, CA: Magnavox Advanced Products and Systems.

Hodgkiss, A. G. 1970. *Maps for books and theses.* Newton Abbot, UK: David and Charles.

———. 1981. *Understanding maps.* Folkestone, UK: Dawson.

Hodgkiss, A. G., and A. F. Tatham. 1986. *Keyguide to information sources in cartography.* New York: Facts on File.

Hoehn, R. P. 1976–1977. *Union list of Sanborn fire insurance maps held by institutions in the United States and Canada.* (Occasional Paper no. 2–3). Santa Cruz, CA: WAML. [Vol. 2 by W. S. Peterson-Hunt and E. L. Woodruff.]

Hofmann-Wellenhof, B. 1994. *Global positioning system: Theory and practice.* 3d rev. ed. Vienna: Springer-Verlag.

Holmes, Nigel. 1991. *Pictorial maps: History, design, ideas, sources.* New York: Watson-Guptill.

Howse, D., and M. Sanderson. 1972. *The sea chart: An historical survey based on the collections of the National Maritime Museum.* New York: McGraw-Hill.

Hutchinson, Scott. 1997. *Inside ArcView GIS.* 2d ed. Santa Fe, NM: OnWord Press.

Hyatt, Edward C. 1988a. Advances in computerized information retrieval in remote sensing. *International Journal of Remote Sensing* 9: 1739–50.

———. 1988b. *Keyguide to information sources in remote sensing.* London: Mansell.

Hyde, Ralph. 1988. *Panoramania!: The art and entertainment of the "all-embracing" view.* London: Trefoil.

Hydrological maps, a contribution to the International Hydrological Decade. 1977. Paris: Unesco.

Imago Mundi, the International Journal for the History of Cartography. 1935– . Various places: various publishers. Currently the access point is Map Library, British Library, London.

IMCOS Journal, Journal of the International Map Collectors Society. 1982?– . Surrey, UK: International Map Collectors Society.

Imhof, E. 1982. *Cartographic relief representation.* New York: Walter de Gruyter.

Information sources in cartography. 1990. London: Bowker-Saur.

Integration of geographic information systems and remote sensing. 1997. Cambridge, UK: Cambridge University Press.

International Cartographic Association. Commission II. 1994. *Multilingual dictionary of technical terms in cartography.* Munich, Germany: Saur.

International Cartographic Association. Commission III: Automation in Cartography. 1973. *Automation terms in cartography*. English ed. Washington, DC: ACSM.

International Cartographic Association. Standing Commission on Education and Training. 1993– . *Basic cartography: For students and technicians*. 2d ed. London: Elsevier.

International Cartographic Association. Standing Commission on Map Production Technology. 1988. *Compendium of cartographic techniques*. London: Elsevier.

International Cartographic Conference. 19___– . *Proceedings*. Various places: various publishers. [Publication done—if at all—by sponsoring country for the conference.] (USGS's National Mapping Division will often have information on this, as will *LCG&M*.)

International classification and mapping of vegetation. 1973. (Ecology and Conservation Series no. 6). New York: Unipub.

International Conference on Geological Information, 1st, 1978, London, England. 1979. *Geoscience information, a state-of-the-art review, proceedings of the first International Conference on Geological Information, London, 10–12 April, 1978*. Heathfield, UK: Broad Oak Press.

International directory of current research in the history of cartography and in carto-bibliography. 1974– . Norwich, UK: Geo Books.

International directory of map dealers. 1988. 2d ed. Tring, U.K.: Map Collector Publications.

International directory of tactile map collections. 1985. Washington, DC: Library of Congress.

International Federation of Library Associations. Geography and Map Libraries Section. 1969?– . *Newsletter*. Various places: Author.

International Hydrographic Organization. 1953. *Limits of oceans and seas*. 3d ed. Monaco: International Hydrographic Organization.

International Journal of Geographical Information Science. 1997– . London: Taylor & Francis.

International Journal of Geographical Information Systems. 1987–1996. London: Taylor & Francis.

International Yearbook of Cartography. 1961– . London: George Philip & Sons [etc.].

Introduction to geographic information systems. 1994. London: HMSO.

Inventory of aerial photography and other remotely sensed imagery of Minnesota. 1978. St. Paul, MN: Legislative Commission on Minnesota.

Ives, Peter B. 1988. State atlases by state agencies: An historical survey. *Government Publications Review* 15: 113–36.

Jahne, B. 1993. *Spatio-temporal image processing: Theory and scientific applications*. Berlin: Springer-Verlag.

————. 1995. *Digital image processing: Concepts, algorithms, and scientific applications*. 3d ed. Berlin: Springer-Verlag.

Jain, A. K. 1989. *Fundamentals of digital image processing*. Englewood Cliffs, NJ: Prentice-Hall.

James, P. 1981. *All possible worlds, a history of geographical ideas*. 2d ed. New York: Wiley.

Jensen, John. 1985. *Introductory digital image processing: A remote sensing perspective*. Englewood Cliffs, NJ: Prentice-Hall.

Johnson, P. L. 1969. *Remote sensing in ecology*. Athens, GA: University of Georgia Press.

Karo, H. A. 1956. World coastline measurements. *International Hydrographic Review* 33: 131–40.

Keates, J. S. 1978. *Cartographic design and production*. New York: Halsted Press.

————. 1996. *Understanding maps*. Harlow, UK: Longman.

Keister, K. 1993. Charts of change. *Historic Preservation* 45: 42–49, 91–92.

Kennedy, M. 1996. *The global positioning system and GIS: An introduction*. Chelsea, MI: Ann Arbor Press.

Kent, Robert B. 1986. National atlases: The influence of wealth and political orientation on content. *Geography* 72: 122–30.

Kent, Robert B.; and Thomas J. Tobias. 1990. State atlases: Funding sources and thematic content. *Professional Geographer* 42: 313–23.

Kidwell, A. M., and P. S. Greer. 1973. *Sites perception and the nonvisual experience: Designing and manufacturing mobility maps*. New York: American Foundation for the Blind.

Kister, K. 1984. *Kister's atlas buying guide, general English-language world atlases available in North America*. Phoenix, AZ: Oryx Press.

Kjellstrom, B. 1976. *Be expert with map and compass: The complete orienteering handbook*. New enl. ed. New York: Scribner's.

Kreis, B. D. 1995. *ARC/INFO quick reference*. 1st ed. Santa Fe, NM: OnWord Press.

Kuchler, A. W. 1965–1970. *International bibliography of vegetation maps*. (University of Kansas Publications, Library Series 45). Lawrence, KS: University of Kansas Libraries. [4 vols.; also 1980– .]

————. 1967. *Vegetation mapping*. New York: Ronald.

Lamb, H. H. 1983. Mapping historical weather and past climates. *SUC Bulletin* 16(l): 25–34.

Land use and land cover classification system for use with remote-sensor data, a revision of the land-use classification system as presented as U.S. Geological Survey Circular 671. 1976. (USGS Professional Paper 964). Washington, DC: GPO.

Land use and natural resource mapping, glossary of terms. 1983. (Open-file Report 83-102). Reston, VA: USGS.

Landsat data users notes. 1978– . Sioux Falls, SD: EROS Data Center.

Langeraar, W. 1984. *Surveying and charting of the seas*. Amsterdam: Elsevier.

Larsgaard, M. L. 1984. *Topographic mapping of the Americas, Australia, and New Zealand*. Littleton, CO: Libraries Unlimited.

————. 1990. Geological maps and remote sensing. In *Information sources in the earth sciences*, 2d ed., 134–71. London: Bowker-Saur.

————. 1993. *Topographic mapping of Africa, Antarctica, and Eurasia*. (Occasional Paper no. 14). Santa Cruz, CA: WAML.

Larson, Catherine A. 1984. *Mineral maps of the United States*. Urbana, IL: Author.

Lawrence, G. R. P. 1972. *Cartographic methods*. London: Methuen.

Lefkowicz, E. J. 1995. Sea charts, sailing directions and maritime history. *AB Bookman's Weekly* 95: 2809–10, 2812–17.

Leick, A. 1995. *GPS satellite surveying*. 2d ed. New York: Wiley.

Lewis, P. 1977. *Maps and statistics*. New York: Wiley.

Lillesand, T. M., and R. W. Kiefer. 1994. *Remote sensing and image interpretation*. 3d ed. New York: Wiley.

Lind, M. 1985. *Using maps and aerial photography in your genealogical research: With supplement on foreign aerial photography*. Cloquet, MN: Linden Tree.

Lobeck, A. K. 1958. *Block diagrams*. 2d ed. Amherst, MA: Emerson-Trussell.

Lock, C. B. M. 1969. *Modern maps and atlases, an outline guide to twentieth century production*. Hamden, CT: Archon Books.

————. 1976. *Geography and cartography: A reference handbook*. 3d ed. rev. and enl. Hamden, CT: Linnet Books.

Lyons, T. R., and T. E. Avery. 1977. *Remote sensing: Handbook for archaeologists and cultural resource managers*. Washington, DC: GPO.

MacEachren, A. M.; and G. B. Johnson. 1987. The evolution, application and implications of strip format travel maps. *Cartographic Journal* 24: 147–55.

MacEathron, S. 1996. A review of atlas reviewing. *SLAG&MD Bulletin* 183: 18–27.

Maltman, A. 1990. *Geological maps, an introduction*. New York: Chapman and Hall.

Manning, M. 1994. Sanborn fire insurance maps: An aid for genealogists. *Illinois Libraries* 76: 101–4.

Manual of detailed geomorphological mapping. 1972. Prague: Academia.

Manual of federal geographic data products. 1993. Falls Church, VA: ViGYAN.

Manual of remote sensing. 3d ed. 1995– . Sewickley, PA: ASPRS. [Issued in CD-ROM; first CD, *Earth observing platforms and sensors*.]

The map collector. 1977–1996. Tring, UK: Map Collector Publications.

Mapline. 1976– . Chicago: Newberry Library, Hermon Dunlap Smith Center for the History of Cartography.

Mappemonde: Revue trimestrielle internationale de cartographie. 1986– . Montpelier, France: Groupement d'interet public RECLUS.

Mapping awareness in the United Kingdom and Ireland. 1994– . London: Longman.

Maps can help you trace your family tree: How to use maps in genealogy. 1991. Reston, VA: USGS.

Maps on file. 1989– . New York: Facts on File.

Maritime boundaries and ocean frontiers. 1987. Totowa, NH: Barnes and Noble.

Mather, P. M. 1978. *Computer processing of remotely sensed images: An introduction*. New York: Wiley.

Mathewson, K. M. 1993. Amazonia: a carto-bibliography. *SLAG&MD Bulletin* 172: 27–40.

McEntyre, J. G. 1978. *Land survey systems*. New York: Wiley.

McGrath, R. J., and W. E. Opalski. [198_?]. *Current automated cartographic production capabilities at the Defense Mapping Agency, Hydrographic Center*. Washington, D.C.: DMA Hydrographic Center.

Mercator's world: The magazine of maps, atlases, globes, and charts. 1996– . Eugene, OR: Aster.

Meynen, E. 1984. *Gazetteers and glossaries of geographical names: Bibliography, 1947–1976.* Wiesbaden, Germany: Franz Steiner.

Microcartography: Applications for archives and libraries. 1981. (Occasional Paper no. 6.) Santa Cruz, CA: WAML.

Minnesota State Planning Agency. 1977. *A directory of Minnesota maps.* St. Paul, MN: Author.

Minnesota University. Wilson Library. Map Division. 1977. *Catalog of aerial photography in the Map Division, Wilson Library, University of Minnesota, Minneapolis, Minnesota.* St. Paul, MN: Minnesota State Planning Agency.

Modelski, A. M. 1984. *Railroad maps of North America, the first hundred years.* Washington, DC: Library of Congress.

Moffat, R. M. 1986. *Map index to topographic quadrangles of the United States, 1882–1940.* (Occasional Paper no. 10). Santa Cruz, CA: WAML.

Moik, J. G. 1980. *Digital processing of remotely sensed images.* (NASA SP-431). Washington, DC: NASA.

Monkhouse, F., and H. R. Wilkinson. 1978. *Maps and diagrams: Their compilation and construction.* 3d ed. rev. and enl. London: Methuen.

Monmonier, M. S. 1977. *Maps, distortion and meaning.* (Resource Paper 75-4). Washington, DC: Association of American Geographers. [Also issued as ED 155 112 from ERIC.]

———. 1996. *How to lie with maps.* 2d ed. Chicago: University of Chicago Press.

Moore, J. A. 1982. Landsat-4 and its Thematic Mapper. *WAML Information bulletin* 14: 47–51.

Moore, W. G. 1975. *A dictionary of geography: Definitions and explanations of terms used in physical geography.* 2d ed. London: Adam and Charles Black.

Moseley, F. 1979. *Advanced geological map interpretation.* London: Edward Arnold.

Muehrcke, P. 1972. *Thematic cartography.* Washington, DC: AAG.

Muehrcke, P. C., and J. O. Muehrcke. 1992. *Map use: Reading, analysis, and interpretation.* 3d ed. Madison, WI: JP Publications.

Multilingual dictionary of remote sensing and photogrammetry. 1984. Falls Church, VA: American Society of Photogrammetry.

Muris, O., and G. Saarmann. 1961. *Der Globus im Wandel der Zeiten eine Geschichte der Globen.* Berlin: Columbus Verlag-Paul Oestergaard K.G.

Murray, J. D. 1994. *Encyclopedia of graphics file formats.* 1st ed. Sebastopol, CA: O'Reilly.

National and regional atlases . . . : Sources, bibliography, articles. 1964?– . (Dokumentacja geograficzna). Warsaw: Institute of Geography, Polish Academy of Sciences.

National Research Council (U.S.). Committee on the Future of the Global Positioning System. 1995. *The global positioning system: A shared national asset, recommendations for technical improvements and enhancements.* Washington, DC: National Academy Press.

National Research Council (U.S.). Highway Research Board. 1950. *Soil explanation and mapping.* (Bulletin no. 50). Washington, DC: Author.

Nautical chart symbols, abbreviations, and terms, chart no. 1, United States of America. 9th ed., Jan. 1990. Rockville, MD: National Ocean Service.

Neumann, J. 1997. *Encyklopädisches wörterbuch kartographie in 25 Sprachen = Encyclopedic dictionary of cartography in 25 languages.* München, Germany: K. G. Saur.

New York Public Library. 1971. *Dictionary catalog of the Map Division.* 10 vols. Boston: G. K. Hall.

New Zealand Map Keepers' Circle. [197_?]– . *Newsletter.* Various places: Author. *See also* New Zealand Map Society journal. [1986?]– . Auckland, New Zealand: New Zealand Map Society.

Nicks, O. W. 1970. *This island Earth.* (NASA SP-250). Washington, DC: GPO.

Nicolson, N. L., and L. M. Sebert. 1981. *The maps of Canada: A guide to official Canadian maps, charts, atlases and gazetteers.* Folkestone, UK: Dawson.

Noe, B. R. 1980. *Facsimiles of maps and atlases: A list of reproductions for sale by various publishers and distributors.* 4th ed. Washington, DC: Library of Congress.

North American Commission on Stratigraphic Nomenclature. 1983. *North American Stratigraphic Code.* American Association of Petroleum Geologists. *Bulletin* 67: 841–75.

Obermeyer, N. J. 1994. *Managing geographic information systems.* New York: Guildford Press.

O'Connor, Maura. 1991. *Map collections in Australia: A directory.* 4th ed. Canberra: National Library of Australia.

Oliver, J. E. 1973. *Climate and man's environment: An introduction to applied climatology.* New York: Wiley.

Omni gazetteer of the United States of America. 1991. Detroit, MI: Omnigraphics, Inc.

Oswald, D. 1997. *Fire insurance maps, their history and application.* College Station, TX: Lacewing Press.

Otness, H. M. 1978. *Index to early twentieth century city plans appearing in guidebooks: Baedeker, Muirhead-Blue Guides, Murray, I. J. G. R., etc.* (Occasional Paper no. 4). Santa Cruz, CA: WAML.

Outline maps on file. 1997. New York: Facts on File.

Ozenda, P. 1986. *La cartographie ecologique et ses applications [Ecological mapping and its applications].* Paris: Masson.

Paine, D. P. 1981. *Aerial photography and image interpretation for resource management.* New York: Wiley.

Pan American Institute of Geography and History. 197_– . *Research guides on Latin America [Guia para investigadores . . .].* Various places: various publishers. Some are part of Publication Series:

    341. Martinson, T. L. 1975. *Research guide to Colombia.* [Also published in 1976 as *Guia para investigadores de Colombia.*] Mexico: PAIGH.

    343. Nicaragua. Instituto Geografico Nacional. 1977. *Guia de recursos basicos contemporaneos para estudios de desarrollo en Nicaragua.* Managua, Nicaragua: Author.

    344. Honduras. Instituto Geografico Nacional. 1986. *Guia para investigadores de Honduras.* 2d ed. Tegucigalpa, Honduras: Author.

    345. Costa Rica. Instituto Geografico Nacional. 1977. *Research guide to Costa Rica.* San Jose, Costa Rica: Author.

    [No series number]. El Salvador. Instituto Geografico Nacional "Ingeniero Pablo Arnoldo Guzman." 1977. *Guia para investigadores republica de El Salvador.* San Salvador, El Salvador: Author.

    341. Panama. Instituto Geografico Nacional "Tommy Guardia." 1985. *Guia para investigadores de Panama.* Panama: Author. [Also published in English as *Guide for research workers of Panama.*]

    319. Guatemala. Instituto Geografico Nacional. 1978. *Guia para investigadores de Guatemala/Research guide to Guatemala.* Guatemala: Author.

    [No series number]. *Guía de la Republica Argentina para investigaciones geográficas.* 1983. Buenos Aires?: PAIGH.

[No series number]. Ecuador. Instituto Geografico Militar. 1982. *Guia para investigadores del Ecuador.* Quito, Ecuador: Author.

[No series number] Peru. Oficina Nacional de Evaluacion de Recursos Naturales. 1979. *Guide to cartographic and natural resources reformation of Peru.* Mexico: PAIGH.

[No series number]. Universidad Catolica de Chile. Instituto de Geografia. 1978. *Guia para investigadores de Chile.* Mexico D.F.: PAIGH.

Parkinson, B. W., and J. J. Spilker. 1996. *Global positioning system: Theory and applications.* 2 vol. Washington, DC: American Institute of Aeronautics and Astronautics.

Penfold, P. A. 1967, 1974. *Maps and plans in the Public Record Office.* [Part 1: British Isles (ca. 1410–1860); Part 2: America and the West Indies.] London: HMSO.

Perry, J. M. 1992. Use of map collections by genealogists, responses to a survey. *SLAG&MD Bulletin* 170: 22–31.

Peterson, M. P. 1987. The mental image in cartographic communication. *Cartographic Journal* 24: 35–41.

Photogrammetric engineering and remote sensing. 1934– . Falls Church, VA: American Society of Photogrammetry. [In 1975, title changed from *Photogrammetric engineering.*]

Podell, D. K. 1994. *Thematic atlases for public, academic, and high school libraries.* Metuchen, NJ: Scarecrow Press.

Post, J. B. 1984. Ward and fire insurance atlases. *SLAG&MD Bulletin* 137: 14–16.

Practical handbook of digital mapping: Terms and concepts. 1994. Boca Raton, FL: CRC Press.

Problems of geomorphological mapping. 1963. Warsaw: Polish Academy of Sciences.

Processes in marine science sensing. 1981. Columbia, SC: University of South Carolina Press.

Proehl, K. H., and B. Shupe. 1984. *Long Island gazetteer: A guide to current and historical place names.* Bayside, NY: LDA Publishers.

Pugliese, P. J. 1987. Maps in time. *American Cartographer* 14: 245–48.

The purpose and use of national and regional atlases. 1979. (Cartographica Monograph no. 23.) Toronto: B. V. Gutsell. [Suppl. no. 1 to *Canadian Cartographer,* no. 16, 1979.]

Putnam, R. 1983. *Early sea charts.* New York: Abbeville Press.

Queen, L. P. 1993. *The basics of geographic information systems.* St. Paul, MN: Minnesota Extension Service, University of Minnesota.

Rabbitt, M. C. 1979– . *Minerals, lands and geology for the common defence and general welfare*. Washington, DC: GPO. [History of USGS: vol. 1 is pre-1879, vol. 2 is 1879–1904.]

Rainville, Alain. 1996. Fire insurance plans in Canada. *The Archivist* 111: 25–38.

Rand McNally and Company. 1993. *The new international atlas*. Anniversary ed. Chicago: Rand McNally.

Raster imagery in geographic information systems. 1st ed. 1996. Santa Fe, NM: OnWord Press.

Ray, R. G. 1960. *Aerial photographs in geologic interpretation and mapping*. (USGS Professional Paper 373). Washington, DC: GPO.

Remote sensing and geographic information systems: An integration of technologies for resource management, a compendium. 1994. Bethesda, MD: ASPRS.

Reps, J. W. 1984. *Views and viewmakers of urban America: Lithographs of towns and cities in the United States and Canada, notes on the artists and publishers, and a union catalog of their world, 1825–1925*. Columbia, MO: University of Missouri Press.

Resources in education. 1974– . Washington, DC: GPO. [From 1966–1974, titled *Research in Education*; has many publications on maps and mapping skills; selected papers of interest to spatial-data librarians are listed below.]

ED 075 266—*Sources of information and materials: Maps and aerial photographs, a reference book*.

ED 088 458—*Federal government map collecting: A brief history*.

ED 096 955—*Map librarianship*.

ED 101 723—*The acquisition of maps and charts published by the United States government*.

ED 104 349—*Map librarianship: Readings*.

ED 104 442—*Planning of map and atlas work in Soviet scientific libraries*.

ED 107 236—*Map resources in San Francisco*.

ED 144 593—*Survey of users at the University of Oregon Map Library*.

ED 174 235—*A written map acquisition policy: The standardized compared with actual map library practices*.

ED 181 882—*Maps: Storage and care self-evaluation form*.

ED 194 436—*Comparative aspects of map collections in the state of Ohio*.

ED 229 036—*Geography and Map Libraries (IFLA) Section. Special Libraries Division. Papers.*

ED 230 482—*A Michigan carto-bibliography: An annotated guide to sources pertaining to Michigan maps, atlases, and related cartographic materials.*

ED 239 652—*Geography and Map Libraries Section. Special Libraries Division (IFLA). Papers.*

Richards, J. A. 1993. *Remote sensing digital image analysis: An introduction.* 2d rev. and enl. ed. Berlin: Springer-Verlag.

Riffel, P. A. 1973. *Reading maps: An introduction to maps using color stereo photographs.* Northbrock, IL: Hubbard Press.

Ringold, P. L.; and J. Clark. 1980. *The coastal almanac for 1980—The year of the coast.* San Francisco: Freeman. [Gives lengths of coastlines.]

Ristow, W. W. 1960. Weather and climate maps. *SLAG&MD Bulletin* 42: 24–35.

———. 1964a. A half-century of oil company road maps. *SLAG&MD Bulletin* 24: 617–37.

———. 1964b. *Three-dimensional maps: An annotated list of references relating to the construction and use of terrain models.* Washington, DC: Library of Congress.

———. 1973. *Guide to the history of cartography: An annotated list of references on the history of maps and mapmaking.* Washington, DC: GPO.

Robinson, A. H. 1982. *Early thematic mapping in the history of cartography.* Chicago: University Press of Chicago.

Robinson, A. H., and B. B. Petchenik. 1976. *The nature of maps.* Chicago: University of Chicago Press.

Rowland, J. B. 1955. *Features shown on topographic maps.* (USGS Circular 368). Washington, DC: GPO.

Sabins, F. F. 1987. *Remote sensing: Principles and interpretation.* 2d ed. New York: Freeman.

Salischev, K. A. 1960. *Atlas nationaux: Histoire, analyse, voies de perfectionnement et edification.* Moscow: Akademia Nauk SSR. [Also as: *National Atlanten. Petermanns,* 1960, no. 1, 77–88; *see also* Fremlin and Sebert 1972 in this appendix.]

Sanborn Map Company. 1960. *Description and utilization of the Sanborn map.* New York: Author.

Scale in remote sensing and GIS. 1997. Boca Raton, FL: Lewis.

Schiff, B. 1989. Aeronautical charts, portraits of the Earth. *AOPA Pilot* (March): 78–80, 82.

Schwartzkopf, R. B. 1989. State atlases from the eighties. *SLAG&MD Bulletin* 155: 21–25.

Scientific and technical, spatial and bibliographic data bases and systems of the U.S. Geological Survey, 1983, including other federal agencies. 1983. Rev. ed. (USGS Circular 817). Reston, VA: USGS.

Sealock, R. B., and P. A. Seely. 1967. *Bibliography of place-name literature: United States and Canada.* 2d ed. Chicago: ALA.

Shalowitz, A. L. 1957. Nautical charting (1807–1957). *Scientific Monthly* 84 (June): 290–301.

Sharing geographic information. 1995. New Brunswick, NJ: Center for Urban Policy Research.

Shkurkin, V. 1993. Sanborn maps: Some personal notes and comments. *WAML Information Bulletin* 24: 99–102.

Short, N. M. 1982. *The Landsat tutorial workbook: Basics of satellite remote sensing.* (NASA Reference Publication 1078). Washington, DC: GPO.

Short, N. M., P. D. Lowman, and S. C. Freden. 1976. *Mission to Earth: Landsat views the world.* (NASA SP-360). Washington, DC: GPO.

Shupe, B., and C. O'Connell. 1983. *Mapping your business.* New York: SLA.

Siegal, B. S., and A. R. Gillespie. 1980. *Remote sensing in geology.* New York: Wiley.

Simpson, B. 1968. *Geological maps.* Oxford, UK: Pergamon Press.

Simpson, E. S. W. 1983. Morphological mapping of the sea floor: The General Bathymetric Chart of the Oceans (GEBCO). *South African Journal of Photogrammetry, Remote Sensing & Cartography* 13: 289–304.

Smith, W. L. 1977. *Remote sensing applications for mineral exploration.* Stroudsburg, PA: Dowden, Hutchinson, and Ross.

Society of University Cartographers. 1967– . *Bulletin.* London: Author.

Sombroek, W. G. 1983. Soil maps and their legends. *Soil Survey and Land Evaluation* 3 (3): 80–87.

Southworth, M., and S. Southworth. 1983. *Maps: A visual survey and design guide.* New York: New York Graphic Society.

Spatial Data Transfer Standard. 1991. Reston, VA: USGS.

Special Libraries Association. Geography and Map Division. 1947– . *Bulletin.* Various places: Author.

————. 1985. *Map collections in the United States and Canada*. 4th ed. New York: SLA.

Spencer, D. D. 1993. *Illustrated computer graphics dictionary*. Ormond Beach, FL: Camelot.

Spencer, E. W. 1993. *Geologic maps: A practical guide to the interpretation and preparation of geologic maps for geologists, geographers, engineers, and planners*. New York: Macmillan.

Stams, W. 1980. *National and regional atlases: A bibliographic survey (up to and including 1978)*. The Netherlands?: International Cartographic Association.

Star, Jeffrey; and John Estes. 1990. *Geographic information systems: An introduction*. Englewood Cliffs, NJ: Prentice-Hall.

Stark, Peter L. 1989. *A cartobibliography of separately published U.S. Geological Survey special maps and river surveys*. (Occasional Paper 12). Santa Cruz, CA: WAML.

State maps on file. 1984– . New York: Facts on File.

Stem, J. E. 1989. *State plane coordinate system of 1983*. (NOAA Manual NOS NGS 5). Rockville, MD: NOAA.

Stephenson, R. W. 1967. *Land ownership maps*. Washington, DC: GPO.

————. 1976. *Civil War maps*. Washington, DC: GPO.

Stevenson, E. L. 1911 (repr. 1971). *Portolan charts, their origin and characteristics with a descriptive list of those belonging to the Hispanic Society of America*. (Publication of the Hispanic Society of America no. 82). New York: Knickerbocker Press.

————. 1921. *Terrestrial and celestial globes: Their history and construction, including a consideration of their value as aids in the study of geography and astronomy*. (Publication of the Hispanic Society of America no. 86). New Haven, CT: Yale University Press. [Reprinted in 2 vols. in 1971.]

Stommel, H. M., and M. Fieux. 1978. *Oceanographic atlases: A guide to their geographic coverage and contents*. Woods Hole, MA: Woods Hole Press.

Stooke, Philip. 1989. Maps of other worlds. *ACML Bulletin* 71: 9–15.

Stoughton, H. W. 1981. *State plane coordinates (1927 NAD and 1983 NAD)*. 2d ed. S.l.: H. W. Stoughton.

Stout, P. W. 1977. Atlas review index 1975. *SLAG&MD Bulletin* 110: 34–48.

Stowe, R. F. 1978. Legal implications of remote sensing. *PERS* 44: 183–88.

Survey of geographic information system and image processing software. 1993. Sioux Falls, SD: United Nations Environment Programme.

Taylor, E. G. R. 1956. *The havenfinding art: Or a history of navigation from Odysseus to Captain Cook.* London: Hollis and Carter.

Thematic cartography and remote sensing. 1992. New Delhi, India: Concept.

Thomas, J. A. 1977. *An introduction to geological maps.* 2d rev. ed. London: Murby.

Thompson, M. M. 1981. *Maps for America.* 2d ed. Washington, DC: GPO.

Thorndale, W. 1987. *Map guide to the U.S. federal censuses, 1790–1920.* Baltimore, MD: Genealogical Publishing.

Thrower, N. J. W. 1996. *Maps & civilization: Cartography in culture and society.* Chicago: University of Chicago Press.

Thrower, N. J. W.; and J. R. Jensen. 1976. The orthophoto and the orthophotomap: Characteristics, development and application. *American Cartographer* 3: 39–56.

Tomlin, C. D. 1990. *Geographic information systems and cartographic modeling.* Englewood Cliffs, NJ: Prentice-Hall.

Tomlinson, R. F. 1976. *Computer handling of geographical data: An examination of selected geographic information systems.* (Natural Resources Research 13). Paris: UNESCO.

Tooley, R. V. 1978. *Maps and map-makers.* 6th ed. London: B. T. Batsford.

———. 1979. *Tooley's dictionary of mapmakers.* [Suppl., 1985.] New York: Alan R. Liss.

Townshend, J. R. G. 1981. *Terrain analysis and remote sensing.* London: Allen and Unwin.

Tufte, Edward R. 1983. *The visual display of quantitative information.* Cheshire, CT: Graphics Press.

———. 1990. *Envisioning information.* Cheshire, CT: Graphics Press.

Tyner, J. A. 1992. *Introduction to thematic cartography.* Englewood Cliffs, NJ: Prentice-Hall.

Ulaby, F., R. K. Moore, and A. K. Fung. 1981. *Microwave remote sensing: Active and passive.* Reading, MA: Addison Wesley.

Understanding GIS: The ARC/INFO method, self-study workbook, version 7 for UNIX and OpenVMS. Redlands, CA: ESRI.

Understanding GPS: Principles and applications. 1996. Boston: Artech House.

United Nations. Department of Social Affairs. 1949. *Modern cartography: Base maps for world needs.* New York: United Nations.

————. 1956. *A chart for all oceans—International cooperation on the seven seas.* New York: United Nations.

United States. Army. Engineer Department. 1944. *Glossary of selected map terms relative to authorities, dates, scales, editions, and locations in foreign text maps.* Washington, DC: Author.

United States. Army. Map Service. 1944. *Glossary of selected map terms relative to authorities, dates, scales, editions, and locations in foreign text maps.* Washington, DC: Author.

————. 1946. *Glossary of Polish map terms.* (Technical Manual no. 13). Washington, DC: Author.

United States. Board on Geographic Names. 1955– . *Gazetteers.* Washington, DC: Author. [Gazetteers for foreign countries are also issued by the DMA; in its previous incarnation as the AMS, gazetteers for foreign countries—often linked to map series that AMS issued—were published.]

United States. Bureau of Land Management. Cadastral Survey Training Staff, Denver Service Center. 1980. *Glossary of BLM surveying and mapping terms.* Denver, CO: Author. [Microfiche versions issued in 1982 and 1983.]

United States. Congress. Senate. Energy and Natural Resources Committee. 1977. *National energy transportation systems.* Washington, DC: GPO.

United States. Copyright Office. 1947– . *Catalog of copyright entries. Third series. Part 6, Maps and atlases.* Washington, DC: Author.

United States. Defense Intelligence Agency. 1972. *Geopolitical data elements and related features.* Washington, DC: Defense Intelligence Agency.

United States. Defense Mapping Agency. [1972?]–1996. *Gazetteers.* Washington, DC: DMA. [*See* United States Board on Geographic Names, and United States Army Map Service (DMA's predecessor) for other gazetteers; it is possible that USNIMA, DMA's successor agency, will issue gazetteers.]

United States. Defense Mapping Agency. Topographic Center. 1973. *Glossary of mapping, charting and geodetic terms.* 3d ed. Washington, DC: DMA. [Also available as AD-775 778/4GI from NTIS (4th ed. 1976).]

United States. Department of the Army. 1964. *Foreign maps.* (Department of the Army Technical Manual, TM5-248). Washington, DC: Department of the Army.

United States. Department of the Army. 1969. *Map reading.* FM 21-26. Washington, DC: Author.

———. 1972?– . *Transportation and travel: Official table of distances, foreign travel*. (Army Regulation 55-61). Washington, DC: Author.

———. 1974?– . *Transportation and travel: Official table of distances, continental United States, Alaska, Hawaii, Canada, Canal Zone, Central America, Mexico, and Puerto Rico* . . . . (Army Regulation 55-60). Washington, DC: Author.

United States. Environmental Data Service. 1975. *Explanation of the "Daily weather map."* Washington, DC: GPO.

United States. Geological Survey. 1907– . *New publications of the U.S. Geological Survey*. Reston, VA: USGS. [Monthly; cumulated annually as *Publications of the U.S. Geological Survey*; in January 1984, the American Geological Institute began producing the publication for the USGS.]

———. 1977– . *APSRS, Aerial photography summary record system*. Reston, VA: USGS.

———. 1979. *Landsat data users handbook*. Rev. ed. Reston, VA: USGS.

———.1982– . *Geographic Names Information System*. Reston, VA: USGS.

———. 1980. *Computer software for spatial data handling*. Washington, DC: GPO.

———. 1982– . *The National Gazetteer of the United States*. (Professional Paper 1200-state). Washington, DC: GPO. [*United States Concise* volume, 1990.]

———. 1984. *Map data catalog*. 2d ed. Washington, DC: GPO.

United States. Library of Congress. Geography and Map Division. 1909–1974. *A list of geographical atlases in the Library of Congress, with bibliographical notes*. Washington, DC: GPO. [Vols. 1–4 by P. L. Phillips; vols. 5–8 by C. E. LeGear.]

———. 1973. *Bibliography of cartography*. Boston: G. K. Hall. [5 vols.; suppl. in 2 vols. 1980.]

———. 1981. *Fire insurance maps in the Library of Congress*. Washington, DC: Author.

———. 1995. *The Geography and Map Division, a guide to its collection and services*. Rev. ed. Washington, DC: GPO. [Abbreviated ed. issued 1981.]

United States. Library of Congress. National Library Service for the Blind and Physically Handicapped. 1987. *Tactile maps: A listing of maps in the National Library Service for the Blind and Physically Handicapped collection*. Washington, DC: Library of Congress.

United States. National Archives and Records Service. 1971. *Guide to cartographic records in the National Archives.* (National Archives Publication 71-16). Washington, DC: GPO.

United States. National Ocean Survey. 1979. *Nautical chart symbols and abbreviations, United States of America.* 7th ed. Washington, DC: DMA Hydrographic/Topographic Center.

United States. Soil Conservation Service. 19__– . *List of published soil surveys.* Washington, D.C.: Author.

Upton, W. B. 1970. *Landforms and topographic maps: Illustrating landforms of the continental United States.* New York: Wiley.

US GeoData: Catalog of digital data. 1989. Reston, VA: USGS.

US GeoData: Digital cartographic and geographic data. 1985. Reston, VA: USGS.

USGS digital cartographic data standards. 1983– . (Circular 895 A through G). Reston, VA: USGS.

A, Overview and USGS activities

B, Digital elevation models

C, Digital line graphs from 1: 24, 000-scale maps

D, Digital line graphs from 1: 2,000,000-scale maps

E, Land use and land cover digital data

F, Geographic Names Information System

G, Digital line graph attribute coding standards [Replaced by: *Data users guide*]

Utility of regional gravity and magnetic anomaly maps. 1985. Tulsa, OK: Society of Exploration Geophysics.

Vacquier, V., et al. 1951. *Interpretation of aeromagnetic maps.* (Memoir no. 47). New York: Geological Society of America.

Van Zandt, F. K. 1976. *Boundaries of the United States and the several states.* (USGS Professional Paper 909). Reston, VA: USGS.

Vanicek, P. 1982. *Geodesy, the concepts.* New York: Elsevier.

Vegetation mapping, from patch to planet. 1996. West Sussex, UK: Wiley.

Verner, C., and B. Stuart-Stubbs. 1979. *The north part of America.* [S.l.]: Academic Press Canada.

Verstappen, H. T. 1977a. *An atlas illustrating the use of aerial photographs in geomorphological mapping.* Enschede, The Netherlands: International Institute for Aerial Survey and Earth Sciences.

———. 1977b. *Remote sensing in geomorphology.* Amsterdam: Elsevier.

Vertical file holdings on mental maps. 1985. *UCLA Map Library Newsletter & Selected Acquisitions* 5(2): 10–12.

Vossmerbaumer, H. 1983. *Geologische karten*. Stuttgart, Germany: E. Schweizerbartsche Verlagsbuchhanlung.

Wagner, H. R. 1937. *The cartography of the northwest coast of America to the year 1800*. 2 vols. Berkeley, CA: University of California Press.

Walsh, J. P. 1973. *General world atlases in print, 1972–1973: A comparative analysis*. 5th ed. New York: R. R. Bowker.

Ward, D. C., M. W. Wheeler, and R. A. Bier. 1981. *Geologic reference sources: A subject and regional bibliography of publications and maps in the geological sciences*. 2d ed. Metuchen, NJ: Scarecrow Press.

Warnecke, L. 1992. *State geographic information activities compendium*. Lexington, KY: Center for Environment, Council of State Governments.

Warner, D. J. 1979. *The sky explored: Celestial cartography, 1500–1800*. New York: Alan R. Liss.

Weather and weather maps: A volume dedicated to the memory of Tor Bergeron. 1981. (Contributions to Current Research in Geophysics vol. 10). Basel, Switzerland: Birkhauser Verlag.

Webster's new geographical dictionary. 1984. Springfield, MA: Merriam.

Weidel, J. W. 1983. *Proceedings of the First International Symposium on Maps and Graphics for the Visually Handicapped*. Washington, DC: AAG.

Western Association of Map Libraries. 1969– . *Information Bulletin*. Various places: WAML. [Index for 1969–1979 is Occasional Paper no. 9: Woodward, F. M. 1983. *Index to the Information Bulletin (vols. 1–10, 1969–1979) of the Western Association of Map Libraries*.]

Wheat, C. I. 1957–1963. *Mapping the Transmississippi West, 1540–1861*. 5 vols. San Francisco, CA: Institute of Historical Cartography.

White, A. G. 1976. *Urban cartography: A selected bibliography*. (Exchange Bibliography no. 1157). Monticello, IL: Council of Planning Libraries.

White, C. A. 1983. *A history of the rectangular survey system*. Washington, DC: GPO.

———. 1996. *Initial points of the rectangular survey system*. Westminster, CO: Publishing House.

White, W. S. 1992. *Geological maps: Portraits of the Earth*. Reston, VA: USGS.

Wilford, J. N. 1981. *The mapmakers*. New York: Alfred A. Knopf.

Will, R. W.; and W. E. Krohn. 1989. *Hand signs for technical terms used in thematic and topographic mapping.* (Circular 1014). Reston, VA: USGS.

Williams, W. R. 1983. *Mine mapping and layout.* Englewood Cliffs, NJ: Prentice-Hall.

Winch, K. L. 1976. *International maps and atlases in print.* 2d ed. London: R. R. Bowker.

Wisconsin soil mapping. 1993. (Guide 4). Madison: State Cartographer's Office, University of Wisconsin.

Wolf, E. W. 1992. *The history of cartography: A bibliography, 1981–1992.* Washington, DC: Washington Map Society in association with Fiat Lux.

Worboys, M. 1995. *GIS: A computing perspective.* London: Taylor & Francis.

World cartography. 1951– . New York: United Nations.

World Chamber of Commerce directory. 1989– . Loveland, CO: World Chamber of Commerce Directory.

World directory of map collections. 1993. (IFLA Publications 63). Munich, Germany: Saur.

World Eagle. 1988. *Asia today: An atlas of reproducible maps.* Wellesley, MA: World Eagle.

———.1989. *Middle East today: An atlas of reproducible maps.* Wellesley, MA: World Eagle.

———. 1990a. *Africa today: An atlas of reproducible pages.* Wellesley, MA: World Eagle.

———. 1990b. *Europe today: An atlas of reproducible pages.* Wellesley, MA: World Eagle.

———. 1990c. *United States today: An atlas of reproducible pages.* Wellesley, MA: World Eagle.

———. 1992. *Latin America today: An atlas of reproducible pages.* Wellesley, MA: World Eagle.

World mapping today. 1987. London: Butterworths.

Worldwide directory of national earth-science agencies and related international organizations. 1984. (Circular 934). Washington, DC: GPO.

Yonge, E. L. 1957. National atlases: A summary. *Geographical Review* 47: 570–78.

———. 1968. *A catalogue of early globes.* New York: American Geographical Society.

Zeiler, Michale. 1994. *Inside ARC/INFO*. 1st ed. Santa Fe, NM: OnWord Press.

Appendix 2B—Projections and Grids

Alpha, T. R. 1982. *The properties and uses of selected map projections*. (Miscellaneous Investigations I-1402). Reston, VA: USGS.

Bibliography of map projections. 1988. (USGS *Bulletin* 1856). Reston, VA: USGS.

Bugayevskiy, L. M. 1995. *Map projections: A reference manual*. London: Taylor & Francis.

Canters, F. 1989. *The world in perspective: A directory of world map collections*. Chichester, UK: Wiley.

Datums, ellipsoids, grids, and grid reference systems. 1990. Washington, DC: DMA.

Freitag, U. 1968. Zeittafel zur Geschichte der Kartennetzlehre. [Chronological table of landmark events in the history of map projections, 550 BC to AD 1957.] *Kartographische Nachrichten* 18(2): 92.

Grids and grid references. 1983. (TM5-241-l). Washington, DC: U.S. Department of the Army.

Hilliard, J. A. 1986. *A projection handbook*. (Paper no. 2). Madison, WI: University of Wisconsin Cartographic Laboratory.

Hinks, A. R. 1921. *Map projections*. 2d ed. rev. and enl. Cambridge, UK: Cambridge University Press.

Keuning, J. 1955. The history of geographical map projections until 1600. *Imago Mundi* 12: 1–24.

Lee, J. E. 1984. *Map projections for use with the geographic information system*. Washington, DC: Western Energy and Land Use Team, Division of Biological Services, Research and Development, Fish and Wildlife Service.

Malin, S. R.1989. *The Greenwich meridian*. Southampton, UK: Ordnance Survey.

Maling, D. H. 1992. *Coordinate systems and map projections*. 2d ed. Oxford, UK: Pergamon Press.

Map projections, which ones best suit your needs? 199_?. Reston, VA: USGS.

Matching the map projection to the need. 1991. Bethesda, MD: ACSM.

McDonnell, P. W. 1979. *Introduction to map projections*. New York: Marcel Dekker.

Melluish, R. K. 1931. *An introduction to the mathematics of map projections*. Cambridge, UK: Cambridge University Press.

Newton, G. D. 1985. *Computer programs for common map projections*. (USGS *Bulletin* 1642). Reston, VA: USGS.

Pearson, F. 1982. *Map projection equations*. (ADA 037 381; NSWCIDL Technical Report 3624). Springfield, VA: NTIS.

———. 1984. *Map projection methods*. Blacksburg, VA: Sigma Scientific.

———. 1990. *Map projections: Theory and applications*. Boca Raton, FL: CRC Press.

Ray, J. M. 1976. Properties of map projections. *SLAG&MD Bulletin* 105: 6–11.

Richardus, P., and R. K. Adler. 1974. *Map projections for geodesists, cartographers and geographers*. Amsterdam: North-Holland Publishing.

Snyder, J. P. 1982. *Map projections used by the U.S. Geological Survey*. (USGS *Bulletin* 1532). Washington, DC: GPO.

———. 1985. *Computer-assisted map projection research*. (USGS *Bulletin* 1629). Reston, VA: USGS.

———. 1987. *Map projections—A working manual*. (USGS *Professional Paper* 1395). Reston, VA: USGS.

———. 1989. *An album of map projections*. (USGS *Bulletin* 1453). Reston, VA: USGS.

———. 1993. *Flattening the Earth: Two thousand years of map projections*. Chicago: University of Chicago Press.

Steers, J. A. 1965. *Study of map projections*. 14th ed. London: University of London Press.

United States. Coast and Geodetic Survey. 1919a. *General theory of polyconic projections*. (Special Publication no. 57). Washington, DC: GPO.

———. 1919b. *A study of map projections in general*. (Special Publication no. 60). Washington, DC: GPO.

———. 1928. *Elements of map projection with applications to map and chart construction*. (Special Publication no. 68). Washington, DC: GPO.

Universal transverse Mercator grid. 1952. (AMS Technical Manual no. 19). Washington, DC: AMS.

Universal transverse Mercator grid. 1973. (Technical Manual 5-241-8). Washington, DC: U.S. Department of the Army.

Universal transverse Mercator grid tables for latitudes 0°–80°, Clarke 1866 spheroid (meters): Transformation of coordinates from geographic to grid. 1949?. (AMS Technical Manual no. 7). Washington, DC: AMS. [Also published in 1959 as U.S. Department of the Army Technical Manual 5-241-11.]

Watts, D. G. 1972. *Map projections are easy.* Milford Haven, Wales: C. I. Thomas.

Appendix 2C—Monographs and Serials Relating to Cataloging

Alpha, T. R. 1979. *Graphs showing linear to fractional scale conversions for maps.* (Miscellaneous Field Studies MF-I 141). Reston, VA: USGS.

Anglo-American cataloguing rules. 1988. 2d ed. rev. Chicago: ALA.

Betz, E. W. 1982. *Graphic materials: Rules for describing original items and historical collections.* Washington, DC: Library of Congress.

Bibliographic guide to maps and atlases. 1980– . Boston: G. K. Hall.

Bibliography of cartographic materials published in the Netherlands [Bibliografie van in Nederland verschenen kartografische materialen]. 1975– . Houten, The Netherlands: Bohn Stafleu van Loghum.

Boggs, S. W., and D. C. Lewis. 1945. *The classification and cataloging of maps and atlases.* New York: SLA.

British Library. 1997. *British Library map catalogue on CD-ROM.* Woodbridge, CT: Primary Source Media.

Brown, L. 1941. *Notes on the care and cataloging of old maps.* Windham, CT: Hawthorn House.

Bruns, P. A. 1981. *National level bibliographic record—Maps.* Washington, DC: Library of Congress.

Cartographic materials: A manual of interpretation for AACR2. 1982. Chicago: ALA.

Cartographic materials in UNIMARC: The proposals of a sub-group of the IFLA Joint Working Group on ISBD(CM). 1979. (Occasional Papers no. 5). London: IFLA International Office for UBC.

Doursther, Horace. 1965. *Dictionnaire universal des poids et mesures anciens et modernes, contenant des tables des monnaies de tous les pays.* Amsterdam: Meridian.

Format integration and its effect on the USMARC bibliographic format. 1992. Washington, DC: LC Cataloging Distribution Service.

Geomatic data sets, cataloguing rules. 1994. Ottawa: Canada General Standards Board and Canadian Library Association.

International Hydrographic Organization. 1953. *Limits of oceans and seas.* 3d ed. Monte-Carlo, Monaco: Imp. Monegasque.

ISBD(CM), International Standard Bibliographic Description for Cartographic Materials. 1987. London: IFLA International Office for UBC.

Johnstone, W. D. 1975. *For good measure: A complete compendium of international weights and measures.* New York: Holt, Rinehart & Winston.

Karrow, Robert W. 1977. *Manual for the cataloging and maintenance of the cartographic collections of the Newberry Library.* 2d draft. Chicago: Newberry Library.

Languages of the world: Cataloging issues and problems. 1993. *Cataloging & Classification Quarterly* 17(1/2). Entire issue.

The Library of Congress Processing Services: Organization and functions. 1979. Washington, DC: Library of Congress.

Mangan, E. U. 1984. *MARC conversion manual—Maps: Content designation conventions and procedures for AACR2.* Washington, DC: LCG&M.

Map classification manual. 1991– . Washington, DC: LCG&M.

Meneely, W. E., and D. McGarry. 1984. *Directory of map catalogers in the United States, 1983.* (Special Publication no. 2). New York: SLAG&M.

Metadata in the geosciences. 1991. Loughborough, UK Group D Publications Ltd.

Military publishers' designations. 1986. (Map Curators' Group Publication no. 2). [Southampton]: British Cartographic Society.

OCLC, Inc. 1986. *Maps format.* 2d ed. Columbus, OH: OCLC.

Ralli, R. A. 1982. *Manual of map cataloguing and classification using AACR 2, Library of Congress class G, Library of Congress subject headings.* Nedlands: University of Western Australia.

UNIMARC manual. 1987. London: IFLA Universal Bibliographic Control and International MARC Programme, British Library Bibliographic Services.

United States. Defense Intelligence Agency. 1977. *Geopolitical data elements and related features.* (DIAM 65-18). Washington, DC: Author.

United States. Library of Congress. 1953–1955. *Library of Congress catalog: A cumulative list of works represented by Library of Congress printed cards: Maps and atlases.* 3 vols. Washington, DC: Author.

———. 1983– . *National union catalog, cartographic materials*. Washington, DC: Author. [In microfiche only; includes indexes for names, titles, subjects, series, and geographic-classification codes.]

United States. Library of Congress. Catalog Publication Division. 1979– . *Name authorities*. Cumulative microform ed. Washington, DC: Author.

United States. Library of Congress. Processing Services. 1978– . *Cataloging service bulletin*. Washington, DC: Library of Congress. [From 1945–1978, titled *Cataloging service*.]

United States. Library of Congress. Subject Cataloging Division. 1976. *Classification, class G*. 4th ed. Washington, DC: Library of Congress. [*LC classification, additions and changes* (1940–) updates it.]

———. 1997. *Library of Congress subject headings*. 20th ed. Washington, DC: Library of Congress. [Updated by cumulative suppls. (quarterly) with annual cumulations, 1979– .]

———. 1996– . *Subject cataloging manual*. 5th ed. Washington, DC: Library of Congress.

Verona, E. 1975. *Corporate headings: Their use in library catalogues and national bibliographies, a comparative and critical study*. London: IFLA Committee on Cataloguing.

Appendix 3

United States Publishers and Distributors of Globes and Three-Dimensional Plastic Raised-Relief Maps

N.B.: Addresses do change, and companies do go out of business or change name. Always check the yellow pages of the telephone book and the Web first.

Cram (George F.) Company
P.O. Box 426
Indianapolis, IN 46206

Farquhar Transparent Globes
426 Sumpter St.
Charlotte, MI 48813

Hammond Incorporated
515 Valley St.
Maplewood, NJ 07040

Hubbard Scientific
Department MP
P.O. Box 2121
Ft. Collins, CO 80522

Kistler Graphics
4000 Dahlia
Denver, CO 80216

National Geographic Society
1145 Seventeenth St., N.W.
Washington, DC 20036

A. J. Nystrom and Company
333 Elston Ave.
Chicago, IL 60618-5898

Panoramic Studios
1104 Churchhill Rd.
Wyndmoor, PA 19118

Rand McNally Map Services Co.
8255 N. Central Park Ave.
Skokie, IL 60076-2970

Relief Technik, Inc.
P.O. Box 91
Morrisville, PA 19067

Replogle Globes
2801 South 25th Ave.
Broadview, IL 60153-4589

World Globes of Seattle
1821 123d Ave. SE
Bellevue, WA 98005

Spherical Concepts
12 Davis Ave.
Frazer, PA 19355

Appendix 4

Free-Request Form

University of Northern South Dakota at Popple
Map Services, Library
Broken Asp, California 00001

DATE:

Please supply a copy of the below title if available free of charge to libraries. If it is not free, please send price and complete ordering information.

THIS IS NOT A PURCHASE ORDER.

Author:

Title:

Please put us on the mailing list for the above title.

THANK YOU!

Sincerely,

Mary Brooks
Spatial-Data Librarian

Appendix 5

Draft of New Cataloging Rules for Spatial Data in Digital Form

—DRAFT ONLY. DO NOT IMPLEMENT—

DIGITAL GRAPHIC REPRESENTATION AREA
3F   Digital graphic representation

3F1   Punctuation
             For instructions on the use of spaces before and after
                   prescribed punctuation, see 0C.
             Precede this area by a full stop, space, dash, space.
             Precede the object type by a colon.
             Precede the format name with a semicolon.
             Enclose each statement on the number of objects in parentheses.
             If both point/vector object count and VPF level are given,
                   precede the VPF level by a semicolon.

3F2   Direct reference method. When the information is readily available,
identify the system of objects used to represent space in a geomatic item
(e.g., raster, vector, point).

3F3   Object type. When the information is readily available, indicate
the specific type of point, raster, vector object type(s) used in the geomatic
item. Separate multiple types by a comma.

             Point: entity point

             Vector: network chain, non-planar graph

             Raster: pixel

3F4   Format. When the information is readily available, indicate the format name and version in which the geomatic item is stored.

>   Raster: pixel; GIF 87

3F5   Object count

>   3F5a   Point/vector object count. When the information is readily available, give the number of point or vector objects for each type of object used in a geomatic item.
>
>   >   Vector: GT-polygon composed of chains (70)
>
>   3F5b   Raster object count. When the information is readily available, give the number of rows x columns x voxels (vertical) in a raster geomatic item. Row and column count are used with rectangular raster items. Voxels are used with rectangular volumetric raster items.
>
>   >   Raster: pixel (128 x 128)
>
>   >   Raster: pixel (5,000 x 5,000)

3F6   Point/vector VPF topology level. When the information is readily available, record the completeness of the topology in the geomatic item in terms of the vector product format level.

>   Vector: edge (70 ; VPF2)

3F7   Indirect reference method. When the information is readily available, describe the types of geographic features, addressing schemes or other means through which locations are referenced.

>   100-year floodplain boundary; 500-year floodplain boundary.

GEOSPATIAL REFERENCE DATA AREA

>   3G   Geospatial reference data
>   3G1   Punctuation
>   >   For instructions on the use of spaces before and after prescribed punctuation, see 0C.
>   >   Precede this area by a full stop, space, dash, space.
>   >   Enclose each set of projection or ellipsoid parameters in parentheses.
>   >   Separate the multiple parameters/statements with a semicolon.

Precede the zone identifier with a semicolon.

Precede the secondary/related reference method with a colon.

3G2 Spatial reference method. When the information is readily available, identify the horizontal and/or vertical referencing system for the encoding of coordinates for a geomatic item.

3G3 Horizontal coordinate system. When the information is readily available, identify the reference method system from which linear or angular quantities are measured and assigned to the position that a point occupies using one of the following methods:

a) geographic

or b) map projection

or c) grid coordinate system

or d) local planar

or e) local

or f) geodetic model

3G3a Geographic. For a geographic reference method, using latitude and longitude to define the position of points with respect to a reference spheroid, give: the latitude resolution (the minimum difference between two adjacent latitude values); the longitude resolution (the minimum difference between two adjacent longitude values); and the unit of measure used for the latitude and longitude values, when the information is readily available.

0.0004; 0.0004; decimal degrees

3G3b Map projection. For a map projection reference method (that is, the systematic representation of the surface of the Earth on a plane), give: the name of the projection and the parameters associated with that projection which define the unique mathematical relationship between the Earth and the plane according to the table in appendix on geomatics, when the information is readily available.

Lambert conformal conic (38.3; 39.4; -77; 37.8333; 800000; 0)

3G3c Grid coordinate system. For a grid coordinate system reference method (that is, a plane-rectangular system usually based on and mathematically adjusted to a map projection, so that geographic positions can be readily transformed to and from plane coordinates), give: the name of the grid system; the zone identifier; and the related projection and its associated parameters, according to the following table, when the information is readily available.

State planar coordinate system 1927; 0405: Polyconic (0.9996; 0; 500000; 0)

3G3d   Local planar. For a local planar system reference method (that is, any planar coordinate system in which the relationship between the planar coordinates and geographic coordinates (latitude and longitude) is not known), give: a description of the local planar system and of the information provided to register the local planar system to the Earth (e.g., control points, satellite ephemeral data, etc.), when the information is readily available.

3G3e   Local. For a local system reference method (that is, any non-planar, non-geographic coordinate system), give: a description of the coordinate system and its orientation to the surface of the Earth and of the information provided to register the local system to the Earth (e.g., control points, satellite ephemeral data, etc.), when the information is readily available.

3G3f   Geodetic model. For a geodetic model reference method (that is, parameters for the shape of the Earth), give: horizontal datum name (the reference system used for defining the coordinate points); ellipsoid name (the established representation of the Earth's shape); the radius of the equatorial axis of the ellipsoid (semi-major axis); and the denominator of the representative fraction of the difference between the equatorial and polar radii of the ellipsoid (flattening ratio), when the information is readily available.

North American datum of 1927: Clarke 1866 (6378206.4; 294.98)

3G4   Vertical coordinate system. When the information is readily available, identify the reference method system from which vertical distances are measured using one of the following methods:
    a) altitude
or b) depth

3G4a   Altitude. For a vertical reference system from which elevations or altitude are measured, give: the altitude datum name (the level surface from which altitudes are measured); the altitude resolution (the minimum distance between two adjacent altitude values); the units of measurement (altitude distance units); and the means used to encode the altitude (vertical encoding method), when the information is readily available.

3G4b   Depth. For a vertical reference system from which depths are measured, give: the depth datum name (the level surface from which depths are measured); the depth resolution (the minimum distance between two adjacent depth values); the units of measurement (depth distance units); and the means used to encode the depth (vertical encoding method), when the information is readily available.

> NGVD 1929; 0.01; feet; explicit depth coordinate included with the horizontal coordinates.

3G5   Planar coordinate information. For geomatic items which use a coordinate reference system on a planar surface (i.e., map projection, grid coordinate system, or local planar), always give the planar coordinate system details in a separate note, when the information is readily available.

Record the means used to represent horizontal positions (planar coordinate encoding method) and the method of encoding the position of a point using one of the following methods:
     a) coordinate representation
or   b) distance and bearing representation

> 3G5a   Coordinate representation. For a geomatic item which encodes the position of a point by measuring its distance from perpendicular reference axes (e.g., coordinate pairs or row and column methods), give: the minimum distance between the "x" or column values of two adjacent points (abscissa resolution); the minimum distance between the "y" or row values of two adjacent points (ordinate resolution); and the unit of measure used for the distances, when the information is readily available.

> Coordinate pair; 22; 22; meters

> Coordinate pair; 0.01; 0.01; U.S. survey feet

> 3G5b   Distance and bearing representation. For a geomatic item which encodes the position of a point by measuring its distance and direction (azimuth angle) from another point give:

> the minimum distance measurable between two points
>   (distance resolution);
> the unit of measure used for the distances;
> the minimum angle measurable between two points
>   (bearing resolution);
> the unit of measure used for angles;
> the direction from which the bearing is measured (bearing
>   reference direction); and
> the axis from which the bearing is measured (bearing
>   reference meridian)
> when the information is readily available.

Distance and bearing; 30.0; U.S. feet; 0.0001; degrees, minutes, and decimal seconds; north; magnetic

3.7B17.5   Entity/attribute information. If the description is of a geomatic item, make a note(s) describing the entity and attribute information, when it is readily available. Provide this information in one of the following ways:

a) a detailed description for each entity and/or attribute

or   b) an overview of the entity/attribute information

or   c) a detailed description and an overview.

7B17.5a   Detailed description. When the information is readily available, indicate the entity and/or attribute label(s) and the definition(s), including the source(s) of the definition(s). Additionally, indicate the type of domain value(s) used for the attribute and the appropriate associated explanations using one of the following methods:

1) for enumerated domains give: the domain value, its definition, the source of the definition; the unit of measurement and resolution; the beginning and ending dates of the values; the accuracy, including an explanation of the accuracy; and the measurement frequency; or

2) for range domains give: the minimum and maximum value; the unit of measurement and resolution; the beginning and ending dates of the values; the accuracy, including an explanation of the accuracy; and the measurement frequency.

Floodplain polygon; 100 and 500 year floodplain zones (FIRM maps [FEMA]); user-id; floodplain zone, USACERL; 100-500; years.

or

3) for codeset domains give: the name of the codeset and its source; the unit of measurement and resolution; the beginning and ending dates of the values; the accuracy, including an explanation of the accuracy; and the measurement frequency;

or

4) for unrepresentable domains give: a description of the values and the reason why they cannot be represented; the unit of measurement and resolution; the beginning and ending dates of the values; the accuracy, including an explanation of the accuracy; and the measurement frequency.

Separate detailed information using semicolons, and enclose source citations in parentheses.

7B17.5b Overview. When the information is readily available, give a detailed summary of the entity(ies) and attributes in a geomatic item and the citation for the complete description of the entity types, attributes, and attribute values for the item. Enclose the citation in parentheses.

> Three observables: Carrier-phase measurements, pseudorange (code) measurements, and observation times, as well as station and antenna information (GPS Bulletin, vol. 3, no. 3, Sept.–Oct. 1990 issue, from the Commission VIII International Coordination of Space Techniques for Geodesy and Geodynamics).

7B17.5c Detailed description and overview. When the information is readily available, give both the detailed description and the overview information for the entity(ies) and attributes related to a geomatic item as separate notes.

Appendix 6

Equipment Manufacturer/Supplier Addresses

N.B.: Addresses do change, and companies do go out of business or change name. Some producers, such as Hamilton and Mayline, deal through regional suppliers. Always check the yellow pages of the telephone book first.

Forestry Suppliers, Inc.
P.O. Box 8397
Jackson, MS 39204

Hamilton Industries
Two Rivers, WI 54241
(now owned by Mayline)

Lenzar
3960 RCA Blvd., Suite 6001
Palm Beach Gardens, CA 33410

Mayline Company
P.O. Box 728
Sheboygan, WI 53082-0728

Multi-Lock Inc.
2027 Harpers Way
Torrance, CA 90501

Plan Hold
17421 Von Karman Ave.
Irvine, CA 92714-6293

Stacor Corporation
285 Emmet St.
Newark, NJ 07114

Ulrich Planfile
2120 Fourth Ave.
Lakewood, NY 14750

Index